D0378786

THE COMPLETE BOOK OF HYMNS

THE COMPLETE BOOK OF

HYMNS

INSPIRING STORIES ABOUT
600 HYMNS AND PRAISE SONGS

WILLIAM J. PETERSEN
& ARDYTHE PETERSEN

Tyndale House Publishers, Inc.
CAROL STREAM, ILLINOIS

Visit Tyndale's exciting Web site at www.tyndale.com

TYNDALE and Tyndale's quill logo are registered trademarks of Tyndale House Publishers, Inc.

The Complete Book of Hymns

Designed by Ron Kaufmann

Library of Congress Cataloging-in-Publication Data

Petersen, William J.
    The complete book of hymns / Bill Petersen and Ardythe E. Petersen.
        p. cm.
    Includes bibliographical references and indexes.
    ISBN-13: 978-1-4143-0933-0 (sc : alk. paper)
    ISBN-10: 1-4143-0933-3 (sc : alk. paper)
    1. Hymns, English—History and criticism.   I. Petersen, Ardythe E.   II. Title.
    BV315.P48 2006
    264'.23—dc22   2006002263

Printed in the United States of America

12   11   10   09   08   07   06
 7   6   5   4   3   2   1

CONTENTS

FOREWORD

God likes music. Maybe that's one reason he created angels.

We like music too—at least certain kinds of music.

Music and Christian worship have grown up together for two thousand years. The apostle Paul wrote of singing psalms, hymns, and spiritual songs, thus recognizing that followers of Jesus can worship God with various musical tastes.

In the past one hundred years, Christians have been introduced, sometimes painfully, to more variety in church music than ever before, and we are still learning music appreciation from younger generations.

Admittedly, the title of this book is not entirely accurate. Probably it should have been called *The Almost Complete Book of Stories about Hymns, Gospel Songs, Contemporary Praise and Worship, Southern Gospel, Spirituals, Etc.* But the publisher thought that might be too cumbersome to put on the cover, so we compromised with the title *The Complete Book of Hymns.*

Of course, this isn't the first book of hymn stories to be written. Mid-nineteenth century author Hezekiah Butterworth may have been one of the first. But no previous book of hymn stories has included as many different styles of Christian music and as many stories—about six hundred—as this book.

I am indebted to the musicologists and compilers who have preceded us—people like Don Hustad, Ken Osbeck, Bill Reynolds, and Lindsay Terry. For a more complete list see the Bibliography in the back.

I am especially indebted to my wife, Ardythe. She played a major role in many of my previous books, but in this one she was indispensable. The task of keeping straight six hundred hymn stories, lyrics, and copyright permissions was awesome. I also want to thank Elizabeth Hess for her help, and I want to thank Al Seawell, Linda Gyrath, Fred Beveridge, Carol Liebert, and others for helping me enjoy the wide spectrum of Christian music.

Bill Petersen

PART I

ADORATION AND PRAISE

They lay their crowns before the throne and say, "You are worthy,

O Lord our God, to receive glory and honor and power. For you created

all things, and they exist because you created what you pleased."

REVELATION 4:10-11

A HYMN OF GLORY LET US SING

The Venerable Bede was not called Venerable because he was so old but because he was so wise and brilliant in many different areas. Living thirteen hundred years ago, he was one of the earliest historians and theologians in the English church. He wrote books on science, nature, and grammar. He is revered as "The Father of English History" because of his book *Ecclesiastical History of the English Nation.*

In the book he describes how the Christian faith came to England. It came, he says, with singing. The early missionaries to England brought a simple lifestyle, and new converts believed, "admiring the simplicity of their innocent life, and the sweetness of their heavenly doctrine." In one city, he wrote, the Christians came together to "meet, to sing, and to pray," and soon the king and ten thousand citizens were baptized.

Bede wrote and sang his hymns accompanied by his Saxon harp. And when he was dying in the year 735, he asked his friends to carry him to the room where he usually prayed. There he sang the "Gloria Patri." When he uttered his last words on earth, he continued his song in the presence of the triune God.

Scriptures: Acts 2:32-33; Philippians 2:8-10; Hebrews 8:1; Hebrews 12:2
Themes: Praise, Eternity, Ascension

A hymn of glory let us sing,
New hymns throughout the world shall ring;
By a new way none ever trod
Christ takes His place—the throne of God.

You are a present joy, O Lord;
You will be ever our reward;
And great the light in You we see
To guide us to eternity.

O risen Christ, ascended Lord,
All praise to You let earth accord,
Who are, while endless ages run,
With Father and with Spirit, One.

THE VENERABLE BEDE (673–735)
Stanzas 1–2 translated by Elizabeth Rundle Charles (1828–1896), altered.
Stanza 3 translated by Benjamin Webb (1819–1885), altered.

ALL CREATURES OF OUR GOD AND KING

Saint Francis of Assisi is perhaps best known as a nature lover. You may recall the painting in which the Italian artist Giotto depicts him feeding the birds. One writer spoke of him this way: "With smiles he met the friendless, fed the poor, freed a trapped bird, led home a child. Although he spoke no word, his text, God's love, the town did not forget."

A soldier in his early years, Francis resolved to imitate the life of Christ. So he renounced his wealth and founded the Franciscan Order of Friars. He and those who followed him became itinerant evangelists, preaching and helping the poor of Italy. He wrote sixty hymns of praise and worship and encouraged church music in every way he could.

The original text of this hymn was probably written by Francis during the last months of his life when he was suffering intense pain and was almost blind.

Scriptures: Psalm 145:10-11; Psalm 148:1, 7-13; Romans 11:36
Themes: Praise, Worship, Adoration

All creatures of our God and King,
Lift up your voice and with us sing,
Alleluia! Alleluia!
Thou burning sun with golden beam,
Thou silver moon with softer gleam!

O praise Him, O praise Him!
Alleluia! Alleluia! Alleluia!

Thou rushing wind that art so strong,
Ye clouds that sail in heaven along,
O praise Him! Alleluia!
Thou rising morn, in praise rejoice,
Ye lights of evening, find a voice!

Thou flowing water, pure and clear,
Make music for thy Lord to hear,
Alleluia! Alleluia!
Thou fire so masterful and bright,
Thou givest man both warmth and light!

And thou, most kind and gentle death,
Waiting to hush our latest breath,
O praise Him! Alleluia!

Thou leadest home the child of God,
And Christ our Lord the way hath trod.

Let all things their Creator bless,
And worship Him in humbleness,
O praise Him! Alleluia!
Praise, praise the Father, praise the Son,
And praise the Spirit, Three in One!

FRANCIS OF ASSISI (1182–1226)
Translated by William H. Draper (1855–1933)

ALL GLORY, LAUD, AND HONOR

When Jesus entered Jerusalem riding on a donkey, a hopeful crowd filled the streets, waving palm branches and praising God. The people believed that the Messiah had finally come to lead a revolt against the Romans. Less than a week later, the same crowd demanded his crucifixion.

Theodulf, who wrote this hymn, had a somewhat similar experience. King Charlemagne had made him Bishop of Orléans in the late 700s, and all the people, as well as the king, praised Theodulf. He was the king's theologian as well as a beloved pastor. But when Charlemagne died, rumors were spread against him. Charlemagne's son charged him with conspiracy and put him in prison. And yet it was while he was in a dark prison that he wrote this hymn, which is still sung more than a thousand years later. It is a favorite Palm Sunday hymn in churches of many denominations.

Scriptures: Psalm 118:25-26; Mark 11:7-10; John 12:12-13
Themes: Palm Sunday, Praise

All glory, laud, and honor
To Thee, Redeemer, King,
To whom the lips of children
Made sweet hosannas ring:
Thou art the King of Israel,
Thou David's royal Son,
Who in the Lord's name comest,
The King and blessed One!

The company of angels
Are praising Thee on high,

And mortal men and all things
Created make reply:
The people of the Hebrews
With palms before Thee went;
Our praise and prayer and anthems
Before Thee we present.

To Thee, before Thy passion,
They sang their hymns of praise;
To Thee, now high exalted,
Our melody we raise:
Thou didst accept their praises—
Accept the praise we bring,
Who in all good delightest,
Thou good and gracious King!

THEODULF OF ORLÉANS (CA. 750–821)
Translated by John Mason Neale (1818–1866)

ALL HAIL, KING JESUS

In 1977, David Moody was giving piano lessons in Vancouver, British Columbia. His students came for their lessons after school was dismissed around 3:30, and on this particular day David had some free time before they were due to arrive. "So," he said, "I went downstairs and began to play and just worship the Lord."

He said that he wasn't really trying to write a song; "I simply wanted to spend time in the presence of the Lord." Then, "quite suddenly, I began to develop a melody that was coming to me—something I had never played before. And just as quickly came some words that I began to sing."

"All Hail, King Jesus" is really a song about the second coming of Christ. David Moody said, "I could just imagine believers all over the world singing this song as Christ returned to earth." Once the song was published, it didn't take long before reports of Christians singing it in Israel, in Russia, in Hungary, and elsewhere were coming back.

Scriptures: Isaiah 7:14; Revelation 19:16; Revelation 22:16-17
Themes: Jesus Christ, Return of Christ, Worship

All hail, King Jesus! All hail, Emmanuel,
King of kings, Lord of lords, Bright Morning star.
And throughout eternity I'll sing Your praises,
And I'll reign with You throughout eternity.

DAVID MOODY (B. 1949)
© 1978 Dayspring Music LLC
All rights reserved. Used by permission.

ALL HAIL THE POWER OF JESUS' NAME

E. P. Scott, a missionary to India, saw an unusual-looking tribesman on the street, and he asked where the man came from. He was told that the man was from a mountain tribe and came only once a year to the major city to trade. Scott also discovered that the gospel had never been taken to that tribe.

After praying about it, he packed up his bags and violin and started in the direction of the mountain village. When Scott told senior missionaries where he was going, they told him, "We will never see you again. It is madness for you to go." But he went anyway.

He traveled for two days and finally found himself in the mountains. Suddenly he was surrounded by spear-carrying tribesmen, and every spear was pointed at him.

Not knowing what else to do, Scott got out his violin and sang and played "All Hail the Power of Jesus' Name," including the verse, "Let every kindred, ev'ry tribe, / On this terrestrial ball, / To Him all majesty ascribe, / And crown Him Lord of all."

The spears had now dropped from the men's hands, and he could see tears in their eyes. He spent the next two-and-a-half years telling them about Jesus and his love for them. When Scott had to leave them because of his health, the tribespeople escorted him forty miles to where he could get other transportation.

Scriptures: Philippians 2:9-11; Colossians 1:15-20; Revelation 5:11-13; Revelation 19:11-13, 16
Themes: Praise, Jesus as Lord, God's Majesty

All hail the pow'r of Jesus' name!
Let angels prostrate fall;
Bring forth the royal diadem,
And crown Him Lord of all;
Bring forth the royal diadem,
And crown Him Lord of all!

Ye chosen seed of Israel's race,
Ye ransomed from the fall,
Hail Him who saves you by His grace,
And crown Him Lord of all;
Hail Him who saves you by His grace,
And crown Him Lord of all!

Let ev'ry kindred, ev'ry tribe,
On this terrestrial ball,
To Him all majesty ascribe,
And crown Him Lord of all;
To Him all majesty ascribe,
And crown Him Lord of all!

O that with yonder sacred throng
We at His feet may fall!
We'll join the everlasting song,
And crown Him Lord of all;
We'll join the everlasting song,
And crown Him Lord of all!

EDWARD PERRONET (1726–1792)
Altered by John Rippon (1751–1836)

ALL NATURE'S WORKS HIS PRAISE DECLARE

All nature continously praises God—only humans require reminders to do so. When Henry Ware's church in Boston prepared to dedicate its new organ, they asked Henry to write a dedicatory hymn. As he wrote, he made sure that he did not speak of the greatness of the instrument. Instead, he emphasized the organ's purpose: to assist Christians in the praise of God. In a way, the hymn is reminiscent of Psalm 150, which speaks of seven or eight different musical instruments, united in the praise of God. Thirteen times that psalm urges us to join in praise. We, too, are created for this purpose, to sing of God's glory.

We can thank God for our church organs and the other instruments that lead us in worship. But how often during the week do we lift our souls to God in the unaccompanied exaltation of our glorious Lord?

Scriptures: Psalm 19:1-4; Psalm 150; Romans 1:20
Themes: Creation, Nature, Praise

All nature's works His praise declare,
To whom they all belong;
There is a voice in every star,
In every breeze, a song.
Sweet music fills the world abroad
With strains of love and power;
The stormy sea sings praise to God,
The thunder and the shower.

To God the tribes of ocean cry,
And birds upon the wing;
To God the powers that dwell on high
Their tuneful tribute bring.
Like them, let man the throne surround,
With them loud chorus raise,
While instruments of loftier sound
Assist his feeble praise.

Great God, to Thee we consecrate
Our voices and our skill;
We bid the pealing organ wait
To speak alone Thy will.
Lord, while the music round us floats,
May earthborn passions die;
O grant its rich and swelling notes
May lift our souls on high!

HENRY WARE JR. (1794–1843)

ALL PEOPLE THAT ON EARTH DO DWELL

This is often called "The Old Hundredth" because it is based on Psalm
100. It is probably the oldest hymn of praise in the English language.
William Kethe, a Scotsman, was a minister of the Church of England.
But during the reign of Queen Mary, which was a reign of terror for
many English Protestants, Kethe fled to Germany and then to Geneva,
Switzerland. In Geneva he was influenced by John Calvin. There he
assisted in the translation of the Geneva Bible and helped to produce a
complete English version of the metrical psalms. From this Psalter, now
more than four hundred years old, "The Old Hundredth" is taken. The
hymn was first published in London in 1561, shortly after Queen Elizabeth I came to the throne.

The music was written by John Calvin's choir director, and the hymn has never been set to any other but the original tune.

Scriptures: Psalm 100:1-4; John 10:11; Hebrews 13:15
Themes: Praise, Worship, Joy

All people that on earth do dwell,
Sing to the Lord with cheerful voice;
Him serve with fear, His praise forth tell,
Come ye before Him and rejoice.

The Lord, ye know, is God indeed;
Without our aid He did us make;
We are His flock, He doth us feed,
And for His sheep He doth us take.

O enter then His gates with praise,
Approach with joy His courts unto;
Praise, laud, and bless His name always,
For it is seemly so to do.

For why? The Lord our God is good,
His mercy is forever sure;
His truth at all times firmly stood,
And shall from age to age endure.

To Father, Son, and Holy Ghost,
The God whom heaven and earth adore,
From earth and from the angel host
Be praise and glory evermore.

WILLIAM KETHE (D. 1593)

ALL PRAISE TO OUR REDEEMING LORD

William Barclay once wrote that a person needs to have three conversions: first, to God; second, to other Christians; and third, to the world. Certainly there are these three crucial aspects to our faith—worship, fellowship, and ministry. Charles Wesley, the prolific Methodist hymnwriter, wrote widely on all three sides of this sacred triangle.

Many churches emphasize one of these aspects and neglect one or two of the others. Some focus on personal growth or outreach but never develop a "body life" in which Christians get to know and love one another. Others are so absorbed in Christian fellowship that they never do anything to reach out to others.

As usual, Wesley's words are rooted in Scripture. The New Testament continually weaves these three threads of Christian life together.

Scriptures: Acts 4:23-24; Ephesians 4:7, 11-13; Hebrews 10:25
Themes: Redemption, Fellowship, Church

All praise to our redeeming Lord,
Who joins us by His grace,
And bids us, each to each restored,
Together seek His face.

The gift which He on one bestows,
We all delight to prove,
The grace through every vessel flows
In purest streams of love.

He bids us build each other up;
And, gathered into one,
To our high calling's glorious hope,
We hand in hand go on.

We all partake the joy of one;
The common peace we feel:
A peace to sensual minds unknown,
A joy unspeakable.

And if our fellowship below
In Jesus be so sweet,
What height of rapture shall we know
When round His throne we meet!

CHARLES WESLEY (1707–1788)

ALL PRAISE TO THEE, MY GOD, THIS NIGHT

In 1673 Anglican bishop Thomas Ken wrote a prayer manual for the students at Winchester College. The book contained a hymn for the morning, one for evening, and one for midnight. Students were admonished to sing the morning and evening hymns devoutly—though apparently the midnight hymn was seldom used! All three hymns concluded with the same stanza, "Praise God, from whom all blessings flow"—the most-sung hymn lyrics in the English language.

Thomas Ken knew well that it is difficult to end some days with a doxology of praise. Orphaned as a boy, he was adopted by a noted scholar and author. He was ordained in the Church of England and became chaplain to Princess Mary of Orange. But when he spoke against the immorality of the royal court, he soon found himself without a job. Later he was imprisoned in the Tower of London by James II for refusing to read the king's Declaration of Indulgence. Still, it is said that Bishop Ken continued to use his morning and evening hymns in his personal devotions.

Years earlier at Winchester College, he told the students, "It is a very good thing to tell of the loving-kindness of God in the morning and of his truth in the night season." And it is a good habit for all of us.

Scriptures: Psalm 3:5; Psalm 22:27-28; Psalm 63:6-8
Theme: Praise, Evening Hymn, Confession

All praise to Thee, my God, this night,
For all the blessings of the light!
Keep me, O keep me, King of kings,
Beneath Thine own almighty wings.

Forgive me, Lord, for Thy dear Son,
The ill that I this day have done,
That with the world, myself, and Thee,
I, when I sleep, at peace may be.

O may my soul on Thee repose,
And with sweet sleep mine eyelids close,
Sleep that may me more vigorous make
To serve my God when I awake.

Praise God, from whom all blessings flow;
Praise Him, all creatures here below;
Praise Him above, ye heavenly host;
Praise Father, Son, and Holy Ghost.

THOMAS KEN (1637–1711)

ALLELUIA

Jerry Sinclair grew up in Calais, Maine, which is just about as far northeast as you can go in the United States. Then he moved to Orange County, California, which is just about as far southwest as you can go in the continental United States. What did he do when he got to California? He wrote a song with one word in it: *alleluia*. That song became famous not only in America but around the world. Sometimes God works in surprising ways.

As a teenager Jerry was a singer in northern Maine, then he moved to Oklahoma before going to California in the 1960s during the Jesus People movement. When worship choruses became popular in the early 1970s, it was Jerry Sinclair's "Alleluia" that led the way. In Scripture, the psalmists apparently thought that *alleluia* was the perfect word for worship. It means "Praise the Lord," and in Psalm 150, the last psalm, the psalmist uses the word *praise* thirteen times in its six verses. In his worship chorus, Sinclair uses the word *alleluia* only eight times.

Scriptures: Psalm 102:18; Psalm 150:1-2; Revelation 19:4-7

Themes: Worship, Praise

> Alleluia, alleluia, alleluia, alleluia, (Repeat.)
> He's my Savior, He's my Savior, (Repeat 6 times.)
> He is worthy (Repeat 7 times.)
> I will praise Him (Repeat 7 times.)

JERRY SINCLAIR (B. 1943)
©1972 Manna Music, Inc. ARR UBP of Manna Music, Inc. (35255 Booten Rd. Pacific City, OR 97135) All rights reserved. Used by permission.

ALLELUIA! SING TO JESUS

This hymn was originally entitled "Redemption through the Precious Blood." It was inspired by Revelation 5:9: "They sung a new song, saying, Thou art worthy . . . for thou wast slain, and hast redeemed us to God by thy blood" (KJV).

William Dix was a Scottish maritime insurance agent when sea travel was still a hazardous affair. He wrote "Alleluia! Sing to Jesus" as a Communion hymn for Ascension Sunday, six weeks after Easter, so it combines two themes: the Lord's Supper and the Lord's ascension into heaven.

The first stanza reminds us of the Revelation scene, where the Lord is portrayed as the King with scepter and the throne; the second recalls Christ's ascension and his comforting words in the upper room: "I will not abandon you as orphans" (John 14:18). The last stanza speaks of the ascended Christ in heaven as the great High Priest, interceding for his children. Here he is called the Bread of Heaven, our Intercessor, our Friend, and our Redeemer. What a wonderful Savior!

Scriptures: John 14:18; Acts 1:9; Revelation 5:9; Revelation 7:9-12
Themes: Praise, Ascension, Communion, Resurrection

Alleluia! sing to Jesus!
His the sceptre, His the throne;
Alleluia! His the triumph,
His the victory alone;
Hark! the songs of peaceful Zion
Thunder like a mighty flood;
"Jesus, out of ev'ry nation
Has redeemed us by His blood."

Alleluia! not as orphans
Are we left in sorrow now;
Alleluia! He is near us,
Faith believes, nor questions how:
Though the clouds from sight received Him
When the forty days were o'er,
Shall our hearts forget His promise,
"I am with you evermore"?

Alleluia! Bread of Heaven,
You on earth our food and stay!
Alleluia! here the sinful
Flee to You from day to day;
Intercessor, Friend of sinners,
Earth's Redeemer, plead for me,
Where the songs of all the sinless
Sweep across the crystal sea.

WILLIAM CHATTERTON DIX (1837–1898)

ANCIENT OF DAYS

In 1886, the city of Albany, New York, celebrated its bicentennial. Episcopal bishop William Croswell Doane wrote this hymn for the occasion, and J. Albert Jeffery, who was in charge of music at St. Agnes School and the recently completed All Saints Cathedral, wrote the music. That new cathedral was the setting for the hymn's introduction, and Bishop Doane himself conducted the singing. It was a memorable day in Albany as the townspeople celebrated the city's own "ancient days."

But the hymn draws our attention further back, to the majesty of the triune God, who existed before all time began. In stanza 1, we see the Ancient of Days, in stanza 2 the Father who leads us through the wilderness, in stanza 3 the Son who calms the storms, in stanza 4 the Holy Spirit who gives life and hope, and in stanza 5 the triune God, who answers our prayers and sustains us day by day. In all these ways, our great God deserves our praise. What a wonderful God we serve!

Scriptures: Isaiah 9:6; Daniel 7:9-10; Titus 3:5
Themes: Trinity, God's Majesty, Worship, Names of God

Ancient of Days, who sittest throned in glory,
To Thee all knees are bent, all voices pray;
Thy love has blessed the wide world's wondrous story
With light and life since Eden's dawning day.

O holy Father, who hast led Thy children
In all the ages with fire and cloud,
Through seas dryshod, through weary wastes
    bewildering,
To Thee in reverent love our hearts are bowed.

O holy Jesus, Prince of Peace and Savior,
To Thee we owe the peace that still prevails,
Stilling the rude wills of men's wild behavior,
And calming passion's fierce and stormy gales.

O Holy Ghost, the Lord and the Life-giver,
Thine is the quickening power that gives increase:
From Thee have flowed, as from a mighty river,
Our faith and hope, our fellowship and peace.

O Triune God, with heart and voice adoring,
Praise we the goodness that doth crown our days;

Pray we that Thou wilt hear us, still imploring
Thy love and favor, kept to us always.
WILLIAM CROSWELL DOANE (1832–1913)

AWESOME GOD

Rich Mullins, the author of this praise song, delighted in doing the unexpected. He was raised in a Quaker church that celebrated quietness and waiting upon God in stillness. But when he went to Bible college, he formed a rock band and, later, a touring group called the Ragamuffin Band. He had a zany sense of humor and at the same time a deep appreciation for St. Thomas of Assisi. Like St. Thomas, Mullins liked to work with poor children, and he spent the last two years of his life on a Navajo Indian reservation in the Southwest.

Once as he was driving across country on his way to a youth conference, he began to doze off. Trying to keep himself awake, Mullins began preaching to himself. The sleepier he got, the more exuberant he got in his preaching; by the time he arrived at the youth conference, he had written a new song called "Awesome God." He didn't think it was a great song, but the kids at the conference loved it, and soon its popularity spread across the country.

Scriptures: Psalm 48:1; Psalm 147:5; Isaiah 40:28
Themes: God the Father, God's Power, Love

Our God is an awesome God.
He reigns from heaven above with wisdom, pow'r, and love.
Our God is an awesome God.
RICH MULLINS (1955–1997)
© 1988 BMG Songs

BE EXALTED, O GOD

There were several turning points in the life of Brent Chambers before he wrote "Be Exalted, O God." The first turning point for this New Zealand lad came when he heard the Beatles for the first time. They inspired him to play the guitar, and he became so obsessed that, because he was left-handed, he learned to play it with the instrument upside down.

The second turning point came when he became a Christian at the age of eighteen, and the third turning point came after a roller coaster ride. On a roller coaster ride, Brent Chambers realized that he had not been living for Christ as he should, so he surrendered himself completely to Christ.

Brent went to Bible college and then to Auckland University, where he majored in the classics. Although he was behind in some of his assignments, he felt he needed some time off. Brent began reading the Psalms, and Psalm 57:9-11 stood out to him. *I'd love to be able to put some music to those words,* he thought, so he picked up his guitar and started singing the Psalm with an improvised tune, creating the song we know today.

Scriptures: Psalm 57:9-11; Psalm 108:3-5; Psalm 113:4-9
Themes: God the Father, Praise, Worship

> I will give thanks to Thee among the people.
> I will sing praises to Thee among the nations.
> For Thy steadfast love is great, is great to the heavens;
> And Thy faithfulness, Thy faithfulness to the clouds.
> Be exalted, O God, above the heavens;
> Let Thy glory be over all the earth.

BRENT CHAMBERS (B. 1955)
© 1977 Scripture in Song (c/o Integrity Music, ASCAP). All rights reserved. Used by permission.

BLESS THE LORD, O MY SOUL

Andrae Crouch's father was managing the family's cleaning business in east Los Angeles when he received a call to become the full-time pastor of a small church. The church didn't have too much to offer. In fact, it didn't even have someone who could play the piano. But he accepted the call.

One Sunday in church, as Andrae recalls it, "Dad called me up in front of the surprised congregation and asked me publicly that, if God would give me the gift of music, would I use it for the rest of my life to his glory?" When young Andrae said yes, his father prayed for him, and that's when his music ministry began. A woman donated a piano to the church, and Andrae began playing some old hymns by ear.

The church had no hymnals and no money to buy them, so Andrae started writing some easy-to-learn and easy-to-sing tunes. One of his earliest was "Bless the Lord, O My Soul," which is a paraphrase of Psalm 103.

Scriptures: Psalm 34:1; Psalm 103:1-2; Psalm 104:1
Themes: Worship, Praise, Prayer

Bless the Lord, O my soul, and all that is within me,
Bless His holy name.
He has done great things, He has done great things,
He has done great things, bless His holy name.
Bless the Lord, O my soul, and all that is within me,
Bless His holy name.

ANDRAE CROUCH (B. 1942)
© Bud John Music, Inc.
All rights reserved. Used by permission.

BLESSED BE THE LORD GOD ALMIGHTY

How would you like to be called by God to serve him in Hawaii? Well, Bob Fitts liked the sound of it, so he, his wife, and their one-year-old headed off to the island of Kona to work with Youth With a Mission. Although his job was to teach in YWAM's Discipleship Training School, Bob hoped he would have some time to write a few songs on the side.

The Fitts family hadn't counted on the poor quality of their housing. The only available housing was a small, run-down shack that had been built for coffee-bean pickers. In fact, the house was called a coffee shack.

It was a difficult situation for the entire family, and day by day they wondered how much more they could take. One Sunday, the local church asked Bob to provide music. Because he couldn't decide on any one piece, he decided to write something, and he wrote "Blessed Be the Lord God Almighty." But when he got up to sing, his mind went blank and he couldn't remember it. However, later that evening in the coffee shack, Bob recalled the tune and recorded it on cassette. Soon Youth With a Mission teams were taking that "coffee shack" tune around the world.

Scriptures: 2 Corinthians 1:3; Ephesians 1:3; Revelation 4:8
Themes: Praise, Worship, God the Father

Father in heaven, how we love You,
We lift Your name in all the earth.
May Your Kingdom be established in our praises
As your people declare Your mighty works.
Blessed be the Lord God Almighty,
Who was and is and is to come.

Blessed be the Lord God Almighty,
Who reigns forevermore.

BLESSED BE THE NAME

In ancient times, names were sacred. Names expressed character. Often we find Old Testament characters changing their names to reflect changes in their lives. Jacob ("the grabber") became Israel ("God's prince") after a divine encounter.

God's name is especially sacred. Ancient Israelite scribes revered the name of God, *Yahweh*, so much that they would not write it. Instead they would call him "Lord." Sometimes they referred to God as "The Name." One of the Ten Commandments is that people should not take the Lord's name in vain. Jesus echoed the idea in the Lord's Prayer: "May your name be kept holy." That is, your name is holy; we acknowledge that you are, by nature, holy.

When Isaiah predicted that the coming Redeemer would "be called Wonderful Counselor, Mighty God, Everlasting Father, Prince of Peace" (Isaiah 9:6, NIV), he was saying that this would be the Messiah's nature. Interesting, isn't it, that these titles are usually associated with different members of the Trinity? Three names, three natures, in one God. So when we bless God's name, we praise God for who he is.

Scriptures: Psalm 138:2; Isaiah 9:6; Philippians 2:9-10; Hebrews 1:3-4

Themes: Praise, Names of God, Worship

All praise to Him who reigns above
In majesty supreme,
Who gave His Son for man to die,
That He might man redeem!

Blessed be the name! blessed be the name!
Blessed be the name of the Lord!
Blessed be the name! blessed be the name!
Blessed be the name of the Lord!

His name above all names shall stand,
Exalted more and more,
At God the Father's own right hand,
Where angel hosts adore.

Redeemer, Savior, Friend of man
Once ruined by the fall,
Thou hast devised salvation's plan,
For Thou hast died for all.

His name shall be the Counselor,
The mighty Prince of Peace,
Of all earth's kingdoms Conqueror,
Whose reign shall never cease.

WILLIAM H. CLARK (19TH CENTURY)
Ralph E. Hudson (1843–1901), refrain

CHILDREN OF THE HEAVENLY KING

John Cennick was a most unlikely candidate to become a child of the heavenly King. He described himself: "My natural temper was obstinate, and my lips full of lies." When John was sixteen, God began working in his life, and for two years he struggled with the fear of going to hell. At eighteen, he began to see that Christ had accomplished his salvation on the cross. "I believed there was mercy for me. . . . I heard the voice of Jesus saying, 'I am thy salvation.' " Cennick was overwhelmed with joy.

After working as a land surveyor, Cennick became involved with the ministry of John and Charles Wesley, later becoming a Moravian minister. Perhaps he is best known today for his table grace: "Be present at our table, Lord." In a hymn that he wrote at the age of twenty-five, he said, "Who can have greater cause to bless, than we the children of the King, than we who Christ possess?" Yes, who indeed?

Scriptures: Romans 8:16-17; Ephesians 5:1; Colossians 3:1-4;
Themes: Praise, Discipleship, Joy

Children of the heavenly King,
As we journey let us sing;
Sing our Savior's worthy praise,
Glorious in His works and ways.

We are traveling home to God,
In the way our fathers trod;
They are happy now, and we
Soon their happiness shall see.

Fear not, brethren; joyful stand
On the borders of our land;
Jesus Christ, our Father's Son,
Bids us undismayed go on.

Lord, obediently we'll go,
Gladly leaving all below;
Only Thou our leader be,
And we still will follow Thee.

Lift your eyes, ye sons of light,
Zion's city is in sight;
There our endless home shall be,
There our Lord we soon shall see.

JOHN CENNICK (1718–1755)

COME, CHRISTIANS, JOIN TO SING

This hymn was originally written as a Sunday school song with the title
"Come, Children, Join to Sing." Since adults liked to sing it, too, the title
was changed to "Come, Christians, Join to Sing."

The words *alleluia* and *amen* are both from the Bible. We find *alleluia*
(or *hallelujah*) frequently in the Psalms. It means "praise the Lord." So
when the book of Psalms ends with "Praise the Lord," it is simply a translation of the Hebrew word *hallelujah*. According to some manuscripts
Revelation, the last book in the New Testament, ends with the word *amen*.
Amen means "assuredly," "indeed," or "so be it." We find *amen* at the end
of prayers, and that's the way we use it today. In the New Testament, we
also find it at the beginning of some of Jesus' statements. Different versions translate it as "verily," "truly," or "assuredly," but it's still *amen*.

The New Testament tells us that all the promises of God are *amen* in
Jesus Christ, and that is enough to make us sing both *alleluia* and *amen*.

Scriptures: Psalm 150; 2 Corinthians 1:20; Ephesians 5:17-20; Revelation 3:14

Themes: Praise, Joy, Resurrection

Come, Christians, join to sing, Alleluia! Amen!
Loud praise to Christ our King; Alleluia! Amen!
Let all, with heart and voice,
Before His throne rejoice;
Praise is His gracious choice: Alleluia! Amen!

Come, lift your hearts on high, Alleluia! Amen!
Let praises fill the sky; Alleluia! Amen!
He is our Guide and Friend;
To us He'll condescend;
His love shall never end: Alleluia! Amen!

Praise yet our Christ again, Alleluia! Amen!
Life shall not end the strain; Alleluia! Amen!
On heaven's blissful shore
His goodness we'll adore,
Singing forevermore, "Alleluia! Amen!"

CHRISTIAN H. BATEMAN (1813–1889)

COME, THOU ALMIGHTY KING

The author of this hymn is anonymous, probably for a good reason. The British national anthem, "God Save Our Gracious King," had just been written. The anthem quickly became popular throughout England. But the king was not popular among Methodists, who did not want to sing praises to their earthly king.

It is thought that Charles Wesley probably wrote the hymn "Come, Thou Almighty King" anonymously to set the priorities straight. It is the King of kings and Lord of lords who deserves our ultimate honor and complete allegiance. Presidents, kings, and other ruling officials should be honored and prayed for, but we must keep our priorities straight. There is an almighty King greater than any earthly ruler.

During the Revolutionary War, a company of British soldiers attended a church on Long Island. They demanded that the congregation sing "God Save Our Gracious King" to honor the king of England. The congregation sang the tune, but the words they used were from "Come, Thou Almighty King."

Scriptures: Psalm 24:7; Psalm 47:7; Psalm 95:1-3; Psalm 103:19; 1 Peter 2:13-15
Themes: Trinity, God the King, God's Majesty

Come, Thou Almighty King,
Help us Thy name to sing,
Help us to praise:
Father! all-glorious,
O'er all victorious,

Come, and reign over us,
Ancient of Days.

Come, Thou Incarnate Word,
Gird on Thy mighty sword,
Our prayer attend!
Come, and Thy people bless,
And give Thy word success:
Spirit of holiness,
On us descend.

Come, Holy Comforter,
Thy sacred witness bear
In this glad hour!
Thou, who almighty art,
Now rule in ev'ry heart
And ne'er from us depart,
Spirit of pow'r.

To Thee, great One in Three,
Eternal praises be,
Hence evermore;
Thy sov'reign majesty
May we in glory see,
And to eternity
Love and adore.

AUTHOR UNKNOWN

COME INTO HIS PRESENCE

While vacationing with his family in Sedona, Arizona, Lynn Baird decided to take a walk on one of the hiking trails that wind their way through the resort area. The verdant wilderness, the mountains, and the little streams put a song in his heart. Before long, he began singing a melody and then added some lyrics. He didn't know where the song came from—God must have given it to him. He hoped he would be able to find his way back to civilization to write it down before he forgot the words and music.

After he wrote it down, he wasn't sure the song was anything special, so he filed it away. About a year later, he played it for a friend. The friend liked the song so much that it was introduced to his church, and the congregation liked the song so much that they sang it almost every Sunday for six years.

Lynn Baird thought that only the people in his home church in Glendale, Arizona, knew about the song, until he heard a praise and worship tape put out by Integrity Music. His song was on the tape, and before long many people were singing "Come into His Presence."

Scriptures: Psalm 95:2; Psalm 100:2; Jeremiah 30:18-22
Themes: Worship, Prayer, Meditation

Come into His presence with thanksgiving in your heart
And give Him praise and give Him praise.
Come into His presence with thanksgiving in your heart
Your voices raise, your voices raise.
Give glory and honor and power unto Him.
Jesus, the name above all names.

LYNN BAIRD (B. 1952)
© 1988 Integrity's Hosanna! Music/ASCAP
All rights reserved. Used by permission.

CROWN HIM WITH MANY CROWNS

Matthew Bridges became a convert to Roman Catholicism at the age of forty-eight and published this hymn three years later under the title "The Song of the Seraphs." Godfrey Thring, an Anglican clergyman, added several stanzas to the hymn about thirty years later, with Bridges's approval. So a Roman Catholic layman and an Anglican cleric, who probably never met, were coauthors of a hymn about heaven, where Christians of every tribe and tongue and denomination will crown him Lord of all.

One aspect that Godfrey Thring felt was missing in the original hymn was a stanza on the Resurrection, and so he added "His glories now we sing / Who died and rose on high, / Who died, eternal life to bring, / And lives, that death may die."

At a large gathering at the Royal Albert Hall in London in 1905, the Bible Society was celebrating its centennial. Congratulatory messages were read from rulers of many lands, including Great Britain and the United States. Then the moderator of the meeting said, "Now that we have read these addresses from earthly rulers, let us turn our mind to the King of kings. We will sing, 'Crown Him with Many Crowns.'"

Scriptures: Romans 14:9; Hebrews 2:9; Revelation 19:11-13
Themes: Praise, Worship, Victory

Crown Him with many crowns,
The Lamb upon His throne;
Hark! how the heavenly anthem drowns
All music but its own.
Awake, my soul, and sing
Of Him who died for thee,
And hail Him as thy matchless King
Through all eternity.

Crown Him the Lord of life,
Who triumphed o'er the grave,
And rose victorious in the strife
For those He came to save;
His glories now we sing
Who died and rose on high,
Who died, eternal life to bring,
And lives, that death may die.

Crown Him the Lord of peace,
Whose power a scepter sways
From pole to pole, that wars may cease,
And all be prayer and praise;
His reign shall know no end,
And round His pierced feet
Fair flowers of paradise extend
Their fragrance ever sweet.

Crown Him the Lord of love;
Behold His hands and side,
Those wounds, yet visible above,
In beauty glorified.
All hail, Redeemer, hail!
For Thou hast died for me;
Thy praise and glory shall not fail
Throughout eternity.

MATTHEW BRIDGES (1800–1894)
Godfrey Thring (1823–1903)

FOR THE BEAUTY OF THE EARTH

Since Roman times, the town of Bath, on the banks of the Avon River in England, has been considered one of the most beautiful spots in the British Isles. Enclosed by an amphitheater of hills and blessed with warm springs, it has been both a pleasure resort and a health spa for the ailing.

Folliot Pierpoint, the author of this hymn, was born in Bath but left to attend Cambridge University, where he became a classical scholar. When he was twenty-nine years old, he returned to his hometown. The beauty of the countryside in the late spring caused his heart to well up with emotion and inspired this hymn.

Each stanza thanks God for a different kind of beauty. In its original form, "For the Beauty of the Earth" was a Communion hymn of eight stanzas. Each stanza concluded with the words "Christ our God, to Thee we raise / This our sacrifice of praise," alluding to Hebrews 13:15.

Scriptures: Psalm 96:1-6; Philippians 4:8; Hebrews 13:15; James 1:17
Themes: Praise, Creation, Joy

For the beauty of the earth,
For the glory of the skies,
For the love which from our birth
Over and around us lies:

Lord of all, to Thee we raise
This our hymn of grateful praise.

For the beauty of each hour
Of the day and of the night,
Hill and vale, and tree and flower,
Sun and moon, and stars of light:

For the joy of ear and eye,
For the heart and mind's delight,
For the mystic harmony
Linking sense to sound and sight:

For the joy of human love,
Brother, sister, parent, child,
Friends on earth, and friends above;
For all gentle thoughts and mild:

For Thy church, that evermore
Lifteth holy hands above,
Offering up on every shore
Her pure sacrifice of love:

For Thyself, best Gift Divine!
To our race so freely given;
For that great, great love of Thine,
Peace on earth, and joy in heaven:

FOLLIOT SANFORD PIERPOINT (1835–1917)

GLORIFY THY NAME

Donna Adkins began singing in public when she was two years old. How did that happen? Her parents were traveling gospel singers, so she was introduced very early to singing in churches. "Glorify Thy Name," however, was written years later when she was thirty-five and had two children of her own.

She and her family had just moved to northern Louisiana. Family moves are always stressful, but Donna looked at the move as a time to start fresh, not just in a new church and a new community, but also with the Lord. She looked at it, she says, "as a needed change of pace and time for me to seek the Lord." She had been reading John 17, which contains Christ's high priestly prayer. The words *glory* and *glorify* (KJV) appear five times in the first five verses.

From those verses she wrote this simple worship chorus which glorifies the Father, Son, and Holy Spirit in successive verses.

Scriptures: John 17:1-5; Romans 15:6; 1 Corinthians 6:20; 2 Thessalonians 1:11-12

Themes: Worship, Praise, Trinity

DONNA ADKINS (B. 1940)

GOD OF THE EARTH, THE SKY, THE SEA

Samuel Longfellow, brother of the famous poet Henry Wadsworth Longfellow, loved nature, especially the seashore. He once compiled a book that included "all the charming bits of poetry in the language about the sea and the seashore."

Like many of the Psalms, this hymn praises God for his involvement in nature. Paul wrote that the invisible qualities of God are clearly seen in what God has created. Longfellow echoes Paul's message here. God's love, life, power, and even his law are seen in the events of nature.

Scriptures: Job 12:10, 13, 22; Psalm 96:11; Romans 1:20
Themes: Creation, God's Omnipotence, Peace

God of the earth, the sky, the sea,
Maker of all above, below,
Creation lives and moves in Thee,
Thy present life through all doth flow.

Thy love is in the sunshine's glow,
Thy life is in the quickening air;
When lightnings flash and storm winds blow,
There is Thy power; Thy law is there.

We feel Thy calm at evening's hour,
Thy grandeur in the march of night;
And when the morning breaks in power,
We hear Thy word, "Let there be light!"

But higher far, and far more clear,
Thee in man's spirit we behold;
Thine image and Thyself are there,
Th'indwelling God, proclaimed of old.

SAMUEL LONGFELLOW (1819–1892)

GREAT IS THE LORD

Michael W. Smith has come a long way since leaving his little hometown of Kenova, West Virginia. The son of an oil refinery worker and a caterer, Michael became a Christian when he was ten, but after high school he turned to drugs and alcohol. When he went to Nashville, he continued the same lifestyle while playing in local bands. At the age of twenty-two, he had an emotional breakdown, but during this time he renewed his commitment to Jesus Christ.

Good things started to happen. As a result of contact with Christian musicians, he began writing Christian music. Then he met Debbie Davis, who became his wife and songwriting partner. Before writing a song, Michael and Debbie read the Bible together and pray. Since Michael works best at night, and since they now have five children, they sometimes use a candle to give them some needed light. That was the setting when they wrote "Great Is the Lord." Debbie, the writer, concentrated on the lyrics, and Michael, the musician, on the music. The song, written in the early 1980s, emphasizes the attributes of God: his holiness; his justice; his power; his love; his faithfulness; his truth; and his mercy. Yes, truly, he is worthy of our praise.

Scriptures: Job 5:9; Psalm 96:4; Psalm 145:3; Romans 11:33

Themes: God the Father, Praise, God's Power

Great is the Lord, He is holy and just;
By His power we trust in His love.
Great is the Lord, He is faithful and true;
By His mercy He proves He is love.

Great is the Lord and worthy of glory!
Great is the Lord and worthy of praise.
Great is the Lord; now lift up your voice,
Now lift up your voice: Great is the Lord! Great is the Lord.

DEBORAH D. SMITH (B. 1958)/MICHAEL W. SMITH (B. 1957)
© Meadowgreen Music Company
All rights reserved. Used by permission.

HE IS EXALTED

Twila Paris, the author of this song, made her first recording, "Little Twila Paris," when she was only four years old. As she grew older, she began asking questions about God's will for her life. She knew she could sing, but she wondered if this was really what God wanted her to do.

After high school she joined a Youth With a Mission drama and music team. As the group toured the country, her singing was very well received. But she continued questioning. She says, "I had to come to the place where I was able to say, 'God, if you don't want me to have a career in music, that's okay.'" She examined her priorities and determined that

Christ had to be exalted in everything she wrote or sang. She felt the Lord wanted her to emphasize worship, praise, and missions. And that is exactly what she did in her song, "He Is Exalted."

Scriptures: Psalm 34:3; Psalm 46:10; Exodus 15:2
Themes: Worship, Praise, God the Father

> He is exalted, the King is exalted on high, I will praise Him.
> He is exalted, forever exalted and I will praise His name.
> He is the Lord, forever His truth shall reign.
> Heaven and earth rejoice in His holy name.
> He is exalted, the King is exalted on high.

TWILA PARIS (B. 1958)
©Mountain Spring Music/Straightway Music. All rights reserved. Used by permission.

HIS MATCHLESS WORTH

As a sailor in the British Royal Navy, Samuel Medley had been leading a life of sin and debauchery. He was seriously wounded in a naval battle, and not long after that he was converted.

Medley became a pastor and soon was called to a Baptist church in the major British port city of Liverpool. Because Medley understood the sea and the people who made their living from overseas commerce, his congregation grew, and soon a much larger building had to be built.

But his goal as a minister was not in getting a larger building; it was in exalting the grace of God. This hymn is a good example. Originally it was called "Praise of Jesus," and that is exactly what it is. Medley talks about Jesus from the beginning, where he mentions Christ's matchless worth, to the end, where he talks about Jesus as our Savior, Brother, and Friend. No one and no thing compares with Jesus.

Scriptures: Psalm 73:25; Romans 8:18; Colossians 1:15-20; Colossians 2:9-10
Themes: Jesus Christ, Deity of Christ, Worship

> O could I speak the matchless worth,
> O could I sound the glories forth which in my Savior shine,
> I'd soar and touch the heavenly strings,
> And vie with Gabriel while he sings
> In notes almost divine, in notes almost divine.

I'd sing the precious blood He spilt,
My ransom from the dreadful guilt of sin, and wrath divine;
I'd sing His glorious righteousness,
In which all-perfect heavenly dress
My soul shall ever shine, my soul shall ever shine.

I'd sing the characters He bears,
And all the forms of love He wears, exalted on His throne;
In loftiest songs of sweetest praise,
I would to everlasting days
Make all His glories known, make all His glories known.

Well, the delightful day will come
When my dear Lord will bring me home, and I shall see His face;
Then with my Savior, Brother, Friend,
A blest eternity I'll spend,
Triumphant in His grace, triumphant in His grace.

SAMUEL MEDLEY (1738–1799)

HOLY GOD, WE PRAISE THY NAME

Any hymn with roots that go as far back as "Holy God, We Praise Thy Name" usually has some legends connected to it, so it is difficult to know the hymn's accurate history. Our version of the hymn is directly traced to eighteenth-century Germany, but the original text is much older. It is a paraphrase of the "Te Deum" of the fourth century, a hymn of praise to God apparently written by Ambrose, the bishop of Milan, around A.D. 387.

One story says that it was written when Augustine was baptized by Ambrose. Some scholars now feel that it was written by a fourth-century missionary bishop, Niceta, in what is now in the Balkan region.

Whatever its origin, Christians have been singing versions of this hymn for more than 1,600 years. The English hymn was produced by Clarence Walworth, a Roman Catholic priest from Albany, New York, who translated it from an Austrian hymnal that had been published nearly a hundred years earlier.

Scriptures: 1 Chronicles 29:11; Psalm 113:1-4; Revelation 15:3
Themes: Praise, Trinity, Worship

Holy God, we praise Thy name;
Lord of all, we bow before Thee;
All on earth Thy scepter claim,
All in heaven above adore Thee.
Infinite Thy vast domain,
Everlasting is Thy reign.

Hark, the glad celestial hymn,
Angel choirs above are raising;
Cherubim and seraphim,
In unceasing chorus praising,
Fill the heavens with sweet accord:
Holy, holy, holy Lord.

Lo! the apostolic train
Joins Thy sacred name to hallow;
Prophets swell the glad refrain,
And the white-robed martyrs follow,
And from morn to set of sun,
Through the church the song goes on.

Holy Father, holy Son,
Holy Spirit: Three we name Thee,
Though in essence only One;
Undivided God we claim Thee,
And adoring bend the knee
While we own the mystery.

ATTRIBUTED TO IGNACE FRANZ (1719–1790)
Translated by Clarence Walworth (1820–1900)

HOSANNA, LOUD HOSANNA

The author of this hymn, Jeannette Threlfall, did not have an ideal child-hood by any means. She was left an orphan, was disabled by an accident, and became a permanent invalid. Jeannette spent most of her life in the homes of relatives, yet her poems and hymns show joy and cheerfulness. You could say that her entire life was a cry of hosanna to her victorious Savior.

In this hymn, she emphasizes the praise of little children on Palm Sunday. The crowd following Jesus were waving palms and singing, "Hosanna!" Apparently the children were exuberant in their praise. The leaders asked Jesus to tell the children to stop such singing. "Do you hear what these children are saying?" they asked Jesus. "Yes," Jesus said, quoting Psalm 8:2, "From the lips of children and infants you have ordained praise" (NIV).

Scriptures: Psalm 8:2; Matthew 21:5-16; John 12:12-13
Themes: Palm Sunday, Praise, Children

Hosanna, loud hosanna
The little children sang;
Through pillared court and temple
The lovely anthem rang;
To Jesus, who had blessed them
Close folded to His breast,
The children sang their praises,
The simplest and the best.

From Olivet they followed
Mid an exultant crowd,
The victor palm branch waving,
And chanting clear and loud;
The Lord of men and angels
Rode on in lowly state,
Nor scorned that little children
Should on His bidding wait.

"Hosanna in the highest!"
That ancient song we sing,
For Christ is our Redeemer,
The Lord of heaven our King.
O may we ever praise Him
With heart and life and voice,
And in His blissful presence
Eternally rejoice!

JEANNETTE THRELFALL (1821–1880)

HOW EXCELLENT IS THY NAME

In Christian contemporary music circles, there are several husband and wife songwriting teams. One such team is Dick and Melodie Tunney, who met while singing with a touring group called Truth. Melodie—whom most people call Mel—was working on a composition in a church classroom when Dick walked in. Dick gave her some suggestions for her song, and although that is sometimes enough to end a friendship, Mel accepted his ideas. Their friendship started, and before long they were married.

About a year after their wedding, they were invited to a cabin on a lake for a fish fry. Afterward, their host, Paul Smith, gave the Tunneys some half-finished lyrics. On their way home, Mel thought about how music she had written several weeks earlier but didn't have any words for might fit. The music fit perfectly with Paul Smith's words, and "How Excellent Is Thy Name" was complete.

Scriptures: Psalm 8:9; Psalm 36:7; Psalm 148:13; Isaiah 12:5
Themes: Worship, Praise, Glory

How excellent is Thy name, O Lord, how excellent is Thy name;
Heaven and earth together proclaim, how excellent is Thy name.
(Repeat.)
I look into the midnight blue and see the work You've done.
Your children raise a perfect praise while enemies hold their tongue.
Creation shows Your splendor, Your reigning majesty
And I find You take the time to care for one like me.
How excellent is Thy name.
One fine day when the trumpets play and the dead in Christ will rise,
The chosen few will gather to proclaim You, Lord most high!
With joyful hallelujahs, the heavenly host will sing;
Ev'ry knee shall bow, ev'ry tongue will shout,
You're the King of kings.
How excellent is Thy name, O Lord, how excellent is Thy name;
Heaven and earth together proclaim how excellent is Thy name.
(Repeat the last 2 lines.)
How excellent is Thy name!

PAUL SMITH/DICK TUNNEY/MELODIE TUNNEY

HOW GREAT THOU ART

In 1885, Carl Boberg, a twenty-six-year-old preacher, wrote a poem titled in Swedish, "*O Store Gud.*" Translated into English, it's "O Great God." Boberg had no thought of his poem's becoming a hymn, so a few years later he was surprised to hear his poem sung to the tune of an old Swedish melody.

A generation later, in the early 1920s, English missionaries Stuart Hine and his wife were ministering in Poland, where they learned the Russian version of Boberg's poem sung to the Swedish melody. Later, Hine created English words for it and arranged the Swedish melody to fit. This is the hymn we now know as "How Great Thou Art."

The first three stanzas were inspired by an experience Stuart Hine had as he ministered in the Carpathian mountains and heard the mighty thunder echoing all around him. As he pushed on, he was deeply impressed by the beauty of the woods and forest glades as well as the singing of the birds. The fourth stanza came after he returned to England.

The song became popular in America in the 1950s, and before long it was the number-one hymn on both sides of the Atlantic.

Scriptures: Deuteronomy 3:24; Job 38:1-7; Psalm 8:1-4; Isaiah 40:26; Romans 1:20
Themes: Worship, Creation, Praise

O Lord my God! When I in awesome wonder
Consider all the worlds Thy hands have made,
I see the stars, I hear the rolling thunder,
Thy power throughout the universe displayed,

Then sings my soul, My Savior, God, to Thee:
How great Thou art! How great Thou art!
Then sings my soul, My Savior, God, to Thee;
How great Thou art! How great Thou art!

When through the woods and forest glades I wander
And hear the birds sing sweetly in the trees,
When I look down from lofty mountain grandeur
And hear the brook and feel the gentle breeze,

And when I think that God, His Son not sparing,
Sent Him to die, I scarce can take it in;
That on the cross, my burden gladly bearing,
He bled and died to take away my sin,

When Christ shall come with shout of acclamation
And take me home, what joy shall fill my heart!
Then I shall bow in humble adoration
And there proclaim, my God, how great Thou art!

STUART K. HINE (1899–1989)

HOW LOVELY SHINES THE MORNING STAR

When Philipp Nicolai was pastor in Unna, Germany, an awful plague hit the town. His window overlooked the cemetery. There were sometimes as many as thirty burials in a single day. In six months he had buried 1,300 people. It seemed that every home in town was mourning a stricken family member. It was a difficult time to be a pastor. How did he get through it?

He gave his answer this way: "There seemed to me nothing more sweet, delightful, and agreeable than the contemplation of the noble, sublime doctrine of Eternal Life obtained through the Blood of Christ. This I allowed to dwell in my heart day and night. . . . Death is not to be feared because death is when we meet our Bridegroom, Jesus Christ. Christ enlarges our scope of vision. We serve Him as much as possible here on earth, but there's another chapter to come, an eternal existence in heaven with Him."

Scriptures: Matthew 4:13-16; Philippians 1:21-26; Revelation 22:16
Themes: Praise, Worship, Names of God

How lovely shines the Morning Star!
The nations see and hail afar
The light in Judah shining.
Thou David's Son of Jacob's race,
My Bridegroom and my King of Grace,
For Thee my heart is pining.
Lowly, Holy, Great and glorious,
Thou victorious Prince of graces,
Filling all the heav'nly places.

Now richly to my waiting heart,
O Thou, my God, deign to impart
The grace of love undying.
In Thy blest body let me be,
E'en as the branch is in the tree,
Thy life my life supplying.
Sighing, crying, for the savor
Of Thy favor; resting never
Till I rest in Thee forever.

Thou, mighty Father, in Thy Son
Didst love me ere Thou hadst begun
This ancient world's foundation.
Thy Son hath made a friend of me,
And when in spirit Him I see,
I joy in tribulation.
What bliss is this! He that liveth
To me giveth Life forever;
Nothing me from Him can sever.

PHILIPP NICOLAI (1556–1608)
Composite Translation

I EXALT THEE

At the age of twenty-six, Pete Sanchez had already been a music director, a youth director, and a musician with a Christian group called One Song. All that was good and exciting, but Pete was newly married and carried baggage, having come from a divorced family.

So he felt the best thing to do was to make sure he was a good husband and father. He withdrew from active ministry and began studying Psalms. He decided that as he meditated on each psalm, he would write a song about it. One day, he came to Psalm 97:9: "For thou, LORD, art high above all the earth: thou art exalted far above all gods" (KJV). It seemed powerful to him, and he went to his piano and played a bit of it. But it didn't seem finished.

For the next eighteen months, Pete kept coming back to the opening lines of his song, "For Thou, O Lord, art high above all the earth," before God gave him the remainder of the song. He says, "The only way I can explain it is that, in a moment, it seemed like I stepped into another place. . . . It was a divine encounter." And the chorus came: "I exalt Thee."

Pete said later, "That song came out of my hunger to be in the Scripture and write something just for the Lord." Well, it seems that the Lord wanted it to be shared with others.

Scriptures: Exodus 18:11; Psalm 95:3; Psalm 97:9; Isaiah 25:1
Themes: Praise, Worship, God the Father

> For Thou, O Lord, art high above all the earth;
> Thou art exalted far above all gods. (Repeat.)
> I exalt Thee, I exalt Thee, I exalt Thee O Lord. (Repeat.)

PETE SANCHEZ JR. (B. 1948)
© 1977 Pete Sanchez, Jr. (Admin. by Gabriel Music Inc.)

I LOVE YOU, LORD

Laurie and Bill Klein had just moved to Oregon with their one-year-old child. Bill was studying forest technology at Central Oregon Community College, and Laurie was cooped up in a mobile home with their baby. Together they were trying to make it on $400 a month. Laurie describes it: "With no friends, money, church home, or driver's license, the days I spent with our one-year-old seemed endless. I was lonely. It was a hopeless time, a very depressed time. I felt the poverty of my own life, both emotionally and physically."

The only person she could talk to was the Lord, and she did plenty of that. Laurie says, "One extra lonely morning I found myself praying, 'Lord, I want to worship you. I'm just so empty inside. Please give me something to sing that you would enjoy hearing.' " She picked up her guitar, and the words and music to the chorus "I Love You, Lord" seemed to come effortlessly. *Maybe I should write these words down,* she thought. We're glad she did.

Scriptures: Psalm 18:1; Psalm 31:23-24; Psalm 47:6-7
Themes: Love, Worship, Praise

LAURIE BRENDEMUEHL KLEIN (B. 1950)

I SING PRAISES TO YOUR NAME

Most people would be nervous about singing in front of a thousand people, but not Terry MacAlmon—not usually. However, this night was different. He was the worship pastor of a large and growing church in Loveland, Colorado, and he and the other staff members met together for prayer before the evening service. In addition to the prayer time together, each person had some quiet time for himself or herself.

It was in this quiet time that Terry softly started to sing a song he had never sung before. He grabbed an offering envelope and jotted down the words as they came to him, and before he left the prayer room, he had written the words to the entire song.

But when he got in front of the congregation of nearly a thousand people, he wasn't sure what he should do with the new song. It seemed that the Lord wanted him to use it, yet he felt (or maybe it was the devil prompting him) the song wasn't ready yet. He hadn't practiced it, and it seemed too simple. Maybe the Lord didn't want Terry to share it with a thousand people. For an embarrassing amount of time, he sat at the piano debating whether to introduce this new and untried song. Finally he told the congregation, "I want to share with you a little chorus. It's called 'I Sing Praises to Your Name.'"

Scriptures: Psalm 9:2; Psalm 18:49; Psalm 68:4
Themes: Praise, Worship, Jesus Christ

I sing praises to Your name, O Lord, praises to Your name O Lord,
For Your name is great and greatly to be praised.
I sing praises to Your name, O Lord, praises to Your name, O Lord,
For Your name is great and greatly to be praised.

I give glory to Your name, O Lord, glory to Your name, O Lord,
For Your name is great and greatly to be praised.
I give glory to Your name, O Lord, glory to Your name, O Lord,
For Your name is great and greatly to be praised.

TERRY MACALMON
© 1989 by Integrity's Hosanna! Music/ASCAP
All rights reserved. Used by permission.

I SING THE MIGHTY POWER OF GOD

Isaac Watts loved children, and he loved the childhood years. As a child, he was precocious. He learned Latin when he was four, Greek when he was eight or nine, French when he was eleven, and Hebrew when he was thirteen. As an adult, he not only wrote books on theology, but on psychology, logic, and astronomy as well. He also wrote a book of children's songs, which included this hymn, although today it is considered a hymn for adults.

His *Divine and Moral Songs for Children* was the first hymnal ever written for children, and it remained popular for more than a hundred years. One song, "Against Quarreling and Fighting," says, "Let dogs delight to bark and bite, for God hath made them so. Let bears and lions growl and fight, for 'tis their nature to. But children, you should never let such angry passions rise. Your little hands were never made to tear each other's eyes."

The first lesson a child should learn is a lesson that adults should never forget: The great God who created this vast universe loves us and keeps us in his care. "I Sing the Mighty Power of God" teaches that lesson.

Scriptures: Job 38:8-11; Psalm 95:3-6; Matthew 7:25-34
Themes: Creation, God's Care, Comfort

I sing the mighty pow'r of God,
That made the mountains rise;
That spread the flowing seas abroad,
And built the lofty skies.
I sing the wisdom that ordained
The sun to rule the day;
The moon shines full at His command,
And all the stars obey.

I sing the goodness of the Lord,
That filled the earth with food;
He formed the creatures with His Word,
And then pronounced them good.
Lord, how Thy wonders are displayed,
Where e're I turn my eye;
If I survey the ground I tread,
Or gaze upon the sky!

There's not a plant or flow'r below,
But makes Thy glories known:

And clouds arise, and tempests blow,
By order from Thy throne;
While all that borrows life from Thee
Is ever in Thy care.
And ev'rywhere that man can be,
Thou, God, art present there.

ISAAC WATTS (1674–1748)

I STAND IN AWE OF YOU

When he was in his teens and early twenties, Mark Altrogge thought of making rock-and-roll music as a career. If the Beatles could do it, why couldn't he? But when, at the age of twenty-four, he became a Christian, he realized that he would have to surrender himself totally to Jesus Christ. Now, his attention was fixed, not on the Beatles, but on the holiness of God, and he was reading books like *The Knowledge of the Holy* by A. W. Tozer and *The Holiness of God* by R. C. Sproul.

God is infinite, and Mark says, "We will never come to an end of learning new things about him." Thinking about the greatness of God, Mark sat down with his guitar and tried to put some of his thoughts into music. Gradually the song was born. He says, " 'I Stand in Awe' was born out of the emotional impact that the doctrine of God's holiness had on me."

Scriptures: Psalm 99:3, 9; Psalm 111:9; 1 Peter 1:15-16

Themes: Worship, God the Father, Holiness of God

You are beautiful beyond description, too marvelous for words,
Too wonderful for comprehension, like nothing ever seen or heard.
Who can grasp Your infinite wisdom?
Who can fathom the depth of Your love?
You are beautiful beyond description, majesty enthroned above.
And I stand, I stand in awe of You,
I stand, I stand in awe of You.
Holy God to whom all praise is due, I stand in awe of You,
I stand in awe of You.

MARK ALTROGGE (B. 1950)

JESUS, NAME ABOVE ALL NAMES

When Naida Hearn of Palmerton, New Zealand, went to do her family's wash, she had to go out to the "wash house" behind their home. One December, Naida was making a list of all the names of Christ that she knew, some from the Old Testament and some from the New Testament.

One day as she went out in the back to do her wash, she took that list with her and placed the list on the windowsill so she could meditate on it as she was doing the wash. As she thought about the list, Naida started singing. She said that the Lord gave her the first line, "Jesus, name above all names," and the rest came as she continued singing.

When Naida finished singing, she thought she had better write the song down before she forgot it, so she interrupted her wash, went back inside, and sat down at her piano to write it out. While she wrote it down, she asked the Lord, "Is that okay, Lord? Is it all right like that?" She thought she felt God saying that it was fine as it was. Naida said, "That was all I wrote, and then I went back to the washing. It was just that simple."

Scriptures: Isaiah 9:6; Matthew 1:23; Philippians 2:9-10
Themes: Jesus Christ, Prophecy, Messiah

> Jesus, name above all names, beautiful Savior, glorious Lord.
> Emmanuel, God is with us, blessed Redeemer, living Word.
>
> NAIDA HEARN (1931–2001)
> © 1974 by Scripture in Song.
> (c/o Integrity Music)/ASCAP. All rights reserved. Used by permission.

JOIN ALL THE GLORIOUS NAMES

Isaac Watts originally wrote twelve stanzas for this hymn, including seventeen different names for Christ. Watts wrote several hymns on the same theme, but his final analysis was, "Earth is too narrow to express His worth, His glory, or His grace."

Another of his hymns—this one with nineteen verses—starts each stanza with a question: "Is He a Rose?" "Is He a Vine?" After eighteen stanzas, Watts concludes, "His beauties we can never trace till we behold Him face to face."

And yet another of his hymns begins, " 'Tis from the treasure of His Word I borrow titles for my Lord. Nor art, nor nature, can supply sufficient forms of majesty." Watts understood that no matter how many titles he might ascribe to Jesus Christ, all of them together would still be inadequate to express his greatness.

Scriptures: Psalm 72:19; Acts 4:12; Ephesians 1:18-21
Themes: Names of Jesus, Praise, Savior

Join all the glorious names
Of wisdom, love, and pow'r,
That ever mortals knew,
That angels ever bore:
All are too poor to speak His worth,
Too poor to set my Savior forth.

Great Prophet of my God,
My tongue would bless Thy name:
By Thee the joyful news
Of our salvation came,
The joyful news of sins forgiv'n,
Of hell subdued and peace with heav'n.

Jesus, my great High Priest,
Offered His blood, and died;
My guilty conscience seeks
No sacrifice beside:
His pow'rful blood did once atone
And now it pleads before the throne.

Thou art my Counselor,
My Pattern, and my Guide,
And Thou my Shepherd art;
O keep me near Thy side;
Nor let my feet e'er turn astray
To wander in the crooked way.

My Savior and my Lord,
My Conqu'ror and my King,
Thy sceptre and Thy sword,
Thy reigning grace, I sing:
Thine is the pow'r; behold I sit
In willing bonds beneath Thy feet.

ISAAC WATTS (1674–1748)

JOYFUL, JOYFUL, WE ADORE THEE

Henry van Dyke was serving as a guest preacher at Williams College, in the Berkshire Mountains of Massachusetts, when he was so moved by the beauty of God's creation that he wrote this hymn of joy. The next morning he handed the poem to the college president. "Here is a hymn for you," he said. "Your mountains were my inspiration. It must be sung to the music of Beethoven's 'Hymn to Joy.' " And it has been ever since.

Van Dyke was not only a Presbyterian minister, but he was also the author of many books, including the best-selling *The Other Wise Man.* He was a professor of literature at Princeton University, navy chaplain during World War I, and an ambassador to Holland and Luxembourg under President Woodrow Wilson.

When van Dyke published this hymn in 1911, he noted that it was to be sung by people who "are not afraid that any truth of science will destroy their religion or that any revolution on earth will overthrow the kingdom of heaven." With such confidence, Christians have much to rejoice about.

Scriptures: Psalm 98; Habakkuk 3:17-19; Philippians 4:4-7
Themes: Creation, Joy, Praise

Joyful, joyful, we adore Thee,
God of glory, Lord of love;
Hearts unfold like flowers before Thee,
Opening to the sun above.
Melt the clouds of sin and sadness;
Drive the dark of doubt away;
Giver of immortal gladness,
Fill us with the light of day!

All Thy works with joy surround Thee,
Earth and heav'n reflect Thy rays,
Stars and angels sing around Thee,
Center of unbroken praise;
Field and forest, vale and mountain,
Flowery meadow, flashing sea,
Chanting bird and flowing fountain,
Call us to rejoice in Thee.

Thou art giving and forgiving,
Ever blessing, ever blest,

Wellspring of the joy of living,
Ocean depth of happy rest!
Thou our Father, Christ our brother,
All who live in love are Thine;
Teach us how to love each other,
Lift us to the joy divine.

Mortals join the mighty chorus,
Which the morning stars began;
Father love is reigning o'er us,
Brother love binds man to man.
Ever singing, march we onward,
Victors in the midst of strife;
Joyful music leads us sunward
In the triumph song of life.

HENRY VAN DYKE (1852–1933)

LET ALL THE WORLD

George Herbert was a renowned seventeenth-century poet whose poetry has been included in British literature texts with Shakespeare's and Milton's works. He was also a minister of the gospel and a musician.

A biographer wrote about Herbert: "He would write his own hymns to the accompaniment of the violin or lute; and at least twice a week he would walk the twelve miles or so to Salisbury Cathedral. Before returning home, he would spend a happy hour with musical friends, song, lute, and strings."

Herbert died before he was forty years old, and on his deathbed, he handed a manuscript to his lawyer, asking him to pass it along to his brother. Herbert suggested that his brother read the manuscript and publish it "if he thought it would be of advantage to any soul—if not, to burn it."

That manuscript contained some of Herbert's greatest works, including this simple, yet profound hymn.

Scriptures: Psalm 97:1; Psalm 148:11-13; Isaiah 52:10
Themes: Worship, Joy, Creation

Let all the world in every corner sing, "My God and King!"
The heavens are not too high, His praise may thither fly;

The earth is not too low, His praises there may grow,
Let all the world in every corner sing, "My God and King!"

Let all the world in every corner sing, "My God and King.!"
The Church with psalms must shout, No door can keep them out;
But above all, the heart must bear the longest part.
Let all the world in every corner sing, "My God and King!"
GEORGE HERBERT (1593–1633)

LOOK YE SAINTS, THE SIGHT IS GLORIOUS

Thomas Kelly, the author of this hymn, was a remarkable man. The son of a judge, he was studying law at the University of Dublin when he had a strong conversion experience. Kelly served for a while in the Anglican church, but when he fell out of favor, he became an independent minister. Although he was a forceful preacher, the people of Ireland knew him most of all because of his generous spirit.

During Ireland's potato famine of 1847, the story of a man comforting his wife was told: "Hold up, Bridget. There's always Mr. Kelly to pull us out of the bog, after we've sunk for the last time."

Yes, Kelly could always be counted on to pull up someone else, but most of all he was interested in lifting up Jesus Christ, as he did in this wonderful hymn on the ascension of Jesus Christ.

Scriptures: Acts 1:9-11; Acts 2:32-33; Philippians 2:9-11
Themes: Deity of Christ, Worship, Return of Christ

Look, ye saints! The sight is glorious; see the Man of Sorrows now;
From the fight returned victorious, ev'ry knee to Him shall bow:
Crown Him! Crown Him! Crowns become the Victor's brow.

Crown the Savior! Angels, crown Him! Rich the trophies Jesus brings;
In the seat of pow'r enthrone Him, while the vault of heaven rings:
Crown Him! Crown Him! Crown the Savior King of kings.

Hark! Those bursts of acclamation! Hark! Those loud triumphant chords!
Jesus takes the highest station—O what joy the sight affords!
Crown Him! Crown Him! King of kings and Lord of lords!
THOMAS KELLY (1769–1855)

LORD, I LIFT YOUR NAME ON HIGH

Rick Founds wanted to major in music at college, but his high school choral teacher talked him out of it. Instead, he got a degree in media technology and began working in research and development at a fiber optics company.

When Rick wrote "Lord, I Lift Your Name on High," he was studying the attributes of God on his electronic Bible. The Lord was bringing all of Rick's gifts and talents together: his interest in technology, his love of music, and his desire to know more of the Lord.

As he marveled at the love of God, he was struck by the divine plan. It was a cycle of events that amazed him, something like the rain that comes down, waters the earth, evaporates into the clouds, and comes again. Likewise Christ came down from heaven to earth, lived among us, died on the cross for us, rose from the dead, and ascended back to heaven to be with his Father. And he is coming again. That is why Rick Founds wrote "Lord, I Lift Your Name on High."

Scriptures: Psalm 145:1-4; John 1:14; Philippians 2:6-11
Themes: Praise, Gospel, Jesus Christ

AUTHOR: RICK FOUNDS

MAJESTIC SWEETNESS SITS ENTHRONED

For nearly fifty years, Samuel Stennett was a pastor of the Baptist Church on Little Wild Street in London. Isn't that a great location for a church— Little Wild Street? His father had been the minister on Little Wild Street before him.

Within five years of taking the pulpit, his reputation was known across England. Though Baptists were not highly regarded, King George III became a friend and admirer. Government leaders joined Stennett's congregation. Offers came from larger churches, but Samuel Stennett did not want to leave, nor did his congregation let him leave.

He wrote nearly forty hymns, but the one for which he is best known is "Majestic Sweetness Sits Enthroned," which is based on the verse in Song of Songs where the Lover is described as "better than ten thousand others."

Scriptures: Song of Songs 5:10-16; Colossians 1:15-18; Hebrews 1:1-3
Themes: Worship, Deity of Christ, Submission

Majestic sweetness sits enthroned
Upon the Savior's brow;
His head with radiant glories crowned,
His lips with grace o'erflow,
His lips with grace o'erflow.

No mortal can with Him compare
Among the sons of men;
Fairer is He than all the fair
Who fill the heav'nly train,
Who fill the heav'nly train.

He saw me plunged in deep distress,
And flew to my relief;
For me He bore the shameful cross
And carried all my grief,
And carried all my grief.

To Him I owe my life and breath
And all the joys I have;
He makes me triumph over death
And saves me from the grave,
And saves me from the grave.

SAMUEL STENNETT (1727–1795)

MAJESTY

Jack and Anna Hayford were vacationing in England in 1977, the year that the country was celebrating the twenty-fifth anniversary of Queen Elizabeth's coronation. Everywhere they traveled, from the south country to the northern parts of Scotland, they noticed the symbols of royalty. But it was after their visit to Blenheim Castle, where Winston Churchill had been born, that Jack Hayford began to think that if we are awestruck by the royalty of earthly kings, how much more should we be in awe of the King of kings.

Pastor Hayford, from Van Nuys, California, then recalls, "As Anna and I drove along together, at once the opening lyrics and melody of 'Majesty' simply came to my heart. I seemed to feel something new of what it meant to be His—to be raised to a partnership with Him on His throne."

When the Hayfords returned to California, he completed the song. He said in his mind "it was not only a description of the gloriously regal nature of our Savior, but also a statement that our worship can align us with His throne so that His kingdom authority flows to us and through us."

Scriptures: Psalm 8:1; Colossians 1:15-17; Hebrews 1:3; Revelation 4:11
Themes: Worship, Deity of Christ, Kingdom of God

Majesty, worship His majesty—
Unto Jesus be all glory, power and praise—
Majesty, kingdom authority flow from His throne
Unto His own, His anthem raise.
So exalt, lift up on high the name of Jesus;
Magnify, come glorify, Christ Jesus, the King.
Majesty, worship His majesty—
Jesus who died, now glorified, King of all kings.

JACK HAYFORD (B. 1934)
© 1980 New Spring (ASCAP)
All rights reserved. Used by permission.

MORE PRECIOUS THAN SILVER

What would you do if you worked at McDonald's, were on a fast, and had been assigned to "fryer duty"? All day long, you will be staring at buckets of potatoes. That was the challenge for Lynn DeShazo.

Lynn, who had just graduated from Auburn University, felt that the Lord wanted her to work on praise and worship music as well as learn something about spiritual disciplines. One of those spiritual disciplines was fasting.

Working at McDonald's when you are fasting is a challenge in itself, but when you have buckets of potatoes in front of you, it's nearly impossible. As the day went on, the temptation grew stronger and stronger. "I began to meditate on those fries," she said. Then, glancing around to see if anyone was looking, she grabbed two fries and gulped them down.

Lynn felt very guilty all the way home. She asked the Lord for forgiveness for not being strong enough to resist the temptation, and for some reason, the Lord put in her mind two verses of Scripture. One was

Colossians 2:3, which says that in Christ are "hidden all the treasures of wisdom and knowledge" (NIV). The other was from Proverbs 8:11, which says that "wisdom is more precious than rubies, and nothing you desire can compare with her" (NIV). Linking those two verses together, and forgetting all about french fries, she began to worship the Lord, and soon the song "More Precious Than Silver" was born.

Scriptures: Proverbs 8:11; Isaiah 45:3; Colossians 2:3
Themes: Jesus Christ, Worship, Praise

> Lord, You are more precious than silver,
> Lord, You are more costly than gold;
> Lord, You are more beautiful than diamonds,
> And nothing I desire compares with You.

LYNN DESHAZO (B. 1956)
© 1992 by Integrity's Hosanna! Music/ASCAP
All rights reserved. Used by permission.

MORNING HAS BROKEN

The unusual story behind this hymn has many twists and turns. Originally, the song was probably a Gaelic hymn. In the 1880s a wandering Highland minstrel was singing the tune in Scotland when someone noted the melody and preserved it for posterity. In 1918 a Scottish poet put words to the melody using the title "Child in the Manger." In the 1920s, the editor of a British hymnal was looking for a light and happy hymn to sing at the beginning of a new day, and he wanted it sung to the old Gaelic tune.

He asked a well-known writer to do it. Eleanor Farjeon was a playwright, novelist, and journalist who had been on a long spiritual journey. Though she was of Jewish descent, Eleanor became an Anglican as a teenager, then dabbled in spiritism and reincarnation. She led a Bohemian lifestyle before she was received into the Roman Catholic Church at the age of seventy.

Eleanor wrote the text based on Genesis 1:5, and she called it "Thanks for the Day."

But the song wasn't widely known until the 1970s, when Cat Stevens, a pop singer and a very active Muslim, made a recording of it that went to the top of the charts.

Scriptures: Genesis 1:1-5; Job 38:7; Psalm 118:24
Themes: Creation, Worship, Wonder

Morning has broken like the first morning,
Blackbird has spoken like the first bird.
Praise for the singing! Praise for the morning!
Praise for them springing fresh from the Word!

Sweet the rain's new fall sunlit from heaven,
Like the first dewfall on the first grass.
Praise for the sweetness of the wet garden,
Sprung in completeness where His feet pass.

Mine is the sunlight! Mine is the morning,
Born of the one light Eden saw play!
Praise with elation, praise ev'ry morning,
God's recreation of the new day!

ELEANOR FARJEON (1881–1965)

MY GOD, HOW WONDERFUL THOU ART

Frederick Faber moved from the Anglican church to the Roman Catholic fold at thirty-one. When he did so, he missed the hymns of Wesley, Newton, and Cowper that had meant so much in his youth. So over the following eighteen years, he wrote 150 hymns, including "Faith of Our Fathers" and "There's a Wideness in God's Mercy," that minister to both Catholics and Protestants alike.

We often use the word *wonderful* quite carelessly, but Faber was speaking of God as "full of wonder." It is only when we take time to consider God's greatness, as Faber does in this hymn, that we truly begin to worship. The hymn takes us step by step through the senses of adoration, fear, love, and devotion, as we see all the great attributes of God displayed. The stanza of consecration, often omitted from our hymnals, reads, "Oh, then, this worse than worthless heart / In pity deign to take, / And make it love Thee for Thyself / And for Thy glory's sake."

Scriptures: Isaiah 57:15; Romans 11:33; 1 Timothy 1:17
Themes: God's Majesty, Worship, Love

My God, how wonderful Thou art,
Thy majesty how bright,
How beautiful Thy mercy seat,
In depths of burning light!

How dread are Thine eternal years,
O everlasting Lord,
By prostrate spirits day and night
Incessantly adored!

O how I fear Thee, living God,
With deepest, tenderest fears,
And worship Thee with trembling hope
And penitential tears!

Yet I may love Thee too, O Lord,
Almighty as Thou art,
For Thou hast stooped to ask of me
The love of my poor heart.

No earthly father loves like Thee;
No mother e'er so mild,
Bears and forbears as Thou hast done
With me, Thy sinful child.

How wonderful, how beautiful,
The sight of Thee must be,
Thine endless wisdom, boundless power,
And aweful purity!

FREDERICK WILLIAM FABER (1814–1863)

MY TRIBUTE

Andrae Crouch has done it all. He has pastored a church, worked with drug addicts and prostitutes, and produced much of the music for Disney's *The Lion King* and Spielberg's *The Color Purple.* He has won eight Grammy awards and has performed in sixty countries.

Most of all, Crouch has enjoyed helping troubled people. Larry was certainly an example of a troubled person. It didn't look as if Larry would ever respond to the gospel. But one day, after a service, Crouch saw Larry weeping, and soon Larry surrendered to Jesus Christ.

Once, Larry phoned Crouch and told him to read Luke 15, the chapter that contains the stories of the lost sheep and the Prodigal Son. Larry was sure Crouch would be inspired to write the greatest song of his career from that chapter. Crouch knew that chapter was a wonderful chapter, but he didn't find a great song in it. The next day the inspiration came. Thinking partly about Larry and partly about the Prodigal Son, Crouch wrote "My Tribute": "To God be the glory for the things He has done."

Scriptures: Psalm 115:1; 1 Corinthians 1:31; Ephesians 3:20-21
Themes: Praise, Love, Worship

> How can I say thanks for the things You have done for me—
> Things so undeserved, yet You give to prove Your love for me?
> The voices of a million angels could not express my gratitude—
> All that I am and ever hope to be, I owe it all to Thee.
>
> To God be the glory, to God be the glory,
> To God be the glory for the things He has done.
> With His blood He has saved me; with His pow'r He hath raised me;
> To God be the glory for the things He has done.
> Just let me live my life; let it be pleasing, Lord, to Thee.
> And should I gain any praise, let it go to Calvary.
> (Repeat the last 4 lines.)

ANDRAE CROUCH (B. 1942)
© Bud John Songs, Inc.
All rights reserved. Used by permission.

O FOR A HEART TO PRAISE MY GOD

It is not surprising that John and Charles Wesley were concerned about the human heart. After all, they had gone through the motions of a heartless Christianity for years. It was not enough, they discovered, for a person to be religious, moral, and orthodox. They had been all that—as ordained clergymen, they knew the gospel well. But their hearts still had to be changed by an encounter with God.

As John Wesley read Luther's commentary of Galatians and then read about "the Son of God, who loved me and gave himself for me" (Galatians 2:20), the personal pronouns struck him. Suddenly he saw the necessity of a personal faith that would change the heart.

This hymn, written by Charles Wesley less than four years after his conversion, is based on Psalm 51:10, "Create in me a clean heart, O God." He knew as well as anyone that this was the only way he could truly be what God wanted him to be.

Scriptures: Psalm 51:10; Ezekiel 11:19-20; Galatians 2:20
Themes: Holiness, Dedication, Sanctification

O for a heart to praise my God,
A heart from sin set free,
A heart that always feels Thy blood
So freely shed for me;

A heart resigned, submissive, meek,
My great Redeemer's throne,
Where only Christ is heard to speak,
Where Jesus reigns alone;

A humble, lowly, contrite heart,
Believing, true, and clean,
Which neither life nor death can part
From Him that dwells within;

A heart in every thought renewed
And full of love divine,
Perfect and right and pure and good,
A copy, Lord, of Thine:

Thy nature, gracious Lord, impart;
Come quickly from above;
Write Thy new name upon my heart,
Thy new, best name of Love.

CHARLES WESLEY (1707–1788)

O JESUS, KING MOST WONDERFUL

Bernard of Clairvaux, the author of this hymn, was a remarkable man of God.

In 1115, at the age of twenty-five, he was sent to start a new monastery in a place called the Valley of Wormwood. Bernard and his followers changed the name to Clairvaux and transformed the desolate land, which had been a haunt for robbers, into a haven of blessing. Peasants were taught about vine culture and other types of agriculture, and the valley began to blossom. Other monasteries were established and other poverty-stricken areas revived—within Bernard's lifetime there were 162 such monasteries established, bringing spiritual and economic health with them.

Above all else, Bernard was a student of Scripture and a lover of Jesus Christ. The hymns ascribed to him—including "Jesus, the Very Thought of Thee" and "Jesus, Thou Joy of Loving Hearts"—indicate the depth of his spiritual life.

Scriptures: 2 Corinthians 3:17-18; Ephesians 3:14-21; Philippians 2:1-11

Themes: Praise, Names of Jesus, Love

O Jesus, King most wonderful!
Thou Conqueror renowned!
Thou Sweetness most ineffable,
In whom all joys are found!

When once Thou visitest the heart,
Then truth begins to shine,
Then earthly vanities depart,
Then kindles love divine.

O Jesus! Light of all below,
Thou Fount of life and fire!
Surpassing all the joys we know,
All that we can desire.

Thy wondrous mercies are untold,
Through each returning day;
Thy love exceeds a thousandfold,
Whatever we can say.

Thee may our tongues forever bless;
Thee may we love alone;
And ever in our lives express
The image of Thine own.

BERNARD OF CLAIRVAUX (1091–1153)
Translated by Edward Caswall (1814–1878)

O LORD OF HEAVEN AND EARTH AND SEA

Any student of English literature knows the name Wordsworth, as in William Wordsworth. But this hymn was written by another Wordsworth—his nephew Christopher. Both men loved nature, but William Wordsworth loved nature for nature's sake; he worshipped nature. Christopher Wordsworth, on the other hand, recognized the Creator of nature.

Originally, this was an offertory hymn. Two extra stanzas, which are now usually omitted, made it very clear that since God has given us so much, putting some money in the offering plate is the least we can do. Without that specific emphasis, however, this becomes an excellent Thanksgiving hymn.

The first two stanzas acknowledge God's gifts in Creation. He has given us a beautiful world to enjoy and beautiful vegetation for nourishment. The third stanza speaks of how God has also given us peace and health, for which we praise him. But in the fourth stanza, Wordsworth remembers God's greatest gift of all, Jesus Christ, who brought us redemption and forgiveness. What it comes down to is that we derive "all" from him—even our ability to give back to him.

Scriptures: Psalm 107:1-3; 1 Timothy 6:17; James 1:5
Themes: Creation, Thanksgiving, Stewardship

O Lord of heaven and earth and sea,
To Thee all praise and glory be!
How shall we show our love to Thee,
Who givest all?

The golden sunshine, vernal air,
Sweet flowers, and fruit Thy love declare;
When harvests ripen, Thou art there,
Who givest all.

For peaceful homes and healthful days,
For all the blessings earth displays,
We owe Thee thankfulness and praise,
Who givest all.

For souls redeemed, for sins forgiven,
For means of grace and hopes of heaven:
What can to Thee, O Lord, be given,
Who givest all?

To Thee, from whom we all derive
Our life, our gifts, our power to give:
O may we ever with Thee live,
Who givest all!

CHRISTOPHER WORDSWORTH (1807–1885)

O MY SOUL, BLESS GOD THE FATHER

This hymn, a recasting of Psalm 103, contains three rich biblical images for us to ponder. The first verses of both the psalm and the hymn call upon us to bless and praise the Lord. There is a totality of worship demanded here.

Later, the psalmist notes that God has removed our sins "as far from us as the east is from the west." East and west are as far apart as you can get. What a vivid reminder that when God forgives us, our sins are truly gone!

The third image is that of a father who cares deeply for his children. Jesus used this same illustration: If a human father gives bread to his hungry child, won't our heavenly Father do this and more? Wise parents know the limitations of their children. We don't ask five-year-old children to compute our taxes and then punish them for missing a few deductions. That would be foolish. In the same way, our heavenly Father understands our limits and has compassion when we fail.

Scriptures: Psalm 103; Isaiah 1:18; 1 John 1:9

Themes: Praise, Forgiveness, God's Mercy

> O my soul, bless God the Father;
> All within me bless His name;
> Bless the Father, and forget not
> All His mercies to proclaim.
>
> Who forgiveth thy transgressions,
> Thy diseases all who heals;
> Who redeems thee from destruction,
> Who with thee so kindly deals.
>
> Far as east from west is distant,
> He hath put away our sin;
> Like the pity of a father
> Hath the Lord's compassion been.
>
> As it was without beginning,
> So it lasts without an end;
> To their children's children ever
> Shall His righteousness extend:
>
> Unto such as keep His covenant
> And are steadfast in His way;
> Unto those who still remember
> His commandments, and obey.

Bless the Father, all His creatures,
Ever under His control;
All throughout His vast dominion
Bless the Father, O my soul.

UNITED PRESBYTERIAN BOOK OF PSALMS, 1871

O SPLENDOR OF GOD'S GLORY BRIGHT

In the fourth century, Ambrose of Milan was a prominent lawyer and government leader. In fact, he was so well respected that he was asked to be a bishop even before he had been baptized.

Ambrose stood against the Roman emperor when the political ruler tried to pressure the church. An edict of banishment was issued against Ambrose, but he refused to accept it. When Ambrose threatened to excommunicate the soldiers who surrounded the church, they left. Ambrose had won.

But Ambrose's biggest battle was theological. His foe was the heresy of Arianism, which held that Jesus Christ was a created being. Despite being condemned by church councils, this false teaching enjoyed continued popularity among the people. Ambrose wrote hymns upholding the deity of Christ so that believers might have the truth embedded in their hearts. "O Splendor of God's Glory Bright" is one of those hymns.

Scriptures: 2 Corinthians 4:5-6; Hebrews 1:1-3; 1 John 1:1-4
Themes: Trinity, Guidance, Light

O splendor of God's glory bright,
O Thou that bringest light from light,
O Light of light, light's living spring,
O Day all days illumining.

O Thou true Sun, on us Thy glance
Let fall in royal radiance;
The Spirit's sanctifying beam
Upon our earthly senses stream.

The Father, too, our prayers implore,
Father of glory evermore;
The Father of all grace and might,
To banish sin from our delight.

To guide whate'er we nobly do,
With love all envy to subdue,
To make ill fortune turn to fair,
And give us grace our wrongs to bear.

AMBROSE OF MILAN (340–397)
Translated by Robert Seymour Bridges (1844–1930)

O WORSHIP THE KING

Sir Robert Grant was acquainted with kings. His father was a member of the British Parliament and later became chairman of the East India Company. Following in his father's footsteps, young Grant was elected to Parliament and led the fight for civil rights for Jewish people. Then he became a director of the East India Company. In 1834 he was appointed governor of Bombay, and in that position he was greatly loved. A medical college in India was named in his honor.

This hymn by Grant is based on Psalm 104, a psalm of praise. The progression of titles for God in the last line is interesting: "Maker, Defender, Redeemer, and Friend." We know God first as our Maker, our Creator. Then, even before our conversion, he is our Defender, our Keeper from harm. We know him then as Redeemer, our personal Savior from sin and its penalty. Finally, as we walk day by day with him, as we commune with him and enjoy his fellowship, we know him also as Friend.

Yes, Sir Robert Grant was acquainted with kings, but he treasured most of all his friendship with the King of kings.

Scriptures: Psalm 47:6-7; Psalm 104:1-4; 1 Timothy 6:15-16

Themes: Worship, Praise, Titles of God

O worship the King, all glorious above,
O gratefully sing His power and His love;
Our Shield and Defender, the Ancient of Days,
Pavilioned in splendor, and girded with praise.

O tell of His might, O sing of His grace,
Whose robe is the light, whose canopy space;
His chariots of wrath the deep thunderclouds form,
And dark is His path on the wings of the storm.

The earth with its store of wonders untold,
Almighty, Thy power hath founded of old,

Hath established it fast by a changeless decree,
And round it hath cast, like a mantle, the sea.

Thy bountiful care, what tongue can recite?
It breathes in the air, it shines in the light;
It streams from the hills, it descends to the plain,
And sweetly distills in the dew and the rain.

Frail children of dust, and feeble as frail,
In Thee do we trust, nor find Thee to fail;
Thy mercies how tender, how firm to the end,
Our Maker, Defender, Redeemer, and Friend.

ROBERT GRANT (1779–1838)

OH THE GLORY OF YOUR PRESENCE

Steve Fry's father, a pastor in San Jose, California, had two goals in his ministry: to glorify the Lord and make worship the church's top priority. So it is not surprising that Steve Fry would seek those two goals as well.

When Steve Fry became the youth pastor in his father's church, he aimed at those goals. In time, he saw the youth group grow from a handful of teens to more than 700 with a teen choir of 120 voices.

Steve was seated in his parents' living room one day when he was overcome by the truth that when you experience the presence of God, you will receive the fullness of everything else you need. He was struck by Psalm 16:11, which says, "In your presence there is fullness of joy; at your right hand are pleasures forevermore" (ESV).

Then Steve began to write, drawing from Solomon's prayer in 2 Chronicles 6, as well as Paul's teaching in 1 Corinthians 3 about how we are the temples of the Lord. The song, "Oh, the Glory of Your Presence," captures the major focus of Steve Fry's ministry.

Scriptures: 2 Chronicles 6:14-19; Psalm 16:11; 1 Corinthians 3:16-17
Themes: Worship, Glory, God the Father

Oh the glory of Your presence
We, Your temple give You rev'rence
So arise from Your rest
And be blessed
By our praise

As we glory in Your embrace,
As Your presence now fills this place.

STEVE FRY

© Birdwing Music/BMG Songs

OUR GOD REIGNS

Lenny Smith couldn't seem to succeed in life. He worked on a master's degree in English from one school, and later a master's degree in theology from another, but he finished neither. He ended up becoming a high school teacher and taught in three Catholic high schools and one public high school. But they all fired him, according to Lenny, because he brought his guitar to school on Fridays and encouraged his students to sing and read the Bible.

Because Lenny couldn't get another teaching job, he tried house painting and carpentry, but that was depressing. One evening, as he read Isaiah 52, he was struck by a verse beginning with, "How beautiful upon the mountains," and ending with the triumphant shout, "Your God reigns" (Isaiah 52:7, ESV).

Through those verses the Lord seemed to be saying to him, "I know you are depressed, and I know you feel like a failure, but I will bring you through this, and you will soon shine as the sun."

Lenny began to weep. He picked up his guitar and began to play what those verses in Isaiah said to him. In the next few days, Lenny played and sang that song over and over again: "Our God reigns, our God reigns." His pastor loved it, and soon it was introduced to other pastors. In only a few years, "Our God Reigns" had reached around the world.

Scriptures: Psalm 93:1; Isaiah 52:7; Romans 10:15

Themes: Prophecy, Jesus Christ, Crucifixion

How lovely on the mountains
Are the feet of him who brings good news,
Good news announcing peace, proclaiming news of happiness,
Our God reigns, our God reigns!

Our God reigns! (Repeat 3 times.)

He had no stately form,
He had no majesty, that we should be drawn to Him.

He was despised and we took no account of Him,
Yet now He reigns with the Most High.

It was our sin and guilt
That bruised and wounded Him. It was our sin that brought Him down.
When we like sheep had gone astray
Our Shepherd came and on His shoulders bore our shame.

Meek as a lamb that's led out to the slaughterhouse,
Dumb as a sheep before its shearer,
His life ran down upon the ground like pouring rain
That we should be born again.

Out of the tomb He came with grace and majesty,
He is alive, He is alive.
God loves us so, see here His hands, His feet, His side,
Yes we know, He is alive.

LEONARD E. SMITH JR. (B. 1942)

PRAISE, MY SOUL, THE KING OF HEAVEN

In 1834 the British clergyman Henry Francis Lyte published a collection of 280 hymns based on the book of Psalms. He called it *The Spirit of the Psalms* because these hymns were not strictly translations (like the old psalters still in use at that time) or even paraphrases (like much of Isaac Watts's work), but texts loosely inspired by the Psalms. This hymn was included as a development of Psalm 103. There are many points of comparison.

The psalmist urges us not to forget the Lord's benefits; Lyte lists those benefits—"ransomed, healed, restored, forgiven." And as the psalmist indicates that God is "slow to chide," Lyte adds that he is also "swift to bless."

Queen Elizabeth II chose this hymn to be sung at her wedding in 1947. It is an apt song for any occasion, as we join our voices in this great "Alleluia!"

Scriptures: 1 Chronicles 29:10-13; Psalm 103:1-5; 1 Timothy 1:17
Themes: Praise, Worship, God's Mercy

Praise, my soul, the King of heaven,
To His feet thy tribute bring;
Ransomed, healed, restored, forgiven,
Evermore His praises sing.
Alleluia! Alleluia! Praise the everlasting King.

Praise Him for His grace and favor
To our fathers in distress;
Praise Him, still the same as ever,
Slow to chide, and swift to bless,
Alleluia! Alleluia! Glorious in His faithfulness.

Fatherlike, He tends and spares us;
Well our feeble frame He knows;
In His hands He gently bears us,
Rescues us from all our foes.
Alleluia! Alleluia! Widely yet His mercy flows.

Angels in the height, adore Him;
Ye behold Him face to face;
Saints triumphant, bow before Him,
Gathered in from every race.
Alleluia! Alleluia! Praise with us the God of grace.

HENRY FRANCIS LYTE (1793–1847)

PRAISE HIM! PRAISE HIM!

A few years ago, *excellent* was the hot word among teenagers. A really great experience was not just good, it was "excellent!" Many of us remember when schoolteachers marked papers with grades of "good," "very good," and "excellent." There was nothing wrong with a "good" paper, but the "excellent" one went beyond expectations. It excelled.

In this hymn, Fanny Crosby urges us to praise God for his "excellent" greatness. Consider who or what, besides God, is the greatest thing in your life. Your family? Your home? Your friends? Your sports team? These may be good, even very good, but God is greater. He excels above all other aspects of our lives. His greatness exceeds our ability to praise him.

It's hard to find a hymn richer in praise and joy. Jesus is hailed as Rock, Redeemer, Prophet, Priest, and King. But just when we begin to think he's so "excellent" that he's out of reach, we see him as a Shepherd, carrying his little ones in his arms.

Scriptures: Psalm 146:2; Hebrews 1:3-8; Revelation 5:11-12
Themes: Praise, Names of Jesus, Joy

Praise Him! praise Him! Jesus, our blessed Redeemer!
Sing, O Earth, His wonderful love proclaim!
Hail Him! hail Him! highest archangels in glory;
Strength and honor give to His holy name!
Like a shepherd Jesus will guard His children,
In His arms He carries them all day long:

Praise Him! praise Him! tell of His excellent greatness;
Praise Him! praise Him! ever in joyful song!

Praise Him! praise Him! Jesus, our blessed Redeemer!
For our sins He suffered, and bled and died;
He our Rock, our hope of eternal salvation,
Hail Him! hail Him! Jesus the Crucified.
Sound His praises! Jesus who bore our sorrows;
Love unbounded, wonderful, deep and strong:

Praise Him! praise Him! Jesus, our blessed Redeemer!
Heav'nly portals loud with hosannas ring!
Jesus, Savior, reigneth forever and ever;
Crown Him! crown Him! Prophet and Priest and King!
Christ is coming! over the world victorious,
Pow'r and glory unto the Lord belong:

FANNY JANE CROSBY (1820–1915)

PRAISE THE LORD! YE HEAVENS ADORE HIM

One Sunday morning in the eighteenth century, Thomas Corin, a retired captain of the Merchant Navy, found an abandoned baby on the steps of St. Andrews Church in the Holborn section of London. He and his wife took the baby home and cared for it. Later he discovered that there were many abandoned babies in London, and most of them were left to die.

Because of his efforts and his Christian commitment, a hospital for destitute and abandoned children was established. It was called the Foundling Hospital in High Holborn. Children in the hospital were all taught to sing, and soon their singing caught public attention. The great composer George Frideric Handel presented the hospital with an organ and conducted a special performance of *Messiah* each year on the hospital's behalf.

Eventually the hospital published its own collection of hymns, called the *Foundling Hospital Collection,* 1796, which included this hymn. The hymnwriter is unknown, but the text is based on Psalm 148.

Scriptures: Job 38:7; Psalm 148; 1 Thessalonians 5:16
Themes: Praise, Worship, Creation

Praise the Lord! ye heav'ns, adore Him;
Praise Him angels in the height;
Sun and moon, rejoice before Him;
Praise Him, all ye stars of light.
Praise the Lord! for He hath spoken;
Worlds His mighty voice obeyed;
Laws which never shall be broken
For their guidance He hath made.

Praise the Lord! for He is glorious;
Never shall His promise fail;
God hath made His saints victorious;
Sin and death shall not prevail.
Praise the God of our salvation!
Hosts on high, His pow'r proclaim;
Heav'n and earth and all creation,
Laud and magnify His name.

Worship, honor, glory, blessing,
Lord, we offer unto Thee;
Young and old, Thy praise expressing,
In glad homage bend the knee.
All the saints in heav'n adore Thee;
We would bow before Thy throne:
As Thine angels serve before Thee,
So on earth Thy will be done.

FOUNDLING HOSPITAL COLLECTION, 1796
Stanza 3 by Edward Osler (1798–1863)

PRAISE THE NAME OF JESUS

What do you do when the going gets tough? Well, you can quit or you can complain or you can do what Roy Hicks did: "Praise the Name of Jesus" in spite of the problems.

Roy Hicks was the pastor of a small, struggling church in Eugene, Oregon. It was a discouraging situation, but one day he began meditating on Psalm 18, which begins, "I will love thee, O LORD, my strength. The LORD is my rock, and my fortress, and my deliverer; my God, my strength, in whom I will trust" (KJV). After reading the psalm, Roy prayed. He says, "The tune and the words came to me during that prayer time." The next Sunday, Roy taught it to his congregation. When the going gets tough, praise the name of Jesus.

Scriptures: Psalm 18:1-3; Romans 15:9-11; Hebrews 13:15
Themes: Praise, Worship, Jesus Christ

> Praise the name of Jesus, Praise the name of Jesus.
> He's my Rock, He's my Fortress, He's my Deliverer,
> In Him will I trust. Praise the name of Jesus.

ROY HICKS JR. (B. 1943)
© Latter Rain Music
All rights reserved. Used by permission.

PRAISE THE SAVIOR, YE WHO KNOW HIM

There was nothing wishy-washy about Thomas Kelly. He was an Irishman through and through, from Kellywatle, Ireland. Kelly studied to be a lawyer like his father, but in the process he began to read Christian doctrine. Under conviction of sin, he struggled to find peace with God through fasting and asceticism, but it didn't work. Eventually, Kelly trusted Jesus Christ for the free gift of salvation through faith. He was ordained a minister in the established church, but because of his strong views on salvation by grace, he moved on to serve in independent chapels.

Most of his hymns were focused on Jesus Christ, praising him for his work on the cross and the glories of heaven. In a way, Kelly writes simply, and yet because his rhyme schemes are unusual, the words become more memorable. This hymn is typical of Kelly, beginning with grateful praise to his Savior and ending with a meditation on heaven.

Scriptures: Psalm 107:1-3; Ephesians 1:11-12; Hebrews 13:15
Themes: Praise, Trust, Hope

Praise the Savior, ye who know Him!
Who can tell how much we owe Him?
Gladly let us render to Him
All we are and have.

Jesus is the name that charms us,
He for conflict fits and arms us;
Nothing moves and nothing harms us
While we trust in Him.

Trust in Him, ye saints forever—
He is faithful, changing never;
Neither force nor guile can sever
Those He loves from Him.

Keep us, Lord, O keep us cleaving
To Thyself, and still believing,
Till the hour of our receiving
Promised joys with Thee.

Then we shall be where we would be,
Then we shall be what we should be;
Things that are not now, nor could be,
Soon shall be our own.

THOMAS KELLY (1769–1855)

PRAISE TO THE LORD, THE ALMIGHTY

As a student in Bremen, Germany, Joachim Neander lived a godless life. Although both his father and grandfather were Lutheran ministers, Neander wasted his teenage years in immorality. Then, when Neander was twenty, a preacher named Under-Eyke came to Bremen. Neander went to the meeting intending to ridicule the preacher, but instead he was converted.

Four years later he became headmaster of a school in Düsseldorf, and during his time there he wrote more than sixty hymns. Because of his strong Christian views and his evangelistic activities, Neander displeased the authorities and was later removed from his position.

Despite the tensions, he went on writing hymns of praise. Neander often wandered through the valleys and hills near Düsseldorf, communing with his Lord. After losing his position at the school, he lived for a time in a cave and continued writing hymns. Neander died very young, at the age of thirty, but he left behind a legacy of praise to God.

Scriptures: Psalm 67:3; Psalm 103:1-5; Colossians 1:15-20
Themes: Praise, Worship, Comfort

Praise to the Lord, the Almighty, the King of creation!
O my soul, praise Him, for He is thy health and salvation!
All ye who hear, now to His temple draw near;
Join me in glad adoration!

Praise to the Lord, who o'er all things so wondrously reigneth,
Shieldeth thee under His wings, yea, so gently sustaineth!
Hast thou not seen how thy desires e'er have been
Granted in what He ordaineth?

Praise to the Lord, who doth prosper thy work and defend thee;
Surely His goodness and mercy here daily attend thee.
Ponder anew what the Almighty can do,
If with His love He befriend thee.

Praise to the Lord! O let all that is in me adore Him!
All that hath life and breath, come now with praises before Him!
Let the amen sound from His people again;
Gladly forever adore Him.

JOACHIM NEANDER (1650–1680)
Translated by Catherine Winkworth (1827–1878)

PRAISE YE THE FATHER

The author of this hymn praising the Trinity was Elizabeth Rundle Charles, a very remarkable nineteenth-century woman. The daughter of a member of British Parliament and the wife of a lawyer, Elizabeth was accomplished in many different fields. She is known as an outstanding church historian, a poet, a translator, a musician, an author, and a painter.

This hymn is not rhymed, and that was unusual in the nineteenth century. The first stanza praises the Father, the second stanza praises the Son, and the third, the Holy Spirit, closing with the words, "Praise ye the Triune God."

Scriptures: 2 Corinthians 13:14; 1 Peter 1:2; Jude 1:20-21
Themes: Trinity, God the Father, Jesus Christ, Holy Spirit

Praise ye the Father for His loving kindness,
Tenderly cares He for His erring children;
Praise Him, ye angels, praise Him in the heavens,
Praise ye Jehovah!

Praise ye the Savior, great is His compassion,
Graciously cares He for His chosen people;
Young men and maidens, ye old men and children
Praise ye the Savior.

Praise ye the Spirit, Comforter of Israel,
Sent of the Father and the Son to bless us;
Praise ye the Father, Son, and Holy Spirit
Praise ye the Triune God!

ELIZABETH RUNDLE CHARLES (1828–1896)

REJOICE, THE LORD IS KING!

The early days of Methodism were filled with persecution and hardship. In such times it would have been natural for Wesley's followers to become discouraged and lose hope. One reason Charles Wesley wrote six thousand hymns was to encourage Methodists to be a singing, joyful people.

Paul's letter to the Philippians provided Wesley's text for this hymn. Paul was imprisoned in Rome under Emperor Nero. But the message to the Philippians is one of joy and encouragement. As Paul concludes his letter, he reminds Christians to "rejoice in the Lord always, and again I say rejoice" in whatever circumstances they find themselves. You can be a victor regardless of the situation because the Lord is King.

This hymn first appeared in Wesley's 1746 collection, *Hymns for Our Lord's Resurrection*. Each stanza adds another dimension to our praise: adoration, thanksgiving, and exultation.

Scriptures: Psalm 95:1-3; Philippians 4:4-9; Hebrews 1:3
Themes: Joy, Praise, Adoration, Easter

Rejoice, the Lord is King!
Your Lord and King adore!
Rejoice, give thanks, and sing,
And triumph evermore:

Lift up your heart, lift up your voice!
Rejoice, again I say, rejoice!

Jesus, the Savior, reigns,
The God of truth and love;
When He had purged our stains,
He took His seat above:

His kingdom cannot fail,
He rules o'er earth and heaven;
The keys of death and hell
Are to our Jesus given:

Rejoice in glorious hope!
Our Lord the judge shall come,
And take His servants up
To their eternal home:

CHARLES WESLEY (1707–1788)

REJOICE, YE PURE IN HEART

This hymn was written in 1865 as the processional for a choir festival at Petersborough Cathedral in England. There are hints in the text of a marching quality ("glorious banner," "as ye go," "lift your standard," "march in firm array"). You can see an army of choir members marching down the aisle—this hymn seems to invite the congregation, and perhaps all Christians everywhere, to join in the song. There is a relentless sense of joy here. One observer commented on the "stately simplicity" of this work.

Edward Plumptre was a noted scholar and author in the Church of England. He wrote a major biography of Bishop Thomas Ken (also a famous hymnwriter), as well as historical works and poetry. Plumptre was also a Bible scholar and worked on a revision of the King James Version. He wrote this hymn at age forty-four, somewhere between "bright youth and snow-crowned age." Perhaps his work as a college professor made him realize that it's not the magnitude of one's scholarship that matters, but the purity of one's heart.

Scriptures: Psalm 20:5-7; Psalm 32:11; Psalm 33:1
Themes: Joy, Praise, Thanksgiving

Rejoice, ye pure in heart;
Rejoice, give thanks and sing;
Your glorious banner wave on high,
The cross of Christ your King.

Rejoice, rejoice,
Rejoice, give thanks and sing.

Bright youth and snow-crowned age,
Strong men and maidens fair,
Raise high your free, exulting song,
God's wondrous praise declare.

With voice as full and strong
As ocean's surging praise,
Send forth the hymns our fathers loved,
The psalms of ancient days.

Yes, on through life's long path,
Still chanting as ye go;
From youth to age, by night and day,
In gladness and in woe.

Still lift your standard high,
Still march in firm array,
As warriors through the darkness toil
Till dawns the golden day.

EDWARD HAYES PLUMPTRE (1821–1891)

RING THE BELLS OF HEAVEN

Pastor William Cushing, the author of this gospel song, was depressed. He had lost his voice not long after his wife died. All the joy had been taken out of his life. His ministry was gone, and he wondered if his life had a purpose any longer.

Then he was asked to write some hymns, and when they were successful, he was asked to write more. Musicians began sending him tunes and asking him to write words to fit. One day he received a tune from George Root, a famous nineteenth-century composer. Root had written the popular Civil War song, "Tramp, Tramp, Tramp, the Boys Are Marching." Now Root had sent Cushing a tune and was requesting words.

Cushing couldn't get the tune out of his mind, but he didn't know what words would fit. Should this be a secular song or a Christian song? Should it be for children or adults? As he played the song, it seemed to be good for Sunday school. Then the words *ring the bells of heaven* seemed to float into his mind. He thought of angels rejoicing over some person turning to Jesus Christ. Later he wrote, "It was a beautiful and blessed experience, and the bells seem ringing yet."

Scriptures: Psalm 148:1-2; Isaiah 61:10; Luke 15:7
Themes: Joy, Conversion, Heaven

Ring the bells of heaven! There is joy today,
For a soul returning from the wild;
See! The Father meets him out upon the way,
Welcoming His weary, wand'ring child.

Glory! glory! How the angels sing!
Glory! glory! How the loud harps ring!
'Tis the ransomed army, like a mighty sea,
Pealing forth the anthem of the free.

Ring the bells of heaven! There is joy today,
For the wand'rer now is reconciled;
Yes, a soul is rescued from his sinful way,
And is born anew a ransomed child.

Ring the bells of heaven! Spread the feast today,
Angels, swell the glad triumphant strain!
Tell the joyful tidings, bear it far away!
For a precious soul is born again.

WILLIAM ORCUTT CUSHING (1823–1902)

SHINE, JESUS, SHINE

The most famous of all contemporary British Christian songwriters is Graham Kendrick. His songs are sung all over England in churches of all denominations. He has been a leader in what are called "Marches of Praise," leading Christians as they march and sing through streets and housing complexes. His March for Jesus movement has involved nearly sixty million people in prayer, praise, and proclamation activities.

"Shine, Jesus, Shine" is his best-known song in America. Kendrick says that the most surprising thing about writing the song was the ordinariness of the circumstances. He says, "My longing for revival in the churches and spiritual awakening in the nation was growing," so he wrote three verses. But the song didn't seem complete, and it wasn't until several months later that he realized it needed a chorus.

He says, "I remember standing in my music room with my guitar slung around my neck trying different approaches, and then the line, 'Shine, Jesus, shine,' came to mind, and within about half an hour I had finished the chorus." Soon it became one of the most popular worship choruses in England, and today it is sung in America as well.

Scriptures: Isaiah 49:6; John 1:9; John 12:46
Themes: Light, Praise, Worship, Witnessing

Lord, the light of Your love is shining,
In the midst of the darkness shining;
Jesus, Light of the world, shine upon us.
Set us free by the truth you now bring us;
Shine on me, shine on me.

Shine, Jesus, shine, fill this land with the Father's glory,
Blaze, Spirit, blaze, set our hearts on fire.
Flow, river, flow, flood the nations with grace and mercy.
Send forth Your Word, Lord, and let there be light.

Lord, I come to Your awesome presence,
From the shadows into Your radiance;
By the blood I may enter Your brightness,
Search me, try me, consume all my darkness,
Shine on me, shine on me.

As we gaze on Your kingly brightness,
So our faces display Your likeness;
Ever changing from glory to glory,
Mirror'd here may our lives tell Your story,
Shine on me, shine on me.

GRAHAM KENDRICK (B. 1950)
©1987 Make Way Music (admin. by Music Services in the Western Hemisphere)
All Rights Reserved. ASCAP. Used by permission.

SHOUT TO THE LORD

Darlene Zschech of Sydney, Australia, had written a worship song, "Shout to the Lord," but she wasn't sure it was any good. Although Darlene is a talented woman, she was going through a dark time, a time of self-doubt. She wondered if God could use anything she did. Then she began reading Psalm 96. As she read it, her depression began to lift and the song "Shout to the Lord" emerged.

When she mentioned it to the music pastor of her church, he insisted on coming to her house to hear it. Now she was really nervous. Her music pastor came with a friend, so she was shakier than ever. Her hands were sweating. She didn't know whether she would be able to play the piano, much less sing the words. So she told the two men to turn and face the wall, looking away from her. She didn't want to see what she thought would be the pained expressions on their faces. When she finished, they said it was wonderful. That was nice, but she was sure they were just being polite.

It wasn't until after her pastor raved about the song that she realized it might have a life beyond her personal devotional time.

Scriptures: 1 Chronicles 16:23-27; Psalm 18:1-3; Psalm 96
Themes: Praise, Worship, Jesus Christ

My Jesus, my Savior, Lord, there is none like You;
All of my days I want to praise the wonders of Your mighty love.
My comfort, my shelter, tower of refuge and strength;
Let every breath, all that I am,
Never cease to worship You.

Shout to the Lord, all the earth, let us sing
Power and majesty, praise to the King;
Mountains bow down and the seas will roar
At the sound of Your name.
I sing for joy at the work of Your hands,
Forever I'll love You, forever I'll stand;
Nothing compares to the promise I have in You.

DARLENE ZSCHECH

SING HALLELUJAH TO THE LORD

Linda Stassen, an Indiana girl, went to California during the Jesus People movement of the early 1970s. Everything seemed to be centered around Calvary Chapel in Costa Mesa, including music classes. So twenty-three-year-old Linda Stassen got involved with a recording group and a music composition class.

It was for an assignment for this class that Linda wrote "Sing Hallelujah to the Lord." The words go back to the times of the early Christian church, but the beautiful call and answer counterpoint is Linda's creation. The simplicity of the words and the beauty of the tune have made it popular in languages around the world, including Chinese, Persian, Eskimo, and various European languages.

Scriptures: Psalm 13:6; Psalm 18:49; Isaiah 12:4-6
Themes: Praise, Worship, Jesus Christ

> Sing hallelujah to the Lord.
> Sing hallelujah to the Lord.
> Sing hallelujah, sing hallelujah,
> Sing hallelujah to the Lord.

LINDA STASSEN-BENJAMIN (B. 1951)

SING PRAISE TO GOD WHO REIGNS ABOVE

One hundred years after Martin Luther, the Lutheran church in Germany needed a revival, and it came through a Lutheran pastor in Frankfurt, Philip Jacob Spener. He started Bible studies in small groups, and he emphasized the importance of a personal commitment to Jesus Christ as well as a continuing devotional life. The movement was called the Pietist movement.

Johann Schütz, a prominent lawyer and legal authority, helped Spener start the movement. Along with Spener, he was concerned that the orthodoxy of the church had become dead orthodoxy. God wasn't personal anymore; he seemed far away.

So the lawyer wrote several hymns emphasizing the nearness of God, including "Sing Praise to God Who Reigns Above." Notice particularly the third stanza: "The Lord is never far away, / But, through all grief distressing, / An ever-present help and stay, / Our peace and joy and blessing."

Scriptures: Psalm 34:18; Psalm 145:18; Isaiah 12:4-6
Themes: Praise, Comfort, God's Power

Sing praise to God who reigns above,
The God of all creation,
The God of pow'r, the God of love,
The God of our salvation.
With healing balm my soul He fills,
And ev'ry faithless murmur stills:
To God all praise and glory!

What God's almighty pow'r hath made
His gracious mercy keepeth,
By morning glow or evening shade
His watchful eye ne'er sleepeth.
Within the kingdom of His might,
Lo! all is just and all is right:
To God all praise and glory!

The Lord is never far away,
But, through all grief distressing,
An ever-present help and stay,
Our peace and joy and blessing.
As with a mother's tender hand
He leads His own, His chosen band:
To God all praise and glory!

Thus all my toilsome way along
I sing aloud His praises,
That men may hear the grateful song
My voice unwearied raises.
Be joyful in the Lord, my heart!
Both soul and body bear your part:
To God all praise and glory!

JOHANN JAKOB SCHÜTZ (1640–1690)
Translated by Frances Elizabeth Cox (1812–1897)

SING TO THE LORD OF THE HARVEST

Athough most Anglican preachers of his day read from carefully prepared texts, John Monsell preached without notes and kept his people
on the edge of their seats with his stirring speaking style.

Like Monsell's preaching, this hymn might have been considered too
informal, almost irreverent. (What is this about seasons "rolling" and
"happy love"? And do we really want to think about hills that "leap up in
gladness" while "the valleys laugh and sing"?) But Monsell didn't care
what the critics thought: "We are too reserved in our praises." He knew
that the church's singing needed to be "more fervent and joyous." If God
is as great as we claim he is, Monsell believed we should show it by the way
we sing.

Scriptures: 1 Chronicles 16:7-8; Psalm 92:1-2; 1 Timothy 4:4-5
Themes: Thanksgiving, Praise, Worship

Sing to the Lord of the harvest,
Sing songs of love and praise;
With joyful heart and voices
Your hallelujahs raise;
By Him the rolling seasons
In fruitful order move;
Sing to the Lord of the harvest
A song of happy love.

By Him the clouds drop fatness,
The deserts bloom and spring,
The hills leap up in gladness,
The valleys laugh and sing;
He filleth with His fullness
All things with large increase;
He crowns the year with goodness,
With plenty and with peace.

Heap on His sacred altar
The gifts His goodness gave,
The golden sheaves of harvest,
The souls He died to save;
Your hearts lay down before Him
When at His feet ye fall,

And with your lives adore Him
Who gave His life for all.

JOHN SAMUEL BEWLEY MONSELL (1811–1875)

STAND UP AND BLESS THE LORD

As a newspaper editor in Sheffield, England, James Montgomery was known as an outspoken advocate for many humanitarian causes. In fact, he was imprisoned twice for his editorials. He wrote against slavery and promoted democracy in government. Though a gentle man by nature, Montgomery was not afraid to champion unpopular causes. He didn't see why anyone who was a Christian should be ashamed to stand up and say so.

In 1824 Montgomery wrote this hymn for a Sunday school anniversary. It is based on Nehemiah 9:5, where the Levites say to the people, "Stand up and praise the LORD your God, who is from everlasting to everlasting" (NIV).

It is one thing to stand up for God in church, or to proclaim God's praise on the steps of the Temple as the Levites did, but it is another thing to proclaim him in the workplace. But that's just what editor James Montgomery did. And so must we.

Scriptures: Nehemiah 9:5-6; Psalm 51:15; 1 Corinthians 15:58
Themes: Praise, Courage, Worship

Stand up and bless the Lord,
Ye people of His choice;
Stand up and bless the Lord your God
With heart and soul and voice.

Though high above all praise,
Above all blessing high,
Who would not fear His holy name,
And laud and magnify?

O for the living flame
From His own altar brought,
To touch our lips, our minds inspire,
And wing to heaven our thought!

God is our strength and song,
And His salvation ours;
Then be His love in Christ proclaimed
With all our ransomed powers.

Stand up and bless the Lord;
The Lord your God adore;
Stand up and bless His glorious name,
Henceforth forevermore.

JAMES MONTGOMERY (1771–1854)

TAKE THE NAME OF JESUS WITH YOU

Although Lydia Baxter was a bedridden invalid for much of her life, people who were depressed came to visit her in order to have their spirits lifted. Christian leaders often met in her home for prayer and Bible study.

Lydia loved to study the Bible and had a special joy in learning the meaning of scriptural names. But the Name above all names to her was Jesus.

When she was asked how she could remain so cheerful, she responded, "I have a very special armor. I have the name of Jesus. When the tempter tries to make me blue or despondent, I mention the name of Jesus, and he can't get through to me anymore. When I feel badly and wonder if I will ever enjoy a good night's sleep again, I take the name of Jesus and ask Him to give me the soothing balm of his presence. He does, and soon I drop off to sleep."

When Lydia was sixty-one years old, she wrote this testimony of her life: "Take the Name of Jesus with You."

Scriptures: Proverbs 18:10; Philippians 2:9-10; Colossians 3:17
Themes: Name of Jesus, Hope, Joy, Comfort

Take the name of Jesus with you,
Child of sorrow and of woe;
It will joy and comfort give you,
Take it, then, where'er you go.

Precious name, O how sweet!
Hope of earth and joy of Heav'n
Precious name, O how sweet! . . .
Hope of earth and joy of Heav'n.

Take the name of Jesus ever,
As a shield from ev'ry snare;
If temptations round you gather,
Breathe that holy name in prayer.

O the precious name of Jesus!
How it thrills our souls with joy,
When His loving arms receive us,
And His songs our tongues employ!

At the name of Jesus bowing,
Falling prostrate at His feet,
King of kings in Heav'n we'll crown Him,
When our journey is complete.

LYDIA BAXTER (1809–1874)

THE LORD IS KING!

Josiah Conder left school in 1802 at the age of thirteen, but he didn't leave the world of books. His father was a bookseller in London, and young Conder joined his father's business. From then on he picked up his education from his father's books and their literary customers. At twenty-five he became the publisher of a magazine and later the editor of a newspaper. As an evangelical, he frequently opposed the actions of the established church and faced determined opposition. He said his best hymns were written in times of trial or change.

When Conder lay dying at the age of sixty-six, he asked to have some of his poems that spoke of Jesus Christ read. The last stanza of one of them, which he asked to have read three times, is "Beset with fears and cares, in Him my heart is strong. All things in life and death are theirs, who to the Lord belong." After the third reading, one of his children said, "Now you can sleep on that."

"Oh yes," responded Josiah, "and die upon it." A few days later he did die, joining the heavenly chorus to sing "The Lord omnipotent is King!"

Scriptures: Psalm 95:3; 1 Timothy 6:15; Revelation 19:5-6
Themes: God's Omnipotence, God the King, Praise

The Lord is King! Lift up thy voice,
O earth; and all ye heav'ns, rejoice:
From world to world the joy shall ring,
"The Lord omnipotent is King!"

The Lord is King! Who then shall dare
Resist His will, distrust His care,
Or murmur at His wise decrees,
Or doubt His royal promises?

The Lord is King! Child of the dust,
The Judge of all the earth is just;
Holy and true are all His ways:
Let ev'ry creature speak His praise.

Alike pervaded by His eye,
All parts of His dominion lie;
This world of ours, and worlds unseen,
And thin the boundary between.

One Lord, one empire, all secures;
He reigns, and life and death are yours:
Through earth and heav'n one song shall ring,
"The Lord omnipotent is King!"

JOSIAH CONDER (1789–1855)

THE TREES OF THE FIELD

In the second half of the twentieth century, Messianic Judaism and Jews for Jesus often made headlines, making both Jews and Christians do some soul-searching. Christians were reminded of the roots of their faith in Judaism and the fulfillment of Old Testament prophecies in Jesus Christ.

A Jews for Jesus group called the Liberated Wailing Wall became popular for its concerts and recordings and introduced Christians to a Hebrew folk music style. Steffi Rubin, one of the early members of Jews for Jesus, wrote "The Trees of the Field" when she was twenty-five years old. It is taken word for word from Isaiah 55:12. The Hebrew folk music was provided by Stuart Dauerman, who also added the Hebrew text so the Liberated Wailing Wall could sing in both Hebrew and English.

Scriptures: 1 Chronicles 16:33; Isaiah 51:11; Isaiah 55:12
Themes: Creation, Joy, Praise

The lyrics are based on Isaiah 55:12.
AUTHOR: STEFFI GEISER RUBIN (B. 1950)

THERE IS A REDEEMER

Melody, raised in a poor beach neighborhood in southern California, was the child of a broken home. As a teenager, she left the Jewish faith in which her mother had raised her and tried Buddhism. But that didn't satisfy her. "I kept coming up empty," she says. She became a hippie and filled her life with drugs of all kinds.

In 1972 she met Keith Green and together they searched for ultimate spiritual fulfillment, which they eventually found in Jesus Christ. Radically changed by their new-birth experience, they sought to rescue others through their music, their messages, and their organization called Last Days Ministries.

It was in 1977, five years after her conversion, that Melody Green wrote "There Is a Redeemer," with the last verse coming from her husband Keith. In 1982, Keith, along with two of their three children, was killed in a plane crash. Melody, at home with their third child, was pregnant with another.

Ten years earlier, she had been a hippie, high on drugs; five years earlier she had written this song of praise to her Redeemer; and then in 1982, despite the devastating tragedy of the death of her husband and two of her children, she could say along with Job in the Old Testament, "I know that my Redeemer lives."

Scriptures: Job 19:25; 1 Peter 1:18; Revelation 5:8-10
Themes: Worship, Salvation, Atonement

There is a Redeemer, Jesus, God's own Son;
Precious lamb of God, Messiah, Holy One.

Thank You O my Father, for giving us Your Son;
And leaving Your Spirit 'til the work on earth is done.

Jesus, my Redeemer, name above all names;
Precious Lamb of God, Messiah, hope for sinners slain.

When I stand in Glory, I will see His face, and
There I'll serve my King forever in that holy place.

MELODY GREEN
© BirdwingMusic/BMG Songs/Ears To Hear Music
All rights reserved. Used by permission.

THERE IS NONE LIKE YOU

Lenny LeBlanc hadn't been to church in twenty years. He figured he didn't need religion. After all, he had signed a big contract with Capitol Records. As a pop artist, he was enjoying one success after another. Pop music was his life.

Then, late one night, he got a phone call from a friend whom Lenny knew as a drug smuggler. The friend said, "Lenny, I got saved. Are you saved?" Lenny had no idea what the word *saved* meant. The friend sent Lenny a Bible and asked him to read it.

Lenny did. He says that two weeks later, "I started crying out to God for forgiveness, and I became born again right there in my house." For a while Lenny was in no-man's-land; he was still under contract to Capitol, but his heart wasn't into writing pop music anymore. Finally, Capitol released him from the contract, and Lenny was free to write praise and worship songs for Jesus Christ. One day, as a tune and lyrics came to him, he began to weep. He called the song, "There Is None Like You."

A few years later he went to Korea, where sixty thousand young people had gathered. Lenny thought he was going to introduce his song to the Korean young people, but they knew it already. They sang it in Korean without his help. Someone later remarked to him, "Didn't you know that your song is one of the most popular Christian songs throughout all of Asia?"

Scriptures: John 6:51; Acts 4:12; Hebrews 1:2-3
Themes: Jesus Christ, Salvation, Conversion

Your mercy flows like a river wide
And healing comes from Your hands;
Suffering children are safe in Your arms,
There is none like You.

There is none like You;
No one else can touch my heart like You do.
I could search for all eternity long
And find there is none like You.

LENNY LEBLANC
© 1991 Integrity's Hosanna! Music/ASCAP
All rights reserved. Used by permission.

THERE'S SOMETHING ABOUT THAT NAME

There is something very special about the name of Jesus, and that is why so many songs and hymns have been written about it. The prophecies in the Old Testament refer to various names of the Messiah, and we sing about them at Christmas. The apostle Paul wrote that, in the future, at the name of Jesus every knee shall bow.

Songwriters Bill and Gloria Gaither were looking at it from a different angle. Gloria says that this song "came out of our personal experience with the effect and power of the name of Jesus in our everyday lives." In the previous few years, their grandparents had died, one by one, and Bill and Gloria were impressed by how often, even in their delirium, the grandparents spoke the name of Jesus.

Then Bill and Gloria became parents. They felt very inexperienced, and when a child woke up crying in the middle of the night with a high fever, they began calling on the name of Jesus, the Great Physician. Yes, there's something about that name.

Scriptures: Matthew 1:21; Acts 4:12; Philippians 2:10
Themes: Messiah, Jesus Christ, Praise

Jesus, Jesus, Jesus; there's just something about that name!
Master, Savior, Jesus, like the fragrance after the rain;
Jesus, Jesus, Jesus, Let all heaven and earth proclaim:
Kings and kingdoms will all pass away,
But there's something about that name!

WILLIAM J. GAITHER (B. 1936) AND GLORIA GAITHER (B. 1942)
© 1970 William J. Gaither, Inc.
All rights controlled by Gaither Copyright Management. Used by permission.

THIS IS MY FATHER'S WORLD

Maltbie Babcock was an athlete. An outstanding baseball pitcher and a champion swimmer, he kept himself in shape by running. When he was pastor of the First Presbyterian Church in Lockport, New York, he would run in the early morning to the brow of a hill two miles away and look over at Lake Ontario. Before he left, he would tell his church staff, "I am going out to see my Father's world." From the brow of the hill, he would run two more miles to a deep ravine where as many as forty different species of birds found sanctuary. Then he would run back.

Babcock loved music as well as athletics and nature. He enjoyed playing the organ, piano, and violin, so it is not strange that he should write a hymn extolling God's handiwork in nature. There are good lines to memorize in this hymn, lines to remember when the world seems to be going haywire: "This is my Father's world, / O let me ne'er forget that though the wrong seems oft so strong, / God is the Ruler yet."

Scriptures: Psalm 24:1-2; Psalm 33:4-8; Psalm 145:1-7; Isaiah 45:18
Themes: Creation, God's Care, Victory

This is my Father's world,
And to my listening ears
All nature sings, and round me rings
The music of the spheres.
This is my Father's world:
I rest me in the thought
Of rocks and trees, of skies and seas—
His hand the wonders wrought.

This is my Father's world,
The birds their carols raise,
The morning light, the lily white,
Declare their Maker's praise.
This is my Father's world:
He shines in all that's fair;
In the rustling grass I hear Him pass,
He speaks to me everywhere.

This is my Father's world,
O let me ne'er forget
That though the wrong seems oft so strong,
God is the Ruler yet.

This is my Father's world:
The battle is not done;
Jesus who died shall be satisfied,
And earth and heav'n be one.

MALTBIE DAVENPORT BABCOCK (1858–1901)

THIS IS THE DAY

There are several reasons why Les Garrett, who wrote this song, doesn't take much credit for it. For one thing, the words are taken mostly from Psalm 118:24; as for the tune, it is derived from a folk melody of the Fiji Islands. Then there's a third reason: In Les's words, "I have very little musical ability and do not play an instrument; therefore, I can only believe that it was a gift from God."

Born in New Zealand, Les Garrett moved to Australia when he was twenty-four and became a traveling evangelist. However, he couldn't do much traveling because he often didn't have enough money to put gas in his car.

As he was feeling sorry for himself, he read Psalm 118:24, the verse that begins, "This is the day the LORD has made," and the tune suddenly came to him. He kept it secret for two years—after all, he wasn't a songwriter. One day in a camp meeting in New Zealand, a woman stood up during a testimony time, and looking at Les, said, "There is someone here who has something that was given to you by the Lord, and you are not sharing it." That evening Les shared his secret song for the first time. It didn't take long for that song to go around the world.

Scriptures: Psalm 96:2; Psalm 118:24; 1 Corinthians 16:2; Philippians 4:4
Themes: Praise, Worship, Joy

This is the day, this is the day that the Lord hath made, that the
  Lord hath made.
We will rejoice, we will rejoice and be glad in it, and be glad in it.
This is the day that the Lord hath made; we will rejoice and be glad in it.
This is the day, this is the day that the Lord hath made.

LESLIE GARRETT (B. 1943)

<caption>THE COMPLETE BOOK OF HYMNS</caption>

THOU ART WORTHY

Pastor Dick Mills was proud of his sixty-four-year-old mother, and he had every right to be. In addition to raising six children, she was a speaker for women's groups and churches, and she had written more than three hundred songs. Sometimes she could write a hymn in just a few minutes after someone suggested a topic or a Bible verse to her.

So one day when Dick Mills knew his mother was coming to visit, he told his congregation at the Foursquare church in Hillsboro, Oregon, that they could suggest a favorite Bible verse to her and she would come up with a song. The only problem was that he had forgotten to tell his mother that he was going to do it. So it was a big surprise.

During the evening service, a member of the congregation suggested Revelation 4:11 as a favorite verse and asked Mrs. Mills to write some music for it. At the close of the service, a service that did not close until after ten o'clock that night, Pauline Mills presented her song and said, "The Lord gave me the music." The song, "Thou Art Worthy," has now been sung around the world.

Scriptures: John 1:3; Revelation 4:11; Revelation 5:9
Themes: Worship, Praise, Creation

Thou art worthy, Thou art worthy, Thou art worthy, O Lord,
To receive glory, glory and honor, glory and honor and pow'r.
For Thou hast created, hast all things created; Thou hast created all things.
And for Thy pleasure they are created; for Thou art worthy, O Lord.

PAULINE MICHAEL MILLS (1898–1991)
© 1963, 1965, 1980 by Fred Bock Music, Inc.
All rights reserved. Used by permission.

WE BRING THE SACRIFICE OF PRAISE

In their church in Grand Prairie, Texas, Kirk and Deby Dearman had just heard a guest speaker talk about bringing a sacrifice of praise to church with them. On the way home, Kirk told Deby that there should be a song about that, so as they were driving down the freeway, Kirk began thinking about how such a song would sound. In five minutes, he had the entire song in his mind, and when they arrived home, he played and sang it for Deby. They now call it their "car tune."

Those were days when life was going well for the Dearmans. Deby was a model, making a thousand dollars a day. Kirk was on staff at a growing church and writing songs on a regular basis. They hardly knew what sacrifice was. But then the Lord called them to be foreign missionaries; they quit their jobs, sold their home, and went from having lots of money to being broke. They spent the next decade in Europe.

Says Kirk, "Our worship is most precious to the Lord when we're in places of affliction."

Scriptures: Psalm 100:1-5; Jeremiah 33:11; Hebrews 13:15
Themes: Praise, Worship, Church

We bring the sacrifice of praise into the house of the Lord;
We bring the sacrifice of praise into the house of the Lord.
And we offer up to You the sacrifices of thanksgiving;
And we offer up to You the sacrifices of joy.

KIRK DEARMAN AND DEBY DEARMAN
© 1984 New Spring (ASCAP)
All rights reserved. Used by permission.

WE PRAISE THEE, O GOD

Ever since her student years, Julia Cady Cory, the writer of this hymn, wrote Christian poems and songs.

When Julia was in her twenties, the organist at Brick Presbyterian Church in New York City asked her to write new words for a traditional Dutch Thanksgiving hymn. She produced "We Praise Thee, O God," and the new words were sung for Thanksgiving at the church.

The original Dutch hymn goes back to the 1600s. Its familiar words, "We gather together to ask the Lord's blessing," are an English rendering of a German version of the Dutch original. Julia Cady Cory's words express the same theme of thanks for God's blessings, but in a fresh way.

Scriptures: 1 Chronicles 16:28-29; Psalm 85:1; 2 Timothy 3:11
Themes: Praise, Worship, Comfort

We praise Thee, O God, our Redeemer, Creator
In grateful devotion our tribute we bring;
We lay it before Thee, we kneel and adore Thee,
We bless Thy holy Name, glad praises we sing.

We worship Thee, God of our fathers, we bless Thee
Thru life's storm and tempest our Guide hast Thou been;
When perils o'ertake us, escape Thou wilt make us,
And with Thy help, O Lord, our battles we win.

With voices united our praises we offer
To Thee, great Jehovah, glad anthems we raise;
Thy strong arm will guide us, our God is beside us,
To Thee, our great Redeemer, forever be praise!

JULIA CADY CORY (1882–1963)

WHEN MORNING GILDS THE SKIES

An anonymous German author wrote the fourteen stanzas of this hymn, which was first printed in *Katholisches Gesangbuch* of Würtzburg in 1828. Only six stanzas were originally translated into English. Three of the others begin like this:

"My tongue shall never tire of chanting with the choir, may Jesus Christ be praised!"

"Be this at meals your grace, in every time and place, may Jesus Christ be praised!"

"And at your work rejoice, to sing with heart and voice, may Jesus Christ be praised!"

The author was pointing out that our praise to God should not be limited to church services but should overflow to our homes and places of work.

The hymn was probably written in the lovely Franconia section of Germany, the home of fairy-tale castles, deep green forests, and lovely mountain ranges. But it matters not whether our surroundings are lovely or gloomy; Jesus Christ always deserves our praise.

Scriptures: Psalm 5:3; Psalm 34:1; 1 Corinthians 10:31–11:1

Themes: Praise, Worship, Devotion

When morning gilds the skies,
My heart awaking cries,
May Jesus Christ be praised!
Alike at work and prayer,
To Jesus I repair;
May Jesus Christ be praised!

The night becomes as day,
When from the heart we say,
May Jesus Christ be praised!
The powers of darkness fear,
When this sweet chant they hear,
May Jesus Christ be praised!

Ye nations of mankind,
In this your concord find,
May Jesus Christ be praised!
Let all the earth around
Ring joyous with the sound,
May Jesus Christ be praised!

Be this, while life is mine,
My canticle divine,
May Jesus Christ be praised!
Be this th' eternal song
Through all the ages long,
May Jesus Christ be praised!

GERMAN HYMN (19TH CENTURY)
Stanzas 1, 2, 4 translated by Edward Caswall (1814–1878)
Stanza 3 translated by Robert Seymour Bridges (1844–1930)

YE SERVANTS OF GOD

In 1744, England was at war with France, and the British were expecting an invasion to dethrone George II and restore the House of Stuart to the throne. People suspected the Methodists of friendship with France and perhaps plotting to overthrow the king. Wesleyan meetings were broken up by mobs, and at times John and Charles Wesley themselves were arrested and hauled into court.

In the middle of the turmoil, the Wesleys published a collection of hymns to encourage their followers. They titled the collection *Hymns for Times of Trouble and Persecution.* This hymn, "Ye Servants of God," was the first song in that little hymnal and it was published under the heading "To Be Sung in a Tumult." The stanzas we have in our hymnals today do not suggest any turmoil, but one that was omitted reads, "Men, devils engage, the billows arise and horribly rage, and threaten the skies; their fury shall never our steadfastness shock, the weakest believer is built on a rock."

Scriptures: Psalm 93:1-4; Mark 10:45; Revelation 7:9-12
Themes: Witness, God's Sovereignty, Praise

Ye servants of God, your Master proclaim,
And publish abroad His wonderful name;
The name all-victorious of Jesus extol;
His kingdom is glorious and rules over all.

God ruleth on high, almighty to save;
And still He is nigh, His presence we have;
The great congregation His triumph shall sing,
Ascribing salvation to Jesus, our King.

"Salvation to God, who sits on the throne!"
Let all cry aloud and honor the Son:
The praises of Jesus the angels proclaim,
Fall down on their faces and worship the Lamb.

Then let us adore and give Him His right,
All glory and power, all wisdom and might,
All honor and blessing, with angels above,
And thanks never ceasing, and infinite love.

CHARLES WESLEY (1707–1788)

PART II

ASSURANCE

He alone is my rock and my salvation, my fortress where I will never be shaken.

PSALM 62:2

A SHELTER IN THE TIME OF STORM

Song leader Ira Sankey discovered this song in a small British newspaper, although it was already well-known in some parts of England. It was said to be a favorite song for fishermen off the northern coast of England, and it is easy to understand why. Winds swept across the coastal areas in northern England, making it treacherous for fishing vessels. When small boats made it into the harbors safely, the fishermen could often be heard singing this song.

The words were written by the headmaster of a London orphanage, but Ira Sankey put a new melody to it, and probably added the rousing chorus as well.

Scriptures: Psalm 32:7; Psalm 94:22; Nahum 1:7
Themes: Safety, Security, Trust

The Lord's our Rock, in Him we hide
A shelter in the time of storm,
Secure whatever ill betide
A shelter in the time of storm.

Oh, Jesus is a Rock in a weary land,
A weary land, a weary land;
Oh, Jesus is a Rock in a weary land
A shelter in the time of storm.

A shade by day, defense by night
A shelter in the time of storm;
No fears alarm, no foes affright
A shelter in the time of storm.

The raging storms may round us beat
A shelter in the time of storm;
We'll never leave our safe retreat
A shelter in the time of storm.

O Rock divine, O Refuge dear
A shelter in the time of storm;
Be Thou our helper ever near
A shelter in the time of storm.

VERNON J. CHARLESWORTH (1838–1915)

BE STILL, MY SOUL

About a hundred years after the time of Martin Luther (1483–1546), Europe was in sad shape. The continent was racked by the Thirty Years' War, which pitted Catholics against Protestants. The Lutheran church had lapsed into formalism and dead orthodoxy. People had stopped going to church.

Then God raised up what is known as the Pietist movement, a movement that was characterized by music, personal holiness, and missionary zeal. In the midst of this time of turmoil and discouragement, Katharina von Schlegel noticed the verse in Psalm 46 that says, "Be still, and know that I am God."

As God spoke to her, she wrote this great hymn. Whatever your circumstances, whatever your problems, you can find comfort in these great words.

Scriptures: Psalm 46:8-11; Philippians 4:7-9
Themes: Peace, Confidence, Trust

> Be still, my soul! the Lord is on thy side;
> Bear patiently the cross of grief or pain;
> Leave to thy God to order and provide;
> In every change He faithful will remain.
> Be still, my soul! thy best, thy heavenly Friend
> Through thorny ways leads to a joyful end.
>
> Be still, my soul! thy God doth undertake
> To guide the future as He has the past.
> Thy hope, thy confidence let nothing shake;
> All now mysterious shall be bright at last.
> Be still, my soul! the waves and winds still know
> His voice who ruled them while He dwelt below.
>
> Be still, my soul! the hour is hastening on
> When we shall be forever with the Lord,
> When disappointment, grief, and fear are gone,
> Sorrow forgot, love's purest joys restored.
> Be still, my soul! when change and tears are past,
> All safe and blessed we shall meet at last.

KATHARINA AMALIA VON SCHLEGEL (1697–?)
Translated by Jane Laurie Borthwick (1813–1897)

BLESSED ASSURANCE

Fanny Crosby wrote more than eight thousand hymns and used more than two hundred pen names. Under contract to a music publisher, she wrote three new hymns each week during much of her adult life. The fact that she was blind didn't diminish her productivity. She would formulate an entire song in her mind and then dictate it to a friend or a secretary.

One of her good friends was Phoebe Palmer Knapp, wife of the founder of Metropolitan Life Insurance Company. One time when Knapp came to Brooklyn to see Crosby, she brought a tune with her that she had composed. "Play it for me on the organ," Crosby requested. Knapp did and then asked, "What does this tune say?" She turned to see Crosby kneeling in prayer. Knapp played it a second time and then a third. Finally the blind woman responded, "That says, 'Blessed assurance, Jesus is mine! O what a foretaste of glory divine!' "

Scriptures: Romans 8:1,16-17; 2 Timothy 1:12; Hebrews 10:18-20; 1 John 5:13
Themes: Assurance, Submission, Praise, Salvation

Blessed assurance, Jesus is mine!
O what a foretaste of glory divine!
Heir of salvation, purchase of God,
Born of His Spirit, washed in His blood.

This is my story, this is my song,
Praising my Savior all the day long;
This is my story, this is my song,
Praising my Savior all the day long.

Perfect submission, perfect delight!
Visions of rapture now burst on my sight;
Angels descending bring from above
Echoes of mercy, whispers of love.

Perfect submission—all is at rest,
I in my Savior am happy and blest;
Watching and waiting, looking above,
Filled with His goodness, lost in His love.

FANNY JANE CROSBY (1820–1915)

CHRIST IS MADE THE SURE FOUNDATION

This hymn is drawn from a Latin meditation on the New Jerusalem. Some scholars think the original work may have been used as a dedication for a new church building. But in this translation, John Neale clearly identifies the "temple" as the people of the church. Christ lives, not in walls of stone, but in the hearts of people whose lives belong to him.

Neale had the title of warden of Sackville College, but it really wasn't a college at all; it was a nursing home for senior citizens. And he wasn't really a warden either; he was a caretaker. Never in good health, he found time in his job to uncover ancient Greek and Latin hymns that had never been translated before. For him it was a wonderful diversion from Sackville College. As a translator of old medieval hymns, he made a wonderful contribution to the Christian church. Many of the hymns he translated are still sung today. Though his own body was a frail temple, he used it tirelessly to strengthen the other temple of God, the church.

Scriptures: 1 Corinthians 3:10-11; Ephesians 4:4-6; 1 Peter 2:4-6
Themes: Church, Praise, Worship

Christ is made the sure foundation,
Christ the head and cornerstone,
Chosen of the Lord and precious,
Binding all the Church in one;
Holy Zion's help forever,
And her confidence alone.

To this temple, where we call Thee,
Come, O Lord of hosts, today!
With Thy wonted loving-kindness
Hear Thy people as they pray;
And Thy fullest benediction
Shed within its walls alway.

Here vouchsafe to all Thy servants
What they ask of Thee to gain:
What they gain from Thee forever
With the blessed to retain,
And hereafter in Thy glory
Evermore with Thee to reign.

Laud and honor to the Father,
Laud and honor to the Son,
Laud and honor to the Spirit,
Ever Three and ever One;
One in might, and One in glory,
While unending ages run.

LATIN HYMN (7TH CENTURY)
Translated by John Mason Neale (1818–1866)

CHRIST LIVETH IN ME

Daniel Webster Whittle, the author of this hymn, had a colorful history. An infantryman in the Civil War, he was converted after being wounded and taken prisoner. A New Testament that his mother had given him was used by God to bring about his salvation. He was promoted to the rank of major, a title he kept even in civilian life. After the army, he became treasurer of the Elgin Watch Company in Elgin, Illinois, but the Lord wanted something more from Major Whittle.

Evangelist Dwight L. Moody asked Whittle to become his assistant, and soon he was a full-fledged evangelist himself, not only speaking, but also writing songs to be used in evangelistic campaigns. In his song-writing, he often used the pen name "El Nathan."

In this hymn Whittle testifies that he was "once far from God and dead in sin," but then moves on to his new life in Christ as found in Galatians 2:20: "I have been crucified with Christ and I no longer live, but Christ lives in me" (NIV).

Scriptures: 2 Corinthians 6:16; Galatians 2:19-20; Colossians 1:27
Themes: Sanctification, Holiness, Consecration

Once far from God and dead in sin, no light my heart could see;
But in God's Word the Light I found. Now Christ liveth in me.

Christ liveth in me.
O what a salvation this, that Christ liveth in me.

As lives the flower, within the seed, as in the cone the tree;
So, praise the God of truth and grace; His Spirit dwelleth in me.

With longing all my heart is filled, that like Him I may be.
As on the wondrous thought I dwell that Christ liveth in me.

DANIEL WEBSTER WHITTLE (1840–1901)

CORNERSTONE

Lari Goss, the man who wrote this song, is not known as a songwriter. He is best known for his music production, his orchestral arranging, and his keyboard artistry. Lari has produced for top music groups, including the Brooklyn Tabernacle Choir and the Gaither Vocal Band. He has provided orchestral arrangements for artists such as Glen Campbell and B. J. Thomas, as well as companies such as RCA and Columbia. In the music community, his name is synonymous with quality, even though he was born in a humble rural village in Georgia and was largely self-taught when it came to music.

The song "Cornerstone" came after Lari had been reading in the Bible about Christ being the Cornerstone. Slowly the song was built, one stone upon another. He says, "Most all of the phrases in the song are straight Scripture." He looked in hymnals to see how older hymns spoke of Christ as the Rock. He studied the hymn "Rock of Ages," and as he meditated, he was impressed with the security of the Christian in the Lord. That led him to the line, "Rock of Ages, so secure, for all time it shall endure."

The New Living Translation puts it this way: "Together, we are his house, built on the foundation of the apostles and the prophets. And the cornerstone is Christ Jesus himself" (Ephesians 2:20).

Scriptures: Psalm 118:22; Ephesians 2:20; 1 Peter 2:4-8
Themes: Jesus Christ, Comfort, Assurance

Jesus is the Cornerstone, came for sinners to atone.
Tho' rejected by His own, He became the Cornerstone;
Jesus is the Cornerstone.
When I am by sin oppressed, On the Stone I am at rest.
When the seeds of truth are sown, He remains the Cornerstone;
Jesus is the Cornerstone.
Rock of Ages cleft for me, Let me hide myself in Thee.
Rock of Ages, so secure, for all time it shall endure
'til the breaking of the dawn, 'til all footsteps cease to roam,
Ever let this truth be known: Jesus is the Cornerstone.
Jesus is the Cornerstone.

FADE, FADE, EACH EARTHLY JOY

In Scotland in the 1800s, virtually everyone knew the name Bonar. Three Bonar brothers were pastors of major churches in Scotland. They had a warm, compassionate style of preaching that made them beloved throughout the British Isles. Two of them were authors. One of them, Horatius Bonar, wrote six hundred hymns, some of which are still being sung today.

Horatius Bonar's wife is sometimes forgotten in the talk about the remarkable Bonar family. But Jane Bonar was also an excellent hymn-writer. In "Fade, Fade, Each Earthly Joy," Jane Bonar is not saying that there are no enjoyments in life. Instead, she is saying that the greatest enjoyment of all is the joy of knowing that "Jesus is mine." Compared to that, everything else pales into insignificance.

Scriptures: John 17:9-10; Philippians 3:20-21; Colossians 3:2-3
Themes: Holiness, Sanctification, Submission

Fade, fade, each earthly joy; Jesus is mine.
Break ev'ry tender tie; Jesus is mine.
Dark is the wilderness, Earth has no resting place,
Jesus alone can bless; Jesus is mine.

Tempt not my soul away; Jesus is mine.
Here would I ever stay; Jesus is mine.
Perishing things of clay, born but for one brief day,
Pass from my heart away; Jesus is mine.

Farewell, ye dreams of night; Jesus is mine.
Lost in this dawning bright, Jesus is mine.
All that my soul has tried left but a dismal void;
Jesus has satisfied; Jesus is mine.

Farewell, mortality; Jesus is mine.
Welcome, eternity; Jesus is mine.
Welcome, O loved and blest, welcome sweet scenes of rest,
Welcome, my Savior's breast; Jesus is mine.

JANE C. BONAR (1821–1884)

FAITH IS THE VICTORY

In Batavia, New York, John Yates was the manager of the local hardware store.

Shortly after he left the hardware store to become editor of a local newspaper, he wrote this hymn, "Faith is the Victory." The key phrase is taken from the King James Version of 1 John 5:4, which says, "And this is the victory that overcometh the world, even our faith."

The imagery of the hymn is drawn from several sections of Scripture. In Ephesians 6, Paul speaks of the Word of God as our sword, salvation as our helmet, and truth as our belt. And faith, Paul says, is our shield. The phrase "His banner over us is love" comes from Song of Songs, and his reference to "white raiment" in the last stanza comes from the book of Revelation, which says, "He that overcometh, the same shall be clothed in white raiment" (3:5, KJV).

No doubt about it, newspaper editor John Yates knew his Scripture, and he knew that it is true that "faith is the victory."

Scriptures: Ephesians 6:10-17; 1 John 5:4; Revelation 3:5
Themes: Faith, World, Conflict

> Encamped along the hills of light, ye Christian soldiers, rise,
> And press the battle ere the night shall veil the glowing skies.
> Against the foe in vales below let all our strength be hurled;
> Faith is the victory, we know, that overcomes the world.
>
> *Faith is the victory! Faith is the victory!*
> *Oh, glorious victory, That overcomes the world.*
>
> His banner over us is love, our sword the Word of God;
> We tread the road the saints above with shouts of triumph trod.
> By faith they, like a whirlwind's breath, swept on o'er ev'ry field;
> The faith by which they conquered Death is still our shining shield.
>
> On ev'ry hand the foe we find drawn up in dread array;
> Let tents of ease be left behind, and onward to the fray.
> Salvation's helmet on each head, with truth all girt about,
> The earth shall tremble 'neath our tread, and echo with our shout.
>
> To him that overcomes the foe, white raiment shall be giv'n;
> Before the angels he shall know His name confessed in heav'n.
> Then onward from the hills of light, our hearts with love aflame;
> We'll vanquish all the hosts of night, in Jesus' conq'ring name.

JOHN H. YATES (1837–1900)

FAITH OF OUR FATHERS

Whether you turn to the Old Testament and see how God called Abraham out of Ur of the Chaldeans or turn to the New Testament and see how God stopped Saul of Tarsus on the road to Damascus, the Bible is filled with events that actually happened. Our Christian faith is rooted in history.

Frederick Faber thought that the new religious movements of his day were dangerous. He felt there was too much emphasis on the experience of the moment. After three years as an Anglican minister, he left that denomination and joined the Roman Catholic Church. He appreciated the continuity with the past that he found there, and he respected the martyrs who had given their lives for Christ. But as a Roman Catholic, he missed the singing he had enjoyed as an Anglican. So he wrote hymns to help fill the void. Today Christians of all denominations sing Faber's hymns, grateful to God for the faith of our spiritual ancestors.

Scriptures: Joshua 1:6; 2 Timothy 4:7-8; Hebrews 11:39-40; Hebrews 12:1
Themes: Faith, Church, Courage

Faith of our fathers! living still
In spite of dungeon, fire, and sword;
O how our hearts beat high with joy
Whene'er we hear that glorious word!

Faith of our fathers, holy faith!
We will be true to thee till death.

Faith of our fathers! we will strive
To win all nations unto thee;
And through the truth that comes from God
Mankind shall then be truly free.

Faith of our fathers! we will love
Both friend and foe in all our strife;
And preach thee, too, as love knows how
By kindly words and virtuous life.

FREDERICK WILLIAM FABER (1814–1863)

HIDING IN THEE

Pastor William Cushing was only forty-seven when his wife died. Then his health began to fail, and paralysis affected his vocal chords. He had to resign his pastorate, and he wondered what he could do.

About that time he received a letter from Ira Sankey, the song leader for evangelist Dwight L. Moody. The letter asked, "Send me something new to help me in my gospel work." Cushing knew what was wanted. Sankey was looking for a new gospel song that could be sung at Moody's revival meetings. He prayed that whatever he wrote would be something that would glorify God.

Cushing recalled, "It was while waiting upon the Lord that 'Hiding in Thee' pressed to make itself known." The song had come from his heart. As he said, "It was the outgrowth of many tears, many heart conflicts and yearnings of which the world could know nothing."

Scriptures: Psalm 32:7; Psalm 78:35; Psalm 94:22
Themes: Comfort, Conflict, Rest

O safe to the Rock that is higher than I,
My soul in its conflicts and sorrows would fly;
So sinful, so weary, Thine, Thine would I be;
Thou blest Rock of Ages, I'm hiding in Thee.

Hiding in Thee, Hiding in Thee,
Thou blest Rock of Ages, I'm hiding in Thee.

In the calm of the noontide, in sorrow's lone hour,
In times when temptation casts o'er me its pow'r;
In the tempests of life, on its wide, heaving sea,
Thou blest Rock of Ages, I'm hiding in Thee.

How oft in the conflict, when pressed by the foe,
I have fled to my Refuge and breathed out my woe;
How often, when trials like sea billows roll,
Have I hidden in Thee, O Thou Rock of my soul.

WILLIAM O. CUSHING (1823–1902)

HOW FIRM A FOUNDATION

When it was first printed, this hymn was simply called "Scripture Promises." In a 1787 hymnal, the words of 2 Peter 1:4 were printed above the first stanza: "Exceeding great and precious promises" (KJV). Each stanza of the hymn emphasizes a different promise in God's Word. The second stanza is based on Isaiah 41:10; the third on Isaiah 43:2; the fourth on 2 Corinthians 12:9; and the fifth on Hebrews 13:5, which concludes "I will never fail you. I will never abandon you."

The final lines of this hymn are among the most memorable in the hymnal: "That soul, though all hell should endeavor to shake, / I'll never, no, never, no, never forsake!" If it still isn't clear, you can add a couple more "no nevers" to it.

Scriptures: Isaiah 41:10; Isaiah 43:2; 2 Corinthians 12:9; Hebrews 13:5; 2 Peter 1:4

Themes: Faith, Promises, Assurance, Trust

How firm a foundation, ye saints of the Lord,
Is laid for your faith in His excellent Word!
What more can He say than to you He hath said,
To you who for refuge to Jesus have fled?

"Fear not, I am with thee; O be not dismayed,
For I am thy God, and will still give thee aid;
I'll strengthen thee, help thee, and cause thee to stand,
Upheld by My righteous, omnipotent hand."

"When through the deep waters I call thee to go,
The rivers of woe shall not thee overflow;
For I will be with thee thy troubles to bless,
And sanctify to thee thy deepest distress."

"When through fiery trials thy pathways shall lie,
My grace, all-sufficient, shall be thy supply;
The flame shall not hurt thee; I only design
Thy dross to consume, and thy gold to refine."

"The soul that on Jesus still leans for repose,
I will not, I will not desert to his foes;
That soul, though all hell should endeavor to shake,
I'll never, no, never, no, never forsake!"

"K" IN RIPPON'S *A SELECTION OF HYMNS*, 1787

IN HEAVENLY LOVE ABIDING

Anna Waring was a shy woman, and the future sometimes frightened her. She was also a brilliant woman; she taught herself Hebrew so she could read the Old Testament in its original language. As Anna grew older, she fought against her shyness and her fears by visiting prisons. Yet she continually struggled with her shyness and fears.

So it is understandable if in this hymn she talks about fear, about storms roaring about her, and about how her heart was laid low. Yet she speaks of her confidence—and ours—"But God is round about me, / And can I be dismayed?"

Scriptures: Psalm 27:1; Isaiah 40:10-11; Matthew 10:31; 2 Timothy 1:7
Themes: Abiding, Trust, Confidence

In heavenly love abiding,
No change my heart shall fear;
And safe is such confiding,
For nothing changes here.
The storm may roar without me,
My heart may low be laid;
But God is round about me,
And can I be dismayed?

Wherever He may guide me,
No want shall turn me back;
My Shepherd is beside me,
And nothing can I lack.
His wisdom ever waketh,
His sight is never dim;
He knows the way He taketh,
And I will walk with Him.

Green pastures are before me,
Which yet I have not seen;
Bright skies will soon be o'er me,
Where darkest clouds have been.
My hope I cannot measure,
My path to life is free;
My Savior has my treasure,
And He will walk with me.

ANNA LAETITIA WARING (1823–1910)

JESUS NEVER FAILS

When he was a boy in elementary school, Arthur Luther wanted to be a foreign missionary. As he got older and realized that he had musical talent, he wanted to write a song that the whole world would sing. He wrote a song that he thought would be popular. In fact, he thought it was pretty good, but apparently no one else did. In his words, "It was a dismal failure."

However, God made both of his dreams come true when Luther wrote the song "Jesus Never Fails." At the time, he was working with an evangelistic team in Kentucky. Then, he says, "I received some very disturbing news from my family some six hundred miles away. Worried and homesick, I sat down at the old square piano in the home where we were staying and as my fingers wandered idly, a simple melody developed beneath them which seemed to sing, 'Jesus Never Fails.' Then and there the words and music of the chorus were born."

This simple little song has been translated into more than a dozen languages, taking it to places that Arthur Luther could never have gone as a missionary. No, Jesus never fails.

Scriptures: Matthew 28:20; Luke 21:33; Hebrews 13:5
Themes: Assurance, Comfort, Jesus

Earthly friends may prove untrue,
Doubts and fears assail;
One still loves and cares for you:
Jesus never fails.

Jesus never fails, Jesus never fails;
Heav'n and earth may pass away but Jesus never fails.

Tho' the sky be dark and drear,
Fierce and strong the gale,
Just remember He is near,
And He will not fail.

In life's dark and bitter hour
Love will still prevail;
Trust His everlasting pow'r,
Jesus will not fail.

ARTHUR A. LUTHER (1891–1960)
© 1927 New Spring (ASCAP)
All rights reserved. Used by permission.

LEANING ON THE EVERLASTING ARMS

Music teacher A. J. Showalter of Hartsville, Alabama, finished his classes for the day and returned to his rooming house. There he found letters from two former students. Amazingly they each told a similar story. Both former students had lost their wives, and both wives had died the same day. Showalter began writing letters of sympathy and condolence to the men.

As he began writing, a Scripture verse from Deuteronomy came to his mind, giving the assurance of God's "everlasting arms" supporting us.

Then he wrote a third letter, this one to a hymnwriter in Pennsylvania, Elisha Hoffman. He even suggested the wording of the chorus. When Hoffman responded quickly with three stanzas, Showalter composed the music.

The theme is simply this: With God's arms beneath us and his love surrounding us, we can find strength in even the most sorrowful situations.

Scriptures: Deuteronomy 33:26-27; Psalm 57:1; Psalm 91:2, 1 John 1:7
Themes: Trust, Comfort, Security

What a fellowship, what a joy divine,
Leaning on the everlasting arms;
What a blessedness, what a peace is mine,
Leaning on the everlasting arms.

Leaning, leaning,
Safe and secure from all alarms;
Leaning, leaning,
Leaning on the everlasting arms.

O, how sweet to walk in this pilgrim way,
Leaning on the everlasting arms;
O, how bright the path grows from day to day,
Leaning on the everlasting arms.

What have I to dread, what have I to fear,
Leaning on the everlasting arms?
I have blessed peace with my Lord so near,
Leaning on the everlasting arms.

ELISHA ALBRIGHT HOFFMAN (1839–1929)

MOMENT BY MOMENT

While Henry Varley and evangelist Daniel Whittle were attending the World's Fair in Chicago, Varley told the evangelist that he didn't like the hymn "I Need Thee Every Hour." Why not? Because, Varley said, "I need Him every moment of the day." That was all Whittle needed to motivate him to write this hymn, "Moment by Moment."

Varley was a unique individual. He had very little education and had drifted to Australia as a teenager. There he dug gold. After a short time in Australia, he returned to England and bought a meat business. As a well-to-do businessman, he met evangelist Dwight L. Moody and told him, "The world has yet to see what God will do with a man fully consecrated to him." Moody couldn't forget those words. Back in Chicago, Moody said, "The very paving stones seemed to be marked with those words." Those words changed Moody's ministry, and a year later he returned to England to thank Henry Varley for saying them.

Varley may have just been a layman in the meat business, but when he said something, people listened, such as the time he told Daniel Whittle, "I need Jesus moment by moment, not just hour by hour."

Scriptures: 1 Thessalonians 5:16-18; Hebrews 4:16
Themes: Submission, Commitment, Holiness

Dying with Jesus, by death reckoned mine;
Living with Jesus, a new life divine;
Looking to Jesus till glory doth shine,
Moment by moment, O Lord, I am Thine.

Moment by moment I'm kept in His love;
Moment by moment I've life from above;
Looking to Jesus till glory doth shine;
Moment by moment, O Lord, I am Thine.

Never a trial that He is not there,
Never a burden that He doth not bear,
Never a sorrow that He doth not share,
Moment by moment, I'm under His care.

Never a heartache, and never a groan,
Never a teardrop and never a moan;
Never a danger but there on the throne,
Moment by moment He thinks of His own.

Never a weakness that He doth not feel,
Never a sickness that He cannot heal;
Moment by moment, in woe or in weal,
Jesus, my Savior, abides with me still.

DANIEL WEBSTER WHITTLE (1840–1901)

MY FAITH LOOKS UP TO THEE

At twenty-two, Ray Palmer was having a tough year. He wanted to go into the ministry but was stuck teaching at a girls' school in New York City. He was lonely, depressed, and sick. One night at his boarding-house, he wrote a poem in a little morocco-bound notebook to bolster his own courage. Later he recalled, "There was not the slightest thought of writing for another eye, least of all writing a hymn for Christian worship."

But two years later, while visiting Boston, he ran across his friend Lowell Mason. Mason, a major figure in American music in the early 1800s, was preparing a new hymnal. He asked Palmer if he'd like to contribute anything. Palmer bashfully showed Mason these verses. Mason hurried into a nearby store, got a piece of paper, and copied the poem. When he handed the notebook back to Palmer, he said, "You may live many years and do many good things, but I think you will be best known to posterity as the author of 'My Faith Looks Up to Thee.'" That night Lowell Mason went home and wrote the music for the words that Ray Palmer had held in his pocket for two years.

Scriptures: Psalm 118:8-9; Isaiah 40:28-29; 2 Corinthians 12:9
Themes: Faith, Guidance, Comfort

My faith looks up to Thee,
Thou Lamb of Calvary,
Savior divine!
Now hear me while I pray,
Take all my guilt away,
O let me from this day
Be wholly Thine!

May Thy rich grace impart
Strength to my fainting heart,
My zeal inspire;
As Thou hast died for me,

O may my love to Thee
Pure, warm, and changeless be,
A living fire!

While life's dark maze I tread
And griefs around me spread,
Be Thou my guide;
Bid darkness turn to day,
Wipe sorrow's tears away,
Nor let me ever stray
From Thee aside.

When ends life's passing dream,
When death's cold, threatening stream
Shall o'er me roll,
Blest Savior, then, in love,
Fear and distrust remove;
O lift me safe above,
A ransomed soul!

RAY PALMER (1808–1887)

NOTHING IS IMPOSSIBLE

Eugene L. Clark, the gifted pianist associated with the Back to the Bible radio broadcast, was also a songwriter, an arranger of choir numbers, and a writer of missionary cantatas. However, he suffered from debilitating arthritis, which gradually affected every part of his body. Soon his eyesight was affected and he became totally blind. Before long, it became impossible for Eugene to continue playing the piano or the organ.

Unwilling to quit, he asked that a dictating machine be brought to his bedside. And he dictated his arrangements by the machine—a note, a rest, a bar, a dot at a time. It was something that neither total blindness nor crippling arthritis could stop.

His best-known song, "Nothing Is Impossible," typifies the life of Eugene Clark.

Scriptures: John 15:5-7; 2 Corinthians 12:9; Philippians 4:13
Themes: Faith, Promises, Hope

Nothing is impossible when you put your trust in God;
Nothing is impossible when you're trusting in His Word.
Hearken to the voice of God to thee: "Is there anything too hard for Me?"
Then put your trust in God alone and rest upon His Word;
For everything, oh everything, yes, everything is possible with God.

EUGENE L. CLARK

O FOR A FAITH THAT WILL NOT SHRINK

Just before Hebrews 11, that great chapter of faith, are two verses that speak of shrinking faith. These verses contrast the righteous person who lives by faith with the one who "shrinks back." That unusual phrase may have prompted this hymn by William Bathurst, but Bathurst wasn't concerned simply about shrinking faith. He was also interested in a growing faith.

At the time Bathurst wrote this hymn, he was working on a sermon called "The Power of Faith." His text was Luke 17:5, where the disciples ask Jesus to increase their faith.

Today our clothing is supposedly "guaranteed not to shrink." In this hymn, William Bathurst writes of a faith that is guaranteed not to shrink. It is, he says, "a faith that shines more bright and clear when tempests rage without, / That, when in danger, knows no fear, in darkness feels no doubt."

Do you have that kind of faith?

Scriptures: Luke 17:5-6; Ephesians 6:16; Hebrews 11:38-39
Themes: Faith, Perseverance, Doubt

O for a faith that will not shrink tho'pressed by many a foe,
That will not tremble on the brink of any earthly woe.

That will not murmur nor complain beneath the chastening rod,
But in the hour of grief or pain will lean upon its God.

A faith that shines more bright and clear when tempests rage without,
That, when in danger, knows no fear, in darkness feels no doubt.

Lord, give me such a faith as this, and then, whate'er may come,
I'll taste e'en now the hallowed bliss of an eternal home.

WILLIAM HILEY BATHURST (1795–1877)

STILL, STILL WITH THEE

When Harriet Beecher Stowe met President Abraham Lincoln in the middle of the Civil War, the president asked, "Is this the little lady who started this big war?" Harriet Beecher Stowe was author of the best-selling *Uncle Tom's Cabin,* the book that energized the antislavery movement in the early 1850s.

But Harriet Beecher Stowe also wrote hymns, and this one was written shortly after her son Charles died of cholera and her husband went into a sanatorium because of poor health. All the problems of managing the home and the other children fell on her shoulders.

Harriet always rose at 4:30 each morning, as she says, "to see the coming of the dawn, hear the singing of the birds, and to enjoy the overshadowing presence of God." One morning she had just read Psalm 139:17 and 18, which say, "How precious also are thy thoughts unto me, O God. . . . When I awake, I am still with thee" (KJV). It was at such a time that she wrote this hymn, "Still, Still with Thee."

Scriptures: Psalm 139:17-18; Philippians 4:6-8; Colossians 3:2-3
Themes: Holiness, Peace, Contentment

Still, still with Thee—when purple morning breaketh,
When the bird waketh and the shadows flee;
Fairer than morning, lovelier than daylight,
Dawns the sweet consciousness—I am with Thee!

Alone with Thee amid the mystic shadows,
The solemn hush of nature newly born;
Alone with Thee in breathless adoration,
In the calm dew and freshness of the morn.

Still, still with Thee—as to each new-born morning
A fresh and solemn splendor still is given;
So doth this blessed consciousness, awaking
Breathe each day nearness unto Thee and heav'n!

So shall it be at last in that bright morning,
When the soul waketh and life's shadows flee;
O in that hour, fairer than daylight dawning,
Shall rise the glorious tho't—I am with Thee!

HARRIET BEECHER STOWE (1811–1896)

STRONG SON OF GOD

The great English poet Alfred, Lord Tennyson had a good friend from his college days at Cambridge. The friend, Arthur Hallam, was engaged to Tennyson's sister. However, on a trip to Austria, just after he had completed his college work, Hallam had a brain aneurysm and died.

Tennyson's faith was shaken, but he fought his way to write the magnificent elegy, "In Memoriam." It is from that poem that this hymn is taken. As the poet struggled to find answers, he found what he called "a faith beyond the forms of faith."

Tennyson's poem is not only a wrestling with his grief, but it is also a response to his colleagues who were turning to science and philosophy and becoming agnostics. Tennyson says that science and philosophy don't have answers to ultimate questions. So he writes, "Our little systems have their day, / They have their day and cease to be: / They are but broken lights of thee, / And Thou, O Lord, are more than they."

Scriptures: Job 9:10-12; Psalm 90:1-12; Hebrews 11:1
Themes: Jesus, Death, Hope

Strong Son of God, immortal love,
When we, that have not seen Thy face,
By faith, and faith alone, embrace,
Believing where we cannot prove;
Thou wilt not leave us in the dust:
Thou madest man, he knows not why,
He thinks he was not made to die;
And Thou hast made him: Thou art just.

Thou seemest human and divine,
The highest, holiest manhood, Thou:
Our wills are ours, we know not how;
Our wills are ours, to make them Thine.
Our little systems have their day,
They have their day and cease to be:
They are but broken lights of Thee,
And Thou, O Lord, art more than they.

ALFRED, LORD TENNYSON (1809–1892)

THE SOLID ROCK

Many of the British hymnwriters were children of clergy or from middle- or upper-class backgrounds. But not Edward Mote. His parents kept a pub in London. Mote said, "My Sundays were spent in the streets; so ignorant was I that I did not know that there was a God." He was apprenticed to a cabinetmaker who took him to church, where he heard the gospel message. Mote himself became a successful cabinetmaker in a London suburb and was active in his local church.

Mote wrote this hymn while he was working as a cabinetmaker. The chorus came to his mind as he was walking to work, and later in the day the stanzas came to him. The following Sunday afternoon, he visited the dying wife of a close friend. Mote didn't know exactly what to say to her, so he quoted the four verses of the hymn he had just written. At the end of each verse, he repeated these words: "On Christ, the solid rock I stand; / All other ground is sinking sand."

Two years later, he published the hymn and titled it "The Immutable Basis of a Sinner's Hope." It is a hymn that combines deep biblical theology with sincere personal experience.

Scriptures: Matthew 7:24-27; 1 Corinthians 3:11; 1 John 1:6-9
Themes: Hope, Salvation, Assurance

My hope is built on nothing less
Than Jesus' blood and righteousness;
I dare not trust the sweetest frame,
But wholly lean on Jesus' name.

On Christ, the solid rock, I stand;
All other ground is sinking sand,
All other ground is sinking sand.

When darkness veils His lovely face,
I rest on His unchanging grace;
In every high and stormy gale,
My anchor holds within the veil.

His oath, His covenant, His blood
Support me in the whelming flood;
When all around my soul gives way,
He then is all my hope and stay.

When He shall come with trumpet sound,
O may I then in Him be found!
Dressed in His righteousness alone,
Faultless to stand before the throne!

EDWARD MOTE (1797–1874)

'TIS SO SWEET TO TRUST IN JESUS

Louisa Stead and her husband were relaxing with their four-year-old daughter on a Long Island beach when they heard a child's desperate cry. A boy was drowning, and Louisa's husband tried to rescue him. In the process, however, the boy pulled Mr. Stead under the water, and both drowned as Louisa and her daughter watched.

Louisa Stead was left with no means of support. She and her daughter experienced dire poverty. One morning, when she had neither funds nor food for the day, she opened the front door and found that someone had left food and money on her doorstep. That day she wrote this hymn.

Sometimes we mouth platitudes about our Christianity—glibly quoting Scripture and singing songs about trusting Jesus. For Stead, there was nothing glib or superficial about it. Her hymn remains a timeless reminder and comfort to all believers who have experienced this same truth: "Jesus, Jesus, how I trust Him! / How I've proved Him o'er and o'er! / Jesus, Jesus, precious Jesus! / O for grace to trust Him more!"

Scriptures: Psalm 91:4; John 14:1-3; Ephesians 1:3-5
Themes: Trust, Confidence, Commitment

'Tis so sweet to trust in Jesus,
Just to take Him at His Word,
Just to rest upon His promise,
Just to know "Thus saith the Lord."

Jesus, Jesus, how I trust Him!
How I've proved Him o'er and o'er!
Jesus, Jesus, precious Jesus!
O for grace to trust Him more!

O how sweet to trust in Jesus,
Just to trust His cleansing blood,
Just in simple faith to plunge me
'Neath the healing, cleansing flood!

Yes, 'tis sweet to trust in Jesus,
Just from sin and self to cease,
Just from Jesus simply taking
Life and rest and joy and peace.

I'm so glad I learned to trust Him,
Precious Jesus, Savior, Friend;
And I know that He is with me,
Will be with me to the end.

LOUISA M. R. STEAD (1850–1917)

'TIS THE PROMISE OF GOD FULL SALVATION TO GIVE

Philip Bliss died while trying to rescue his wife from a fire following a train crash. He was only thirty-eight, but those thirty-eight years were filled with activity. He had been a farmworker, a sawmill operator, and a cook in a lumber camp before Dwight L. Moody urged him to become a singing evangelist. He became a gifted song leader and soloist and also an accomplished songwriter. Many were converted as they sang one of his gospel songs.

One of those converts was an eight-year-old German immigrant lad living in Peoria, Illinois. Later, this boy wrote a letter explaining how his conversion happened. He wrote, "I can say I was converted when they were singing the second hymn, 'Hallelujah, 'Tis Done.' In singing the chorus of it, I thought, Do I believe on the Son? and so . . . I was among the lot that rose. It was Thanksgiving night at the Centennial Hall, in which I was converted. I was eight years old."

Scriptures: John 3:16; John 5:24; Acts 16:31

Themes: Salvation, Promises, Assurance

'Tis the promise of God, full salvation to give
Unto him who on Jesus, His Son, will believe.

Hallelujah, 'tis done! I believe on the Son;
I am saved by the blood of the crucified One.

Tho' the pathway be lonely, and dangerous too,
Surely Jesus is able to carry me through

Many loved ones have I in yon heavenly throng,
They are safe now in glory, and this is their song:

There's a part in that chorus for you and for me,
And the theme of our praises forever will be.

PHILIP PAUL BLISS (1838–1876)

TRUSTING JESUS

A minister was visiting a woman with an incurable illness. She was depressed and deeply distressed. "The future is so dark," she said.

The minister asked, "Can't you trust yourself in God's hands?"

"Not for long," she said. "And I can't leave myself there."

Her pastor repeated the chorus of this song: "Trusting as the moments fly, trusting as the days go by; / Trusting Him whate'er befall, trusting Jesus, that is all." And then he sang it for her. The change that came over her was wonderful, the pastor said later. And she never lost that trust. She had the page in her hymnbook turned down so that anyone who visited her could read it to her again. "Trusting Jesus, that is all."

Scriptures: Psalm 37:3; Psalm 84:12; Nahum 1:7; 2 Corinthians 1:9-10
Themes: Trust, Assurance, Rest

Simply trusting ev'ry day,
Trusting through a stormy way;
Even when my faith is small,
Trusting Jesus, that is all.

Trusting as the moments fly, trusting as the days go by;
Trusting Him whate'er befall, trusting Jesus, that is all.

Brightly doth His Spirit shine
Into this poor heart of mine;
While He leads I cannot fall;
Trusting Jesus, that is all.

Singing if my way is clear,
Praying if the path be drear;
If in danger, for Him call;
Trusting Jesus, that is all.

Trusting Him while life shall last,
Trusting Him till earth be past;
Till within the jasper wall,
Trusting Jesus, that is all.

EDGAR PAGE STITES (1836–1921)

PART III

ATONEMENT AND THE CROSS

He forgave all our sins. He canceled the record of the charges against

us and took it away by nailing it to the cross.

COLOSSIANS 2:13-14

ALAS! AND DID MY SAVIOR BLEED?

This hymn by Isaac Watts has certainly touched the hearts of millions through the centuries. After drawing the stark contrasts between the sacrificial death of the mighty Maker and the unworthiness of the sinful creature, he concludes with the consecration, "Here, Lord, I give myself away—'tis all that I can do."

A young man who lived in the West wrote his former Sunday school teacher: "Do you remember that old hymn, 'Alas! And Did My Savior Bleed'? I thought it rubbish at the time, but its lines have followed me like a detective. I haven't been able to shake off the question: 'Was it for crimes that I have done?' So I finally decided to surrender my life to Him. 'Here, Lord, I give myself away—/ 'Tis all that I can do.' "

And then there was a thirty-year-old blind woman who heard a revival choir sing this simple hymn. Stanza after stanza stirred her heart, but when the choir came to the line "Here, Lord, I give myself away," she gave herself away to the Lord as well. When she did, she said, her "soul flooded with celestial light." That blind woman was Fanny Crosby, who went on to become the great writer of hundreds of gospel songs.

Scriptures: Psalm 22:6; Isaiah 53:4-6; Romans 5:8
Themes: Cross, Salvation, Consecration

> Alas! and did my Savior bleed
> And did my Sovereign die?
> Would He devote that sacred head
> For sinners such as I?
>
> Was it for sins that I have done
> He suffered on the tree?
> Amazing pity! grace unknown!
> And love beyond degree!
>
> Well might the sun in darkness hide
> And shut His glories in,
> When Christ, the great Redeemer, died
> For man the creature's sin.
>
> Thus might I hide my blushing face
> While His dear cross appears,
> Dissolve my heart in thankfulness,
> And melt mine eyes to tears.

But drops of grief can ne'er repay
The debt of love I owe;
Here, Lord, I give myself away—
'Tis all that I can do.

ISAAC WATTS (1674–1748)

AT CALVARY

William R. Newell was best known as a Bible teacher and as the writer of a commentary on the book of Romans. But one day while on his way to teach a class at Moody Bible Institute in Chicago, the words of this hymn began to form in his mind. He didn't want to forget these ideas, so he went into an unoccupied classroom and scribbled the words on the back of an envelope. Continuing on to his class, he met the school's director of music, Daniel B. Towner, and gave him the envelope on which he had scribbled the words. By the time Newell finished teaching his class an hour later, Towner had finished composing the music for this gospel song.

The verses of the song follow the outline of the book of Romans. The first stanza deals with our sinfulness, the second with God's law and with the Cross, the third with our salvation, and the fourth with praise to God for his goodness.

Scriptures: Romans 5:8-11; Romans 11:33; Ephesians 1:5-7; Colossians 1:19-23
Themes: Cross, Salvation, God's Mercy

Years I spent in vanity and pride,
Caring not my Lord was crucified,
Knowing not it was for me He died
On Calvary.

Mercy there was great and grace was free,
Pardon there was multiplied to me,
There my burdened soul found liberty—
At Calvary.

By God's Word at last my sin I learned—
Then I trembled at the law I'd spurned,
Till my guilty soul imploring turned
To Calvary.

Now I've giv'n to Jesus ev'rything,
Now I gladly own Him as my King,
Now my raptured soul can only sing
Of Calvary.

O the love that drew salvation's plan!
O the grace that bro't it down to man!
O the mighty gulf that God did span
At Calvary.

WILLIAM REED NEWELL (1868–1956)

AT THE LAMB'S HIGH FEAST

Scripture speaks of several Passover (or paschal) feasts. The first was celebrated by the Israelites in Egypt. After the lamb was slain and blood was put on the doorposts, the Israelite families feasted while the angel of death passed over their houses. This is the Passover that continues to be celebrated in Jewish homes today.

In the upper room just prior to his death, Jesus, the Lamb of God, observed the Last Supper with his disciples. This Passover meal took on special meaning because of Jesus. This is the Eucharist—or Communion—that the Christian Church continues to celebrate today.

Revelation 19 speaks of the wedding supper of the Lamb, the consummation of the Paschal feast. The Lamb that was slain, Jesus, has now been glorified. The Victim is now the Victor. Thus this ancient hymn, translated from Latin, weaves the three feasts together into a triumphant climax.

Scriptures: Exodus 12:24-27; Matthew 26:26-28; 1 Corinthians 11:23-26; Revelation 19:7-9
Themes: Crucifixion, Praise, Communion

At the Lamb's high feast we sing
Praise to our victorious King,
Who hath washed us in the tide
Flowing from His pierced side;
Praise we Him, whose love divine
Gives His sacred Blood for wine,
Gives His Body for the feast,
Christ the victim, Christ the priest.

Where the Paschal Blood is poured,
Death's dark angel sheathes his sword;
Israel's hosts triumphant go
Through the wave that drowns the foe.
Praise we Christ, whose Blood was shed,
Paschal victim, Paschal bread;
With sincerity and love
Eat we manna from above.

Mighty Victim from the sky,
Hell's fierce powers beneath Thee lie;
Thou hast conquered in the fight,
Thou hast brought us life and light;
Now no more can death appall,
Now no more the grave enthrall;
Thou hast opened paradise,
And in Thee Thy saints shall rise.

Paschal triumph, Paschal joy,
Sin alone can this destroy;
From sin's power do Thou set free
Souls new-born, O Lord, in Thee.
Hymns of glory, songs of praise,
Father, unto Thee we raise:
Risen Lord, all praise to Thee
With the Spirit ever be.

LATIN HYMN
Translated by Robert Campbell (1814–1868)

BENEATH THE CROSS OF JESUS

Elizabeth Clephane spent her whole life in Scotland. The daughter of a county sheriff, she grew up in the village of Melrose. She suffered from poor health most of her life, but that didn't keep her from serving others. Elizabeth regularly helped the poor and those with disabilities, even selling a horse and carriage to give more money. Her cheery attitude and selfless spirit earned her the nickname "The Sunbeam of Melrose."

Elizabeth wrote eight hymns in her short life of thirty-nine years. Her hymns were filled with biblical images. In this hymn, she begins with Isaiah 32:1, which speaks of a righteous king coming. This king will refresh his people like the cool shadow of a large rock in a hot and weary land.

She finds the fulfillment of this prophecy in Jesus Christ and in the cross. Thus the cross becomes a rock that offers shade to the desert traveler. It's a home in the wilderness, a rest stop for the exhausted wanderer.

In the last stanza, this woman who was nicknamed "The Sunbeam," writes, "I ask no other sunshine / Than the sunshine of His face . . . My sinful self my only shame, / My glory all the cross."

Scriptures: Psalm 63:1; Isaiah 4:6; Isaiah 32:1-2; Galatians 6:14
Themes: Cross, Love of Christ, Devotion

Beneath the cross of Jesus
I fain would take my stand—
The shadow of a mighty Rock
Within a weary land;
A home within the wilderness,
A rest upon the way,
From the burning of the noontide heat,
And the burden of the day.

Upon that cross of Jesus
Mine eye at times can see
The very dying form of One
Who suffered there for me;
And from my smitten heart with tears
Two wonders I confess—
The wonders of redeeming love
And my unworthiness.

I take, O cross, thy shadow
For my abiding place;
I ask no other sunshine than
The sunshine of His face;
Content to let the world go by,
To know no gain nor loss,
My sinful self my only shame,
My glory all the cross.

ELIZABETH CECELIA CLEPHANE (1830–1869)

BURDENS ARE LIFTED AT CALVARY

While working at the Seaman's Chapel in Glasgow, Scotland, John Moore received a phone call from a large shipping firm. They asked him to visit a young merchant seaman who was critically ill. Moore made the hospital visit, and after talking with the sailor, he reached into his briefcase for a gospel tract. What he pulled out of his case was a tract based on *Pilgrim's Progress.* The front page showed Christian coming to the cross with a huge burden on his back.

Moore told the merchant seaman the story of how Christian had come to the cross and how his burden had been rolled away. Then he asked the young man, "Do you feel this burden on your back today?" The seaman nodded his head, so they prayed together. Moore said, "Never will I forget the smile of peace and assurance that lit up his face when he said that his burden was lifted."

That night, with the experience still fresh in his mind, John Moore wrote the song, "Burdens Are Lifted at Calvary."

Scriptures: Psalm 147:3; Matthew 11:28; Luke 4:17-18
Themes: Comfort, Salvation, Joy

Days are filled with sorrow and care; hearts are heavy and drear;
Burdens are lifted at Calvary—Jesus is very near.

Burdens are lifted at Calvary, Calvary, Calvary,
Burdens are lifted at Calvary; Jesus is very near.

Cast your care on Jesus today; Leave your worry and fear;
Burdens are lifted at Calvary, Jesus is very near.

Troubled soul, the Savior can see ev'ry heartache and tear;
Burdens are lifted at Calvary, Jesus is very near.

JOHN M. MOORE (B. 1925)
© 1952 New Spring (ASCAP)
All rights reserved. Used by permission.

GO TO DARK GETHSEMANE

Step by step, James Montgomery takes us through Christ's passion. We go with our Lord to the garden of Gethsemane. While his disciples drifted off to sleep, Jesus fought the temptation to avoid the Cross. It was a difficult time, and in the simple text of this hymn we feel each drop of sweat.

At Jesus' trial—a shabby excuse for justice if ever there was one—he bore the beating and badgering without speaking a word. He was carrying our sins with him to the Cross. At the cross we can only fall at his feet in worship.

When we finally reach the tomb in the last verse, we find he is not there. There is a moment of confusion—who has taken him?—before the truth dawns on us. He is risen!

At each point of this journey we have much to learn from our Savior. We can learn to pray when tempted and to endure suffering with patience. And Christ teaches us to rise in newness of life, to live in a way that honors him, and ultimately to join him in glory.

Scriptures: Matthew 26:36-38; Matthew 27:28-29; John 19:30
Themes: Suffering of Christ, Crucifixion, Passion

Go to dark Gethsemane,
Ye that feel the tempter's power;
Your Redeemer's conflict see;
Watch with Him one bitter hour;
Turn not from His griefs away;
Learn of Jesus Christ to pray.

See Him at the judgment hall,
Beaten, bound, reviled, arraigned;
See Him meekly bearing all!
Love to man His soul sustained.
Shun not suffering, shame, or loss;
Learn of Christ to bear the cross.

Calvary's mournful mountain climb;
There adoring at His feet,
Mark that miracle of time,
God's own sacrifice complete;
"It is finished!" hear Him cry;
Learn of Jesus Christ to die.

Early hasten to the tomb
Where they laid His breathless clay:
All is solitude and gloom;
Who hath taken Him away?
Christ is risen! He meets our eyes.
Savior, teach us so to rise.

JAMES MONTGOMERY (1771–1854)

I GAVE MY LIFE FOR THEE

Twenty-two-year-old Frances Havergal was traveling in Europe with friends. In Düsseldorf, Germany, she visited an art gallery. She soon became exhausted and sat down in front of a painting by Sternberg. It was a painting of Christ on the cross, and under it were the words "This have I done for thee; what hast thou done for Me?"

Tears came to her eyes as she thought about those words. Then the lines of this hymn came to her, and she wrote them down with a pencil on a scrap of paper. When she got back to England, she read the poem and thought the poetry was bad. So she tossed the lines into a stove.

Though the paper was scorched, it didn't get all the way into the stove. Instead, it floated away from the flames and onto the floor, where her father found it later. He liked the poem and encouraged her to write a few more verses for it. It was the first hymn she wrote but not the last. For the last 150 years, the Christian Church has been singing her hymns.

Scriptures: Romans 5:8; Romans 12:1-2; 2 Corinthians 5:15
Themes: Commitment, Atonement, Submission

I gave My life for thee, My precious blood I shed,
That thou might'st ransomed be, and quickened from the dead;
I gave, I gave My life for thee, what hast thou giv'n for Me?

My Father's house of light, My glory circled throne I left for earthly night,
For wand'rings sad and lone; I left, I left it all for thee,
Hast thou left aught for Me?

I suffered much for thee, More than thy tongue can tell,
Of bitt'rest agony, To rescue thee from hell; I've borne,
I've borne it all for thee, What hast thou borne for Me?

And I have brought to thee, down from My home above,
Salvation full and free, My pardon and My love;
I bring, I bring rich gifts to thee, what hast thou brought to Me?
FRANCES RIDLEY HAVERGAL (1836–1879)

I SAW ONE HANGING ON A TREE

All his life John Newton marveled at God's grace. It wasn't the fact that Jesus died on the cross; it was the fact that Jesus had died for him. And that amazing fact was what caused Newton to write "Amazing Grace," as well as this hymn with its chorus, "Can it be upon a tree the Savior died for me?"

Newton never forgot that he had lived a wild life of wretchedness and degradation as a slave trader. A headstrong young man, Newton had to be tamed by the Lord as if he were a wild beast. His language was so vile and his lifestyle so immoral that even the other sailors couldn't take it any more. He was put ashore in Africa, where he wandered about, utterly destitute until he became a servant to slaves.

His rescue was miraculous and his conversion even more so. He went into the ministry when he was thirty-nine years old and, through his hymns and his sermons, continued to express his amazement at God's marvelous grace for the rest of his life.

Each one of us should look at the Cross with the same wonder—that Jesus would die for you and me.

Scriptures: Romans 5:8; 2 Corinthians 5:21; Titus 3:5-6
Themes: Atonement, Worship, Salvation

I saw One hanging on a tree, in agony and blood,
He fixed His loving eyes on me, as near the cross
   I stood.

O, can it be, upon a tree, the Savior died for me?
My soul is thrilled, my heart is filled,
*   To think He died for me!*

Sure, never till my latest breath, can I forget that look;
It seemed to charge me with His death, though not a word
   He spoke.

My conscience felt and owned the guilt, and plunged me in despair;
I saw my sins His blood had spilt and helped to nail Him there.

A second look He gave, which said, "I freely all forgive;
This blood is for your ransom paid, I die that you may live."

JOHN NEWTON (1725–1807)

IN THE CROSS OF CHRIST I GLORY

John Bowring was a genius. He was one of the greatest linguists who ever lived. He could converse in a hundred different languages. He was knighted by the queen of England. He sat in the English Parliament. He was the British consul to China, and later he was named governor of Hong Kong. He wrote a book on commerce, a book of Russian poetry, a book of morals for young people, and a book on travel to the Far East.

But it was while he was governor of Hong Kong that he wrote the hymn "In the Cross of Christ I Glory." It was inspired by Galatians 6:14, which in the King James Version reads, "God forbid that I should glory, save in the cross of our Lord Jesus Christ." Another influence on him, according to some sources, was the sight of a huge cross on the ruins of a cathedral at Macao on the south China coast. Apparently the cathedral, built by Portuguese colonists, had been leveled by a typhoon, but the wall with its bronze cross remained standing. The scene so impressed Bowring that he wrote this memorable hymn of the cross towering o'er the wrecks of time. The first line of the hymn is on his tombstone.

Scriptures: 1 Corinthians 2:1-5; Galatians 6:14; Ephesians 2:16
Themes: Cross, Comfort, Confidence

In the cross of Christ I glory,
Towering o'er the wrecks of time;
All the light of sacred story
Gathers round its head sublime.

When the woes of life o'ertake me,
Hopes deceive, and fears annoy,
Never shall the cross forsake me:
Lo! it glows with peace and joy.

When the sun of bliss is beaming
Light and love upon my way,
From the cross the radiance streaming
Adds more luster to the day.

Bane and blessing, pain and pleasure,
By the cross are sanctified;
Peace is there, that knows no measure,
Joys that through all time abide.

In the cross of Christ I glory,
Towering o'er the wrecks of time;
All the light of sacred story
Gathers round its head sublime.

JOHN BOWRING (1792–1872)

JESUS, I MY CROSS HAVE TAKEN

As the daughter of a wealthy English merchant, Mary Bosenquet enjoyed the finest of clothing and jewelry. But Mary went to some Methodist meetings and was converted, her father disinherited her, and she had to move from the large family home to a two-room house furnished with a borrowed table and chairs. Because she was a Methodist, she was personally threatened, and the windows of her house were frequently broken. Yet her faith remained strong.

It was probably her story that inspired Henry Lyte, an Anglican minister, to write this hymn. Some of the language may be archaic, but the words are powerful.

Scriptures: Matthew 16:24; Mark 8:34-35; 1 Peter 2:21
Themes: Cross, Dedication, Discipleship

Jesus, I my cross have taken,
All to leave and follow Thee;
Destitute, despised, forsaken,
Thou, from hence, my all shalt be.
Perish every fond ambition,
All I've sought or hoped or known;
Yet how rich is my condition:
God and heaven are still my own!

Let the world despise and leave me;
They have left my Savior, too.
Human hearts and looks deceive me;
Thou art not, like man, untrue.
And, while Thou shalt smile upon me,
God of wisdom, love, and might,
Foes may hate, and friends may shun me;
Show Thy face, and all is bright.

Man may trouble and distress me,
'Twill but drive me to Thy breast;
Life with trials hard may press me;
Heaven will bring me sweeter rest.
O 'tis not in grief to harm me
While Thy love is left to me;
O 'twere not in joy to charm me,
Were that joy unmixed with Thee.

Haste thee on from grace to glory,
Armed by faith and winged by prayer;
Heaven's eternal day's before thee,
God's own hand shall guide thee there.
Soon shall close thy earthly mission;
Swift shall pass thy pilgrim days;
Hope shall change to glad fruition,
Faith to sight, and prayer to praise.

HENRY FRANCIS LYTE (1793–1847)

JESUS, KEEP ME NEAR THE CROSS

Which comes first, the words or the music? In most cases, the words come first and then a musician composes the tune. The blind hymnwriter Fanny Crosby, who wrote eight thousand hymn texts, worked both ways. She often wrote the lyrics first and then sent them to a musician for him or her to set the lyrics to music. But sometimes she worked the other way.

In the case of this hymn, William Doane wrote the music first and asked Crosby if the music said anything to her. In such times, she would often say, "That tune says to me . . ." and then she would write a stirring text.

This hymn's tune reminded Crosby of the Cross and its importance in our lives. She knew that the Cross of Christ is the central point of history. Without the Cross, there would be no salvation, no eternal life, no hope. If we don't stay near the Cross, we lose our focus in life. Sometimes, although we acknowledge that the Cross is essential for salvation, we lose sight of the fact that it is also essential for our daily living.

Scriptures: Galatians 6:14-15; Colossians 1:20-21; Hebrews 12:2
Themes: Cross, Jesus' Death, Redemption

Jesus, keep me near the cross—
There a precious fountain,
Free to all, a healing stream,
Flows from Calv'ry's mountain.

In the cross, in the cross
Be my glory ever,
Till my raptured soul shall find
Rest, beyond the river.

Near the cross, a trembling soul,
Love and mercy found me;
There the Bright and Morning Star
Sheds its beams around me.

Near the cross! O Lamb of God,
Bring its scenes before me;
Help me walk from day to day
With its shadow o'er me.

Near the cross I'll watch and wait,
Hoping, trusting ever,
Till I reach the golden strand
Just beyond the river.

FANNY JANE CROSBY (1820–1915)

JESUS PAID IT ALL

Elvina Hall wrote this hymn when she should have been listening to her pastor preach. Instead, she was sitting in the choir loft of her Baltimore church, looking for paper to write on. Finding no paper, she started scribbling on the flyleaf of her hymnal, and she ended up writing four stanzas—but not the chorus—of the hymn: "Jesus Paid It All."

John T. Grape, the church organist and a successful coal merchant in the city, composed the music. He said that he only dabbled in music. But one day as he dabbled, he came up with a tune that he liked. He called it "All to Christ I Owe." Grape gave a copy to his pastor, who wasn't too impressed with it. However, when Hall gave the pastor the hymn she had written on the flyleaf of the hymnal, he remembered the organist's music. Surprisingly, Grape's music fit Hall's words, except that Grape had a refrain with his tune. So Hall added a refrain to fit: "Jesus paid it all, / All to him I owe; / Sin had left a crimson stain—/ He washed it white as snow."

Scriptures: Isaiah 1:18; Romans 5:6-8; 1 Corinthians 6:11; Ephesians 2:1-9
Themes: Salvation, Cross, Redemption

I hear the Savior say,
"Thy strength indeed is small!
Child of weakness, watch and pray,
Find in Me thine all in all."

Jesus paid it all,
All to Him I owe;
Sin had left a crimson stain—
He washed it white as snow.

Lord, now indeed I find
Thy pow'r, and Thine alone,
Can change the leper's spots
And melt the heart of stone.

For nothing good have I
Whereby Thy grace to claim—
I'll wash my garments white
In the blood of Calv'ry's Lamb.

And when before the throne
I stand in Him complete,
"Jesus died my soul to save,"
My lips shall still repeat.

ELVINA MABEL HALL (1820–1889)

LEAD ME TO CALVARY

Not much is known about the writer of this hymn, Jennie Hussey, but you can connect the dots and get a pretty good picture. Jennie Hussey lived all her life in rural New Hampshire, and for most of it, she took care of her invalid sister. Although this certainly restricted her in some ways, Jennie was known for her cheerful and courageous attitude.

Jennie was a member of the Society of Friends, the Quakers. In fact, she was a fourth-generation Quaker, which takes her Quaker roots back to the eighteenth century, almost back to the time of William Penn, the remarkable man who brought the Quakers to America and founded the colony of Pennsylvania.

Besides founding Pennsylvania, William Penn is also remembered for a Quaker classic entitled "No Cross, No Crown." Maybe this explains why Jennie began her hymn with the words, "King of my life, I crown thee now," and ended it with the words, "Lead me to Calvary."

Scriptures: Galatians 2:20; Galatians 6:14; Philippians 3:10-11
Themes: Crucifixion, Commitment, Submission

King of my life, I crown Thee now,
Thine shall the glory be;
Lest I forget Thy thorn-crowned brow,
Lead me to Calvary.

Lest I forget Gethsemane; Lest I forget Thine agony;
Lest I forget Thy love for me, Lead me to Calvary.

Show me the tomb where Thou wast laid,
Tenderly mourned and wept;
Angels in robes of light arrayed
Guarded Thee whilst Thou slept.

Let me like Mary, thro' the gloom,
Come with a gift to Thee;
Show to me now the empty tomb,
Lead me to Calvary.

May I be willing, Lord, to bear
Daily my cross for thee;
Even Thy cup of grief to share,
Thou hast borne all for me.

JENNIE EVELYN HUSSEY (1874–1958)

MUST JESUS BEAR THE CROSS ALONE?

When Thomas Shepherd wrote this hymn, he was struggling with two issues. The first was a minor one: He was preaching a sermon on Simon Peter and couldn't find many hymns about Peter. The second was a major one: He was a minister in the Church of England, but he was unhappy about what was going on in the church. But to leave the church would mean losing his security and prestige as well as leaving the beauty of his handsome church.

To solve the minor problem, Shepherd wrote a hymn. He was thinking of the tradition that says Simon Peter was crucified in Rome upside down because he considered himself unworthy to die in the same way as his Lord, so he began his hymn with "shall Simon bear the cross alone, and other saints be free?" Later the hymn was changed to refer to Jesus bearing the cross, but the message is the same: There is a cross for all of us. Cross bearing precedes crown wearing.

Later, Thomas Shepherd answered the call of his own hymn. He left his comfortable parish church and began preaching in a Nottingham barn as an independent preacher.

Scriptures: Matthew 16:24-25; Galatians 2:20; Philippians 3:10; 1 Peter 2:21-24
Themes: Cross, Discipleship, Commitment

Must Jesus bear the cross alone
And all the world go free?
No, there's a cross for ev'ryone,
And there's a cross for me.

The consecrated cross I'll bear
Till death shall set me free,
And then go home my crown to wear,
For there's a crown for me.

Upon the crystal pavement, down
At Jesus' pierced feet,
Joyful I'll cast my golden crown
And His dear name repeat.

O precious cross! O glorious crown!
O resurrection day!
Ye angels, from the stars come down
And bear my soul away.

THOMAS SHEPHERD (1665–1739)

NEAR THE CROSS

Fanny Crosby, the blind songwriter, wrote more than eight thousand hymns. Often she would write a hymn and send it off to a musician friend to supply the melody. Sometimes musicians would give her a tune and ask her for words to fit. That's the way it worked with "Near the Cross."

The composer of the tune was William H. Doane, a prominent Cincinnati businessman who owned the Fay Woodworking Machinery Company. He was Sunday school superintendent of the Mount Auburn Baptist Church for twenty-five years as well as the choir director for the church. In his spare time he wrote tunes for Fanny Crosby. In fact, he became her principal collaborator. He wrote more than 2,200 gospel-song tunes, many of which we are still singing.

He did well in business, too, and left a fortune at his death. Some of his money was used to construct the Doane Memorial Music Building at the Moody Bible Institute in Chicago. William Doane knew what his priorities were, and he honored the Lord in every aspect of his life.

Scriptures: Galatians 6:14; Philippians 2:8; Colossians 1:19-20
Themes: Crucifixion, Forgiveness, Hope

Jesus, keep me near the cross,
There a precious fountain
Free to all, a healing stream,
Flows from Calv'ry's mountain.

In the cross, in the cross, be my glory ever;
Till my raptured soul shall find rest beyond the river.

Near the cross, a trembling soul,
Love and mercy found me;
There the Bright and Morning Star
Sheds its beams around me.

Near the cross! O Lamb of God,
Bring its scenes before me;
Help me walk from day to day,
With its shadows o'er me.

Near the cross I'll watch and wait,
Hoping, trusting ever,
Till I reach the golden strand,
Just beyond the river.

FANNY JANE CROSBY (1820–1915)

O SACRED HEAD, NOW WOUNDED

Bernard of Clairvaux was one of the most influential Christians of the Middle Ages. He settled disputes between kings, and he influenced the selection of popes. Yet he remained single-minded in his devotion to Christ. He is honored by Protestants as well as by Roman Catholics. The great reformer Martin Luther, who disliked many of the medieval theologians, said, "Bernard loved Jesus as much as anyone can."

In his own day, he was known as a preacher and a churchman; today he is remembered for his hymns of devotion to Christ. "O Sacred Head, Now Wounded" comes from a poem of seven sections, each section focusing on a wounded part of the crucified Savior's body—his feet, knees, hands, side, chest, heart, and head. The words compel us to look at the cross until the depth of God's love overwhelms us.

Scriptures: Isaiah 53:4-6; Matthew 27:29-30; 1 Peter 3:18
Themes: Cross, Suffering of Christ

O sacred Head, now wounded,
With grief and shame weighed down,
Now scornfully surrounded
With thorns Thine only crown:
How pale Thou art with anguish,
With sore abuse and scorn!
How does that visage languish
Which once was bright as morn!

What Thou, my Lord, has suffered
Was all for sinners' gain;
Mine, mine was the transgression,
But Thine the deadly pain.
Lo, here I fall, my Savior!
'Tis I deserve Thy place;
Look on me with Thy favor,
Vouchsafe to me Thy grace.

What language shall I borrow
To thank Thee, dearest Friend,
For this Thy dying sorrow,
Thy pity without end?
O make me Thine forever;
And should I fainting be,

Lord, let me never, never
Outlive my love to Thee.

ATTRIBUTED TO BERNARD OF CLAIRVAUX (1091–1153)
Translated from Latin into German by Paul Gerhardt (1607–1676)
Translated into English by John Waddell Alexander (1804–1859)

ROOM AT THE CROSS FOR YOU

Ira Stanphill was seventeen when he wrote his first gospel song, and he kept on writing country gospel music for the rest of his life. As a child, he traveled with his parents by covered wagon from Arkansas to New Mexico, and he was immersed in country music from his earliest years.

As he traveled to evangelistic meetings, Stanphill would often ask people to suggest some titles for him and he would write a song based on one of those titles during the meeting. In 1946 someone in one of his meetings suggested the title, "There's Room at the Cross for You." Stanphill didn't have time in the meeting to work on it, but when he got home, he found the title stuffed in his pocket on a scrap of paper. He liked the idea and soon the song was written.

Stanphill says, "The basic reason I have written songs is that I love God and Christ has loved me. Most of my songs are the outgrowth of real experiences with Christ. I think they appeal to people because I have had trials, heartaches, and sorrow in my own life, and I know what I write about."

Scriptures: John 6:37; Romans 10:13; 1 Timothy 1:15

Themes: Crucifixion, Invitation, Atonement

The cross upon which Jesus died
Is a shelter in which we can hide;
And its grace so free is sufficient for me,
And deep is its fountain—as wide as the sea.

There's room at the cross for you;
Tho' millions have come,
There's still room for one,
Yes, there's room at the cross for you.

Tho' millions have found Him a friend
And have turned from the sins they have sinned,
The Savior still waits to open the gates
And welcome a sinner before it's too late.

The hand of my Savior is strong,
And the love of my Savior is long;
Through sunshine or rain, through loss or in gain,
The blood flows from Calv'ry to cleanse every stain.

Writer: Ira Stanphill
©1946 New Spring (ASCAP)
All rights reserved. Used by permission.

TEN THOUSAND ANGELS

Ray Overholt was making it big in show business. At thirty-six, he had his own TV show and had been on Kate Smith's nationally broadcast program. Now he was moving into the nightclub circuit.

But something was missing, and he knew it. He told his wife he was going to clean up his act. Things were going to change. He decided to read the Bible, which was a good place to start. He began to read about the Crucifixion. He says, "I read where Jesus told Peter that he could ask his Father and he would send twelve legions of angels." He hadn't heard that before.

Overholt had written secular songs, but he thought that a good title for a religious song would be "He Could Have Called Ten Thousand Angels." However, if he were going to write a song about Jesus, he needed to know more about him, so he did a little research. While playing in a nightclub in Battle Creek, Michigan, he began writing the song.

News got around about this nightclub singer writing a spiritual song, and a small church invited him to sing it. After his solo, he listened to the sermon. Overholt says, "It gripped my heart. I knew I needed Christ, so I knelt there and accepted as my Savior, the One whom I had been singing and writing about."

Scriptures: Psalm 91:11; Matthew 26:53; 2 Thessalonians 1:7
Themes: Crucifixion, Jesus Christ, Angels

They bound the hands of Jesus in the garden where He prayed.
They led Him through the streets in shame.
They spat upon the Savior, so pure and free from sin.
They said, "Crucify Him! He's to blame."

He could have called ten thousand angels
To destroy the world and set Him free.

He could have called ten thousand angels,
But He died alone for you and me.

Upon His precious head they placed a crown of thorns;
They laughed and said, "Behold the King!"
They struck Him and they cursed Him, and mocked His holy name,
All alone He suffered everything.

When they nailed Him to the Cross, His mother stood nearby;
He said, "Woman, behold thy son!"
He cried, "I thirst for water," but they gave Him none to drink.
Then the sinful work of man was done.

To the howling mob He yielded; He did not for mercy cry.
The cross of shame He took alone.
And when He cried, "It's finished," He gave himself to die.
Salvation's wondrous plan was done.

THE OLD RUGGED CROSS

From 1925 to 1960 "The Old Rugged Cross" was America's favorite gospel hymn. Each year when a poll was taken, it finished in the number-one position. The song emerged when George Bennard was going through some personal spiritual struggles. He decided to reflect on the meaning of the Cross, what John 3:16 was all about, and what the apostle Paul meant when he talked about entering into the fellowship of Christ's sufferings. Then one day, he said, "I saw the Christ of the cross as if I were seeing John 3:16 leave the printed page, take form, and act out the meaning of redemption." He became convinced that the Cross was "the very heart of the gospel." And then, he said, "The words of the finished hymn were put into my heart in answer to my own need."

Thus George Bennard's personal struggles were the seed of one of the most popular gospel songs of the twentieth century.

Scriptures: John 3:16; Philippians 3:10; Hebrews 12:2; 1 Peter 2:23-25
Themes: Cross, Salvation

On a hill far away stood an old rugged cross,
The emblem of suffering and shame;
And I love that old cross where the dearest and best
For a world of lost sinners was slain.

So I'll cherish the old rugged cross,
'Til my trophies at last I lay down;
I will cling to the old rugged cross,
And exchange it some day for a crown.

O that old rugged cross, so despised by the world,
Has a wondrous attraction for me;
For the dear Lamb of God left His glory above
To bear it to dark Calvary.

In the old rugged cross, stained with blood so divine,
A wondrous beauty I see;
For 'twas on that old cross Jesus suffered and died
To pardon and sanctify me.

To the old rugged cross I will ever be true,
Its shame and reproach gladly bear;
Then He'll call me some day to my home far away,
Where His glory forever I'll share.

GEORGE BENNARD (1873–1958)

THERE IS A FOUNTAIN FILLED WITH BLOOD

William Cowper suffered from deep depression for most of his life. In 1764 he found himself in an institution for the mentally ill. There in the asylum, William Cowper found Christ through reading the Bible.

Despite his emotional pain, or perhaps because of it, Cowper produced literature of amazing insight. He is still renowned in literary circles as one of England's greatest poets.

"There Is a Fountain Filled with Blood" is based on Zechariah 13:1, which says, "On that day a fountain will be opened to the house of David . . . to cleanse them from sin and impurity" (NIV). Cowper grabbed any assurance of God's forgiveness that he could find. He always felt guilty, unworthy of Christ's love. But like the dying thief, he found that the precious fountain could wash all his sins away. Cowper would certainly be surprised that the work of "this poor lisping, stammering tongue" has filled the mouths of millions who claim the blood of Christ as their atonement.

Scriptures: Psalm 36:5-7, 9; Zechariah 13:1; Ephesians 1:7; Hebrews 9:12-14
Themes: Cross, Salvation, Justification

There is a fountain filled with blood
Drawn from Emmanuel's veins,
And sinners, plunged beneath that flood,
Lose all their guilty stains,
Lose all their guilty stains;
And sinners, plunged beneath that flood,
Lose all their guilty stains.

The dying thief rejoiced to see
That fountain in his day;
And there may I, though vile as he,
Wash all my sins away,
Wash all my sins away;
And there may I, though vile as he,
Wash all my sins away.

E'er since, by faith, I saw the stream
Thy flowing wounds supply,
Redeeming love has been my theme,
And shall be till I die,
And shall be till I die;
Redeeming love has been my theme,
And shall be till I die.

Then in a nobler, sweeter song,
I'll sing Thy pow'r to save,
When this poor lisping, stammering tongue
Lies silent in the grave,
Lies silent in the grave;
When this poor lisping, stammering tongue
Lies silent in the grave.

WILLIAM COWPER (1731–1800)

THERE IS A GREEN HILL FAR AWAY

Cecil Alexander, the writer of this hymn loved children. In fact, many of the hymns that she wrote were written to help her Sunday school class of ragamuffin boys learn Christian doctrine. Alexander also visited their homes, sewing, mending, cooking, and caring for the sick. But what concerned her the most was that the youngsters in her class didn't know anything about the basics of Christianity. So she started to teach the Apostles' Creed to the boys, and when she came to the phrase, "Suffered under Pontius Pilate, was crucified, dead and buried," she realized that her class had no idea what it meant to be crucified. So she wrote the song "There is a Green Hill Far Away."

Her husband became an archbishop in the Anglican church. Shortly before he died, he said that in the future he would be remembered only as the husband of the woman who wrote, "There Is a Green Hill Far Away."

Scriptures: John 19:15-18: Ephesians 1:7; Titus 2:14
Themes: Cross, Jesus' Death, Redemption

There is a green hill far away,
Without a city wall,
Where the dear Lord was crucified,
Who died to save us all.

Oh, dearly, dearly has He loved,
And we must love Him too,
And trust in His redeeming blood,
And try His works to do.

We may not know, we cannot tell
What pains He had to bear;
But we believe it was for us
He hung and suffered there.

He died that we might be forgiv'n,
He died to make us good,
That we might go at last to heav'n,
Saved by His precious blood.

There was no other good enough
To pay the price of sin;
He only could unlock the gate
Of heav'n, and let us in.

CECIL FRANCES ALEXANDER (1818–1895)

WERE YOU THERE?

This spiritual comes from a rich American tradition, developed in the early 1800s by African-American slaves. The words are simple, seizing one central theme.

Spirituals often have a lot of emotional appeal. As a result, this hymn, like few others, puts the singer "there." "Were you there?" it asks. We experience the "tremble" as we sing it. And in the triumphant final stanza, we experience the glory of a risen Lord. No longer is it just a Christian discussion; now it is stark reality. We hear the nails pounded into the cross, we see the onlookers wagging their heads, we smell the burial spices, and we feel the rumble of the stone rolling away. And we tremble . . . tremble . . . tremble.

Scriptures: Psalm 22:15-18; Isaiah 53:4-7; Luke 23:45-47; 1 Peter 2:24
Themes: Crucifixion, Burial, Resurrection

Were you there when they crucified my Lord?
Were you there when they crucified my Lord?
O! Sometimes it causes me to tremble, tremble, tremble!
Were you there when they crucified my Lord?

Were you there when they nailed Him to the tree?
Were you there when they nailed Him to the tree?
O! Sometimes it causes me to tremble, tremble, tremble!
Were you there when they nailed Him to the tree?

Were you there when they laid Him in the tomb?
Were you there when they laid Him in the tomb?
O! Sometimes it causes me to tremble, tremble, tremble!
Were you there when they laid Him in the tomb?

Were you there when He rose up from the dead?
Were you there when He rose up from the dead?
O! Sometimes I feel like shouting glory, glory, glory!
Were you there when He rose up from the dead?

TRADITIONAL SPIRITUAL

WHAT WONDROUS LOVE IS THIS?

This hymn has always been associated with the Appalachian area. Like most spirituals, it has been passed down through the generations and exists in several different versions. The melody, based on a six-tone scale, sounds minor to modern ears and has a haunting effect. The text adds to the effect. This is the question of the ages. What made him do it? What made him do it for me?

Every so often you'll read about a disaster where someone makes a heroic but fatal effort to save others. A man jumps into icy water to save a drowning victim. He puts the lifeline in the person's hand, but he himself drowns. We marvel at the selflessness of such a person. What made him do it? Christ bore "the dreadful curse" for our soul, and we can ponder that for the rest of our lives. We can also resolve to devote our lives to him, to please him, and to praise him through all eternity.

Scriptures: Jeremiah 31:3; John 3:16; Galatians 3:13-14; Revelation 1:5-6
Themes: Love, Cross, Atonement

> What wondrous love is this, O my soul, O my soul,
> What wondrous love is this, O my soul!
> What wondrous love is this that caused the Lord of bliss
> To bear the dreadful curse for my soul, for my soul,
> To bear the dreadful curse for my soul?
>
> What wondrous love is this, O my soul, O my soul,
> What wondrous love is this, O my soul!
> What wondrous love is this that caused the Lord of life
> To lay aside His crown for my soul, for my soul,
> To lay aside His crown for my soul?
>
> AMERICAN FOLK HYMN

WHEN I SURVEY THE WONDROUS CROSS

Whenever Isaac Watts wanted a hymn to go with a sermon or a special service that he was leading, he would write one. He ended up writing more than six hundred hymns; today he is known as "The Father of English Hymnody."

So when he needed a hymn for a Communion service one Sunday morning, he wrote "When I Survey the Wondrous Cross." Some have called it "the finest hymn in the English language." The words vividly depict the scene at Calvary and the dying Savior. And the rich, grave tones of the music impress upon us the seriousness of Christ's sacrificial death. What shall we offer to God in grateful return for his gracious gift? All that we are and have is but a small offering in return for such great love.

Scriptures: John 19:17-18; Galatians 6:14; Philippians 3:7-9
Themes: Cross, God's Love, Dedication

> When I survey the wondrous cross
> On which the Prince of glory died,
> My richest gain I count but loss,
> And pour contempt on all my pride.
>
> Forbid it, Lord, that I should boast,
> Save in the death of Christ, my God;
> All the vain things that charm me most—
> I sacrifice them to His blood.
>
> See, from His head, His hands, His feet,
> Sorrow and love flow mingled down;
> Did e'er such love and sorrow meet,
> Or thorns compose so rich a crown?
>
> Were the whole realm of nature mine,
> That were a present far too small:
> Love so amazing, so divine,
> Demands my soul, my life, my all.
>
> ISAAC WATTS (1674–1748)

PART IV

BIBLE

Your word is a lamp to guide my feet and a light for my path.

PSALM 119:105

ACCORDING TO THY GRACIOUS WORD

Newspaper editor James Montgomery, the author of this hymn, remembered the poor and downtrodden. He worked hard for the abolition of slavery and was imprisoned twice for his strong editorials. He also remembered his parents, Moravian missionaries who had given their lives for the people of the West Indies. But most of all, he remembered his Lord, who had given his life for Montgomery.

It would have been easy for Montgomery to get so caught up in the issues of the day that he forgot the issues of eternity. But he resolved that he would never become so busy that he'd forget what Jesus Christ had done for him.

Earthly concerns press upon our lives. Family concerns may overwhelm us. In fact, they can seem so important that they overshadow eternal issues. Along with James Montgomery, let us resolve to remember the Lord.

Scriptures: Luke 22:17-20; Luke 23:42; 1 Corinthians 11:23-28
Themes: Commitment, Atonement, Christian Living

According to Thy gracious word,
In meek humility,
This will I do, my dying Lord,
I will remember Thee.

Thy body, broken for my sake,
My bread from heaven shall be;
Thy testamental cup I take,
And thus remember Thee.

Remember Thee, and all Thy pains,
And all Thy love to me;
Yea, while a breath, a pulse remains,
Will I remember Thee!

And when these failing lips grow dumb,
And mind and memory flee,
When Thou shalt in Thy kingdom come,
Then, Lord, remember me!

JAMES MONTGOMERY (1771–1854)

ALMIGHTY GOD, THY WORD IS CAST

This hymn was written to be sung by a congregation immediately after the sermon was preached. It alludes to the parable of the sower and the seed and serves as a reminder to pray that the sermon just preached (which presumably contained the "seed" of God's Word) might fall on good ground and produce a good crop.

John Cawood, the author of this hymn, grew up on a farm, so he knew all about planting seeds and harvesting crops. Although he wrote many hymns, he was too shy to publish any with his name on them.

In our day God's Word goes forth in many different ways, in ways that Cawood would never have imagined. It is broadcast on radio and TV, presented in movies and recordings, and transmitted through the phone lines to our personal computers. God's Word is cast in many new ways, but hearts still need to be ready to receive it.

Our own hearts need to be tilled like good soil for the truth that God is casting there. That is why many Christians observe a "quiet time" for their personal Bible reading. It's not just a verse or two grabbed on the run, but a seed received, planted, surrounded with the soil of prayer.

Scriptures: Matthew 13:3-5, 7-9; 1 Corinthians 3:6; 2 Corinthians 9:8-11
Themes: Word of God; Church; Obedience;

Almighty God, Thy word is cast
Like seed into the ground;
Now let the dew of heav'n descend
And righteous fruits abound.

Let not the foe of Christ and man
This holy seed remove,
But give it root in ev'ry heart,
To bring forth fruits of love.

Let not the world's deceitful cares
The rising plant destroy,
But let it yield a hundredfold
The fruits of peace and joy.

Oft as the precious seed is sown,
Thy quick'ning grace bestow,
That all whose souls the truth receive
Its saving pow'r may know.

JOHN CAWOOD (1775–1852)

k8

THE COMPLETE BOOK OF HYMNS

BREAK THOU THE BREAD OF LIFE

Mary Lathbury was better known as a commercial artist than as a hymnwriter, and her illustrations appeared regularly in popular American magazines. But she was concerned about superficial Christianity. So many Christians didn't seem to have any depth. Their Bible reading only scratched the surface, and they had no understanding of how culture and education could enrich their Christian lives.

During the summers, Lathbury often vacationed at Lake Chautauqua in New York and shared her burden with others who vacationed there. Soon the Chautauqua movement was founded. Mixing Christian inspiration, culture, and education, the movement spread rapidly across the country. Knowing Mary Lathbury's concern that people study the Bible to get into a deeper relationship with Jesus Christ, the leader of the movement asked her to write a hymn.

This hymn is often sung as a Communion hymn because of its mention of bread, but Mary Lathbury wrote it to encourage Bible readers to go "beyond the sacred page" and let Jesus reveal himself to them as they read.

Scriptures: Psalm 63:1; Jeremiah 15:16; Luke 24:30-31; John 6:35
Themes: Word of God, Bread, Communion, Bible Study

Break Thou the bread of life,
Dear Lord, to me,
As Thou didst break the loaves
Beside the sea;
Beyond the sacred page
I seek Thee, Lord;
My spirit pants for Thee,
O living Word!

Bless Thou the truth, dear Lord,
To me, to me,
As Thou didst bless the bread
By Galilee;
Then shall all bondage cease,
All fetters fall;
And I shall find my peace,
My all-in-all.

MARY ARTEMISIA LATHBURY (1841–1913)

148

HOLY BIBLE, BOOK DIVINE

Sunday schools were introduced to England in 1780 by Robert Raikes, and they quickly spread across the country. There was no public school system, and most children could not read. Many had never even seen a Bible.

One of the first questions the founders of Sunday schools had to answer was, "What shall we teach?" Some thought it best to have the children memorize catechisms, but Raikes and a young Sunday school teacher named John Burton taught the Bible. And if they needed to teach children to read, they did that, too.

In 1803, when he was thirty, Burton published this hymn for children in his little book, *Youth's Monitor in Verse, A Series of Tales, Emblems, Poems and Songs.* Three years later he included it in a second book, *Hymns for Sunday Schools.* You can almost picture a small boy, on his one day off from a rough factory job, proudly clutching a Bible to his chest and singing heartily, "Holy Bible, book divine, / Precious treasure, thou art mine!" Such an image should keep us from taking God's Word for granted.

Scriptures: Psalm 119:97; 2 Timothy 3:16-17; Hebrews 4:12
Themes: Bible, Comfort, Guidance

Holy Bible, book divine,
Precious treasure, thou art mine;
Mine to tell me whence I came;
Mine to teach me what I am.

Mine to chide me when I rove;
Mine to show a Savior's love;
Mine thou art to guide and guard;
Mine to punish or reward.

Mine to comfort in distress,
Suff'ring in this wilderness;
Mine to show, by living faith,
Man can triumph over death.

Mine to tell of joys to come,
And the rebel sinner's doom;
O thou Holy Book divine,
Precious treasure, thou art mine.

JOHN BURTON (1773–1822)

STANDING ON THE PROMISES

When you are "standing on the promises," you can be secure regardless of the premises. That was certainly true in the life of the author of this hymn, Kelso Carter.

Kelso Carter was a hard man to keep track of because he kept moving around. A star athlete, he returned to college after his graduation to become a professor of chemistry, natural science, civil engineering, and mathematics. Then he moved out West and raised sheep in California. After that, he practiced a different kind of shepherding and was ordained into the Methodist ministry. He spoke frequently in Methodist camp meetings when he wasn't writing novels or mathematics and science textbooks. Later he returned to his home state of Maryland, studied medicine, and became a practicing physician in Baltimore.

When the Christian and Missionary Alliance asked him to help compile a hymnal for use in their churches, Carter gladly did so, personally contributing more than fifty poems and tunes to the hymnal.

Some people feel insecure when they are thrust into new jobs, new locations, or new circumstances, but not Kelso Carter. Regardless of the premises, he was "standing on the promises of God."

Scriptures: Psalm 119:49; Isaiah 40:8; 2 Peter 1:4
Themes: Assurance, Security, Promises

> Standing on the promises of Christ my King,
> Thro' eternal ages let His praises ring;
> Glory in the highest, I will shout and sing,
> Standing on the promises of God.
>
> *Standing, standing, standing on the promises of God
>   my Savior.*
> *Standing, standing, I'm standing on the promises of God.*
>
> Standing on the promises that cannot fail,
> When the howling storms of doubt and fear assail,
> By the living word of God I shall prevail,
> Standing on the promises of God.
>
> Standing on the promises of Christ the Lord,
> Bound to Him eternally by love's strong cord,
> Overcoming daily with the Spirit's sword,
> Standing on the promises of God.

Standing on the promises I cannot fall,
List'ning ev'ry moment to the Spirit's call,
Resting in my Savior, as my all in all,
Standing on the promises of God.

R. KELSO CARTER (1849–1928)

THY WORD HAVE I HID IN MY HEART

Ernest Sellers, the writer of this gospel song, started out as a civil engineer and the superintendent of public works in Lansing, Michigan, and ended up having a music building named after him at New Orleans Baptist Theological Seminary. In between he got a Bible education, worked for the YMCA, taught Christian education at the Moody Bible Institute in Chicago, and was director of the music department of the Baptist Bible Institute in New Orleans.

This unique song is derived from Psalm 119, the longest chapter in the Bible. The first stanza is taken from verse 105; the second stanza from verses 89 and 90; the third from verses 44, 62, and 164; and the fourth from verse 41. Then the chorus is directly from Psalm 119:11.

Ernest Sellers did many different things in his life and went to many different places, but he made sure that whatever he did and wherever he went that his life, like this song, revolved around God's Word.

Scriptures: Psalm 119:11; Luke 11:28; 1 Peter 1:23
Themes: Scripture, Growth, Guidance

Thy word is a lamp to my feet, a light to my path always,
To guide and to save me from sin, and show me the heavenly way.

Thy word have I hid in my heart,
That I might not sin against Thee;
That I might not sin, that I might not sin,
Thy word have I hid in my heart.

Forever, O Lord, is Thy word established and fixed on high;
Thy faithfulness unto all men abideth forever nigh.

At morning, at noon, and at night I ever will give Thee praise;
For Thou art my portion, O Lord, and shall be thro' all my days!

Thro' Him whom Thy word hath foretold, the Savior and Morning Star,
Salvation and peace have been bro't to those who have strayed afar.

ERNEST ORLANDO SELLERS (1869–1952)

THY WORD IS LIKE A GARDEN, LORD

When nineteen-year-old Edwin Hodder sailed from England to New Zealand, his job was to do sociological research among the Maori aboriginal tribes there. It was an exciting time for Hodder, and it was exciting for New Zealand, too. The British crown had just made a treaty with forty-six Maori chiefs, although the Maori tribespeople were already having second thoughts. Besides that, gold had just been discovered, and mining was starting to change the face of the land.

But Hodder must have stared wide-eyed at the trees and flowers that were there. Foliage was everywhere. It must have looked like the Garden of Eden. Hodder stayed in New Zealand only five years before returning to England at the age of twenty-four. Two years later he wrote a hymn—possibly the only hymn he wrote in his entire life—about the Bible being a lush, verdant garden and a deep, deep mine with jewels rich and rare. Somehow the Bible reminded him of New Zealand, and just as he had been amazed when he saw that country for the first time, so he prayed that he might be amazed with God's Word, too.

Scriptures: Psalm 119:14,18; Isaiah 51:3; 2 Timothy 3:16-17

Themes: Scripture, Contentment, Commitment

Thy Word is like a garden, Lord, with flowers bright and fair;
And everyone who seeks may pluck a lovely cluster there.
Thy Word is like a deep, deep mine, and jewels rich and rare
Are hidden in its mighty depths for ev'ry searcher there.

Thy Word is like a starry host—a thousand rays of light
Are seen to guide the traveler and make his pathway bright.
Thy Word is like an armory where soldiers may repair
And find, for life's long battle-day all needful weapons there.

O may I love Thy precious Word, may I explore the mine;
May I its fragrant flowers glean, may light upon me shine.
O may I find my armor there, Thy Word my trusty sword!
I'll learn to fight with ev'ry foe the battle of the Lord!

EDWIN HODDER (1837–1904)

WONDERFUL WORDS OF LIFE

As a child raised in a rural log cabin in Pennsylvania, Philip Bliss loved music. The only musical instrument he owned was a flute his father had whittled for him from a cane. Philip hoped to buy a cheap violin, so he picked a basket of berries in the swamps and sold them door-to-door. Hearing the music of a piano coming from one house, Philip went to the door and listened, but the pianist told the barefoot ten-year-old to go away.

Two decades later, Philip Bliss was directing the music in evangelist Dwight L. Moody's evangelistic campaigns, where Bliss had become known for his singing voice and for the gospel songs he wrote.

When Moody's brother-in-law, Fleming H. Revell, was launching a new religious periodical, to be called *Words of Life,* he asked Philip Bliss to write a song for the first issue. Revell suggested both the title "Words of Life" and the text, John 6:67-68. In these verses Jesus sees many of his followers walking away and asks his inner core of twelve: "You do not want to go away also, do you?" Peter replies, "Lord, to whom shall we go? You have words of eternal life" (NASB). As Revell requested, Bliss wrote the gospel song, "Wonderful Words of Life."

Scriptures: Psalm 119:103-105; John 6:67-68; John 8:31-32
Themes: Scripture, Salvation, Comfort

Sing them over again to me,
Wonderful words of Life;
Let me more of their beauty see,
Wonderful words of Life.
Words of Life and beauty,
Teach me faith and duty:

Beautiful words, wonderful words,
Wonderful words of Life. (Repeat.)

Christ, the blessed One, gives to all,
Wonderful words of Life;
Sinner, list to the loving call,
Wonderful words of Life.
All so freely given,
Wooing us to Heaven:

Sweetly echo the gospel call,
Wonderful words of Life;
Offer pardon and peace to all,
Wonderful words of Life.
Jesus, only Savior, Sanctify forever.

PHILIP PAUL BLISS (1838–1876)

PART V

CHILDREN AND YOUTH

Jesus said, "Let the children come to me. . . . For the Kingdom of

Heaven belongs to those who are like these children."

MATTHEW 19:14

ALL THINGS BRIGHT AND BEAUTIFUL

When Cecil Alexander wanted to teach the children in her Sunday school class about the Apostles' Creed, she wrote hymns for them to sing. She and her husband, William Alexander, a parish minister in Londonderry, Ireland, served in a rural area. Cecil visited the poor families and gathered the children around her for instruction in the Bible, the catechism, and the Apostles' Creed. When she published a collection of her songs, almost all for children, she donated the profits to support disabled children in her area.

"All Things Bright and Beautiful" was written to help children understand the phrase, "I believe in God the Father, Maker of heaven and earth." Often when we think of God the Creator, we consider the vast galaxies of space and the mighty billowing oceans, but this hymn, written for boys and girls, talks of little flowers with glowing colors, little birds with tiny wings, purple-headed mountains, ripe fruits in the garden, and meadows where we play. God created these things, not only so we would marvel at his greatness, but also so we could enjoy them. Make this a day to play in the goodness of God's creation.

Scriptures: Genesis 1:1; John 1:1-3; Hebrews 1:2
Themes: Creation, Praise

Each little flow'r that opens up,
Each little bird that sings,
He made their glowing colors and
He made their tiny wings.

All things bright and beautiful,
All creatures great and small,
And all things wise and wonderful;
The Lord God made them all.

The purple-headed mountain,
The river running by,
The sunset and the morning light
That brightens up the sky.

The cold wind in the wintertime,
The pleasant summer sun,
The ripe fruits in the garden now,
He made them ev'ry one.

He gave us eyes to see them all,
And lips that we might tell
How great is the Almighty God
Who has made all things well.

CECIL FRANCES ALEXANDER (1818–1895)

BRIGHTEN THE CORNER WHERE YOU ARE

For Ina Ogdon it was the chance of a lifetime. She had been selected to travel on the prestigious Chautauqua speaking circuit, and on the tour she would be speaking all across the country to thousands of people.

She was packed and ready to go when she got word that her father had been seriously injured in an automobile accident. She wondered what she should do. But she had no choice. She had to cancel the speaking tour; she had to care for her father.

At first she was bitter about it. A chance like that would never come again. Although Ina wondered why God had allowed it to happen, she finally decided that God must have a reason even if she would never know it. Maybe one person, somewhere, would be helped if she would simply brighten the corner where she was.

So she wrote the song, "Brighten the Corner Where You Are." It was set to music and it became the theme song of the Billy Sunday evangelistic campaigns. More than twenty-five million copies of the song were printed. Every Billy Sunday campaign began with the singing of the song, and since more than one hundred million people came to his campaigns, you can be sure that Ina Ogdon brightened a lot of corners where she was.

Scriptures: Matthew 5:16; Philippians 2:15; 1 Peter 2:12
Themes: Joy, Service, Witness

Do not wait until some deed of greatness you may do.
Do not wait to shed your light afar.
To the many duties ever near you now be true;
Brighten the corner where you are.

Brighten the corner where you are!
Brighten the corner where you are!
Someone far from harbor you may guide across the bar
Brighten the corner where you are!

Just above are clouded skies that you may help to clear;
Let not narrow self your way debar.
Tho' into one heart alone may fall your song of cheer,
Brighten the corner where you are.

Here for all your talent you may surely find a need,
Here reflect the Bright and Morning Star.
Ever from your humble hand the Bread of Life may feed;
Brighten the corner where you are.

INA DULEY OGDON (1877–1964)

DARE TO BE A DANIEL

Two British missionaries were surveying some of the major cities in China to see how much missionary work had been done there. When they got to one city, they found a young Chinese boy walking down the street, singing at the top of his voice, "Dare to be a Daniel, dare to stand alone!" They followed him at a distance and saw him stop in front of a peanut vendor and ask, "Did you know that there is only one God and one Lord Jesus Christ?"

"No," said the peanut vendor.

The boy said, "It's true," and then he continued down the street singing, "Dare to have a purpose firm! Dare to make it known."

That Chinese lad had learned the meaning of the song very well.

Scriptures: Daniel 1:8; Daniel 6:10-11; Acts 16:25-28
Themes: Courage, Commitment, Strength

Standing by a purpose true,
Heeding God's command,
Honor them, the faithful few!
All hail to Daniel's Band!

Dare to be a Daniel, dare to stand alone!
Dare to have a purpose firm! Dare to make it known!

Many mighty men are lost,
Daring not to stand,
Who for God had been a host,
By joining Daniel's Band!

Many giants, great and tall,
Stalking thro' the land,
Headlong to the earth would fall,
If met by Daniel's Band!

Hold the gospel banner high!
On to vict'ry grand!
Satan and his host defy,
And shout for Daniel's Band!

PHILIP PAUL BLISS (1838–1876)

GENTLE JESUS, MEEK AND MILD

The story is told of a little girl named Becca, who lived in an institution for troubled children. She had never spoken, and her behavior was quite violent. She terrorized the other children, hitting them and stomping on their toys.

This was in the 1800s, when treatment for emotional problems was still quite primitive. But there was a nurse who loved this little girl. And slowly Becca calmed down. She began to show affection for the nurse, and she would even sit quietly with the other children as they learned to sing. Still, she wouldn't speak.

One summer evening, the nurse put Becca to bed early. The sun had just gone down, and some birds were singing outside. Then the nurse heard another voice along with the birds. It was Becca. Alone in her room she was singing a song she had heard the other children sing: "Gentle Jesus, meek and mild, / Look upon a little child; / Pity my simplicity, / Suffer me to come to Thee."

Scriptures: Luke 18:15-17; Ephesians 5:1-2; Philippians 2:1-3
Themes: Children's Hymn, Lamb of God, Humility

Gentle Jesus, meek and mild,
Look upon a little child;
Pity my simplicity,
Suffer me to come to Thee.

Lamb of God, I look to Thee;
Thou shalt my example be:
Thou art gentle, meek and mild;
Thou wast once a little child.

Fain I would be as Thou art;
Give me Thine obedient heart:
Thou art pitiful and kind;
Let me have Thy loving mind.

Loving Jesus, gentle Lamb,
In Thy gracious hands I am;
Make me, Savior, what Thou art,
Live Thyself within my heart.

CHARLES WESLEY (1707–1788)

JESUS BIDS US SHINE

Two sisters, Susan and Anna Warner, lived together on Constitution Island, a small island in the Hudson River. Across from them, on the mainland, was West Point Military Academy.

Both Susan and Anna were writers. Susan was a novelist; many of her novels had biblical settings, and some of them made the best-selling lists of the time.

Today, Anna is better known because of one song she wrote: "Jesus Loves Me." Susan's well-known song is "Jesus Bids Us Shine."

Susan and Anna enjoyed their island home, but they were aware that they needed to be shining as candles for Jesus as well. So every Sunday for years they sent a boat to West Point to pick up cadets for a Bible study at their island home. Each week after the study they had dessert with the cadets.

Susan and Anna Warner were loved by the cadets of West Point, so much so that when the sisters died they were allowed to be buried at West Point. As the song says, their candles were burning in the night.

Scriptures: Matthew 5:14-16; Ephesians 5:8; Philippians 2:15-16
Themes: Childhood, Witnessing, Commitment

Jesus bids us shine with a pure, clear light,
Like a little candle burning in the night;
In this world of darkness we must shine,
You in your small corner, and I in mine.

Jesus bids us shine, first of all for Him;
Well He sees and knows it if our light is dim;
He looks down from heaven, to see us shine,
You in your small corner, and I in mine.

Jesus bids us shine, then, for all around
Many kinds of darkness in this world abound,
Sin and want, and sorrow; so we must shine,
You in your small corner, and I in mine.

Jesus bids us shine, as we work for Him,
Bringing those that wander from the paths of sin;
He will ever help us, if we shine,
You in your small corner, and I in mine.

SUSAN WARNER (1819–1885)

JESUS LOVES EVEN ME

Philip Bliss, the author of this gospel song, had attended a service in which the song, "Oh, How I Love Jesus" had been sung over and over again. He had nothing against that song, but he thought, *Haven't I been singing enough about my poor love for Jesus? Shouldn't I rather sing of his great love for me?* Then thinking about Romans 5:5, which speaks of how dearly God loves us, he wrote "Jesus Loves Even Me."

A few years later, a woman in Scotland told of how God had used this hymn to win her husband to Christ. Her three-year-old daughter couldn't remember much of the song, but she remembered the line, "Jesus loves even me." The mother had tried to get her husband to attend an evangelistic meeting, but he refused. Then one day when he came home from work, he was met by his little daughter. He picked her up, and she threw her arms around him, saying, "Daddy, Jesus loves even me." She paused and then added, "And Daddy, Jesus loves even you." The father was touched by the simple words. He attended the meetings and gave his heart to Jesus.

Scriptures: John 15:9; Romans 5:5-8; Romans 8:39
Themes: Love, Jesus Christ, Assurance

I am so glad that our Father in heaven
Tells of His love in the Book He has given;
Wonderful things in the Bible I see,
This is the dearest, that Jesus loves me,

I am so glad that Jesus loves me, Jesus loves me, Jesus love me.
I am so glad that Jesus loves me, Jesus loves even me.

Though I forget Him and wander away,
Still He doth love me wherever I stray;

Back to His dear loving arms would I flee
When I remember that Jesus loves me,

O if there's only one song I can sing
When in His beauty I see the great King,
This shall my song through eternity be:
"O what a wonder, that Jesus loves me!"

PHILIP PAUL BLISS (1838–1876)

JESUS LOVES ME

Anna Warner and her sister, Susan, grew up near West Point Military
Academy, where they became known for leading Sunday school services
for the young men there. After the death of their father, a New York lawyer, the sisters supported themselves with their various literary endeav-
ors. Susan became known as a best-selling novelist. Anna also wrote
novels and published two collections of poems. She wrote this simple
hymn in 1860 to be included in one of her sister's novels. In the story, it
was a poem of comfort spoken to a dying child.

Today millions of voices around the world sing, "Yes, Jesus loves me!"
Once, when asked to summarize the essential truths of the Christian
faith, the great Swiss theologian Karl Barth gave this simple answer:
"Jesus loves me, this I know, / For the Bible tells me so." This profound
yet simple truth is certainly worth singing about!

Scriptures: Matthew 11:25; Mark 10:16; John 3:16-17
Themes: Love, Children's Hymn, Bible

Jesus loves me! this I know,
For the Bible tells me so;
Little ones to Him belong,
They are weak but He is strong.

Yes, Jesus loves me!
Yes, Jesus loves me!
Yes, Jesus loves me!
The Bible tells me so.

Jesus loves me! He who died
Heaven's gate to open wide;
He will wash away my sin,
Let His little child come in.

Jesus loves me! He will stay
Close beside me all the way;
Thou hast bled and died for me,
I will henceforth live for Thee.

ANNA BARTLETT WARNER (1820–1915)

JEWELS (WHEN HE COMETH)

Pastor William Cushing liked children, and he wanted to write a song just for the children of his own Sunday school. One day he saw a special verse in the last book of the Old Testament, Malachi: "And they shall be mine, saith the LORD of hosts, in that day when I make up my jewels" (3:17, KJV). As Cushing thought about the verse, he thought of his Sunday school children as jewels for the crown of Jesus.

The difference between an ordinary stone and a jewel is belief in Jesus, and Cushing could imagine the little children, shining like the stars of the morning, bright gems for his crown.

Scriptures: Malachi 3:17; Matthew 18:2; Mark 10:14
Themes: Return of Christ, Childhood, Love

When He cometh, when He cometh to make up His jewels,
All His jewels, precious jewels, His loved and His own.

Like the stars of the morning,
His bright crown adorning,
They shall shine in their beauty,
Bright gems for His Crown.

He will gather, He will gather the gems for His kingdom;
All the pure ones, all the bright ones, His loved and His own.

Little children, little children, who love their Redeemer,
Are the jewels, precious jewels, His loved and His own.

WILLIAM O. CUSHING (1823–1902)

SHEPHERD OF EAGER YOUTH

This is the oldest Christian hymn of which the authorship is known. It was written by Clement of Alexandria sometime between A.D. 202 and

A.D. 220 and was apparently written to instruct new believers who had just converted from heathenism.

Clement of Alexandria was a scholar of the first order. He was probably born to pagan parents, but came to believe in Christ through his studies. He was very familiar with the secular philosophies of his day. In Alexandria he ran a philosophical school that employed both Christian and non-Christian teachers. There he taught a young man named Origen, who later became one of the greatest thinkers in Christian history.

We may see a hint of Clement's love of philosophy in the line "The all-subduing Word." In the marketplace of ideas, Jesus, the all-subduing Word, had truly conquered all other attempts to explain the nature of God.

Scriptures: John 1:1-5, 14; John 10:14; Colossians 1:27-28
Themes: Shepherds, Word of God, Guidance

Shepherd of eager youth,
Guiding in love and truth
Through devious ways—
Christ, our triumphant King,
We come Thy name to sing;
Hither Thy children bring
Tributes of praise.

Thou art our Holy Lord,
The all-subduing Word,
Healer of strife;
Thou didst Thyself abase
That from sin's deep disgrace
Thou mightest save our race
And give us life.

Ever be near our side,
Our shepherd and our guide,
Our staff and song;
Jesus, Thou Christ of God,
By Thy enduring Word
Lead us where Thou hast trod,
Make our faith strong.

CLEMENT OF ALEXANDRIA (CA. 170–CA. 220)
Translated by Henry Martyn Dexter (1821–1890)

PART VI

CHRISTIAN LIFE AND DISCIPLESHIP

Since God chose you to be the holy people he loves, you must clothe

yourselves with tenderhearted mercy, kindness, humility,

gentleness, and patience.

COLOSSIANS 3:12

A CHARGE TO KEEP I HAVE

If we wanted to write a hymn, most of us would not turn to the book of Leviticus for inspiration. But Charles Wesley wrote sixteen hymns derived from that Old Testament book. This hymn was composed after he had been reading Matthew Henry's commentary on Leviticus 8:35.

In that verse, the Hebrew priests were commanded to be faithful in their duties in the tabernacle. "Keep the charge of the LORD, that ye die not," Moses had said (KJV). Matthew Henry commented: "We have every one of us a charge to keep, an eternal God to glorify, an immortal soul to provide for, a needful duty to be done, our generation to serve, and it must be our daily care to keep this charge, for it is the charge of the Lord our Master, who will shortly call us to an account about it, and it is our utmost peril if we neglect it."

Scriptures: Leviticus 8:35; 2 Timothy 4:1-5; 1 Peter 4:10-11
Themes: Service, Christian Living, Holiness

A charge to keep I have,
A God to glorify,
A never-dying soul to save,
And fit it for the sky.

To serve the present age,
My calling to fulfill;
O may it all my powers engage
To do my Master's will!

Arm me with jealous care,
As in Thy sight to live,
And O, Thy servant, Lord, prepare
A strict account to give!

Help me to watch and pray,
And on Thyself rely,
Assured, if I my trust betray,
I shall forever die.

CHARLES WESLEY (1707–1788)

AM I A SOLDIER OF THE CROSS?

When Isaac Watts was preaching in England in the eighteenth century, he frequently would write a hymn to illustrate his sermon. After preaching the sermon, he (or a clerk in the church) would teach the congregation the hymn by singing two lines and then having the congregation repeat those lines.

One Sunday in 1727, Watts was preaching a sermon entitled "Holy Fortitude, or Remedies against Fear." The text was 1 Corinthians 16:13, "Be on guard. Stand firm in the faith." At that time many Nonconformist believers were imprisoned for their views, even as Watts's own father had been. In his sermon, Watts urged his congregation to "practice unfashionable virtues, plead the cause of the oppressed, be courageous before infidels and scoffers." Then, as he closed the sermon, he began the hymn, "Am I a Soldier of the Cross?"

Scriptures: 1 Corinthians 16:13; Ephesians 6:10-20; 2 Timothy 2:3-4
Themes: Cross, Consecration, Discipleship

Am I a soldier of the cross?
A foll'wer of the Lamb?
And shall I fear to own His cause
Or blush to speak His name?

Must I be carried to the skies
On flow'ry beds of ease,
While others fought to win the prize
And sailed through bloody seas?

Are there no foes for me to face?
Must I not stem the flood?
Is this vile world a friend to grace,
To help me on to God?

Sure I must fight if I would reign—
Increase my courage, Lord!
I'll bear the toil, endure the pain,
Supported by Thy Word.

ISAAC WATTS (1674–1748)

ANOTHER YEAR IS DAWNING

Admittedly, most verses on greeting cards are not very memorable, so sometimes Frances Ridley Havergal, the well-known British hymnwriter, sent a New Year's poem to her friends that she had written herself. In 1872, when she was thirty-six years old, she wrote "Another Year Is Dawning," printed it on a specially designed greeting card, and sent it to her friends. Over it was the caption, "A Happy New Year! Ever such may it be!"

Havergal always gave God the credit for her work, and she liked to refer to God as her King. When she was asked about the process by which she wrote her hymns, she replied, "I believe my King suggests a thought, and whispers me a musical line or two, and then I look up and thank him delightedly and go on with it. This is how my hymns come."

Scriptures: Exodus 33:13-14; Joshua 1:9; Psalm 90:12
Themes: New Year's, Seasonal, Hope

Another year is dawning; dear Father, let it be,
In working or in waiting, another year with Thee;
Another year of progress, another year of praise,
Another year of proving Thy presence all the days.

Another year of mercies, of faithfulness and grace;
Another year of gladness in the shining of Thy face;
Another year of leaning upon Thy loving breast;
Another year of trusting, of quiet, happy rest.

Another year of service, of witness for Thy love;
Another year of training for holier work above,
Another year is dawning; dear Father, let it be,
On earth or else in heaven, another year for Thee.

FRANCES RIDLEY HAVERGAL (1836–1879)

AS THE DEER PANTETH FOR THE WATER

Marty Nystrom, a twenty-four-year-old schoolteacher in Seattle, wanted to get to know a young woman a lot better. Since she was going to be at a school in Dallas, Texas, that summer, he decided to enroll in the same six-week program.

However, after arriving in Texas, he discovered that things were not going to work out with the young woman, and he was stuck in a program he didn't want during a very hot Dallas summer. Since Marty was both broke and heartbroken, a roommate decided he should go on a fast to get his priorities straightened out again. So Marty did. During the fast, all he drank was water. Marty says, "To be honest, I could not say that my soul thirsted for more of God."

But as he fasted, he says, "I noticed that earthly desires and physical lusts began to wane. My spirit became more and more hungry for communion with God." After fasting for nineteen days, he sat down at a piano in the men's dorm. A Bible was open on the piano. Since it was open to Psalm 42, Marty began singing through the psalm. He recalls the time: "God gave me a melody for Psalm 42:1. I just began to sing right off the page, literally."

Ten years later, Marty was in Seoul, Korea, attending a worship conference that had attracted 100,000 Koreans. To open the conference, the huge audience sang Marty's song, "As the Deer Panteth for the Water."

Scriptures: Psalm 42:1-2; Isaiah 55:1; John 4:13-14
Themes: Worship, Holiness, Prayer

AUTHOR: MARTY NYSTROM (B. 1957)

CHANNELS ONLY

The original meaning of *channel* was a waterway, like the English Channel. It's related to the word *canal*. Over the years it gained a figurative meaning as any route of communication or authority; for example, in government and business, it's important to "go through the right channels" to get something done. Now it also refers to electronic frequencies that TV stations use to get their signals to your set.

So how are we to be "channels"? We are conduits for the living water of Christ. The Spirit flows within us and through us to others. Note that a channel is not the source of the water it carries. We do not create goodness or power; we merely receive it and channel it forward. When your friends tune in to your "channel," what kind of signal do they get? Is it the clear programming of Christ? Or is there static, interference on the line? Let the gospel flow freely through you in all you say and do.

Scriptures: 2 Corinthians 12:10; Galatians 2:20; 2 Timothy 2:20-21
Themes: Holy Spirit, Consecration, Holiness

How I praise Thee, precious Savior,
That Thy love laid hold of me;
Thou hast saved and cleansed and filled me
That I might Thy channel be.

Channels only, blessed Master,
But with all Thy wondrous pow'r
Flowing thro' us, Thou canst use us
Ev'ry day and ev'ry hour.

Emptied that Thou shouldest fill me,
A clean vessel in Thy hand;
With no pow'r but as Thou givest
Graciously with each command.

Witnessing Thy pow'r to save me,
Setting free from self and sin;
Thou who boughtest to possess me,
In Thy fullness, Lord, come in.

Jesus, fill now with Thy Spirit
Hearts that full surrender know;
That the streams of living water
From our inner man may flow.

MARY E. MAXWELL (1837–1915)

CLOSE TO THEE

A Scottish minister once told Fanny Crosby that it was too bad God had allowed her to become blind. Crosby quickly responded, "If I had been given a choice at birth, I would have asked to be blind . . . for when I get to heaven, the first face I will see will be the One who died for me." That desire to see Jesus, to be close to him, was always foremost in her mind.

When Silas Jones Vail, a Long Island hatter by trade, said he had a tune for Crosby, she asked him to sit down at the piano and play it for her. As he was playing it, Crosby said, "That refrain said 'Close to Thee, close to Thee, close to Thee, close to Thee.' "

"Thou my everlasting portion" is a frequent allusion in Psalms. The

Old Testament Levites did not inherit any land in Canaan because the Lord was to be their portion. Similarly, Fanny Crosby was not given sight, but she felt blessed because the Lord was her portion.

Scriptures: Psalm 73:26; Hebrews 4:16; Hebrews 10:21-22
Themes: Devotion, Holiness, Prayer

Thou my everlasting portion,
More than friend or life to me;
All along my pilgrim journey,
Savior, let me walk with Thee.
Close to Thee, close to Thee,
Close to Thee, close to Thee;
All along my pilgrim journey,
Savior, let me walk with Thee.

Not for ease or worldly pleasure,
Nor for fame my prayer shall be;
Gladly will I toil and suffer,
Only let me walk with Thee.
Close to Thee, close to Thee,
Close to Thee, close to Thee;
Gladly will I toil and suffer,
Only let me walk with Thee.

Lead me through the vale of shadows,
Bear me o'er life's fitful sea;
Then the gate of life eternal
May I enter, Lord, with Thee.
Close to Thee, close to Thee,
Close to Thee, close to Thee;
Then the gate of life eternal
May I enter, Lord, with Thee.

FANNY JANE CROSBY (1820–1915)

DEAR LORD AND FATHER OF MANKIND

John Greenleaf Whittier was an outstanding American poet who belonged to the Quakers, a group that did not practice hymn singing at the time. Whittier confessed, "I am really not a hymnwriter, for the good reason that I know nothing of music." Nevertheless, several of his poems have found their way into church hymnals.

The stanzas that make up this hymn are taken from his longer poem "The Brewing of Soma," beginning with the twelfth stanza. In the earlier stanzas, Whittier writes about an intoxicating drink called *soma* that was brewed by a Hindu sect in India. Soma was drunk by worshippers in order "to bring the skies more near, or lift men up to heaven." Whittier was disturbed to see Christians using emotionalism the same way. So he asked God to forgive our feverish ways, and instead "let our ordered lives confess the beauty of Thy peace." He was calling Christians back to simplicity and purity in worship.

Scriptures: Psalm 46:8-10; Matthew 1:16-20; Matthew 6:19-23
Themes: Peace, Worship, Prayer

Dear Lord and Father of mankind,
Forgive our fev'rish ways!
Reclothe us in our rightful mind;
In purer lives Thy service find,
In deeper rev'rence, praise.

In simple trust like theirs who heard,
Beside the Syrian Sea,
The gracious calling of the Lord,
Let us, like them, without a word,
Rise up and follow Thee.

O Sabbath rest by Galilee!
O calm of hills above,
Where Jesus knelt to share with thee
The silence of eternity,
Interpreted by love.

Drop Thy still dews of quietness
Till all our strivings cease;
Take from our souls the strain and stress,
And let our ordered lives confess
The beauty of Thy peace.

Breathe thru the heats of our desire
Thy coolness and Thy balm;
Let sense be dumb, let flesh retire;
Speak thru the earthquake, wind, and fire,
O still small voice of calm!

JOHN GREENLEAF WHITTIER (1807–1892)

DEEPER AND DEEPER

Later in his life, Oswald J. Smith would become a noted Canadian pastor and international missionary statesman. But when he was only twenty-one, on his way to a church in Woodstock, Ontario, the melody of this hymn, he said, "sang itself into my heart and with it the words, 'Into the heart of Jesus deeper and deeper I go.'" Smith hoped that he would remember the music and the words until the service was over. So in the afternoon, he said, "The first thing I did was to write out the melody as God had given it to me."

But writing the verses was harder. It was three years later, when he was a pastor in South Chicago, that he wrote the verses. He said, "I doubt if I have ever written anything more profound since."

In the hymn he refers to going "deeper and deeper" into the heart, the joy, and the love of Jesus. Smith always enjoyed the last verse most of all, which ends, "O how He loved! O how He loved! Jesus, my Lord and King!"

Scriptures: Psalm 40:8; Ephesians 3:17-18; Colossians 3:12-15
Themes: Christlikeness, Holiness, Submission

Into the heart of Jesus deeper and deeper I go,
Seeking to know the reason why He should love me so
Why He should stoop to lift me up from the miry clay,
Saving my soul, making me whole, tho' I had wandered away.

Into the joy of Jesus deeper and deeper I go,
Rising, with soul enraptured, far from the world below;
Joy in the place of sorrow, peace in the midst of pain,
Jesus will give, Jesus will give—He will uphold and sustain!

Into the love of Jesus deeper and deeper I go,
Praising the One who brought me out of my sin and woe;

And thru eternal ages gratefully I shall sing,
"O how He loved! O how He loved! Jesus, my Lord and King!"

OSWALD J. SMITH (1889–1986)

FROM EVERY STORMY WIND

In 1857 in the Punjab province of northern India, fourteen Presbyterian missionaries were imprisoned during the Sepoy Mutiny in the area. One day eight of them and two of their young children were taken from prison and were ordered to be put to death. On their way they sang this hymn: "From ev'ry stormy wind that blows, from ev'ry swelling tide of woes, / There is a calm, a sure retreat—'Tis found beneath the mercy seat."

About thirty years earlier, Hugh Stowell, just out of college, had written the hymn and called it "Peace at the Mercy Seat." In the Old Testament, the high priest entered once a year on the Day of Atonement into the Holy of Holies of the Tabernacle and sprinkled sacrificial blood on the "mercy seat," which was the lid of the Ark of the Covenant. The mercy seat was thought of as the place where law and mercy met, thus finding its fulfillment in Jesus Christ and his atoning blood. That is why the missionaries, on the brink of death, could find a calm and safe retreat there—beneath the mercy seat.

Scriptures: Leviticus 16:15; Isaiah 43:2-3; Hebrews 4:15-16
Themes: Prayer, Peace, Comfort

From ev'ry stormy wind that blows, from ev'ry swelling tide of woes,
There is a calm, a sure retreat—'Tis found beneath the mercy seat.

There is a place where Jesus sheds the oil of gladness on our heads,
A place than all besides more sweet—It is the blood-bought mercy seat.

There is a scene where spirits blend, where friend holds fellowship
    with friend;
Tho'sundered far, by faith they meet around one common mercy seat.

Ah! Whither could we flee for aid when tempted, desolate, dismayed,
Or how the hosts of hell defeat, had suff'ring saints no mercy seat?

Ah! There on eagle wings we soar, and sin and sense molest no more;
And heaven comes down our souls to greet, while glory crowns
    the mercy seat.

HUGH STOWELL (1799–1865)

HAPPY THE HOME WHEN GOD IS THERE

On a recent television show, two ministers disagreed over the influence of the media on children. Then the host skeptically asked, "Can a three-year-old really know anything about Jesus?" Suddenly the ministers were in complete agreement. "Yes!" said both; and one added, "My children learned early on that Jesus loved them."

Christians may have serious debates over how we should relate to the world around us. But let us all agree on this: The home should be a place bathed in the love of Christ. Let us teach our children early that Jesus loves them. Let them "lisp His fame" from an early age.

The author, Henry Ware, was a minister in Boston, Massachusetts, in the nineteenth century. For a while, the noted American poet Ralph Waldo Emerson served as his assistant.

As this hymn indicates, when parents exhibit a genuine love for the Lord, children will see and learn. They will still have to make their own choices, but at least they will have lived in a home where God was an important part of the family. That memory will stay with them for the rest of their lives.

Scriptures: Deuteronomy 6:4-7; Proverbs 22:6; Colossians 3:16-21
Themes: Home, Word of God, Love

Happy the home when God is there,
And love fills every breast;
When one their wish, and one their prayer,
And one their heavenly rest.

Happy the home where Jesus' name
Is sweet to every ear;
Where children early lisp His fame,
And parents hold Him dear.

Happy the home where prayer is heard,
And praise is wont to rise;
Where parents love the sacred Word
And all its wisdom prize.

Lord, let us in our homes agree
This blessed peace to gain;
Unite our hearts in love to Thee,
And love to all will reign.

HENRY WARE JR. (1794–1843)

HE GIVETH MORE GRACE

Annie Flint, the author of this hymn, understood something of God's grace. Her mother died in childbirth, and her father died shortly afterwards from an incurable disease. Before his death, Annie's father left Annie and her baby sister with a childless Christian couple, the Flints, who adopted them.

Annie wanted to become a teacher, but in her second year of teaching, she began experiencing the symptoms of arthritis. The disease grew worse until she could hardly walk. Then the death of both adoptive parents left Annie and her sister alone again. Annie went to a sanatorium, but the doctors said there was nothing they could do for her.

She began writing from experience. Her fingers were bent, her joints were swollen, and often she could write only a few lines at a time. But she continued writing, praying that others might be helped through her experience. Her poems were published in magazines across the country. Sometimes the publisher would mention Annie's physical condition, and readers would donate funds to help her.

Annie learned what the apostle Paul had learned when God told him, "My grace is sufficient for you, for my power is made perfect in weakness" (2 Corinthians 12:9, NIV). And she also learned that "He giveth more grace when the burden grows greater."

Scriptures: Romans 5:1-6; 1 Corinthians 10:13; 2 Corinthians 12:8-9; James 1:2-5
Themes: Grace, Comfort, Love

He giveth more grace when the burden grows greater;
He sendeth more strength when the labors increase.
To added affliction He addeth His mercy;
To multiplied trials, His multiplied peace.

His love has no limit;
His grace has no measure;
His pow'r has no boundary known unto men.
For out of His infinite riches in Jesus,
He giveth, and giveth, and giveth again!

When we have exhausted our store of endurance,
When our strength has failed ere the day is half done,
When we reach the end of our hoarded resources,
Our Father's full giving is only begun.

ANNIE JOHNSON FLINT (1866–1932)

I AM HIS, AND HE IS MINE

Too many Christians miss out on the full joy that Christ wants to give us. Jesus said, "My purpose is to give them a rich and satisfying life" (John 10:10).

Jesus came, not just to give us heaven, but also to make a difference in our lives now. Life as a Christian is infinitely richer, more joyful, and more secure. Those who do not know Christ can know only part of the blessings that God bestows on the world. Christians know the Creator, and that changes everything.

The sky is bluer, the grass greener, the birds cheerier, the flowers more beautiful. Why? Because we belong to the Creator.

"I am His, and He is mine." Not only does that deepen our enjoyment of his Creation, but it also gives us a new security and contentment in daily living. As the last line indicates, "But while God and I shall be, / I am His, and He is mine."

Scriptures: Song of Songs 6:3; John 10:27-28; John 15:9-11
Themes: Assurance, Peace, Joy, Comfort, Security

Loved with everlasting love,
Led by grace that love to know;
Spirit, breathing from above,
Thou hast taught me it is so!
Oh, this full and perfect peace!
Oh, this transport all divine!
In a love which cannot cease,
I am His, and He is mine.

Heav'n above is softer blue,
Earth around is sweeter green!
Something lives in ev'ry hue
Christless eyes have never seen:
Birds with gladder songs o'erflow,
Flow'rs with deeper beauties shine,
Since I know, as now I know,
I am His, and He is mine.

Things that once were wild alarms
Cannot now disturb my rest;
Closed in everlasting arms,
Pillowed on the loving breast.

Oh, to lie forever here,
Doubt, and care, and self resign,
While He whispers in my ear—
I am His, and He is mine.

His forever, only His;
Who the Lord and me shall part?
Ah, with what a rest of bliss,
Christ can fill the loving heart!
Heav'n and earth may fade and flee,
First born light in gloom decline;
But while God and I shall be,
I am His, and He is mine.

GEORGE WADE ROBINSON (1838–1877)

I NEED THEE EVERY HOUR

You don't often think of hymns being written by a thirty-seven-year-old homemaker from Brooklyn, but that's the story behind this hymn. Annie Hawks was busy with household chores when the words came to her. Later she recalled the day, "I was so filled with a sense of nearness to my Master that . . . these words, 'I need Thee every hour,' were flashed into my mind." It was a bright June day, so she sat by an open window, picked up her pencil, and wrote the entire hymn. She gave the words to her pastor, who wrote the music and the chorus.

When evangelist Dwight L. Moody discovered the simple hymn and began using it in his meetings, the hymn became famous, much to the amazement of Annie Hawks, a simple homemaker from Brooklyn.

Scriptures: Psalm 86:1-4; Psalm 109:22; Philippians 4:19
Themes: Prayer, Meditation

I need Thee ev'ry hour,
Most gracious Lord;
No tender voice like Thine
Can peace afford.

I need Thee, O I need Thee;
Ev'ry hour I need Thee!
O bless me now, my Savior,
I come to Thee.

I need Thee ev'ry hour,
Stay Thou nearby;
Temptations lose their pow'r
When Thou art nigh.

I need Thee ev'ry hour,
In joy or pain;
Come quickly, and abide,
Or life is vain.

I need Thee ev'ry hour,
Teach me Thy will,
And Thy rich promises
In me fulfill.

ANNIE SHERWOOD HAWKS (1835–1918)
Robert Lowry (1826–1899), refrain

I WANT TO WALK AS A CHILD OF THE LIGHT

You might think that Episcopalian Kathleen Thomerson would be best known for her classical music. After all, she had studied organ in Antwerp and Paris and had taught organ at Southern Illinois University. In addition, she was an organ recitalist in both America and Europe.

But it is this simple and yet profound hymn for which she is best known. It was written during the rather dismal summer of 1966. Kathleen's mother was visiting with her in St. Louis, but after a power shortage restricted air-conditioning, Kathleen decided to take her mother back to her home in Houston. Then came another problem—an airline strike. Since they couldn't fly, they drove; as they drove, Kathleen wrote "I Want to Walk as a Child of the Light."

The song is rich in biblical imagery. Concepts like the brightness of God, run with patience, the Lamb as the light, and the absence of darkness, come straight from God's Word.

When they arrived in Houston, Kathleen dedicated the song, both words and music, to the Episcopal Church of the Redeemer there.

Scriptures: Ephesians 5:8; Hebrews 1:1-3; Hebrews 12:1; Revelation 21:23
Themes: Light, Guidance, Growth

I want to walk as a child of the light;
I want to follow Jesus.

God set the stars to give light to the world;
The star of my life is Jesus.

In Him there is no darkness at all;
The night and the day are both alike.

The Lamb is the light of the city of God;
Shine in my heart, Lord Jesus.

KATHLEEN ARMSTRONG THOMERSON (B. 1934)
© 1970, 1975 by Celebration
All rights reserved. Used by permission.

I WOULD BE TRUE

Howard Walter, the author of this hymn, seemed to be living a charmed life. When he graduated from Princeton, the seminary bulletin said, "He romped through Princeton clutching class and scholastic honors right and left, graduating cum laude." At Hartford Seminary he garnered every prize in sight, including the fellowship, which he used for one year in Glasgow, Edinburgh, and Marburg.

In between his studies at Princeton and Hartford, he took a year off to go to a university in Japan and teach English to Japanese students. While he was there, he wrote this poem, which was later published in *Harper's Magazine.* Yes, he lived a charmed life.

But then he felt a call to go to India as a missionary to Muslim students. Before going, he had a physical exam; a heart specialist told him he would probably not live more than five years. His reply was, "That makes it all the more essential that I get back to work at once." He died in India six years later at the age of thirty-five. His last words were, "O Christ, I am ready."

Scriptures: Psalm 119:30; Isaiah 58:6-8; Philippians 4:8
Themes: Conscience, Character, Commitment

I would be true, for there are those who trust me;
I would be pure, for there are those who care.

I would be strong, for there is much to suffer;
I would be brave, for there is much to dare.

I would be friend of all—the foe, the friendless;
I would be giving, and forget the gift.

I would be humble, for I know my weakness;
I would look up, and laugh, and love, and lift.

I would be prayerful thru each busy moment;
I would be constantly in touch with God,

I would be tuned to hear His slightest whisper;
I would have faith to keep the path Christ trod.

HOWARD A. WALTER (1883–1918)

LIVING FOR JESUS

Charles Lowden of Camden, New Jersey, had a music business and
wrote music for gospel songs. His church had asked him to compose a
gospel song for a children's day service, and he was happy to do it. However, after it was performed, he wasn't pleased with it. He thought the
music was okay, but the words weren't right, so he put the song on the
shelf.

About two years later, he heard that, due to poor health and poor
finances, a well-known Christian songwriter, Thomas Chisholm, was
moving from Indiana to Vineland, New Jersey. Lowden looked forward
to meeting him and wondered if they could team up for a song.

Then he remembered the music he had written two years earlier. He
asked Chisholm if he could write some new words for it—maybe something along the theme of living for Jesus. Chisholm wasn't so sure; he
didn't know whether he could fit words to a tune. But he said that he
would try, and two weeks later Lowden got the words he wanted from
Chisholm: "Living for Jesus."

Scriptures: Romans 12:1-2; Ephesians 4:20-24; Colossians 3:1-10
Themes: Christlikeness, Commitment, Submission

Living for Jesus a life that is true,
Striving to please Him in all that I do,
Yielding allegiance, glad-hearted and free,
This is the pathway of blessing for me.

O Jesus, Lord and Savior, I give myself to Thee,
For Thou in Thine atonement didst give Thyself for me,
I own no other Master—my heart shall be Thy throne;
My life I give, henceforth to live, O Christ, for Thee alone.

Living for Jesus who died in my place,
Bearing on Calv'ry my sin and disgrace
Such love constrains me to answer His call,
Follow His leading and give Him my all.

Living for Jesus thru earth's little while,
My dearest treasure the light of His smile,
Seeking the lost one He died to redeem
Bringing the weary to find rest in Him.

THOMAS OBEDIAH CHISHOLM (1866–1960)

LORD, I WANT TO BE A CHRISTIAN

It isn't easy to trace the source of most spirituals, but "Lord, I Want to Be a Christian" seems to have originated in Virginia sometime around 1750. A Presbyterian named William Davies was preaching there when a slave came up to him and said that he wanted to learn more about how to become a Christian. He also wanted to learn more about Jesus Christ and how to live for him. Soon after that, this song appeared and became popular among African Americans in the South. Since the middle of the twentieth century it has been used in churches of all denominations.

Scriptures: Acts 16:30-31; Philippians 1:6; 1 Thessalonians 1:6-10
Themes: Conversion, Holiness, Christlikeness

Lord, I want to be a Christian in my heart, in my heart.
Lord, I want to be a Christian in my heart
In my heart, in my heart.
Lord, I want to be a Christian in my heart.

Lord, I want to be more loving in my heart, in my heart.
Lord, I want to be more loving in my heart
In my heart, in my heart.
Lord, I want to be more loving in my heart.

Lord, I want to be more holy in my heart, in my heart.
Lord, I want to be more holy in my heart.
In my heart, in my heart.
Lord, I want to be more holy in my heart.

Lord, I want to be like Jesus in my heart, in my heart.
Lord, I want to be like Jesus in my heart.

In my heart, in my heart.
Lord, I want to be like Jesus in my heart.
WILLIAM DAVIES (18TH CENTURY)

O FOR A CLOSER WALK WITH GOD

Poet William Cowper liked to walk. It was good therapy for him. He had tried to commit suicide three times and had been hospitalized twice for insanity. During his hospitalization, he became a Christian, and after his release he became a good friend of John Newton, the author of "Amazing Grace," who also enjoyed walking. Besides their mutual love of walking, they both had a sense of humor and liked to write poetry. John Newton encouraged Cowper to write hymns, and they had a friendly hymnwriting competition. When they walked together, Cowper moved at a fast pace, but he also loved to stroll slowly through the little town of Olney, where he visited the poor and chatted with the children.

Sometimes they would read the Bible together in Newton's garden. One morning Cowper was reading the passage in Genesis that talks about Enoch walking with God. Sometimes he thought there was nothing better than to walk with John Newton, but he knew walking with God was better yet. That thought inspired him to write this hymn.

Scriptures: Genesis 5:24; Colossians 2:6; Hebrews 11:5-6; 1 John 2:6
Themes: Consecration, Holy Spirit, Holiness

O for a closer walk with God,
A calm and heav'nly frame,
A light to shine upon the road
That leads me to the Lamb.

Where is the blessedness I knew
When first I saw the Lord?
Where is the soul-refreshing view
Of Jesus and His Word?

Return, O holy Dove, return,
Sweet messenger of rest;
I hate the sins that made Thee mourn
And drove Thee from my breast.

The dearest idol I have known,
What e'er that idol be,

Help me to tear it from Thy throne
And worship only Thee.

So shall my walk be close with God,
Calm and serene my frame;
So purer light shall mark the road
That leads me to the Lamb.

WILLIAM COWPER (1731–1800)

O MASTER, LET ME WALK WITH THEE

Washington Gladden believed that Christians should be involved in the world's problems—and he wasn't afraid to say so. A newspaperman-turned-clergyman, he crusaded against injustice. He fought against the infamous Tweed Ring that controlled New York City politics. He objected to John D. Rockefeller's gift to his denomination's foreign mission board because of the millionaire's policies at Standard Oil. In his various churches, he often preached a social gospel, trying to rouse his congregation to the social and labor problems that were engulfing the country.

When Gladden wrote this hymn in 1879, he said the poem had no theological significance but was an honest cry of human need and of the need for divine companionship. If our friendship with Jesus does not lead us to concern for others—not only spiritually, but in every other way as well—then we'd better check to see how closely we are walking with the Master.

Scriptures: Amos 5:21-24; Micah 6:8; Ephesians 5:1-2
Themes: Service, Social Concern, Prayer

O Master, let me walk with Thee
In lowly paths of service free;
Tell me Thy secret; help me bear
The strain of toil, the fret of care.

Help me the slow of heart to move
By some clear, winning word of love;
Teach me the wayward feet to stay,
And guide them in the homeward way.

Teach me Thy patience; still with Thee
In closer, dearer company,
In work that keeps faith sweet and strong,
In trust that triumphs over wrong.

In hope that sends a shining ray
Far down the future's broadening way,
In peace that only Thou canst give,
With Thee, O Master, let me live.

WASHINGTON GLADDEN (1836–1918)

ONCE TO EVERY MAN AND NATION

Later in life, James Russell Lowell would achieve fame as a great American poet, as the editor of *The Atlantic Monthly,* and as an American diplomat. But when he was twenty-six years old, he wrote a poem, which later became the hymn "Once to Every Man and Nation."

The year was 1845, and a new president had just been installed after a very hotly contested election. The key issues were slavery and the possibility of a war with Mexico. Lowell was concerned that people were making choices not on the basis of right and wrong or of truth versus falsehood but on the basis of which choice would be better economically.

The question of slavery, Lowell argued, must not be settled based on what is expedient or profitable. It must be settled on the basis of what is right and what is wrong.

As Christian citizens we have a responsibility to be courageous for the truth.

Scriptures: Joshua 24:14-15; 1 Kings 18:21; Esther 4:13-14
Themes: Decision, Truth, Courage

Once to every man and nation comes the moment to decide,
In the strife of truth with falsehood, for the good or evil side;
Some great cause, some great decision, off'ring each the bloom or blight,
And the choice goes by forever 'twixt that darkness and that light.

Then to side with truth is noble, when we share her wretched crust,
Ere her cause bring fame and profit, and 'tis prosperous to be just;
Then it is the brave man chooses while the coward stands aside,
Till the multitude make virtue of the faith they had denied.

Though the cause of evil prosper, yet the truth alone is strong;
Though her portion be the scaffold, and upon the throne be wrong,
Yet that scaffold sways the future, and behind the dim unknown,
Standeth God within the shadow, keeping watch above His own, Amen.

JAMES RUSSELL LOWELL (1819–1891)

ONWARD, CHRISTIAN SOLDIERS

Ever since the apostle Paul told the Ephesian Christians to put on the armor of God, Christian writers have used the symbolism of the soldier as a call for preparedness and courage. But when Sabine Baring-Gould, a thirty-one-year-old preacher and schoolteacher, wrote "Onward, Christian Soldiers," he simply wanted to write a marching song for his schoolchildren. Later, he apologized for the hymn: "It was written in great haste, and I am afraid that some of the rhymes are faulty."

Whitmonday was a festival day for schoolchildren in Yorkshire, and Baring-Gould's youngsters in the mill town of Horbury had to walk to a neighboring town to join other children for the celebration. "I wanted the children to sing when marching from one village to the other, but couldn't think of anything quite suitable," Baring-Gould commented, "so I sat up at night and resolved to write something myself." Christians have been singing it ever since.

Scriptures: Ephesians 6:10-17; 1 Timothy 6:12; 2 Timothy 2:3
Themes: Victory, Joy, Unity

Onward, Christian soldiers!
Marching as to war,
With the cross of Jesus
Going on before.
Christ, the royal Master,
Leads against the foe;
Forward into battle,
See His banners go!

Onward, Christian soldiers,
Marching as to war,
With the cross of Jesus
Going on before.

Like a mighty army
Moves the Church of God;
Brothers, we are treading
Where the saints have trod;
We are not divided,
All one body we,
One in hope and doctrine,
One in charity.

Onward, then, ye people,
Join our happy throng,
Blend with ours your voices
In the triumph song;
Glory, laud, and honor
Unto Christ the King;
This through countless ages
Men and angels sing.

SABINE BARING-GOULD (1834–1924)

SOLDIERS OF CHRIST, ARISE

The early Methodists took their lives in their hands when they announced themselves as followers of John and Charles Wesley. According to one writer, "They were outrageously treated—stoned, mauled, ducked, hounded with bulldogs, threatened, homes looted, businesses ruined. Anyone who walked through a town could pick out by their ruinous condition the houses where Methodists lived."

Charles Wesley wrote this hymn under the title "The Whole Armor of God" in order to confirm new converts. He was not writing about hitting back at the enemy in a physical way; he was writing about overcoming the powers of darkness by putting on the whole armor of God.

Scriptures: 1 Corinthians 15:57-58; Ephesians 6:10-13; 1 Timothy 6:12
Themes: Christian Warfare, Victory, Conflict

Soldiers of Christ, arise,
And put your armor on,
Strong in the strength which God supplies
Through His eternal Son;
Strong in the Lord of hosts,
And in His mighty power,
Who in the strength of Jesus trusts
Is more than conqueror.

Stand, then, in His great might,
With all His strength endued;
But take, to arm you for the fight,
The panoply of God:
That, having all things done,
And all your conflicts passed,

Ye may o'ercome through Christ alone,
And stand entire at last.

From strength to strength go on,
Wrestle and fight and pray;
Tread all the powers of darkness down,
And win the well-fought day.
Still let the Spirit cry,
In all His soldiers, "Come!"
Till Christ the Lord descends from high,
And takes the conquerors home.

CHARLES WESLEY (1707–1788)

STAND UP, STAND UP FOR JESUS

In 1858, churches throughout Philadelphia united in a citywide evangelistic effort. Every morning and evening, services were held in churches,
convention halls, and theaters. Dudley Tyng, a twenty-nine-year-old
Episcopalian preacher, spoke to five thousand men, and one thousand
responded to the gospel invitation.

Four days later, however, Tyng was tragically injured while watching a
corn-threshing machine in a barn on the family farm. He caught his
loose sleeve between the cogs, and his arm was severely torn. A main
artery was cut, and he lost a great deal of blood. As he lay dying, he whispered to his father, "Stand up for Jesus, Father, and tell my brethren of
the ministry to stand up for Jesus."

A friend, Presbyterian minister George Duffield, preached the next
Sunday on the text "Stand therefore" and in conclusion read a poem that
he had just written entitled "Stand Up, Stand Up for Jesus." The verses of
the hymn first appeared as a leaflet for Sunday school children, then later
were set to music.

Scriptures: John 17:14-19; Ephesians 6:10-12; James 1:12
Themes: Courage, Victory, Evangelism

Stand up, stand up for Jesus,
Ye soldiers of the cross;
Lift high His royal banner,
It must not suffer loss:
From vict'ry unto vict'ry
His army shall He lead,

Till every foe is vanquished
And Christ is Lord indeed.

Stand up, stand up for Jesus,
The trumpet call obey;
Forth to the mighty conflict
In this His glorious day:
Ye that are men, now serve Him
Against unnumbered foes;
Let courage rise with danger,
And strength to strength oppose.

Stand up, stand up for Jesus,
Stand in His strength alone;
The arm of flesh will fail you;
Ye dare not trust your own.
Put on the gospel armor;
Each piece put on with prayer.
Where duty calls, or danger,
Be never wanting there.

Stand up, stand up for Jesus,
The strife will not be long.
This day the noise of battle;
The next, the victor's song.
To him that overcometh,
A crown of life shall be;
He with the King of Glory
Shall reign eternally.

GEORGE DUFFIELD JR. (1818–1888)

STEPPING IN THE LIGHT

There are at least two reasons why Eliza Hewitt wrote this gospel song. As a thirty-six-year-old schoolteacher in Phildelphia, she was struck with a heavy slate by one of her students and suffered severe spinal injuries. After being confined to her home throughout the winter, she was permitted by her doctor to take short walks outside during the spring.

Being able to get out into the spring sunshine did much for her spirits. It also was an inspiration for her songwriting. It was then that she wrote "There Is Sunshine in My Soul Today" and, two years later, "Stepping in the Light." You can imagine the delight she felt as she took each slow step in the sunshine. "How beautiful to walk," she writes, and it was especially beautiful for her.

A second reason behind this song is that during her convalescence she spent time studying the promises of God in Scripture. "Live as people of light," Paul told the Ephesians, "and carefully determine what pleases the Lord." Eliza spent a long time "trying to walk."

Scriptures: Ephesians 5:8-9; Colossians 2:6; 1 John 1:7
Themes: Light, Obedience, Christlikeness

Trying to walk in the steps of the Savior,
Trying to follow our Savior and King;
Shaping our lives by His blessed example,
Happy, how happy, the songs that we bring.

How beautiful to walk in the steps of the Savior,
Stepping in the light, stepping in the light;
How beautiful to walk in the steps of the Savior,
led in paths of light.

Pressing more closely to Him who is leading,
When we are tempted to turn from the way;
Trusting the arm that is strong to defend us,
Happy, how happy, our praises each day.

Walking in footsteps of gentle forbearance,
Footsteps of faithfulness, mercy, and love,
Looking to Him for the grace freely promised,
Happy, how happy, our journey above.

Trying to walk in the steps of the Savior,
Upward, still upward we'll follow our Guide;
When we shall see Him, "the King in His beauty,"
Happy, how happy, our place at His side.

ELIZA EDMUNDS HEWITT (1851–1920)

SWEETER AS THE YEARS GO BY

Lelia moved with her parents, brothers, and sisters to the small town of Malta, Ohio, when she was four years old. It was there that she grew up, went to school, fell in love, and got married. When she got married, Lelia moved across the Ohio River to McConnelsville, where she lived with her husband for the next forty-seven years.

Lelia Naylor Morris didn't discover that God had given her the ability to write hymns until she was thirty years old, and once she started, she couldn't stop. She started going blind in her early fifties, but that didn't stop her either. She used a twenty-eight-foot-long blackboard with large musical staffs on it to help her with her hymnwriting. By the time she died at sixty-seven, she had written more than a thousand hymns.

Three years after she went totally blind, she wrote a hymn that contained these lines: "Walking by faith where my eyes cannot see; I will follow Jesus; Holding the hand that was wounded for me; I will follow Jesus."

Scriptures: Psalm 90:4-10; Psalm 92:12-15; John 15:10-11
Themes: Love, Jesus Christ, Life of Christ

Of Jesus' love that sought me,
When I was lost in sin;
Of wondrous grace that brought me
Back to His fold again;
Of heights and depths of mercy,
Far deeper than the sea,
And higher than the heavens,
My theme shall ever be.

Sweeter as the years go by, sweeter as the years go by;
Richer, fuller, deeper, Jesus' love is sweeter,
Sweeter as the years go by.

He trod in old Judea
Life's pathway long ago;
The people thronged about Him,
His saving grace to know;
He healed the broken-hearted,
And caused the blind to see;
And still His great heart yearneth
In love for even me.

'Twas wondrous love which led Him
For us to suffer loss
To bear without a murmur,
The anguish of the cross;
With saints redeemed in glory,
Let us our voices raise,
Till heav'n and earth re-echo
With our Redeemer's praise.

LELIA NAYLOR MORRIS (1862–1929)

TAKE TIME TO BE HOLY

William Longstaff never considered himself a hymnwriter. In fact, "Take Time to Be Holy" may have been the only poem he ever wrote. The son of a wealthy ship merchant, Longstaff was treasurer of his church and gave liberally to Christian causes. When evangelists Dwight L. Moody and Ira Sankey came to England, he assisted them financially, and he also wrote reports of the meetings for the Christian press.

A few years later, Longstaff heard a sermon on the text "Be ye holy; for I am holy" (1 Peter 1:16, KJV) and wrote down what holiness meant to him. A businessman at heart, Longstaff wrote no flowery or pious-sounding verses, but these down-to-earth thoughts.

The hymn appeared in a Christian newspaper in 1882 and was promptly forgotten. But years later gospel composer George Stebbins, who was leading music in India in connection with evangelistic services there, remembered the poem when he was asked if there was a good hymn on living a holy life. Retrieving the newspaper clipping he had saved, he set the poem to music.

Scriptures: Leviticus 20:7-8; 2 Corinthians 7:1; 1 Thessalonians 5:14-22; 1 Peter 1:15-16
Themes: Holiness, Christian Living, Prayer

Take time to be holy,
Speak oft with thy Lord;
Abide in Him always,
And feed on His Word.
Make friends of God's children;
Help those who are weak;
Forgetting in nothing
His blessing to seek.

Take time to be holy,
The world rushes on;
Much time spend in secret
With Jesus alone;
By looking to Jesus,
Like Him thou shalt be;
Thy friends in thy conduct
His likeness shall see.

Take time to be holy,
Let Him be thy guide,
And run not before Him
Whatever betide;
In joy or in sorrow
Still follow the Lord,
And, looking to Jesus,
Still trust in His Word.

Take time to be holy,
Be calm in thy soul;
Each thought and each motive
Beneath His control;
Thus led by His Spirit
To fountains of love,
Thou soon shalt be fitted
For service above.

WILLIAM DUNN LONGSTAFF (1822–1894)

TEACH ME, MY GOD AND KING

George Herbert was a brilliant and privileged young man who gave his all for God's glory. From a noted Welsh family, he went to Cambridge University at age fifteen and specialized in rhetoric and oratory. Herbert became a country priest and wrote about his experiences. He also wrote poetry, focusing on the Christian's heart as a temple of God.

Shortly before his death, he sent a manuscript of his poems to a fellow churchman. He asked him to publish the poems if he thought anybody could benefit. But if not, he told him to burn them. He concluded, "I and [the poems] are the least of God's mercies."

The last stanza here alludes to the medieval belief in a "philosopher's stone" that would touch a baser metal and turn it to gold. Herbert says that doing things for God's sake is that stone, because God takes what is offered to him and makes it precious. That was the story of George Herbert's life.

Scriptures: 1 Corinthians 10:31–11:1; Ephesians 5:1-2; Colossians 3:1-2, 16-17

Themes: Service, Consecration, Obedience

Teach me, my God and King,
In all things Thee to see,
And what I do in anything,
To do it as for Thee.

A man that looks on glass,
On it may stay his eye,
Or, if he pleaseth, through it pass,
And then the heav'n espy.

All may of Thee partake:
Nothing can be so mean
Which with this motive, "For Thy sake,"
Will not grow bright and clean.

This is the famous stone
That turneth all to gold;
For that which God doth touch and own
Cannot for less be told.

GEORGE HERBERT (1593–1633)

WALK IN THE LIGHT

For forty years Bernard Barton, the author of this hymn, worked as a bank clerk in England. After he had been there thirty-three years, he said, "I took my seat on the identical stool I now occupy at the desk to the wood of which I have now well-nigh grown, and there I have sat . . . without one month's respite in all that time. I often wonder that my health has stood this sedentary probation as it has and that my mental faculties have survived three and thirty years of putting down figures in three rows, casting them up and carrying them forward, ad infinitum."

But that isn't all Bernard Barton did. He was known as the Quaker poet, and he enjoyed the friendship of authors such as Lord Byron, Walter Scott, and Charles Lamb. He published several books of poetry while working at the bank.

This hymn, which presents the key Quaker doctrine of the "inner light," is based on 1 John 1:7: "If we walk in the light, as he is in the light, we have fellowship one with another" (KJV).

Scriptures: John 1:4-5; 2 Corinthians 4:6; 1 John 1:7
Themes: Light, Fellowship, Holiness

Walk in the light! So shalt thou know that fellowship of love
His Spirit only can bestow, who reigns in light above.

Walk in the light! And thou shalt find thy heart made truly His,
Who dwells in cloudless light enshrined, in Whom no darkness is.

Walk in the light! And thou shalt own thy darkness passed away,
Because that light hath on thee shone in which is perfect day.

Walk in the light! And thine shall be a path, though thorny, bright:
For God, by grace, shall dwell in thee, and God Himself is light.

BERNARD BARTON (1784–1849)

WE GIVE THEE BUT THINE OWN

London's East End housed the slums of the city. That is exactly where William Walsham How wanted to serve. He had worked faithfully as pastor of the Anglican church in his farming village of Whittington for a quarter century. He repeatedly turned down advancements and opportunities to serve as bishop in such places as South Africa, New Zealand,

and Jamaica. He was not a scholar, and some people thought he lacked ambition, but when the opportunity came to serve in London's East End, he took it.

He became known as the poor man's bishop. He rode public buses rather than private coaches. He always did whatever he could to raise funds to alleviate the poverty around him. His ambition was "not to be remembered but to be helpful." He was called "a most unselfish man, with a tender fondness for children."

William How was a man who practiced what he preached, as he writes in the last verse of this hymn: "Whate'er for Thine we do, O Lord, / We do it unto Thee."

Scriptures: 1 Chronicles 29:10-17; Psalm 96:8; Ephesians 2:6-10
Themes: Giving, Stewardship, Service

We give Thee but Thine own,
Whate'er the gift may be:
All that we have is Thine alone,
A trust, O Lord, from Thee.

May we Thy bounties thus
As stewards true receive,
And gladly, as Thou blessest us,
To Thee our first fruits give.

To comfort and to bless,
To find a balm for woe,
To tend the lone and fatherless,
Is angels' work below.

And we believe Thy word,
Though dim our faith may be:
Whate'er for Thine we do, O Lord,
We do it unto Thee.

WILLIAM WALSHAM HOW (1823–1897)

WHERE CROSS THE CROWDED WAYS OF LIFE

When Frank Mason North was asked to write a missionary hymn for the Methodist hymnal, he protested. "I'm not a hymnwriter," he said. He was a New York City man. He had been born there and had served as a pastor there. He knew New York City inside and out, but what did he know about hymnwriting?

North was, however, an excellent choice to present a changing missionary picture. In 1903 he was an officer of both the New York City Mission and the National City Evangelical Mission, so he knew city missions as few others did.

North realized that the city was a great mission field. Most missionary hymns talked about Greenland's icy mountains or the heathen who lived in distant lands, but North finally accepted the challenge of presenting the city as a mission field. He decided to write about the city as he saw it, about "haunts of wretchedness" and "shadowed thresholds dark with fears." He wrote of Wall Street–like paths that "hide the lures of greed."

North's stirring words were published first by the Methodist City Missionary Society and later appeared in the Methodist hymnal.

Scriptures: Matthew 9:36; Matthew 10:42; Matthew 25:34-36
Themes: Missions, Compassion, Social Concern

Where cross the crowded ways of life,
Where sound the cries of race and clan,
Above the noise of selfish strife,
We hear Thy voice, O Son of man!

In haunts of wretchedness and need,
On shadowed thresholds dark with fears,
From paths where hide the lures of greed,
We catch the vision of Thy tears.

From tender childhood's helplessness,
From woman's grief, man's burdened toil,
From famished souls, from sorrow's stress
Thy heart has never known recoil.

The cup of water given for Thee
Still holds the freshness of Thy grace;
Yet long these multitudes to see
The sweet compassion of Thy face.

O Master, from the mountainside,
Make haste to heal these hearts of pain;
Among these restless throngs abide,
O tread the city's streets again.

Till sons of men shall learn Thy love
And follow where Thy feet have trod;
Till, glorious from Thy heaven above,
Shall come the city of our God!

FRANK MASON NORTH (1850–1935)

WHO IS ON THE LORD'S SIDE?

For someone who struggled with illness much of her life, Frances Ridley Havergal wrote a remarkable number of vigorous, robust hymns. The last manuscript she worked on was *Starlight through the Shadows,* a book for invalids. She died at the age of forty-three, before she could complete the book, but her sister added the final chapter from Havergal's unpublished papers. That chapter is entitled "Marching Orders" and concludes with the words of this hymn.

The hymn itself was written October 13, 1877, and is based on 1 Chronicles 12:1-18. In the biblical text, the early followers of David are listed: archers and slingers, experts in running and swimming. David asked them whose side they were on, and they responded: "Thine are we, David, and on thy side, thou son of Jesse" (1 Chronicles 12:18, KJV). Frances Havergal put the refrain like this: "We are on the Lord's side, Savior, we are Thine."

Scriptures: Joshua 24:15; 1 Chronicles 12:1-18; Ephesians 6:13
Themes: Service, Consecration, Commitment

Who is on the Lord's side? Who will serve the King?
Who will be His helpers, other lives to bring?
Who will leave the world's side? Who will face the foe?
Who is on the Lord's side? Who for Him will go?
By Thy call of mercy, by Thy grace divine,
We are on the Lord's side, Savior, we are Thine.

Not for weight of glory, not for crown and palm,
Enter we the army, raise the warrior psalm;
But for love that claimeth lives for whom He died;
He whom Jesus nameth must be on His side.
By Thy love constraining, by Thy grace divine,
We are on the Lord's side, Savior, we are Thine.

Jesus, Thou hast bought us, not with gold or gem,
But with Thine own lifeblood, for Thy diadem.
With Thy blessing filling each who comes to Thee,
Thou hast made us willing, Thou hast made us free.
By Thy grand redemption, by Thy grace divine,
We are on the Lord's side, Savior, we are Thine.

Fierce may be the conflict, strong may be the foe,
But the King's own army none can overthrow.
Round His standard ranging; vict'ry is secure;
For His truth unchanging makes the triumph sure.
Joyfully enlisting by Thy grace divine,
We are on the Lord's side, Savior, we are Thine.

FRANCES RIDLEY HAVERGAL (1836–1879)

PART VII

CHRISTMAS

"Don't be afraid!" [the angel] said. "I bring you good news that

will bring great joy to all people."

LUKE 2:10

ALL PRAISE TO THEE, ETERNAL LORD

Five hundred years ago, a fourteen-year-old boy was sent away to school at Magdeburg, Germany. His father was too poor to support him, so the boy earned his bread by singing ballads in the street.

That boy never stopped singing. His name: Martin Luther. His own experience of the power of song in boyhood led him to give it a very high place in the Reformation. Luther often gathered a group of musicians in his house, and they arranged the hymns he gave them and set them to the favorite tunes of the German people; then he had the hymns and the tunes printed and circulated all over the land.

Many of the hymns were ones he had written; some of them were adapted from earlier poems. This Christmas hymn, which appeared originally in Latin, may have been the work of Gregory the Great in the sixth century. Despite Luther's disagreements with the Roman church, he realized that its hymns and traditions contained much value. Luther's translation of this Latin hymn into German illustrates his mission to give hymn singing back to the people.

Scriptures: Matthew 1:23; Luke 2:9-14; John 1:14
Themes: Birth of Christ, Love, Angels

All praise to Thee, eternal Lord,
Clothed in a garb of flesh and blood;
Choosing a manger for Thy throne,
While worlds on worlds are Thine alone.

Once did the skies before Thee bow,
A Virgin's arms contain Thee now;
Angels, who did in Thee rejoice,
Now listen for Thine infant voice.

A little child, Thou art our guest,
That weary ones in Thee may rest;
Forlorn and lowly is Thy birth,
That we may rise to heaven from earth.

Thou comest in the darksome night,
To make us children of the light,
To make us in the realms divine,
Like Thine own angels, 'round Thee shine.

All this for us Thy love hath done,
By this to Thee our love is won,
For this we tune our cheerful lays,
And shout our thanks in ceaseless praise.

MARTIN LUTHER (1483–1546)
Translator Unknown, 1858

ANGELS, FROM THE REALMS OF GLORY

James Montgomery, a newspaperman in London, had been imprisoned twice for his controversial editorials. But there was no controversy when he ran this poem in his newspaper column on Christmas Eve, 1816.

Other than Isaac Watts and Charles Wesley, probably no writer contributed more to the development of Christian hymns than this unique journalist who championed the cause of the poor and downtrodden, as well as foreign missions. It is fitting that the music was composed by a blind organist, Henry Smart, the designer and builder of some of England's finest organs and one of the outstanding musicians of his day.

In writing this hymn, Montgomery referred, not only to the Gospel accounts of Christ's birth, but also to the messianic prophecies of the Old Testament, where the Messiah is called the desired of all nations (Haggai 2:7, NIV), who would come suddenly to his Temple (Malachi 3:1).

Scriptures: Haggai 2:7; Malachi 3:1; Luke 2:10-12
Themes: Birth of Christ, Prophecy, Worship, Angels

Angels, from the realms of glory,
Wing your flight o'er all the earth;
Ye who sang creation's story
Now proclaim Messiah's birth:

Come and worship, come and worship,
Worship Christ, the newborn King.

Shepherds, in the field abiding,
Watching o'er your flocks by night,
God with man is now residing;
Yonder shines the infant light:

Sages, leave your contemplations;
Brighter visions beam afar;

Seek the great Desire of nations;
Ye have seen His natal star:

Saints, before the altar bending,
Watching long in hope and fear,
Suddenly the Lord, descending,
In His temple shall appear:

JAMES MONTGOMERY (1771–1854)

ANGELS WE HAVE HEARD ON HIGH

This traditional French carol puts to music the shepherds' story as recorded in the Gospel of Luke. It tells about the angelic chorus, the trip to Bethlehem, the meeting with Mary and Joseph, and the adoration of the baby Jesus.

Luke 2:17-20 tells of the reaction of the shepherds after they had been to Bethlehem's manger. They spread the word, and all who heard were amazed at what the shepherds said. Then the shepherds "went back to their flocks, glorifying and praising God for all they had heard and seen."

Sometimes our Christmas season ends with the viewing of the manger scene. We never get to the glorifying and praising, joining the angel chorus in the fullness of *Gloria in excelsis Deo*—"Glory to God in the highest." Make Christmas complete this year by following the shepherds' example, giving glory to our Redeemer God.

Scriptures: Matthew 9:8; Luke 2:8-20; Revelation 5:11
Themes: Birth of Christ, Angels, Shepherds

Angels we have heard on high
Sweetly singing o'er the plains,
And the mountains in reply
Echoing their joyous strains.

Gloria in excelsis Deo,
Gloria in excelsis Deo.

Shepherds, why this jubilee?
Why your joyous strains prolong?
What the gladsome tidings be
Which inspire your heavenly song?

Come to Bethlehem and see
Him whose birth the angels sing;
Come, adore on bended knee
Christ the Lord, the newborn King.

See Him in a manger laid,
Whom the choirs of angels praise;
Mary, Joseph, lend your aid,
While our hearts in love we raise.

JAMES CHADWICK (1813–1882)

AS WITH GLADNESS, MEN OF OLD

William Dix was an insurance man, specializing in maritime insurance. He knew all about the rigors of travel and the joy of bringing gifts from a foreign land.

So Dix had a natural interest in the coming of the wise men to Bethlehem. On Epiphany Sunday in 1860, when his minister was scheduled to preach about the wise men, Dix became ill and could not go to church. While he was home in bed, he decided to write a new Christmas carol, one that applied the message of the wise men to people of his day.

In his carol, instead of focusing on the costliness of the magi's gifts, he emphasized their finding what they sought and their worship of the Christ child. The pattern of the wise men—following, adoring, giving—is a pattern that is just as relevant today as it was then.

Scriptures: Matthew 2:10-11; 2 Corinthians 9:7
Themes: Epiphany, Gifts, Magi, Christmas

As with gladness, men of old
Did the guiding star behold;
As with joy they hailed its light,
Leading onward, beaming bright;
So, most gracious Lord, may we
Evermore be led to Thee.

As with joyous steps they sped
To that lowly manger bed,
There to bend the knee before
Him whom heaven and earth adore;

So may we with willing feet
Ever seek Thy mercy seat.

As they offered gifts most rare
At the manger rude and bare,
So may we with holy joy,
Pure and free from sin's alloy,
All our costliest treasures bring,
Christ, to Thee, our heavenly King.

Holy Jesus, every day
Keep us in the narrow way;
And, when earthly things are past,
Bring our ransomed souls at last
Where they need no star to guide,
Where no clouds Thy glory hide.

In the heavenly country bright
Need they no created light;
Thou its light, its joy, its crown,
Thou its sun which goes not down,
There forever may we sing
Hallelujah to our King.

WILLIAM CHATTERTON DIX (1837–1898)

AWAY IN A MANGER

Children enjoy Christmas more than any other time of year, and adults share that special joy. "Away in a Manger" is usually considered a children's carol, yet its beauty and power are loved equally by people of all ages. All of us can pray, "I love you, Lord Jesus! Stay close to me tonight."

For many years this hymn was attributed to Martin Luther, but Luther was probably not its author. The first two verses of the carol appeared for the first time in a Lutheran hymnal in 1885. The next publisher to pick it up called it "Luther's Cradle Hymn," assuming that since it was anonymous and in a Lutheran hymnal, it must be Luther's. The third verse was added by a Methodist minister in the early 1900s.

Regardless of its author, the beauty of this carol is the beauty of Christmas. It is simple. Christmas is not the gold and glitter, the wrappings and trappings. It is the story of God humbling himself to become a baby, born in crude circumstances to a young woman in ancient Palestine. Sing this carol softly. It is what Christmas is all about.

Scriptures: Isaiah 53:1-3; Matthew 8:20; Luke 2:7
Themes: Birth of Christ, Childhood, Comfort

Away in a manger, no crib for a bed,
The little Lord Jesus laid down His sweet head;
The stars in the sky looked down where He lay,
The little Lord Jesus, asleep on the hay.

The cattle are lowing, the Baby awakes,
But little Lord Jesus no crying He makes,
I love Thee, Lord Jesus, look down from the sky,
And stay by my cradle till morning is nigh.

Be near me, Lord Jesus, I ask Thee to stay
Close by me forever, and love me, I pray.
Bless all the dear children in Thy tender care,
And fit us for heaven, to live with Thee there.

STANZAS 1 AND 2, UNKNOWN

STANZA 3 BY JOHN THOMAS MCFARLAND (1851–1913)

BRIGHTEST AND BEST

Reginald Heber was a twenty-eight-year-old pastor in the village of Hodnot in western England when he wrote this carol.

In the autumn of 1811, Heber had an idea for a hymn. Before the idea escaped him, he grabbed his daughter's small composition book, went to his study, dipped his pen in an inkwell, and began writing the five stanzas of the hymn.

As Heber envisioned the nativity scene and saw shepherds and wise men worshipping the Christ child, he asked the question, What kind of worship is most acceptable to God? The gold, incense, and myrrh of the three kings? No, says Heber, "Richer by far is the heart's adoration, / Dearer to God are the prayers of the poor."

Scriptures: Psalm 51:17; Isaiah 60:1-3; Matthew 2:10-11
Themes: Birth of Christ, Joy, Worship

Brightest and best are the stars of the morning,
Dawn on our darkness and come to our aid;
Star of the east, the horizon adorning,
Guide where our infant redeemer is laid.

What shall we give him, in costly devotion?
Shall we bring incense and offerings divine,
Gems of the mountains and pearls of the ocean,
Myrrh from the forest or gold from the mine?

Vainly we offer each lavish oblation,
Vainly with gifts would his favor secure;
Richer by far is the heart's adoration,
Dearer to God are the prayers of the poor.

Brightest and best are the stars of the morning,
Dawn on our darkness and come to our aid;
Star of the east, the horizon adorning,
Guide where our infant Redeemer is laid!

REGINALD HEBER (1783–1826)

CALM ON THE LISTENING EAR OF NIGHT

Edmund Sears had just finished college in New York and was planning to go on to law school, but somehow in the noise of the world, he heard a quiet voice that urged him to go into the ministry. He did.

At the age of twenty-four, just one year out of college, he wrote this carol. Like his other carol, "It Came upon a Midnight Clear," it emphasizes the contrast between the angels' song and the noise of the world. One stanza of this hymn, which is not usually included in hymnals, has the line, "O hush the noise, ye men of strife, / And hear the angels sing."

He wrote this carol in 1834, and the noise of Christmas has increased every year since then. As we celebrate Christmas, we are challenged to hush the noise and hear the angels sing.

Scriptures: Isaiah 2:1-4; Luke 1:76-79; Luke 2:8-14
Themes: Birth of Christ, Angels, Prophecy

Calm on the listening ear of night
Come heaven's melodious strains,
Where wild Judea stretches forth
Her silver mantled plains;
Celestial choirs from courts above
Shed sacred glories there,
And angels, with their sparkling lyres,
Make music on the air.

The answering hills of Palestine
Send back the glad reply,
And greet from all their holy heights
The Day-Spring from on high;
O'er the blue depths of Galilee,
There comes a holier calm,
And Sharon waves, in solemn praise,
O'er silent groves of palm.

"Glory to God!" the lofty strain
The realm of ether fills;
How sweeps the song of solemn joy
O'er Judah's sacred hills!
"Glory to God!" the sounding skies
Loud with their anthems ring,
"Peace on the earth; good will to men
From heaven's Eternal King."

Light on thy hills, Jerusalem!
The Savior now is born,
And bright on Bethlehem's joyous plains
Breaks the first Christmas morn,
And brightly on Moriah's brow
Crowned with her temple spires,
Which first proclaim the new-born light,
Clothed with its orient fires.

EDMUND HAMILTON SEARS (1810–1876)

CHILD OF THE STABLE'S SECRET BIRTH

This carol was originally written as a family Christmas card. Because it was well received by the author's friends, Timothy Dudley-Smith included the carol in the magazine that he edited. Others liked it, and soon it was put to a tune by Christopher Dearnley and published in a British hymnal.

The idea of the carol is simple enough, but it still makes us wonder in amazement. A weak and helpless baby born in a stable is the Almighty God's greatest gift to this earth. Yet that divine Gift was rejected by the very men and women whom he came to redeem.

Scriptures: Luke 2:7; John 1:11-12; Galatians 4:4
Themes: Birth of Christ, Meekness, Humility of Christ

Child of the stable's secret birth,
The Lord by right of the lords of earth,
Let angels sing of a King newborn,
The world is weaving a crown of thorn;
A crown of thorn for that infant head
Cradled soft in the manger bed.

Eyes that shine in the lantern's ray;
A face so small in its nest of hay,
Face of a child who is born to scan
The world he made through the eyes of man:
And from that face in the final day
Earth and heaven shall flee away.

Voice that rang through the courts on high,
Contracted now to a wordless cry,
A voice to master the wind and wave,
The human heart and the hungry grave:
The voice of God through the cedar trees
Rolling forth as the sound of seas.

Infant hands in a mother's hand,
For none but Mary may understand
Whose are the hands and the fingers curled
But his who fashioned and made the world;
And through these hands in the hour of death
Nails shall strike to the wood beneath.

Child of the stable's secret birth,
The Father's gift to a wayward earth,
To drain the cup in a few short years
Of all our sorrows, our sins, and tears—
Ours the prize for the road he trod:
Risen with Christ; at peace with God.

TIMOTHY DUDLEY-SMITH (B. 1926)

CHRISTIANS, AWAKE, SALUTE THE HAPPY MORN

If it weren't for young Dolly Byrom, this carol would never have been written. When her father, John Byrom, asked her what she wanted for Christmas, she replied, "Please write me a poem."

So on Christmas morning 1749 in Manchester, England, Dolly came to the breakfast table and found a sheet of paper under her plate. On it was written, "Christmas Day for Dolly," and underneath it was the poem, "Christians, Awake, Salute the Happy Morn."

But that's only half the story. John Byrom, a surgeon by profession, had many friends in the area, one of whom was John Wainwright, the organist of a church in a neighboring community. Somehow Wainwright was given a copy of Dolly's Christmas poem and wrote music for it. Then early on Christmas morning 1750, Wainwright brought his entire church choir to Dr. Byrom's house. Quietly, they gathered outside the Byroms' bedroom windows and then burst into song, "Christians, awake, salute the happy morn."

Scriptures: Psalm 57:8; Isaiah 26:19; Ephesians 5:14
Themes: Birth of Christ, Joy, Wonder

Christians, awake, salute the happy morn
Whereon the savior of the world was born;
Rise to adore the mystery of love,
Which hosts of angels chanted from above;
With them the joyful tidings first begun
Of God incarnate and the virgin's Son.

Then to the watchful shepherds it was told,
Who heard th' angelic herald's voice, "Behold
I bring good tidings of a savior's birth
To you and to all nations upon earth;
This day hath God fulfilled His promised word;
This day is born a savior, Christ the Lord."

He spake; and straightway the celestial choir
In hymns of joy, unknown before, conspire;
The praises of redeeming love they sang,
And heaven's whole orb with alleluias rang;
God's highest glory, was their anthem still,
Peace upon earth, and unto men good will.

Then may we hope, the angelic hosts among,
To sing, redeemed, a glad triumphal song;
He that was born upon this joyful day
Around us all His glory shall display;
Saved by His love, forever we shall sing,
Eternal praise to heaven's Almighty King.

JOHN BYROM (1692–1763)

COME, THOU LONG-EXPECTED JESUS

Although prolific hymnwriter Charles Wesley penned eighteen Christ-mas songs, he was never content with simply painting the picture of the manger scene. He needed to go deeper. In this hymn, he begins by allud-ing to scriptural prophecies of Christ. Moving on to personal applica-tion, he continues: Christ is not only the "desire of every nation"; he is the "joy of every longing heart." He is not only the child born with the "government . . . on his shoulders" (Isaiah 9:6); he is also "born to reign in us forever."

Such personal application was a hallmark of the Wesleys' ministry. Charles and his brother John challenged the staid Anglican traditions of their time. The church of their day had great scholarship; its theology was orthodox. Christians sang hymns straight from Scripture. But the Wesleys asked, "Does this mean anything to you? Is the biblical story about long-ago events or about what is going on in your life?" They urged people to meet Christ personally and to include him in every part of their lives—even their hymn singing.

Scriptures: Daniel 7:13-14; Haggai 2:7; Luke 1:32-35
Themes: Birth of Christ, Prophecy, Hope

Come, Thou long-expected Jesus,
Born to set Thy people free;
From our fears and sins release us;
Let us find our rest in Thee.
Israel's strength and consolation,
Hope of all the earth Thou art;
Dear desire of every nation,
Joy of every longing heart.

Born Thy people to deliver,
Born a child and yet a King,

Born to reign in us forever,
Now Thy gracious kingdom bring.
By Thine own eternal spirit
Rule in all our hearts alone;
By Thine all sufficient merit,
Raise us to Thy glorious throne.

CHARLES WESLEY (1707–1788)

COMFORT, COMFORT YE MY PEOPLE

It shouldn't surprise us that Johannes Olearius based this hymn on Isaiah 40:1-8. Olearius was an influential church leader, well connected in the noble courts of Germany. He compiled and wrote for the major hymnal used in Germany in his time. He also wrote devotional books and a commentary on the Bible. In many ways, he was similar to the prophet Isaiah, who apparently had a connection with Judah's royal court in his day. Isaiah, too, wrote both poetry and prose, both words of devotion and theology. And Isaiah's world, like that of Olearius, was shattered by war.

From our perspective, we see that Isaiah's words go past Babylon to John the Baptist, announcing the arrival of Jesus the Messiah. They are words of hope and comfort that again rang out in seventeenth-century Germany and still ring out today. People in darkness can see the light as they focus their faith on Jesus Christ.

Scriptures: Isaiah 40:1-3; Matthew 3:3; Luke 3:4-6
Themes: Birth of Christ, Prophecy, Comfort

Comfort, comfort ye My people
Speak ye peace, thus saith our God;
Comfort those who sit in darkness,
Mourning 'neath their sorrow's load.
Speak ye to Jerusalem
Of the peace that waits for them;
Tell her that her sins I cover,
And her warfare now is over.

Yea, her sins our God will pardon,
Blotting out each dark misdeed;
All that well deserved His anger

He no more will see or heed.
She hath suffered many a day
Now her griefs have passed away;
God will change her pining sadness
Into ever-springing gladness.

For the herald's voice is crying
In the desert far and near,
Bidding all men to repentance,
Since the kingdom now is here.
O that warning cry obey!
Now prepare for God a way;
Let the valleys rise to meet Him,
And the hills bow down to greet Him.

Make ye straight what long was crooked,
Make the rougher places plain;
Let your hearts be true and humble,
As befits His holy reign.
For the glory of the Lord
Now o'er earth is shed abroad;
And all flesh shall see the token,
That His Word is never broken.

JOHANNES OLEARIUS (1611–1684)
Translated by Catherine Winkworth (1827–1878)

EARTH HAS MANY A NOBLE CITY

Aurelius Clemens Prudentius grew up in Spain, becoming a lawyer and a judge. In 379, he was invited to Rome to join the emperor's staff. He was fascinated by Rome with its new Christian churches and the tombs of martyrs. Christianity had been legalized earlier that century and was now the official religion of the empire. Perhaps Rome was the "noble city" on which he began this meditation.

Despite his early enthusiasm, Prudentius soon grew weary of public life. He felt he had become too self-centered, so in 395 he forsook his worldly position and entered a monastery. There he wrote several devotional and practical works. A few fragments such as this one have been translated and set to music.

Scriptures: Isaiah 9:1-7; Isaiah 60:1-3; Matthew 2:1-5
Themes: Birth of Christ, Messiah, Worship

Earth has many a noble city;
Bethlehem, thou dost all excel;
Out of thee the Lord from heaven
Came to rule His Israel.

Fairer than the sun at morning
Was the star that told His birth,
To the world its God announcing
Seen in fleshly form on earth.

Eastern sages at His cradle
Make oblations rich and rare;
See them give, in deep devotion,
Gold and frankincense and myrrh.

Sacred gifts of mystic meaning:
Incense doth their God disclose;
Gold the King of kings proclaimeth;
Myrrh His sepulcher foreshows.

Jesus, whom the Gentiles worshiped
At Thy glad epiphany,
Unto Thee, with God the Father
And the Spirit, glory be.

AURELIUS CLEMENS PRUDENTIUS (348–CA. 413)
Translated by Edward Caswall (1814–1878)

FROM HEAVEN ABOVE TO EARTH I COME

The coming of Christ at Christmas is in vain unless we allow him to come and dwell in our hearts as well. This simple and glorious message is captured beautifully in this Christmas hymn by the great reformer Martin Luther. He wrote it for his young son Hans, to be sung at a family Christmas celebration. Just as God communicated with us by sending his Son that first Christmas night, Luther sought to communicate the life-transforming message of Christ to his son.

What a beautiful reminder that Christ's coming at Christmas is for everyone—old and young, rich and poor, wise and simple. It was such an amazing event: heralded by angels in the heavens, yet witnessed by animals in a pungent stable; beyond the understanding of the wise, yet presented in an event even children can grasp. God became a human being to reveal his loving and gracious character to us.

Scriptures: Luke 1:30-33; Luke 2:10-14; Hebrews 10:7-9
Themes: Birth of Christ, Childhood, Joy

From heaven above to earth I come
To bear good news to every home;
Glad tidings of great joy I bring,
Whereof I now will say and sing.

To you this night is born a child
Of Mary, chosen mother mild;
This little child, of lowly birth,
Shall be the joy of all the earth.

Were earth a thousand times as fair,
Beset with gold and jewels rare,
She yet were far too poor to be
A narrow cradle, Lord, to Thee.

Ah, dearest Jesus, Holy Child,
Make Thee a bed, soft undefiled,
Within my heart, that it may be
A quiet chamber kept for Thee.

"Glory to God in highest heaven,
Who unto man His Son hath given,"
While angels sing with pious mirth
A glad new year to all the earth.

MARTIN LUTHER (1483–1546)
Translated by Catherine Winkworth (1827–1878)

FROM HEAVEN YOU CAME (THE SERVANT KING)

Graham Kendrick was planning to become a teacher, but after college he decided to take a year off and tour schools and colleges with a group of Christian musicians. It also gave him a chance to try out some of the praise and worship songs he had been writing.

Before long, his songs were being sung all over England in churches of every variety. He began leading outdoor singing and helped organize

"Marches of Praise" and "Make Way" marches through streets and housing complexes.

This song, "From Heaven You Came," emphasizes Christ's role as both a servant and as the king. It challenges us to follow him and to put others before ourselves as we learn servanthood from the King of kings.

Scriptures: Matthew 20:26-28; John 13:14; Philippians 2:7
Themes: Birth of Christ, Servanthood, Worship

From heaven you came, helpless Babe,
Entered our world, Your glory veiled;
Not to be served, but to serve,
And give your life that we might live.

This is our God, the servant King,
He calls us now to follow Him;
To bring our lives as a daily offering
Of worship to the servant King.

There in the garden of tears,
My heavy load He chose to bear;
His heart with sorrow was torn,
"Yet not my will, but yours," He said.

Come see His hands and His feet,
The scars that speak of sacrifice;
Hands that flung stars into space,
To cruel nails surrendered.

So let us learn how to serve,
And in our lives enthrone Him;
Each other's needs to prefer,
For it is Christ we're serving.

Words by: Graham Kendrick
©Thankyou Music
All rights reserved. Used by permission.

GENTLE MARY LAID HER CHILD

Joseph Cook entered a Christmas carol-writing contest in 1919. He was not known as a poet, but he had some ideas that he thought should be presented in a Christmas carol. Many of the Protestant carols seemed to neglect Mary, he thought, so he wrote a carol to give her proper honor.

After all, the angel had announced to her, "Greetings, favored one! The Lord is with you" (Luke 1:28, NASB), and Mary's Magnificat in the first chapter of Luke is one of the most beautiful songs in the Bible. Joseph Cook put the spotlight on the verse in Luke that says, "She gave birth to her first child, a son. She wrapped him snugly in strips of cloth and laid him in a manger, because there was no lodging available for them" (Luke 2:7).

By the way, Joseph Cook's entry won the Christmas carol-writing competition.

Scriptures: Luke 1:26-33, 46-55; Luke 2:6-7
Themes: Birth of Christ, Angels, Comfort

> Gentle Mary laid her child lowly in a manger;
> There He lay, the undefiled, to the world a stranger;
> Such a Babe in such a place, can He be the Savior?
> Ask the saved of every race who have found His favor.
>
> Angels sang about His birth; wise saw and found Him;
> Heaven's star shone brightly forth, glory all around Him;
> Shepherds saw the wondrous sight, heard the angels singing;
> All the plains were lit that night, all the hills were ringing.
>
> Gentle Mary laid her child lowly in a manger;
> He is still the undefiled, but no more a stranger;
> Son of God, of humble birth, beautiful the story;
> Praise His name in all the earth, hail the King of glory!
>
> JOSEPH SIMPSON COOK (B. 1859)

GO TELL IT ON THE MOUNTAIN

The popular musical *The Sound of Music* speaks of the hills in Austria being alive with the sound of music, but long before that musical was written, the Appalachian Mountains in America were alive with the sound of music. John Work was a professor of Latin and Greek, but he spent much of his life roaming the Appalachian Mountains with his brother Frederick Work, collecting, arranging, and promoting music that he found in those mountains.

"Go Tell It on the Mountain" was first published in 1907, when John Work added the stanzas to the chorus that had long been sung throughout Appalachia.

Scriptures: Isaiah 40:9; Isaiah 52:7; Romans 10:14-15
Themes: Evangelism, Birth of Christ, Joy

While shepherds kept their watching o'er silent flocks by night,
Behold, throughout the heavens there shone a holy light.

Go tell it on the mountain, over the hills and ev'rywhere.
Go tell it on the mountain that Jesus Christ is born.

The shepherds feared and trembled when lo above the earth
Rang out the angel chorus that hailed our Savior's birth.

Down in a lowly manger the humble Christ was born,
And God sent us salvation that blessed Christmas morn.

TRADITIONAL SPIRITUAL

STANZAS BY JOHN WESLEY WORK JR. (1872–1925)

GOD REST YE MERRY, GENTLEMEN

This carol was first published in 1827, but even then it was introduced as "an ancient carol, sung in the streets of London." In fact, old London had municipal watchmen who were licensed to perform certain tasks, including the singing of Christmas carols. This was one of their songs.

In *A Christmas Carol* by Charles Dickens, Ebenezer Scrooge hears this song sung joyously in the street and tells the singer he'll hit him with a ruler unless he stops singing. Of course that was not the intended response to this carol. The point is that joy reigns on Christmas Day because of God's great gift of his Son, Jesus Christ. We can "rest merry" in the knowledge that Christ has paid our penalty for going astray and has set us free from the power of evil.

Scriptures: Isaiah 40:1-2; Matthew 1:18-20; Luke 2:10
Themes: Birth of Christ, Joy, Comfort

God rest ye merry, gentlemen,
Let nothing you dismay,
For Jesus Christ our Savior
Was born upon this day,
To save us all from Satan's power
When we were gone astray.

O tidings of comfort and joy, comfort and joy;
O tidings of comfort and joy!

In Bethlehem in Jewry
This blessed babe was born,
And laid within a manger
Upon this blessed morn:
The which His mother Mary
Did nothing take in scorn.

From God our heavenly Father
A blessed angel came,
And unto certain shepherds
Brought tidings of the same,
How that in Bethlehem was born
The Son of God by name.

The shepherds at those tidings
Rejoiced much in mind,
And left their flocks afeeding
In tempest, storm, and wind,
And went to Bethlehem straightway,
The blessed babe to find.

Now to the Lord sing praises,
All you within this place,
And with true love and brotherhood
Each other now embrace;
This holy tide of Christmas
All other doth deface.

TRADITIONAL ENGLISH CAROL (18TH CENTURY)

GOOD CHRISTIAN MEN, REJOICE

Both text and music for this hymn go back many centuries. In 1601, Bartholomaeus Gesius adapted the previously existing music and called it *In Dulci Jubilo*, which means "With Sweet Shouting." Later Bach arranged it for the organ, and later still John Stainer did a choral version. The words come from Latin, but very early the Germans had translated it, adding some thoughts to it. Many other language groups have freely adapted this song as well. Though the great translator John Neale standardized the hymn in English, it is truly a folk song with many different forms and traditions.

It is reported that in Bethlehem, Pennsylvania, in 1745 a gathering of

Moravian missionaries sang this carol in thirteen different European and Native American languages.

Scriptures: Isaiah 49:13; Luke 1:77-79; 1 Peter 1:8
Themes: Birth of Christ, Joy, Salvation

Good Christian men, rejoice,
With heart and soul and voice;
Give ye heed to what we say:
Jesus Christ is born today.
Ox and ass before Him bow,
He is in the manger now.
Christ is born today,
Christ is born today!

Good Christian men, rejoice,
With heart and soul and voice;
Now ye hear of endless bliss;
Jesus Christ was born for this!
He hath oped the heavenly door,
And man is blessed evermore.
Christ was born for this,
Christ was born for this!

Good Christian men, rejoice,
With heart and soul and voice;
Now ye need not fear the grave;
Jesus Christ was born to save!
Calls you one and calls you all,
To gain His everlasting hall,
Christ was born to save,
Christ was born to save!

LATIN HYMN (14TH CENTURY)
Paraphrase by John Mason Neale (1818–1866)

GOOD KING WENCESLAS

Wenceslas was one of the early Christian rulers of Bohemia. When he was five, his father was killed in battle and his mother became the head of state, ruling the country with a firm hand. Wenceslas became king when he was eighteen and was known as a wise and diplomatic ruler.

He was invited to a banquet where his enemies had planned to assassinate him. Although weapons were drawn, the official historian wrote, "God did not permit them to strike." The next morning, he went to church, where the plotters were waiting. At the age of twenty-two, he was murdered on the church steps.

Wenceslas sought to rule as Christ would rule. He helped the poor, he improved the cultural standards of the people, and today in Prague, although it is a millennium after his death and although the country has passed through various governments, he is still remembered by a statue of him on horseback in the middle of Wenceslas Square.

Scriptures: Psalm 72:4; Psalm 82:4; Luke 2:7
Themes: Birth of Christ, Joy, Poverty

Good King Wenceslas looked on the Feast of Stephen
When the snow lay round about, deep and crisp and even.
Brightly shone the moon that night, tho' the frost was cruel
When the poor man came in sight, gathering winter fuel.

Hither, page. And stand by me, if thou knows it telling,
Yonder peasant, where is he, where and what his dwelling.
Sire, he lives a good league hence, underneath the mountain;
Right against the forest fence, by St. Agnes' fountain.

Bring me flesh and bring me wine; bring me pine logs hither;
Thou and I will see him dine when we bear them thither.
Page and monarch forth they went, forth they went together,
Through the rude winds' wild lament, and the bitter weather.

Sire, the night is darker now, and the wind blows stronger;
Fails my heart, I know not how I can go no longer.
Mark my footsteps, my good page, tread thou in them boldly,
Thou shalt find the winter's rage, freeze thy blood less coldly.

In his master's steps he trod where the snow lay dinted;
Heat was in the very sod which the saint had printed.
Therefore, Christian men, be sure wealth of rank possessing,
Ye who now will bless the poor, shall yourself find blessing.

JOHN MASON NEALE (1818–1866)

HAIL TO THE LORD'S ANOINTED

In April 1822, James Montgomery was speaking in Liverpool at a Methodist missionary meeting. It was a time when the British were waking up to foreign missions, and numerous meetings like this one were presenting worldwide needs and commissioning new workers. Montgomery, a noted hymnwriter, loved to promote missionary zeal wherever he could.

As the hymnwriter spoke, the building suddenly went dark, and a loud crash followed. For a moment it seemed that mass panic might ensue. But then the chairman of the meeting called out, "There is still light within," and Montgomery resumed speaking. The crowd calmed down, listening in the darkness. Montgomery concluded his words by reciting this newly written hymn, "Hail to the Lord's Anointed," which is really a paraphrase of Psalm 72.

Scriptures: Psalm 72:1-14; Isaiah 9:7; Isaiah 60:1-3
Themes: Birth of Christ, Prophecy, Blessing

Hail to the Lord's Anointed,
Great David's greater Son!
Hail in the time appointed,
His reign on earth begun!
He comes to break oppression,
To set the captive free;
To take away transgression,
And rule in equity.

He comes with succor speedy
To those who suffer wrong;
To help the poor and needy,
And bid the weak be strong;
To give them songs for sighing,
Their darkness turn to light,
Whose souls, condemned and dying,
Are precious in His sight.

He shall come down like showers
Upon the fruitful earth;
Love, joy, and hope, like flowers,
Spring in His path to birth.
Before Him, on the mountains,
Shall peace, the herald, go,

And righteousness, in fountains,
From hill to valley flow.

To Him shall prayer unceasing
And daily vows ascend;
His kingdom still increasing,
A kingdom without end.
The tide of time shall never
His covenant remove;
His name shall stand forever;
That name to us is love.

JAMES MONTGOMERY (1771–1854)

HARK! A THRILLING VOICE IS SOUNDING

This ancient hymn depicts the full story of Christ from the prediction of his first arrival, through his second coming, and on into glory. Like many good works of poetry, it is not easy to understand—it takes a little thinking to sort out.

What is the "thrilling voice" that's sounding? If we read this in chronological order, it must be the voices of the Old Testament prophets, culminating in John the Baptist. In many ways they announced to their people, "Christ is nigh!" and urged the people to reform their ways. The mention of Christ as "our sun" in the second stanza may allude to Malachi 4:2, the last of the messianic prophecies in the Old Testament.

The third stanza, of course, refers to Christ in his first coming as the Lamb who came to be our sacrifice. We find forgiveness as we come to him. At his next coming, as the world shudders with fear, we will receive mercy and love. And we'll join in the eternal praise invoked by the final stanza.

Scriptures: Malachi 4:2; Matthew 3:1-3; 1 Thessalonians 5:2-5
Themes: Birth of Christ, Prophecy, Messiah

Hark! a thrilling voice is sounding.
"Christ is nigh," it seems to say;
"Cast away the works of darkness,
O ye children of the day."

Wakened by the solemn warning,
From earth's bondage let us rise;

Christ, our sun, all sloth dispelling,
Shines upon the morning skies.

Lo! the Lamb, so long expected,
Comes with pardon down from heaven;
Let us haste, with tears of sorrow,
One and all to be forgiven;

So when next He comes with glory,
And the world is wrapped in fear,
May He with His mercy shield us,
And with words of love draw near.

Honor, glory, might, and blessing
To the Father and the Son,
With the everlasting Spirit
While unending ages run.

LATIN HYMN (6TH CENTURY)
From Hymns Ancient and Modern, *1861, altered*

HARK THE GLAD SOUND!

Three days after Christmas in 1735, Philip Doddridge was planning to preach a sermon called "Christ's Message from Luke 4:18-19." Doddridge was known as a hymnwriter, and he would often introduce one of his hymns at the conclusion of a sermon. As was the custom in that day, the hymn was sung line by line from the pulpit, and then repeated line by line by the congregation. Since some of these hymns had ten or twelve stanzas, it took a long time for them to be sung from the pulpit and repeated by the congregation.

This hymn is usually called a Christmas carol. After all, the title is "Hark the Glad Sound," and it was introduced three days after Christmas, but it really isn't a Christmas carol. It's a hymn about the start of Christ's ministry, and it is a paraphrase of Isaiah 61:1-2 and Luke 4:18-19. In these verses Christ announces his mission to bring good news to the poor, to heal the brokenhearted, to bring deliverance to captives, and to heal the blind and the wounded. Good news, indeed! The Savior has come.

Scriptures: Isaiah 61:1-2; Luke 4:18-19; Luke 7:18-22
Themes: Life of Christ, Miracles of Christ, Joy

Hark, the glad sound! The Savior comes, the Savior promised long;
Let every heart prepare a throne and every voice a song.

He comes the pris'ners to release, in Satan's bondage held.
The gates of brass before Him burst, the iron fetters yield.

He comes the broken heart to bind, the bleeding soul to cure,
And with the treasures of His grace to enrich the humble poor.

Our glad Hosannas, Prince of Peace, Your welcome shall proclaim,
And heav'n's eternal arches ring with Your beloved name.

PHILIP DODDRIDGE (1702–1751)

HARK! THE HERALD ANGELS SING

Charles Wesley wrote over six thousand hymn texts, but this may have
been his best. In singing this hymn, we not only join the shepherds under
a canopy of singing angels, we also learn about the Jesus they proclaimed. We discover who he is and what his coming means.

Wesley's carol is filled with powerful scriptural ideas; a month could
be spent exploring these stanzas. But let's focus now on the last four
lines: "Mild He lays His glory by, born that man no more may die, born
to raise the sons of earth, born to give them second birth." These are the
reasons why Jesus came: so we would not have to face eternal death; so
he could raise us with him; and so he could regenerate us into children of
God. For these and so much more, he deserves our praise. "Glory to the
newborn King!"

Scriptures: Luke 1:34-35; Luke 2:9-11; Galatians 4:4
Themes: Birth of Christ, Angels, Prophecy

Hark! the herald angels sing,
"Glory to the newborn King;
Peace on earth, and mercy mild,
God and sinners reconciled!"
Joyful, all ye nations, rise,
Join the triumph of the skies;
With th' angelic host proclaim,
"Christ is born in Bethlehem!"

Hark! the herald angels sing,
"Glory to the newborn King!"

Christ, by highest heaven adored;
Christ, the everlasting Lord!
Late in time behold Him come,
Offspring of the virgin's womb.
Veiled in flesh the Godhead see;
Hail th' incarnate Deity,
Pleased as man with men to dwell,
Jesus, our Emmanuel.

Hail the heaven-born Prince of Peace!
Hail the Sun of Righteousness!
Light and life to all He brings,
Risen with healing in His wings,
Mild He lays His glory by,
Born that man no more may die,
Born to raise the sons of earth,
Born to give them second birth.

CHARLES WESLEY (1707–1788)
Altered by George Whitefield (1714–1770)

HIS NAME IS WONDERFUL

Audrey Mieir began writing hymns when she was sixteen. Soon she became a pianist; then a choir director; and by the time she was thirty, she had founded the Mieir Choir Clinic in Hollywood.

This song, "His Name Is Wonderful," was inspired by her church's annual Christmas program. Perhaps the Christmas program at Bethel Union Church in Duarte, California, was basically not much different from other years. A nervous teenage girl played the part of Mary, young boys were supposedly the angels, and the organist played Christmas carols in the background. But there seemed to be an unusual electricity about that program; when it was over, the pastor stood and declared, "His name is Wonderful. His name is Wonderful. His name is Wonderful."

Those words would make a great worship song, Audrey thought, so she jotted them on the back page of her Bible. That afternoon she wrote the song, and in the evening she sang it for the church's young people, little thinking that the simple song would become famous in only a few years.

Scriptures: Isaiah 9:6-7; Philippians 2:9-11; 1 Timothy 6:15
Themes: Birth of Christ, Prophecy, Promises

His name is wonderful, His name is wonderful,
His name is wonderful, Jesus, my Lord;
He is the mighty King, Master of everything,
His name is wonderful, Jesus, my Lord.

He's the great Shepherd, the Rock of all ages,
Almighty God is He;
Bow down before Him, love and adore Him,
His name is wonderful, Jesus, my Lord.

AUDREY MIEIR (B. 1916)

I HEARD THE BELLS ON CHRISTMAS DAY

Christmas Day 1863 was not a day of "peace on earth, good will to men" in the United States. The bloody Civil War was being waged. At Gettysburg, only six months earlier, forty thousand men were killed, wounded, or missing. The long siege of Vicksburg resulted in thirty thousand Confederate soldiers being taken as prisoners. And there was no end in sight.

No wonder the poet Henry Wadsworth Longfellow "bowed his head" in despair and said, "There is no peace on earth." The entire country, both North and South, was bowed in despair. But there was something about Christmas that helped Longfellow see beyond the carnage of the present and realize that God is not dead and that right would prevail.

The birth of Jesus Christ brings hope. Christmas doesn't mean that all problems disappear, but it does assure you that God is not dead, nor does he sleep. Even the darkness of Good Friday is followed by the dawn of Easter. Yes, the bells of Christmas are still ringing, singing on their way.

Scriptures: Micah 5:5; Luke 2:13-14; Luke 19:42
Themes: Birth of Christ, Peace, Violence

I heard the bells on Christmas day their old familiar carols play,
And wild and sweet the words repeat of peace on earth, good will to men.

I thought how as the day had come, the belfries of all Christendom
Had rolled along th'unbroken song of peace on earth, good will to men.

And in despair I bowed my head: "There is no peace on earth," I said,
"For hate is strong, and mocks the song of peace on earth,
   good will to men."

Yet pealed the bells more loud and deep: "God is not dead,
   nor does he sleep;
The wrong shall fail, the right prevail, with peace on earth,
   good will to men."

Then ringing, singing on its way, the world revolved
   from night to day—
A voice, a chime, a chant sublime of peace on earth, good will to men.

HENRY WADSWORTH LONGFELLOW (1807–1882)

I WONDER AS I WANDER

Kentuckian John Jacob Niles started collecting Appalachian folk music when he was fifteen years old. He collected a lot of it and he wrote a lot of it. In fact, he became so associated with the folk music style that it is hard to tell what he collected and what he wrote. "I Wonder As I Wander" was probably written by Niles about 1930. But Niles was more than a folk singer. He had studied music in Paris, was an opera singer, and taught at noted music schools such as Juilliard and Eastman. Yet he was best known as an authority on music of the southern Appalachians and for this simple, though powerful, carol, "I Wonder As I Wander."

Scriptures: Isaiah 9:6; Matthew 15:31; Mark 6:51; Luke 2:18
Themes: Birth of Christ, Worship, Wonder

AUTHOR: JOHN JACOB NILES

IMMANUEL, TO THEE WE SING

Isaiah prophesied that a virgin would bear a child and name him Immanuel. But in the Christmas story we find that Mary named her baby Jesus! What's all this about Immanuel?

It helps to understand how names were used in Bible times and what the name *Immanuel* means. A name was not just what someone was called, it was *who they were*. A name was an indication of a person's nature. Immanuel means "God with us," and that is probably the best description of Jesus that can be given. Jesus was indeed God, but "with us" in human flesh, facing our struggles.

Paul Gerhardt, the German author of this hymn, needed that understanding of who Jesus Christ is. He had suffered much in the Thirty Years' War. Four of his children died in infancy. His wife died after only thirteen years of marriage. In times of sorrow and suffering, he needed, as we all do, the knowledge that Jesus is Immanuel—God with us.

Scriptures: Isaiah 7:14; Matthew 1:22-23; Matthew 28:20

Themes: Birth of Christ, Jesus Christ, Waiting on God

Immanuel, to Thee we sing,
Thou Prince of life, almighty King;
That Thou, expected ages past,
Didst come to visit us at last.

For Thee, since first the world was made,
Men's hearts have waited, watched and prayed;
Prophets and patriarchs, year by year,
Have longed to see Thy light appear.

All glory, worship, thanks and praise,
That Thou art come in these our days!
Thou heavenly Guest, expected long,
We hail Thee with a joyful song.

PAUL GERHARDT (1607–1676)
Translated by Ludolph Ernst Schlicht (1714–1769)

IN THE BLEAK MIDWINTER

Christina Rossetti came from a remarkable family. Her father, a political refugee from Italy, became professor of Italian at Oxford. Christina, her sister, and two brothers all became writers. Her brother Dante gained recognition as a painter. As a poet, Christina was compared to Elizabeth Barrett Browning. By all accounts her beauty was quite stunning, but she never married because of religious differences with her fiancés.

This poem—set to music twelve years after Rossetti's death—is disarming in its simplicity. Powerful notions are presented in the starkest of images. "Snow on snow" shows the bleakness of the earth, which stands "hard as iron." We see the angels "thronged" in the winter sky; we are then immediately transported to the stable, where Mary worships her beloved Son as any new mother would—with a kiss.

Scriptures: Psalm 51:16-17; Luke 2:4-7; Hebrews 10:22
Themes: Birth of Christ, Gifts, Worship

> In the bleak midwinter,
> Frosty wind made moan,
> Earth stood hard as iron,
> Water like a stone;
> Snow had fallen, snow on snow,
> Snow on snow,
> In the bleak midwinter,
> Long ago.
>
> Our God, heaven cannot hold Him,
> Nor earth sustain;
> Heaven and earth shall flee away
> When He comes to reign;
> In the bleak midwinter
> A stable place sufficed
> The Lord God Almighty,
> Jesus Christ.
>
> Angels and archangels
> May have gathered there,
> Cherubim and seraphim
> Thronged the air;
> But His mother only,
> In her maiden bliss,

Worshiped the beloved
With a kiss.

What can I give Him,
Poor as I am?
If I were a shepherd,
I would bring a lamb;
If I were a wise man,
I would do my part;
Yet what I can I give Him:
Give my heart.

CHRISTINA G. ROSSETTI (1830–1894)

INFANT HOLY, INFANT LOWLY

Our Christmas carols come from many countries. "Infant Holy, Infant Lowly" is an old Polish carol. Its English paraphrase was first published in 1921 in a magazine called *Music and Youth,* edited by Edith Reed. The title of the tune it is sung to is a Polish phrase, which we would translate as "in a manger lies."

The text and the music fit beautifully together, starting softly, but crescendoing in the last line: "Christ the babe was born for you."

Scriptures: Luke 2:7, 20; Revelation 19:16
Themes: Birth of Christ, Joy, Worship

Infant holy, infant lowly, for his bed a cattle stall;
Oxen lowing, little knowing Christ the babe is Lord of all.
Swift are winging angels singing, noels ringing, tidings bringing;
Christ the babe is Lord of all.

Flocks are sleeping, shepherds keeping vigil till the morning new
Saw the glory, heard the story, tidings of a gospel true.
Thus rejoicing, free from sorrow, praises voicing, greet the morrow;
Christ the babe was born for you.

OLD POLISH CAROL, PARAPHRASED BY EDITH E. M. REED

IT CAME UPON THE MIDNIGHT CLEAR

Although he was a Unitarian minister, Edmund Sears believed in the deity of Christ. He also believed in the angels' message of "peace on earth."

This hymn, written in Massachusetts in 1849, focuses on the angels' song of "peace on the earth." Like many other hymns written in America during the mid-1800s, it might be called a "horizontal hymn." Such hymns called people to live well, to be at peace, and to honor God. It seeks to encourage people who are bent "beneath life's crushing load," as the third stanza says, to stop and hear the message of Christmas sung by the angels.

Peace was a timely topic when Sears penned these words. Tensions were rising in America, leading toward the Civil War. But the peace promised by the angels is not only national; it is personal as well.

Scriptures: Isaiah 2:4; Isaiah 9:6-7; Luke 2:13-14
Themes: Birth of Christ, Peace, Angels

It came upon the midnight clear,
That glorious song of old,
From angels bending near the earth
To touch their harps of gold:
"Peace on the earth, goodwill to men,
From heav'n's all-gracious King!"
The world in solemn stillness lay
To hear the angels sing.

Still through the cloven skies they come
With peaceful wings unfurled,
And still their heav'nly music floats
O'er all the weary world:
Above its sad and lowly plains
They bend on hov'ring wing,
And ever o'er its Babel sounds
The blessed angels sing.

And ye, beneath life's crushing load,
Whose forms are bending low,
Who toil along the climbing way
With painful steps and slow,
Look now! for glad and golden hours

Come swiftly on the wing:
O rest beside the weary road
And hear the angels sing.

For lo, the days are hast'ning on,
By prophets seen of old,
When with the ever-circling years
Shall come the time foretold,
When the new heav'n and earth shall own
The Prince of Peace their King,
And the whole world send back the song
Which now the angels sing.

EDMUND HAMILTON SEARS (1810–1876)

JOY TO THE WORLD!

When is a Christmas carol not *really* a Christmas carol? When it doesn't focus on the birth of Christ, perhaps?

Take "Joy to the World," for instance. Isaac Watts based this text on the last half of Psalm 98, which celebrates the coming of the Lord to judge the world in righteousness. The psalmist calls on all creation to sing and shout for joy at the Lord's coming. There is nothing in the psalm or in Watts's paraphrase that specifically mentions the birth of Christ, just the Lord's return in judgment.

So should we stop singing this at Christmas? Not at all! This hymn celebrates God's involvement with his people—and this work of God began at the stable in Bethlehem. At Christmas we need bifocal vision. We need to look back and praise God for the glorious gift of his Son, Jesus. But we should also look forward to Christ's return, when God will bring a righteous conclusion to all things. Then we will begin to fully enjoy the "wonders of His love" for all eternity.

Scriptures: Psalm 98; Isaiah 40:3-5; Luke 2:10
Themes: Birth of Christ, Joy, Return of Christ

Joy to the world! the Lord is come;
Let earth receive her King;
Let ev'ry heart prepare Him room,
And heav'n and nature sing,
And heav'n and nature sing,

And heav'n, and heav'n and nature sing.

Joy to the earth! the Savior reigns;
Let men their songs employ;
While fields and floods, rocks, hills, and plains
Repeat the sounding joy,
Repeat the sounding joy,
Repeat, repeat the sounding joy.

No more let sins and sorrows grow,
Nor thorns infest the ground;
He comes to make His blessings flow
Far as the curse is found,
Far as the curse is found,
Far as, far as the curse is found.

He rules the world with truth and grace,
And makes the nations prove
The glories of His righteousness,
And wonders of His love,
And wonders of His love,
And wonders, wonders of His love.

ISAAC WATTS (1674–1748)

LET ALL MORTAL FLESH KEEP SILENCE

Is this hymn about Jesus' first coming or his second? Perhaps both. The first line comes from Zechariah 2:13, "Be silent, O all flesh, before the LORD: for he is raised up out of his holy habitation" (KJV). As the Lord comes to be with us on earth, we respond with fear and trembling. Even so, he comes with "blessing in His hand."

The third verse refers to a host of angels. It is only right that angels attend him. They are the bringers of news, and this is news indeed. They are heralds of judgment, and here he acts to judge the earth. Angels are also eternal worshippers, and we can all join them in paying homage to the King of kings.

This hymn may go back to the fifth-century Eastern church and is based on the "Cherubic Hymn" from the *Liturgy of St. James* of Jerusalem. It is still used frequently in Eastern Orthodox churches.

Scriptures: Zechariah 2:13; John 1:1-3; 2 Thessalonians 1:7
Themes: Birth of Christ, Worship, Holiness

Let all mortal flesh keep silence,
And with fear and trembling stand;
Ponder nothing earthly minded,
For with blessing in His hand,
Christ our God to earth descendeth,
Our full homage to demand.

King of kings, yet born of Mary,
As of old on earth He stood,
Lord of lords, in human vesture,
In the body and the blood,
He will give to all the faithful
His own self for heavenly food.

Rank on rank the host of heaven
Spreads its vanguard on the way,
As the Light of light descendeth
From the realms of endless day,
That the powers of hell may vanish
As the darkness clears away.

At His feet the six-winged seraph,
Cherubim, with sleepless eye,
Veil their faces to the presence,
As with ceaseless voice they cry,
Alleluia, Alleluia,
Alleluia, Lord most high!

LITURGY OF ST. JAMES
Translated by Gerard Moultrie (1829–1885)

LIFT UP YOUR HEADS, YE MIGHTY GATES

The words King David used in Psalm 24 to celebrate the arrival of God's presence in Jerusalem inspired this beautiful Christmas hymn. Georg Weissel recognized that Jesus' birth in Bethlehem was the ultimate fulfillment of the ancient psalmist's praise. On that first Christmas, God came to be with us in a new way. He was Immanuel—"God with us."

Weissel was a German scholar, teacher, and pastor who died at the height of the Thirty Years' War—a period of unspeakable horror in Germany. Due to the war, repeated plagues, and other disasters, the population of sixteen million dwindled to only six million in thirty short years. Despite the horrors that surrounded him, Weissel found a reason for rejoicing because of God's arrival in our world in the person of Jesus Christ. It was the birth of Jesus at Christmas that made it possible for God to enter each of our hearts, beginning the transformation of our lives and our world from the inside out.

Scriptures: Psalm 24:7-10; Isaiah 26:2; Isaiah 60:1-3, 11
Themes: Birth of Christ, Prophecy, Commitment

Lift up your heads, ye mighty gates:
Behold, the King of glory waits!
The King of kings is drawing near,
The Savior of the world is here.

O blest the land, the city blest,
Where Christ the ruler is confessed!
O happy hearts and happy homes
To whom this King of triumph comes!

Fling wide the portals of your heart:
Make it a temple, set apart
From earthly use for heav'n's employ,
Adorned with prayer and love and joy.

Redeemer, come! I open wide
My heart to Thee: here, Lord, abide!
Let me Thy inner presence feel:
Thy grace and love in us reveal.

So come, my Sov'reign, enter in!
Let new and nobler life begin!
Thy Holy Spirit guide us on,
Until the glorious crown be won.

GEORG WEISSEL (1590–1635)
Translated by Catherine Winkworth (1827–1878)

LO, HOW A ROSE E'ER BLOOMING

"I am a rose of Sharon," says Song of Songs 2:1 (NIV). Medieval interpreters assigned these words to Christ, and *Rose* became another name for our Lord. In Isaiah 11:1, one of the best-known messianic prophecies speaks of a shoot coming up from "the stump of Jesse" (NIV).

This beautiful hymn, which may go back as far as the fourteenth century, takes the rose image and the branch prophecy and weaves a lovely meditation. The repeated "half-spent was the night" gives us the sense of a beautiful event going almost unnoticed. It also suggests a more theological point, that the night is still with us. This Rose sprouted and blossomed in the middle of the night, and its fragrance is wafting through the world. But the world will not see it in all its beauty until morning, when Christ is fully revealed as Ruler of all.

Scriptures: Song of Songs 2:1; Isaiah 11:1-4; Isaiah 35:1-2
Theme: Birth of Christ, Prophecy, Hope

Lo, how a Rose e'er blooming
From tender stem hath sprung!
Of Jesse's lineage coming
As men of old have sung.
It came, a Flower bright,
Amid the cold of winter,
When half-spent was the night.

Isaiah 'twas foretold it,
The Rose I have in mind;
With Mary we behold it,
The virgin mother kind.
To show God's love aright
She bore to men a Savior,
When half-spent was the night.

This Flower, whose fragrance tender
With sweetness fills the air,
Dispels with glorious splendor
The darkness everywhere.
True man, yet very God,
From sin and death He saves us
And lightens every load.

GERMAN CAROL (16TH CENTURY)
Stanzas 1 and 2 translated by Theodore Baker (1851–1934)
Stanza 3 translated by Harriet Krauth Spaeth (1845–1925)

O COME, ALL YE FAITHFUL

John Francis Wade made his living copying manuscripts by hand, and he became famous for his artistic calligraphy. Because he sometimes copied music as well, scholars have been unsure whether or not Wade wrote "O Come, All Ye Faithful."

The song was originally written in Latin as "Adeste Fidelis." But that was no problem for Wade. He was a Roman Catholic, and all services in the church at that time were conducted in Latin. Apparently, in 1750 he slipped this hymn into a manuscript he was copying for the English Roman Catholic College in Lisbon, Portugal. Over thirty years later, in 1785, it was sent to the Portuguese Chapel in London, and the tune became known as the "Portuguese Hymn." The Duke of Leeds heard it sung there and included it in the repertoire of his own singing group. It soon became known around the world.

Scriptures: Matthew 2:1-2; Luke 2:15-18; John 1:1-14
Themes: Birth of Christ, Worship, Angels

O come, all ye faithful, joyful and triumphant,
O come ye, O come ye to Bethlehem;
Come and behold Him, born the King of angels;

O come, let us adore Him,
O come, let us adore Him,
O come, let us adore Him,
Christ, the Lord!

Sing, choirs of angels, sing in exultation,
O sing, all ye citizens of heaven above!
Glory to God, all glory in the highest;

Yea, Lord, we greet Thee, born this happy morning,
Jesus, to Thee be all glory given;
Word of the Father, now in flesh appearing;

LATIN HYMN (18TH CENTURY)
Attributed to John Francis Wade (1711–1786)
Translated by Frederick Oakeley (1802–1880) and others

O COME, O COME, EMMANUEL

This hymn is ancient, not only in its text, but also in its music. While the tune used today was not really finalized until the 1800s, it is based on plainsong, the type of music used in the church during medieval times. The lack of strict rhythmic measures gives the tune a free-flowing style. You can almost imagine the simple intervals echoing through a stone cathedral.

The text developed without the chorus as a series of liturgical phrases used during Advent. Each stanza concentrates on a different biblical name for Christ, making this hymn a rich source for Christian meditation. Jesus is Emmanuel—"God with us," "Wisdom from on high," "Desire of nations," and "Dayspring."

Scriptures: Isaiah 7:14; Luke 1:32-33, 76-78
Themes: Birth of Christ, Prophecy, Joy

O come, O come, Emmanuel,
And ransom captive Israel,
That mourns in lonely exile here
Until the Son of God appear.

Rejoice! Rejoice! Emmanuel
Shall come to thee, O Israel!

O come, Thou Wisdom from on high,
And order all things, far and nigh;
To us the path of knowledge show,
And cause us in her ways to go.

O come, Desire of nations, bind
All peoples in one heart and mind;
Bid envy, strife, and quarrels cease;
Fill the whole world with heaven's peace.

O come, Thou Dayspring, come and cheer
Our spirits by Thine advent here;
Disperse the gloomy clouds of night,
And death's dark shadows put to flight.

LATIN HYMN (12TH CENTURY)
Stanzas 1 and 4 translated by John Mason Neale (1818–1866)
Stanzas 2 and 3 translated by Henry S. Coffin (1877–1954)

O LITTLE TOWN OF BETHLEHEM

Phillips Brooks was a giant of a man and a prince of a preacher. When his six-foot-six frame filled the pulpit, the people of his churches learned and responded. He served Episcopal congregations in Pennsylvania and Massachusetts.

In 1865, Brooks went to the Holy Land and was especially impressed by a Christmas Eve service at Bethlehem's Church of the Nativity, the traditional site of Jesus' birth. Three years later he needed a Christmas song for the children's service at his church in Philadelphia. Since he loved children, Brooks decided to write the song himself. For inspiration, he thought back to his experience in the Holy Land and wrote "O Little Town of Bethlehem."

It is said that after Brooks died, one five-year-old girl of the church was upset because she hadn't seen him recently. Her mother told her gently that Bishop Brooks had gone to heaven. The girl's face brightened as she said, "Oh, Mama, how happy the angels will be!"

Scriptures: 1 Samuel 16:1-4; Micah 5:2-4; Luke 2:4
Themes: Birth of Christ, Peace, Worship

O little town of Bethlehem,
How still we see thee lie!
Above thy deep and dreamless sleep
The silent stars go by.
Yet in thy dark streets shineth
The everlasting light;
The hopes and fears of all the years
Are met in thee tonight.

For Christ is born of Mary,
And gathered all above,
While mortals sleep, the angels keep
Their watch of wond'ring love.
O morning stars, together
Proclaim the holy birth!
And praises sing to God the King,
And peace to men on earth.

How silently, how silently
The wondrous gift is giv'n!
So God imparts to human hearts

The blessings of His heav'n.
No ear may hear His coming,
But in this world of sin,
Where meek souls will receive Him still
The dear Christ enters in.

O holy Child of Bethlehem!
Descend to us, we pray;
Cast out our sin, and enter in;
Be born in us today.
We hear the Christmas angels
The great glad tidings tell;
O come to us, abide with us,
Our Lord Emmanuel.

PHILLIPS BROOKS (1835–1893)

ONCE IN ROYAL DAVID'S CITY

We don't think of this carol as a children's song, but originally it was. Cecil Alexander loved children. She wrote about four hundred hymns, and most of them were for children. She wrote a series of hymns to teach children about the Apostles' Creed. For instance, "All Things Bright and Beautiful," was written to illustrate the first phrase of the creed, about God the Father, "maker of heaven and earth." This hymn teaches about the phrase "conceived by the Holy Ghost, born of the Virgin Mary." Later, "There Is a Green Hill Far Away" was written for "suffered under Pontius Pilate . . ." Alexander had a knack for taking major biblical themes and boiling them down into four or six easy-to-understand lines.

In this carol Alexander wanted to teach children why we celebrate Christmas, telling them not only what happened on the first Christmas but also why it happened and what it means to us today.

Scriptures: Micah 5:2; Luke 1:27; Luke 2:4
Themes: Birth of Christ, Humanity of Christ, Life of Christ

Once in royal David's city
Stood a lowly cattle shed,
Where a mother laid her baby,
In a manger for His bed.
Mary was that mother mild,
Jesus Christ her little Child.

He came down to earth from heaven
Who is God and Lord of all,
And His shelter was a stable,
And His cradle was a stall.
With the poor, and mean, and lowly
Lived on earth, our Savior holy.

And through all His wondrous childhood
He would honor and obey,
Love, and watch the lowly mother
In whose gentle arms He lay.
Christian children all must be
Mild, obedient, good as He.

For He is our childhood's pattern:
Day by day like us He grew;
He was little, weak, and helpless;
Tears and smiles like us He knew;
And He feeleth for our sadness,
And He shareth in our gladness.

And our eyes at last shall see Him,
Through His own redeeming love;
For that child so dear and gentle
Is our Lord in heav'n above;
And He leads His children on
To the place where He is gone.

Not in that poor lowly stable,
With the oxen standing round,
We shall see Him, but in heaven,
Set at God's right hand on high,
When, like stars, His children crowned,
All in white shall wait around.

CECIL FRANCES ALEXANDER (1818–1895)

SILENT NIGHT, HOLY NIGHT

In their village high in the Austrian Alps, a Catholic priest and his organist often talked about the hymns their church sang. They agreed that the perfect Christmas hymn had not yet been written. Then, just before Christmas in 1818, the church organ broke down. Suddenly, they needed a new hymn that could be easily sung by the congregation, even without a booming organ to lead the way.

Joseph Mohr, the priest, took up the challenge and quickly wrote the words for "Silent Night." He handed them to Franz Grüber, the organist, who said, "You have found it—the right song—God be praised!" Then Grüber wrote a tune that could be effective with guitar accompaniment.

The hymn might have remained an obscure Alpine folk song if it weren't for the organ repairman. A few days after Christmas, he got a copy of the song and began sharing it with others. Soon touring groups began to sing it in concerts, spreading its popularity even further. Today it is one of the most beloved of all Christmas songs.

Scriptures: Matthew 2:1-2; Luke 2:11, 16-18
Themes: Birth of Christ, Messiah, Love

Silent night, holy night,
All is calm, all is bright
Round yon virgin mother and Child.
Holy Infant so tender and mild,
Sleep in heavenly peace,
Sleep in heavenly peace.

Silent night, holy night,
Shepherds quake at the sight.
Glories stream from heaven afar,
Heavenly hosts sing alleluia;
Christ the Savior is born!
Christ the Savior is born!

Silent night, holy night,
Son of God, love's pure light
Radiant beams from Thy holy face,
With the dawn of redeeming grace,
Jesus, Lord, at Thy birth,
Jesus, Lord, at Thy birth.

JOSEPH MOHR (1792–1848)
Translated by John Freeman Young (1820–1885)

SONGS OF PRAISE THE ANGELS SING

James Montgomery's early years were not happy ones. His parents, who were missionaries to the West Indies, both died when James was a teenager. At school he was expelled because he was a dreamer. He went to work at a bakery, but that lasted for only eighteen months. He liked to write poetry, and he took a collection of his poems to a publisher in London. But the publisher was not enthusiastic.

He got a job with a newspaper, a rather radical newspaper for its time. When the editor had to flee the area to avoid persecution, young Montgomery, then twenty-three years old, became the editor. A few years later, he wrote and published a song honoring the French Revolution, and he was in trouble again. The jury found him to be a "wicked, malicious, and seditious person," and he was put in jail for three months, where he found ample time to write more poetry.

When he got out, he returned to his newspaper work and continued as editor for thirty-one years. Later in life, he became one of England's finest hymnwriters. This hymn, "Songs of Praise the Angels Sing," was written when he was in his mid-forties.

Scriptures: Job 38:7; Luke 2:8-14; Ephesians 4:8
Themes: Birth of Christ, Joy, Angels

Songs of praise the angels sang,
Heaven with alleluias rang,
When creation was begun,
Then God spake and it was done.

Songs of praise awoke the morn
When the Prince of Peace was born;
Songs of praise arose when He
Captive led captivity.

Heaven and earth must pass away,
Songs of praise shall crown that day;
God will make new heavens and earth,
Songs of praise shall hail their birth.

And shall man alone be dumb
Till that glorious kingdom come?
No! the church delights to raise
Psalms and hymns and songs of praise.

Saints below, with heart and voice,
Still in songs of praise rejoice,
Learning here, by faith and love,
Songs of praise to sing above.

Borne upon their latest breath,
Songs of praise shall conquer death,
Then, amidst eternal joy,
Songs of praise their powers employ.

JAMES MONTGOMERY (1771–1854)

SWEET LITTLE JESUS BOY

Most people think of "Sweet Little Jesus Boy" as a Negro spiritual from the South in the mid-1800s. The lyrics certainly make you think of America at the time of the Civil War. But actually this was written by Robert MacGimsey in 1934.

MacGimsey was asked once to comment on the song, and he responded, "This is not so much a song as just a meaning. You have to imagine an aging Negro standing off in the middle of a field just giving his heart to Jesus in the stillness."

Scriptures: Luke 2:7; John 1:10-11; Philippians 2:6-9
Themes: Birth of Christ, Suffering of Christ, Wonder

Sweet little Jesus Boy, they made You be born in a manger.
Sweet little Holy Child, they didn't know who You was.
Didn't know You come to save us, Lord; to take our sins away.
Our eyes was blind, we couldn't see, we didn't know who You was.

Long time ago, You was born. Born in a manger low,
Sweet little Jesus Boy.
The world treat You mean, Lord; treat me mean too,
But that's how things is down here, we didn't know 'twas You.

You done showed us how, we is trying.
Master, You done showed us how, even when you's dying.
Just seem like we can't do right, look how we treated You.
But please, sir, forgive us Lord, we didn't know 'twas You.

Sweet little Jesus Boy, born long time ago
Sweet little Holy Child, and we didn't know who You was.

ROBERT MACGIMSEY (1898–1979)

TELL OUT, MY SOUL

Timothy Dudley-Smith, an Anglican bishop as well as a talented hymnwriter, wrote this hymn shortly after he and his wife moved into their first home. He had been reading a modern translation of the Magnificat, the song of the Virgin Mary, in the first chapter of Luke's Gospel. It begins with the words, "Tell out, my soul, the greatness of the Lord." Deeply impressed, Dudley-Smith started writing a hymn beginning with the same words.

Each stanza of the hymn begins by referring to the greatness of the Lord, echoing the words of Mary. The second verse talks about the great things he has done; the third verse refers to the coming of his Kingdom, and the final verse talks about the great promises of the Lord, which are fulfilled in Jesus Christ.

Scriptures: 1 Samuel 2:1-10; Psalm 34:2-3; Luke 1:46-56
Themes: Birth of Christ, Thankfulness, Joy

Tell out, my soul, the greatness of the Lord!
Unnumbered blessings give my spirit voice;
Tender to me the promise of His Word;
In God my savior shall my heart rejoice.

Tell out, my soul, the greatness of His name!
Make known His might, the deeds His arm has done;
His mercy sure, from age to age the same;
His holy name, the Lord, the Mighty One.

Tell out, my soul, the greatness of His might!
Pow'rs and dominions lay their glory by.
Proud hearts and stubborn wills are put to flight,
The hungry fed, the humble lifted high.

Tell out, my soul, the glories of His word!
Firm is His promise, and His mercy sure.
Tell out, my soul, the greatness of the Lord
To children's children and forevermore!

TIMOTHY DUDLEY-SMITH (B. 1926)

THAT BEAUTIFUL NAME

No one knows anything about the author of this hymn, Jean Perry. In fact, some believe that Mabel Johnston Camp, who wrote the music, also wrote the words under a pen name. Mabel Camp was certainly a talented woman, and she might have written both the words and the music.

The daughter of a banker, she was a gifted contralto soloist. She was also an accomplished pianist. She married a young lawyer, and it looked as if the two would become rich and famous in the secular world. But that changed when her husband began attending a Bible class and then was converted. Soon Mabel became a Christian as well. When her husband became a Bible teacher and evangelist, Mabel encouraged him in his new work. When he traveled, she was active on Chicago's Gold Coast, raising money for Chicago's underprivileged children. She wrote other hymns, and perhaps she wrote this one, too.

Scriptures: Isaiah 9:6; Matthew 1:21; Philippians 2:9-11
Themes: Birth of Christ, Angels, Messiah

I know of a Name, a beautiful Name,
That Jesus brought down to earth;
They whispered it low, one night long ago,
To a maiden of lowly birth.

That beautiful Name, that beautiful Name
From sin has pow'r to free us!
That beautiful Name, that wonderful Name,
That matchless Name is Jesus.

I know of a Name, a beautiful Name,
That unto a Babe was given;
The stars glittered bright throughout that glad night,
And angels praised God in heaven.

The one of that Name my Savior became,
My Savior of Calvary;
My sins nailed Him there; my burdens He bare,
He suffered all this for me.

I love that blest Name, that wonderful Name,
Made higher than all in heav'n;
'Twas whispered, I know, in my heart long ago,
To Jesus my life I've given.

JEAN PERRY (1865–1935)

THE FIRST NOEL

Noel is a French word that may have come either from the Latin *natalis,* meaning "birth," or from the Latin *novella,* meaning "new." In one sense *noel* refers to the whole Christmas season; in another it refers to the good news that Jesus Christ has come. The first Noel, this song says, was sung by an angel to poor shepherds. The chorus rings out like a corner paperboy—"News! News! News! Hear all about it! King of Israel born today!"

Early folk carols such as this one often had a memorable chorus and many stanzas, each presenting some new aspect of the story. An individual or group could sing a stanza, perhaps one newly made up, and the whole crowd would join in the refrain. "The First Noel" was first published in its present form by William Sandys in 1833.

It is inspiring to think of "us all" in the last stanza as crossing the boundaries of time. We modern believers join with earlier Christians to praise our Lord, who bought us all with his blood.

Scriptures: Isaiah 60:1-3; Matthew 2:1-12; Luke 2:8
Themes: Birth of Christ, Worship, Angels

The first Noel, the angel did say,
Was to certain poor shepherds in fields as they lay;
In fields where they lay keeping their sheep,
On a cold winter's night that was so deep.

Noel, Noel, Noel, Noel,
Born is the King of Israel.

They looked up and saw a star
Shining in the east, beyond them far,
And to the earth it gave great light,
And so it continued both day and night.

And by the light of that same star
Three wise men came from country far;
To seek for a king was their intent,
And to follow the star wherever it went.

This star drew nigh to the northwest,
O'er Bethlehem it took its rest,
And there it did both stop and stay,
Right over the place where Jesus lay.

Then entered in those wise men three,
Full rev'rently upon their knee,
And offered there in His presence
Their gold, and myrrh, and frankincense.

Then let us all with one accord
Sing praises to our heav'nly Lord,
That hath made heav'n and earth of naught,
And with His blood mankind hath bought.

TRADITIONAL ENGLISH CAROL

THE FRIENDLY BEASTS

This children's carol may go back as far as the twelfth century. It is a meditation on the animals that may have been present at Jesus' birth. What would each of them have given as a birthday gift to the Christ child?

We don't know for sure that Joseph and Mary traveled on a donkey, but they might have. The Bible doesn't say anything about cattle, although Jesus was laid in a manger, which was a feed bin for cattle. The shepherds were tending sheep, but did they bring them to see Jesus? Were there doves in the rafters? We don't know.

While we don't know for sure that there were animals present at the birth of Christ, there is a biblical tradition of animals serving God. A donkey challenged Balaam to obey God, and ravens fed Elijah in the wilderness. A great fish swallowed Jonah whole and delivered him back to shore. The Psalms speak freely of all creation joining in the praise of God, and Romans says that all things await their final redemption. The future of donkeys, cattle, sheep, and doves is somehow wrapped up with ours, so they would have good reason to honor the Messiah's birth.

Scriptures: Psalm 148:10-13; Isaiah 1:2-3; Luke 2:8
Themes: Birth of Christ, Animals, Childhood

Jesus our brother, strong and good,
Was humbly born in a stable rude;
And the friendly beasts around Him stood,
Jesus our brother, strong and good.

"I," said the donkey, shaggy and brown,
"I carried His mother up hill and down;

I carried her safely to Bethlehem town,
I," said the donkey, shaggy and brown.

"I," said the cow, all white and red,
"I gave Him my manger for His bed;
I gave Him my hay to pillow His head,
I," said the cow, all white and red.

"I," said the sheep with the curly horn,
"I gave Him my wool for His blanket warm.
He wore my coat on Christmas morn,
I," said the sheep with the curly horn.

"I," said the dove from rafters high,
"I cooed Him to sleep so He would not cry,
We cooed Him to sleep, my mate and I,
I," said the dove from rafters high.

And every beast, by some good spell,
In the stable dark was glad to tell,
Of the gift he gave Emmanuel,
The gift he gave Emmanuel.

TRADITIONAL ENGLISH CAROL

THE PEOPLE THAT IN DARKNESS SAT

The prophecy of Isaiah expounded in this hymn is quite astonishing. Isaiah was writing in the southern kingdom of Judah when it was being threatened by the northern kingdom of Israel. God was promising Judah that he would remove the threat and that he would punish the northern kingdom by bringing the mighty Assyrians to defeat them.

But even in this harsh judgment there was hope. Isaiah 9 opens with a promise to honor the region of Galilee—which was in the northern kingdom! Isaiah's readers in the south might have expected great promises to Jerusalem and Judah, but Galilee? Yet these are "the people walking in darkness" (Isaiah 9:2, NIV)—northerners who would see the light of Christ.

Jesus fulfilled this prophecy, conducting most of his public ministry around the Sea of Galilee. He was the Child born to recover David's kingdom, not physically but spiritually.

Scriptures: Isaiah 9:1, 6-7; Matthew 4:15-16
Themes: Birth of Christ, Prophecy, Worship

The people that in darkness sat
A glorious light have seen;
The light has shined on them who long
In shades of death have been.

For unto us a child is born,
To us a son is given,
And on His shoulder ever rests
All power on earth and heaven.

His name shall be the Prince of Peace
Forevermore adored,
The Wonderful, the Counselor,
The great and mighty Lord.

His righteous government and power
Shall over all extend;
On judgment and on justice based,
His reign shall have no end.

JOHN MORISON (1750–1798)
Scottish Paraphrases, *1781*

THERE'S A SONG IN THE AIR

Josiah Holland, born and raised in western Massachusetts, had a hard time figuring out what to do with his life. A high school dropout because of poor health, he thought he could be a photographer. When that didn't work, he somehow enrolled in medical school and earned a degree. After practicing medicine a few years, he quit to become a newspaper editor and later helped to start a national magazine.

Although Josiah Holland dabbled in many different professions, he is best remembered for this carol, "There's a Song in the Air."

Scriptures: Matthew 2:10; Luke 2:13; Revelation 22:16
Themes: Birth of Christ, Light, Joy

There's a song in the air! There's a star in the sky!
There's a mother's deep prayer and a baby's low cry!
And the star rains its fire while the beautiful sing,
For the manger of Bethlehem cradles a King!

There's a tumult of joy o'er the wonderful birth,
For the Virgin's sweet Boy is the Lord of the earth.
Ay the star rains its fire while the beautiful sing,
For the manger of Bethlehem cradles a King!

In the light of that star lie the ages impearled,
And that song from afar has swept over the world.
Ev'ry hearth is aflame—and the beautiful sing
In the homes of the nations that Jesus is King.

We rejoice in the light, and we echo the song
That comes down through the night from the heavenly throng.
Ay! We shout to the lovely evangel they bring,
And we greet in His cradle our Savior and King!

JOSIAH GILBERT HOLLAND (1819–1881)

THOU DIDST LEAVE THY THRONE

Emily Elliott had a special concern for those who were sick. She wrote many poems and hymn texts especially for the infirm, publishing forty-eight of them in a book called *Under the Pillow*. She may have been influenced by her aunt, Charlotte Elliott, who wrote "Just As I Am." Charlotte, also a prolific poet, was sickly for much of her life.

This particular hymn was written for children to teach them about Jesus' birth. It has a simple construction—each of the first four stanzas presents a contrast beginning with the word *but*. Given the first two lines of each stanza, you might expect the world to welcome Christ, but no—it had no room for him. The chorus is a natural response to the predicament, something that even a child could understand. Although the world had no room for the Lord, we have room for him in our hearts.

The last stanza provides a stirring conclusion. The Lord, once rejected and displaced, will soon come in victory—and we should all be waiting.

Scriptures: John 1:10-12; 2 Corinthians 8:9; Philippians 2:5-11
Themes: Birth of Christ, Deity of Christ, Commitment

Thou didst leave Thy throne and Thy kingly crown
When Thou camest to earth for me;
But in Bethlehem's home was there found no room
For Thy holy nativity.

O Come to my heart, Lord Jesus—
There is room in my heart for Thee!

Heaven's arches rang when the angels sang,
Proclaiming Thy royal decree;
But of lowly birth didst Thou come to earth,
And in great humility.

The foxes found rest, and the birds their nest
In the shade of the forest tree;
But Thy couch was the sod, O Thou Son of God,
In the deserts of Galilee.

Thou camest, O Lord, with the living Word
That should set Thy people free;
But with mocking scorn and with crown of thorn
They bore Thee to Calvary.

When the heav'ns shall ring and the angels sing
At Thy coming to victory,
Let Thy voice call me home, saying, "Yet there is room—
There is room at My side for thee."

My heart shall rejoice, Lord Jesus,
When Thou comest and callest for me!

EMILY ELIZABETH STEELE ELLIOTT (1836–1879)

WATCHMAN, TELL US OF THE NIGHT

This is an unusual hymn from an unusual man. John Bowring was a brilliant linguist, scholar, and politician. Later in life he became a British governor of Hong Kong. Here he displays his flair for poetry.

This hymn is unusual in that it shows more than it tells. Most hymns are instructional or devotional. In either case they tell things about the nature of God or about personal experience or about how to live. Bowring himself did that sort of thing in his hymn "In the Cross of Christ I Glory." This hymn, in contrast, offers a single image and builds it for dramatic effect.

Bowring borrows the watchman from an obscure reference in Isaiah. The watchman—perhaps representing the longing soul, perhaps the watchful wise men, or perhaps the prophet himself—watches for the coming of the day as heralded by the morning star. This is a lovely Advent hymn because it presents the expectancy as well as the fulfillment of Christ's first coming.

Scriptures: Isaiah 21:11-12; Matthew 2:10; Romans 13:12
Themes: Birth of Christ, Prophecy, Hope

Watchman, tell us of the night,
What its signs of promise are.
Traveler, o'er yon mountain's height
See that glory-beaming star!
Watchman, doth its beauteous ray
Aught of joy or hope foretell?
Traveler, yes; it brings the day,
Promised day of Israel.

Watchman, tell us of the night;
Higher yet that star ascends.
Traveler, blessedness and light,
Peace and truth, its course portends.
Watchman, will its beams alone
Gild the spot that gave them birth?
Traveler, ages are its own;
See, it bursts o'er all the earth!

Watchman, tell us of the night,
For the morning seems to dawn.
Traveler, darkness takes its flight;
Doubt and terror are withdrawn.
Watchman, let thy wandering cease;
Hide thee to thy quiet home!
Traveler, lo, the Prince of Peace,
Lo, the Son of God is come!

JOHN BOWRING (1792–1872)

WE THREE KINGS OF ORIENT ARE

Everyone knows that the wise men brought gifts, but what was the significance of those gifts?

John Henry Hopkins, an Episcopalian minister, pondered this question in 1857 and then wrote this popular Christmas carol.

Gold was a gift for a king. Frankincense was brought by priests as they worshipped God in the Temple. Myrrh was a spice used in burial. Thus, the wise men honored Jesus as King, God, and Sacrifice.

The hymnwriter clearly spells this out in verses two, three, and four. How then are we to approach the Babe of Bethlehem? What can we bring the King of kings? What incense can we offer as priests of our God? How can we recognize the divine Sacrifice in our daily lives?

Scriptures: Matthew 2:1-2; John 19:39; 1 Timothy 1:17; 1 Timothy 6:15; Revelation 19:16
Themes: Christmas, Star, Gifts

We three kings of Orient are;
Bearing gifts we traverse afar,
Field and fountain, moor and mountain,
Following yonder star.

O star of wonder, star of night,
Star with royal beauty bright,
Westward leading, still proceeding,
Guide us to thy perfect light.

Born a King on Bethlehem's plain,
Gold I bring to crown Him again,
King forever, ceasing never
Over us all to reign.

Frankincense to offer have I;
Incense owns a Deity nigh;
Prayer and praising all men raising,
Worship Him, God on high.

Myrrh is mine. Its bitter perfume
Breathes a life of gathering gloom:
Sorrowing, sighing, bleeding, dying,
Sealed in the stone-cold tomb.

Glorious now behold Him arise,
King and God and sacrifice;
Alleluia, Alleluia!
Sounds through the earth and skies.

JOHN HENRY HOPKINS JR. (1820–1891)

WHAT CHILD IS THIS?

The tune for this Christmas hymn was sung long before its words were written. "Greensleeves" is an English folk song that can be traced back as far as the 1500s. Shakespeare even mentioned it in one of his plays.

The author of the hymn, William Dix, was an Anglican layman, born in Bristol, England. He settled in Glasgow, Scotland, where he became a successful insurance salesman. As a young man of twenty-nine, Dix was stricken by a serious illness and was confined to bed. He suffered deep depression during this time, but through it all he met God in a very personal way. His spiritual experience led to the composition of this hymn and many others.

This insightful text was originally part of a longer Christmas poem called "The Manger Throne." The words mesh with the lilting melody to present a lovely picture of baby Jesus in the manger.

Scriptures: Matthew 1:20-23; Matthew 2:10-11; Luke 1:30-35
Themes: Birth of Christ, Shepherds, Angels

What child is this, who, laid to rest,
On Mary's lap is sleeping?
Whom angels greet with anthems sweet,
While shepherds watch are keeping?

This, this is Christ the King,
Whom shepherds guard and angels sing;
Haste, haste to bring Him laud,
The babe, the son of Mary.

Why lies He in such mean estate
Where ox and ass are feeding?
Good Christian, fear, for sinners here
The silent Word is pleading.

So bring Him incense, gold, and myrrh,
Come, peasant, king, to own Him;
The King of kings salvation brings,
Let loving hearts enthrone Him.

WILLIAM CHATTERTON DIX (1837–1898)

WHILE BY THE SHEEP

Sometimes, as we read the Christmas story, we slide over the verses that refer to how excited the shepherds must have been. After the angels had told them about the baby in a manger, the shepherds said to one another, "Let's go. . . . Let's see this thing" (Luke 2:15). After they had gone to Bethlehem and seen the Christ child, they went back, glorifying and praising God.

Years ago, probably in the 1600s, a German songwriter tried to recreate the scene. He tells it almost as if the shepherds were telling it to their family and neighbors: "While by the sheep we watched at night." But after they said a sentence, their excitement must have gotten the best of them, and they burst out, "How great our joy! Joy, joy, joy! / Praise we the Lord in heaven on high." And the other shepherds echoed their excitement.

Scriptures: Isaiah 40:11; Jeremiah 31:7-10; Luke 2:20
Themes: Birth of Christ, Shepherds, Joy

While by the sheep we watched at night,
Glad tidings brought an angel bright.

How great our joy! (echo) Great our joy!
Joy, joy, joy, (echo) joy, joy, joy!
Praise we the Lord in heaven on high!
(echo) Praise we the Lord in heaven on high!

There shall be born, so He did say,
In Bethlehem a Child today.

There shall the Child lie in a stall,
This Child who shall redeem us all.

This gift of God we'll cherish well,
That ever joy our hearts shall fill.

TRADITIONAL GERMAN CAROL

WHILE SHEPHERDS WATCHED THEIR FLOCKS

Along with his friend Nicholas Brady, Nahum Tate was a pioneer in church music. At the end of the seventeenth century, the Church of England still did most of its singing from the Psalter compiled by Sternhold and Hopkins in 1562. Tate and Brady recast the Psalms in more "modern" language, publishing the *New Version of the Psalter* in 1696. Even though the old Psalter was often unpoetic and hard to sing, many resisted attempts to change it and resented Tate and Brady for trying to improve it.

Eventually, though, King William III of England endorsed Tate and Brady's *New Version,* and it became the standard Psalter in both England and America. Ironically, many people later protested when translators tried to improve on Tate and Brady!

In 1700 Tate and Brady published a supplement of sixteen new hymns to go along with their psalms. This Christmas carol, a paraphrase of the shepherds' story as found in Luke 2:8-14, was in that collection.

Scriptures: Isaiah 57:18-19; Luke 2:8-14; Acts 5:19-20

Themes: Birth of Christ, Angels, Joy

While shepherds watched their flocks by night,
All seated on the ground,
The angel of the Lord came down,
And glory shone around,
And glory shone around.

"Fear not!" said he; for mighty dread
Had seized their troubled mind,
"Glad tidings of great joy I bring
To you and all mankind,
To you and all mankind.

"To you, in David's town this day,
Is born of David's line,
The Savior who is Christ the Lord,
And this shall be the sign:
And this shall be the sign:

"The heav'nly Babe you there shall find
To human view displayed,
All meanly wrapped in swathing bands,

And in a manger laid;
And in a manger laid.

"All glory be to God on high,
And to the earth be peace:
Good will henceforth from heav'n to men,
Begin and never cease,
Begin and never cease."

NAHUM TATE (1625–1715)

WHO IS HE IN YONDER STALL?

The author of this song, Benjamin Hanby, died at the age of thirty-four. His career as a musician was just getting started. He had written a few secular songs that had become quite successful; he had also written a few Sunday school songs, and had helped to edit a book of gospel songs. But throughout his short life he desired above all to tell the wondrous story of the Lord, the King of glory.

As we trace the life of Jesus on earth in this song, we see a baby in a stable, whisked off to Egypt to avoid danger. We see a man fasting in the desert, then moving on after overcoming temptation. We see him weeping at the tomb of Lazarus, then praying in Gethsemane as his friends sleep. We see him die, rise, and ascend to heaven. In the vast sweep of history we catch only a short, though unforgettable, glimpse of Jesus. We may ask, "Who is he?"

This song answers the question in its strong refrain. Jesus is the King of glory, Lord of all. He was born, he served and taught, and he died and rose again "to heal and help and save" us.

Scriptures: Ephesians 3:20-21; Philippians 2:9-11; Revelation 19:11-16
Themes: Birth of Christ, Meekness, Worship

Who is He in yonder stall,
At whose feet the shepherds fall?
Who is He in deep distress,
Fasting in the wilderness?

'Tis the Lord! O wondrous story!
'Tis the Lord! The King of glory!
At His feet we humbly fall,
Crown Him, crown Him, Lord of all!

Who is He the people bless
For His words of gentleness?
Who is He to whom they bring
All the sick and sorrowing?

Who is He that stands and weeps
At the grave where Lazarus sleeps?
Who is He the gath'ring throng
Greet with loud triumphant song?

Lo at midnight, who is He
That prays in dark Gethsemane?
Who is He on yonder tree
Dies in grief and agony?

Who is He that from the grave
Comes to heal and help and save?
Who is He that from His throne
Rules through all the world alone?

BENJAMIN RUSSELL HANBY (1833–1867)

PART VIII

CHURCH AND FELLOWSHIP

Make every effort to keep yourselves united in the Spirit,

binding yourselves together with peace.

EPHESIANS 4:3

BLESSED JESUS, AT THY WORD

The author of this hymn did not know peace until he was nearly thirty. The Thirty Years' War began the year before he was born, and it tore Europe apart. It was a time of princes wrestling for power, claiming religion as their motive, yet displacing innocent residents of disputed territories. In spite of all the turmoil, this period is rich with hymnody, as true believers launched their prayers and praises to the only Ruler who would listen.

This is a gathering hymn, bringing believers out of the murky world and into the presence of the Lord. It shows a justifiable cynicism about all things earthly. All the "knowledge" that was gained as Europe crawled out of the Dark Ages had merely created chaos. There was a desperate need for the Spirit to shine his light on human affairs. God's people were "wandering," but they knew they were headed for a heavenly homeland. And the experience of worship gave them a glimpse of that home.

Scriptures: Matthew 22:35-39; Acts 2:46-47; Hebrews 10:25
Themes: Trinity, Word of God, Church

Blessed Jesus, at Thy Word
We are gathered all to hear Thee;
Let our hearts and souls be stirred
Now to seek and love and fear Thee,
By Thy teachings, sweet and holy,
Drawn from earth to love Thee solely.

All our knowledge, sense, and sight
Lie in deepest darkness shrouded
Till Thy Spirit breaks our night
With the beams of truth unclouded.
Thou alone to God canst win us;
Thou must work all good within us.

Glorious Lord, Thyself impart,
Light of Light, from God proceeding;
Open Thou our ears and heart,
Help us by Thy Spirit's pleading;
Hear the cry Thy people raise,
Hear and bless our prayers and praises.

Father, Son, and Holy Ghost,
Praise to Thee and adoration!
Grant that we Thy Word may trust
And obtain true consolation
While we here below must wander,
Till we sing Thy praises yonder.

TOBIAS CLAUSNITZER (1619–1684)
Translated by Catherine Winkworth (1827–1878)

BLEST BE THE DEAR UNITING LOVE

J. B. Gough, a famous nineteenth-century American orator, tells the story of how he left England when he was only twelve to come to America. His parents were poor and unable to apprentice him to learn a trade. So they sent him to America with neighbors who were emigrating there.

While in America, he strayed from his parents' faith. Though he was able to make money, he was a spiritual pauper. He said, "I was forever digging deep wells to quench my maddening thirst, and forever bringing up nothing but the hot dry sand." But he could not forget his mother who was "poor in purse, but rich in piety." Nor could he forget the Christian friends who had sung "Blest Be the Dear Uniting Love" as he left them. This hymn by Charles Wesley stuck in his mind. And he could not forget a Bible verse that his mother had taught him: "He is able also to save them to the uttermost that come unto God by him" (Hebrews 7:25, KJV).

Is there salvation even for me? Gough wondered. Then he quoted to himself the first three words of the Bible verse: "He is able. . . ." A hymn and a Bible verse led to his conversion.

Scriptures: Ephesians 4:1-6; Philippians 2:1-2; 1 Peter 1:22
Themes: Church, Unity, Love

Blest be the dear uniting love
That will not let us part;
Our bodies may far off remove,
We still are one in heart.

Joined in one spirit to our Head,
Where He appoints we go;
And still in Jesus' footsteps tread,
And show His praise below.

O may we ever walk in Him,
And nothing know beside,
Nothing desire, nothing esteem,
But Jesus crucified!

Partakers of the Savior's grace,
The same in mind and heart,
Nor joy, nor grief, nor time, nor place,
Nor life, nor death can part.

CHARLES WESLEY (1707–1788)

BLEST BE THE TIE THAT BINDS

Orphaned when he was twelve, then forced to work fourteen hours a day in a sweatshop, John Fawcett learned to read by candlelight. He was converted at sixteen under the preaching of George Whitefield, and he was ordained a Baptist minister at the age of twenty-five. He began his ministry at a poor church in Wainsgate in northern England. The small congregation could afford to pay him only a minimal salary, partly in potatoes and wool.

After seven years of ministry, Fawcett received a call to the prestigious Carter's Lane Church in London. All his personal belongings were packed onto the wagons outside the church. But as he was saying his farewells, he saw the tears on the faces of his people. As a result, he changed his mind and decided to stay.

Not long afterward, he wrote this hymn for the congregation at Wainsgate. He recognized that the bond of love he experienced there was worth more than any material wealth. He and his wife, Mary, ministered in that small church for fifty-four years.

Scriptures: Psalm 133; Ephesians 4:1-6; Hebrews 13:1
Themes: Love, Body of Christ, Unity

Blest be the tie that binds
Our hearts in Christian love:
The fellowship of kindred minds
Is like to that above.

Before our Father's throne
We pour our ardent prayers;

Our fears, our hopes, our aims are one,
Our comforts and our cares.

We share each other's woes,
Our mutual burdens bear,
And often for each other flows
The sympathizing tear.

When we asunder part,
It gives us inward pain;
But we shall still be joined in heart,
And hope to meet again.

JOHN FAWCETT (1740–1817)

BRETHREN, WE HAVE MET TO WORSHIP

What does it mean to meet for worship? One part of worship involves adoring the Lord our God, which includes the idea of gazing lovingly. We come to meet our God and to consider how wonderful he is.

Our worship also usually involves preaching and prayer. This hymn presents these two aspects of worship together. Prayer unleashes the power of God, and preaching wields and displays that power. Preaching is more than just the transmittal of information. It is the powerful display of truth, and it can carve our souls like a sharp saber.

And what is the result of prayerful worship? We are blessed by "holy manna"—bread from heaven. In the Old Testament, God provided the Israelites with manna as they wandered in the wilderness. In the New Testament, Jesus gave his body as the Bread of Life, through which we can receive spiritual nourishment. As we worship, we participate in the eternal banquet of Christ's presence. We celebrate God's provision and thank him for it.

Scriptures: 1 Chronicles 16:25-26; Psalm 107:32; Hebrews 10:25
Themes: Worship, Prayer, Church

Brethren, we have met to worship
And adore the Lord our God;
Will you pray with all your power,
While we try to preach the Word?
All is vain unless the Spirit
Of the Holy One comes down;

Brethren, pray, and holy manna
Will be showered all around.

Brethren, see poor sinners round you
Slumbering on the brink of woe;
Death is coming, hell is moving—
Can you bear to let them go?
See our fathers and our mothers
And our children sinking down;
Brethren, pray, and holy manna
Will be showered all around.

Sisters, will you join and help us?
Moses' sister aided him;
Will you help the trembling mourners
Who are struggling hard with sin?
Tell them all about the Savior—
Tell them that He will be found;
Sisters, pray, and holy manna
Will be showered all around.

Let us love our God supremely,
Let us love each other too;
Let us love and pray for sinners
Till our God makes all things new.
Then He'll call us home to heaven,
At His table we'll sit down;
Christ will gird Himself and serve us
With sweet manna all around.

GEORGE ATKINS (18TH CENTURY)

FOR ALL THE SAINTS

In 1864 Bishop William How wrote this hymn for All Saints' Day. He cited Hebrews 12:1 in his original title, but he drew on Hebrews 11 for inspiration. That's the famous "faith chapter," which praises the faithful deeds of a score of Old Testament heroes.

The author might be considered a hero of the faith himself. He was a man of the people, regularly reaching out to minister to the poor and needy in his area. Once, he listed the characteristics that a minister should have; among them was being "wholly without thought of self."

Those who knew him said that Bishop How was like that, selflessly caring for others.

His son wrote his biography, saying, "It is the fate of a hymnwriter to be forgotten. The hymn remains; the name of the writer passes away." But that would have been acceptable to Bishop How. "To be praised is the ambition of the world," his son wrote, "but to be a blessing is the abundant satisfaction of those who find their joy in loving service of their fellow man."

Scriptures: Ephesians 2:19-22; Hebrews 12:1; Revelation 7:9
Themes: Church, Praise, Fellowship

For all the saints, who from their labors rest,
Who Thee by faith before the world confessed,
Thy name, O Jesus, be forever blest.
Alleluia, Alleluia!

Thou wast their rock, their fortress, and their might;
Thou, Lord, their captain in the well-fought fight;
Thou, in the darkness drear, their one true light.
Alleluia, Alleluia!

O may Thy soldiers, faithful, true, and bold,
Fight as the saints who nobly fought of old,
And win with them the victor's crown of gold.
Alleluia, Alleluia!

O blest communion, fellowship divine!
We feebly struggle, they in glory shine;
Yet all are one in Thee, for all are Thine.
Alleluia, Alleluia!

And when the strife is fierce, the warfare long,
Steals on the ear the distant triumph song,
And hearts are brave again, and arms are strong.
Alleluia, Alleluia!

From earth's wide bounds, from ocean's farthest coast,
Through gates of pearl streams in the countless host,
Singing to Father, Son, and Holy Ghost.
Alleluia, Alleluia!

WILLIAM WALSHAM HOW (1823–1897)

GLORIOUS THINGS OF THEE ARE SPOKEN

Stonewall Jackson was a legendary Confederate general in the Civil War. He had a long beard, he rarely combed his hair, his boots were never polished, and he wore an old slouch hat and a faded uniform with missing buttons. But he was a military genius and a wonderful Christian. His men said of him, "When he ain't a-fightin' he's a-prayin'."

And when he wasn't fighting or praying, he was singing hymns. But he couldn't carry a tune. He had no note-sense whatsoever, even when he was singing his favorite hymn, "Glorious Things of Thee Are Spoken."

One night in 1862, his army bivouacked in the Shenandoah Valley. The soldiers had marched fifty-two miles that day, and they were exhausted. When they awoke the next morning, they heard a strange sound. They eventually discovered that the sound was Stonewall Jackson singing. There on the hill the general had watched over his men all night, with his old slouch hat in his hands. But now he was singing his favorite hymn, with his bearded face looking heavenward: "On the Rock of Ages founded, / What can shake thy sure repose? / With salvation's walls surrounded, / Thou may'st smile at all thy foes."

Scriptures: Psalm 48:1-3; Psalm 87:3; Isaiah 33:20-24
Themes: Church, Security, Hope

Glorious things of thee are spoken,
Zion, city of our God;
He whose word cannot be broken
Formed thee for His own abode:
On the Rock of Ages founded,
What can shake thy sure repose?
With salvation's walls surrounded,
Thou may'st smile at all thy foes.

See, the streams of living waters,
Springing from eternal love,
Well supply thy sons and daughters,
And all fear of want remove.
Who can faint while such a river
Ever flows their thirst to assuage?
Grace which, like the Lord, the Giver,
Never fails from age to age!

Round each habitation hovering,
See the cloud and fire appear

For a glory and a covering,
Showing that the Lord is near!
Thus deriving from their banner
Light by night and shade by day,
Safe they feed upon the manna
Which He gives them when they pray.

JOHN NEWTON (1725–1807)

HERE, O MY LORD, I SEE THEE FACE TO FACE

Horatius Bonar was probably Scotland's finest hymnwriter. He was one of three sons of an Edinburgh tax collector, and all three went into the ministry. In the Church of Scotland, the Communion service is a very special occasion because it occurs only once or twice a year. Because it was so special, Horatius made it his custom to go and assist his brother John at his annual Communion service.

One year John asked Horatius to bring a hymn for the communion service, and he agreed. Bonar wrote most of his hymns as he walked across the Scottish hills. He always carried a notebook with him, and when an idea came to him for a poem, he would jot it down. His notebook was also full of funny faces and doodling.

Bonar's hymns are always filled with solid biblical truth, and in this one, he emphasizes that the important thing in the Communion service is a personal encounter with Jesus Christ.

Scriptures: Song of Songs 2:4; 1 Corinthians 11:23-25; 1 John 1:1-3;
Themes: Communion, Death of Christ, Fellowship

Here, O my Lord, I see Thee face to face;
Here would I touch and handle things unseen,
Here grasp with firmer hand eternal grace,
And all my weariness upon Thee lean.

This is the hour of banquet and of song;
This is the heavenly table spread for me;
Here let me feast, and feasting, still prolong
The hallowed hour of fellowship with Thee.

Here would I feed upon the bread of God,
Here drink with Thee the royal wine of heaven.

Here would I lay aside each earthly load,
Here taste afresh the calm of sin forgiven.

Too soon we rise: the symbols disappear;
The feast, though not the love, is past and gone.
The bread and wine remove: but Thou art here,
Nearer than ever, still my shield and sun.

Feast after feast thus comes and passes by;
Yet, passing, points to the glad feast above,
Giving sweet foretaste of the festal joy,
The Lamb's great bridal feast of bliss and love.

HORATIUS BONAR (1808–1889)

HOLY GROUND

In many ways, Geron Davis was just a typical teenager in the small town of Savannah, Tennessee. But he was a pastor's kid who liked to write songs. When the time came for the dedication of the new church building, Geron's dad asked him to write a song for the special occasion. Geron agreed, but he realized he had two months to write it. Every week or two his father asked him for a progress report, and Geron had to admit that he hadn't done it yet.

The night before the dedication, his father asked again, and Geron replied, "No, sir, but I'm fixin' to."

It was almost midnight. Geron went into the new sanctuary, dimmed the lights, and sat down at the new piano. He asked himself, "What do we want to say when we come into this building tomorrow for our first worship service?" The words came to him rather quickly—in fifteen minutes he had written the entire song.

Early the next morning, he taught it to his younger brother and sister, and the three sang it together at the church service.

Nineteen-year-old Geron had no idea what was going to happen to that song. Then governor of Arkansas, Bill Clinton heard it and liked it. After he became President, he had it sung at his mother's funeral. That's when Barbara Streisand heard it and asked if she could put it on her next CD.

Says Geron Davis, who is still amazed at what has happened to that song, "It doesn't matter how powerful, how big, how popular, how wealthy, how well-known you are. When we come into God's presence, we're all on level ground. And it's holy ground."

Scriptures: Psalm 5:7; Psalm 29:2; Psalm 65:4; 2 Corinthians 10:17
Themes: Church, Worship, Holiness

We are standing on holy ground,
And I know that there are angels all around.
Let us praise Jesus now,
We are standing in His presence on holy ground.
Words: Geron Davis
© Meadowgreen Music Company/Songchannel Music Co.
All rights reserved. Used by permission.

I LOVE THY KINGDOM, LORD

Timothy Dwight was a brilliant scholar just like his grandfather, theologian Jonathan Edwards. When he was six, he could read Latin. He graduated from Yale at seventeen, began teaching there at nineteen, and wrote his first book at twenty. Dwight was so popular as a teacher that, when he was twenty-five, his students wanted to petition the trustees to appoint him president of the college. He asked them not to.

Instead, he enlisted in the Continental Army in 1777 as a chaplain, where he became known for writing songs to encourage the troops. After the Revolutionary War, he served as a pastor in Connecticut. Finally, in 1795, he accepted the trustees' invitation to become president of Yale.

When Dwight returned to Yale, there were probably as few as five professing Christians on campus. But with Dwight came a new spiritual emphasis, and revival soon swept over the university. This hymn, written during the revival at Yale, is the earliest American hymn in use today.

Scriptures: Ephesians 2:19-22; Colossians 1:25-26; Hebrews 10:24-25
Themes: Church, Worship, Prayer

I love Thy kingdom, Lord,
The house of Thine abode,
The Church our blest Redeemer saved
With His own precious blood.

I love Thy Church, O God!
Her walls before Thee stand
Dear as the apple of Thine eye,
And graven on Thy hand.

For her my tears shall fall,
For her my prayers ascend,
To her my cares and toils be given,
Till toils and cares shall end.

Beyond my highest joy
I prize her heavenly ways,
Her sweet communion, solemn vows,
Her hymns of love and praise.

Sure as Thy truth shall last,
To Zion shall be given
The brightest glories earth can yield,
And brighter bliss of heaven.

TIMOTHY DWIGHT (1752–1817)

IN CHRIST THERE IS NO EAST OR WEST

John Oxenham's real name was William Arthur Dunkerley. He ran a successful wholesale grocery company and served as a deacon in a Congregational church. He was also a writer, working for newspapers and magazines. Like many journalists, he longed to do more creative work. Perhaps a bit embarrassed about these efforts, he used the name Julian Ross when he wrote some short stories. He also borrowed the name John Oxenham from an adventure novel and used it for his poems and hymns. Many of his friends never knew about his triple identity.

Oxenham's writing was very popular. In fact, he was asked to write this hymn to be included in a missionary exhibition presented by the London Missionary Society in 1908. Viewed by over a quarter million people, the presentation was called "The Pageant of Darkness and Light." Afterward, when he couldn't find a publisher for the text, he published it himself, including it in a book called *Bees in Amber,* which sold 286,000 copies!

Whatever name he used—Oxenham, Dunkerley, or Ross—this author was ahead of his time in presenting sentiments against racial prejudice. We still struggle with racial and national divisions today, and we still need to hear this message of unity.

Scriptures: Acts 10:34-35; Galatians 3:28-29; Ephesians 4:3-4
Themes: Missions, Unity, Church

In Christ there is no east or west,
In Him no south or north;
But one great fellowship of love
Throughout the whole wide earth.

In Him shall true hearts everywhere
Their high communion find;
His service is the golden cord
Close binding all mankind.

Join hands, then, brothers of the faith,
Whate'er your race may be.
Who serves my Father as a son
Is surely kin to me.

In Christ now meet both east and west,
In Him meet south and north;
All Christly souls are one in Him
Throughout the whole wide earth.

JOHN OXENHAM (1852–1941)

LET US BREAK BREAD TOGETHER

Some say that this spiritual was the password used to call slaves to secret, forbidden worship meetings in Virginia. Originally, the first line probably was, "Let us praise God together on our knees." Whether secret or not, the song now calls Christians to gather and celebrate the Lord's Supper.

The posture is significant. Some churches have participants kneel to take the elements of Communion, others have them sit or stand. Whatever posture the body takes, the attitude of the heart is worship. We come in reverence before our Lord, the host of this dinner party.

At the Lord's Table we have Communion not only with our Lord but also with one another. J. B. Phillips wrote, "Holy Communion is surely always falling short of its true purpose if it fails to produce some sense of solidarity with our fellow worshipers."

"The rising sun" could refer to an ancient custom of worshipping toward the east. However, in one of the last verses in the Old Testament, Malachi prophesied that the "Sun of Righteousness will rise with healing in his wings" (Malachi 4:2), which is usually understood as a reference to the coming Christ.

Scriptures: Psalm 133:1; Malachi 4:2; Acts 2:42-44; Romans 15:5-6
Themes: Communion, Praise, Fellowship

Let us break bread together on our knees;
Let us break bread together on our knees;
When I fall on my knees
With my face to the rising sun,
O Lord, have mercy on me.

Let us drink the cup together on our knees;
Let us drink the cup together on our knees;
When I fall on my knees
With my face to the rising sun,
O Lord, have mercy on me.

Let us praise God together on our knees;
Let us praise God together on our knees;
When I fall on my knees
With my face to the rising sun,
O Lord, have mercy on me.

TRADITIONAL SPIRITUAL

LET US LOVE, AND SING, AND WONDER

Much has been made of John Newton's move from the slave trade to the church. It was a turnaround that rivaled that of the apostle Paul, and Newton always recognized the depths of sin from which he had come. The "wretch like me" that he mentions in his hymn "Amazing Grace" was no exaggeration. Newton knew that he had sinned greatly; he also knew the greatness of God's redeeming grace.

"Let Us Love, and Sing, and Wonder," however, comes from later years, when Newton was a renowned preacher. It is rich with theology and biblical images. Christ has "hushed the Law's loud thunder," says Newton, evoking images of Mount Sinai. For centuries the Law stood strong and unkeepable. "You're not good enough!" it rumbled. But Christ silenced that rumble with the sweet promise of his own righteousness.

Grace and justice join in Christ, says Newton. Normally these two words don't belong in the same sentence, but when our trust is in Christ's righteousness, both are satisfied—"justice smiles and asks no more."

Scriptures: Psalm 96:1-3; 1 Corinthians 6:20; Revelation 1:5-6
Themes: Praise, Love, Worship

Let us love, and sing, and wonder,
Let us praise the Savior's name!
He has hushed the Law's loud thunder,
He has quenched Mount Sinai's flame;
He has washed us with His blood,
He has brought us nigh to God.

Let us love the Lord who bought us,
Pitied us when enemies,
Called us by His grace, and taught us,
Gave us ears, and gave us eyes:
He has washed us with His blood,
He presents our souls to God.

Let us sing, though fierce temptations
Threaten hard to bear us down!
For the Lord, our strong salvation,
Holds in view the conqu'ror's crown,
He who washed us with His blood,
Soon will bring us home to God.

Let us wonder; grace and justice
Join, and point to mercy's store;
When through grace in Christ our trust is,
Justice smiles and asks no more:
He who washed us with His blood,
Has secured our way to God.

Let us praise, and join the chorus
Of the saints enthroned on high;
Here they trusted Him before us,
Now their praises fill the sky:
"Thou hast washed us with Thy blood;
Thou art worthy, Lamb of God!"

JOHN NEWTON (1725–1807)

LORD JESUS CHRIST, BE PRESENT NOW

Where is Jesus? There are several ways to answer that question: As God, he is omnipresent, all around us. He said that he was somehow present in the poor and needy people that we meet. Scripture also speaks of him sitting at the right hand of the Father. This is a place of honor, where he waits for the right time to return to earth in triumph. Through his Spirit, he is present in our hearts.

If Jesus is in all these places, why should we invite him to "be present now"? Well, there are several other Scriptures to take note of. Jesus said that where two or three gather in his name, he would be there with them. That happens each time we worship. Another verse says that the Lord inhabits his people's praise. And Christ is also wonderfully present when we observe the Lord's Supper.

This hymn is a call to worship, inviting Christ to inspire, inhabit, and enjoy our praise. It also serves to remind us that Christ has promised to join us on such occasions.

Scriptures: Matthew 18:20; Luke 22:19; John 14:24-26
Themes: Communion, Trinity, Holy Spirit

Lord Jesus Christ, be present now,
Our hearts in true devotion bow,
Thy Spirit send with grace divine,
And let Thy truth within us shine.

Unseal our lips to sing Thy praise,
Our souls to Thee in worship raise,
Make strong our faith, increase our light
That we may know Thy name aright.

Until we join the hosts that cry,
"Holy art Thou, O Lord, most high!"
And in the light of that blest place
Fore'er behold Thee face to face.

Glory to God the Father, Son,
And Holy Spirit, Three in One!
To Thee, O blessed Trinity,
Be praise throughout eternity!

GERMAN HYMN
Cantionale Sacrum, *1651*
Translated by Catherine Winkworth (1827–1878)

MAY THE GRACE OF CHRIST, OUR SAVIOR

The apostle Paul concluded one of his letters to the troubled Corinthian church with this benediction: "May the grace of the Lord Jesus Christ, and the love of God, and the fellowship of the Holy Spirit be with you all" (2 Corinthians 13:14, NIV). It is a remarkable verse because it mentions the work of God on our behalf through each person of the Trinity—Father, Son, and Holy Spirit.

John Newton, the former slave trader whose life was touched by God's amazing grace, became a loving pastor. He loved his congregation, and they loved him. He had special services for children and special services for senior citizens, teaching the Bible faithfully and singing songs that he had written.

One writer said, "Newton was more remarkable for his goodness than for his greatness." Newton would have loved that assessment.

Scriptures: 2 Corinthians 13–14; Galatians 2:20-21; Ephesians 6:23-24
Themes: Trinity, Grace, Unity, Benediction

> May the grace of Christ, our Savior,
> And the Father's boundless love,
> With the Holy Spirit's favor,
> Rest upon us from above.
>
> Thus may we abide in union
> With each other and the Lord,
> And possess, in sweet communion,
> Joys which earth cannot afford.
>
> JOHN NEWTON (1725–1807)

O DAY OF REST AND GLADNESS

Christopher Wordsworth was a distinguished athlete in college and a recognized Greek scholar in his adult life, but he is remembered as the author of "O Day of Rest and Gladness."

He once said, "It is the first duty of a hymn to teach sound doctrine and thence to save souls." The second stanza of this hymn is a good example of the way Wordsworth used his hymns to teach doctrine. As he makes his case for Sunday being the Lord's Day and a day of rest, he says that, first of all, it was on the first day of the week that God created light; second, that it was on the first day of the week that Christ arose from the dead; and third, that it was on the first day of the week that the Holy Spirit was given at Pentecost. Thus, Sunday is a day honored three times—by the Father, by the Son, and by the Holy Spirit.

The verse that inspired Wordsworth was Psalm 118:24, "This is the day which the LORD hath made; we will rejoice and be glad in it" (KJV).

Scriptures: Genesis 1:3-5; Psalm 118:24; Isaiah 58:13-14; Luke 24:1; John 4:23-24; Revelation 1:10
Themes: Sunday, Trinity, Praise

O day of rest and gladness,
O day of joy and light,
O balm of care and sadness,
Most beautiful, most bright:
On thee the high and lowly,
Through ages joined in tune,
Sing holy, holy, holy,
To the great God Triune.

On thee, at the creation,
The light first had its birth;
On thee for our salvation
Christ rose from depths of earth;
On thee our Lord victorious
The Spirit sent from heaven,
And thus on thee most glorious
A triple light was given.

Today on weary nations
The heavenly manna falls;
To holy convocations
The silver trumpet calls,
Where Gospel light is glowing
With pure and radiant beams,
And living water flowing
With soul-refreshing streams.

New graces ever gaining
From this our day of rest,
We reach the rest remaining
To spirits of the blest.
To Holy Ghost be praises,
To Father, and to Son;

The Church her voice upraises
To Thee, blest Three in One.

CHRISTOPHER WORDSWORTH (1807–1885)

RISE UP, O MEN OF GOD

This hymn has been criticized because it speaks only of men of God and not women of God. Many contemporary hymnals have changed the words to "saints of God" or "church of God." Yet William Merrill's notion was not to discriminate against women, but to challenge men. Women in his day had numerous church organizations and groups, but there was not much for men.

Merrill had been trying to strengthen the men's brotherhood in his Presbyterian denomination when a magazine editor suggested that he write a special hymn for the brotherhood. It was an interesting idea, Merrill thought, but he didn't know what to write.

A short time later, as Merrill was returning to his church in Chicago on board a Lake Michigan steamer, he was reading a Christian magazine. In it he noticed an article entitled, "The Church of the Strong Men," and that gave him his inspiration. Before the steamer was tied up at the dock in Chicago, he had written this brotherhood hymn.

The hymn is full of exclamation points and military-sounding commands. The Christian message still comes to us—both men and women—with exclamation points and definite commands. Followers of Christ are called to be soldiers, not merely passive recipients of God's blessings.

Scriptures: 1 Corinthians 16:13; Ephesians 4:7, 11-13; Philippians 1:27-28
Themes: Courage, Service, Dedication

Rise up, O men of God!
Have done with lesser things;
Give heart and soul and mind and strength
To serve the King of kings.

Rise up, O men of God!
His kingdom tarries long;
Bring in the day of brotherhood
And end the night of wrong.

Rise up, O men of God!
The Church for you doth wait,

Her strength unequal to her task:
Rise up and make her great.

Lift high the cross of Christ,
Tread where His feet have trod;
As brothers of the Son of man,
Rise up, O men of God!

WILLIAM PIERSON MERRILL (1867–1954)

SHALL WE GATHER AT THE RIVER?

The summer of 1864 was a summer Robert Lowry would have liked to forget. An epidemic was sweeping New York, and the heat that summer was oppressive. As a Baptist pastor in Brooklyn, Lowry had buried many of his church members, and others were near death. He was exhausted, but he knew he had to keep on giving comfort to the families that were left behind.

Late one afternoon, Lowell comforted a family with a verse in Revelation that speaks of heaven and of a river in heaven called the river of the water of life. Although he had heard people refer to the river of death and crossing Jordan, he hadn't known of a hymn about the river of life.

So, thinking of his church members who had succumbed to the epidemic and those who were sorrowing, he said, "The words began to construct themselves." They came first as a question: "Shall we gather?" and then they broke out in a joyous answer, "Yes, we'll gather at the river," and at that river we will see our loved ones again.

Scriptures: Ezekiel 47:1-7; John 7:37-39; Revelation 22:1
Themes: Heaven, Joy, Hope

Shall we gather at the river,
Where bright angel feet have trod;
With its crystal tide forever
Flowing by the throne of God?

Yes, we'll gather at the river, The beautiful, the beautiful river,
Gather with the saints at the river that flows by the throne of God.

On the bosom of the river,
Where the Savior-King we own,
We shall meet, and sorrow never,
'Neath the glory of the throne.

Ere we reach the shining river,
Lay we ev'ry burden down;
Grace our spirits will deliver,
And provide a robe and crown.

Soon we'll reach the shining river,
Soon our pilgrimage will cease;
Soon our happy hearts will quiver
With the melody of peace.

ROBERT LOWRY (1826–1899)

SURELY THE PRESENCE OF THE LORD

When Lanny Wolf wrote songs, he would scribble a few words on any piece of paper that he could find or just keep the words in his head until he met with the other members of the Lanny Wolf Trio. Then he would sing them to the group, and they would fine-tune both the words and the melody.

But "Surely the Presence of the Lord" happened much more spontaneously than that. The Lanny Wolf Trio was in Columbia, Mississippi, for the dedication of a new church building. The mayor was there, along with other officials.

As the trio was waiting to sing, Lanny felt the Lord was giving him a new song. He quickly grabbed a scrap of paper and jotted down the words. There was no time to go over them with the other members of the trio.

When the time came for the trio to sing, Lanny went to the piano and began singing the chorus. As he taught it to the audience, he was also teaching it to his trio. Lanny's scribbled notes are still hanging in the foyer of that church, reminding church members of the birth of the song.

Scriptures: Acts 2:1-2; Acts 4:31; Ephesians 4:1-6
Themes: Church, Holy Spirit, Unity

Surely the presence of the Lord is in this place,
I can feel His mighty power and His grace.
I can hear the brush of angels' wings, I see glory on each face;
Surely the presence of the Lord is in this place.

LANNY WOLF

THE CHURCH'S ONE FOUNDATION

Windsor on the Thames, with its royal castle, is one of England's most popular tourist attractions. Samuel Stone's ministry was located here, among the poorer people at the outskirts of town.

Samuel Stone was a fighter. He stood up for what he believed, and if local "toughs" threatened the neighborhood, he was not afraid to take them on. In the Church of England, Stone was regarded as a fundamentalist, opposing the liberal theological tendencies of his day.

When he was twenty-seven, he wrote a collection of hymns based on the Apostles' Creed. This hymn, taken from that collection, is based on the article in the creed regarding the church as the body of Christ.

Two years later, Anglicans from around the world met to discuss the crucial theological issues that were raging in the church. Significantly, they chose Stone's hymn as the processional for their historic conference.

Scriptures: 1 Corinthians 3:11; Ephesians 2:19-22; Ephesians 5:23; Colossians 1:18
Themes: Church, Jesus, Mission

The Church's one foundation is Jesus Christ her Lord;
She is His new creation by water and the word.
From heaven He came and sought her to be His holy bride;
With His own blood He bought her, and for her life He died.

Elect from every nation, yet one o'er all the earth,
Her charter of salvation, one Lord, one faith, one birth;
One holy name she blesses, partakes one holy food,
And to one hope she presses, with every grace endued.

Mid toil and tribulation, and tumult of her war,
She waits the consummation of peace forevermore;
Till, with the vision glorious, her longing eyes are blest,
And the great Church victorious shall be the Church at rest.

Yet she on earth hath union with God the Three in One,
And mystic sweet communion with those whose rest is won.
O happy ones and holy! Lord, give us grace that we,
Like them, the meek and lowly, on high may dwell with Thee.

SAMUEL JOHN STONE (1839–1900)

THE FAMILY OF GOD

Well-known gospel songwriters Bill and Gloria Gaither were home for Easter and attending their home church in Anderson, Indiana. They heard of a young man in the community who had been severely burned when an explosion demolished the garage where he worked. Doctors did not expect him to live through the night.

A church prayer chain was activated, and church members prayed all night for the young man. When church members gathered to celebrate Easter the next day, they received word that the young man was recovering. The pastor reported that he had just spoken to the doctor, who told him the young man had a good chance of pulling through. They rejoiced in the answer to prayer.

As Bill and Gloria Gaither went home after the church service, they talked about what a wonderful thing it is to be a part of a family of believers and to be able to pray together to our Father in heaven. Before long, a new gospel song was born: "The Family of God."

Scriptures: 1 Corinthians 12:13; Galatians 3:28; Ephesians 2:19-22
Themes: Fellowship, Joy, Salvation

I'm so glad I'm a part of the family of God—
I've been washed in the fountain, cleansed by His blood!
Joint heirs with Jesus as we travel this sod,
For I'm part of the family, the family of God.

GLORIA GAITHER (B. 1942) AND WILLIAM J. GAITHER (B. 1936)
© Copyright 1970 William J. Gaither, Inc.
All rights controlled by Gaither Copyright Management. Used by permission.

THERE'S A QUIET UNDERSTANDING

Tedd Smith is perhaps best known as the pianist for many of the Billy Graham Evangelistic Association's crusades, but he has also been a recording artist for RCA Victor and the writer and composer of many hymns.

In 1972, after a crusade service in Oakland, California, several members of the Graham team gathered together for an informal Communion service. Smith recalls the time this way: "As we sat in a circle on the floor sharing Communion, the feeling of being strangers disappeared and there seemed to come this quiet understanding of each other, a feeling of being with brothers and sisters and sensing the oneness Christ promised whenever two or three gather in his name."

Following that time of fellowship and Communion, Tedd Smith went back to his room and wrote this song, "There's a Quiet Understanding."

Scriptures: Psalm 133:1; Matthew 18:20; John 17:20-21
Themes: Fellowship, Unity, Communion

There's a quiet understanding when we're gathered in the Spirit,
It's a promise that He gives us, when we gather in His name.
There's a love we feel in Jesus, there's a manna that He feeds us
It's a promise that He gives us when we gather in His name.
And we know when we're together, sharing love and understanding,
That our brothers and our sisters feel the oneness that He brings.
Thank You, thank You, thank You, Jesus, for the way You love and feed us,
For the many ways You lead us, thank You, thank You, Lord.

TEDD SMITH

WE ARE GOD'S PEOPLE

Bryan Leech, the author of this hymn, came to America from England in 1955. He says that what is unusual about the hymn is that it was written by a Britisher on a dreary Independence Day. Leech wrote it, of course, not to celebrate America's independence from England, but to celebrate the body of Christ, the Church. He says, "We have had so few popular hymns relating to the church."

The tune is adapted from the last movement of Brahms's Symphony No. 1 in C minor. In the hymn, the church is referred to by several biblical phrases: "God's people," "the chosen of the Lord," "the bride of Christ," the Body of Christ, and the Temple of the Holy Spirit.

Scriptures: Ephesians 1:22-23; Ephesians 2:21-22; 1 Peter 2:9
Themes: Church, Fellowship, Unity

We are God's people, the chosen of the Lord,
Born of His Spirit, established by His word;
Our cornerstone is Christ alone, and strong in Him we stand:
O let us live transparently, and walk heart to heart and hand in hand.

We are God's loved ones, the bride of Christ our Lord,
For we have known it, the love of God outpoured;
Now let us learn how to return the gift of love once given:
O let us share each joy and care, and live with a zeal that
    pleases Heaven.

We are the body of which the Lord is Head,
Called to obey Him, now risen from the dead;
He wills us be a family diverse yet truly one:
O let us give our gifts to God, and so shall His work on earth be done.

We are a temple, the Spirit's dwelling place,
Formed in great weakness, a cup to hold God's grace;
We die alone, for on its own each ember loses fire:
Yet joined in one the flame burns on to give warmth and light,
    and to inspire.

BRYAN JEFFERY LEECH

ZION, TO THY SAVIOR SINGING

Thomas Aquinas is listed among the greatest Christian thinkers in the history of the church. During the Middle Ages, he anchored Christian theology to Aristotle's philosophy and recovered the role of reason in church life. In this way, he paved the way for the Reformation and the Renaissance.

Not everyone agrees with all aspects of his theology. His teachings were suspect within the church at first, and later the Reformers took issue with some of his assertions. But he remains one of the most influential Christian thinkers of all time, an intellectual light during the Dark Ages.

Despite Aquinas's intellectual brilliance, this hymn is not bathed in intellectualism. It is a simple Communion hymn, a meditation on the Lord's Table. After speaking of the surpassing wonder of Christ, he marvels that Christ offers his own body and blood for us. Christ himself is our Passover meal, protecting us from the angel of death and delivering us from slavery.

Scriptures: Exodus 12:23-28; John 6:56-58; 1 Corinthians 11:23-25
Themes: Communion, Praise, Worship

Zion, to thy Savior singing,
To thy Prince and Shepherd bringing

Sweetest hymns of love and praise,
Thou wilt never reach the measure
Of His worth, by all the treasures
Of thy most ecstatic lays.

Of all wonders that can thrill thee,
And with adoration fill thee,
What than this can greater be,
That Himself to thee He giveth?
He that eateth ever liveth,
For the Bread of Life is He.

Fill thy lips to overflowing
With sweet praise, His mercy showing
Who this heav'nly table spread:
On this day so glad and holy,
To each longing spirit lowly
Giveth He the living Bread.

Here the King hath spread His table,
Whereon eyes of faith are able
Christ our Passover to trace:
Shadows of the law are going,
Light and life and truth inflowing,
Night to day is giving place.

O Good Shepherd, Bread life-giving,
Us, Thy grace and life receiving,
Feed and shelter evermore;
Thou on earth our weakness guiding,
We in heav'n with Thee abiding
With all saints will Thee adore.

THOMAS AQUINAS (CA. 1225–1274)
Translated by Alexander R. Thompson (1822–1895)

PART IX

COMFORT AND PEACE

Jesus said, "Come to me, all of you who are weary and carry

heavy burdens, and I will give you rest."

MATTHEW 11:28

ABIDE WITH ME

It was the author of this hymn who coined the phrase, "It is better to wear out than to rust out." For most of his adult life, Henry Lyte was the pastor of a poor church in a fishing village in Devonshire, England. It was a discouraging pastorate, but he kept at it. When he wrote this hymn, he knew he was dying of tuberculosis and asthma, and he felt very much alone.

Lyte was inspired by the words of the two disciples on the road to Emmaus. They were met by Jesus on the day of his resurrection, and they invited him to stay with them because it was getting late. "Abide with us," they said, "for it is toward evening" (Luke 24:29, KJV).

The aging pastor knew that it was getting "toward evening" in his life, but he determined that he would wear out rather than rust out. Shortly after he wrote this hymn, he preached his last sermon; he was so ill that he practically crawled to the pulpit to do so. The hymn concludes, "In life, in death, O Lord, abide with me."

Scriptures: Psalm 27:4; Luke 24:28-31; John 15:5; 1 John 3:24
Themes: Comfort, Death, Hope, Confidence

Abide with me; fast falls the eventide;
The darkness deepens; Lord, with me abide!
When other helpers fail and comforts flee,
Help of the helpless, O abide with me.

Swift to its close ebbs out life's little day;
Earth's joys grow dim; its glories pass away;
Change and decay in all around I see;
O Thou who changest not, abide with me.

I need Thy presence every passing hour;
What but Thy grace can foil the tempter's power?
Who, like Thyself, my guide and stay can be?
Through cloud and sunshine, Lord, abide with me.

I fear no foe, with Thee at hand to bless;
Ills have no weight, and tears no bitterness.
Where is death's sting? Where, grave, thy victory?
I triumph still, if Thou abide with me.

Hold Thou Thy cross before my closing eyes;
Shine through the gloom and point me to the skies;

Heaven's morning breaks, and earth's vain shadows flee;
In life, in death, O Lord, abide with me.
HENRY FRANCIS LYTE (1793–1847)

ART THOU WEARY, ART THOU LANGUID?

Whether this hymn should be credited to John Neale in 1862 or to Stephen the Sebaite in the eighth century is hard to tell. At least we can say that the hymn Neale produced for the modern church was inspired by the life and writings of this Greek monk, who lived in the Mar Sabas monastery near the Dead Sea. Neale specialized in discovering old Greek and Latin hymns and translating or paraphrasing them.

By the eighth century, Islam had overrun the Middle East and North Africa. Many Christians fled to desolate areas, where monasteries were set up. Stephen was one of these Christians. At Mar Sabas, he became choirmaster for a community of monks and composed the hymn on which this one is based.

The beauty of the hymn lies in the contrast between the first couplet of each stanza (our human question or concern) and the second (Christ's divine answer). The questions posed by this ancient hymn are still relevant today—and the answers, still true.

Scriptures: Psalm 55:22; Matthew 11:28-30; Revelation 22:17
Themes: Discipleship, Comfort, Guidance

Art thou weary, art thou languid,
Art thou sore distressed?
"Come to me," saith One, "and, coming,
Be at rest."

Hath He marks to lead me to Him,
If He be my guide?
In His feet and hands are wound prints,
And His side.

Hath He diadem, as monarch,
That His brow adorns?
Yea, a crown, in very surety,
But of thorns.

If I find Him, if I follow,
What His guerdon here?

Many a sorrow, many a labor,
Many a tear.

If I still hold closely to Him,
What hath He at last?
Sorrow vanquished, labor ended,
Jordan passed.

If I ask Him to receive me,
Will He say me nay?
Not till earth and not till heaven
Pass away.

Finding, following, keeping, struggling,
Is He sure to bless?
Saints, apostles, prophets, martyrs,
Answer yes.

STEPHEN THE SEBAITE (734–794)
Translated by John Mason Neale (1818–1866)

BLESSED QUIETNESS

On the stormy Sea of Galilee, Jesus commanded the winds and waves, "Peace, be still" (Mark 4:39, KJV), and immediately there was calm. Later in the upper room, as Jesus told his disciples that he would leave them, he promised them the Holy Spirit and peace.

Manie Payne, born in Carlow, Ireland, was a Christian, but she did not know peace. She struggled with her sinful nature until she began to experience the fullness of the Holy Spirit. This is the "blessed quietness" that she wrote about. Now, she was so happy she could hardly contain herself. Indeed, joy was flowing like a river in her life.

Later she married T. P. Ferguson and founded Peniel Missions, with branches in Egypt, China, and the United States.

Scriptures: Luke 4:29-30; John 14:25-27; Galatians 5:22
Themes: Holy Spirit, Peace, Assurance

Joys are flowing like a river
Since the Comforter has come.
He abides with us forever,
Makes the trusting heart His home.

Blessed quietness, holy quietness,
What assurance in my soul!
On the stormy sea He speaks peace to me,
How the billows cease to roll!

Bringing life and health and gladness
All around this heav'nly Guest
Banished unbelief and sadness,
Changed our weariness to rest.

Like the rain that falls from heaven,
Like the sunlight from the sky,
So the Holy Ghost is given,
Coming on us from on high.

See, a fruitful field is growing,
Blessed fruit of righteousness;
And the streams of life are flowing
In the lonely wilderness.

What a wonderful salvation,
Where we always see His face!
What a perfect habitation,
What a quiet resting place!

MANIE PAYNE FERGUSON (1850–1932)

CHILDREN OF THE HEAVENLY FATHER

When Carolina Sandell was a child, she was stricken with a mysterious paralysis and was bedridden. Her doctors could do nothing for her, and they believed her case was hopeless. One Sunday morning when she was twelve years old, her parents went to church and left her at home so she could rest. She spent the time praying.

When her parents returned home, they were astonished to find her dressed and walking around the house. From that time on, she wrote hymns and poems. At the age of sixteen, she published her first collection of poetry.

Throughout her life she retained her childlike trust in God and her appreciation of God's comfort even in the darkest hours. The final stanza of this hymn assures us "more secure is no one ever / Than the loved ones of the Savior."

Scriptures: Psalm 121:3; Matthew 6:26; 1 John 3:1-2
Themes: Comfort, Security, Assurance

Children of the heav'nly Father
Safely in His bosom gather;
Nestling bird nor star in heaven
Such a refuge e'er was given.

God His own doth tend and nourish,
In His holy courts they flourish;
From all evil things He spares them,
In His mighty arms He bears them.

Neither life nor death shall ever
From the Lord His children sever;
Unto them His grace He showeth,
And their sorrows all He knoweth.

Praise the Lord in joyful numbers,
Your protector never slumbers;
At the will of your Defender
Ev'ry foe-man must surrender.

Though He giveth or He taketh,
God His children ne'er forsaketh;
His the loving purpose solely
To preserve them pure and holy.

More secure is no one ever
Than the loved ones of the Savior;
Not yon star on high abiding
Nor the bird in home-nest hiding.

CAROLINA SANDELL BERG (1832–1903)
Translated by Ernst W. Olson (1870–1958)
© Copyright Board of Publication Lutheran Church in America
by permission.

COME, YE DISCONSOLATE

Irish poet Thomas Moore is best known for his ballads such as "The Last Rose of Summer" and "Believe Me If All Those Endearing Young Charms." One writer called Moore "one of the strangest of all men to write hymns." The son of a Dublin grocer, Moore was educated at Trinity College in Dublin, but he could not graduate because he was Roman

Catholic. After a short career in government, he devoted himself to writing and became known as the "Voice of Ireland." Many were surprised when Moore published his *Sacred Song-Duets* in 1824.

"Come, Ye Disconsolate," which was originally titled "Relief in Prayer," has undergone some revision since Moore wrote it, but the original version contained the same message. The third stanza is now completely different from Moore's rendering, which was "Go ask the infidel what boon he brings us, / What charm for aching hearts he can reveal? . . . / Earth has no sorrow that heaven cannot heal."

Scriptures: Psalm 30:11; Jeremiah 29:13; 1 Peter 5:7; Revelation 21:3-4
Themes: Comfort, Sorrow, Prayer

Come, ye disconsolate, where'er ye languish,
Come to the mercy seat, fervently kneel.
Here bring your wounded hearts, here tell your anguish:
Earth has no sorrow that heaven cannot heal.

Joy of the desolate, light of the straying,
Hope of the penitent, fadeless and pure!
Here speaks the Comforter, tenderly saying,
"Earth has no sorrow that heaven cannot cure."

Here see the Bread of Life; see waters flowing
Forth from the throne of God, pure from above.
Come to the feast of love; come, ever knowing
Earth has no sorrow but heaven can remove.

THOMAS MOORE (1779–1852)
Altered by Thomas Hastings (1784–1872)

DAY BY DAY AND WITH EACH PASSING MOMENT

Even during our most painful experiences God is with us. Carolina Sandell Berg understood this truth personally. Because she was never strong as a child, she spent much time in her father's study rather than playing outside. Carolina grew very close to her father. When she was twenty-six, she accompanied her father on a voyage to Göteborg, Sweden. As they stood together on deck, the boat lurched and her father fell overboard. The crew tried to save him, but they couldn't. He drowned as Carolina looked on.

At the loss of her earthly father, Carolina drew even closer to her heavenly Father. She discovered that even during the times of greatest loss, God's comforting presence was near. At times she wondered how she could make it through the next week or month, but day by day the Lord gave her the strength she needed.

Scriptures: Deuteronomy 33:25; Joshua 1:9; Psalm 55:22; 2 Corinthians 4:8-11; Hebrews 4:16
Themes: Trust, Rest, Hope

Day by day and with each passing moment,
Strength I find to meet my trials here;
Trusting in my Father's wise bestowment,
I've no cause for worry or for fear.
He whose heart is kind beyond all measure
Gives unto each day what He deems best—
Lovingly, its part of pain and pleasure,
Mingling toil with peace and rest.

Ev'ry day the Lord Himself is near me
With a special mercy for each hour;
All my cares He fain would bear, and cheer me,
He whose name is Counsellor and Pow'r.
The protection of His child and treasure
Is a charge that on Himself He laid;
"As thy days, thy strength shall be in measure,"
This the pledge to me He made.

Help me then in ev'ry tribulation
So to trust Thy promises, O Lord,
That I lose not faith's sweet consolation
Offered me within Thy holy Word.
Help me, Lord, when toil and trouble meeting,
E'er to take, as from a father's hand,
One by one, the days, the moments fleeting,
Till I reach the promised land.

CAROLINA SANDELL BERG (1832–1903)
Translated by Andrew L. Skoog (1856–1934)

DOES JESUS CARE?

Frank Graeff had a wonderful nickname—"The Sunshine Minister." He loved little children and became famous for the stories he told them. He was also called "a spiritual optimist," and people were drawn to him because he had "a holy magnetism."

But inside, Frank Graeff was going through some spiritual struggles. Today we might call it a midlife crisis. Struggling with physical problems, he fell into depression and had some spiritual doubt. It all hit "The Sunshine Minister" at the same time.

He turned to the Scriptures, searching for a verse that he could really hold onto, and he found it in 1 Peter 5:7: "Casting all your care upon him; for he careth for you" (KJV).

That verse not only guided him through his "downtime," but it also inspired him to write the song "Does Jesus Care?"

Scriptures: Psalm 23:4; Matthew 28:20; 1 Peter 5:7
Themes: Comfort, Encouragement, Hope

Does Jesus care when my heart is pained
Too deeply for mirth and song;
As the burdens press, and the cares distress,
And the way grows weary and long?

O yes, He cares; I know He cares, His heart is touched with my grief;
When the days are weary, the long nights dreary, I know my Savior cares.

Does Jesus care when my way is dark
With a nameless dread and fear?
As the daylight fades into deep nightshades,
Does He care enough to be near?

Does Jesus care when I've tried and failed
To resist some temptation strong;
When for my deep grief I find no relief,
Tho' my tears flow all the night long?

Does Jesus care when I've said "good-bye"
To the dearest on earth to me.
And my sad heart aches till it nearly breaks—
Is it aught to Him? Does He see?

FRANK E. GRAEFF (1860–1919)

GOD BE WITH YOU

Jeremiah Rankin was intrigued by the thought that the word *good-bye* was simply a contraction of the phrase "God be with you," so he wrote this hymn. He explained, "It was called forth by no person or occasion," but was simply written to remind his congregation and others what saying good-bye really meant. After writing the hymn, he sent it to two composers and asked each of them to come up with a tune. One was a famous composer; the other was "wholly unknown and not thoroughly educated in music." He selected the composition of William Tomer, who was unknown in the music world.

Unlike Tomer, Rankin was quite well-known. He was a powerful speaker and pastor of the First Congregational Church of Washington, D.C. A few years later he was chosen to be president of Howard University.

"God Be with You" caught on quickly. Evangelist Dwight L. Moody began using it in his meetings. Christian Endeavor Conventions used it around the world and translated it into many languages. Perhaps "God Be with You," along with "Blest Be the Tie that Binds," has closed more Christian services than any other hymns.

Scriptures: Act 20:32; Romans 15:33; Romans 16:20
Themes: Encouragement, Hope, Blessing

God be with you till we meet again,
By His counsels guide, uphold you,
With His sheep securely fold you,
God be with you till we meet again.

Till we meet, till we meet,
Till we meet at Jesus' feet,
Till we meet, till we meet—
God be with you till we meet again.

God be with you till we meet again,
'Neath His wings protecting hide you,
Daily manna still provide you,
God be with you till we meet again.

God be with you till we meet again,
When life's perils thick confound you,
Put His arms unfailing round you—
God be with you till we meet again.

God be with you till we meet again,
Keep love's banner floating o'er you,
Smite death's threatening wave before you—
God be with you till we meet again.

JEREMIAH E. RANKIN (1828–1904)

GOD WILL TAKE CARE OF YOU

W. Stillman Martin had accepted an invitation to preach at a church a few hours away from his home. When his wife became ill that Sunday morning, he thought he should cancel the engagement. But then his young son spoke up: "Father, don't you think that if God wants you to preach today, he will take care of Mother while you are away?"

Because of his son's question, he kept the engagement and preached at the church. When he returned that night, his wife was feeling better and had written this hymn, inspired by their son's words. Later that evening, Martin composed the music for his wife's text.

God will take care of you. It's a lesson we all need to learn.

Scriptures: Job 23:10; Psalm 57:1; Psalm 91:1-4; Philippians 4:6; 1 Peter 5:7
Themes: Trust, God's Protection, Providence

Be not dismayed whate'er betide,
God will take care of you;
Beneath His wings of love abide,
God will take care of you.

God will take care of you,
Through every day, o'er all the way;
He will take care of you,
God will take care of you.

Through days of toil when heart doth fail,
God will take care of you;
When dangers fierce your path assail,
God will take care of you.

All you may need He will provide,
God will take care of you;
Nothing you ask will be denied,
God will take care of you.

No matter what may be the test,
God will take care of you;
Lean, weary one, upon His breast,
God will take care of you.

CIVILLA DURFEE MARTIN (1866–1948)

HE HIDETH MY SOUL

As a blind person, Fanny Crosby faced daily insecurity, which is why she found so much comfort in the book of Psalms and why so many of her hymns point to the security we have in the Lord.

This gospel song was one of her favorites. Like David in the desert, she sometimes felt alone and vulnerable. In the words of Scripture, she prayed, "Hide me," and she delighted in Psalm 32:7, which says, "You are my hiding place."

But the verse that inspired this song is from Exodus. Seeking to know God was with the Israelites in the wilderness, Moses asked the Lord to show him his presence. God acquiesced to Moses' request and assured him, "I will put you in a cleft in the rock and cover you with my hand" (Exodus 33:22, NIV).

In the New Testament we find that Jesus is the cornerstone who was rejected for us, and thus we who are Christians are hidden in the cleft of the Rock. When we consider how the hand of God covers us and shields us from harm, we, too, can join in praise to God: "O glory to God / For such a Redeemer as mine!"

Scriptures: Exodus 33:22; Psalm 27:4-5; Psalm 32:7; Isaiah 51:16
Themes: Security, Salvation, Comfort

A wonderful Savior is Jesus my Lord,
A wonderful Savior to me;
He hideth my soul in the cleft of the rock,
Where rivers of pleasure I see.

He hideth my soul in the cleft of the rock
That shadows a dry, thirsty land;
He hideth my life in the depths of His love,
And covers me there with His hand,
And covers me there with His hand.

A wonderful Savior is Jesus my Lord,
He taketh my burden away;
He holdeth me up, and I shall not be moved,
He giveth me strength as my day.

With numberless blessings each moment He crowns,
And, filled with His fulness divine,
I sing in my rapture, "O glory to God
For such a Redeemer as mine!"

When clothed in His brightness transported I rise,
To meet Him in clouds of the sky,
His perfect salvation, His wonderful love,
I'll shout with the millions on high.

FANNY JANE CROSBY (1820–1915)

I HEARD THE VOICE OF JESUS SAY

Horatius Bonar loved to doodle as he wrote his hymns. On the sheet where this hymn first took shape, the lines are abbreviated, edited, and added to, and several doodles are scratched in the margins. Many of Bonar's ideas came to him during long country walks in his native Scotland, and he often fleshed out his ideas while riding a train. All told, Bonar wrote more than six hundred hymns and became known as "The Prince of Scottish Hymnwriters."

Bonar began writing hymns for the children in his church. As a student assistant in the church, he had become close with the Sunday school pupils and began writing hymns that they could sing to popular melodies.

When Bonar wrote this hymn, he intended it for children, but adults soon appreciated its message as well. The invitation of Christ to "come" is simple enough for a child and profound enough for an adult to respond to. But after we accept that invitation, it takes a lifetime to probe the depths of what it means to come to him, to drink the living water, and to walk in the Light.

Scriptures: Isaiah 55:1; Matthew 11:28; John 8:12
Themes: Invitation, Comfort, Salvation

I heard the voice of Jesus say,
"Come unto Me and rest;
Lay down, thou weary one, lay down

Thy head upon My breast."
I came to Jesus as I was,
Weary and worn and sad;
I found in Him a resting place,
And He has made me glad.

I heard the voice of Jesus say,
"Behold, I freely give
The living water; thirsty one,
Stoop down and drink and live."
I came to Jesus, and I drank
Of that life-giving stream;
My thirst was quenched, my soul revived,
And now I live in Him.

I heard the voice of Jesus say,
"I am this dark world's light;
Look unto Me, thy morn shall rise,
And all thy day be bright."
I looked to Jesus, and I found
In Him my star, my sun;
And in that light of life I'll walk
Till traveling days are done.

HORATIUS BONAR (1808–1889)

IN TIMES LIKE THESE

Late in 1943, Ruth Caye Jones, mother of five and wife of a busy pastor, was reading 2 Timothy 3:1, which says, "In the last days perilous times shall come" (KJV). As she read the Pittsburgh papers, saw the World War II casualty lists, and watched the slow progress of Allied troops moving up the boot of Italy, it seemed that perilous times had already come. Rationing was hitting hard; discouragement was everywhere. How long could people continue in times like these?

Ruth took out a small notepad from her apron pocket and started writing some words. A melody came to her as she wrote. She had no formal music training, and she wasn't trying to do something to make herself famous, but it was the right song for the right time. Soon people around the world were singing it.

Years later, when she watched a Billy Graham telecast and heard George Beverly Shea sing it, tears came to her eyes and she said, "I can't believe I had any part in writing this song. I just feel that God gave it to me, and I gave it to the world."

Scriptures: Isaiah 26:3-4; 2 Timothy 3:1; Hebrews 6:19
Themes: Assurance, Hope, Trust

In times like these you need a Savior,
In times like these you need an anchor;
Be very sure, be very sure your anchor holds and grips the Solid Rock!

This Rock is Jesus, yes, He's the One;
This Rock is Jesus, the only One!
(1&2) Be very sure, be very sure
Your anchor holds and grips the Solid Rock!
(3) I'm very sure, I'm very sure
My anchor holds and grips the Solid Rock!

In times like these you need the Bible,
In times like these O be not idle;
Be very sure, be very sure your anchor holds and grips the Solid Rock!

In times like these I have a Savior,
In times like these I have an anchor;
I'm very sure, I'm very sure my anchor holds and grips the Solid Rock!

Written by: Ruth Caye Jones
© 1944 New Spring (ASCAP)
All rights reserved. Used by permission.

IT IS WELL WITH MY SOUL

The year had been filled with tragedy when Horatio Spafford, a forty-three-year-old Chicago businessman, penned this hymn. He and his wife were still grieving over the death of their son when the Great Chicago Fire struck and caused them financial disaster. He realized that his family needed to get away, so that fall he decided to take his wife and four daughters to England. His wife and daughters went ahead on the SS *Ville du Havre;* he planned to follow in a few days.

But on the Atlantic the *Ville du Havre* was struck by another ship and sank within twelve minutes. More than two hundred lives were lost, including the Spaffords' four daughters. When the survivors were brought to shore at Cardiff, Wales, Mrs. Spafford cabled her husband with the words, "Saved alone."

303

He booked passage on the next ship. It was while crossing the Atlantic that Spafford penned the words to the hymn: "When sorrows like sea-billows roll . . . / 'It is well, it is well with my soul.' "

Scriptures: Psalm 31:14; Psalm 46:1; Romans 5:2-4; 1 Peter 4:19
Themes: Assurance, Comfort, Hope, Peace

When peace like a river attendeth my way,
When sorrows like sea-billows roll;
Whatever my lot, Thou hast taught me to say,
"It is well, it is well with my soul."

It is well with my soul,
It is well, it is well with my soul.

Though Satan should buffet, tho' trials should come,
Let this blest assurance control,
That Christ has regarded my helpless estate,
And hath shed His own blood for my soul.

My sin—O, the bliss of this glorious thought,
My sin—not in part but the whole,
Is nailed to the cross and I bear it no more,
Praise the Lord, praise the Lord, O my soul!

And, Lord, haste the day when the faith shall be sight,
The clouds be rolled back as a scroll,
The trump shall resound and the Lord shall descend,
"Even so"—it is well with my soul.

HORATIO GATES SPAFFORD (1828–1888)

JESUS, I AM RESTING, RESTING

In 1901, J. Hudson Taylor, the founder of the China Inland Mission, kept getting messages of his missionaries being assassinated by Chinese terrorists. His mission had nearly one thousand missionaries in the country, and one by one they were being killed in the Boxer Rebellion. A total of 189 Protestant missionaries were killed.

There wasn't anything Taylor could do, except pray and sing. Sing? Yes, day after day his coworkers heard Taylor singing softly the words to this, his favorite hymn: "Jesus, I am resting, resting in the joy of what Thou art."

It isn't easy to rest in the midst of disaster, but as we do, Jesus gives an inner peace and satisfaction, and we will, as the hymn says, find out the greatness of his loving heart.

Scriptures: Psalm 23:2; Isaiah 30:15; Isaiah 32:17; Matthew 11:28; Hebrews 4:9
Themes: Comfort, Assurance, Trust

Jesus, I am resting, resting
In the joy of what Thou art;
I am finding out the greatness
Of Thy loving heart.
Thou hast bid me gaze upon Thee,
And Thy beauty fills my soul,
For by Thy transforming power,
Thou hast made me whole.

Jesus, I am resting, resting
In the joy of what Thou art;
I am finding out the greatness
Of Thy loving heart.

O, how great Thy loving-kindness,
Vaster, broader than the sea!
O, how marvelous Thy goodness,
Lavished all on me!
Yes, I rest in Thee, Beloved,
Know what wealth of grace is Thine,
Know Thy certainty of promise,
And have made it mine.

Simply trusting Thee, Lord Jesus,
I behold Thee as Thou art,
And Thy love, so pure, so changeless,
Satisfies my heart;
Satisfies its deepest longings,
Meets, supplies its every need,
Compasseth me round with blessings:
Thine is love indeed!

Ever lift Thy face upon me
As I work and wait for Thee;

Resting 'neath Thy smile, Lord Jesus,
Earth's dark shadows flee.
Brightness of my Father's glory,
Sunshine of my Father's face,
Keep me ever trusting, resting,
Fill me with Thy grace.

JEAN SOPHIA PIGOTT (1845–1882)

JESUS, THOU JOY OF LOVING HEARTS

Bernard of Clairvaux knew what he was talking about. A nobleman by birth, he gave up his life of luxury to follow Christ and become a monk. So when he writes about being "unfilled" by "the best bliss that earth imparts," we can see he knew.

The monastic life was often one of withdrawal. Monks had their own communities, which were largely self-sufficient. Thus they could work and pray in relative solitude, focusing exclusively on Jesus and his joy. But Bernard broke out of that mold. If Jesus was going to "chase the dark night of sin away" and "shed o'er the world [His] holy light," he would surely use devoted Christians working in the world.

Bernard became an unusually public figure for a monk. He challenged popes and political leaders to live righteously. He urged professors to teach truth. He launched evangelistic campaigns, and many were won to Christ as a result.

We can learn much from Bernard's example. We do need time for "calm and bright" moments alone with Christ. But we also need to let him send us forth in service.

Scriptures: John 6:35; John 15:11; Philippians 3:7-8
Themes: Joy, Consecration, Love

Jesus, Thou joy of loving hearts!
Thou fount of life! Thou light of men!
From the best bliss that earth imparts,
We turn unfilled to Thee again.

Thy truth unchanged hath ever stood;
Thou savest those that on Thee call;
To them that seek Thee, Thou art good;
To them that find Thee, all-in-all.

We taste Thee, O Thou living bread,
And long to feast upon Thee still;
We drink of Thee, the fountainhead,
And thirst our souls from Thee to fill!

Our restless spirits yearn for Thee
Where'er our changeful lot is cast,
Glad, when Thy gracious smile we see,
Blest, when our faith can hold Thee fast.

O Jesus, ever with us stay;
Make all our moments calm and bright;
Chase the dark night of sin away;
Shed o'er the world Thy holy light!

ATTRIBUTED TO BERNARD OF CLAIRVAUX (1091–1153)
Translated by Ray Palmer (1808–1887)

LIKE A RIVER GLORIOUS

The world is filled with violence, terrorism, and senseless crime. How is it possible to enjoy inner peace when there is so much turmoil all around us?

By drawing on two passages from the prophet Isaiah, the hymnwriter Frances Ridley Havergal tells how. In Isaiah 48:18, God promises peace like a river. And in Isaiah 26:3 Isaiah writes, "You will keep in perfect peace him whose mind is steadfast, because he trusts in you" (NIV).

In one of her last letters, Havergal quoted Romans 5:1: "We have peace with God." Then she added as a note to her friend, "It is yours already, purchased for you, made for you, sealed for you, pledged to you, by the word of the Father and the precious blood of Jesus." It is not merely peace that God promises, but perfect peace—perfected, completed in Christ.

Scriptures: Isaiah 26:3; Isaiah 48:18; John 14:27; John 16:33; Romans 5:1
Themes: Peace, Protection

Like a river glorious
Is God's perfect peace,
Over all victorious
In its bright increase;
Perfect, yet it floweth

Fuller ev'ry day,
Perfect, yet it groweth
Deeper all the way.

Stayed upon Jehovah,
Hearts are fully blest—
Finding as He promised
Perfect peace and rest.

Hidden in the hollow
Of His blessed hand,
Never foe can follow,
Never traitor stand;
Not a surge of worry,
Not a shade of care,
Not a blast of hurry
Touch the spirit there.

Ev'ry joy or trial
Falleth from above,
Traced upon our dial
By the sun of love;
We may trust Him fully
All for us to do—
They who trust Him wholly
Find Him wholly true.

FRANCES RIDLEY HAVERGAL (1836–1879)

NO, NOT ONE

Many hymns are somewhat autobiographical. The blind songwriter Fanny Crosby writes of looking forward to that day in heaven when she will see Jesus face-to-face. The former slave captain John Newton writes of God's amazing grace that saved "a wretch like me."

You might wonder about Johnson Oatman writing "No, Not One." The insurance business in which he worked wasn't satisfying to him. Although he was an ordained Methodist minister, he couldn't get a church, apparently because he wasn't a good preacher. He liked to sing, but everyone compared him to his father who was one of the best singers in the state. So even though he had above-average abilities in singing, he didn't know where he fit in. That's why he needed a friend like Jesus.

We all need that kind of friend. You don't have to be down and out or in the hospital to sing this song. We all go through times of stress and loneliness. We are all in need of a friend, and Jesus knows that.

Scriptures: Proverbs 17:17; Proverbs 18:24; John 15:15; Galatians 4:6-7
Themes: Comfort, Hope, Help

There's not a friend like the lowly Jesus,
No, not one! no, not one!
None else could heal all our soul's diseases,
No, not one! no, not one!

Jesus knows all about our struggles, He will guide till the day is done;
There's not a friend like the lowly Jesus, No, not one! no, not one!

No friend like Him is so high and holy,
No, not one! no, not one!
And yet no friend is so meek and lowly,
No, not one! no, not one!

There's not an hour that He is not near us,
No, not one! no, not one!
No night so dark but His love can cheer us,
No, not one! no, not one!

Did ever saint find this Friend forsake him?
No, not one! no, not one!
Or sinner find that He would not take him?
No, not one! no, not one!

Was e'er a gift like the Savior given?
No, not one! no, not one!
Will He refuse us a home in heaven?
No, not one! no, not one!

JOHNSON OATMAN JR. (1856–1922)

O GOD, OUR HELP IN AGES PAST

In 1714, Queen Anne of England lay dying, and she had no son or daughter to succeed her. Who would be the new ruler? All of Britain was concerned.

Isaac Watts had reason to worry. His father had been imprisoned under the previous regime because his views did not please the ruling family. As a young child, Isaac had been carried by his mother to visit his father in jail. Queen Anne had brought a new tolerance and had given freedom to Isaac's father. But now what?

Isaac Watts turned to Psalm 90 for his answers, and he wrote a hymn about time. God stands above time, and in him all our anxieties can be laid to rest. When the events of the day bring worry and concern, the God of the ages remains our eternal refuge.

Scriptures: Psalm 33:20; Psalm 90:1-4; Isaiah 26:4
Themes: Security, Providence, Protection

> O God, our help in ages past,
> Our hope for years to come,
> Our shelter from the stormy blast,
> And our eternal home!
>
> Under the shadow of Thy throne
> Still may we dwell secure;
> Sufficient is Thine arm alone,
> And our defense is sure.
>
> Before the hills in order stood,
> Or earth received her frame,
> From everlasting Thou art God,
> To endless years the same.
>
> A thousand ages in Thy sight
> Are like an evening gone;
> Short as the watch that ends the night,
> Before the rising sun.
>
> Time, like an ever-rolling stream,
> Bears all its sons away;
> They fly, forgotten, as a dream
> Dies at the opening day.

O God, our help in ages past,
Our hope for years to come;
Be Thou our guide while life shall last,
And our eternal home.

ISAAC WATTS (1674–1748)

PEACE, PERFECT PEACE

In 1875, while Edward Bickersteth was vacationing in Harrowgate, England, he heard a sermon on Isaiah 26:3, "Thou wilt keep him in perfect peace, whose mind is stayed on thee" (KJV). The minister explained that the original Hebrew read, "Thou wilt keep him in peace, peace. . . ." In Hebrew, the repetition of a word indicates intensity or perfection.

That afternoon Bickersteth visited a dying relative. When he found the man deeply distressed, he withdrew for a while and wrote this hymn. Then he returned to read Scripture and to share the comforting lines he had written.

As we read the first line of each stanza, we are pummeled by the problems of our modern society. Headlines are filled with violence; hectic lifestyles frustrate and worry us; discouragements overwhelm us; loneliness causes heartache. But while problems are found in the first line of each stanza, there is one word that appears consistently in the second line—*Jesus*. His presence in our problems and heartaches makes all the difference.

Scriptures: Isaiah 26:3; John 16:31-33; Philippians 4:7
Themes: Peace, Comfort, Victory

Peace, perfect peace, in this dark world of sin?
The blood of Jesus whispers peace within.

Peace, perfect peace, by thronging duties pressed?
To do the will of Jesus, this is rest.

Peace, perfect peace, with sorrows surging round?
On Jesus' bosom naught but calm is found.

Peace, perfect peace, our future all unknown?
Jesus we know, and He is on the throne.

Peace, perfect peace, death shadowing us and ours?
Jesus has vanquished death and all its powers.

It is enough: earth's struggles soon shall cease,
And Jesus, call us to heav'n's perfect peace.
EDWARD HENRY BICKERSTETH (1825–1906)

PEACE IN THE VALLEY

Thomas Dorsey, the author of "Precious Lord, Take My Hand," became the best known African American composer of gospel music in America. And his work gained acceptance in churches of both the North and the South.

It was in 1939 that "Peace in the Valley" was written. Dorsey said, "It was just before Hitler sent his war chariots into western Europe. I was on a train going through southern Indiana on the way to Cincinnati. . . . I passed through a valley on the train. Horses, cows, and sheep were all grazing together in this little valley. A little brook was running through the valley. . . . Everything seemed so peaceful. . . . It made me wonder. . . . What's the matter with mankind?"

Soon he scribbled words to a song, and the tune he set it to seemed to combine gospel, blues, and country in a unique way. Country singers picked it up and by the 1960s it had become one of the ten best-known country gospel songs of all-time.

Scriptures: Psalm 34:14; Proverbs 3:17; Isaiah 66:12; John 14:27
Themes: Heaven, Contentment

AUTHOR: THOMAS A. DORSEY (1899–1993)

PRECIOUS PROMISE

When people commute to work on a train or bus, some sleep, some read a newspaper, some read a book, some do crossword puzzles, and some just stare out the window and daydream.

Nathaniel Niles, the author of this hymn, was a New York City lawyer who commuted by train from Morristown, New Jersey, every day. One day he had bought his newspaper and was prepared to read it, but he couldn't get Psalm 32:8 out of his mind. Perhaps he had read it that morning, or perhaps his pastor had preached on it the week before. We don't know. In the King James Version, Psalm 32:8 says simply, "I will guide thee with mine eye." A beautiful promise.

Niles looked for a blank piece of paper, but he didn't have any with him, so he took his newspaper and started scribbling in the margin. By the time the train pulled into the station in New York City, he had completed the song.

Scriptures: Psalm 32:8; Psalm 33:18; Proverbs 3:5-6
Themes: Promises, Guidance, Hope

Precious promise God hath given
To the weary passerby,
On the way from earth to heaven,
"I will guide thee with Mine eye."

I will guide thee, I will guide thee,
I will guide thee with Mine eye;
On the way from earth to heaven,
I will guide thee with Mine eye.

When temptations almost win thee,
And thy trusted watchers fly,
Let this promise ring within thee,
"I will guide thee with Mine eye."

When thy secret hopes have perished
In the grave of years gone by,
Let this promise still be cherished,
"I will guide thee with Mine eye."

When the shades of life are falling,
And the hour has come to die,
Hear the trusty Pilot calling,
"I will guide thee with Mine eye."

NATHANIEL NILES IN *SUNSHINE FOR SUNDAY SCHOOLS*, 1873

ROCK OF AGES

It may seem strange that such a sedate hymn as "Rock of Ages" was written by a feisty, pugnacious man named Augustus Toplady. Converted under a Methodist evangelist while attending the University of Dublin, Toplady decided to prepare for the ministry. Although he was impressed with the spirit of Methodism, Toplady strongly disagreed with the Wesleyan theology and waged a running battle with the Wesleys through tracts, sermons, and even hymns. "Wesley," said Toplady, "is guilty of

Satan's shamelessness." Wesley retorted, "I do not fight with chimney sweeps!"

Toplady wrote "Rock of Ages" to conclude a magazine article in which he emphasized that, just as England could never repay its national debt, so humans through their own efforts could never satisfy the eternal justice of God. He died of tuberculosis and overwork at the age of thirty-eight, two years after he published his own hymnal, in which "Rock of Ages" and Charles Wesley's "Jesus, Lover of My Soul" were placed side by side.

Scriptures: Exodus 33:17-23; Psalm 62:5-8; 1 Corinthians 10:1-4
Themes: Salvation, Refuge, Forgiveness

Rock of Ages, cleft for me,
Let me hide myself in Thee;
Let the water and the blood,
From Thy wounded side which flowed,
Be of sin the double cure,
Save from wrath and make me pure.

Could my tears forever flow,
Could my zeal no languor know,
These for sin could not atone;
Thou must save, and Thou alone.
In my hand no price I bring;
Simply to Thy cross I cling.

While I draw this fleeting breath,
When my eyes shall close in death,
When I rise to worlds unknown,
And behold Thee on Thy throne,
Rock of Ages, cleft for me,
Let me hide myself in Thee.

AUGUSTUS TOPLADY (1740–1778)

SUN OF MY SOUL, THOU SAVIOR DEAR

When someone asked Alfred, Lord Tennyson what Jesus Christ meant to him, he pointed to an open flower and responded, "What the sun is to that flower, Jesus Christ is to my soul. He is the Sun of my soul." The prophet Malachi called the Messiah the Sun of righteousness, who would rise with healing in his wings.

So John Keble was using a familiar title for Jesus when he wrote this poem. Keble first published "Sun of my Soul, Thou Savior Dear" in a book called *The Christian Year,* which included poems to be used by believers for worship throughout the church year. An extremely modest man, Keble published this book anonymously. He used the proceeds from the sale of his book to maintain the small village church near Oxford in which he served for more than three decades.

Throughout his ministry, Keble was known as an outstanding preacher and a careful Bible scholar. This hymn was inspired by Luke 24:29, where two disciples on the way to Emmaus were met by Jesus. They begged him to stay with them because it was getting late. Maybe it was getting late, but if the "Sun of my soul" was with them, it would never get dark.

Scriptures: Psalm 27:1-4; Psalm 84:11-12; Luke 1:77-79
Themes: Devotion, Prayer, Security

Sun of my soul, Thou Savior dear,
It is not night if Thou be near;
O may no earthborn cloud arise
To hide Thee from Thy servant's eyes.

When the soft dews of kindly sleep
My wearied eyelids gently steep,
Be my last thought, how sweet to rest
Forever on my Savior's breast.

Abide with me from morn till eve,
For without Thee I cannot live;
Abide with me when night is nigh,
For without Thee I dare not die.

If some poor wandering child of Thine
Has spurned, today, the voice divine,
Now, Lord, the gracious work begin;
Let him no more lie down in sin.

Watch by the sick; enrich the poor
With blessings from Thy boundless store;
Be every mourner's sleep tonight,
Like infants' slumbers, pure and light.

Come near and bless us when we wake,
Ere through the world our way we take,
Till in the ocean of Thy love
We lose ourselves in heaven above.

JOHN KEBLE (1792–1866)

SUNSHINE IN MY SOUL TODAY

Schoolteaching has never been an easy profession. Eliza Hewitt found that out from personal experience. As a young schoolteacher in Philadelphia, she was disciplining a student who responded by striking her across the back with a heavy slate. For six months she was in a heavy cast. All winter long she was confined to her room.

Finally she was released and allowed to take a short walk outside. It was a bright spring day, a day she would never forget. After she took her short walk, enjoying the azaleas of the springtime, she returned to write the joyful gospel song in praise to her Savior, "Sunshine in My Soul Today."

Scriptures: Nehemiah 8:10; Psalm 148:1-3; Luke 1:77-79
Themes: Joy, Peace, Salvation

There's sunshine in my soul today,
More glorious and bright
Than glows in any earthly sky,
For Jesus is my light.

O there's sunshine, blessed sunshine,
When the peaceful, happy moments roll;
When Jesus shows His smiling face,
There is sunshine in my soul.

There's music in my soul today,
A carol to my King,
And Jesus, listening, can hear
The songs I cannot sing.

There's springtime in my soul today,
For, when the Lord is near,
The dove of peace sings in my heart,
The flow'rs of grace appear.

There's gladness in my soul today,
And hope and praise and love,
For blessings which He gives me now,
For joys "laid up" above.

ELIZA EDMUNDS HEWITT (1851–1920)

THE KING OF LOVE MY SHEPHERD IS

The twenty-third Psalm has been sung in hundreds of different forms since King David wrote the words some three thousand years ago. It isn't only because the psalm is so beautiful and expresses the Lord's handling of his sheep so well, but also because Christians have found so much to appreciate in Jesus as the Good Shepherd.

The version from the 1650 *Scottish Psalter,* "The Lord's My Shepherd, I'll Not Want," has certainly stood the test of time. But when Henry Baker, an Anglican clergyman, was asked to compile a new hymnal for his church, he added this hymn, a paraphrase of Psalm 23, to the appendix of the hymnal. The fact that his hymnal sold more than sixty million copies indicates he did his job well.

As Baker was dying, his last words came from the third stanza of this hymn: "Perverse and foolish, oft I strayed, / But yet in love He sought me, / And on His shoulder gently laid, / And home, rejoicing, brought me."

Scriptures: Psalm 23; Psalm 95:7; John 10:9
Themes: Shepherds, Love, Comfort

The King of love my Shepherd is,
Whose goodness faileth never;
I nothing lack if I am His,
And He is mine forever.

Where streams of living water flow,
My ransomed soul He leadeth,
And where the verdant pastures grow,
With food celestial feedeth.

Perverse and foolish, oft I strayed,
But yet in love He sought me,
And on His shoulder gently laid,
And home, rejoicing, brought me.

In death's dark vale I fear no ill
With Thee, dear Lord, beside me;
Thy rod and staff my comfort still,
Thy cross before to guide me.

Thou spread'st a table in my sight;
Thy unction grace bestoweth;
And O what transport of delight
From Thy pure chalice floweth!

And so through all the length of days
Thy goodness faileth never:
Good Shepherd, may I sing Thy praise
Within Thy house forever.

HENRY WILLIAMS BAKER (1821–1877)

THERE IS A BALM IN GILEAD

What is a "balm in Gilead"?

In Genesis the story of Joseph is told. Joseph's brothers beat him up and threw him into a pit. Then they sold him to a caravan passing through. The merchants were traveling from Gilead to Egypt with spices, balms, and myrrh. Gilead, the area just east of the Jordan near Galilee, was famous for its medicinal balms.

Later on in the Old Testament, we read of Jeremiah crying out for the healing of his people. "Is there no balm in Gilead?" he asks (8:22, NIV). He was looking for a cure for Israel in Gilead but he found none. It would be like going to the local drugstore and finding no medicine to treat your illness. Of course, the problem that Israel had was not a physical ailment but a spiritual one. The disease was sin. We all suffer from "sin-sick souls." We are unable to live righteous lives in our own strength. This is the human condition.

Fortunately, this song answers Jeremiah's question with a resounding *yes.* There is a balm in Gilead, and it is found in the simple truth that Jesus died for all, and that he alone can heal the soul sick with sin. Jesus himself is the balm of Gilead.

Scriptures: Jeremiah 8:21-22; Matthew 9:12; Matthew 11:2-4; Romans 5:8; 2 Corinthians 5:15
Themes: Comfort, Encouragement

Sometimes I feel discouraged,
And think my work's in vain,
But then the Holy Spirit
Revives my soul again.

There is a balm in Gilead
To make the wounded whole;
There is a balm in Gilead
To heal the sin-sick soul.

If you cannot preach like Peter,
If you cannot pray like Paul,
You can tell the love of Jesus,
And say, "He died for all."

TRADITIONAL SPIRITUAL

THERE SHALL BE SHOWERS OF BLESSING

As a teenager, Daniel Whittle was a cashier at the Wells Fargo Bank in Chicago, but when the Civil War erupted, he enlisted and soon became a soldier in General Grant's Union Army. Just before he left, his mother put a New Testament in his kit, where it stayed unread. In 1863 during the siege of Vicksburg, in which nearly twenty thousand soldiers lost their lives, young Whittle was wounded and taken prisoner by Confederate troops. His right arm had to be amputated. In the hospital he finally discovered the New Testament in his kit and began to read it.

One day an orderly came and told Whittle that a man was dying in the next room and needed someone to pray with him. Whittle protested. Just because he was reading his Bible didn't mean he was a Christian, and he didn't know how to pray. But because of the urgency of the situation, Whittle went to talk with him. When the man said, "Pray for me, and ask God to forgive me," Whittle asked God to forgive his fellow soldier and then prayed for forgiveness for himself as well. Whittle got up from his knees and discovered that the soldier had died while he was praying. As for himself, Whittle had entered into new life; he had become a new creation. His mother's prayers had been answered

Whittle wrote many popular gospel songs later in his life, including

"There Shall Be Showers of Blessing." This gospel song is derived from Ezekiel 34:26 in which God promises showers of blessing upon the land.

Scriptures: Psalm 72:6; Ezekiel 34:11-26; Zechariah 8:13
Themes: Blessing, Revival, Prayer

"There shall be showers of blessing":
This is the promise of love;
There shall be seasons refreshing,
Sent from the Savior above.

Showers of blessing, showers of blessing we need:
Mercy-drops round us are falling, but for the showers we plead.

"There shall be showers of blessing"
Precious reviving again;
Over the hills and the valleys,
Sound of abundance of rain.

"There shall be showers of blessing":
Send them upon us, O Lord;
Grant to us now a refreshing,
Come, and now honor Thy Word.

"There shall be showers of blessing":
Oh, that today they might fall,
Now as to God we're confessing,
Now as on Jesus we call!

DANIEL WEBSTER WHITTLE (1840–1901)

UNDER HIS WINGS I AM SAFELY ABIDING

When William O. Cushing suddenly lost his voice, he was distraught. He didn't know what to do. He had been a pastor of several churches in New York and had enjoyed fruitful ministry. Then a paralysis affected his voice so he could no longer preach. He wondered how he could continue to serve the Lord if he couldn't preach.

He cried out to God, "O Lord, give me something to do for you." Not yet fifty years old, Cushing wondered how God could possibly use him. But God did. In the following years, Cushing wrote texts for more than three hundred hymns and gospel songs and teamed up with some of the best-known gospel composers of the day. They supplied the music, and he wrote the words. The evangelistic team of Moody and Sankey spread Cushing's songs around the world.

When he was seventy-three, this prolific hymnwriter was moved by the words of Psalm 17:8, "Hide me in the shadow of your wings," and thought about God's care for him even when everything seemed dark. This song was the result. Although he could not speak with an audible voice, God multiplied his words for generations to come.

Scriptures: Deuteronomy 33:27; Psalm 36:7; Psalm 91:1-4
Themes: Security, Comfort, Abiding

Under His wings I am safely abiding;
Though the night deepens and tempests are wild,
Still I can trust Him—I know He will keep me;
He has redeemed me and I am His child.

Under His wings, under His wings,
Who from His love can sever?
Under His wings my soul shall abide,
Safely abide forever.

Under His wings, what a refuge in sorrow!
How the heart yearningly turns to His rest!
Often when earth has no balm for my healing,
There I find comfort and there I am blest.

Under His wings, O what precious enjoyment!
There will I hide till life's trials are o'er;
Sheltered, protected, no evil can harm me;
Resting in Jesus I'm safe evermore.

WILLIAM ORCUTT CUSHING (1823–1902)

WHAT A FRIEND WE HAVE IN JESUS

Not far from Port Hope, Ontario, stands a monument with this inscription: "Four miles north, in Pengally's Cemetery, lies the philanthropist and author of this great masterpiece, written at Port Hope, 1857." Above the inscription are the words of the beloved hymn, "What a Friend We Have in Jesus." Joseph Scriven, its author, was a man who had experienced the friendship of Jesus through a life filled with personal tragedy.

When Scriven was a young man in Ireland, his fiancée accidentally drowned on the eve of their wedding. Soon after this, he set sail for Canada. He seemed destined to live his life alone, with Jesus as his only close friend. In Canada, he determined to be a friend to those in need, and he became known as the "Good Samaritan of Port Hope."

Scriven never intended to publish this hymn. He wrote the words to accompany a letter to his mother in Ireland when she became ill. He had no material resources to send her—only a reminder that the most perfect of friends, Jesus himself, was nearby.

Later, when Scriven himself was ill, a visiting friend noticed the hymn scribbled on scratch paper near his bed. "Did you write this?" asked the friend. "Well, not completely," Scriven answered, "The Lord and I did it between us."

Scriptures: Proverbs 18:24; John 15:13-16; Philippians 4:6-7
Themes: Comfort, Prayer, Jesus as Friend

What a Friend we have in Jesus,
All our sins and griefs to bear!
What a privilege to carry
Everything to God in prayer!
O what peace we often forfeit,
O what needless pain we bear,
All because we do not carry
Everything to God in prayer!

Have we trials and temptations?
Is there trouble anywhere?
We should never be discouraged,
Take it to the Lord in prayer.
Can we find a friend so faithful
Who will all our sorrows share?
Jesus knows our every weakness,
Take it to the Lord in prayer.

Are we weak and heavy-laden,
Cumbered with a load of care?
Precious Savior, still our refuge—
Take it to the Lord in prayer.
Do thy friends despise, forsake thee?
Take it to the Lord in prayer;
In His arms He'll take and shield thee,
Thou wilt find a solace there.

JOSEPH MEDLICOTT SCRIVEN (1819–1886)

WHEN ALL THY MERCIES, O MY GOD

Joseph Addison, the author of this hymn, was one of the finest essayists in English literature. In fact, he and Richard Steele perfected the essay as a literary form. Not only was he famous as a writer, but he was also elected to Parliament and eventually became Secretary of State.

These words were probably written after he had been rescued from a shipwreck off the coast of Genoa, Italy. It was published in 1712 in the London daily newspaper he edited. Addison had written an essay on gratitude and concluded it with this poem. Just before the poem, he wrote, "If gratitude is due from man to man, how much more from man to his Maker. . . . Any blessing which we enjoy . . . is the gift of Him who is the great author of good and the Father of mercies."

Scriptures: Isaiah 63:9; Ephesians 2:4; James 1:17
Themes: Grace, Comfort, Wonder

When all Thy mercies, O my God, my rising soul surveys,
Transported with the view I'm lost in wonder, love and praise.

Unnumbered comforts to my soul Thy tender care bestowed
Before my infant heart conceived from Whom those comforts flowed.

When worn with sickness, oft hast Thou with health renewed my face;
And, when in sins and sorrows bowed, revived my soul with grace.

Thru ev'ry period of my life Thy goodness I'll pursue,
And after death, in distant worlds, the glorious theme renew.

JOSEPH ADDISON (1672–1719)

YOU ARE MY HIDING PLACE

Michael Ledner, the author of this song, was going through a low point in his life. Separated from his wife, he was living in a small, rented room in Tucson, Arizona.

Seated on his bed, with his guitar on his lap and his Bible, open to Psalms, beside him, he looked for something to sing about. His eyes stopped at Psalm 32:7: "You are my hiding place." Then he recalled a phrase in Psalm 56 that says, "When I am afraid, I will put my trust in you." That was enough to get him started on a new song, "You Are My Hiding Place."

After it was finished, he had second thoughts. Looking at the words, he thought it might be too sissy. The words, *afraid, hiding,* and *weak,* were not manly sounding words at all. Then he recalled that people like David, Moses, and Paul all talked about hiding, being afraid, and being weak, and they were real men. Gradually, as he worked through his emotions, he realized that his own song was teaching him about the true nature of manliness and, indeed, of being human. After all, the apostle Paul told us that God's strength is made perfect in our weakness.

Scriptures: Psalm 32:7; Psalm 56:3; 2 Corinthians 12:9-10

Themes: Fear, Hope, Comfort

AUTHOR: MICHAEL LEDNER (B. 1952–)

COMMITMENT AND INVITATION

[Jesus said,] "Anyone who wants to be my disciple must follow me."

JOHN 12:26

ALL FOR JESUS, ALL FOR JESUS!

In studying this hymn, perhaps it's best to start with the last stanza and meditate on the wonder of it. "Jesus, glorious King of kings, deigns to call me His beloved." Frequently we recall the names of our Lord. His titles are many and glorious. But it is equally amazing to see what God calls us in Scripture. We are called saints, joint heirs, friends, and coworkers. But what most impressed this hymnwriter was that, over and over in the Bible, we are called God's beloved.

The New Testament speaks of the mystery of marriage, husband and wife belonging to each other; it's a picture of Christ and the church. He has given himself to us in remarkable love. Because of his selfless sacrifice, all the privileges of royalty belong to us. And we belong to him completely.

Scriptures: Romans 6:12-13; Colossians 3:1; Hebrews 12:1-4
Themes: Dedication, Surrender, Holiness

> All for Jesus, all for Jesus!
> All my being's ransomed pow'rs:
> All my tho'ts and words and doings,
> All my days and all my hours.
> All for Jesus! all for Jesus!
> All my days and all my hours;
> All for Jesus! all for Jesus!
> All my days and all my hours.
>
> Let my hands perform His bidding,
> Let my feet run in His ways;
> Let my eyes see Jesus only,
> Let my lips speak forth His praise.
> All for Jesus! all for Jesus!
> Let my lips speak forth His praise;
> All for Jesus! all for Jesus!
> Let my lips speak forth His praise.
>
> Since my eyes were fixed on Jesus,
> I've lost sight of all beside;
> So enchained my spirit's vision,
> Looking at the Crucified.
> All for Jesus! all for Jesus!
> Looking at the Crucified;

All for Jesus! all for Jesus!
Looking at the Crucified.

Oh, what wonder! how amazing!
Jesus, glorious King of kings,
Deigns to call me His beloved,
Lets me rest beneath His wings.
All for Jesus! all for Jesus!
Resting now beneath His wings;
All for Jesus! all for Jesus!
Resting now beneath His wings.

MARY D. JAMES (1810–1883)

ALMOST PERSUADED

When the apostle Paul was on trial before King Agrippa, he gave a strong witness to his faith, and Agrippa responded, "Do you think you can persuade me to become a Christian so quickly?" He was almost persuaded.

Philip Bliss, the author of this hymn, heard a preacher end a sermon with the words, "He who is almost persuaded is almost saved, and to be almost saved is to be entirely lost." Bliss couldn't forget those words, and he soon wrote the hymn "Almost Persuaded."

It has been used as an invitation hymn in bringing many to Jesus Christ. One young man in London said, "God used that song in drawing me to Jesus. I had been afraid. . . . For six weeks that hymn was ringing in my ears, till I accepted the invitation. I came, and am now rejoicing in the Lord, my Savior."

Scriptures: Acts 26:28; 2 Corinthians 5:17; Revelation 3:20
Themes: Invitation, Salvation, Decision

"Almost persuaded," now to believe;
"Almost persuaded," Christ to receive;
Seems now some soul to say,
"Go Spirit, go Thy way,
Some more convenient day
On Thee I'll call."

"Almost persuaded," come, come today;
"Almost persuaded," turn not away;
Jesus invites you here,

Angels are ling'ring near,
Prayers rise from hearts so dear,
O wand'rer, come.

"Almost persuaded," harvest is past!
"Almost persuaded," doom comes at last!
"Almost" cannot avail;
"Almost" is but to fail!
Sad, sad, that bitter wail,
"Almost," but lost.

PHILIP PAUL BLISS (1838–1876)

ARE YE ABLE?

In 1924, the Boston University School of Religious Education had a contest to develop a school song. No one remembers the tune that won, but another song, written by graduate student Harry Mason, has stuck in the minds of many.

In fact, a year after the contest, when Earl Marlatt, a professor at the school, was asked to write a hymn for a consecration service, he thought of Harry Mason's tune and decided to write some words to fit it. On the previous Sunday, he had preached a sermon on Matthew 20:22, so that text came to his mind, along with Mason's melody. In Matthew 20:22, Jesus asked the question: "Are you able to drink the cup that I am to drink?" And the disciples responded, "We are able" (ESV).

Scriptures: Matthew 20:22; Luke 14:27; 2 Timothy 1:7-10
Themes: Consecration, Discipleship, Courage

"Are ye able," said the Master, "to be crucified with me?"
"Yea," the sturdy dreamers answered, "To the death we follow Thee":

"Lord, we are able"—our spirits are Thine;
Remold them—make us like Thee, divine:
Thy guiding radiance above us shall be
A beacon to God, his love and loyalty.

Are ye able to remember, when a thief lifts up his eyes,
That his pardoned soul is worthy of a place in paradise?

"Are ye able?" still the Master whispers down eternity,
And heroic spirits answer now as then in Galilee:

EARL MARLATT (1892–1976)

CHRIST RECEIVETH SINFUL MEN

Although this song sounds as if it were written more recently, it really dates back to 1718, when Erdmann Neumeister, the pastor of a Lutheran church in Hamburg, Germany, wrote it. He wrote the hymn to be sung at the end of a sermon on Luke 15:2. That verse tells about the Pharisees and scribes grumbling, "This man [meaning Jesus] receives sinners and eats with them" (ESV).

About 150 years later, Emma Bevan, a British woman who was the wife of a prominent banker and fluent in German, translated this old hymn into English.

The third step came about thirty years later when James McGranahan, who pioneered developing men's choirs in meetings, took this old hymn and gave it a lilt that men would like to sing, and shortly after that the same McGranahan melody was arranged as a church hymn.

Although this hymn has gone through changes, the message has remained the same. Jesus still receives sinful men—and sinful women, too.

Scriptures: Isaiah 55:7; Luke 15:2; Romans 5:8
Themes: Salvation, Forgiveness, Repentance

Sinners Jesus will receive; sound this word of grace to all
Who the heav'nly pathway leave, all who linger, all who fall.

Sing it o'er and o'er again; Christ receiveth sinful men;
Make the message clear and plain:
Christ receiveth sinful men.

Come, and He will give you rest, trust Him, for His word is plain;
He will take the sinfulest; Christ receiveth sinful men.

Now my heart condemns me not, pure before the lot I stand;
He who cleansed me from all spot, satisfied its last demand.

Christ receiveth sinful men, even me with all my sin;
Purged from every spot and stain, Heav'n with Him I enter in.

ERDMANN NEUMEISTER (1671–1756)
Translated by Emma Bevan

COME, YE SINNERS, POOR AND NEEDY

London-born Joseph Hart struggled against God for years. When he attended church, he went to find fault. After he heard a sermon by John Wesley, he responded by writing a tract, "The Unreasonableness of Religion." He was a language teacher by profession, but spiritually he was (in his own words) a "loose backslider, an audacious apostle, and a bold-faced rebel." Then he came under conviction. At times he was afraid to sleep, fearing he would "awake in hell." He went from church to church to find peace, but as he said, "Everything served only to condemn me."

Finally, at the age of forty-five, he wandered into a Moravian chapel in London and heard words of hope. On returning home he knelt in prayer.

Three years later, he became a minister and began writing hymns to touch the hearts of others who had experienced similar spiritual struggles. The words of his hymns come from the heart of someone who has been there.

Scriptures: Mark 2:16-17; Romans 5:8-10; Ephesians 2:1-8
Themes: Salvation, Jesus' Love, Grace

Come, ye sinners, poor and needy,
Weak and wounded, sick and sore;
Jesus ready stands to save you,
Full of pity, love, and power;
He is able, He is able,
He is willing; doubt no more.

Now, ye needy, come and welcome;
God's free bounty glorify;
True belief and true repentance,
Every grace that brings you nigh;
Without money, without money,
Come to Jesus Christ and buy.

Let not conscience make you linger,
Nor of fitness fondly dream;
All the fitness He requireth
Is to feel your need of Him:
This He gives you, this He gives you;
'Tis the Spirit's glimmering beam.

Come, ye weary, heavy laden,
Bruised and mangled by the Fall;
If you tarry till you're better,
You will never come at all;
Not the righteous, not the righteous;
Sinners Jesus came to call.

JOSEPH HART (1712–1768)

COME INTO THE HOLY OF HOLIES

John Sellers, the writer of this worship chorus, was raised in the Salvation Army, so he knew about church music. He says, "Just as soon as you could breathe and sit up, you had a horn in your mouth."

As he grew older, he began studying what the Bible had to say about praise and worship. Having a personal relationship with God that goes beyond simple head knowledge was thrilling to him. In the Old Testament he read of how the high priest went into the Holy of Holies in the Temple once a year. No one else was allowed in. A rope was tied to the leg of the high priest so he could be dragged out in case he was overcome in the performance of his duties.

Then Sellers read in the New Testament that at Jesus' crucifixion the veil of the Temple was ripped in two. That meant believers could enter the Holy of Holies and approach God directly. This is what Jesus' ministry was all about, Sellers says: "the ripping of the veil." Once he saw that biblical truth, he wrote "Come into the Holy of Holies."

Scriptures: Leviticus 16:1-5; Luke 23:45; Hebrews 10:19-23
Themes: Prayer, Communion, Worship

Come into the Holy of Holies. Enter by the blood of the Lamb.
Come into His presence with singing,
Worship at the throne of God.
Lifting holy hands to the King of kings. Worship Jesus.

JOHN SELLERS
© 1984 by Integrity's Hosanna! Music/ASCAP

DEPTH OF MERCY!

Sometimes when Charles Wesley wrote a hymn, there was no stopping him. You might think that after writing six or seven thousand hymns, he would slow down or at least start to write some shorter choruses. But he didn't.

This hymn, "Depth of Mercy," is an example. It was written with thirteen stanzas, but modern hymnals usually condense the hymn to four stanzas. Wesley originally entitled the hymn "After a Relapse into Sin," and he had much to say about man's sinfulness and God's wonderful grace.

In the four stanzas printed below, the plight of the wanderer is depicted in the first three stanzas. After wandering away from God's love over and over again, the Christian asks, "Depth of mercy! can there be / Mercy still reserved for me?" The fourth verse concludes with the answer: "God is love! I know, I feel, / Jesus weeps and loves me still."

Scriptures: Romans 8:38-39; Ephesians 2:4-6; 1 John 1:9
Themes: God's Mercy, Forgiveness, Love of God

Depth of mercy! can there be
Mercy still reserved for me?
Can my God His wrath forbear,
Me, the chief of sinners, spare?

I my Master have denied;
I afresh have crucified,
Oft profaned His hallowed name,
Put Him to an open shame.

Now incline me to repent;
Let me now my sins lament;
Now my foul revolt deplore,
Weep, believe, and sin no more.

There for me the Savior stands,
Holding forth His wounded hands;
God is love! I know, I feel,
Jesus weeps and loves me still.

CHARLES WESLEY (1707–1788)

GIVE OF YOUR BEST TO THE MASTER

The Old Testament prophet Malachi had a problem. The people were bringing substandard sacrifices to the Temple, and the Lord didn't like it (Malachi 1:6-14). "When you give blind animals as sacrifices, isn't that wrong?" the Lord asked. It wasn't that the people were too poor to afford healthy animals, they just didn't think sacrifices to the Lord were all that important. "You say, 'It's too hard to serve the LORD,' and you turn up your noses at my commands" the Lord charged. He went on to say that he deserved better treatment from them.

The New Testament echoes this principle and expands it. Our whole lives are offerings to God. Paul told the slaves at Colosse, "Whatever you do, work at it with all your heart, as working for the Lord, not for men" (Colossians 3:23, NIV). Whoever your earthly master may be, you are ultimately serving the Lord.

Scriptures: Malachi 1:6-14; Luke 21:2; Colossians 3:23; 1 Peter 2:21-24
Themes: Dedication, Stewardship, Surrender

Give of your best to the Master,
Give of the strength of your youth;
Throw your soul's fresh, glowing ardor
Into the battle for truth.
Jesus has set the example—
Dauntless was He, young and brave;
Give Him your loyal devotion,
Give Him the best that you have.

Give of your best to the Master;
Give of the strength of your youth;
Clad in salvation's full armor,
Join in the battle for truth.

Give of your best to the Master,
Give Him first place in your heart;
Give Him first place in your service;
Consecrate every part.
Give, and to you shall be given—
God His beloved Son gave;
Gratefully seeking to serve Him,
Give Him the best that you have.

Give of your best to the Master,
Naught else is worthy His love;
He gave Himself for your ransom,
Gave up His glory above;
Laid down His life without murmur,
You from sin's ruin to save;
Give Him your heart's adoration,
Give Him the best that you have.

HOWARD BENJAMIN GROSE (1851–1939)

HAVE THINE OWN WAY, LORD

At forty, Adelaide Pollard was trying unsuccessfully to raise support to go to Africa as a missionary. She wondered why the Lord could so burden her with the needs of Africa, but not make it possible for her to go. During this time of discouragement, she attended a small prayer meeting where an elderly woman prayed, "Lord, it doesn't matter what You bring into our lives, just have Your way with us."

That night, Pollard went home and read the story of Jeremiah's visit to the potter's house, and later that evening she wrote this hymn. She said that she had always felt the Lord was molding her and preparing her for his service. Then all of a sudden, he seemed to have deserted her.

"Perhaps," she reasoned, "my questioning of God's will shows a flaw in my life. So God decided to break me, as the potter broke the defective vessel, and then to mold my life again in his own pattern."

Scriptures: Jeremiah 18:3-6; Romans 9:20-21; Galatians 2:20
Themes: Consecration, Confession, Humility

Have Thine own way, Lord! Have Thine own way!
Thou art the potter; I am the clay.
Mold me and make me after Thy will,
While I am waiting, yielded and still.

Have Thine own way, Lord! Have Thine own way!
Search me and try me, Master, today!
Whiter than snow, Lord, wash me just now,
As in Thy presence humbly I bow.

Have Thine own way, Lord! Have Thine own way!
Wounded and weary, help me, I pray!

Power, all power, surely is Thine!
Touch me and heal me, Savior divine!

Have Thine own way, Lord! Have Thine own way!
Hold o'er my being absolute sway!
Fill with Thy Spirit till all shall see
Christ only, always, living in me!

ADELAIDE ADDISON POLLARD (1862–1934)

HIS WAY WITH THEE

He didn't know how much longer he could take it. Cyrus Nusbaum was a young Methodist pastor struggling to care for seven congregations. It was hard on him and maybe even harder on his wife. He wrote, "It has been a most difficult task, strenuous and discouraging, and the income pitifully small."

When Nusbaum and his wife went to the annual denominational conference that year, they were praying that he would be appointed to a better charge. But he wasn't. He was sent back to the same place.

When he got the news, he stayed up late. This is how he described his feelings: "I was very unhappy and a spirit of rebellion seemed to possess me. About midnight, I finally knelt in prayer beside my chair. After some struggle, a deep peace came stealing into my heart. I told the Lord that I would be willing to let him have his way with me regardless of the cost."

Then the inspiration for the song came to him, and he wrote "His Way with Thee."

Scriptures: Romans 12:1-2; 1 Corinthians 6:19-20; 1 Peter 5:6
Themes: Surrender, Consecration, Service

Would you live for Jesus and be always pure and good?
Would you walk with Him within the narrow road?
Would you have Him bear your burden, carry all your load?
Let Him have His way with thee.

His power can make you what you ought to be;
His blood can cleanse your heart and make you free;
His love can fill your soul, and you will see
'Twas best for Him to have His way with thee.

Would you have Him make you free and follow at His call?
Would you know the peace that comes by giving all?

Would you have Him save you, so that you need never fall?
Let Him have His way with thee.

Would you in His kingdom find a place of constant rest?
Would you prove Him true in providential test?
Would you in His service labor always at your best?
Let Him have His way with thee.

CYRUS SILVESTER NUSBAUM (1861–1937)

HOLD THE FORT

Shortly after the Civil War, Philip Bliss, the author of this gospel song, heard Major W. D. Whittle give an illustration he couldn't forget. The text was Revelation 2:25, which closes with the words "Hold fast till I come" (KJV). Major Whittle told the story of a small group of Federal soldiers who were given the task of guarding a vital storage area during the Civil War. The troops were under heavy attack from the Confederate Army, which was much larger and stronger. They received a message asking them to surrender, but just at that time they got another message. It was just one short sentence from their commander, General Sherman: "Hold the fort, for I am coming. Sherman."

The captain of the small group signaled back, "Sir, we will." Then Major Whittle said, "And they certainly did, with the result that the supplies and the soldiers were saved."

After he heard the story, Philip Bliss couldn't get to sleep. He pictured Jesus in the distance signaling to the Christian Church, "Hold the fort, for I am coming." So he got up and wrote this gospel song.

Scriptures: Joshua 1:5-7; Ephesians 6:10-20; 1 Timothy 6:12; Revelation 2:25
Themes: Conflict, Perseverance, Strength

Ho, my comrade! See the signal Waving in the sky!
Reinforcements now appearing, victory is nigh.

"Hold the fort, for I am coming," Jesus signals still;
Wave the answer back to heaven, "By Thy grace we will."

See the mighty host advancing, Satan leading on;
Mighty men around us falling, Courage almost gone!

See the glorious banner waving! Hear the trumpet blow!
In our Leader's name we triumph over ev'ry foe.

Fierce and long the battle rages, but our help is near;
Onward comes our great Commander, cheer, my comrades, cheer!

PHILIP PAUL BLISS (1838–1876)

I AM THINE, O LORD

The composer of the music to this gospel song was known for many things other than gospel music. He was an inventor, a businessman who owned a large woodworking machinery plant in Cincinnati, and a respected civic leader. He was on his way to accumulating a fortune. But what William Doane enjoyed most was serving as Sunday school superintendent at his church and writing music. He became Fanny Crosby's principal collaborator in writing gospel songs.

One evening as Fanny Crosby visited his home in Cincinnati, they were talking about what a wonderful thing it is to enjoy the nearness of God, to feel his presence, to delight in his love. Suddenly Fanny Crosby, the famous blind songwriter, stopped and said she had an idea for a song. Line by line, verse by verse, she dictated it to him. The next morning, Doane added the music.

Fanny Crosby found delight in writing gospel songs; William Doane found delight serving as a Christian businessman. But both agreed that there was no delight that equaled the delight of enjoying the presence of God.

Scriptures: Psalm 73:28; Romans 12:1-2; Hebrews 10:22; James 4:7-8
Themes: Consecration, Prayer

I am Thine, O Lord, I have heard Thy voice,
And it told Thy love to me;
But I long to rise in the arms of faith,
And be closer drawn to Thee.

Draw me nearer, nearer, nearer, blessed Lord,
To the cross where Thou hast died;
Draw me nearer, nearer, nearer, blessed Lord,
To Thy precious, bleeding side.

Consecrate me now to Thy service, Lord,
By the pow'r of grace divine;
Let my soul look up with a steadfast hope,
And my will be lost in Thine.

O, the pure delight of a single hour
That before Thy throne I spend,
When I kneel in prayer, and with Thee, my God,
I commune as friend with friend!

There are depths of love that I cannot know
Till I cross the narrow sea;
There are heights of joy that I may not reach
Till I rest in peace with Thee.

FANNY JANE CROSBY (1820–1915)

I KNOW WHOM I HAVE BELIEVED

"It's not what you know, it's who you know." That's what we say when job hunting, but it's also a foundational Christian truth. You can study an entire lifetime to try to discover who God is and how to reach him. But it all comes down to one question: Do you know Jesus?

As a POW during the Civil War, Daniel Whittle began reading the New Testament his mother had given him as he marched off to war, and he committed his life to Jesus Christ.

After the war, Whittle was promoted to the rank of major and then became a successful businessman. In 1873 he began preaching in evangelistic services, and for a quarter century he led revivals throughout the United States. He also encouraged some of the leading songwriters of his time and wrote many hymns himself, including "Showers of Blessing" and "Moment by Moment." Whittle penned this hymn in 1883, perhaps thinking back to questions he had asked during his imprisonment. There were still many things he didn't know, but he certainly did know Jesus.

Scriptures: John 14:6; Romans 8:38; 2 Timothy 1:12
Themes: Confidence, Trust, Faith

I know not why God's wondrous grace
To me He hath made known,
Nor why, unworthy, Christ in love
Redeemed me for His own.

But "I know whom I have believed,
And am persuaded that He is able
To keep that which I've committed
Unto Him against that day."

I know not how this saving faith
To me He did impart,
Nor how believing in His Word
Wrought peace within my heart.

I know not how the Spirit moves,
Convincing men of sin,
Revealing Jesus through the Word,
Creating faith in Him.

I know not when my Lord may come,
At night or noonday fair,
Nor if I'll walk the vale with Him,
Or "meet Him in the air."

DANIEL WEBSTER WHITTLE (1840–1901)

I SURRENDER ALL

Many Christians have sung this song with their fingers crossed. Or perhaps in the emotion of the church service they meant it, but they didn't realize the corners they would turn or the new opportunities they would face in the coming days. J. W. Van De Venter, the author of this hymn, meant it. He was a schoolteacher by profession but an artist at heart. Teaching school allowed him to make a living while he continued his study of drawing and painting. After evangelistic meetings in his church, friends saw his gifts in counseling and working with people and urged him to become an evangelist. For five years he wavered between his love of art and what seemed to be God's calling to evangelistic ministry.

He later recalled, "At last the pivotal hour of my life came and I surrendered all. A new day was ushered into my life. I became an evangelist and discovered down deep in my soul a talent hitherto unknown to me." A few years later, Van De Venter, remembering that decisive moment, wrote this hymn.

Scriptures: Matthew 10:38-39; Romans 12:1; Philippians 3:7-8
Themes: Surrender, Consecration, Holiness

All to Jesus I surrender,
All to Him I freely give;
I will ever love and trust Him,
In His presence daily live.

I surrender all,
I surrender all.
All to Thee, my blessed Savior,
I surrender all.

All to Jesus I surrender,
Humbly at His feet I bow,
Worldly pleasures all forsaken,
Take me, Jesus, take me now.

All to Jesus I surrender,
Make me, Savior, wholly Thine;
May Thy Holy Spirit fill me,
May I know Thy pow'r divine.

All to Jesus I surrender,
Lord, I give myself to Thee;
Fill me with Thy love and power,
Let Thy blessing fall on me.

JUDSON W. VAN DE VENTER (1855–1939)

I'VE A MESSAGE FROM THE LORD

William Ogden, the author of this hymn, had an ear for music. He enrolled in singing school when he was only eight, and soon he could not only read music but he could also write the tune down after hearing it once. At eighteen, he became the choir director of his church. During the Civil War, he served in the Indiana Volunteer Infantry, but he was proudest of organizing a choir of soldiers that became well-known in the Army of the Cumberland.

As a Christian, he loved to write gospel songs, and as he thought about the simplicity of salvation, he was reminded of a story in the Old Testament. The Israelites were bitten by poisonous snakes. God told Moses to put the image of a snake on top of a pole, so those who were bitten could be healed and live simply by looking at the pole. Jesus referred to this story in John 3 and said that he, too, would be lifted up, and that everyone who looks and believes will have eternal life.

So songwriter Ogden urges, "Look and live . . . / Look to Jesus now and live."

Scriptures: Numbers 21:8-9; John 3:14-15; Hebrews 12:2
Themes: Salvation, Conversion, Prophecy

I've a message from the Lord, Hallelujah!
The message unto you I'll give;
'Tis recorded in His Word, Hallelujah!
It is only that you "look and live."

"Look and live," my brother, live,
Look to Jesus now and live.
'Tis recorded in His word, Hallelujah!
It is only that you "look and live."

I've a message full of love, Hallelujah!
A message, O my friend, for you;
'Tis a message from above, Hallelujah!
Jesus said it, and I know 'tis true.

Life is offered unto you, Hallelujah!
Eternal life thy soul shall have,
If you'll only look to Him, Hallelujah!
Look to Jesus who alone can save.

I will tell you how I came, Hallelujah!
To Jesus when He made me whole;
'Twas believing on His name, Hallelujah!
I trusted and He saved my soul.

WILLIAM AUGUSTINE OGDEN (1841–1897)

JESUS, I COME

William Sleeper was a church planter who started a church in Worcester, Massachusetts, and three churches in Maine. Church planters have to have a special kind of temperament. Once they get a church started in one place, it is time to move to another town where a church is needed.

Eventually he returned to Worcester, Massachusetts, to be pastor of the first church he had planted. When he was nearly sixty years old, an evangelistic crusade came to town. George Stebbins, the young song leader of the crusade, had an idea, as well as the melody, for an invitation song. He went to William Sleeper and asked for help with the words. In a few days the words were written, and the song, "Ye Must Be Born Again," was used immediately in the meetings.

A few years later, Sleeper had an idea for an invitation song himself, but he needed help with the music. It would start, "Out of my bondage, sorrow and night" and have a chorus, "Jesus, I come." He wrote out the words and sent them to his young friend Stebbins to provide the music. Another gospel song was born.

Scriptures: Isaiah 1:18; Matthew 11:28; Revelation 22:17

Themes: Confession, Conversion, Salvation

Out of my bondage, sorrow and night, Jesus, I come, Jesus, I come;
Into Thy freedom, gladness and light, Jesus, I come to Thee;
Out of my sickness into Thy health, out of my want and into Thy wealth,
Out of my sin and into Thyself, Jesus, I come to Thee.

Out of my shameful failure and loss, Jesus, I come, Jesus, I come;
Into the glorious gain of Thy cross, Jesus, I come to Thee;
Out of earth's sorrows into Thy balm, out of life's storms and into Thy calm,
Out of distress to jubilant psalm, Jesus, I come to Thee.

Out of unrest and arrogant pride, Jesus, I come, Jesus, I come;
Into They blessed will to abide, Jesus, I come to Thee;
Out of myself to dwell in Thy love, out of despair into raptures above,
Upward for aye on wings like a dove, Jesus, I come to Thee.

Out of the fear and dread of the tomb, Jesus, I come, Jesus, I come;
Into the joy and light of Thy home, Jesus, I come to Thee;
Out of the depth of ruin untold, into the peace of Thy sheltering fold,
Ever Thy glorious face to behold, Jesus, I come to Thee.

WILLIAM TRUE SLEEPER (1809–1904)

JESUS CALLS US

Most of the hymns that Cecil Alexander wrote were written for children, and many of her best children's hymns were written before she was twenty years old.

When Cecil was thirty-two, she married William Alexander, a parish minister in an impoverished rural area of northern Ireland. She loved the people. One writer says, "From one house to another, from one bed of sickness to another, from one sorrow to another she went." Another describes her life this way: "Day after day she rode over the wet moorlands in all weathers, carrying food, warm clothing, medical supplies to the impoverished and sick."

One day her husband asked her to write a hymn for adults. He would be preaching on the call of Andrew by Jesus on the shores of Galilee, and he needed a hymn to go along with his sermon. So she wrote "Jesus Calls Us," a simple hymn with a powerful application. It was one of the few hymns that she wrote for adults.

Scriptures: Exodus 3:10-12; Matthew 4:18-20; Luke 9:23
Themes: Discipleship, Dedication, Service

> Jesus calls us; o'er the tumult
> Of our life's wild, restless sea,
> Day by day His sweet voice soundeth,
> Saying, "Christian, follow Me."
>
> Jesus calls us from the worship
> Of the vain world's golden store,
> From each idol that would keep us,
> Saying, "Christian, love Me more."
>
> In our joys and in our sorrows,
> Days of toil and hours of ease,
> Still He calls in cares and pleasures,
> "Christian, love Me more than these."
>
> Jesus calls us: by Thy mercies,
> Savior, may we hear Thy call,
> Give our hearts to Thine obedience,
> Serve and love Thee best of all.
>
> CECIL FRANCES ALEXANDER (1818–1895)

JESUS IS TENDERLY CALLING

A blind sixty-year-old songwriter, Fanny Crosby, and a thirty-four-year-old musician, George Stebbins, teamed up to produce this tender invitation hymn. Fanny Crosby spent most of her life in New York City, where she went to rescue missions in the Bowery neighborhood to "tenderly call" alcoholics, homeless people, and wayward youth back to the Savior.

George Stebbins had been raised on a farm and had been introduced to music by learning to play an accordion. Soon he began a new trend in church music by arranging songs for male quartets. When evangelist

Dwight L. Moody went to England and Scotland, he took young Stebbins with him, and Stebbins saw thousands respond to the tender call of Jesus Christ.

Shortly after Stebbins returned from England, he was given the words that Fanny Crosby had written, and he wrote the music. God sometimes speaks through thunder and lightning, but more often he speaks to our hearts tenderly with a still, small voice, saying, "Come home."

Scriptures: Matthew 11:28; John 1:39-43; Revelation 22:17
Themes: Invitation, Salvation, Conversion

Jesus is tenderly calling thee home—
Calling today, calling today;
Why from the sunshine of love wilt thou roam
Farther and farther away?

Calling today, calling today,
Jesus is calling, is tenderly calling today.

Jesus is calling the weary to rest—
Calling today, calling today;
Bring Him thy burden and thou shalt be blest:
He will not turn thee away.

Jesus is waiting; O come to Him now—
Waiting today, waiting today;
Come with thy sins; at His feet lowly bow;
Come, and no longer delay.

Jesus is pleading; O list to His voice:
Hear Him today, hear Him today;
They who believe on His name shall rejoice;
Quickly arise and away.

FANNY JANE CROSBY (1820–1915)

JUST AS I AM

Charlotte Elliott seemed to have everything going for her as a young woman. She was gifted as a portrait artist and also as a writer of humorous verse. Then in her early thirties she suffered a serious illness that left her weak and depressed. During her illness, a noted minister, Dr. Caesar Malan of Switzerland, came to visit her. Noticing her depression, he asked if she had peace with God. She resented the question and said she did not want to talk about it.

But a few days later she apologized to Dr. Malan. She said that she wanted to clean up some things in her life before becoming a Christian. Malan looked at her and answered, "Come just as you are." That was enough for Charlotte Elliott, and she yielded herself to the Lord that day.

Fourteen years later, remembering those words spoken to her by Caesar Malan in Brighton, England, she wrote this simple hymn that has been used to touch the hearts of millions who have also responded to Christ's invitation to come just as they are.

Scriptures: Psalm 51:1-2; John 1:29; John 3:16; John 6:35-38
Themes: Surrender, Dedication, Invitation, Salvation

Just as I am, without one plea,
But that Thy blood was shed for me,
And that Thou bidd'st me come to Thee,
O Lamb of God I come! I come!

Just as I am, and waiting not
To rid my soul of one dark blot,
To Thee, whose blood can cleanse each spot,
O Lamb of God I come! I come!

Just as I am, tho' tossed about
With many a conflict, many a doubt,
Fightings within, and fears without,
O Lamb of God I come! I come!

Just as I am, poor, wretched, blind,
Sight, riches, healing of the mind,
Yea, all I need, in Thee to find,
O Lamb of God I come! I come!

Just as I am, Thou wilt receive,
Wilt welcome, pardon, cleanse, relieve;

Because Thy promise I believe,
O Lamb of God I come! I come!

Just as I am, Thy love unknown
Hath broken ev'ry barrier down;
Now to be Thine, yea Thine alone,
O Lamb of God I come! I come!

Just as I am, of that free love
The breadth, length, depth, the height to prove,
Here for a season then above,
O Lamb of God I come! I come!

CHARLOTTE ELLIOTT (1789–1871)

LET JESUS COME INTO YOUR HEART

Lelia and her husband, Charles Morris, were active in Methodist and Holiness camp meetings in Ohio and Maryland. In 1898 at a camp meeting in Mountain Lake Park, Maryland, a refined woman responded to the altar call, and Lelia Morris went to talk with her. The woman had doubts and questions; Lelia put her arm around the woman's shoulders and told her to give her doubts to Jesus. As Lelia recalled it, she actually said, "Just now, your doubtings give o'er." The song leader had joined them and added the next phrase: "Just now, reject him no more." It was then that the evangelist added a third: "Just now, throw open the door," and then Lelia Morris put in the closer: "Let Jesus come into your heart."

Not only did the woman "let Jesus come into her heart," but Lelia Morris went home, wrote the verses to the song, and added the music. It was a song that almost wrote itself.

Scriptures: Acts 16:31; Romans 10:9-10; 2 Corinthians 6:2
Themes: Invitation, Conversion, Salvation

If you are tired of the load of your sin,
Let Jesus come into your heart;
If you desire a new life to begin,
Let Jesus come into your heart.

Just now, your doubtings give o'er; just now, reject Him no more;
Just now, throw open the door; let Jesus come into your heart.

If 'tis for purity now that you sigh,
Let Jesus come into your heart;
Fountains for cleansing are flowing nearby,
Let Jesus come into your heart.

If there's a tempest your voice cannot still,
Let Jesus come into your heart;
If there's a void this world never can fill,
Let Jesus come into your heart.

If you would join the glad songs of the blest,
Let Jesus come into your heart;
If you would enter the mansions of rest,
Let Jesus come into your heart.

LELIA NAYLOR MORRIS (1862–1929)

LORD, I'M COMING HOME

You don't usually find a hymn that was written for an individual. But "Lord, I'm Coming Home" was.

William Kirkpatrick was leading the singing at a camp meeting in rural Pennsylvania. The soloist was a man with a great voice, but he was not a Christian. Every day as the camp meeting continued, Kirkpatrick prayed for the soloist. One morning as he was praying, these words came to him: "Coming home, coming home, nevermore to roam."

Kirkpatrick continued to write the entire invitation song, and that evening he gave the manuscript to the soloist to sing. The soloist sang it while the invitation was being given, but after he finished his solo, he went down and joined the others at the altar, seeking salvation.

Kirkpatrick never dreamed that his song, which was written for one man, would bring thousands of others to the Lord through the years, but it has. Its message is universal: "I've wandered far away from God, / Now I'm coming home."

Scriptures: Genesis 31:3; Luke 15:17-21; John 1:11-12
Themes: Invitation, Salvation, Conversion

I've wandered far away from God,
Now I'm coming home;
The paths of sin too long I've trod,
Lord, I'm coming home.

Coming home, coming home, nevermore to roam,
Open wide Thine arms of love, Lord, I'm coming home.

I've wasted many precious years,
Now I'm coming home;
I now repent with bitter tears,
Lord, I'm coming home.

I'm tired of sin and straying, Lord,
Now I'm coming home;
I'll trust Thy love, believe Thy word,
Lord, I'm coming home.

My soul is sick, my heart is sore,
Now I'm coming home;
My strength renew, my hope restore,
Lord, I'm coming home.

WILLIAM JAMES KIRKPATRICK (1838–1921)

MORE LOVE TO THEE, O CHRIST

Elizabeth Payson Prentiss came from a godly home. Her father, Edward Payson, was a brilliant Bible teacher and a loving father. Her husband, a gifted Presbyterian minister, later became a seminary professor.

But despite her many blessings, Prentiss's life was not easy. She suffered from severe headaches and chronic insomnia. One of her children suddenly died, and a short time later a second child died. One evening, after putting flowers on the graves of her children, Prentiss cried out in anguish, "Our home is broken up, our lives wrecked, our hopes shattered, our dreams dissolved. I don't think I can stand living for another moment." Her husband tried to comfort her and said quietly to her, "In times like these, God loves us all the more."

In her room with a Bible and hymnal in hand, Prentiss sought comfort. She stopped at Sarah Adams's hymn "Nearer, My God, to Thee" and read it several times. As she prayed, words came to her: "More love to Thee, O Christ, more love to Thee."

Scriptures: John 15:12-15; Philippians 1:9-11; James 1:12
Themes: Love, Prayer, Dedication

More love to Thee, O Christ,
More love to Thee!
Hear Thou the prayer I make
On bended knee;
This is my earnest plea:
More love, O Christ, to Thee,
More love to Thee,
More love to Thee!

Once earthly joy I craved,
Sought peace and rest;
Now Thee alone I seek,
Give what is best;
This all my prayer shall be:
More love, O Christ, to Thee,
More love to Thee,
More love to Thee!

Then shall my every breath
Sing out Your praise;
This be the only song
My heart shall raise;
This still my prayer shall be:
More love, O Christ, to Thee,
More love to Thee,
More love to Thee!

ELIZABETH PAYSON PRENTISS (1818–1878)

MY JESUS, AS THOU WILT

This hymn was written in 1709 when Pastor Benjamin Schmolk was thirty-seven years old. We don't know much about the actual writing, but we know a little about the author.

After Martin Luther died, Germany was divided up by a treaty between Lutherans and Catholics. Some districts were Lutheran and some Catholic. Schmolk was the pastor of the only legal Lutheran church in a formerly Protestant area—now, by the treaty, a Catholic district. His church served thirty-six villages and was under severe restrictions. For instance, his church could not have a steeple, and he could not serve Communion to a dying parishioner unless he got permission from the Catholic priest.

But for thirty-five years he faithfully served there. Discouraging? Certainly. Yet he wrote this hymn, "My Jesus, As Thou Wilt!"

Scriptures: Psalm 40:8; Matthew 6:10; Luke 22:39-42
Themes: Submission, Comfort, Sorrow

My Jesus, as Thou wilt! O may Thy will be mine!
Into Thy hand of love I would my all resign.
Through sorrow or through joy, conduct me as Thine own;
And help me still to say, "My Lord, Thy will be done."

My Jesus, as Thou wilt! Though seen through many a tear,
Let not my star of hope grow dim or disappear.
Since Thou on earth hast wept, and sorrowed oft alone,
If I must weep with Thee, my Lord, Thy will be done.

My Jesus, as Thou wilt! All shall be well for me;
Each changing future scene I gladly trust with Thee.
Straight to my home above I travel calmly on.
And sing, in life or death, "My Lord, Thy will be done."

BENJAMIN SCHMOLK (1672–1737)
Translated by Jane Laurie Borthwick (1813–1897)

MY JESUS, I LOVE THEE

Sixteen-year-old William Featherston of Montreal wrote this simple hymn shortly after his conversion in 1862. He died before his twenty-seventh birthday, and this is apparently the only hymn he wrote.

Young Featherston sent the poem to his aunt in Los Angeles, who then sent it to England, where it appeared in *The London Hymnbook* in 1864. Back in Boston, Massachusetts, a Baptist minister, A. J. Gordon, was preparing a hymnal for Baptist congregations when he saw "My Jesus, I Love Thee" in the British hymnal. He didn't like the music the words were set to, and he later wrote that "in a moment of inspiration, a beautiful new air sang itself to me." The simple tune he wrote perfectly complemented the simple words, and soon the hymn was being sung across America.

A. J. Gordon had a remarkable ministry in New England. He wrote several books and started a college and seminary. But putting music to this hymn written by a teenage boy may be the accomplishment in A. J. Gordon's life that has touched the most lives of all.

Scriptures: Ephesians 2:4-5; 1 Peter 1:8; 1 John 4:9-11, 19
Themes: Love, Devotion, Commitment

My Jesus, I love Thee, I know Thou art mine—
For Thee all the follies of sin I resign;
My gracious Redeemer, my Savior art Thou:
If ever I loved Thee, my Jesus, 'tis now.

I love Thee because Thou hast first loved me
And purchased my pardon on Calvary's tree;
I love Thee for wearing the thorns on Thy brow:
If ever I loved Thee, my Jesus, 'tis now.

I'll love Thee in life, I will love Thee in death,
And praise Thee as long as Thou lendest me breath;
And say when the death-dew lies cold on my brow,
"If ever I loved Thee, my Jesus, 'tis now."

In mansions of glory and endless delight,
I'll ever adore Thee in heaven so bright;
I'll sing with the glittering crown on my brow,
"If ever I loved Thee, my Jesus, 'tis now."

WILLIAM RALPH FEATHERSTON (1846–1873)

NOTHING BETWEEN

Charles Tindley, the author of this hymn, was single-minded, no doubt about that. Born to slave parents before the Civil War, he taught himself to read and write. He attended night school, finished seminary by correspondence school, and went into the ministry. He began writing gospel songs, including one that started as "I'll Overcome Some Day" and later became famous as the theme song of the Civil Rights movement: "We Shall Overcome."

But Tindley wasn't after fame and fortune. He didn't want anything to get between him and his Savior. When church leaders wanted to rename his church in his honor, he resisted it strenuously. He knew that Satan wants to get anything and everything between the Christian and the Lord. In this song he mentions pleasures: "habits of life though harmless they seem," pride, friends, delusive dreams, and self.

"Keep the way clear!" he says. Be single-minded for the Lord.

Scriptures: Romans 12:1-2; Colossians 3:1-3; Hebrews 12:1-2
Themes: Separation, Holiness, Conscience

Nothing between my soul and the Savior,
Naught of this world's delusive dream;
I have renounced all sinful pleasure,
Jesus is mine; there's nothing between.

Nothing between my soul and the Savior,
So that His blessed face may be seen;
Nothing preventing the least of His favor,
Keep the way clear! Let nothing between.

Nothing between, like worldly pleasure,
Habits of life though harmless they seem,
Must not my heart from Him e'er sever,
He is my all; there's nothing between.

Nothing between, like pride or station,
Self or friends shall not intervene,
Tho' it may cost me much tribulation,
I am resolved; there's nothing between.

Nothing between e'en many hard trials,
Tho' the whole world against me convene;
Watching with prayer and much self-denial,
I'll triumph at last, with nothing between.

CHARLES A. TINDLEY (1851–1933)

O JESUS, I HAVE PROMISED

In Hebrews 10:23 there is an important parenthetical clause that reads, "He who promised is faithful" (NIV). In other words, there is no question that God will do what he says. There is a question, however, about whether we will do what we say. Yet God invites us to make promises to him.

When John Bode served the parish of Castle Camps, near Cambridge, England, in the middle of the nineteenth century, he had the privilege of officiating at the confirmation of his daughter and two sons. He wrote this hymn specifically for this occasion, and originally the first line was "O Jesus, *we* have promised" because all three children were making this dedication of themselves to the Lord.

While Bode wrote the hymn for young people and referred to the alluring temptations of the world, its message applies to Christians of any age. As the second stanza declares, "My foes are ever near me, / Around me and within." It is easy to blame our problems on external influences, but often our greatest foe is within.

Scriptures: Colossians 3:23-24; Hebrews 6:10-12; Hebrews 10:23
Themes: Commitment, Dedication, Consecration

O Jesus, I have promised
To serve Thee to the end;
Be Thou forever near me,
My Master and my Friend:
I shall not fear the battle
If Thou art by my side,
Nor wander from the pathway
If Thou wilt be my guide.

O let me feel Thee near me,
The world is ever near;
I see the sights that dazzle,
The tempting sounds I hear:
My foes are ever near me,
Around me and within;
But, Jesus, draw Thou nearer,
And shield my soul from sin.

O Jesus, Thou hast promised
To all who follow Thee,
That where Thou art in glory,
There shall Thy servant be;
And, Jesus, I have promised
To serve Thee to the end;
O give me grace to follow,
My Master and my Friend.

JOHN ERNEST BODE (1816–1874)

O JESUS, THOU ART STANDING

Holman Hunt's famous painting *Light of the World* shows Jesus, lantern in hand, knocking at a door. When the painting first went on display at Keble College, Oxford, England, it created quite a stir. Some thought it was inappropriate for Jesus, who is the Light of the world, to be carrying a lantern.

The famous British essayist, John Ruskin, wrote an explanation of the painting to mute the criticism. It was that explanation by Ruskin as well as a poem entitled "Two Brothers and a Sermon" that prompted William How to write the hymn "O Jesus, Thou Art Standing."

Interestingly, How addresses his hymn to Christians. While we usually think of Christ knocking at the door of a non-Christian's heart, How's hymn talks of Christians who stubbornly refuse to open the door and let Christ take complete control.

Scriptures: John 1:4-5; John 9:5; Revelation 3:20

Themes: Jesus Christ, Conviction of Sin, Commitment

> O Jesus, Thou art standing outside the fast-closed door,
> In lowly patience waiting to pass the threshold o'er.
> Shame on us, Christian brothers, His name and sign who bear,
> O shame, thrice shame upon us, to keep Him standing there!
>
> O Jesus, Thou art knocking; and, lo! That hand is scarred,
> And thorns Thy brow encircle, and tears Thy face have marred.
> O love that passeth knowledge, so patiently to wait!
> O sin that hath no equal, so fast to bar the gate!
>
> O Jesus, Thou art pleading in accents meek and low,
> "I died for you, my children, and will ye treat me so?"
> O Lord, with shame and sorrow we open now the door;
> Dear Savior, enter, enter, and leave us nevermore.

WILLIAM WALSHAM HOW (1823–1897)

O LORD, HOW SHALL I MEET THEE?

If Martin Luther was the mind of German hymnwriting, Paul Gerhardt was its heart. Gerhardt wrote devotional songs of love and commitment—133 hymns in all.

Not that Gerhardt's life was all peaceful contemplation. Far from it!

Like other hymnwriters of his era, he faced the Thirty Years' War, which devastated Germany. Four of his children died in infancy, and he lost his wife after only thirteen years of marriage. Gerhardt also walked a rocky road professionally. He was a popular Lutheran pastor, but after defying an order of the secular ruler, Elector Frederick, William I, Gerhardt was banished from his thriving ministry in Berlin.

In spite of his troubles, his hymns ring with love for the Lord. He seemed truly to strive "to do in spirit lowly / All that may please" the Lord.

Scriptures: Matthew 25:1-6; Colossians 3:17; Revelation 3:20
Themes: Comfort, Hope, Love

O Lord, how shall I meet Thee,
How welcome Thee aright?
Thy people long to greet Thee,
My Hope, my heart's Delight!
O kindle, Lord most holy,
Thy lamp within my breast
To do in spirit lowly
All that may please Thee best.

Love caused Thine incarnation,
Love brought Thee down to me;
Thy thirst for my salvation
Procured my liberty.
O love beyond all telling,
That led Thee to embrace,
In love all love excelling,
Our lost and fallen race!

Rejoice, then, ye sad-hearted,
Who sit in deepest gloom,
Who mourn o'er joys departed
And tremble at your doom.
Despair not, He is near you,
Yea, standing at the door,
Who best can help and cheer you
And bids you weep no more.

Sin's debt, that fearful burden,
Let not your souls distress;

Your guilt the Lord will pardon
And cover by His grace.
He comes, for men procuring
The peace of sin forgiv'n,
For all God's sons securing
Their heritage in heav'n.

PAUL GERHARDT (1607–1676)
Composite Translation

ONLY TRUST HIM

John Stockton, a Methodist minister in southern New Jersey, struggled with poor health for much of his life. Although he wanted to enter the ministry, he didn't do it until he was forty-four years old. But his health kept breaking down, and he had to take a leave of absence. When he was getting his strength back, he wrote hymns, hymns such as this one and "Glory to His Name."

Often when he finished a hymn, he would send it to Ira Sankey, who was Dwight L. Moody's music director and soloist. Sankey would put it in his "musical scrapbook," which was sort of a bottomless pit that Sankey would reach into from time to time to find a new song.

In 1873, Sankey was crossing the Atlantic for meetings in England and had time to examine his musical scrapbook. It was then he rediscovered this hymn from John Stockton. He liked it except for the chorus which, in the original, began "Come to Jesus, come to Jesus." Sankey changed it to "Only trust him, only trust him" and began using it in England. When Moody and Sankey returned to Philadelphia, a very frail John Stockton helped Sankey lead the congregation in singing this invitation hymn.

Scriptures: Jeremiah 17:7; Acts 16:31; Ephesians 1:12-13
Themes: Invitation, Salvation, Decision

Come, ev'ry soul by sin oppressed,
There's mercy with the Lord,
And He will surely give you rest
By trusting in His word.

Only trust Him, only trust Him, only trust Him now.
He will save you, He will save you, He will save you now.

For Jesus shed His precious blood,
Rich blessings to bestow;
Plunge now into the crimson flood
That washes white as snow.

Yes, Jesus is the Truth, the Way,
That leads you into rest:
Believe in Him without delay,
And you are fully blest.

Come, then, and join this holy band,
And on to glory go,
To dwell in that celestial land,
Where joys immortal flow.

JOHN HART STOCKTON (1813–1877)

PASS ME NOT, O GENTLE SAVIOR

Cincinnati businessman William Doane liked to write gospel music, so he searched out Fanny Crosby, who could write words to a song at the drop of a hat. Despite her blindness, she already had a reputation, and Doane wanted to see if they could work together on some songs. He was surprised when he found her living in a dilapidated tenement in Manhattan's lower west side.

A few days later, he returned and asked her to write lyrics for a song that would begin, "Pass me not, O gentle Savior." He didn't have a tune yet, and he didn't have any ideas for more words.

Fanny Crosby usually came up with hymn lyrics quite quickly, but this stumped her for several weeks. Then one day she went, as she did regularly, to speak at services in a prison near her tenement. The room was full of angry criminals as Fanny began to speak. Then she heard one prisoner cry out, "Good Lord! Do not pass me by!" These men were now forgotten by society, but this man didn't want to be forgotten by God.

With that in mind, Fanny went home, wrote the hymn, and sent it to William Doane for the music. It was the first hymn on which they collaborated. After that, they worked together on many more.

Scriptures: Mark 10:46-48; Luke 18:13; John 6:37
Themes: Invitation, Prayer, Conversion

Pass me not, O gentle Savior,
Hear my humble cry;
While on others Thou art calling,
Do not pass me by.

Savior, Savior, hear my humble cry;
While on others Thou art calling, do not pass me by.

Let me at a throne of mercy
Find a sweet relief;
Kneeling there in deep contrition,
Help my unbelief.

Trusting only in Thy merit,
Would I seek Thy face;
Heal my wounded, broken spirit,
Save me by Thy grace.

Thou the Spring of all my comfort,
More than life to me,
Whom have I on earth beside Thee?
Whom in Heav'n but Thee?

FANNY JANE CROSBY (1820–1915)

REVIVE US AGAIN

At first, the words of this hymn may not seem to go together. Is the hymn a prayer for personal revival or is it a hymn of praise? The first three stanzas are outbursts of praise to the triune God, so the natural response is "Hallelujah, Thine the glory." Only the chorus and the last stanza tie in with the title, "Revive Us Again."

But the author, William P. Mackay, a Scottish physician-turned-minister, knew what he was doing. The hymn was first published in 1875 under the inscription, "O Lord, Revive Thy Work." It is based on Habakkuk 3:2, which combines awe and wonder for the amazing things God has done with a prayer for revival. Psalm 85:6 asks, "Will you not revive us again, that your people may rejoice in you?" (NIV). In commenting on this psalm, Charles Haddon Spurgeon wrote, "A genuine revival without joy in the Lord is as impossible as spring without flowers or daydawn without light." When surrounded by discouragement and fear, it is good for us to sing praise to the One "who has borne all our sins / And has cleansed ev'ry stain."

Scriptures: 2 Chronicles 7:14; Psalm 85:6; Habakkuk 3:2; Titus 3:4-8
Themes: Praise, Worship, Revival

We praise Thee, O God,
For the Son of Thy love,
For Jesus who died
And is now gone above.

Hallelujah, Thine the glory!
Hallelujah, amen!
Hallelujah, Thine the glory!
Revive us again.

We praise Thee, O God,
For Thy Spirit of light,
Who has shown us our Savior
And scattered our night.

All glory and praise
To the Lamb that was slain,
Who has borne all our sins
And has cleansed ev'ry stain.

Revive us again—
Fill each heart with Thy love;
May each soul be rekindled
With fire from above.

WILLIAM PATON MACKAY (1839–1885)

SOFTLY AND TENDERLY JESUS IS CALLING

Will Thompson was called the "Bard of Ohio." Leaving his home in East Liverpool, Ohio, he went to New York City to sell some of the secular songs he had written. Music dealers picked them up, and soon people across the country were singing "My Home on the Old Ohio" and "Gathering Shells from the Seashore." He made so much money from his compositions that newspapers called him "the millionaire songwriter."

But Thompson was a Christian, and he soon began concentrating on hymnwriting. After he set up his own firm for publishing hymnals, he sold two million copies of his gospel-quartet books. Sometime around

1880, when Thompson was thirty-three years old, he wrote this invitation hymn, "Softly and Tenderly Jesus Is Calling."

Recognizing that many people in the smaller towns of America would never hear evangelists like Moody or singers like Sankey, "the millionaire songwriter" loaded an upright piano on a two-horse wagon and drove into the Ohio countryside to sing his gospel songs in the hamlets and villages of his state.

"Come home, come home, ye who are weary, come home." The invitation still stands.

Scriptures: Isaiah 30:15: Isaiah 55:1-2; Matthew 11:28-30
Themes: Invitation, Salvation, Redemption

Softly and tenderly Jesus is calling,
Calling for you and for me;
See, on the portals He's waiting and watching,
Watching for you and for me.

Come home, come home,
Ye who are weary, come home;
Earnestly, tenderly, Jesus is calling,
Calling, O sinner, come home!

Why should we tarry when Jesus is pleading,
Pleading for you and for me?
Why should we linger and heed not His mercies,
Mercies for you and for me?

Time is now fleeting, the moments are passing,
Passing from you and from me;
Shadows are gathering, death's night is coming,
Coming for you and for me.

O for the wonderful love He has promised,
Promised for you and for me!
Though we have sinned, He has mercy and pardon,
Pardon for you and for me.

WILLIAM LAMARTINE THOMPSON (1847–1909)

TAKE MY LIFE AND LET IT BE

In December 1873, Frances Ridley Havergal surrendered herself completely to Jesus Christ. She wrote, "I just yielded myself to Him, and utterly trusted Him to keep me."

Two months later, she went for a five-day visit to a place where there were several non-Christians. Before going, she prayed, "Lord, give me all in that house." And that's what happened. She was so happy on the last night she couldn't sleep. As she praised the Lord, the words of this hymn came to her mind. The next morning she wrote it, finishing with "Ever, only, ALL for Thee." As she wrote the words, she capitalized the word *ALL.*

Scriptures: Matthew 22:37; Romans 12:1-2; 1 Corinthians 10:31
Themes: Surrender, Yielding, Stewardship

Take my life and let it be
Consecrated, Lord, to Thee;
Take my moments and my days—
Let them flow in ceaseless praise,
Let them flow in ceaseless praise.

Take my hands and let them move
At the impulse of Thy love;
Take my feet and let them be
Swift and beautiful for Thee,
Swift and beautiful for Thee.

Take my voice and let me sing
Always, only, for my King;
Take my lips and let them be
Filled with messages from Thee,
Filled with messages from Thee.

Take my silver and my gold—
Not a mite would I withhold;
Take my intellect and use
Ev'ry pow'r as Thou shalt choose,
Ev'ry pow'r as Thou shalt choose.

Take my will and make it Thine—
It shall be no longer mine;
Take my heart—it is Thine own,

It shall be Thy royal throne,
It shall be Thy royal throne.

Take my love—my Lord, I pour
At Thy feet its treasure store;
Take myself—and I will be
Ever, only, all for Thee,
Ever, only, all for Thee.

FRANCES RIDLEY HAVERGAL (1836–1879)

TAKE THE WORLD, BUT GIVE ME JESUS

Many people have heard about Fanny Crosby, the blind songwriter. She wrote more than 8,500 hymns, even though she didn't get started until she was forty-four. She was the first woman ever to speak before the Senate, and she became a friend of several presidents. Besides being a poet, she was also a concert singer, organist, and harpist. She was much in demand as a speaker, partly because she had a delightful sense of humor. Yet she lived in a New York City tenement and spent several days a week in the missions of the Bowery district of New York City.

At the age of ninety she said, "I am living in the sight of Eternity's sunrise. . . . My simple trust in God's goodness has never failed me during these many years. There is nothing in this wide world that gives me so much joy as telling the story of my Savior's loving mercy." So she wrote "Take the World, but Give Me Jesus."

Scriptures: Mark 8:36-37; 1 Corinthians 1:27-28; 1 John 2:15-17
Themes: Commitment, Holiness, World

Take the world, but give me Jesus,
All its joys are but a name;
But His love abideth ever,
Thro' eternal years the same.

Oh, the height and depth of mercy!
Oh, the length and breadth of love!
Oh, the fullness of redemption,
Pledge of endless life above!

Take the world, but give me Jesus,
Sweetest comfort of my soul;

With my Savior watching o'er me,
I can sing though billows roll.

Take the world, but give me Jesus,
Let me view His constant smile;
Then thro'out my pilgrim journey
Light will cheer me all the while.

Take the world, but give me Jesus,
In His cross my trust shall be;
Till, with clearer, brighter vision,
Face to face my Lord I see.

FANNY JANE CROSBY (1820–1915)

THE SAVIOR IS WAITING

If you recall the verse in Revelation 3:20 that begins "Behold, I stand at the door, and knock" (KJV), or if you remember the famous painting of Christ standing outside and knocking at the heart's door, you'll get the context of this invitation song.

The composer, Ralph Carmichael, has written almost every kind of music imaginable. He has arranged music for pop singers like Nat King Cole and Bing Crosby. He has worked with top TV shows and written folk rock musicals. When it came to writing his autobiography, he decided the best title would be his testimony, so he called it, *He's Everything to Me.*

This song, "The Savior Is Waiting," is one of Ralph Carmichael's earlier songs, written when his pastor asked him for a hymn to be used at evangelistic services.

Scriptures: 2 Corinthians 6:2; Hebrews 3:15; Revelation 3:20
Themes: Invitation, Conversion, Salvation

The Savior is waiting to enter your heart—
Why don't you let Him come in?
There's nothing in this world to keep you apart—
What is your answer to Him?

*Time after time He has waited before,
And now He is waiting again
To see if you're willing to open the door—
O how He wants to come in.*

If you'll take one step toward the Savior
You'll find His arms open wide;
Receive Him and all of your darkness will end,
Within your heart He'll abide.

RALPH CARMICHAEL (B. 1927)
© 1958 Spiritquest Music. All rights controlled by Gaither Copyright Management.
Used by permission.

TRUST AND OBEY

The order we pick up items in a grocery store doesn't really matter. But order is important when it comes to our Christian faith. Our obedience will never save us, nor will it enable us to trust. Instead, our vain attempts at obedience will bring only frustration. But when trust comes first, obedience follows out of love.

This song was written after a Dwight L. Moody evangelistic meeting in Brockton, Massachusetts. Daniel Towner was the song leader that night in 1886, and he asked the people to share how they had been saved. Several stood and spoke of how certain they felt of their salvation. But then a young man rose and said, "I am not quite sure, but I am going to trust, and I am going to obey."

Towner couldn't forget that testimony. He jotted it down and sent it to John Sammis, who had recently left a career in business to enter the ministry. Towner asked Sammis to write a hymn text on trusting and obeying. Sammis wrote the chorus first and then the five stanzas. Later, Towner supplied the tune. To be happy in Jesus, we need to trust first, and then obey.

Scriptures: John 14:23; James 2:14-16; 1 John 5:1-3
Themes: Trust, Obedience, Joy, Salvation

When we walk with the Lord in the light of His Word,
What a glory He sheds on our way!
While we do His good will He abides with us still,
And with all who will trust and obey.

Trust and obey, for there's no other way
To be happy in Jesus, but to trust and obey.

Not a shadow can rise, not a cloud in the skies,
But His smile quickly drives it away;
Not a doubt nor a fear, not a sigh nor a tear,
Can abide while we trust and obey.

Not a burden we bear, not a sorrow we share,
But our toil He doth richly repay;
Not a grief nor a loss, not a frown nor a cross,
But is blest if we trust and obey.

But we never can prove the delights of His love
Until all on the altar we lay;
For the favor He shows and the joy He bestows
Are for them who will trust and obey.

Then in fellowship sweet we will sit at His feet,
Or we'll walk by His side in the way;
What He says we will do, where He sends we will go—
Never fear, only trust and obey.

JOHN H. SAMMIS (1846–1919)

TURN YOUR EYES UPON JESUS

Helen Lemmel was already a noted Christian singer and voice teacher when a missionary friend of hers handed her a gospel tract titled "Focus." Helen wondered why someone was handing her a tract.

The tract said that if you focus on Jesus, if you look full into His face, "you will find that the things of earth will acquire a strange new dimness."

Those words had an impact on Helen Lemmel. "Suddenly," she said later, "as if commanded to stop and listen, I stood still, and singing in my soul and spirit was the chorus, with not one conscious moment of putting word to word to make rhyme, or note to note to make melody." Later the same year the song was published, and soon it became a favorite of Christians in America, in England, and around the rest of the world.

It's so easy to lose focus. Focus on Jesus, and the tawdry things of this world will lose their glamour "in the light of His glory and grace."

Scriptures: Matthew 6:33; John 1:36-37; Colossians 3:1-2; Hebrews 12:2
Themes: Consecration, Trust

O soul, are you weary and troubled?
No light in the darkness you see?
There's light for a look at the Savior,
And life more abundant and free!

Turn your eyes upon Jesus,
Look full in His wonderful face,
And the things of earth will grow strangely dim
In the light of His glory and grace.

Through death into life everlasting
He passed, and we follow Him there;
Over us sin no more hath dominion—
For more than conquerors we are!

His word shall not fail you—He promised;
Believe Him, and all will be well:
Then go to a world that is dying,
His perfect salvation to tell!

HELEN HOWARTH LEMMEL (1864–1961)

WHOSOEVER WILL

Once when evangelist Dwight L. Moody was preaching in England, a young British preacher, Henry Moorhouse, filled Moody's pulpit in Chicago for a week of meetings. Moorhouse was a converted pickpocket, and Moody didn't know him too well, so he was eager to get a full report when he returned home. He asked his wife what Moorhouse had preached about.

"John 3:16," she replied.

Moody then asked what he preached on the second night. The answer was the same: John 3:16; and the third night: John 3:16. Moody asked, "Did he preach on John 3:16 every night?" His wife said that he had the same text every night, and then added, "He preaches a little different from you. He preaches that God loves sinners."

From then on, Moody also preached that God loved sinners.

The song leader for the entire week of meetings was Philip Bliss. What had impressed him in Moorhouse's messages on John 3:16 was the word *whosoever*. After the meetings, he wrote this song, "Whosoever Will."

Scriptures: John 3:16; Romans 10:9-11; 1 John 4:15-17
Themes: Invitation, Salvation, Grace

"Whosoever heareth," shout, shout the sound!
Spread the blessed tidings all the world around;
Tell the joyful news wherever man is found,
"Whosoever will may come."

"Whosoever will, whosoever will!"
Send the proclamation over vale and hill;
'Tis a loving Father calls the wand'rer home:
"Whosoever will may come."

Whosoever cometh, need not delay,
Now the door is open, enter while you may;
Jesus is the true, the only Living Way:
"Whosoever will may come."

"Whosoever will," the promise is secure;
"Whosoever will," forever must endure;
"Whosoever will," 'tis life forevermore;
"Whosoever will may come."

PHILIP PAUL BLISS (1838–1876)

WITHOUT HIM

When seventeen-year-old Mylon LeFevre wrote "Without Him" in 1963, he didn't know that he would try to live the next seventeen years of his life "without Him." A few months after Mylon wrote the song, a singer named Elvis Presley recorded it, then more than a hundred other vocalists also recorded the song. Soon the teenage Mylon had so much money that he felt he could actually live "without Him." He didn't need Jesus anymore.

Mylon recorded with all the big names, from the Beatles to the Rolling Stones, and he started using drugs because "everyone else" was doing it. He became a heroin addict, and it looked as if the teenager who wrote that "without Him life would be hopeless" was proving it.

But in 1980 a Christian musical group helped Mylon get back on track. He begged the Lord for forgiveness and said that, from that time on, he wanted to live with him and not without him. His message was now about his newfound hope and about the dangers of trying to live without Jesus.

Scriptures: Proverbs 3:5-6; John 15:5; 2 Corinthians 12:9
Themes: Submission, Prayer, Salvation

Without Him I could do nothing, without Him I'd surely fail;
Without Him I would be drifting like a ship without a sail.

Jesus, O Jesus! Do you know Him today? Do not turn Him away.
O Jesus, O Jesus, without Him, how lost I would be.

Without Him I would be dying, without Him I'd be enslaved;
Without Him life would be hopeless, but with Jesus, thank God, I'm saved.

MYLON LEFEVRE (B. 1946)

PART XI

GOD THE FATHER

*The L*ORD *of Heaven's Armies is here among us;*

the God of Israel is our fortress.

PSALM 46:7

A MIGHTY FORTRESS IS OUR GOD

The poet Samuel Coleridge said of Martin Luther, "He did as much for the Reformation by his hymns as he did by his translation of the Bible."

Martin Luther's grandest hymn is this one, inspired by the forty-sixth psalm. It became the battle cry of the Reformation. Martin Luther probably wrote it at a time when evangelical leaders were delivering their protest against the attack on their liberties at the Diet of Speyer. And incidentally, the meaning of the word *protestant* was no doubt derived from that meeting when these leaders delivered their protest.

Martin Luther had posted his Ninety-five Theses on the door of the Wittenberg Church in October 1517, about thirteen years earlier. Despite his excommunication from the Roman church, Luther came to know the gracious power of God's sheltering hand. He faced continual threats to his life and freedom, and times of intense spiritual battle as well. But in the comforting words of Psalm 46, Luther found the inspiration for this hymn: "A mighty fortress is our God!"

Scriptures: Deuteronomy 33:27; 2 Samuel 22:2; Psalm 20:7; Psalm 46:1-3
Themes: Security, Trust, Confidence

A mighty fortress is our God, a bulwark never failing;
Our helper He amid the flood of mortal ills prevailing.
For still our ancient foe doth seek to work us woe—
His craft and pow'r are great, and, armed with cruel hate,
On earth is not His equal.

Did we in our own strength confide, our striving would be losing,
Were not the right man on our side, the man of God's own choosing.
Dost ask who that may be? Christ Jesus, it is He—
Lord Sabaoth His name, from age to age the same,
And He must win the battle.

And though this world, with devils filled, should threaten
    to undo us,
We will not fear, for God hath willed His truth to triumph through us.
The prince of darkness grim, we tremble not for him—
His rage we can endure, for lo! his doom is sure:
One little word shall fell him.

That word above all earthly pow'rs, no thanks to them, abideth;
The Spirit and the gifts are ours through Him who with us sideth.

Let goods and kindred go, this mortal life also—
The body they may kill; God's truth abideth still:
His kingdom is forever.

MARTIN LUTHER (1483–1546)
Translated by Frederick H. Hedge (1805–1890)

COME, THOU FOUNT OF EVERY BLESSING

Robert Robinson had always been prone to wander. Apprenticed to a barber at fourteen, he spent more time reading and playing with friends than cutting hair. He became the leader of a notorious gang, and he shamed his family so much that they practically disowned him. Then, still a teen, he went to a George Whitefield meeting, intending to ridicule it; instead, he almost fell asleep in it. But then the preacher shouted out a Bible verse: "O generation of vipers; who hath warned you to flee from the wrath to come" (Matthew 3:7, KJV). That evening Robinson was converted. After his apprenticeship was over, Robinson went into the ministry. He wrote this hymn at the age of twenty-three as he served at the Calvinistic Methodist Church in Norfolk, England.

Late in life, Robinson did stray from the faith and drifted far from the Fount of every blessing. One day he was riding in a stagecoach and sitting by a woman who was reading a hymnbook. She showed him the hymn, "Come, Thou Fount of Every Blessing," saying how wonderful it was. He tried to change the subject but couldn't. Finally he said, "Madam, I am the poor man who wrote that hymn many years ago, and I would give a thousand worlds to enjoy the feelings I had then."

Scriptures: 1 Samuel 7:10-12; Zechariah 13:1; 1 Peter 2:23-25
Themes: Praise, Redemption, Grace

Come, Thou Fount of ev'ry blessing,
Tune my heart to sing Thy grace;
Streams of mercy never ceasing,
Call for songs of loudest praise:
Teach me some melodious sonnet,
Sung by flaming tongues above;
Praise the mount—O fix me on it,
Mount of God's unchanging love.

Here I raise mine Ebenezer;
Hither by Thy help I'm come;

And I hope, by Thy good pleasure,
Safely to arrive at home:
Jesus sought me when a stranger,
Wand'ring from the fold of God;
He, to save my soul from danger,
Interposed His precious blood.

O, to grace how great a debtor
Daily I'm constrained to be!
Let that grace, Lord, like a fetter,
Bind my wand'ring heart to Thee.
Prone to wander, Lord, I feel it;
Prone to leave the God I love;
Here's my heart; Lord, take and seal it;
Seal it for Thy courts above.

ROBERT ROBINSON (1735–1790)

COME, WE THAT LOVE THE LORD

Unless songwriters compose the music themselves, they usually have no control over what music accompanies their texts. The prolific hymn-writer Isaac Watts wrote "Come, We That Love the Lord" and published it in 1707. In 1763, Aaron Williams put it together with a tune called "St. Thomas." However, in many denominations in the United States, the hymn underwent a transformation. Perhaps because of the popularity of Negro spirituals, gospel songs of the nineteenth and early twentieth centuries emphasized a chorus, just as the spirituals did. So the old Watts stanzas were attached to a chorus called "Marching to Zion" and set to a rousing gospel tune by Brooklyn clergyman Robert Lowry.

Lowry had a brilliant idea—let the adults sing the complicated hymn stanzas, and let the children join in on the familiar and lilting chorus, "We're marching to Zion, beautiful city of Zion." So children and their parents were united in worship, led by an innovative reworking of a classic hymn text.

Scriptures: Psalm 149:1-4; Isaiah 35:10; Hebrews 12:22
Themes: Joy, Praise, Victory

Come, we that love the Lord,
And let our joys be known;

Join in a song with sweet accord,
And thus surround the throne.

Let those refuse to sing
Who never knew our God;
But children of the heav'nly King
May speak their joys abroad.

The men of grace have found
Glory begun below;
Celestial fruit on earthly ground
From faith and hope may grow.

The hill of Zion yields
A thousand sacred sweets
Before we reach the heav'nly fields,
Or walk the golden streets.

Then let our songs abound,
And every tear be dry;
We're marching thro' Emmanuel's ground
To fairer worlds on high.

ISAAC WATTS (1674–1748)

EL SHADDAI

Michael Card's father was a jazz trombonist, and his mother played classical violin. As a teenager, Michael enjoyed jam sessions with Randy Scruggs and the Nitty Gritty Dirt Band. When you combine that background with the fact that he grew up in Nashville, one might guess that he would have a career in music.

But where did he end up? Card went to Western Kentucky University, majoring in biblical studies and concentrating on Old Testament rabbinics. While at the university, he attended a small Presbyterian church and was asked to write a song each week to go along with the pastor's message. With that collection of Sunday morning worship songs and his connections with the Nashville recording industry, Michael Card soon became known as both a performer and a songwriter.

Card has a range of styles from bluegrass to rock, hymns to ballads, but he is rooted in Scripture. "El Shaddai" uses several Old Testament names for God. In Hebrew, *El Shaddai* means "God Almighty"; *El Elyon* means "The Most High God"; *na Adonai* means "O Lord." And the phrase *Erkahmkana* means "We will love you."

Scriptures: Genesis 17:1; Psalm 7:17; Psalm 18:1; Psalm 90:1

Themes: Worship, God the Father, Joy

> El Shaddai, El Shaddai, El Elyon na Adonai,
> Age to age You're still the same by the power of the name.
> El Shaddai, El Shaddai Erkahmka na Adonai,
> We will praise and lift you high El Shaddai.

MICHAEL CARD/JOHN THOMPSON
©1982 Mole End Music (Administered by Word Music, LLC)

FATHER, I ADORE YOU

Many people find that driving in the car is a great time to worship the Lord. It's also a good time to sing because no one except the Lord can hear you and he already knows what kind of voice you have.

Terrye Coelho and her sister were driving home from a wonderful Christian-life conference, worshipping God as they traveled. Terrye started composing a new worship song, "Father, I Adore You," and her sister joined in. By the time they arrived home, the entire song, text and tune, was completed. Terrye had just become a Christian the year before, and at the age of twenty, she was worshipping the Lord with music.

A different Person of the Trinity is praised in each of the three short verses, but when the worship chorus is sung as a round, the Trinity is praised simultaneously.

Scriptures: Psalm 18:1; Psalm 57:9-11; Matthew 12:30

Themes: Worship, Trinity, God the Father

AUTHOR: TERRYE COELHO STROM (B. 1952)

FATHER, WHATE'ER OF EARTHLY BLISS

The writer of this hymn, Anne Steele, didn't know a great deal about earthly bliss. Her mother died when Anne was only three years old. When she was nineteen, she suffered a serious injury to her hip that made her an invalid, and for days at a time she was confined to her bed.

She became engaged to a young man and the couple set a date for the wedding, but the evening before the wedding, her fiancé drowned. After that experience, she wrote the hymn "Father, Whate'er of Earthly Bliss." She originally entitled the hymn, "Desiring Resignation and Thankfulness."

Because her hymns were often quite personal, she hesitated to have them printed. But after she was forty years old, she mailed off her first collection of poems to a publisher. Soon she became the leading Baptist hymnwriter of the eighteenth century and opened the way for other women to have their writings published.

Scriptures: Psalm 34:4-8; Psalm 37:3-5; Philippians 4:6-9
Themes: Submission, Contentment, Peace

Father, whate'er of earthly bliss Thy sovereign will denies,
Accepted at Thy throne of grace, Let this petition rise.

Give me a calm, a thankful heart, from every murmur free;
The blessings of Thy grace impart, and make me live to Thee.

Let the sweet hope that Thou art mine my life and death attend:
Thy presence through my journey shine, and crown my journey's end.

ANNE STEELE (1716–1788)

GOD OF GRACE AND GOD OF GLORY

What a diversity of people God has used to bring music to his church.

Harry Emerson Fosdick, one of the leaders of the liberal Protestant movement of the 1920s and 1930s, was denounced by many conservatives, some of whom now sing this hymn he wrote. In 1930, when the new building for the Riverside Church in New York City was dedicated, this hymn was sung as the dedicatory hymn.

It is a prayer of dedication that can be uttered any day. Some days in our lives are obvious turning points—a church dedication, the birth of a child, a wedding—but every day has its crucial moments. The prayer of our hearts should constantly be "Grant us wisdom, / Grant us courage, / For the facing of this hour."

Scriptures: Joshua 1:7-9; Psalm 31:24; Proverbs 3:5-6
Themes: Courage, Strength, Prayer

God of grace and God of glory,
On Thy people pour Thy power;
Crown Thine ancient Church's story,
Bring her bud to glorious flower.
Grant us wisdom,
Grant us courage,
For the facing of this hour,
For the facing of this hour.

Lo! the hosts of evil round us
Scorn Thy Christ, assail His ways!
From the fears that long have bound us,
Free our hearts to faith and praise.
Grant us wisdom,
Grant us courage,
For the living of these days,
For the living of these days.

Cure Thy children's warring madness;
Bend our pride to Thy control;
Shame our wanton, selfish gladness,
Rich in things and poor in soul.
Grant us wisdom,
Grant us courage,
Lest we miss Thy kingdom's goal,
Lest we miss Thy kingdom's goal.

Set our feet on lofty places,
Gird our lives that they may be
Armored with all Christlike graces
In the fight to set men free.
Grant us wisdom,
Grant us courage,
That we fail not man nor Thee,
That we fail not man nor Thee.

HARRY EMERSON FOSDICK (1878–1969)

GOD OF OUR FATHERS, KNOWN OF OLD

Rudyard Kipling is not known as a hymnwriter. In the 1890s, he became famous for his poetry and for books such as *Barrack-Room Ballads* and *The Jungle Book*. In 1897, when England was celebrating the Diamond Jubilee of Queen Victoria's reign, the *Times* of London asked Rudyard Kipling to write a special poem for the occasion.

Kipling said, "That poem gave me more trouble than anything I ever wrote. When it came due I had nothing that satisfied me." But finally the poem was written, and when it was released, it created quite a stir. Instead of praising his country's military strength, Kipling sounded like an Old Testament prophet calling for mercy from a just and righteous God.

It seemed uncharacteristic for Kipling, who was associated with British colonialism, to write, "All our pomp of yesterday / Is one with Nineveh and Tyre!" Kipling's hymn serves as a powerful sermon to all who are tempted to elevate the glory and power of their nation above that of the sovereign Creator.

Scriptures: Psalm 51:17; Daniel 4:30-32; Zephaniah 2:13
Themes: Patriotic, God's Omnipotence, Humility

God of our fathers, known of old,
Lord of our far-flung battle-line,
Beneath whose awful hand we hold
Dominion over palm and pine;
Lord God of hosts, be with us yet,
Lest we forget—lest we forget!

The tumult and the shouting dies;
The captains and the kings depart;
Still stands Thine ancient sacrifice,
An humble and a contrite heart.
Lord God of hosts, be with us yet,
Lest we forget—lest we forget!

Far-called, our navies melt away;
On dune and headland sinks the fire:
Lo, all our pomp of yesterday
Is one with Nineveh and Tyre!
Judge of the nations, spare us yet,
Lest we forget—lest we forget!

If, drunk with sight of power, we loose
Wild tongues that have not Thee in awe,
Such boastings as the Gentiles use,
Or lesser breeds without the law—
Lord God of hosts, be with us yet,
Lest we forget—lest we forget!

For heathen heart that puts her trust
In reeking tube and iron shard,
All valiant dust that builds on dust,
And, guarding, calls not Thee to guard,
For frantic boast and foolish word—
Thy mercy on Thy people, Lord!

RUDYARD KIPLING (1865–1936)

GOD THE OMNIPOTENT!

There was no war in 1842 when Henry F. Chorley, music critic of the *London Athenaeum,* wrote this hymn under the title "In Time of War." Twenty-eight years later, John Ellerton added additional stanzas as the Franco-Prussian War was being waged in Europe.

But the prayer "Give to us peace in our time, O Lord" has been uttered since the beginning of history. Wars and rumors of wars, civic unrest, riots, looting, and rampant crime have increased as humanity has supposedly become more educated and civilized.

External peace may not come, despite our efforts and our prayers. But internal peace can be a reality because our rest and our trust are in a God who is omnipotent, all-merciful, all-righteous, and all-wise. Our God is greater than the armies and armaments of nations. The dreaded forces of Nazism and Communism both rose and fell in the twentieth century; terrorism still threatens us, but the omnipotent God remains, and he continues to reign.

Scriptures: Zechariah 9:9-10; 1 Timothy 1:17; Revelation 19:6
Themes: Peace, God's Omnipotence, Prayer

God the omnipotent! King, who ordainest
Thunder Thy clarion, the lightning Thy sword;
Show forth Thy pity on high where Thou reignest;
Give to us peace in our time, O Lord.

God the all-merciful! Earth hath forsaken
Meekness and mercy, and slighted Thy Word;
Let not Thy wrath in its terrors awaken;
Give to us peace in our time, O Lord.

God the all-righteous One! Man hath defied Thee;
Yet to eternity standeth Thy Word;
Falsehood and wrong shall not tarry beside Thee;
Give to us peace in our time, O Lord.

So shall Thy people, with thankful devotion,
Praise Him who saved them from peril and sword,
Singing in chorus from ocean to ocean,
Peace to the nations, and praise to the Lord.

STANZAS 1–2 BY HENRY FOTHERGILL CHORLEY (1808–1872)

STANZAS 3–4 BY JOHN ELLERTON (1826–1893)

GREAT GOD OF WONDERS

About two hundred years ago England had a prison colony in the South Seas called Van Diemen's Land. It was where England's most incorrigible prisoners were sent. One writer commented, "With no companions but other convicts like themselves, they grew to be almost fiends." Yet by the mercy of God some of these men were converted and began meeting together to pray and sing hymns.

Their favorite hymn was "Great God of Wonders," with its majestic refrain, "Who is a pard'ning God like Thee? / Or who has grace so rich and free?"

The hymn they loved was written by American Samuel Davies, a Presbyterian evangelist who became president of Princeton, succeeding Jonathan Edwards.

Scriptures: 1 Chronicles 29:11; Job 36:5; Psalm 145:3; Micah 7:18-19
Themes: God's Omnipotence, Grace, Pardon

Great God of wonders! all Thy ways
Are matchless, Godlike, and divine;
But the fair glories of Thy grace
More Godlike and unrivaled shine,
More Godlike and unrivaled shine.

Who is a pard'ning God like Thee?
Or who has grace so rich and free?
Or who has grace so rich and free?

In wonder lost, with trembling joy
We take the pardon of our God;
Pardon for crimes of deepest dye,
A pardon bought with Jesus' blood;
A pardon bought with Jesus' blood.

O may this strange, this matchless grace,
This Godlike miracle of love,
Fill the whole earth with grateful praise,
And all th' angelic choirs above,
And all th' angelic choirs above.

SAMUEL DAVIES (1723–1761)

HOLY, HOLY, HOLY

Reginald Heber was always trying to improve the music at the Anglican church he served in Hodnet, England. Though his superiors frowned on the use of anything but metrical psalms, Heber introduced hymns by Newton and Cowper and even wrote new hymns of his own. Many of our hymnals still carry three or four of Heber's hymns, including "Holy, Holy, Holy," which the poet Alfred, Lord Tennyson called the world's greatest hymn.

After serving sixteen years as a parish priest in England, Heber accepted the call to become the bishop of Calcutta, India. He served in Calcutta for only three years before he died at the age of forty-three. Whether in England, as he surveyed the prevalence of vice, or in India, where he was surrounded by the worship of false gods, Heber was impressed with the holiness of God. "Only Thou art holy," he wrote. The tune to which this hymn is usually sung is called "Nicaea," named after the church council that met in 325 A.D. which formulated the Nicene Creed and affirmed the doctrine of the Trinity.

Scriptures: Psalm 145:9-13; Isaiah 6:1-7; Revelation 4:8-11
Themes: Holiness of God, Trinity, Worship

Holy, holy, holy! Lord God Almighty!
Early in the morning our song shall rise to Thee;
Holy, holy, holy! merciful and mighty!
God in three Persons, blessed Trinity!

Holy, holy, holy! all the saints adore Thee,
Casting down their golden crowns around the glassy sea;
Cherubim and seraphim falling down before Thee,
Which wert and art and evermore shalt be.

Holy, holy, holy! though the darkness hide Thee,
Though the eye of sinful man Thy glory may not see;
Only Thou art holy—there is none beside Thee,
Perfect in pow'r, in love and purity.

Holy, holy, holy! Lord God Almighty!
All Thy works shall praise Thy name in earth and sky and sea;
Holy, holy, holy! merciful and mighty!
God in three Persons, blessed Trinity!

REGINALD HEBER (1783–1826)

IMMORTAL, INVISIBLE, GOD ONLY WISE

British hymnologist Erik Routley calls this hymn "full of plump polysyllables." Another scholar called it a flowery attempt to express the inexpressible. The hymn was inspired by the apostle Paul's words to young Timothy: "Now unto the King eternal, immortal, invisible, the only wise God, be honour and glory for ever and ever" (1 Timothy 1:17, KJV). The writer of the hymn, Walter Chalmers Smith, was a pastor in the Free Church of Scotland for forty-four years (1850–1894). Though he wrote many hymns, this is the only one still in use today.

In our day of casual Christianity and almost flippant prayer, we desperately need to catch glimpses of God's incredible character. In these wonderful stanzas, we who "wither and perish" come face-to-face with our immortal, invisible, unchanging God. And amazingly, this great God, whom even polysyllables cannot adequately describe, loves us dearly.

Scriptures: Psalm 36:5-6; Colossians 1:15-17; 1 Timothy 1:17; Hebrews 13:8
Themes: God's Character, Worship, Light

Immortal, invisible, God only wise,
In light inaccessible hid from our eyes,
Most blessed, most glorious, the Ancient of Days,
Almighty, victorious, Thy great name we praise.

Unresting, unhasting, and silent as light,
Nor wanting, nor wasting, Thou rulest in might.
Thy justice like mountains high soaring above
Thy clouds which are fountains of goodness and love.

To all, life Thou givest, to both great and small;
In all life Thou livest, the true life of all.
We blossom and flourish as leaves on the tree,
And wither and perish, but naught changeth Thee.

Great Father of glory, pure Father of light,
Thine angels adore Thee, all veiling their sight.
All praise we would render: O help us to see
'Tis only the splendor of light hideth Thee.

WALTER CHALMERS SMITH (1824–1908)

LORD OF ALL BEING, THRONED AFAR

Oliver Wendell Holmes went to Harvard University to study law but ended up studying medicine. His fame, however, came from his literary efforts. After writing "Old Ironsides" at the age of twenty-one and launching The Autocrat of the Breakfast-Table series at twenty-two, he quickly gained fame as a writer. Because of his quick wit, some regarded him as irreverent, but there was nothing irreverent about his hymns.

In a letter to Harriet Beecher Stowe, Holmes wrote that the first words of the Lord's Prayer—Our Father—described well his understanding of God. In December 1859, the last of his papers making up The Professor at the Breakfast-Table appeared. He concluded with these words: "And so my year's record is finished. . . . Peace to all such as may have been vexed in spirit by any utterance the pages have repeated. They will doubtless forget for the moment the difference in the lines . . . and join in singing this hymn to the source of the light we all need to lead us."

Then he printed this hymn, which has been called "the finest statement of God's omnipresence in the English language."

Scriptures: Genesis 1:3; Psalm 19:1-6; Hebrews 12:28-29
Themes: Praise, Creation, Omnipresence

Lord of all being, throned afar,
Thy glory flames from sun and star;
Center and soul of every sphere,
Yet to each loving heart how near!

Sun of our life, Thy quickening ray
Sheds on our path the glow of day;
Star of our hope, Thy softened light
Cheers the long watches of the night.

Our midnight is Thy smile withdrawn;
Our noontide is Thy gracious dawn;
Our rainbow arch Thy mercy's sign;
All, save the clouds of sin, are Thine!

Lord of all life, below, above,
Whose light is truth, whose warmth is love,
Before Thy ever-blazing throne
We ask no luster of our own.

Grant us Thy truth to make us free,
And kindling hearts that burn for Thee;
Till all Thy living altars claim
One holy light, one heavenly flame.

OLIVER WENDELL HOLMES (1809–1894)

O GOD OF EARTH AND ALTAR

G. K. Chesterton, the noted British author and journalist, blended the realms of earth and altar. He was known for writing both detective stories and profound Christian apologetics; humorous essays such as "On Running after One's Hat" and deep polemical works such as *Orthodoxy;* hilarious nonsense poems and hymns for worship. He always kept a sense of humor about him, whether in writing his personal testimony, which he called "My Elephantine Adventures in Pursuit of the Obvious," or in this hymn, where he asked God to "Tie in a living tether the prince and priest and thrall."

Chesterton calls for unity between the political and the spiritual, reminding us that political freedom can find its source only in God. Only as the hearts of political leaders, religious leaders, and citizens are turned to him can a nation become "aflame with faith, and free."

Scriptures: 2 Chronicles 7:14; Isaiah 59:1-3, 20; 1 Peter 2:13-14
Themes: Prayer for the Nation, Deliverance, Unity

O God of earth and altar,
Bow down and hear our cry,
Our earthly rulers falter,
Our people drift and die;
The walls of gold entomb us,
The swords of scorn divide,
Take not Thy thunder from us,
But take away our pride.

From all that terror teaches,
From lies of tongue and pen,
From all the easy speeches
That comfort cruel men,
From sale and profanation
Of honor, and the sword,
From sleep and from damnation,
Deliver us, good Lord!

Tie in a living tether
The prince and priest and thrall,
Bind all our lives together,
Smite us and save us all;
In ire and exultation
Aflame with faith, and free,
Lift up a living nation,
A single sword to Thee.

GILBERT KEITH CHESTERTON (1874–1936)

TO GOD BE THE GLORY

It was hard to discourage Fanny Crosby. Joy was a characteristic of her life. When English hymnwriter Frances Havergal asked someone about Crosby, she received the reply, "She is a blind lady whose heart can see splendidly in the sunshine of God's love." Crosby herself acknowledged, "Darkness may throw a shadow over my outer vision, but there is no cloud that can keep the sunlight of hope from a trustful soul."

Probably written in 1872, this song was taken to England by Ira Sankey, who led the singing for Dwight L. Moody's evangelistic campaigns. The hymn immediately became popular in England and remained well-known there. But it was published in only a few American hymnals, so it was relatively unknown in the United States and Canada. During their 1952 British crusade, it was introduced to members of the Billy Graham team and soon became Billy Graham's British crusade theme hymn. The words, they said, expressed their praise to God, who was doing wondrous things in Britain. A short time later, Graham introduced the hymn in his Nashville crusade, and it became as popular in America as it had been in England.

Scriptures: Psalm 115:1; Psalm 145:1-4; Mark 5:19-20; Ephesians 3:21
Themes: Praise, Redemption, Worship

To God be the glory—great things He hath done!
So loved He the world that He gave us His Son,
Who yielded His life an atonement for sin,
And opened the life-gate that all may go in.

Praise the Lord, praise the Lord,
Let the earth hear His voice!
Praise the Lord, praise the Lord,
Let the people rejoice!
O come to the Father through Jesus the Son,
And give Him the glory—great things He hath done!

O perfect redemption, the purchase of blood!
To ev'ry believer the promise of God;
The vilest offender who truly believes,
That moment from Jesus a pardon receives.

Great things He hath taught us, great things He hath done,
And great our rejoicing through Jesus the Son;
But purer, and higher, and greater will be
Our wonder, our transport, when Jesus we see.

FANNY JANE CROSBY (1820–1915)

PART XII

GUIDANCE AND CARE

He is our God forever and ever, and he will guide us until we die.

PSALM 48:14

A PERFECT HEART

Dony and Reba McGuire call this their "lake song" because it was "caught" at Center Hill Lake in Tennessee. Friends of theirs who had a houseboat on the lake invited Dony and Reba to vacation with them on the houseboat. The McGuires accepted the invitation as long as they could have time to work on some songs and a musical they wanted to write.

Toward the end of the week, Dony went fishing for catfish, and when he came back he had a strange look on his face. Reba says, "Some people come down with a cold, but Dony comes down with a song," and she knew it from the expression on his face. They had an electric piano on the houseboat, and Dony played it while Reba was writing down lyrics as fast as she could. The music and the words came so fast they were amazed. It became, Reba says, "our little lake song." She says it was as if God was saying to them, "I'm going to give you something just because I have the power to do so."

Scriptures: Psalm 51:10; Psalm 119:10; Ezekiel 36:26
Themes: Praise, Holiness, Worship

Bless the Lord, who reigns in beauty;
Bless the Lord, who reigns in wisdom and with pow'r;
Bless the Lord, who reigns my life with so much love,
He can make a perfect heart.

DONY MCGUIRE/REBA RAMBO
© Bud John Songs, Inc./Makanume Music/Ooh's and Ah's Music
All rights reserved. Used by permission.

ALL THE WAY MY SAVIOR LEADS ME

Fanny Crosby, a blind hymnwriter who lived a century ago, trusted the Lord to lead her and to provide for her each step of the way. One day she needed five dollars and didn't know where she would get it. So she prayed about it. A few minutes later a stranger knocked at her door. When she answered it, the man gave her a five-dollar bill and then turned around and left.

Crosby was amazed at the Lord's marvelous timing. Later she wrote, "I have no way of accounting for this except to believe that God, in answer to my prayer, put it into the heart of this good man to bring the money to me. My first thought was, *It is so wonderful the way the Lord leads me.*"

That day she wrote this hymn: "All the way my Savior leads me; / What have I to ask beside?"

Scriptures: Psalm 48:14; Psalm 78:13-16; Isaiah 49:10; Mark 7:37
Themes: Guidance, Trust, Confidence

All the way my Savior leads me;
What have I to ask beside?
Can I doubt His tender mercy,
Who through life has been my guide?
Heav'nly peace, divinest comfort,
Here by faith in Him to dwell!
For I know whate'er befall me,
Jesus doeth all things well;
For I know whate'er befall me,
Jesus doeth all things well.

All the way my Savior leads me;
Cheers each winding path I tread,
Gives me grace for ev'ry trial,
Feeds me with the living bread:
Though my weary steps may falter,
And my soul athirst may be,
Gushing from the Rock before me,
Lo! a spring of joy I see;
Gushing from the Rock before me,
Lo! a spring of joy I see.

All the way my Savior leads me;
Oh, the fullness of His love!
Perfect rest to me is promised
In my Father's house above:
When my spirit, cloth'd immortal,
Wings its flight to realms of day,
This my song through endless ages:
Jesus led me all the way;
This my song through endless ages:
Jesus led me all the way.

FANNY JANE CROSBY (1820–1915)

GOD LEADS US ALONG

The author of this hymn, George Young, was a carpenter and a pastor. He didn't make much money in either profession. Most of his life was spent in small farming communities. Finally, however, he and his wife were able to build their own home, and they moved in. Shortly afterwards, while the Youngs were holding meetings in another small town, someone set fire to their house, and it was reduced to ashes.

It was probably out of that experience that George Young wrote this hymn and ended the chorus with these words: "Some thru great sorrow but God gives a song, / In the night season and all the day long."

Scriptures: Job 35:10; 2 Corinthians 1:3-7; James 1:2-4
Themes: Encouragement, Hope, Perseverance

In shady, green pastures, so rich and so sweet,
God leads His dear children along;
Where the water's cool flow bathes the weary one's feet,
God leads His dear children along.

Some thru the waters, some thru the flood,
Some thru the fire, but all thru the blood;
Some thru great sorrow, but God gives a song,
In the night season and all the day long.

Sometimes on the mount where the sun shines so bright,
God leads His dear children along;
Sometimes in the valley, in the darkest of night,
God leads His dear children along.

Tho' sorrows befall us and Satan oppose,
God leads His dear children along,
Thru grace we can conquer, defeat all our foes,
God leads His dear children along.

GEORGE A. YOUNG (19TH CENTURY)

GOD MOVES IN A MYSTERIOUS WAY

"God moves in a mysterious way," and he certainly did in the life of William Cowper, who wrote this hymn. Cowper was afflicted with mental illness, and it is easy to understand why: His mother died when he was six. He was teased and ridiculed at school. His father prevented him from marrying the girl he loved. He was forced to study law, but he didn't like it. When he learned he would have his bar exam before the House of Lords in London, he tried to commit suicide and was committed to an insane asylum.

After a year, he was released into the care of a Christian couple, and soon he discovered that his best therapy came by writing poetry. He wrote many hymns, and his secular poetry is included in most collections of great English literature. He became one of England's finest poets.

In this hymn you see some of the lessons that Cowper himself had to learn as he talks about the clouds that hang overhead (in the third stanza) and the frowning providence (in the fourth stanza). These are lessons that all of us need to learn as well.

Scriptures: Exodus 34:5-6; Proverbs 16:9; Matthew 6:34; Matthew 10:30-31
Themes: God, Guidance, Comfort

God moves in a mysterious way
His wonders to perform;
He plants His footsteps in the sea,
And rides upon the storm.

Deep in unfathomable mines
Of never-failing skill,
He treasures up His bright designs,
And works His sovereign will.

Ye fearful saints, fresh courage take;
The clouds ye so much dread
Are big with mercy, and shall break
With blessing on your head.

Judge not the Lord by feeble sense,
But trust Him for His grace;
Behind a frowning providence
He hides a smiling face.

His purposes will ripen fast,
Unfolding every hour;

The bud may have a bitter taste,
But sweet will be the flower.

Blind unbelief is sure to err,
And scan His work in vain;
God is His own interpreter,
And He will make it plain.

WILLIAM COWPER (1731–1800)

GOD UNDERSTANDS

In the twentieth century, Oswald Smith of Toronto, Canada, was known as a missionary statesman. His own church, Peoples Church of Toronto, sent millions of dollars to world missions, and Smith encouraged other churches to do likewise.

Oswald Smith's sister went as a missionary to Peru with her husband, Clifford Bicker. The Bickers were just about to sail home on their first missionary furlough when Clifford Bicker was killed instantly in a car crash. Only twenty-six years old, Mrs. Bicker became a widow, and her two young children were fatherless.

She buried the body of her husband in Peru and was about to sail home with her two children when she received this poem from her brother, Oswald Smith. It gave her the reminder that "God understands," and it pointed her to the promise of Jesus: "I will never leave you nor forsake you" (Hebrews 13:5, ESV).

Scriptures: Psalm 56:8; Hebrews 13:5; 1 Peter 5:7

Themes: Comfort, Peace, Hope

God understands your sorrow, He sees the falling tear,
And whispers, "I am with thee," then falter not nor fear.
God understands your heartache, He knows the bitter pain;
O, trust Him in the darkness, you cannot trust in vain.

God understands your weakness, He knows the tempter's pow'r;
And He will walk beside you however dark the hour.
He understands your longing, your deepest grief He shares;
Then let Him bear your burden, He understands, and cares.

B. D. ACKLEY/OSWALD J. SMITH
©1937 Word Music, LLC

GREAT IS THY FAITHFULNESS

Thomas Chisholm certainly had his share of disappointments in life. Born in a crude log cabin in Kentucky, he never had a chance to attend high school or college. His health was fragile, forcing him to resign as a Methodist minister after only one year. He began writing, but received more than his share of rejection letters. Even when his poems were published, he seldom received any money for them.

At the age of fifty-seven, he wrote the hymn "Great Is Thy Faithfulness," based on the verses in Lamentations that say, "His compassions fail not. They are new every morning: great is thy faithfulness" (3:22-23, KJV). Later, when he was asked how he came to write the hymn, he said there were no special circumstances surrounding it, but he simply wrote about God's faithfulness from studying the Bible.

Scriptures: Psalm 36:5-7; Lamentations 3:22-25; James 1:17
Themes: Faithfulness, God's Mercy, Assurance

Great is Thy faithfulness, O God my Father,
There is no shadow of turning with Thee;
Thou changest not, Thy compassions they fail not;
As Thou hast been Thou forever wilt be.

Great is Thy faithfulness!
Great is Thy faithfulness!
Morning by morning new mercies I see;
All I have needed Thy hand hath provided—
Great is Thy faithfulness, Lord, unto me!

Summer and winter, and springtime and harvest,
Sun, moon and stars in their courses above
Join with all nature in manifold witness
To Thy great faithfulness, mercy and love.

Pardon for sin and a peace that endureth,
Thy own dear presence to cheer and to guide;
Strength for today and bright hope for tomorrow,
Blessings all mine, with ten thousand beside!

THOMAS OBEDIAH CHISHOLM (1866–1960)

GUIDE ME, O THOU GREAT JEHOVAH

The author of this hymn, William Williams, had been preparing for a career in medicine, but one Sunday morning he heard a man preaching in a Welsh churchyard. He responded in faith, and his life was drastically changed. For forty-three years, he preached and sang throughout Wales and became known as the poet laureate of the Welsh revival. Soon all Wales was singing their way to the coal mines and the soccer matches, and this became their favorite marching song.

In the hymn, Williams compares the Christian life to the Israelites' trek through the wilderness. He refers to God feeding the children of Israel with manna, leading them with fire and a cloudy pillar, and finally guiding them across the Jordan River into Canaan.

Scriptures: Exodus 13:22; Exodus 16:15; Psalm 48:14; Isaiah 58:11
Themes: Guidance, Deliverance, Security

Guide me, O Thou great Jehovah,
Pilgrim through this barren land;
I am weak, but Thou art mighty;
Hold me with Thy powerful hand;
Bread of heaven, Bread of heaven,
Feed me till I want no more,
Feed me till I want no more.

Open now the crystal fountain,
Whence the healing stream doth flow;
Let the fire and cloudy pillar
Lead me all my journey through;
Strong deliverer, strong deliverer,
Be Thou still my strength and shield,
Be Thou still my strength and shield.

When I tread the verge of Jordan,
Bid my anxious fears subside;
Death of death and hell's destruction,
Land me safe on Canaan's side;
Songs of praises, songs of praises
I will ever give to Thee,
I will ever give to Thee.

WILLIAM WILLIAMS (1717–1791)
Stanza 1 translated from Welsh by Peter Williams (1722–1796)
Stanzas 2 and 3 probably translated by the author

HE LEADETH ME!

It was the time of the Civil War, and people were losing hope. The war seemed to be endless, and the casualties were mounting. Joseph Gilmore, pastor of Philadelphia's First Baptist Church, wanted to bring some hope to his congregation, so he turned to Psalm 23. The important thing, he told his congregation, is to know that God is leading—no matter *how* or *where* he leads us.

After the service, he went to a deacon's home and continued the conversation about how God leads his children. As they were talking, he started scribbling some thoughts, and soon the words of the hymn were written. He gave the hymn to his wife and forgot all about it.

Three years later, when he was a pastoral candidate for a church in Rochester, New York, he began leafing through the church hymnal and spotted the hymn "He Leadeth Me"—his own hymn. What he didn't know was that his wife had submitted the hymn to a Christian periodical and that it had been set to music. He discovered that, when you are led by the Lord, there may be some delightful surprises.

Scriptures: Psalm 23:2-4; Psalm 31:3; Isaiah 48:17
Themes: Guidance, Comfort, Rest

He leadeth me! O blessed thought!
O words with heav'nly comfort fraught!
Whate'er I do, where'er I be,
Still 'tis God's hand that leadeth me!

He leadeth me, He leadeth me,
By His own hand He leadeth me:
His faithful follower I would be,
For by His hand He leadeth me.

Lord, I would clasp Thy hand in mine,
Nor ever murmur nor repine,
Content, whatever lot I see,
Since 'tis Thy hand that leadeth me!

And when my task on earth is done,
When, by Thy grace, the vict'ry's won,
E'en death's cold wave I will not flee,
Since God through Jordan leadeth me!

JOSEPH HENRY GILMORE (1834–1918)

HEAVENLY SUNLIGHT

Henry Zelley, a Methodist pastor in southern New Jersey, served nineteen different churches in his forty-year ministry. He also found time to write about 1,500 poems, hymns, and gospel songs, including the only song that is sung today, "Heavenly Sunlight."

"Heavenly Sunlight" might have been forgotten too, had it not been for radio pioneer Charles E. Fuller, who changed the word from *sunlight* to *sunshine* and featured the song every Sunday on his *Old Fashioned Revival Hour* program. Aired nationally on the Mutual Broadcasting System, Fuller's program opened with the singing of "Heavenly Sunshine." Thanks to his very popular radio program, Charles Fuller was said to have told the gospel story to more people than any other person in history up until the time of evangelist Billy Graham. Closely associated with Fuller was this gospel song, written by a Methodist pastor who served nineteen small churches in a forty-year ministry.

Scriptures: Psalm 16:11; Romans 12:12; Philippians 4:4

Themes: Joy, Thankfulness, Hope

Walking in sunlight all of my journey;
Over the mountains, thro' the deep vale;
Jesus has said "I'll never forsake thee,"
Promise divine that never can fail.

Heavenly sunlight, heavenly sunlight,
Flooding my soul with glory divine;
Hallelujah, I am rejoicing,
Singing His praises,
Jesus is mine.

Shadows around me, shadows above me,
Never conceal my Savior and Guide;
He is the light, in Him is no darkness;
Ever I'm walking close to His side.

In the bright sunlight, ever rejoicing,
Pressing my way to mansions above;
Singing His praises gladly I'm walking,
Walking in sunlight, sunlight of love.

HENRY J. ZELLEY (1859–1942)

I KNOW WHO HOLDS TOMORROW

Ira Stanphill had an international ministry as a singing evangelist and writer of about four hundred gospel songs. But in the 1940s he felt his ministry might be finished. His wife had walked out on him, and he felt his life had been shattered. He had an exciting ministry in a large church and school of music, but now he wondered if he should give it all up and get out of Christian work altogether. He sank deeper and deeper into depression.

Then one day he began humming a tune. He didn't know where it came from. Then he started putting words to the tune, words about not knowing the future but realizing that God knew.

When he got to the church that day, he rushed to a piano and started writing "I Know Who Holds Tomorrow." He hadn't written anything for months while in his depression, but now the words and the melody flowed out of him. Suddenly he felt at peace.

His questions weren't all answered, but he was content to leave them with the One who holds tomorrow, the One who was walking with him each step of the way, the One who was holding his hand.

Scriptures: Job 19:25; Romans 8:18; James 4:14-15
Themes: Hope, Trust, Faith

I don't know about tomorrow,
I just live from day to day;
And I don't borrow the sunshine
'cause the skies might turn to gray.

There are things about tomorrow
That I don't seem to understand;
But I know who holds tomorrow
And I know He holds my hand.

And I don't worry about the future
'cause I know what Jesus said;
And today I'm gonna walk right beside Him
'cause He's the one who knows what lies ahead.

And each step is getting brighter
As these golden stairs I climb;
And every burden is getting lighter,
And all the clouds, they're silver lined.

And over there the sun it's always shining;
There no tears will dim the eye.
And at the ending of the rainbow
Where the mountains touch the sky.

Written by Ira Stanphill

© 1950 New Spring (ASCAP)
All rights reserved. Used by permission.

IF THOU BUT SUFFER

While on his way to study law at the University of Konigsberg in Germany, Georg Neumark was robbed. All his savings were taken, and he had no money for further education. The next few years were difficult for him as he struggled to find employment. He wondered if God had forsaken him.

"How long, O Lord?" he asked. "Why do I have to wait so long to get on with my life?" But during that time he wrote hymns telling what he had learned in the process of waiting. The last verse of this hymn concludes, "God never yet forsook at need / The soul that trusted him indeed."

Scriptures: Psalm 13:1; Psalm 55:16-17, 22; Romans 5:3-4; James 1:3-4
Themes: Trust, Guidance, Prayer

If thou but suffer God to guide thee,
And hope in Him through all thy ways,
He'll give thee strength, whate'er betide thee,
And bear thee through the evil days;
Who trusts in God's unchanging love
Builds on the Rock that nought can move.

Only be still, and wait His leisure
In cheerful hope, with heart content
To take whate'er thy Father's pleasure
And all discerning love hath sent;
Nor doubt our inmost wants are known
To Him who chose us for His own.

Sing, pray, and swerve not from His ways,
But do thine own part faithfully;
Trust His rich promises of grace,

398

So shall they be fulfilled in thee;
God never yet forsook at need
The soul that trusted Him indeed.

GEORG NEUMARK (1621–1681)
Translated by Catherine Winkworth (1827–1878)

IN HIS TIME

As camp director of a conference center in northern California and the mother of four kids ages ten to fourteen, Diane Ball worked on a schedule. Everything was planned to the minute, including the family vacation. They were scheduled to leave at ten because she had a speaking engagement (during her vacation) at noon. But her husband, who was the maintenance man for the conference grounds, had a last-minute emergency, so he wasn't ready to go until eleven.

In Diane's words, "I was furious." She fretted and stewed and finally asked the Lord to give her some peace. Suddenly she heard the words *In His time.* She repeated them over and over and then heard more—*He makes everything beautiful—in His time.*

When she finally arrived for her speaking engagement, she had written the entire song, "In His Time." Not only that, but because of some unexpected problems, the luncheon had been delayed, so as it worked out, Diane and her husband and family arrived "just in time."

Scriptures: Psalm 31:15; Psalm 37:7; John 11:5-10

Themes: Contentment, Comfort, Submission

AUTHOR: DIANE BALL (B. 1941)

JESUS, SAVIOR, PILOT ME

Edward Hopper, the writer of this hymn, was born in New York City; went to school at New York University and Union Theological Seminary, both in New York City; and spent his life ministering to churches in New York City, except for eleven years when he served a church on Long Island.

Hopper's favorite ministry was a small church near New York Harbor called the Church of the Sea and Land. It was a ministry to sailors who used the harbor. Hopper was a quiet and humble man, hardly the type you would think could minister effectively to boisterous men of the sea.

Most of his hymns were written anonymously—he didn't acknowledge this hymn until seven years after it was published.

At Hopper's funeral, it was said that he had entered the heavenly port, "safely piloted by that never-failing friend, Jesus, whose divine voice was still tenderly whispering to him, 'Fear not, I will pilot thee.'"

Scriptures: Psalm 107:23-30; Jonah 2:1-9; Matthew 8:23-27
Themes: Comfort, Assurance, Peace

Jesus, Savior, pilot me
Over life's tempestuous sea;
Unknown waves before me roll,
Hiding rock and treacherous shoal;
Chart and compass came from Thee:
Jesus, Savior, pilot me.

As a mother stills her child,
Thou canst hush the ocean wild;
Boisterous waves obey Thy will
When Thou say'st to them "Be still!"
Wondrous Sov'reign of the sea,
Jesus, Savior, pilot me.

When at last I near the shore,
And the fearful breakers roar
'Twixt me and the peaceful rest,
Then, while leaning on Thy breast,
May I hear Thee say to me,
"Fear not, I will pilot thee."

EDWARD HOPPER (1818–1888)

LEAD, KINDLY LIGHT!

In 1833, John Henry Newman, a prominent minister in the Church of England, went to visit Catholic leaders in Italy. After he contracted Sicilian fever, he boarded a ship back to England. A lack of wind kept the ship motionless in the Mediterranean, and a dense fog left them unable to navigate. Restless and sick, Newman penned the words of this hymn. Along with his desire for the recovery of his physical health, he wanted to see spiritual recovery in the Church of England. And he wanted the ship to get moving.

Finally, the ship's captain pointed heavenward and said, "The star is shining tonight. If a wind rises, we can chart our course. At night one little star is sufficient."

Newman later wrote that he had been looking for dazzling sunlight to guide him through his life, "but He sent me the kindly light of a star to show me the way one step at a time."

Scriptures: Psalm 23:2-3; Psalm 31:3; Psalm 32:8; Psalm 48:14; John 8:12; Ephesians 5:14; 1 John 1:7
Themes: Guidance, Light, Leading

Lead, kindly Light! amid th'encircling gloom,
Lead Thou me on;
The night is dark, and I am far from home,
Lead Thou me on;
Keep Thou my feet: I do not ask to see
The distant scene; one step enough for me.

I was not ever thus, nor prayed that Thou
Shouldst lead me on;
I loved to choose and see my path; but now
Lead Thou me on;
I loved the garish day, and, spite of fears,
Pride ruled my will. Remember not past years.

So long Thy pow'r has blessed me, sure it still
Will lead me on
O'er moor and fen, o'er crag and torrent, till
The night is gone;
And with the morn those angel faces smile
Which I have loved long since, and lost awhile!

JOHN HENRY NEWMAN (1801–1890)

LEAD ON, O KING ETERNAL

In 1887 Ernest Shurtleff was graduating from seminary, and his graduating class asked him to write the class poem. Instead of writing a poem, he wrote a hymn, and he asked the entire graduating class to sing it on commencement day. He introduced it with these words: "We've been spending days of preparation here at seminary. Now the day of march has come, and we must go out to follow the leadership of the King of kings, to conquer the world under His banner."

His words apply to all of us at any time. Every day is a commencement, and the Lord calls us to step through the open door and face the world in his strength.

Scriptures: Joshua 1:9-11; Psalm 43:3; Proverbs 6:22; 1 Timothy 1:17
Themes: Guidance, Future, Warfare

> Lead on, O King eternal,
> The day of march has come;
> Henceforth in fields of conquest
> Thy tents shall be our home.
> Through days of preparation
> Thy grace has made us strong,
> And now, O King eternal,
> We lift our battle song.
>
> Lead on, O King eternal,
> Till sin's fierce war shall cease,
> And holiness shall whisper
> The sweet amen of peace.
> For not with swords' loud clashing,
> Nor roll of stirring drums,
> With deeds of love and mercy
> The heavenly kingdom comes.
>
> Lead on, O King eternal,
> We follow, not with fears,
> For gladness breaks like morning
> Where'er Thy face appears.
> Thy cross is lifted o'er us;
> We journey in its light;
> The crown awaits the conquest;
> Lead on, O God of might.

ERNEST WARBURTON SHURTLEFF (1862–1917)

LORD, IT BELONGS NOT TO MY CARE

From this hymn and the books he wrote, such as *The Saints' Everlasting Rest*, it would be easy to assume that Richard Baxter was a docile gentleman who lived quietly in a British country manor. But that was far from the case for this seventeenth-century English clergyman. Too Puritan for the Anglican bishops and too Episcopalian for the Presbyterians, he was always getting into trouble. And the Puritans didn't like him because he was a champion of church music.

At the age of seventy, Baxter was brought before a judge and accused of writing a paraphrase of the New Testament. The judge called him "an old rogue, a hypocritical villain, a fanatical dog, and a sniveling Presbyterian." He proceeded to have Baxter whipped and jailed in the Tower of London.

This hymn was written as an expansion of Philippians 1:21—"For to me, to live is Christ and to die is gain" (NIV). It was dedicated to Baxter's wife, who had died a few years earlier after a long and painful illness. Baxter's life was full of constant struggle, but he was content to leave matters in the hands of the Lord.

Scriptures: Matthew 6:25-34; Philippians 1:21; Philippians 4:11-13
Themes: Guidance, Discipleship, Assurance

Lord, it belongs not to my care
Whether I die or live;
To love and serve Thee is my share,
And this Thy grace must give.

If life be long, I will be glad
That I may long obey;
If short, yet why should I be sad
To soar to endless day?

Christ leads me through no darker rooms
Than He went through before;
He that into God's kingdom comes
Must enter by this door.

Come, Lord, when grace hath made me meet
Thy blessed face to see;
For if Thy work on earth be sweet,
What will Thy glory be?

My knowledge of that life is small;
The eye of faith is dim;
But 'tis enough that Christ knows all,
And I shall be with Him.

RICHARD BAXTER (1615–1691)

NO ONE EVER CARED FOR ME LIKE JESUS

Charles Weigle spent most of his life as an evangelist, and that meant he was on the road a great deal. One day after returning home from an evangelistic crusade, he found a note written by his wife. She had had enough of being an evangelist's wife. She couldn't take it anymore. She said she was leaving him and taking their young daughter to live in a distant city.

Weigle was despondent. What could he do to restore the marriage? How could he continue to serve the Lord when he couldn't even make his marriage work? He thought of suicide; he had ruined his wife's life and ruined his own life. No one really cared for him, he thought.

And then he felt sustained by the grace of God. The simple truth that Jesus still loved him brought him through. Sitting at the piano, he started writing some thoughts and some notes about how God's love hadn't changed. Despite everything, Jesus had not forsaken him. No one ever cared for him like Jesus.

Scriptures: Jeremiah 31:3; Ephesians 3:19; 1 Peter 5:7

Themes: Love, Comfort, Assurance

I would love to tell you what I think of Jesus
Since I found in Him a friend so strong and true;
I would tell you how He chang'd my life completely.
He did something that no other friend could do.

No one ever cared for me like Jesus,
There's no other friend so kind as He;
No one else could take the sin and darkness from me
O how much He cared for me.

All my life was full of sin when Jesus found me,
All my heart was full of misery and woe;
Jesus placed His strong and loving arms around me,
And He led me in the way I ought to go.

Ev'ry day He comes to me with new assurance,
More and more I understand His words of love;
But I'll never know just why He came to save me,
Till some day I see His blessed face above.

Written by: Charles F. Weigle
© 1932 New Spring (ASCAP)
All rights reserved. Used by permission.

SAVIOR, LIKE A SHEPHERD LEAD US

Of all the names and titles given to Jesus, perhaps the most beloved is Shepherd, a title Jesus gave himself in John 10. The Good Shepherd knows his sheep, guards his sheep, and even gives his life for his sheep. Scripture also says that he knows his sheep by name.

On Christmas Eve 1875, Ira Sankey, the gospel singer who accompanied evangelist Dwight L. Moody, was traveling with friends by steamboat up the Delaware River. He was asked to sing for the other passengers, but instead of singing a Christmas carol, he felt he should sing, "Savior, like a Shepherd Lead Us." Afterward, another passenger asked him if he had been doing picket duty on a particular night at a particular place during the Civil War. Sankey agreed that he was. The other passenger said, "I, too, was on duty that night; I was serving in the Confederate Army, and I saw you and raised my musket to take aim. And then you began to sing. It was the same hymn you sang tonight. I remembered my mother singing that hymn to me, and I could not shoot you."

On board the steamboat, Sankey put his arm around the man and introduced him to the Good Shepherd, who gave his life for his sheep.

Scriptures: Psalm 23:1; John 10:14-15; 1 Corinthians 6:20
Themes: Guidance, Protection, Shepherds, Names of Jesus

Savior, like a shepherd lead us,
Much we need Thy tender care;
In Thy pleasant pastures feed us,
For our use Thy folds prepare:
Blessed Jesus, blessed Jesus!
Thou hast bought us, Thine we are.

We are Thine, do Thou befriend us,
Be the guardian of our way;
Keep Thy flock, from sin defend us,
Seek us when we go astray:
Blessed Jesus, blessed Jesus!
Hear, O hear us, when we pray.

Thou hast promised to receive us,
Poor and sinful though we be;
Thou hast mercy to relieve us,
Grace to cleanse and power to free:

Blessed Jesus, blessed Jesus!
Early let us turn to Thee.

Early let us seek Thy favor,
Early let us do Thy will;
Blessed Lord and only Savior,
With Thy love our bosoms fill:
Blessed Jesus, blessed Jesus!
Thou hast loved us, love us still.

HYMNS FOR THE YOUNG, 1836
Attributed to Dorothy A. Thrupp (1779–1847)

SEEK YE FIRST

Karen Lafferty always seemed to be coming in second. She kept reaching for the brass ring, but it always seemed to elude her grasp. She had graduated from Eastern New Mexico University with a degree in choral music and oboe, and by that time she also played piano, saxophone, and guitar. She entered the Miss New Mexico contest and ended up as first runner-up. Thinking that she could climb the ladder in show business, she started singing in saloons in New Orleans. But as a Christian, she recognized that this was not the right place for her to be. "I was faced with a strong decision," she said. "Either I'm going to live for Christ or I'm not."

She renewed her commitment to the Lord and decided to use her talents for him. But when she auditioned for Campus Crusade's music ministry, she was turned down; they didn't think she was mature enough as a Christian. "I was crushed," she says. She decided to give guitar lessons, but got only three students—not enough to support herself. When she was at the lowest point of her life, she went to a Bible study. "That evening," she says, "we studied from Matthew 6, about how God takes care of the birds of the air, and there was that verse, 'Seek ye first the kingdom of God, and His righteousness.'"

That evening she went home and began plucking on her guitar. Suddenly this verse and melody came out. "That was it," she says. "I went to bed and slept in peace, confident that God would do something."

Scriptures: Psalm 23:1; Matthew 6:33; Philippians 4:19
Themes: Stewardship, Commitment, Blessing

AUTHOR: KAREN LAFFERTY (B. 1948)

SURELY GOODNESS AND MERCY

Alfred B. Smith, music publisher and songwriter, received a letter one day from one of the descendants of Philip Bliss, a nineteenth-century gospel composer. It told the story of how Philip Bliss learned the Twenty-third Psalm before he could read or write. His teacher's name was Miss Murphy, and little Philip learned the psalm this way: "Surely, good Miss Murphy shall follow me all the days of my life." Sometimes the inspiration for a gospel song comes in strange ways!

At the time, Smith was associated with composer John W. Peterson in one of the largest gospel-music companies of the mid-twentieth century. One day John was improvising on the piano as Al Smith came into the room. "For no particular reason that I can remember," John says, "we started to develop a new song."

They thought about a new approach to Psalm 23. Al apparently was thinking of "Good Miss Murphy," and John's mind went back to his days in the air force during World War II when he often gave thanks for the Good Shepherd who cares for his sheep. So the song was born, emphasizing God's goodness and mercy, as well as God's guidance through cold nights and lonesome valleys.

Scriptures: Psalm 23; Isaiah 40:11; John 10:14
Themes: Shepherds, Guidance, Comfort

A pilgrim was I, and a wand'ring, in the cold night of sin I did roam,
When Jesus the kind Shepherd found me, and now I am on
   my way home.

Surely goodness and mercy shall follow me all the days of my life;
And I shall dwell in the house of the Lord forever,
And I shall feast at the table spread for me.
Surely goodness and mercy shall follow me all the days,
All the days of my life.

He restoreth my soul when I'm weary, He giveth me strength
   day by day;
He leads me beside the still waters; He guards me each step of the way.

When I walk thru the dark lonesome valley, my Savior will walk with me
there;
And safely His great hand will lead me to the mansions
   He's gone to prepare.

JOHN WILLARD PETERSON (B. 1921) AND ALFRED BARNEY SMITH (1916–2001)

THE GOD OF ABRAHAM PRAISE

Tommy Olivers had the worst reputation of all the young men in his eighteenth-century English neighborhood. Orphaned at a young age, he was headed to a life of debauchery. But then one day in Bristol, England, he heard George Whitefield preach on Zechariah 3:2: "Is not this a brand plucked out of the fire?" (KJV).

Tommy felt he was headed straight for fire and brimstone, and he wanted to be plucked out of it. That day he was converted, and he became an evangelist.

One day Tommy walked into a Jewish synagogue in London and heard the cantor sing a doxology. Impressed by both the music and the words, he adapted them for Christian worship. Some of the stanzas are not in our hymnals. There is one that Olivers regarded as his own personal testimony. It ends, "He calls a worm His friend; He calls Himself my God! / And He shall save me to the end through Jesus' blood."

Scriptures: Exodus 3:14; Psalm 99:1-3; John 8:58; Hebrews 13:8
Themes: Praise, God the Father, Adoration

The God of Abraham praise,
Who reigns enthroned above;
Ancient of everlasting days,
And God of love.
Jehovah, great I AM,
By earth and heaven confessed;
I bow and bless the sacred name,
Forever blest.

The God of Abraham praise,
At whose supreme command
From earth I rise, and seek the joys
At His right hand.
I all on earth forsake,
Its wisdom, fame, and power;
And Him my only portion make,
My shield and tower.

He by Himself hath sworn,
I on His oath depend,
I shall, on eagles' wings upborne,
To heaven ascend;

I shall behold His face,
I shall His power adore,
And sing the wonders of His grace
Forevermore.

The whole triumphant host
Give thanks to God on high;
"Hail, Father, Son and Holy Ghost!"
They ever cry.
Hail, Abraham's God and mine!
I join the heavenly lays;
All might and majesty are Thine,
And endless praise.

THOMAS OLIVERS (1725–1799)

THE LORD JEHOVAH REIGNS

In the churches of seventeenth-century England, worshippers sang the Psalms. There was no choice. Isaac Watts paraphrased them so some of them didn't sound like Psalms. Few people realize today, for instance, that "Joy to the World" is really Isaac Watts's paraphrase of Psalm 98. "The Lord Jehovah Reigns" is his paraphrase of Psalm 97.

It begins by speaking of God's power and majesty, then reminds us of God's hand in nature. But in the last verse, Watts goes beyond the psalm and tells us how our sovereign God, who made the universe, condescends to become "My Father and my Friend." It is a great conclusion. No wonder Watts could add, "I love His name, I love His Word; / Join all my powers to praise the Lord."

Yes, our God is an awesome God, and because of Jesus, this awesome God is our Friend.

Scriptures: Psalm 96:10-11; Psalm 97:1-5; John 15:14-15
Themes: God's Power, Creation, God's Love

The Lord Jehovah reigns,
His throne is built on high;
The garments He assumes
Are light and majesty;
His glories shine with beams so bright,
No mortal eye can bear the sight.

The thunders of His hand
Keep the wide world in awe;
His wrath and justice stand
To guard His holy law;
And where His love resolves to bless,
His truth confirms and seals the grace.

Through all His mighty works
Amazing wisdom shines,
Confounds the powers of hell,
And breaks their dark designs;
Strong is His arm, and shall fulfill
His great decrees and sovereign will.

And will this sovereign King
Of glory condescend;
And will He write His name
My Father and my Friend?
I love His name, I love His Word;
Join all my powers to praise the Lord!

ISAAC WATTS (1674–1748)

THE LORD'S MY SHEPHERD, I'LL NOT WANT

In the seventeenth century, Scottish Bibles often had psalms in meter printed after the book of Revelation. In most of the humble cottages of Scotland, the metrical psalms were sung twice a day, thus becoming more familiar to the people than the Bible text itself.

Francis Rous, a member of the British Parliament, was dissatisfied with the accuracy of the translations, so he prepared his own metrical version of Psalms, which he said was a more faithful paraphrase of the original. Rous's Psalter became very popular and was authorized by the Westminster Assembly, which developed the Westminster Catechism and Confession in the mid-seventeenth century.

Scriptures: Psalm 23; John 10:11; Hebrews 13:20
Themes: Comfort, Guidance, Provision

The Lord's my Shepherd, I'll not want;
He makes me down to lie
In pastures green; He leadeth me
The quiet waters by.

My soul He doth restore again;
And me to walk doth make
Within the paths of righteousness,
E'en for His own name's sake.

Yea, though I walk through death's dark vale,
Yet will I fear no ill;
For Thou art with me, and Thy rod
And staff me comfort still.

My table Thou hast furnished
In presence of my foes;
My head Thou dost with oil anoint,
And my cup overflows.

Goodness and mercy all my life
Shall surely follow me;
And in God's house forevermore
My dwelling place shall be.

FRANCIS ROUS, FROM THE *SCOTTISH PSALTER*, 1650

THE NINETY AND NINE

In 1874, evangelist Dwight L. Moody and song leader Ira Sankey had just finished a series of meetings in Glasgow, Scotland, and were taking the train to Edinburgh for more meetings. Ira Sankey picked up a newspaper, glanced through it, found nothing of interest, and put it down. But just before they reached Edinburgh, he picked up the newspaper again and noticed a small poem in a corner of a page. He read it to Dwight L. Moody, but Moody wasn't listening; he was absorbed in something else. Sankey cut out the poem anyway and tucked it away. The poem was called "The Ninety and Nine."

In Edinburgh, Moody's message was on "The Good Shepherd," and afterwards Sankey was asked to sing something appropriate. Sankey said he was "greatly troubled" because he could think of nothing. Then he seemed to hear a voice saying, "Sing the hymn you found on the train." *Impossible*, thought Sankey, *there's no music for it*. But the feeling he had came stronger than ever: "Sing it anyway." So, Sankey said, "I lifted my heart in prayer, asking God to help me. Laying my hands upon the organ I struck the key of A-flat and began to sing. Note by note the tune was given, which has not been changed from that day."

The audience was moved. Moody had tears in his eyes and so did Sankey. Thus the gospel song "The Ninety and Nine" was born.

Scriptures: Psalm 23; Isaiah 53:6; Luke 15:2-7; John 10:11
Themes: Shepherds, Parables, Love

There were ninety and nine that safely lay
In the shelter of the fold,
But one was out on the hills away,
Far off from the gates of gold—
Away on the mountains wild and bare,
Away from the tender Shepherd's care,
Away from the tender Shepherd's care.

"Lord, Thou hast here Thy ninety and nine;
Are they not enough for Thee?"
But the Shepherd made answer:
"This of mine has wandered away from me,
And altho' the road be rough and steep,
I go to the desert to find my sheep,
I go to the desert to find my sheep."

But none of the ransomed ever knew
How deep were the waters crossed;
Nor how dark was the night that the Lord passed thro'
Ere He found His sheep that was lost.
Out in the desert He heard its cry,
Sick and helpless, and ready to die;
Sick and helpless, and ready to die.

"Lord, whence are those blood drops all the way
That mark out the mountain's track?"
"They were shed for one who had gone astray
Ere the Shepherd could bring him back."
"Lord, whence are Thy hands so rent and torn?"
"They're pierced tonight by many a thorn;
They're pierced tonight by many a thorn."

But all thro' the mountains, thunder-riv'n,
And up from the rocky steep,
There arose a glad cry to the gates of heav'n,
"Rejoice! I have found My sheep!"
And the angels echoed around the throne,

"Rejoice, for the Lord brings back His own!
Rejoice, for the Lord brings back His own!"

ELIZABETH CECILIA CLEPHANE (1830–1869)

THERE'S A WIDENESS IN GOD'S MERCY

Brought up as an Anglican, Frederick Faber was ordained in the Church of England. But at the age of thirty-one, he converted to Roman Catholicism and became a Catholic priest. In 1849, Faber decided to open an oratory—a place of prayer in London. The word *oratory* comes from the Latin *oratorio*, which is often used to describe a composition uniting a biblical text with music. When Faber opened his oratory, it soon became a place of both prayer and music, much like the famous Oratory in Rome.

Faber was concerned that British Roman Catholics did not have a heritage of hymnwriters like Isaac Watts, Charles Wesley, and John Newton. So he began writing hymns so that Catholics, too, could be a hymn-singing people. Just as there is "a wideness in God's mercy," so was there a breadth to Faber's hymns, which soon became more familiar to Protestants than to Catholics.

Scriptures: Psalm 86:15; Psalm 100:3-5; Ephesians 1:6-8
Themes: God's Mercy, Redemption, Love

There's a wideness in God's mercy,
Like the wideness of the sea;
There's a kindness in His justice,
Which is more than liberty.
There is welcome for the sinner,
And more graces for the good;
There is mercy with the Savior;
There is healing in His blood.

For the love of God is broader
Than the measure of man's mind;
And the heart of the Eternal
Is most wonderfully kind.
If our love were but more simple,
We should take Him at His word;
And our lives would be all sunshine
In the sweetness of our Lord.

FREDERICK WILLIAM FABER (1814–1863)

WHEREVER HE LEADS I'LL GO

The missionary R. S. Jones was speaking at a Sunday school convention in Clanton, Alabama. After many years of missionary service in Brazil, he had been forced to return home; doctors said that he could not return to the mission field.

B. B. McKinney, a leading Southern Baptist hymnwriter, was leading the singing that night, and after the meeting, he talked with Jones and asked him about his future plans.

"I don't know," said the missionary, "but wherever he leads, I'll go."

McKinney couldn't get those words out of his mind. He went to his room and wrote the words and music for this hymn. R. S. Jones was speaking again at the closing session of the convention, and after his message, McKinney told Jones's story and then sang the new hymn, "Wherever He Leads, I'll Go," to the congregation.

Scriptures: Matthew 10:38; Mark 1:17-18; John 12:25
Themes: Guidance, Submission, Missions

"Take up thy cross and follow Me," I heard my Master say;
"I gave My life to ransom thee, surrender your all today."

Wherever He leads I'll go,
Wherever He leads I'll go,
I'll follow my Christ who loves me so,
Wherever He leads I'll go.

He drew me closer to His side, I sought His will to know,
And in that will I now abide, wherever He leads I'll go.

It may be thro' the shadows dim, or o'er the stormy sea,
I take the cross and follow Him, wherever He leadeth me.

My heart, my life, my all I bring to Christ who loves me so;
He is my Master, Lord, and King, wherever He leads I'll go.

BAYLUS BENJAMIN MCKINNEY (1886–1952)

PART XIII

HOLY SPIRIT

"You will receive power when the Holy Spirit comes upon you. And you will be my witnesses, telling people about me everywhere."

ACTS 1:8

BREATHE ON ME, BREATH OF GOD

Edwin Hatch, the writer of this hymn, was a learned man. He could string together sentences filled with polysyllabic words. He was a distinguished lecturer in ecclesiastical history at Oxford and a professor of classics at Trinity College in Quebec. His lectures "On the Organization of Early Christian Churches" were translated into German by the noted theologian Harnack. Few other English theologians had won European recognition for original research.

But when it came to expressing his faith, Hatch was "as simple and unaffected as a child." This hymn is filled with one-syllable words and is a simple, heartfelt prayer.

Hatch knew that, while the words of his hymn were simple, the meaning was profound. At man's creation, God breathed and man "became a living being" (Genesis 2:7, NIV). At our re-creation through Jesus, the breath of God brings spiritual life and power.

Scriptures: Genesis 2:7; John 20:22; Romans 8:11-12, 14
Themes: Holy Spirit, Holiness, Sanctification

Breathe on me, Breath of God,
Fill me with life anew,
That I may love what Thou dost love,
And do what Thou wouldst do.

Breathe on me, Breath of God,
Until my heart is pure,
Until with Thee I will one will,
To do and to endure.

Breathe on me, Breath of God,
Till I am wholly Thine,
Till all this earthly part of me
Glows with Thy fire divine.

Breathe on me, Breath of God,
So shall I never die,
But live with Thee the perfect life
Of Thine eternity.

EDWIN HATCH (1835–1889)

COME, GRACIOUS SPIRIT, HEAVENLY DOVE

Jesus told his disciples that the Father would send the Holy Spirit to guide them and to guard them. He would be the Paraclete, the Counselor, sent to help them and us. He would lead us into truth, Jesus said, and bring glory to Christ through us.

Hymnwriter Simon Browne often found it easier to write things on paper than to know them experientially. He wrote an English dictionary, completed the memorable commentary of Matthew Henry after that great scholar passed away, and wrote beautiful hymns.

But he struggled with the painful memory of an event that happened when he was forty years old. Browne was attacked by a highwayman, and in self-defense, he struck the man, knocking him down and killing him. Convinced that he was a murderer, Browne could never forgive himself; he felt God had taken his soul from him. The prayer of his tortured heart is captured in the first line of this hymn, "Come, gracious Spirit, heav'nly Dove, / With light and comfort from above."

Scriptures: John 14:15-18; John 16:13-15; 1 John 4:13
Themes: Holy Spirit, Holiness, Guidance

Come, gracious Spirit, heav'nly Dove,
With light and comfort from above;
Be Thou our Guardian, Thou our Guide;
O'er ev'ry thought and step preside.

To us the light of truth display,
And make us know and choose Thy way;
Plant holy fear in ev'ry heart,
That we from God may ne'er depart.

Lead us to holiness, the road
Which we must take to dwell with God;
Lead us to Christ, the living way;
Nor let us from His pastures stray.

Lead us to God, our final rest,
To be with Him forever blest;
Lead us to heav'n, its bliss to share,
Fullness of joy forever there.

SIMON BROWNE (1680–1732)

COME, HOLY GHOST, OUR HEARTS INSPIRE

This hymn uses two Scripture passages: the very first biblical reference to the Holy Spirit and one of the last. In Genesis 1:2, we find the Spirit involved in Creation, "hovering over the surface of the waters." The earth has just been described as "formless and empty," but the Spirit oversees the ordering of our world. Light shines in the next verse, at God's command, and the rest of the chapter details the molding of a Creation that God pronounced "good."

Toward the end of the New Testament, 2 Peter 1:19-21 urges readers to pay attention to the word of the prophets, "like a lamp shining in a dark place." The prophets, Peter says, were not just making this stuff up. No, they were inspired by God, "moved by the Holy Spirit."

As usual, Charles Wesley has woven solid theology into his hymn. The Spirit brings order out of our chaos. He shines light into our dark places. He often does this through the Scriptures. He unlocks the truth spoken by the ancient prophets so it makes sense in modern times.

Scriptures: Genesis 1:2; 1 Corinthians 2:9-10; 2 Peter 1:19-21
Themes: Holy Spirit, Guidance, Holiness

Come, Holy Ghost, our hearts inspire,
Let us Thine influence prove:
Source of the old prophetic fire,
Fountain of life and love.

Come, Holy Ghost, for moved by Thee
The prophets wrote and spoke;
Unlock the truth, Thyself the key,
Unseal the sacred book.

Expand Thy wings, celestial Dove,
Brood o'er our nature's night;
On our disordered spirits move,
And let there now be light.

God, through Himself, we then shall know
If Thou within us shine,
And sound with all Thy saints below,
The depths of love divine.

CHARLES WESLEY (1707–1788)

COME, HOLY GHOST, OUR SOULS INSPIRE

The Holy Spirit is often associated with fire. John the Baptist spoke of Jesus baptizing people with the Holy Spirit and with fire. Sure enough, when the Holy Spirit came at Pentecost, he appeared as tongues of fire resting on each believer. It's a reminder of the many Old Testament appearances of the Lord as a fiery presence—in the burning bush, leading Israel through the desert, inhabiting the Tabernacle and the Temple. Was this the Spirit's "celestial fire"?

The Latin original of this hymn dates back to the ninth or tenth century and was probably written by the archbishop of Mainz, Rhabanus Maurus. Consequently, it has been used in worship for more than a thousand years.

There are seven gifts of the Spirit mentioned in Romans 12:6-8. This may be behind the "sevenfold gifts" of this hymn's first stanza. Note that the Holy Spirit is called "the anointing Spirit." In Scripture, anointing had two purposes: Ritually, it was used as a sign of God's special empowerment for kings, prophets, and priests. But in everyday life, it was a way of refreshing and cleansing. The Spirit does all that for us, empowering us to serve God as well as offering spiritual refreshment.

Scriptures: Acts 10:38; Acts 13:2-4; Romans 12:6-8; 2 Corinthians 3:17-18
Themes: Holy Spirit, Trinity, Power

Come, Holy Ghost, our souls inspire,
And lighten with celestial fire;
Thou the anointing Spirit art,
Who dost Thy sevenfold gifts impart.

Thy blessed unction from above
Is comfort, life, and fire of love;
Enable with perpetual light
The dullness of our blinded sight.

Anoint and cheer our soiled face
With the abundance of Thy grace;
Keep far our foes; give peace at home;
Where Thou art guide, no ill can come.

Teach us to know the Father, Son,
And Thee, of both, to be but One;
That through the ages all along
This, this may be our endless song:

Praise to Thy eternal merit
Father, Son, and Holy Spirit.

ATTRIBUTED TO RHABANUS MAURUS (CA. 776–856)
Translated by John Cosin (1594–1672)

COME, HOLY SPIRIT, DOVE DIVINE

Adoniram Judson and his wife, Ann, served in Burma as missionaries for a long time before they saw their first converts. During those years, Adoniram worked to translate the Bible into the Burmese language. Both Adoniram and Ann printed tracts and prepared curriculum, but after five years of evangelistic efforts, there were no visible results. Finally, one Burmese man responded. You can sense the hesitation in Adoniram's journal as he wrote, "I begin to think that the grace of God has reached his heart."

The next step was to prepare the man for baptism, and Adoniram prayed, "Oh, may it prove the beginning of a series of baptisms in the Burman Empire which shall continue in uninterrupted succession to the end of time." When more Burmese became Christians and asked to be baptized, Judson wrote this baptismal hymn.

By the time of Judson's death, seven thousand Burmese had come to Christ. The waiting was worth it.

Scriptures: Luke 3:22; Romans 6:3-4; Romans 8:11
Themes: Holy Spirit, Baptism, Lamb of God

Come, Holy Spirit, Dove divine,
On these baptismal waters shine,
And teach our hearts, in highest strain,
To praise the Lamb for sinners slain.

We love Thy name, we love Thy laws,
And joyfully embrace Thy cause;
We love Thy cross, the shame, the pain,
O Lamb of God for sinners slain.

We sink beneath the water's face,
And thank Thee for Thy saving grace;
We die to sin and seek a grave
With Thee, beneath the yielding wave.

And as we rise with Thee to live,
O let the Holy Spirit give

The sealing unction from above,
The joy of life, the fire of love.

ADONIRAM JUDSON (1788–1850)

COME, HOLY SPIRIT, HEAVENLY DOVE

Isaac Watts was disturbed with "business-as-usual" Christianity. He knew that the only way Christians could be shaken out of their lethargy was if they had a fresh touch of the Spirit. Just as Jesus is described as both a meek lamb and a fearsome lion, so the Holy Spirit is described as both a dove and a fire. Sometimes Christians need to experience the Holy Spirit as a gentle dove, but often we need to know him as a roaring fire.

One stanza that is often omitted from this hymn is "Father, and shall we ever live / At this poor dying rate, / Our love so faint, so cold to Thee, / And Thine to us so great?" It was this contrast between our love for God and God's love for us that disturbed Watts. He knew that only the fire of the Spirit could kindle our hearts into deeper love.

Scriptures: Mark 1:10; John 16:8-11; Acts 2:2-4
Themes: Holy Spirit, Revival, Consecration

Come, Holy Spirit, Heav'nly Dove,
With all Thy quick'ning pow'rs;
Kindle a flame of sacred love
In these cold hearts of ours.

Look, how we grovel here below,
Fond of these earthly toys;
Our souls, how heavily they go,
To reach eternal joys.

In vain we tune our formal songs,
In vain we strive to rise;
Hosannas languish on our tongues,
And our devotion dies.

Father, and shall we ever live
At this poor dying rate,
Our love so faint, so cold to Thee,
And Thine to us so great?

Come, Holy Spirit, Heav'nly Dove,
With all Thy quick'ning pow'rs;
Come, shed abroad a Savior's love,
And that shall kindle ours.

ISAAC WATTS (1674–1748)

COME DOWN, O LOVE DIVINE

Six hundred years ago, Bianco da Siena, while living in Venice, Italy, wrote this hymn, which he entitled "The Holy Spirit Desired." It was one of ninety-two hymns he wrote for a hymnbook he called *Spiritual Praise*. In the nineteenth century, Richard Littledale—a man of broad interests who had a special interest in writing and translating hymns—discovered the hymn and translated it from Italian into English. He published it in *The People's Hymnal* in 1867. The amazing thing about Littledale is that he also translated hymns from Danish, Swedish, Greek, Latin, Syrian, and German.

This hymn is a lovely, sensitive invitation to the Holy Spirit to enter our hearts and consume all our earthly passions, transforming us into the people God wants us to be.

Scriptures: Psalm 51:10-13; John 16:7-11; Romans 8:5-6
Themes: Holy Spirit, Holiness, Consecration

Come down, O Love divine,
Seek Thou this soul of mine,
And visit it with Thine own ardor glowing;
O Comforter, draw near,
Within my heart appear,
And kindle it, Thy holy flame bestowing.

O let it freely burn,
Till earthly passions turn
To dust and ashes in its heat consuming;
And let Thy glorious light
Shine ever on my sight,
And clothe me round the while my path illuming.

And so the yearning strong,
With which the soul will long,
Shall far outpass the power of human telling;

For none can guess its grace,
Till he become the place
Wherein the Holy Spirit makes His dwelling.

BIANCO DA SIENA (?–1434)
Translated by Richard F. Littledale (1833–1890)

EVEN ME

As Elizabeth Codner was reading her Bible, she noticed a verse in Ezekiel that said, "I will cause the shower to come down in his season; there shall be showers of blessing" (34:26, KJV).

She was still thinking about that verse when a group of church young people came to her door. They had just returned from a mission trip to Ireland and were excited about what they had experienced. A spiritual awakening was going on, and they had to tell her about it.

But she wondered whether these young people were just spectators to the revival, or if they had experienced the outpouring of God in their own lives. So with the verse in Ezekiel still fresh in her mind, she said, "While the Lord is pouring out such showers of blessing upon others, pray that some drops will fall on you."

A few days later, she wrote "Even Me," which begins with the words, "Lord, I hear of show'rs of blessing."

Scriptures: Psalm 72:6; Psalm 85:6; Ezekiel 34:26
Themes: Blessing, Revival, Seeking God

Lord, I hear of show'rs of blessing Thou art scatt'ring full and free;
Show'rs the thirsty land refreshing—let some drops now fall on me.

Even me, even me, let Thy blessing fall on me.

Love of God so pure and changeless, blood of Christ so rich and free,
Grace of God so strong and boundless magnify them all in me.

Pass me not! Thy lost one bringing, bind my heart, O Lord, to Thee;
While the streams of life are springing, blessing others, O bless me.

ELIZABETH CODNER (1824–1919)

GRACIOUS SPIRIT, DWELL WITH ME

Pastor Thomas Lynch of London, England, included this hymn in a collection of hymns he published in 1855. He never anticipated the violent response he received. Some said that the hymns were too personal; others said they might have been written by a man who had never seen a Bible. The attacks were so persistent that some of the foremost ministers of England came to his defense and published a protest against the attackers.

But Lynch seemed to be unruffled. After all, he had just written this hymn, which begins, "Gracious Spirit, dwell with me; I myself would gracious be." Did he respond? Oh, yes, he did. He answered this way: "The air will be all the clearer for the storm. We must conquer our foes by suffering them to crucify us, rather than by threatening them with crucifixion."

Scriptures: Romans 8:11; 1 Corinthians 6:19-20; Galatians 5:22-25
Themes: Holy Spirit, Grace, Holiness

Gracious Spirit, dwell with me; I myself would gracious be;
And with words that help and heal would Thy life in mine reveal;
And with actions bold and meek would for Christ my Savior speak.

Truthful Spirit, dwell with me: I myself would truthful be;
And with wisdom kind and clear let Thy life in mine appear;
And with actions brotherly speak my Lord's sincerity.

Mighty Spirit, dwell with me: I myself would mighty be;
Mighty so as to prevail where unaided man must fail:
Ever by a mighty hope pressing on and bearing up.

Holy Spirit, dwell with me: I myself would holy be;
Separate from sin, I would choose and cherish all things good,
And whatever I can be, give to Him who gave me Thee!

THOMAS T. LYNCH (1818–1871)

GREATER IS HE THAT IS IN ME

Composer Lanny Wolf was driving through Nevada one day on his way to Montana, a trip that gives plenty of time for composing. Wolf remembers it this way: "I was just riding in my car and I had a moment of truth of the Scripture that I had read all my life. It was just a realization of what that Scripture really meant."

The Scripture was 1 John 4:4: "Ye are of God, little children, and have overcome them: because greater is he that is in you, than he that is in the world" (KJV). As Christians, we have the Holy Spirit indwelling us, and the Holy Spirit gives us the confidence and courage we need to face any obstacle.

Scriptures: Luke 12:11-12; Romans 8:11; 1 John 4:4
Themes: Courage, Power, Holy Spirit

Satan's like a roaring lion roaming to and fro:
Seeking whom he may devour, the Bible tells me so.
Many souls have been his prey to fall in some weak hour,
But God has promised us today His overcoming pow'r.

Greater is He that is in me,
Greater is He that is in me,
Greater is He that is in me
Than he that is in the world!

On the day of Pentecost a rushing mighty wind
Blew into the upper room and baptized all of them
With a power greater than to any earthly foe,
And I'm so glad I've got it, too, I'm gonna let the whole world know.

LANNY WOLF (B. 1942)

HOLY GHOST, WITH LIGHT DIVINE

When the light of the Holy Spirit shines in our darkened hearts, things start to happen. There is cleansing power, there is joy, and there is an abiding peace. In addition, the Holy Spirit begins to accomplish his purpose through us.

This hymn's tune is entitled "Mercy," and that is what the Holy Spirit accomplished through Andrew Reed, the hymn's author. A Congregational pastor in London, Reed founded six hospitals for the sick and helpless in London, including the London Orphan Asylum, the Asylum for Fatherless Children, the Hospital for Incurables, and the Asylum for Idiots. While the names of the institutions may seem strange to modern ears, they were all much-needed missions of mercy.

Andrew Reed's son wanted to write a biography of his father and asked for some biographical information. Andrew responded with these words, "I was born yesterday; I shall die tomorrow; I must not spend today in telling what I have done, but in doing what I may for him who has done so much for me."

Scriptures: John 14:16-21; Romans 5:8-9; Romans 8:12-14
Themes: Holy Spirit, Power, Consecration

Holy Ghost, with light divine,
Shine upon this heart of mine;
Chase the shades of night away,
Turn my darkness into day.

Holy Ghost, with pow'r divine,
Cleanse this guilty heart of mine;
Long hath sin without control
Held dominion o'er my soul.

Holy Ghost, with joy divine,
Cheer this saddened heart of mine;
Bid my many woes depart,
Heal my wounded, bleeding heart.

Holy Spirit, all divine,
Dwell within this heart of mine;
Cast down ev'ry idol throne,
Reign supreme and reign alone.

ANDREW REED (1787–1862)

HOLY SPIRIT, FAITHFUL GUIDE

Marcus Wells was a farmer, and this is the way he told the story of writing this hymn: "On a Saturday afternoon in October 1858, while at work in my cornfield near Hartwick, New York, the sentiment of this hymn came to me. The next day I finished the hymn and wrote a tune for it."

Not many hymns are written by farmers working in their cornfields, but it is obvious that Marcus Wells considered the Holy Spirit an ever-present Friend, whether he was plowing a furrow or writing a hymn. In this hymn he speaks of the Holy Spirit as a faithful Guide. Each verse closes with the same words: "Follow Me, I'll guide thee home."

Scriptures: John 14:16; Romans 8:14, 26-27; Galatians 5:16-18
Themes: Holy Spirit, Comforter, Hope

> Holy Spirit, faithful Guide, ever near the Christian's side,
> Gently lead us by the hand, pilgrims in a desert land;
> Weary souls fore'er rejoice, while they hear that sweetest voice
> Whisp'ring softly, "Wand'rer come! Follow Me,
>   I'll guide thee home."
>
> Ever-present, truest Friend, ever near Thine aid to lend,
> Leave us not to doubt and fear, groping on in darkness drear;
> When the storms are raging sore, hearts grow faint,
>   and hopes give o'er,
> Whisp'ring softly, "Wand'rer come! Follow Me,
>   I'll guide thee home."
>
> When our days of toil shall cease, waiting still for sweet release,
> Nothing left but heav'n and prayer, knowing that our names
>   are there,
> Wading deep the dismal flood, pleading naught but Jesus' blood,
> Whisp'ring softly, "Wand'rer come! Follow Me,
>   I'll guide thee home."

MARCUS M. WELLS (1815–1895)

HOLY SPIRIT, TRUTH DIVINE

Samuel Longfellow, a Unitarian minister and brother to the famous American poet Henry Wadsworth Longfellow, compiled a hymnbook that included this hymn he had recently written, "Holy Spirit, Truth Divine." Though Samuel was a minister in the Unitarian church, as he grew older he refused to be called a Unitarian.

The hymn itself is one that is acceptable to all Christians. The Holy Spirit is praised as truth, love, power, and right. The last stanza reminds us of the words in the Gospel of John that say the Holy Spirit would convict the world of sin, righteousness, and judgment. The Spirit carries on this ministry within us as the still, small voice that shows us the way. As

Longfellow wrote, may we pray that the Holy Spirit reign as king within our consciences.

Scriptures: John 16:13-14; Acts 1:8; Galatians 5:16-18
Themes: Holy Spirit, Love, Power

Holy Spirit, Truth divine,
Dawn upon this soul of mine;
Word of God and inward light,
Wake my spirit, clear my sight.

Holy Spirit, Love divine,
Glow within this heart of mine;
Kindle every high desire;
Perish self in Thy pure fire.

Holy Spirit, Power divine,
Fill and nerve this will of mine;
By Thee may I strongly live,
Bravely hear and nobly strive.

Holy Spirit, Right divine,
King within my conscience reign;
Be my Lord, and I shall be
Firmly bound, forever free.

SAMUEL LONGFELLOW (1819–1892)

LET THE RIVER FLOW

Darrell Evans wrote this song when he was working at a pancake house in Tulsa. It was a slow day, and Darrell was talking to the manager when the melody came to him like a pancake flipped in the air.

Darrell had spent a year at Oral Roberts University, then began leading worship at a Tulsa church. As he looked around at the church members he knew, he felt that, although there were a lot of Christians, not many of them were enjoying a deep, personal relationship with Jesus Christ. So Darrell was praying for revival—not a surface revival, but one that would really bring Christians into a new intimacy with Christ.

Darrell had thought through some of the lyrics, but he hadn't been making much headway until that day in the pancake house. Then it came to him. He said, "Excuse me," to the manager, walked over to the pie station to get a sheet of paper, and wrote down the words for "Let the

River Flow." All day long he kept humming the tune or singing the words so he wouldn't forget them.

The following Sunday he introduced the song to his congregation. "It was incredible," he said. "People were really crying out to the Lord."

Scriptures: Ezekiel 47:5-9; John 7:37-38; Revelation 22:1-2
Themes: Revival, Conversion, Sanctification

Let the poor man say, I am rich in Him;
Let the lost man say, I am found in Him;
Let the river flow. Let the river flow.

Let the river flow, let the river flow.
Holy Spirit come; move in power.
Let the river flow.

Let the blind man say, I can see again;
Let that dead man say, I am born again:
Let the river flow. Let the river flow.

DARRELL PATTON EVANS
© 1995 Mercy/Vineyard Publishing
Admin. In North America by Music Services
o/b/o Vineyard Music Global Inc. (ASCAP)
All rights reserved. Used by permission.

OLD TIME POWER

Paul Rader, author of this hymn, was a dynamo who energized everyone he came in contact with. He was a whirlwind that could not be harnessed. His résumé listed him as an ex-bellboy, ex-cowboy, ex-prospector, ex-football player, and ex-pugilist. Though he was the son of a Methodist minister, he had turned away from God as a youth and had become a defeated, discouraged man. Wandering along Broadway in New York City one day, he was convicted by the Holy Spirit and returned to the Lord.

A powerful evangelistic speaker, Rader became pastor of Moody Church in Chicago for six years, then served as president of the Christian and Missionary Alliance. He started his own church, the Chicago Gospel Tabernacle, and helped to start Tabernacle Publishing Company.

Yet, along with his constant energy, Rader was a man deeply committed to prayer, and he realized that God's work, if it is to be effective, must be immersed in prayer.

Scriptures: Habakkuk 3:2; Acts 1:8; Acts 2:1-2
Themes: Prayer, Holy Spirit, Revival

We are gathered for thy blessing,
We will wait upon our God;
We will trust in Him who loved us,
And who bought us with His blood.

Spirit, now melt and move all of our hearts with love,
Breathe on us from above with old-time pow'r.

We will glory in Thy power,
We will sing of wondrous grace;
In our midst, as Thou hast promised,
Come, O come, and take Thy place.

Bring us low in prayer before Thee,
And with faith our souls inspire,
Till we claim, by faith, the promise
Of the Holy Ghost and fire.

PAUL RADER (1879–1938)

SPIRIT OF GOD, DESCEND UPON MY HEART

One of the most significant days in the church year is Pentecost, celebrating the coming of the Holy Spirit to indwell and empower believers.

George Croly, who wrote this hymn, came from Ireland to minister in a small parish church in London. During his twenty-five years of service there, he had much time for writing and became known for poems, novels, biographies, and plays. When he was fifty years old, he was asked to reopen a church in one of London's worst slums. The church had been closed for more than a century. Croly's preaching soon attracted crowds. At the age of seventy-four, he prepared a new hymnal for the congregation, including this hymn, under the title "Holiness Desired."

Croly had spent twenty-five years interacting with culture and almost the same amount of time dealing with society's ills in London's slums. But to Croly what mattered most was not what a person was on the outside, but what he was on the inside. So in this hymn he asks for a fresh filling of the Spirit.

Scriptures: Romans 8:5-6, 26; Galatians 5:22-25; Ephesians 4:29-30
Themes: Holy Spirit, Pentecost, Consecration, Holiness

Spirit of God, descend upon my heart;
Wean it from earth; through all its pulses move;
Stoop to my weakness, mighty as Thou art,
And make me love Thee as I ought to love.

I ask no dream, no prophet ecstasies,
No sudden rending of the veil of clay,
No angel visitant, no opening skies;
But take the dimness of my soul away.

Hast Thou not bid me love Thee, God and King?
All, all Thine own, soul, heart and strength and mind.
I see Thy cross; there teach my heart to cling:
O let me seek Thee, and O let me find!

Teach me to feel that Thou art always nigh;
Teach me the struggles of the soul to bear,
To check the rising doubt, the rebel sigh;
Teach me the patience of unanswered prayer.

Teach me to love Thee as Thine angels love,
One holy passion filling all my frame;
The kindling of the heaven descended Dove,
My heart an altar, and Thy love the flame.

GEORGE CROLY (1780–1860)

SWEET, SWEET SPIRIT

Doris Akers started playing the piano when she was five and wrote her first song when she was ten. She has won many awards for singing, songwriting, and choir directing, but she never had any formal music training. She said that she learned her trade the best way—by practical experience.

It was through a personal experience that "Sweet, Sweet Spirit" was born. She was leading a preservice prayer meeting with her choir one Sunday morning when she sensed something special happening. She described it this way:

"The Holy Spirit came down on me and my choir in a sweet gentle sense of powerful presence. I could see Him displayed on the choir members' warm expressions! I didn't know how the prayer meeting could conclude and wondered whether I should send word to the waiting pastor and congregation in the church sanctuary." But finally she had to tell the choir that it was time to go. It was hard to break up the prayer time because there was a sweet, sweet Spirit in that place.

Scriptures: Romans 8:14-17; Galatians 5:25; Ephesians 5:18
Themes: Holy Spirit, Fellowship, Love

There's a sweet, sweet Spirit in this place,
And I know that it's the Spirit of the Lord.

Sweet Holy Spirit, sweet heavenly Dove,
Stay right here with us, filling us with Your love;
And for these blessings we lift our hearts in praise:
Without a doubt we'll know that we have been revived,
When we shall leave this place.

There are sweet expressions on each face,
And I know that it's the presence of the Lord.

DORIS MAE AKERS (B. 1922)
© 1962, Renewed 1990 Manna Music, inc. ARR UBP of Manna Music, Inc.
(35255 Brooten Rd. Pacific City, OR 97135) All rights reserved. Used by permission.

THE COMFORTER HAS COME

Few verses in the New Testament have been translated in as many ways as John 14:16. In the King James Version, which the songwriter Frank Bottome used, Jesus tells his disciples, "I will pray the Father, and he shall give you another Comforter, that he may abide with you for ever." The Greek word translated "Comforter" is *parakletos*. Other versions have translated the word as "Counselor," "Advocate," "Encourager," "Helper," "Friend," or "Someone to stand beside you." Putting them all together, we get the idea of what the Holy Spirit can do for us.

This songwriter was not concerned about which one was the correct translation. He simply wanted to share the excitement that the Holy Spirit has come, dwells in us, and is ready to help us and guide us. Just as the Holy Spirit transformed those fearful disciples into bold witnesses for Jesus Christ, so can he transform us. Yes, it is exciting news that the Comforter has come.

Scriptures: John 7:39; John 14:16; Acts 2:1
Themes: Holy Spirit, Hope, Comforter

O spread the tidings 'round, wherever man is found,
Wherever human hearts and human woes abound;
Let ev'ry Christian tongue proclaim the joyful sound;
The Comforter has come!

The Comforter has come, the Comforter has come!
The Holy Ghost from heav'n—the Father's promise giv'n;
O spread the tidings round, wherever man is found—
The Comforter has come!

The long, long night is past; the morning breaks at last,
And hushed the dreadful wail and fury of the blast,
As o'er the golden hills the day advances fast!
The Comforter has come!

O boundless love divine! How shall this tongue of mine
To wondering mortals tell the matchless grace divine—
That I, a child of hell, should in His image shine!
The Comforter has come!

FRANK BOTTOME (1823–1894)

PART XIV

HOPE AND HEAVEN

[Jesus said,] "Don't let your hearts be troubled.

Trust in God, and trust also in me. There is more than enough

room in my Father's home.

If this were not so, would I have told you that I am going

to prepare a place for you?"

JOHN 14:1-2

AFTER

Evangelist N. B. Vandall got news that his son Paul had been struck by a car and was critically injured. Vandall rushed to the hospital and found that the prognosis was bleak. There was little hope for recovery.

Vandall later told the story: "For one hour and fifteen minutes I held out in prayer while they cleaned and sewed up the head wounds and set the broken bones. Wearily I made my way back to my home. I tried to comfort my wife. . . . I fell on my knees and tried to pray, saying only, 'O God.'

"It seemed to me that Jesus knelt by my side and I could feel his arms around me. He seemed to say, 'Never mind, my child. In the afterward to come, these things shall not be. . . . In heaven, all tears will be wiped away.' "

The word *after* stuck in Vandall's mind; and he went to the piano and through his tears composed the song "After." His son recovered from the accident.

Scriptures: Psalm 30:5; John 14:3; 2 Corinthians 5:1
Themes: Heaven, Hope, Comfort

After the toil and the heat of the day, after my troubles are past,
After the sorrows are taken away, I shall see Jesus at last.

He shall be waiting for me—Jesus so kind and true;
On His beautiful throne, He will welcome me home,
After the day is through.

After the heartaches and sighing shall cease, after the cold winter's blast,
After the conflict comes glorious peace—I shall see Jesus at last.

After the shadows of evening shall fall, after my anchor is cast,
After I list to my Savior's last call, I shall see Jesus at last.

N. B. VANDALL (1896–1970)
© 1934 New Spring (ASCAP)
All rights reserved. Used by permission.

ALL MY HOPE ON GOD IS FOUNDED

Joachim Neander, the writer of this hymn, became a Christian when he was twenty and died at the age of thirty. But during his decade of faith, this German high school teacher displayed great evangelistic zeal. All Neander's hymns are notably rich in content and deep in meaning. Perhaps his best-known hymn is "Praise to the Lord, the Almighty."

Robert Bridges, who adapted this hymn from German, was Britain's poet laureate for a time. Wanting to raise the standard of British hymns, he translated many hymns from German and adapted numerous German melodies for British worshippers. He couldn't understand why he should have to sing something in church that insulted his intelligence.

This Neander hymn, as translated by Bridges, is a noble blending of the talents and dedication of these two godly men. Though the towers and temples of this world fall to dust, as the hymn says, we can found our hope on God, who alone is worthy of trust.

Scriptures: Psalm 33:18-22; Romans 4:18; Hebrews 6:19
Themes: Trust, Eternity

All my hope on God is founded;
He doth still my trust renew,
Me through change and chance He guideth,
Only good and only true,
God unknown, He alone
Calls my heart to be His own.

Mortal pride and earthly glory,
Sword and crown betray our trust;
Though with care and toil we build them,
Tower and temple fall to dust.
But God's power, hour by hour,
Is my temple and my tower.

God's great goodness e'er endureth,
Deep His wisdom passing thought:
Splendor, light, and life attend Him,
Beauty springeth out of naught.
Evermore from His store
Newborn worlds rise and adore.

Daily doth the almighty Giver
Bounteous gifts on us bestow;

His desire our soul delighteth,
Pleasure leads us where we go.
Love doth stand at His hand;
Joy doth wait on His command.

Still from earth to God eternal
Sacrifice of praise be done,
High above all praises praising
For the gift of Christ, His Son.
Christ doth call one and all:
Ye who follow shall not fall.

JOACHIM NEANDER (1650–1680)
Translated by Robert Seymour Bridges (1844–1930)

BEULAH LAND

You won't find the name Beulah in most versions of the Bible, but it
appeared once in the King James Version. That was enough for many
parents to name their daughters Beulah and for people to write songs
about Beulah land. Isaiah 62:4 speaks of the future time when the New
Jerusalem would be known as the City of God's Delight and the Bride of
God. The word translated "Bride of God" or "married" in some versions
is the word *Beulah.*

Edgar Page Stites, the author of "Beulah Land," had been a soldier in
the Civil War, a riverboat pilot, a home missionary, and a local businessman in Cape May, New Jersey. He wrote hymns as a hobby.

He wrote "Beulah Land" in 1876. Stites said, "I could only write two
verses and the chorus when I was overcome and fell on my face. I could
write no more. A week later I wrote the third and fourth verses, and
again I was so influenced by emotion that I could only pray and weep."

Scriptures: Deuteronomy 34:1; Isaiah 62:4; Jeremiah 32:40-43
Themes: Heaven, Hope, Joy

I've reached the land of corn and wine,
And all its riches freely mine;
Here shines undimmed one blissful day,
For all my night has passed away.

O Beulah Land, sweet Beulah Land, as on thy highest mount I stand,
I look away across the sea, where mansions are prepared for me
And view the shining glory-shore, my Hav'n, my home forevermore!

My Savior comes and walks with me,
And sweet communion here have we;
He gently leads me by His hand,
For this is Heaven's border land.

A sweet perfume upon the breeze
Is borne from ever-vernal trees,
And flow'rs, that never-fading grow,
Where streams of life forever flow.

The zephyrs seem to float to me,
Sweet sounds of Heaven's melody,
As angels with the white-robed throng
Join in the sweet Redemption song.

EDGAR PAGE STITES (1836–1921)

BEYOND THE SUNSET

At dinner in Winona Lake, Indiana, Virgil Brock and his wife, Blanche, were admiring a beautiful sunset with Mr. and Mrs. Horace Burr. Just above the setting sun was a large thundercloud with flashing lightning. Conversation stopped as claps of thunder roared in the distance. Then the sun's rays disappeared, and all that could be seen were the storm clouds.

At that point Virgil Brock remembered that Horace Burr was blind, and while the other three were admiring the brilliance of the sunset, Horace Burr could see nothing.

But it was Burr who was the first to speak. "That was the most beautiful sunset I have ever seen," he said.

There was an awkward silence before he spoke again. "I see through other people's eyes, and I think I often see more; I see beyond the sunset."

Brock was struck by the phrase "beyond the sunset" and spontaneously began singing a tune with these words. Then, Brock recalls, "We went to the piano nearby and completed the first verse. Before the evening meal was finished, all four stanzas had been written and we sang the whole song together"—a song of hope and anticipation.

Scriptures: John 14:2-3; 1 Corinthians 13:12; 1 John 3:2-3
Themes: Future, Heaven, Anticipation

Beyond the sunset, O blissful morning,
When with the Savior heaven is begun;

Earth's toiling ended, O glorious dawning,
Beyond the sunset, when day is done.

Beyond the sunset, no clouds will gather,
No storms will threaten, no fears annoy;
O day of gladness, O day unending,
Beyond the sunset, eternal joy!

Beyond the sunset, O glad reunion,
With our dear loved ones who've gone before;
In that fair homeland we'll know no parting,
Beyond the sunset, forever more!

DAY IS DYING IN THE WEST

Mary Lathbury was an artist by training and an art teacher by profession, but she kept hearing the Lord asking for something more from her. What God was saying to her went something like this: "Remember, my child, that you have a gift of weaving fancies into verse and a gift with the pencil of producing visions that come to your heart. I want you to consecrate these to Me as thoroughly as you do your inmost spirit."

Today, she is regarded as one of the founders of the Chautauqua movement, which began as a Christian summer conference on Lake Chautauqua in western New York. The movement spread across the country in the nineteenth century, providing both Christian education and cultural development to thousands of believers.

At Chautauqua in 1877, Lathbury was asked to write an appropriate evening hymn for the conference. As she sat watching the sun disappear behind the trees, she was inspired to write the first two stanzas of this hymn. The third and fourth stanzas were written two years later. She had, indeed, consecrated her pencil to the Lord.

Scriptures: Psalm 69:34; Psalm 104:19-23; Isaiah 6:3
Themes: Worship, Praise, Creation

Day is dying in the west;
Heaven is touching earth with rest;
Wait and worship while the night

Sets her evening lamps alight
Through all the sky.

Holy, holy, holy, Lord God of Hosts!
Heaven and earth are full of Thee!
Heaven and earth are praising Thee,
O Lord most high!

Lord of life, beneath the dome
Of the universe, Thy home,
Gather us who seek Thy face
To the fold of Thy embrace,
For Thou art nigh.

While the deepening shadows fall,
Heart of love enfolding all,
Through the glory and the grace
Of the stars that veil Thy face,
Our hearts ascend.

When forever from our sight
Pass the stars, the day, the night,
Lord of angels, on our eyes
Let eternal morning rise
And shadows end.

MARY ARTEMISIA LATHBURY (1841–1913)

FACE TO FACE WITH CHRIST, MY SAVIOR

It didn't seem possible that Carrie Breck, the author of "Face to Face," was a hymnwriter. She couldn't carry a tune and had no natural sense of pitch at all. She loved to write poetry. She said, "I penciled verses under all conditions: over a mending basket, with a baby on my arm, and sometimes even when sweeping or washing dishes." During her life Breck wrote more than two thousand poems. One of them was "Face to Face with Christ, My Savior."

When she finished the poem, she sent it to Grant Tullar, a friend who lived in Rutherford, New Jersey. Tullar had just written a tune for another song, but he wasn't happy with it. Then the mail came with Carrie Breck's poem. Amazingly, her poem perfectly fit the tune that he had written the night before. Nothing had to be changed.

Scriptures: 2 Corinthians 4:16-18; 1 Thessalonians 4:14-17; 1 John 3:2-3
Themes: Heaven, Hope, Joy

Face to face with Christ, my Savior, face to face—what will it be?
When with rapture I behold Him, Jesus Christ who died for me!

Face to face I shall behold Him, far beyond the starry sky;
Face to face, in all His glory, I shall see Him by and by!

Only faintly now I see Him, with the darkling veil between,
But a blessed day is coming, when His glory shall be seen.

What rejoicing in His presence, when are banished grief and pain,
When the crooked ways are straightened and the dark things shall be plain.

Face to face—O blissful moment! Face to face—to see and know;
Face to face with my Redeemer, Jesus Christ who loves me so.

CARRIE E. BRECK (1855–1934)

FARTHER ALONG

Late in the nineteenth century, W. B. Stevens, a preacher in the little crossroads village of Queen City, Missouri, was struggling. His young son had died suddenly, and he was devastated. He had counseled many people who had lost loved ones. He had given them the right Bible verses, and he had prayed with them and comforted them, but this sorrow struck home.

He wondered if he could keep preaching; recently his sermons seemed hollow. How could a loving God allow such a horrible thing to happen? Why do good people suffer and bad people prosper? Why me, God, why me?

Stevens wrote down his thoughts in a poem. He had no easy answers—only the assurance that "we'll understand it all by and by." Little did he know that his simple poem expressing a father's heartache would become one of the best-known gospel songs to comfort others with heavy hearts.

Scriptures: Psalm 56:8-9; 2 Corinthians 1:2-7; 2 Corinthians 4:7-12; Revelation 21:4
Themes: Comfort, Faith, Hope

Tempted and tried, we're oft made to wonder
Why it should be thus all the day long

While there are others living about us
Never molested though in the wrong.

Farther along we'll know all about it
Farther along we'll understand why
Cheer up my brother, live in the sunshine
We'll understand it all by and by.

J. R. BAXTER/W. B. STEVENS
© 1937 Bridge Building (BMI)
All rights reserved. Used by permission.

HE THE PEARLY GATES WILL OPEN

Fredrick Blom remembered well the day when prison gates clanged shut behind him and he was incarcerated. He deserved it, and he knew it. As a minister of the gospel there was no excuse for him.

He had emigrated from Sweden to America, joined the Salvation Army, and later became a minister in the Evangelical Covenant Church. Then he fell into sin. He wrote about it later: "I drifted from God and became embittered with myself, the world, and not the least with ministers who looked on me with suspicion because I was a member of the Socialist party."

It took a term in prison to remind him of God's great and wondrous love. God could still forgive, even the sin of a pastor who had betrayed his calling. Shortly after he was let out of prison he wrote this hymn about the gates of heaven, pearly gates that would open, even for someone like Fredrick Blom.

Scriptures: 2 Corinthians 5:1-2; 1 John 1:9; Revelation 21:21
Themes: Love, Redemption, Forgiveness

Love divine, so great and wondrous,
Deep and mighty, pure, sublime;
Coming from the heart of Jesus—
Just the same through tests of time.

He the pearly gates will open,
So that I may enter in;
For He purchased my redemption,
And forgave me all my sin.

Like a dove when hunted, frightened,
As a wounded fawn was I,
Broken hearted, yet He healed me—
He will heed the sinner's cry.

Love divine, so great and wondrous,
All my sins He then forgave,
I will sing His praise forever,
For His blood, His pow'r to save.

In life's eventide, at twilight,
At His door I'll knock and wait;
By the precious love of Jesus,
I shall enter heaven's gate.

FREDRICK A. BLOM (1867–1927)
Translated by Nathaniel Carlson (1879–1937)

I'LL FLY AWAY

The son of tenant farmers in the Indian Territory that is now Oklahoma, Albert Brumley quit school after tenth grade and didn't have much of a future to look forward to—except to pick cotton for the rest of his life. Then, when he was sixteen years old, he attended a singing school in his farm community of Rock Island and discovered he could sing better than most adults and he could harmonize, too.

So at nineteen he went to a music school in the Ozark Mountains to learn how to write music. He dropped out after a year and went back to picking cotton. One day while picking cotton, he started singing a popular song called "The Prisoner's Song." *I was like that prisoner,* he thought. When he saw a bird flying away to a better place, young Albert got an idea for a new song. He returned to music school and continued to struggle with his idea for a song. Seven years later, he felt the song was ready to be published. Immediately, it became a favorite.

In time, Brumley became known as the world's most recorded songwriter, but none of his songs rivaled the popularity of "I'll Fly Away."

Scriptures: 2 Corinthians 5:8; Philippians 1:23; 1 Thessalonians 4:16-18
Themes: Heaven, Hope, Death

Some glad morning when this life is o'er, I'll fly away;
To a home on God's celestial shore, I'll fly away.

I'll fly away, O glory, I'll fly away;
When I die, hallelujah, by and by, I'll fly away.

When the shadows of this life have gone, I'll fly away;
Like a bird from prison bars has flown, I'll fly away.

Just a few more weary days and then, I'll fly away;
To a land where joys shall never end, I'll fly away.

ALBERT E. BRUMLEY (1905–1977)

JESUS IS COMING AGAIN

When Japanese troops forced General Douglas MacArthur out of the Philippines at the beginning of World War II, he made the promise, "I will return." Those words brought hope to American troops in the Pacific theater during the darkest days of the war.

At times it looked as if MacArthur's promise would never be fulfilled. But MacArthur did return to the Philippines. He kept his promise.

During World War II John W. Peterson, a pilot in the U.S. Army Air Force, was flying dangerous missions over Southeast Asia. He was well aware of Someone else who had made a promise that he would return.

Back in the States again, John Peterson became a gospel songwriter after World War II, and "Jesus Is Coming Again" was one of his earlier songs. Jesus' promise that he would return is much more certain of fulfillment than the promise that MacArthur made. And that promise gives us hope and assurance for the future.

Scriptures: John 14:3; Acts 1:11; 1 Corinthians 15:51-52
Themes: Return of Christ, Hope, Assurance

Marvelous message we bring, glorious carol we sing,
Wonderful word of the King—Jesus is coming again.

Coming again, coming again;
Maybe morning, maybe noon, maybe evening and maybe soon!
Coming again, coming again;
Oh what a wonderful day it will be—Jesus is coming again!

Forest and flower exclaim, mountain and meadow the same,
All earth and heaven proclaim—Jesus is coming again.

Standing before Him at last, trial and trouble all past,
Crowns at His feet we will cast—Jesus is coming again.

JOHN W. PETERSON

JESUS IS COMING TO EARTH AGAIN

Until she turned thirty, Lelia Naylor Morris thought she would be spending the rest of her life sitting behind a sewing machine making dresses for women in the river town of McConnellsville, Ohio. Lelia was quite young when her father died, so her mother had started a millinery shop to support the five children. It was there that Lelia learned to knit, sew, crochet, and darn; and since a church was nearby, she also learned to play the little church organ.

Then one day when she was thirty, Lelia said that she "opened her heart to let the Holy Spirit come in," and soon she was writing songs and tunes. During the next four decades she wrote more than a thousand hymns.

In many of her hymns she uses the words *now* or *today*. There is an immediacy in her songs. And so this gospel song on the Second Coming does more than affirm that Jesus is coming to earth in the future; Lelia Morris goes on to ask the question, "What if it were today?"

Scriptures: Matthew 24:36-42; 1 Thessalonians 5:2-6; 2 Peter 3:10-12
Themes: Return of Christ, Joy, Kingdom of God

Jesus is coming to earth again, What if it were today?
Coming in power and love to reign, What if it were today?
Coming to claim His chosen Bride, All the redeemed and purified,
Over this whole earth scattered wide, What if it were today?

Glory, glory! Joy to my heart 'twill bring
Glory, glory! When we shall crown Him King:
Glory, Glory! Haste to prepare the way
Glory, Glory! Jesus will come some day.

Satan's dominion will then be o'er, O that it were today!
Sorrow and sighing shall be no more, O that it were today!
Then shall the dead in Christ arise, Caught up to meet Him in the skies,
When shall these glories meet our eyes? What if it were today?

Faithful and true would He find us here If He should come today?
Watching in gladness and not in fear, If He should come today?
Signs of His coming multiply, Morning light breaks in eastern sky,
Watch, for the time is drawing nigh, What if it were today?

LELIA NAYLOR MORRIS (1862–1929)

LO! HE COMES, WITH CLOUDS DESCENDING

This hymn was truly a team effort. The original version was penned by John Cennick, a land surveyor from Reading, England, who became a Moravian preacher. Hymnwriter Charles Wesley adapted the Cennick version, and then it was finished by two of Wesley's followers. One of them was Thomas Olivers, who had been a London cobbler; the other was Martin Madan, who loved to embellish Wesley's hymns and probably added the *hallelujahs.*

As we await the coming of our Lord, about which this hymn is written, God's Kingdom continues to grow, just as this hymn once grew. Preachers, cobblers, land surveyors, and those who embellish with *hallelujahs* build on one another's efforts for the glory of God. They are just a few of the "thousand, thousand saints attending."

Scriptures: Acts 1:10-11; 2 Peter 3:13-14; Revelation 1:7
Themes: Second Coming, Praise, Worship

Lo! He comes, with clouds descending,
Once for favored sinners slain;
Thousand, thousand saints attending
Swell the triumph of His train;
Hallelujah! Hallelujah! Hallelujah!
God appears on earth to reign,
God appears on earth to reign.

Every eye shall now behold Him,
Robed in dreadful majesty;
Those who set at naught and sold Him,
Pierced and nailed Him to the tree,
Deeply wailing, deeply wailing, deeply wailing,
Shall the true Messiah see,
Shall the true Messiah see.

The dear tokens of His passion
Still His dazzling body bears;
Cause of endless exultation
To His ransomed worshipers;
With what rapture, with what rapture, with what rapture,
Gaze we on those glorious scars!
Gaze we on those glorious scars!

Yea, Amen! Let all adore Thee,
High on Thy eternal throne;
Savior, take the power and glory,
Claim the kingdom for Thine own;
Hallelujah! Hallelujah! Hallelujah!
Everlasting God, come down!
Everlasting God, come down!

CHARLES WESLEY (1707–1788)

MANSION OVER THE HILLTOP

A local businessman was on the platform telling how he had lost everything: He had let many of his employees go; he was going deeper and deeper into debt. There seemed to be no way out, and he had begun to question God. So one day he got into his car and drove. He didn't know where he was going. He finally found himself on a narrow trail, unable to turn around. He came to an old shack that seemed abandoned.

But it wasn't. There was a little girl in front of the shack, playing with a broken doll. She had a big smile on her face and was obviously very happy.

The businessman got out of his car and asked why she was so happy. "My daddy," she said, "is going to build a big house over the hill out there, and I can't wait to get there."

Hearing that story in the audience was songwriter Ira Stanphill, who thought of John 14:2: "In my Father's house are many mansions" (KJV). That evening after he got home, he wrote the gospel song "Mansion over the Hilltop."

Scriptures: John 14:2; 1 Thessalonians 4:17; Revelation 21:21-24
Themes: Heaven, Hope, Assurance

I'm satisfied with just a cottage below,
A little silver and a little gold;

But in that city where the ransomed will shine,
I want a gold one that's silver lined.

I've got a mansion just over the hilltop,
In that bright land where I'll never grow old;
And some day yonder we will never more wander
But walk the streets that are purest gold.

Tho' often tempted, tormented and tested
And like the prophet my pillow a stone;
And tho' I find here no permanent dwelling,
I know He'll give me a mansion my own.

Don't think me poor or deserted or lonely,
I'm not discouraged, I'm heaven bound;
I'm just a pilgrim in search of a city.
I want a mansion, a harp and a crown.

IRA STANPHILL (1914–1993)
© 1949 New Spring (ASCAP)

MY SAVIOR FIRST OF ALL

As a six-week-old baby, Fanny Crosby had an eye inflammation. Since their family physician was away, a substitute came. His treatment caused Fanny Crosby to lose her sight.

Was she bitter? No. Fanny Crosby said that at an early age, she resolved "to leave all care to yesterday and to believe that the morning would bring forth its own peculiar joy."

A well-meaning minister once told her that it was a pity she didn't have her sight.

She responded, "If at birth I had been able to make one petition to my Creator, it would have been that I should be born blind."

"Why?" asked the minister.

She replied, "Because when I get to heaven, the first sight that shall ever gladden my eyes will be that of my Savior."

She wrote several hymns that speak of seeing her Savior face-to-face in heaven, but this one is especially poignant, saying, "I shall know my Redeemer when I reach the other side, / And His smile will be the first to welcome me."

Scriptures: 2 Corinthians 4:16-18; Philippians 3:20-21; 1 John 3:2-3
Themes: Heaven, Jesus Christ, Joy

When my lifework is ended, and when I cross the swelling tide,
When the bright and glorious morning I shall see;
I shall know my Redeemer when I reach the other side,
And His smile will be the first to welcome me.

I shall know Him, I shall know Him,
And redeemed by His side I shall stand,
I shall know Him, I shall know Him
By the print of the nails in His hand.

Oh, the soul-thrilling rapture when I view His blessed face,
And the luster of His kindly beaming eye;
How my full heart will praise Him for the mercy, love, and grace,
That prepare for me a mansion in the sky.

Oh, the dear ones in glory, how they beckon me to come,
And our parting at the river I recall;
To the sweet vales of Eden they will sing my welcome home;
But I long to meet my Savior first of all.

Thro' the gates to the city in a robe of spotless white,
He will lead me where no tears will ever fall;
In the glad song of ages I shall mingle with delight;
But I long to meet my Savior first of all.

FANNY JANE CROSBY (1820–1915)

O THAT WILL BE GLORY

Songwriter Charles Gabriel had a good friend named Ed Card, who was superintendent of the Sunshine Rescue Mission in St. Louis, Missouri. Card was one of those exuberant people who always had a smile on his face. In fact, his smiling face earned him his nickname, "Old Glory Face."

If he was blessed by a sermon or a prayer, he would shout out, "Glory!" whereas others might just mumble, "Amen" under their breaths. Apparently, he got his inspiration from Psalm 29:9, which says, "In his Temple everyone shouts, 'Glory!'"

When Card prayed, he often closed his prayer with a reference to heaven, then he would add, "And that will be glory for me." As Charles

Gabriel thought about his friend, he was motivated to write a gospel song about glory.

Of course, the focus of this hymn is not on getting glory for ourselves, but on the glorious experience of arriving in heaven and seeing Jesus Christ face-to-face. I am sure that "Old Glory Face" will be saying, "Glory!" when we get there.

Scriptures: Psalm 29:9; 2 Corinthians 3:18; 1 John 3:2; Revelation 5:12
Themes: Joy, Heaven, Hope

When all my labors and trials are o'er,
And I am safe on that beautiful shore,
Just to be near the dear Lord I adore,
Will thro' the ages be glory for me . . .

O that will be glory for me, glory for me, glory for me;
When by His grace I shall look on His face,
That will be glory, be glory for me.

When, by the gift of His infinite grace,
I am accorded in Heaven a place,
Just to be there and to look on His face,
Will thro' the ages be glory for me . . .

Friends will be there I have loved long ago;
Joy like a river around me will flow;
Yet, just a smile from my Savior, I know,
Will thro' the ages be glory for me . . .

CHARLES HUTCHINSON GABRIEL (1856–1932)

ON JORDAN'S STORMY BANKS I STAND

The banks of the Jordan River are hardly ever stormy, so some have wanted to change this title to "On Jordan's Muddy Banks" or "On Jordan's Rugged Banks." But Samuel Stennett, who wrote the song, had never seen the Jordan River. The song, of course, is not really about the literal Jordan River, but what the Jordan represents: the river that separates us from glory.

On the other side of Jordan is the promised land, Canaan, where our possessions lie. For the Christian it is not a fearsome place; it is an anticipated place. Another hymn, "Guide Me, O Thou Great Jehovah," refers to it this way: "When I tread the verge of Jordan, . . . / Land me safe on Canaan's side."

Even as the children of Israel looked forward to crossing Jordan after forty years of wandering in the wilderness, so the Christian realizes that this life is only a wilderness compared to what lies ahead.

Scriptures: Numbers 14:7-9; Isaiah 35:8-10; 2 Corinthians 5:1-7
Themes: Heaven, Hope, Invitation

On Jordan's stormy banks I stand, and cast a wishful eye
To Canaan's fair and happy land, where my possessions lie.

I am bound for the promised land, I am bound for the promised land;
O who will come and go with me? I am bound for the promised land.

O'er all those wide, extended plains shines one eternal day;
There God, the Son, forever reigns, and scatters night away.

No chilling winds, nor pois'nous breath, can reach that healthful shore;
Sickness and sorrow, pain and death, are felt and feared no more.

When shall I reach that happy place, and be forever blest?
When shall I see my Father's face, and in His bosom rest?

SAMUEL STENNETT (1727–1795)

SAVED BY GRACE

Fanny Crosby, the blind hymnwriter who wrote more than eight thousand texts, wrote this hymn when she was seventy-one years old. Fanny Crosby always said that when she got to heaven and got her sight again, the first thing she wanted to see was Jesus. The chorus of this gospel song says, "And I shall see Him face to face."

She had sent the poem to her publishers thinking they would put it to music and publish it quickly. But they didn't; they forgot about it. Three years later, when Fanny Crosby was attending a conference in Massachusetts, word got around that she was in the audience, and she was requested to speak to the crowd. Although she was an excellent speaker, she knew there were many eloquent ministers at the conference, so she was reluctant. Finally, she agreed to speak, and in the middle of her talk, she quoted the lines of this hymn. The entire audience was in tears when she finished.

Music director Ira Sankey contacted composer George Stebbins to write music for Crosby's text, and the hymn was published soon after.

Scriptures: Psalm 17:15; Ecclesiastes 12:6; Romans 3:24; Ephesians 2:8-9
Themes: Salvation, Heaven, Death

Some day the silver cord will break,
And I no more as now shall sing;
But O, the joy when I shall wake
Within the palace of the King!

And I shall see Him face to face,
And tell the story—Saved by grace;
And I shall see Him face to face,
And tell the story—Saved by grace.

Some day my earthly house will fall,
I cannot tell how soon 'twill be,
But this I know—my All in All
Has now a place in Heav'n for me.

Some day, when fades the golden sun
Beneath the rosy-tinted west,
My blessed Lord will say, "Well done!"
And I shall enter into rest.

Some day: till then I'll watch and wait,
My lamp all trimmed and burning bright,
That when my Savior opens the gate,
My soul to Him may take its flight.

FANNY JANE CROSBY (1820–1915)

SOME GOLDEN DAYBREAK

C. A. Blackmore preached a series of radio messages about the Second Coming of Jesus Christ. A woman who had been bedridden for twenty-three years wrote in to ask, "Will I really be well in heaven? Will all pain and sorrow actually be gone?"

Blackmore responded, "Yes, my friend, some glorious day, when Jesus comes, you will leap from that bed with all the vigor of youth and never know pain again."

Blackmore's son, Carl, was impressed with his father's series and wrote the chorus, "Some Golden Daybreak." Then he said to his father, "Dad, you should write some verses for this chorus."

A short time later, Blackmore awoke early one morning. Unable to go back to sleep, he began to pray and then meditate on the return of Christ. Then came the words to the verses of "Some Golden Daybreak."

Scriptures: Acts 1:9-11; 1 Corinthians 15:51-52; 1 Thessalonians 4:16-18
Themes: Return of Christ, Hope, Victory

Some glorious morning sorrow will cease,
Some glorious morning all will be peace;
Heartaches all ended, school days all done,
Heaven will open—Jesus will come.

Some golden daybreak Jesus will come;
Some golden daybreak, battles all won,
He'll shout the victory, break thro' the blue,
Some golden daybreak, for me, for you.

Sad hearts will gladden, all shall be bright,
Goodbye forever to earth's dark night;
Changed in a moment, like Him to be,
Oh, glorious daybreak, Jesus I'll see.

Oh, what a meeting, there in the skies,
No tears nor crying shall dim our eyes;
Loved ones united eternally,
Oh, what a daybreak that morn will be.

C. A. BLACKMORE AND CARL BLACKMORE
© 1934 Word Music, LLC
All rights reserved. Used by permission.

SOMETIME WE'LL UNDERSTAND

The author of this gospel song, Maxwell Cornelius, was a building contractor in Pittsburgh when his leg was crushed in a construction accident. The nineteenth-century doctors decided that amputation would be necessary to save his life. On the day of the operation he asked to have his violin brought to him, and he played what he thought would be his last song. However, the operation went well, and he came out of it safely.

Cornelius decided to go back to college, and after getting his degree, he felt God's call into the ministry. Because of his wife's health, he moved to Pasadena, California, where he built the large Presbyterian Church. Soon after the church was completed his wife died. Although he was grieving, he preached the funeral sermon himself and finished his message by reading the words of this hymn that he had written.

The poem was printed in a West Coast newspaper and then made its way to a composer, James McGranahan, who provided the music. The chorus was written later by an associate of evangelist Dwight L. Moody: "Then trust in God through all thy days; / Fear not! For He doth hold thy hand; / Though dark the way, still sing and praise; / Sometime, sometime, we'll understand."

Scriptures: Psalm 34:18; Isaiah 43:10; Habakkuk 3:17-19
Themes: Sorrow, Hope, Suffering

Not now, but in the coming years,
It may be in the better land,
We'll read the meaning of our tears,
And there, some time, we'll understand.

Then trust in God thro' all the days;
Fear not, for He doth hold thy hand;
Though dark thy way, still sing and praise,
Some time, some time, we'll understand.

We'll catch the broken thread again,
And finish what we here began;
Heav'n will the mysteries explain,
And then, ah, then, we'll understand.

We'll know why clouds instead of sun
Were over many a cherished plan;
Why song has ceased when scarce begun;
'Tis there, some time, we'll understand.

God knows the way, He holds the key,
He guides us with unerring hand;
Some time with tearless eyes we'll see;
Yes, there, up there, we'll understand.

MAXWELL N. CORNELIUS (19TH CENTURY)

SOON AND VERY SOON

Without a doubt, Andrae Crouch has contributed a great deal to praise and worship music across America. Yet when Andrae was a boy, his parents didn't know if he would be able to do anything for the Lord. He was dyslexic and stuttered badly, so he most likely wouldn't be preaching. His father began praying that Andrae would be able to play the piano. There were no musicians in the family, so Andrae was shocked by the prayer. He says it was as if his father had asked, "Would you like to be an astronaut?"

But his parents bought him a cardboard keyboard to use for practice and three weeks later Andrae's father called him to come forward in a church service. Motioning to the upright piano, he said, "If you're gonna play, play." Andrae has played the piano ever since.

Many of the old spirituals emphasize heaven and the second coming of Christ, and with "Soon and Very Soon," Andrae Crouch has added a powerful gospel song to that collection, combining anticipation, excitement, and joy.

Scriptures: 2 Timothy 4:8; Revelation 21:4; Revelation 22:20
Themes: Return of Christ, Joy, Hope

> Soon and very soon, we are going to see the King;
> Soon and very soon, we are going to see the King;
> Soon and very soon, we are going to see the King;
> Hallelujah! Hallelujah! We're going to see the King.
>
> No more crying there, we are going to see the King; (Repeat 2 Times.)
> Hallelujah! Hallelujah! We're going to see the King.
>
> No more dying there, we are going to see the King; (Repeat 2 Times.)
> Hallelujah! Hallelujah! We're going to see the King.

Writer: Andrae Crouch
© Bud John Songs, Inc./Crouch Music

THE KING IS COMING

For Bill and Gloria Gaither, this is a different kind of song. Many of their songs are sing-along types, but this one is more of an anthem expressing praise and gladness about Christ's return. Bill and Gloria loved to write songs of personal testimony and happy songs that brought together the family of God.

Gloria had heard an evangelist speak on the joy of the second coming of Christ. "Previously," she said, "I had tended to think of the end of the world as a time of judgment." But after hearing the sermon, she began to think "of Jesus as the Master of Restoration—of marriages He had put back together, relationships His hand had mended, and generation gaps His Spirit had bridged. I saw an image of the coronation of a King, who walked down the corridor of history; I could see lining the corridor throngs of witnesses to His redeeming grace."

She wrote the words for "The King Is Coming" and gave them to her husband to supply the music. The result is a hymn combining simplicity and power, looking ahead to a time of rejoicing with the King of glory.

Scriptures: 1 Thessalonians 3:16-17; Revelation 5:9-13; Revelation 22:20
Themes: Second Coming, Victory, Assurance

> O the King is coming, the King is coming!
> I just heard the trumpets sounding, and now His face I see;
> O the King is coming, the King is coming!
> He's coming for me!

CHARLES MILLHUFF, WILLIAM J. GAITHER (B. 1936) AND GLORIA GAITHER (B. 1942)
© 1970 William J. Gaither, Inc. All rights controlled by Gaither Copyright Management.
Used by permission.

THE SWEET BY AND BY

Sanford Bennett owned a pharmacy in Elkhorn, Wisconsin. One of his regular customers was Joseph Webster, who was prone to depression. Bennett regularly supplied some pills to Webster to help him out of his melancholy. But since they both liked music, Bennett found something else that worked better than pills. Bennett said, "I had learned his peculiarities so well that on meeting him I could tell at a glance if he was in one of his melancholy moods, and I found that I could rouse him from them by giving him a new song or hymn to work on."

One day when Webster walked in, Bennett asked, "Webster, what's the matter now?"

Webster answered, "It is no matter; it will be all right by and by."

Bennett said quickly, "The sweet by and by. Wouldn't that make a good hymn?"

"Maybe," said Webster. Bennett went back to his desk, not to fill a prescription, but to write the words of a song. In less time than it takes to fill a prescription, the song was written. Webster liked it, and he asked for a violin that Bennett had in the store so he could start writing the music. Both men sang the song together as the other customers listened. One of the customers said, "That hymn is immortal." Within two weeks children on the streets were singing it.

Scriptures: 1 Corinthians 2:9; 1 Thessalonians 4:17-18; Hebrews 13:14

Themes: Heaven, Joy, Assurance

There's a land that is fairer than day,
And by faith we can see it afar;
For the Father waits over the way,
To prepare us a dwelling place there.

In the sweet by and by, we shall meet on that beautiful shore;
In the sweet by and by, we shall meet on that beautiful shore.

We shall sing on that beautiful shore
The melodious songs of the blest,
And our spirits shall sorrow no more,
Not a sigh for the blessing of rest.

To our bountiful Father above,
We will offer our tribute of praise,
For the glorious gift of His love,
And the blessings that hallow our days.

SANFORD F. BENNETT (1836–1898)

THE UNCLOUDED DAY

Josiah Alwood was one of those legendary circuit-riding preachers. Associated with the United Brethren denomination, he traveled on horseback to small churches in isolated areas, sometimes through swamps and creeks, then preaching in wet clothing. His territory was northwest Ohio, southern Michigan, and northeast Indiana.

One August night in 1879, Alwood was returning after midnight from a meeting in Spring Hill, Ohio, to his home in southern Michigan, and he saw a rainbow. The sky was clear except for one dark storm cloud. From that storm cloud came a heavy shower of rain, and through that shower the rays of the moon were streaming A rainbow at night is an unusual sight, and Alwood said later, "You can scarcely imagine the feeling of solemn joy which came over me as I gazed upon the rainbow of promise."

When he awoke the next morning, he was still in awe from the experience. He went to the small pump organ in his home and with one finger drummed out the tune. Then he wrote the words as quickly as he could. He remembered the tune, so the next time a music teacher came to the area, Josiah Alwood asked the teacher to write down the music for him.

Scriptures: John 14:2; Hebrews 4:9-11; Revelation 7:16-17
Themes: Hope, Heaven, Assurance

O they tell me of a home far beyond the skies;
O they tell me of a home far away.
O they tell me of a home where no storm clouds rise;
O they tell me of an unclouded day.

O the land of cloudless day.
O the land of an unclouded day.
O they tell me of a home where no storm clouds rise;
O they tell me of an unclouded day.

O they tell me of a home where my friends have gone;
O they tell me of that land far away,
Where the tree of life in eternal bloom
Sheds its fragrance through the unclouded day.

O they tell me of a King in His beauty there;
And they tell me that mine eyes shall behold
Where He sits on the throne that is whiter than snow
In the city that is made of gold.

O they tell me that He smiles on His children there;
And the smile drives their sorrows all away.
And they tell me that no tears ever come again,
In that lovely land of unclouded day.

JOSIAH KELLY ALWOOD (1828–1909)

THERE'LL BE NO DARK VALLEY

The author of this gospel song, a pastor named William Cushing, knew all about dark valleys. Soon after the death of his wife, he became ill and lost his voice, which meant he had to give up preaching. But it was while he was in this valley that he discovered he had a gift for writing gospel songs, and he wrote more than three hundred.

A few years after the song was written, it was being sung in the British

Isles, and an inner-city missionary wrote, "Thank you for this song because it presents death in such a glorious way. The old Welsh people used to speak and sing of death as something very fearful—a dark river, great waves and so on. I remember my dear mother singing all the Welsh hymns referring to death until I shuddered. But, praise the Lord, I know now that it is different."

Scriptures: 1 Corinthians 15:55-57; 1 Thessalonians 4:16-17; Revelation 22:5
Themes: Death, Resurrection, Heaven

> There'll be no dark valley when Jesus comes;
> There'll be no dark valley when Jesus comes;
> There'll be no dark valley when Jesus comes
>   to gather His loved ones home.
>
> *To gather His loved ones home, to gather His loved ones home;*
> *There'll be no dark valley when Jesus comes to gather His loved ones home.*
>
> There'll be no more sorrow when Jesus comes,
> There'll be no more sorrow when Jesus comes,
> But a glorious morrow when Jesus comes to gather His loved ones home.
>
> There'll be songs of greeting when Jesus comes;
> There'll be songs of greeting when Jesus comes;
> And a joyful meeting when Jesus comes to gather His loved ones home.

WILLIAM ORCUTT CUSHING (1823–1902)

THIS WORLD IS NOT MY HOME

When, as a boy, Albert Brumley was out in the cotton fields picking cotton, he knew that wasn't the life for him. He wanted to write songs for the Lord. So he did.

Albert had grown up in poverty and witnessed two world wars and the Great Depression. Life wasn't easy, but he saw that it became a lot easier when you had Jesus as your friend walking alongside you.

Two themes seem to pop up in Albert's songs over and over again. One is the theme of heaven. Life here may be rough, but glory is up ahead. The second theme is that Jesus Christ is the only way to heaven. Establishing a personal relationship with him now can bring a touch of heaven to earth.

For the Christian, our citizenship is not ultimately here on earth, but in heaven. It's the plain teaching of Scriptures: "This World is Not My Home."

Scriptures: Philippians 3:20; Hebrews 11:13; Hebrews 13:14
Themes: Heaven, Hope, Assurance

This world is not my home, I'm just a passing through;
My treasures are laid up somewhere beyond the blue.
The angels beckon me from heaven's open door,
And I can't feel at home in this world anymore.

O Lord, you know, I have no friend like you,
If heaven's not my home, then, Lord, what will I do?
The angels beckon me from heaven's open door,
And I can't feel at home in this world anymore.

ALBERT E. BRUMLEY (1905–1977)
Copyright © 1936, renewed 1964. Albert P. Brumley and Sons (Administered by Integrated Copyright Group, Inc. Used by permission.)

UNTIL THEN

Stuart Hamblen started as an entertainer when he was radio's first singing cowboy. For more than two decades, his radio programs kept him on top of the West Coast popularity charts.

Although he was the son of a traveling Methodist preacher and the husband of a devoutly Christian wife, Hamblen was boisterous and his world was filled with drinking, cheating, and lying. However, his wife didn't give up on him. She kept praying that her husband would be converted.

At a Billy Graham crusade, Hamblen was converted, and he began to write songs to glorify God. As a Christian he recognized that he didn't have answers to a lot of questions: Why is there suffering? Why is there so much evil? Why isn't the pathway smoother? But Hamblen was content to leave such questions in God's hands. Some day we will understand, but until then . . .

Scriptures: 1 Corinthians 13:12; Hebrews 11:1; James 1:12
Themes: Hope, Heaven, Assurance

My heart can sing when I pause to remember,
A heartache here is but a stepping stone
Along a trail that's winding always upwards,
This troubled world is not my final home.

But until then my heart will go on singing,
Until then with joy I'll carry on,
Until the day my eyes behold the city,
Until the day God calls me home.

The things of earth will dim and lose their value
If we recall they're borrowed for awhile;
And things of earth that cause the heart to tremble,
Remembered there will only bring a smile.

This weary world with all its toil and struggle
May take its toll of misery and strife;
The soul of man is like a waiting falcon,
When it's released it's destined for the skies.

STUART HAMBLEN (1908–1989)
Copyright © 1958 by Hamblen Music Co.
All rights reserved. Used by permission.

WE SHALL BEHOLD HIM

In southern gospel circles, there is no one like Dottie Rambo, who started writing songs when she was just a child. Some of the songs have come from the hardships of her life, and others were born out of very ordinary circumstances.

Dottie wrote "We Shall Behold Him" in 1981 during revival meetings in Ohio. She and a young woman were driving from a motel to the large tent where the meetings were being held. As she drove, she noticed an unusual cloud formation. She said, "I saw colors that I had never seen in my lifetime." And then the clouds parted, and she said, "There seemed to be a straight passageway through the formation."

She began to weep, and she asked her partner to take over the driving. As Dottie continued looking at the cloud formation, she seemed to see the Savior coming with trumpets sounding. As they stopped by the side of the road, Dottie composed the song. Dottie had no paper to write it on, but she said that she didn't need paper, because "it was written on my heart." Dottie played it on her guitar for her friend, and both of them were in tears.

That night at the revival meeting, Dottie officially introduced the song, "We Shall Behold Him," and many more were in tears.

Scriptures: Acts 1:9-11; 1 Thessalonians 4:16-17; Revelation 1:7
Themes: Return of Christ, Hope, Joy

The sky shall unfold, preparing His entrance;
The stars shall applaud Him with thunders of praise.
The sweet light in His eyes shall enhance those awaiting;
And we shall behold Him then face to face.

And we shall behold Him, we shall behold Him
Face to face in all of His glory. O we shall behold Him,
We shall behold Him face to face, our Savior and Lord.

The angel shall sound the shout of His coming;
The sleeping shall rise from their slumbering place.
And those who remain shall be changed in a moment;
And we shall behold Him then face to face.

DOTTIE RAMBO (B. 1934)
© 1980 New Spring (ASCAP)
All rights reserved. Used by permission.

WE'LL SOON BE DONE WITH TROUBLES AND TRIALS

Cleavant Derricks experienced many "troubles and trials."An African-American pastor in Alabama, he grew up in the first half of the twentieth century when racial discrimination against blacks was rampant.

Derricks wrote this song, "We'll Soon Be Done with Troubles and Trials," when he was a young pastor. He still had lots of troubles and trials ahead of him. He sold the rights for this song to a music publisher in exchange for some hymnals for his church. During World War II, this song became one of America's most popular gospel songs. Both black and white groups recorded it and sold their recordings for big profits. But Derricks didn't get a penny from it. In fact, no one knew who he was.

Derricks was a humble man who didn't want the spotlight. He knew that in God's eternity everything will be made right and "we'll soon be done with troubles and trials."

Scriptures: Philippians 1:21-25; Hebrews 13:13-14; 1 Peter 3:17
Themes: Comfort, Hope, Heaven

One of these days I'm going home
Where no sorrows ever come,
We'll soon be done with troubles and trials;
Safe from heartaches, pain and care,
We shall all that glory share

Sit down beside my Jesus,
Sit down and rest a little while.

We'll soon be done with troubles and trials,
Yes, in that home on the other side,
Shake glad hands with the elders,
Tell my kindred good morning,
Sit down beside my Jesus,
Gonna sit down and rest a li'l while.

Kindred and friends now wait for me,
Soon their faces I shall see,
We'll soon be done with troubles and trials;
'Tis a home of life so fair
And we'll all be gathered there,
Sit down beside my Jesus,
Sit down and rest a little while.

I shall behold His blessed face,
I shall feel His matchless grace,
We'll soon be done with troubles and trials;
O what peace and joy sublime
In that home of love divine,
Sit down beside my Jesus,
Sit down and rest a little while.

CLEAVANT DERRICKS (1910–1977)
© 1934, Renewed 1962. Stanzas—Baxter Music (Admin. by Brentwood-Benson Music Publishing Inc. Franklin, TN 37067.

WHAT A DAY THAT WILL BE

An orphan girl and a mother-in-law were the two inspirations for James Hill when he wrote this song. Hill never forgot an orphan girl who had come to sing at his Baptist church years earlier. She ended her song with the words, "What a day that will be."

But the immediate influence was Hill's mother-in-law, who was paralyzed by a stroke when she was only fifty years old. Hill couldn't understand why this had happened to such a wonderful woman. One day as he was sitting on his porch, thinking about his mother-in-law, he wrote this song.

He had never written a song before, so he wasn't sure how good it was. But the next time he, his wife, and his wife's sister went to visit his mother-in-law, they sang it all the way to her home. When they got there, they sang it again. And as they sang, for the first time in three years, his mother-in-law smiled and showed signs of excitement.

To Jim that was a sign that the song was going to be blessed by God. Since that time it has been recorded by more than a thousand singing groups and individuals.

Scriptures: Isaiah 35:10; John 14:1-3; Revelation 21:4

Themes: Heaven, Hope, Comfort

There is coming a day when no heartaches shall come,
No more clouds in the sky, no more tears to dim the eye;
All is peace forevermore on that happy, golden shore.
What a day, glorious day that will be!

What a day that will be when my Jesus I shall see,
And I look upon His face, the One who saved me by His grace!
When He takes me by the hand, and leads me through the Promised Land,
What a day, glorious day that will be!

There'll be no sorrow there, no more burdens to bear,
No more sickness, no pain, no more parting over there;
And forever I will be with the One who died for me.
What a day, glorious day that will be!

JAMES VAUGHN HILL

© 1955. Renewed 1983, Ben Speer Music/SESAC (Admin. by ICG).
All rights reserved. Used by permission.

WHEN HE SHALL COME

Her husband, Rowan Pearce, was a Bible teacher with an emphasis on prophecy, so Almeda Pearce understood what the Bible taught about the future. Yet this hymn did not come from her husband's teachings, but rather from a personal experience when she was forty years old.

Pearce was a hemophiliac, and she needed a blood transfusion. She thought her husband's blood would work, but it was the wrong type and it did not help. She felt she was dying. Later Pearce told of going through "the valley of the shadow" and of seeing the hand of the Lord vividly and feeling the Lord's presence. She was given a second transfusion that worked, but at this point Pearce really didn't want to "come back" because she felt she was in the presence of the Lord and a part of "a vast crowd," as prophesied in the book of Revelation, "too great to count, from every nation and tribe and people and language" (Revelation 7:9).

This song comes out of that deep experience. She and her husband continued a radio ministry for three decades after her near-death experience.

Scriptures: Revelation 3:4; Revelation 6:11; Revelation 7:9
Themes: Return of Christ, Last Things, Hope

When He shall come, resplendent in His glory,
To take His own from out this vale of night,
O may I know the joy at His appearing
Only at morn to walk with Him in white!

When I shall stand within the court of heaven
Where white-robed pilgrims pass before my sight—
Earth's martyred saints and blood-washed overcomers—
These then are they who walk with Him in white!

When He shall call, from earth's remotest corners,
All who have stood triumphant in His might,
O to be worthy then to stand beside them,
And in that morn to walk with Him in white!

ALMEDA J. PEARCE (1893–1966)
© 1934, renewed 1962, Jeanne P. Hopkins
All rights reserved. Used by permission.

WHEN THE MORNING COMES OR (WE'LL UNDERSTAND IT BETTER BY AND BY)

Charles Tindley didn't have answers for all the questions of life.

He was born a slave, his mother died when he was young, and his father was sold and separated from him. He plowed fields fourteen hours a day, six days a week and then ran ten miles to night school so he could learn to read.

When he moved north to Philadelphia, Tindley started working as a church janitor, then he felt the Lord wanted him in the ministry. He loved to sing, and he often combined songs with sermons.

One Sunday morning in 1904, he spoke of the twelve disciples who were always trying to put Jesus on their timetable. They wanted Jesus to set up his Kingdom now. They wanted Jesus to call down fire from heaven now. They wanted answers now. They didn't know why they had to wait.

Tindley told his congregation that we want our answers now too. But sometimes we have to wait. How long? For some of the answers we may have to wait until the morning comes, and then "We'll Understand It Better By and By."

Scriptures: Psalm 30:5; 1 Corinthians 13:12; Galatians 6:9
Themes: Hope, Heaven, Assurance

We are often tossed and driv'n on the restless sea of time,
Somber skies and howling tempests oft succeed a bright sunshine,
In that land of perfect day, when the mists have rolled away
We will understand it better by and by.

By and by when the morning comes,
When the saints of God are gathered home,
We'll tell the story how we've overcome;
For we'll understand it better by and by.

We are often destitute of the things that life demands,
Want of food and want of shelter, thirsty hills and barren lands,
We are trusting in the Lord, and according to His word,
We will understand it better by and by.

Trials dark on ev'ry hand, and we cannot understand,
All the ways that God would lead us to that blessed promised land;
But He guides us with His eye and we'll follow till we die,
For we'll understand it better by and by.

Temptations, hidden snares, often take us unawares,
And our hearts are made to bleed for many a thoughtless word or deed,
And we wonder why the test when we try to do our best,
But we'll understand it better by and by.

CHARLES A. TINDLEY (1851–1933)

WHEN THE ROLL IS CALLED UP YONDER

As president of his church's young people's society, James Black called the roll each week. He was glad to see a particular young teenager become a regular member of the group. A few weeks earlier, Black had seen her sitting on the front steps of her house, and he had invited her to come. He knew her father was a drunkard and that she had no Christian training at home.

But one Sunday evening, she didn't answer to the roll call. He called her name a second time and soon learned that she had become seriously ill.

Black later recalled, "I spoke of what a sad thing it would be when our names are called from the Lamb's Book of Life, if one of us should be absent."

That night when he went home, the words of the gospel song came to him very quickly. In not much more than fifteen minutes, he had written all three verses.

The missing girl had been stricken with pneumonia, and ten days later she died. She missed the roll call of her youth group, but James Black trusted that she will be present at the great roll call in heaven.

Scriptures: John 6:40; Philippians 4:3; 1 Thessalonians 4:15
Themes: Heaven, Hope, Salvation

When the trumpet of the Lord shall sound, and time shall be no more,
And the morning breaks, eternal, bright and fair;
When the saved of earth shall gather over on the other shore,
And the roll is called up yonder, I'll be there.

When the roll is called up yonder,
When the roll is called up yonder,
When the roll is called up yonder,
When the roll is called up yonder, I'll be there.

On that bright and cloudless morning when the dead in Christ shall rise,
And the glory of His resurrection share;
When His chosen ones shall gather to their home beyond the skies,
And the roll is called up yonder, I'll be there.

Let us labor for the Master from the dawn till setting sun,
Let us talk of all His wondrous love and care;
Then when all of life is over, and our work on earth is done,
And the roll is called up yonder, I'll be there.

JAMES M. BLACK (1856–1938)

WHEN WE ALL GET TO HEAVEN

Retreats and conferences can be mountaintop experiences. Sometimes we come away from such a time and say, "Heaven can't be much better than this." Of course, it will be, but that was the feeling Eliza Hewitt and Emily Wilson had at the Ocean Grove Conference Grounds in New Jersey.

Eliza Hewitt was a Presbyterian and a schoolteacher. Emily Wilson was a Methodist and a pastor's wife. They both lived in Philadelphia, but the time that they looked forward to was the time in the summer when they would meet in Ocean Grove. It was almost like heaven.

One summer when they got together, Eliza Hewitt brought along a poem she had written. She thought it might be a good song for their Sunday schools to sing. Since Emily was a musician, Eliza asked her to write the music for it.

We may have mountaintop experiences here on earth, but we still look forward to the time when we all get to heaven and see Jesus. "What a day of rejoicing that will be!"

Scriptures: 2 Corinthians 4:17-18; 1 Thessalonians 4:17-18; 1 John 3:2
Themes: Heaven, Joy, Fellowship

Sing the wondrous love of Jesus,
Sing His mercy and His grace;
In the mansions bright and blessed,
He'll prepare for us a place.

When we all get to heaven,
What a day of rejoicing that will be!
When we all see Jesus,
We'll sing and shout the victory.

While we walk the pilgrim pathway,
Clouds will over-spread the sky;
But when trav'ling days are over,
Not a shadow, not a sigh.

Let us then be true and faithful,
Trusting, serving ev'ry day;
Just one glimpse of Him in glory
Will the toils of life repay.

Onward to the prize before us!
Soon His beauty we'll behold;
Soon the pearly gates will open,
We shall tread the streets of gold.

ELIZA EDMUNDS HEWITT (1851–1920)

PART XV

JESUS

Jesus told him, "I am the way, the truth, and the life."

JOHN 14:6

AND CAN IT BE?

Charles Wesley had strict religious training at home, started "Holy Clubs" in college to promote righteous living, and went as a missionary to Native Americans after college. But he was not converted. Charles had no peace in his heart. One day in 1738, he met with a group of Moravians in Aldersgate Hall in London, and there he came to realize that salvation was by faith alone. In his journal of May 21, he wrote, "At midnight I gave myself to Christ." His brother John was converted shortly after.

Two days later, he began writing two hymns. Both of them told of his conversion. At first he wasn't sure he should finish them. Was it pride, he wondered, to talk about his own experience? But then, he said, "I prayed Christ to stand by me, and finished the hymns." Yes, it may have described his own experience, but it is also the experience of millions of others who have come by faith to Jesus Christ.

In his lifetime he wrote between five and six thousand hymns, but this hymn stands as one of his most powerful and most profound.

Scriptures: Romans 5:8; Romans 8:1-3; Hebrews 9:11-12; 1 Peter 1:18-19
Themes: Conversion, Love, Grace, Forgiveness

And can it be that I should gain
An interest in the Savior's blood?
Died He for me, who caused His pain?
For me, who Him to death pursued?
Amazing love! How can it be
That Thou, my God, shouldst die for me?

He left His Father's throne above,
So free, so infinite His grace!
Emptied Himself of all but love,
And bled for Adam's helpless race!
'Tis mercy all, immense and free,
For, O my God, it found out me.

'Tis mystery all! th' Immortal dies!
Who can explore His strange design?
In vain the firstborn seraph tries
To sound the depths of love divine.
'Tis mercy all! let earth adore;
Let angel minds inquire no more.

Long my imprisoned spirit lay
Fast bound in sin and nature's night.
Thine eye diffused a quickening ray;
I woke—the dungeon flamed with light!
My chains fell off, my heart was free,
I rose, went forth, and followed Thee.

No condemnation now I dread;
Jesus, and all in Him is mine;
Alive in Him, my living Head,
And clothed in righteousness divine,
Bold I approach th' eternal throne,
And claim the crown, through Christ my own.

CHARLES WESLEY (1707–1788)

ARISE, MY SOUL, ARISE

One minister said he knew of more than two hundred people who had come to Christ through singing this hymn. The story of one young boy is typical of many. He had gone to a revival meeting, and when the sermon was over, he dropped to his knees. "I knew I was sorry for my sins," he said later, "and I wanted Jesus to forgive me." The congregation sang this hymn of Charles Wesley, and the boy listened carefully. Some of the stanzas he did not understand very well, but when they came to the last stanza, joy exploded inside him.

The words "with confidence I now draw nigh" changed his life. "It was just like being introduced to someone," he said. "From a penitent, weeping boy, I arose happy and smiling." And that's what Jesus does. He brings us to the point of denouncing our sinful lives but then gives us confidence to enter a relationship with him.

Scriptures: Romans 8:5-8; Galatians 4:6-7; Ephesians 3:11-12
Themes: Grace, Forgiveness, Redemption

Arise, my soul, arise; shake off thy guilty fears;
The bleeding sacrifice in my behalf appears:
Before the throne my surety stands,
Before the throne my surety stands,
My name is written on His hands.

He ever lives above, for me to intercede;
His all-redeeming love, His precious blood, to plead:
His blood atoned for all our race,
His blood atoned for all our race,
And sprinkles now the throne of grace.

Five bleeding wounds He bears, received on Calvary;
They pour effectual prayers; they strongly plead for me:
"Forgive him, O forgive," they cry,
"Forgive him, O forgive," they cry,
"Nor let the ransomed sinner die!"

The Father hears Him pray, His dear anointed One;
He cannot turn away the presence of His Son:
His spirit answers to the blood,
His spirit answers to the blood,
And tells me I am born of God.

My God is reconciled; His pardoning voice I hear;
He owns me for His child; I can no longer fear:
With confidence I now draw nigh,
With confidence I now draw nigh,
And, "Father, Abba, Father," cry.

CHARLES WESLEY (1707–1788)

AT THE NAME OF JESUS

As a young woman, Caroline Noel tried to write poems, but she gave it up by the age of twenty. When she was bedridden with a serious illness at age forty, she took up her pen once again. Eventually, her poetry was published in a book called *At the Name of Jesus, and Other Verses for the Sick and Lonely.*

You might think the tone of her work would be comforting and devotional, but this hymn is more theological in nature. It focuses attention on Jesus and his power, rather than on sickness and loneliness. Actually, the poem is a beautiful paraphrase of Philippians 2:4-11, an early-church hymn that shows Jesus humbling himself on earth and being glorified in heaven.

During times of suffering we can easily become self-centered. Caroline Maria Noel, on her own sickbed, penned this lovely hymn that instead lifts our eyes away from self-pity and self-concern to the One who deserves our constant praise.

Scriptures: Isaiah 45:22-24; Philippians 2:5-9; 1 Peter 2:21
Themes: Humility, Worship, Praise

At the name of Jesus
Every knee shall bow,
Every tongue confess Him
King of glory now;
'Tis the Father's pleasure
We should call Him Lord,
Who from the beginning
Was the mighty Word.

At His voice creation
Sprang at once to sight,
All the angel faces,
All the hosts of light,
Thrones and dominations,
Stars upon their way,
All the heavenly orders,
In their great array.

Humbled for a season,
To receive a name
From the lips of sinners
Unto whom He came,
Faithfully He bore it
Spotless to the last,
Brought it back victorious
When from death He passed.

In your hearts enthrone Him;
There let Him subdue
All that is not holy,
All that is not true:
Crown Him as your captain
In temptation's hour;
Let His will enfold you
In its light and power.

CAROLINE MARIA NOEL (1817–1877)

BLESSED REDEEMER

Usually, the text of a hymn is written before the tune, but in this case, it was the other way around. Harry Dixon Loes was a music student in Chicago. One day Loes heard a sermon on Christ's atonement entitled "Blessed Redeemer." Inspired by the sermon, he composed a tune that he thought would be appropriate. Then he sent the melody and the title to his friend Avis Christiansen, a twenty-five-year-old poet. She had already written a few hymns that had been published, and Loes felt she could do well with the material he sent her.

She responded with the three verses and chorus that we have today. Avis Christiansen continued to write lyrics for hundreds of hymns, and Loes wrote some three thousand hymn tunes.

Scriptures: Isaiah 54:5-8; John 19:17-18; Colossians 2:13-15
Themes: Cross, Atonement, Redemption

Up Calvary's mountain, one dreadful morn,
Walked Christ my Savior, weary and worn;
Facing for sinners death on the cross,
That He might save them from endless loss.

Blessed Redeemer, precious Redeemer!
Seems now I see Him on Calvary's tree
Wounded and bleeding, for sinners pleading—
Blind and unheeding—dying for me!

"Father, forgive them!" thus did He pray,
E'en while His life-blood flowed fast away;
Praying for sinners while in such woe—
No one but Jesus ever loved so.

O how I love Him, Savior and Friend!
How can my praises e'er find end!
Thru years unnumbered on heaven's shore,
My tongue shall praise Him forevermore.

AVIS B. CHRISTIANSEN (1895–1985)

CHRIST RETURNETH

In the nineteenth century, Christians rediscovered the truth that Jesus is coming again. Of course, the Second Coming has always been a doctrine of the Church, but in earlier centuries, other doctrines seemed to crowd out this one.

In the twentieth century, Christians spent so much time arguing about the Tribulation and the Millennium that some churches decided it was best not to talk about the Second Coming at all.

But Jesus is coming again—yes, he is. This hymn comes to us from the nineteenth century, and it emphasizes what Christians agree on: Jesus is coming again, and we should be ready because we don't know when that will be.

Scriptures: Matthew 24:36; John 14:3; 1 Thessalonians 2:19; 1 Thessalonians 3:13
Themes: Second Coming, Hope, Joy

It may be at morn, when the day is awaking,
When sunlight thro' darkness and shadow is breaking,
That Jesus will come in the fullness of glory,
To receive from the world "His own."

O Lord Jesus, how long, how long ere we shout the glad song,
Christ returneth! Hallelujah! Hallelujah! Amen, Hallelujah! Amen.

It may be at midday, it may be at twilight,
It may be, perchance, that the blackness of midnight
Will burst into light in the blaze of His glory,
When Jesus receives "His own."

While its hosts cry Hosanna, from heaven descending,
With glorified saints and the angels attending,
With grace on His brow, like a halo of glory,
Will Jesus receive "His own."

Oh joy! oh, delight! should we go without dying,
No sickness, no sadness, no dread and no crying,
Caught up thro' the clouds with our Lord into glory,
When Jesus receives "His own."

H. L. TURNER (19TH CENTURY)

FAIREST LORD JESUS

This is sometimes called "The Crusader's Hymn," even though it was probably not sung until several hundred years after the Crusades. It may have first been sung around 1400 by followers of reformer John Hus, who lived near Prague. In an anti-Reformation purge, Hussites were expelled from Bohemia and went into Silesia, where they became weavers and cobblers, maintaining their faith in secret. But they had a strong tradition of hymn singing, and the most reliable tradition says that this hymn came from these humble Christians.

The hymn contains no comments on persecution, but only praise to a wonderful Savior. Whoever wrote the hymn was close to nature and adored God's creation but recognized that even fairer than the creation is the Creator. God has given his vast creation for us to enjoy, but we must never forget that Jesus is fairer and purer than all the blooming garb of spring.

Scriptures: Psalm 148:1-6; Colossians 1:16; Hebrews 1:2-3

Themes: Nature, Creation, Beauty, Praise

Fairest Lord Jesus,
Ruler of all nature,
O Thou of God and man the son,
Thee will I cherish,
Thee will I honor,
Thou, my soul's glory, joy, and crown.

Fair are the meadows,
Fairer still the woodlands,
Robed in the blooming garb of spring:
Jesus is fairer,
Jesus is purer,
Who makes the woeful heart to sing.

Fair is the sunshine,
Fairer still the moonlight,
And all the twinkling starry host:
Jesus shines brighter,
Jesus shines purer,
Than all the angels heaven can boast.

MÜNSTER GESANGBUCH, 1677
Translator Unknown

GRACE GREATER THAN OUR SIN

Grace is one of the hardest lessons for us to learn about God. Some show their ignorance of God's grace by working hard to be good enough. They pay lip service to the idea of God's grace but don't really understand it. Others display their misunderstanding of God's grace by concluding it's inaccessible to them. They know they cannot be good enough for God, so they despair of ever having a relationship with him.

It is this second group that Julia Johnston was writing for. She knew how important it was to understand and experience the simple, yet difficult, truth of God's gracious forgiveness. Johnston, who lived in Peoria, Illinois, was a Sunday school teacher and became a noted expert in Sunday school curriculum. Though she penned texts for more than five hundred hymns, this is the only one widely known. It powerfully teaches this essential Christian truth: God's grace is far greater than any sin you have committed. All you have to do is receive it.

Scriptures: Romans 3:24-26; Romans 5:16-17; 2 Corinthians 8:9
Themes: Grace, Forgiveness, Salvation

Marvelous grace of our loving Lord,
Grace that exceeds our sin and our guilt!
Yonder on Calvary's mount outpoured—
There where the blood of the Lamb was spilt.

Grace, grace, God's grace,
Grace that will pardon and cleanse within,
Grace, grace, God's grace,
Grace that is greater than all our sin!

Sin and despair, like the sea waves cold,
Threaten the soul with infinite loss;
Grace that is greater—yes, grace untold—
Points to the refuge, the mighty cross.

Dark is the stain that we cannot hide—
What can avail to wash it away?
Look! there is flowing a crimson tide—
Whiter than snow you may be today.

Marvelous, infinite, matchless grace,
Freely bestowed on all who believe!

You that are longing to see His face,
Will you this moment His grace receive?

JULIA HARRIETTE JOHNSTON (1849–1919)

HAIL, THOU ONCE DESPISED JESUS

No one knows much about John Bakewell, the author of this hymn, except that he died when he was ninety-eight years old and that he was a pastor for seventy years. The fact that he was a Methodist pastor indicates that he himself knew something about being despised, for Methodist pastors were ridiculed and persecuted in eighteenth-century England.

In the Old Testament, Isaiah prophesied that the Messiah would be despised and rejected and that he would be a man of sorrows, acquainted with bitter grief. Isaiah goes on to say that "because of his experience, my righteous servant [the Messiah] will make it possible for many to be counted righteous, for he will bear all their sins" (Isaiah 53:11).

But there is more, as hymnwriter John Bakewell knew very well. As the obedient Son of God, Jesus has been given a name that is above every name, and every knee will one day bow to him. The rejection of the past will become the glory of the future, and Jesus Christ, the One who was despised and rejected, will be hailed for his sacrificial suffering. As the last stanza of the hymn says, "Worship, honor, power, and blessing, / Christ is worthy to receive."

Scriptures: Isaiah 53:3-6; Matthew 27:29-31; Ephesians 1:19-21; Revelation 5:11-13
Themes: Jesus, Lamb of God, Crucifixion

Hail, Thou once despised Jesus!
Hail, Thou Galilean King!
Thou didst suffer to release us;
Thou didst free salvation bring.
Hail, Thou universal Savior,
Who hast borne our sin and shame!
By Thy merits we find favor;
Life is given through Thy name.

Paschal Lamb, by God appointed,
All our sins on Thee were laid;
By almighty love appointed,
Thou hast full atonement made.
Every sin may be forgiven,

Through the virtue of Thy blood;
Opened is the gate of heaven;
Peace is made twixt man and God.

Worship, honor, power, and blessing
Christ is worthy to receive;
Loudest praises, without ceasing,
Meet it is for us to give.
Help, ye bright angelic spirits,
Bring your sweetest, noblest lays;
Help to sing of Jesus' merits,
Help to chant Emmanuel's praise!

ATTRIBUTED TO JOHN BAKEWELL (1721–1819)
Translation attributed to Martin Madan (1726–1790)

HALLELUJAH, WHAT A SAVIOR!

Philip Bliss was one of the most prominent hymnwriters in the heyday of gospel hymnwriting. Though he grew up working on a farm and in lumber camps, he eventually became a music teacher. He sold his first song at age twenty-six and later worked for a hymn publisher. Dwight L. Moody urged Bliss to become a singing evangelist, so he did, beginning in 1874. This hymn was published in 1875. In 1876, while traveling through Ohio on his way to Moody's tabernacle in Chicago, he and his family were involved in a train wreck. When Bliss went back into the fiery train to save his wife, both he and his wife died.

It was a tragedy for hymn lovers around the world, but you might say that Bliss just changed his address. Certainly he continues, even now, creating new praises for our wonderful Savior in glory.

The first four stanzas of the hymn focus on the Cross and the atonement for sin. The last verse has a different mood, as we look ahead to eternity with our glorious King.

Scriptures: Isaiah 53:1-3; Philippians 2:7-11; 1 Peter 2:24
Themes: Cross, Passion, Atonement

"Man of Sorrows!" what a name
For the Son of God, who came
Ruined sinners to reclaim!
Hallelujah, what a Savior!

Bearing shame and scoffing rude,
In my place condemned He stood—
Sealed my pardon with His blood:
Hallelujah, what a Savior!

Guilty, vile and helpless we,
Spotless Lamb of God was He;
Full atonement! can it be?
Hallelujah, what a Savior!

Lifted up was He to die,
"It is finished!" was His cry;
Now in heav'n exalted high:
Hallelujah, what a Savior!

When He comes, our glorious King,
All His ransomed home to bring,
Then anew this song we'll sing:
Hallelujah, what a Savior!

PHILIP PAUL BLISS (1838–1876)

HOW SWEET THE NAME OF JESUS SOUNDS

At the age of eighty, John Newton was quite deaf and almost blind, but he still continued to preach. For his final messages, Newton brought an aide to the pulpit. The aide would read the next point of Newton's sermon outline, and Newton would then expound on that point.

On one particular Sunday, not long before Newton's death, the assistant read the first point, and Newton said to the congregation, "Jesus Christ is precious." He paused and waited until the aide read the second point. Newton said again, "Jesus Christ is precious."

The aide reminded Newton that he had already said that. "Yes, I said it twice," the aged pastor replied, this time with a shout, "and I'll say it again! Jesus Christ is precious." Then he asked the congregation to sing the hymn he had written many years before, "How Sweet the Name of Jesus Sounds."

Scriptures: Song of Songs 1:3; Philippians 2:5-11; 1 Peter 2:7
Themes: Name of Jesus, Comfort, Praise

How sweet the name of Jesus sounds
In a believer's ear!
It soothes his sorrows, heals his wounds,
And drives away his fear.

It makes the wounded spirit whole
And calms the troubled breast;
'Tis manna to the hungry soul
And to the weary, rest.

Dear name! the rock on which I build,
My shield and hiding place;
My never-failing treasure, filled
With boundless stores of grace!

Jesus, my Shepherd, Brother, Friend,
My Prophet, Priest, and King,
My Lord, my Life, my Way, my End,
Accept the praise I bring.

Till then I would Thy love proclaim
With ev'ry fleeting breath;
And may the music of Thy name
Refresh my soul in death.

JOHN NEWTON (1725–1807)

I LOVE TO TELL THE STORY

Kate Hankey, the daughter of a prosperous British banker, grew up in a stylish London suburb. She started a Bible class for girls in her neighborhood, and when she was only eighteen, Hankey went to London to teach a Bible class of "factory girls." In her twenties, she started other Bible classes for factory girls.

When she was in her early thirties, Kate Hankey became seriously ill. Doctors said she needed a year of bed rest. She was forbidden to teach her Bible classes for twelve months. During her long, slow recovery, she wrote two lengthy poems. The first, at the beginning of her convalescence, later became the hymn "Tell Me the Old, Old Story." The second, written ten months later, was "I Love to Tell the Story."

After ten months she felt strong enough to leave her bed. She soon returned to her Bible classes in London and continued teaching for many years. When she became too old to teach the factory girls regularly, she started a prison ministry in London—even then she continued to tell the story of Jesus.

Scriptures: Acts 1:8; Acts 4:12; 1 Peter 3:15
Themes: Jesus' Ministry, Evangelism, Salvation

I love to tell the story of unseen things above,
Of Jesus and His glory, of Jesus and His love;
I love to tell the story because I know 'tis true,
It satisfies my longings as nothing else can do.

I love to tell the story!
'Twill be my theme in glory—
To tell the old, old story
Of Jesus and His love.

I love to tell the story—'tis pleasant to repeat
What seems, each time I tell it, more wonderfully sweet;
I love to tell the story, for some have never heard
The message of salvation from God's own holy Word.

I love to tell the story, for those who know it best
Seem hungering and thirsting to hear it like the rest;
And when in scenes of glory I sing the new, new song,
'Twill be the old, old story that I have loved so long.

ARABELLA CATHERINE HANKEY (1834–1911)

IN JESUS

James Procter, the author of this song, had been raised in a Christian home, but as a teenager he began reading the writings of agnostics and infidels. Soon he started attending some meetings of a group that called itself the Free Thinkers. He now doubted his parents' Christian views and renounced Christianity. In time he became the president of the Free Thinkers.

However, when he became seriously ill and it was thought that he might not live, he asked to see a Christian minister. The minister came and prayed with him, and James Procter, responding in faith, was converted.

Later when his sister came to visit him, he asked her to look in his dresser to find a poem he had written. Then he dictated to her two closing verses that he wanted his friends in the Free Thinkers' group to read. So the hymn was completed: "There's love in all His words and deeds; /

There's all a guilty sinner needs." Good advice, whether you are a free-thinker or not.

Scriptures: Acts 4:12; Acts 10:43; 1 Timothy 2:3-6
Themes: Jesus Christ, Salvation, Hope

> I've tried in vain a thousand ways
> My fear to quell, my hopes to raise;
> But what I need, the Bible says,
> Is ever, only Jesus.
>
> My soul is night, my heart is steel—
> I cannot see, I cannot feel;
> For light, for life I must appeal
> In simple faith to Jesus.
>
> He died, He lives, He reigns, He pleads;
> There's love in all His words and deeds;
> There's all a guilty sinner needs
> Forevermore in Jesus.
>
> Tho' some should sneer, and some should blame,
> I'll go with all my guilt and shame;
> I'll go to Him because His name,
> Above all names, is Jesus.
>
> JAMES PROCTER

I'VE FOUND A FRIEND, O SUCH A FRIEND

Sometimes the buddy-buddy approach to Christianity causes our concept of God's holiness to be diminished. But when Christ's friendship is depicted as James Small depicts it here, Christ is exalted.

Small, a minister in the Scottish Free Church, loved to write hymns. His first book was *Hymns for Youthful Voices,* published in 1859. This hymn, originally called "Jesus the Friend," was published four years later in *The Revival Hymnbook.*

The hymn is full of great theological truths. From our standpoint, we sing, "I've found a Friend," but the truth is "He loved me ere I knew Him," and "He drew me with the cords of love." Obviously it is Jesus who initiates this friendship. The final stanza concludes with lines that recall Romans 8:35: "Who shall separate us from the love of Christ?"

(KJV). Small concludes, "I am His forever." Such a Friend is truly worth singing about!

Scriptures: Hosea 11:4; John 15:15; Romans 8:35
Themes: Friend, Jesus, Assurance

I've found a Friend, O such a Friend!
He loved me ere I knew Him;
He drew me with the cords of love,
And thus He bound me to Him.
And round my heart still closely twine
Those ties which naught can sever;
For I am His, and He is mine,
Forever and forever.

I've found a Friend, O such a Friend!
He bled, He died to save me;
And not alone the gift of life,
But His own self He gave me.
Naught that I have my own I call,
I hold it for the Giver;
My heart, my strength, my life, my all,
Are His, and His forever.

I've found a Friend, O such a Friend!
So kind and true and tender;
So wise a Counselor and Guide,
So mighty a Defender!
From Him who loves me now so well,
What pow'r my soul shall sever?
Shall life or death, shall earth or hell?
No; I am His forever.

JAMES GRINDLAY SMALL (1817–1888)

IVORY PALACES

Henry Barraclough was secretary to a member of the British Parliament when evangelist J. Wilbur Chapman came to town. Chapman needed a pianist, and since Barraclough had studied piano and organ from the age of five, the evangelistic team added Barraclough as its musician when it returned to America.

The following year, Chapman was preaching at the Montreat conference grounds in North Carolina. He chose Psalm 45:8 as his text: "All thy garments smell of myrrh, and aloes, and cassia, out of the ivory palaces, whereby they have made thee glad" (KJV). Chapman said it was a messianic psalm, telling us how Christ left the ivory palaces of heaven to come to this sinful world and die to redeem us.

Barraclough was moved by the message. On the way to the Blue Ridge YMCA that night, they stopped at a little village store. Barraclough bought a small card and wrote out the three stanzas of "Ivory Palaces," following the sermon outline of Evangelist Chapman. The next day the new hymn was sung for the first time. Chapman liked it but suggested a fourth verse, referring to the time when Christ will come again. That is the hymn as we now have it.

Scriptures: Psalm 45:8; John 1:14; 2 Corinthians 2:14-15; Hebrews 10:5-7
Themes: Messiah, Prophecy, Love

My Lord has garments so wondrous fine,
And myrrh their texture fills;
Its fragrance reached to this heart of mine,
With joy my being thrills.

Out of the ivory palaces into a world of woe,
Only His great eternal love made my Savior go.

His life had also its sorrows sore,
For aloes had a part;
And when I think of the cross He bore,
My eyes with teardrops start.

His garments too were in cassia dipped,
With healing in a touch;
Each time my feet in some sin have slipped,
He took me from its clutch.

In garments glorious He will come,
To open wide the door;
And I shall enter my heav'nly home,
To dwell forevermore.

HENRY BARRACLOUGH (1891–1983)

JESUS, LOVER OF MY SOUL

Two years before his conversion, Charles Wesley was crossing the Atlantic. When a storm arose, he was terrified. He wrote in his journal, "The sea streamed in at the sides; . . . it was as much as four men could do by continual pumping to keep her above water. I rose and lay down by turns, but could remain in no posture long; strove vehemently to pray, but in vain." Later in the afternoon as the storm reached its peak, he said, "In this dreadful moment, I found the comfort of hope."

After he returned from America, Charles was converted. One year after his conversion, he wrote this hymn, one of the most famous of the six thousand hymns that he wrote.

The hymn speaks about the tempest and about seeking a refuge from the storm. Charles found that refuge, that safe haven in Jesus Christ, and he speaks about it in the last stanza: "Plenteous grace with Thee is found, grace to cover all my sin."

Scriptures: Psalm 17:6-8; Psalm 91:2-4; Nahum 1:7
Themes: Comfort, Grace, Mercy

Jesus, Lover of my soul, let me to Thy bosom fly,
While the nearer waters roll, while the tempest still is high;
Hide me, O my Savior, hide, till the storm of life is past;
Safe into the haven guide; O receive my soul at last!

Other refuge have I none; hangs my helpless soul on Thee;
Leave, ah! leave me not alone, still support and comfort me.
All my trust on Thee is stayed; all my help from Thee I bring;
Cover my defenseless head with the shadow of Thy wing.

Thou, O Christ, art all I want; more than all in Thee I find:
Raise the fallen, cheer the faint, heal the sick, and lead the blind.
Just and holy is Thy name; I am all unrighteousness;
False and full of sin I am; Thou art full of truth and grace.

Plenteous grace with Thee is found, grace to cover all my sin;
Let the healing streams abound; make and keep me pure within.
Thou of life the fountain art; freely let me take of Thee:
Spring Thou up within my heart; rise to all eternity.

CHARLES WESLEY (1707–1788)

JESUS, MY LORD, MY GOD, MY ALL

Henry Collins wrote this moving prayer-hymn the year he graduated from Oxford and began his ministry as an Anglican clergyman. One writer said that it was "almost too intimate to sing in a great congregation."

But the depth of the hymn is worth exploring. The second and third stanzas ask unanswerable questions: "How can I love Thee as I ought?" and "What did Thou find in me that Thou has dealt so lovingly?"

In the apostle John's first epistle, we are reminded that God's love precedes ours: "We love each other because he loved us first" (1 John 4:19). But when we start asking why God loves us, there are no answers except in the character of God himself. In Ephesians 3:19, Paul reminds us that God's love "surpasses knowledge" (NIV).

In response, our love is always a dim reflection, like the moon. Our love is always tainted by our own self-interest. Yet even that imperfect love is valued by God, and we join Henry Collins in singing, "Jesus, my Lord, I Thee adore; / Oh, make me love Thee more and more."

Scriptures: Psalm 73:25-26; Ephesians 3:19; 1 John 4:19
Themes: Love, Worship, Devotion

Jesus, my Lord, my God, my All,
Hear me, blest Savior, when I call;
Hear me, and from Thy dwelling-place
Pour down the riches of Thy grace:

Jesus, my Lord, I Thee adore;
Oh, make me love Thee more and more.

Jesus, too late I Thee have sought;
How can I love Thee as I ought?
And how extol Thy matchless fame,
The glorious beauty of Thy name?

Jesus, what did Thou find in me
That Thou has dealt so lovingly?
How great the joy that Thou has brought,
So far exceeding hope or thought!

Jesus, of Thee shall be my song;
To Thee my heart and soul belong;
All that I have or am is Thine,
And Thou, blest Savior, Thou art mine:

HENRY COLLINS (1827–1919)

JESUS! THE NAME HIGH OVER ALL

Mrs. Turner was a quiet woman who had only recently come to faith in Christ. She met Charles Wesley in her brother's home when Wesley came there physically ill and needing a place to recover. Shyly, Mrs. Turner told him how she had come to personal faith in Christ. Then she said boldly to Charles Wesley, "In the name of Jesus of Nazareth, arise and believe, and thou shalt be healed of thine infirmities!" That was the turning point for Charles, and he recovered from his illness.

Several years later, when Charles Wesley was preaching among the miners of Cornwall, England, a drunken man stood up, began swearing at Wesley, and shouted against his preaching. Wesley responded, "Who is this that pleads for the devil?" and in the name of Jesus he rebuked the man.

That night Wesley went to bed thinking about the name of Jesus. The hymn he wrote during the night refers to that experience in the first stanza. But as he wrote the second stanza, he was probably thinking of what shy Mrs. Turner had told him years earlier when she said, "In the name of Jesus of Nazareth, arise and believe!"

Scriptures: Luke 10:17-20; Ephesians 1:20-21; Philippians 2:9-11
Themes: Worship, Victory, Praise

Jesus! the name high over all,
In hell or earth or sky;
Angels and men before it fall,
And devils fear and fly.

Jesus! the name to sinners dear,
The name to sinners given;
It scatters all their guilty fear;
It turns their hell to heaven.

O that the world might taste and see
The riches of His grace!
The arms of love that compass me
Would all mankind embrace.

Thee I shall constantly proclaim,
Though earth and hell oppose,
Bold to confess Thy glorious name
Before a world of foes.

His only righteousness I show,
His saving grace proclaim;

'Tis all my business here below
To cry, "Behold the Lamb!"

Happy, if with my latest breath
I may but gasp His name;
Preach Him to all and cry in death,
"Behold, behold the Lamb!"

CHARLES WESLEY (1707–1788)

JESUS, THE VERY THOUGHT OF THEE

This hymn was written nearly a thousand years ago in the middle of the time we sometimes call the Dark Ages. It was a dark time because it was riddled with extensive corruption among leaders of the nations as well as leaders of the church. In such a time, the life of Bernard of Clairvaux shines brightly. "Knowing God," he said, "is a matter of the heart." It was a truth that dominated his life. At a very early age he was drawn to spiritual things, largely influenced by the piety of his mother. At the age of twenty-two he entered a monastery at Citeaux, and three years later he founded a monastery at Clairvaux and served as its spiritual leader until he died in 1153.

In spite of his many pressing responsibilities and frequent travel, Bernard never lost sight of what he prized most—the love of Jesus. God's love was Bernard's lifeblood, pulsing through everything he said and did. His knowledge of God was deeply personal, a mystical love affair that not only gave meaning to his life on earth but formed his vision of heaven. As Bernard said, "[God] is Himself the reward of those who love Him, the eternal reward of those who love Him for eternity."

Scriptures: Psalm 42:1-2; Jeremiah 17:7; 1 Corinthians 2:1-5
Themes: Jesus, Worship, Devotion

Jesus, the very thought of Thee
With sweetness fills my breast;
But sweeter far Thy face to see,
And in Thy presence rest.

Nor voice can sing, nor heart can frame,
Nor can the mem'ry find
A sweeter sound than Thy blest name,
O Savior of mankind!

O Hope of every contrite heart,
O Joy of all the meek,
To those who fall, how kind Thou art!
How good to those who seek!

But what to those who find? Ah, this
Nor tongue nor pen can show:
The love of Jesus, what it is
None but His loved ones know.

Jesus, our only joy be Thou,
As Thou our prize wilt be:
Jesus, be Thou our glory now,
And through eternity.

ATTRIBUTED TO BERNARD OF CLAIRVAUX (1091–1153)
Translated by Edward Caswall (1814–1878)

JESUS, THY BLOOD AND RIGHTEOUSNESS

Count Nicolaus von Zinzendorf was one of the most remarkable persons in church history. He was born into a wealthy family in Saxony, Germany; educated at the best universities; and named counselor of the State of Saxony. But he chose instead to be associated with the persecuted Moravians, devout believers who had been exiled from Austria. When the Moravians had no place they could call home, the count provided a refuge for them.

Of the two thousand hymns he wrote, this is perhaps the best known. He completed it on his return from visiting Moravian missionaries in the West Indies. His hymns were personal because he was a passionate promoter of what he called "Christianity of the heart." They were also Christ-centered because his life motto was, "I have but one passion, and that is He and only He."

Scriptures: Hebrews 7:25; 1 Peter 1:18-19; 2 Peter 3:9
Themes: Atonement, Forgiveness, Salvation

Jesus, Thy blood and righteousness
My beauty are, my glorious dress;
Midst flaming worlds, in these arrayed,
With joy shall I lift up my head.

Bold shall I stand in Thy great day,
For who aught to my charge shall lay?
Fully absolved through these I am,
From sin and fear, from guilt and shame.

Lord, I believe Thy precious blood,
Which, at the mercy seat of God,
Forever doth for sinners plead,
For me, e'en for my soul, was shed.

Lord, I believe were sinners more
Than sands upon the ocean shore,
Thou hast for all a ransom paid,
For all a full atonement made.

NICOLAUS VON ZINZENDORF (1700–1760)
Translated by John Wesley (1703–1791)

JESUS! WHAT A FRIEND FOR SINNERS

Jesus' detractors accused him of being a friend of tax collectors and sinners. They couldn't have been more right. By sinners they meant those who had stopped trying to keep the law, those who had given up on the religious games of the Pharisees. Such "sinners" were shunned by the religious leaders, but Jesus spoke to them, ate with them, and befriended them.

In defense of his actions, Jesus said cryptically, "Wisdom is shown to be right by its results" (Matthew 11:19). Certainly he backed this up with his own actions. As he said later, "There is no greater love than to lay down one's life for one's friends" (John 15:13). That is precisely what he did for his friends, the sinners. Jesus gave his life so everyone can experience freedom from sin's powerful grip.

As an evangelist, J. Wilbur Chapman knew the joy of seeing scores of sinners open their hearts to the Lord. As a pastor, he preached with great sympathy. He knew firsthand the joy of a sinner finding a friend in Christ, because it was as a college student that he himself had received Jesus as his Friend.

Scriptures: Luke 5:30-32; John 15:13-16; Ephesians 1:3-5
Themes: Friend, Salvation, Comfort

Jesus! what a Friend for sinners!
Jesus! Lover of my soul;
Friends may fail me, foes assail me,
He, my Savior, makes me whole.

Jesus! what a Strength in weakness!
Let me hide myself in Him;
Tempted, tried, and sometimes failing,
He, my Strength, my vict'ry wins.

Jesus! what a Help in sorrow!
While the billows o'er me roll,
Even when my heart is breaking,
He, my Comfort, helps my soul.

Jesus! what a Guide and Keeper!
While the tempest still is high,
Storms about me, night o'ertakes me,
He, my Pilot, hears my cry.

Jesus! I do now receive Him,
More than all in Him I find,
He hath granted me forgiveness,
I am His, and He is mine.

J. WILBUR CHAPMAN (1859–1918)

LORD JESUS, THINK ON ME

Synesius was a native of Cyrene in northern Africa, the hometown of the Simon who had carried the cross for Jesus. Synesius was more famous as a philosopher than as a Christian leader. Most of his writings come from his pre-Christian days, including a humanist eulogy on baldness; a speech depicting the ideal Roman emperor; and a paper, *De Insomniis*, on the causes and meaning of dreams.

When he was thirty-three, Synesius married a Christian and later became a Christian himself. Yet he struggled with how to reconcile his philosophy with Christian doctrine. Eventually he was consecrated a bishop in the church, but his philosophical struggle continued.

This hymn was derived from an ode written by Synesius, and in it can be seen his sincere desire for God to shed light on his path. "Through darkness and perplexity," he prayed, "point Thou the heavenly way."

Scriptures: Luke 23:26; John 17:20; 2 Timothy 1:11-12
Themes: Prayer, Confession, Dedication

Lord Jesus, think on me,
And purge away my sin;
From earthborn passions set me free,
And make me pure within.

Lord Jesus, think on me,
With care and woe oppressed;
Let me Thy loving servant be,
And taste Thy promised rest.

Lord Jesus, think on me,
Amid the battle's strife;
In all my pain and misery
Be Thou my health and life.

Lord Jesus, think on me,
Nor let me go astray;
Through darkness and perplexity
Point Thou the heavenly way.

Lord Jesus, think on me,
That when this life is past,
I may th'eternal brightness see,
And share Thy joy at last.

Lord Jesus, think on me,
That I may sing above
To Father, Spirit, and to Thee,
The strains of praise and love.

SYNESIUS OF CYRENE (CA. 375–430)
Translated by Allen W. Chatfield (1808–1896)

MORE ABOUT JESUS

Eliza Hewitt wrote this hymn as she was studying the promises of God that had been fulfilled in Jesus Christ. The more she studied, the more excited she became as she saw Scripture fulfilled in every aspect of Christ's life. All Scripture, she discovered, focused on Jesus Christ.

It is especially significant that Hewitt was so faithfully seeking God at this point in her life. At the time, she was recovering from a severe spinal injury. A Philadelphia schoolteacher, Hewitt had been struck with a heavy slate by one of her students.

Hewitt was never again able to teach in the public schools, but she continued to be involved with Sunday school. There she was able to combine the two great loves of her life: children and Jesus.

Scriptures: Ephesians 3:16-19; Philippians 3:10; 2 Peter 1:2-4
Themes: Jesus, Salvation, Word of God

More about Jesus would I know,
More of His grace to others show,
More of His saving fullness see,
More of His love who died for me.

More, more about Jesus,
More, more about Jesus;
More of His saving fullness see,
More of His love who died for me!

More about Jesus let me learn,
More of His holy will discern;
Spirit of God, my teacher be,
Showing the things of Christ to me.

More about Jesus; in His Word,
Holding communion with my Lord,
Hearing His voice in ev'ry line,
Making each faithful saying mine.

More about Jesus on His throne,
Riches in glory all His own,
More of His kingdom's sure increase,
More of His coming—Prince of Peace.

ELIZA EDMUNDS HEWITT (1851–1920)

O CHRIST, OUR KING, CREATOR, LORD

"Keep on seeking, and you will find," says Jesus (Matthew 7:7). "Seek the LORD while you can find him," says Isaiah (55:6). And God says in Amos, "Come back to me and live!" (5:4). The Bible encourages people to look for the Lord, and as this hymn puts it, God is "to them who seek [him] ever near."

Gregory the Great, who wrote this hymn, was the pope who taught the church how to sing. He established a music school in Rome and sent monks throughout what is now Germany and England to spread his style of singing. Once when his city was struck by a disastrous plague, Gregory organized musical processions through the plague-stricken streets, followed by choirs singing litanies. His music calmed the terror of the people and helped to spark a religious revival.

Scriptures: Matthew 27:50-54; John 1:14; Hebrews 1:3
Themes: Creator, Salvation, Victory

O Christ, our King, Creator, Lord,
Savior of all who trust Thy Word,
To them who seek Thee ever near,
Now to our praises bend Thine ear.

In Thy dear cross a grace is found—
It flows from every streaming wound—
Whose pow'r our inbred sin controls,
Breaks the firm bond, and frees our souls.

Thou didst create the stars of night;
Yet Thou hast veiled in flesh Thy light,
Hast deigned a mortal form to wear,
A mortal's painful lot to bear.

When Thou didst hang upon the tree,
The quaking earth acknowledged Thee;
When Thou didst there yield up Thy breath,
The world grew dark as shades of death.

Now in the Father's glory high,
Great Conqueror, nevermore to die,
Us by Thy mighty pow'r defend,
And reign through ages without end.

GREGORY THE GREAT (540–604)
Translated by Ray Palmer (1808–1887)

O CHRIST, OUR TRUE AND ONLY LIGHT

This hymn reminds us that God seeks those who are lost. Jesus told the story of the Prodigal's father, who watched for the return of his runaway son. God is like that, gently seeking those who have strayed, offering his healing to those who will receive it.

This may be the earliest missionary hymn we have. Johann Heermann was a Lutheran pastor in the German village of Köben. This town was at the center of conflict during the Thirty Years' War, which pitted Protestants against Catholics throughout central Europe. Historians estimate that half the population of Germany died in the fighting.

And there, as the smoke cleared, Heermann was calling for lost souls to come to the Savior. We might have expected an introspective hymn, something that called on God for relief in trying times. Other hymnwriters wrote such hymns during that conflict. But Heermann longed to see others brought into the fold of God's care.

Scriptures: Isaiah 60:1-3; Luke 15:1-7; John 10:14-16
Themes: Missions, Evangelism, Praise

O Christ, our true and only Light,
Illumine those who sit in night;
Let those afar now hear Thy voice,
And in Thy fold with us rejoice.

And all who else have strayed from Thee,
O gently seek; Thy healing be
To ev'ry wounded conscience giv'n;
And let them also share Thy heav'n.

O make the deaf to hear Thy Word;
And teach the dumb to speak, dear Lord,
Who dare not yet the faith avow,
Though secretly they hold it now.

Shine on the darkened and the cold;
Recall the wand'rers from Thy fold;
Unite those now who walk apart;
Confirm the weak and doubting heart.

So they with us may evermore
Such grace with wond'ring thanks adore,
And endless praise to Thee be giv'n
By all the church in earth and heav'n.

JOHANN HEERMANN (1585–1647)
Translated by Catherine Winkworth (1827–1878)

O DEAREST JESUS

Jean de Fécamp was a Benedictine monk who lived and wrote nearly a thousand years ago. For about a half century, Fécamp was the head of a monastic colony in Normandy. Then late in his life, he went to the Holy Land, where he was arrested and imprisoned by the ruling Turks.

Perhaps you can imagine him in that dank Turkish jail, as he remembered Jesus Christ imprisoned in Jerusalem a thousand years earlier. Fécamp asks the question in this hymn: "O dearest Jesus, what law hast Thou broken / That such sharp sentence should on Thee be spoken?"

This Latin hymn was translated by Lutheran pastor Johann Heermann in the seventeenth century. The message of the hymn was very appropriate for his German town that was being ravaged by the Thirty Years' War at the time.

Scriptures: Isaiah 53:9-11; 2 Corinthians 5:21; 1 Peter 2:21-23
Themes: Cross, Redemption, Grace

O dearest Jesus, what law hast Thou broken
That such sharp sentence should on Thee be spoken?
Of what great crime hast Thou to make confession,
What dark transgression?

They crown Thy head with thorns, they smite, they scourge Thee;
With cruel mockings to the cross they urge Thee;
They give Thee gall to drink, they still decry Thee;
They crucify Thee.

Whence come these sorrows, whence this mortal anguish?
It is my sins for which Thou, Lord, must languish;
Yea, all the wrath, the woe, Thou dost inherit,
This I do merit.

What punishment so strange is suffered yonder!
The Shepherd dies for sheep that loved to wander;
The Master pays the debt His servants owe Him,
Who would not know Him.

JEAN DE FÉCAMP (CA. 1000–1079)
Johann Heermann (1585–1647)
Translated by Catherine Winkworth (1827–1878)

O, WHAT A SAVIOR THAT HE DIED FOR ME

One evening many years ago, a woman in London decided to visit some friends. When she knocked at the door of one house, she was disappointed to find her friends not at home. She called on some other friends nearby, but they also had gone out. She decided to go home, but on the way she passed a large auditorium, where she heard singing inside. She went in and heard a song she had never heard before. The words were "O, what a Savior, that He died for me!"

She went home that night but couldn't get the song out of her mind. She finally got to sleep and dreamt that she was singing the song along with others in the auditorium: "O, what a Savior, that He died for me!" Her first words on awaking were the next words of the song: "From condemnation he hath made me free."

James McGranahan, the author of this gospel song, wrote many hymns, but those he enjoyed the most were the songs, like this one, that come directly from Scripture. This one is taken from John 6:47, which says, "Verily, verily, I say unto you, He that believeth on me hath everlasting life" (KJV).

Scriptures: John 3:36; John 5:24; John 6:47
Themes: Salvation, Faith, Conversion

O, what a Savior, that He died for me!
From condemnation He hath made me free;
"He that believeth on the Son," saith He,
"Hath everlasting life."

"Verily, verily, I say unto you,"
"Verily, verily," message ever new;
"He that believeth on the Son,"
'Tis true, "Hath everlasting life."

All my iniquities on Him were laid,
All my indebtedness by Him was paid;
All who believe on Him, the Lord hath said,
"Hath everlasting life."

Though poor and needy I can trust my Lord,
Though weak and sinful I believe His Word;
Oh, glad message! Ev'ry child of God
"Hath everlasting life."

Though all unworthy, yet I will not doubt,
For him that cometh, He will not cast out;
"He that believeth," oh, the good news shout,
"Hath everlasting life!"

JAMES MCGRANAHAN (1840–1907)

O WORD OF GOD INCARNATE

There was a down-to-earth simplicity about William Walsham How. He confessed that he was not a good student in college. Science, he said, baffled him. But he went on to become a minister. He served a rural congregation on the Welsh border for twenty-eight years and then ministered in the slums of London's East End, serving ordinary folk. William How became known as the "Poor Man's Bishop." His ambition in life, he said, was not "to be remembered, but to be helpful."

He loved children and wrote hymns for them. One of these hymns began like this: "It is a thing most wonderful, almost too wonderful to be, that God's own Son should come from heaven, and die to save a child like me."

William How also loved the Bible. On his symbolic pastoral staff, he engraved the words, "Feed with the Word, feed with the Life." So it is not surprising that he should write a hymn that combines praise to the written Word of God with praise to the Incarnate Word of God.

Scriptures: Psalm 119:33-37; John 1:1-14; 2 Timothy 3:16-17
Themes: Word of God, Jesus Christ, Church

O Word of God incarnate, O Wisdom from on high,
O Truth unchanged, unchanging, O Light of our dark sky:
We praise Thee for the radiance that from the hallowed page,
A lantern to our footsteps, shines on from age to age.

The Church from Thee, her Master, received the gift divine,
And still that light she lifteth o'er all the earth to shine,
It is the sacred casket where gems of truth are stored;
It is the heaven-drawn picture of Thee, the living Word.

It floateth like a banner before God's host unfurled;
It shineth like a beacon above the darkling world.
It is the chart and compass that o'er life's surging sea,
Mid mists and rocks and quicksands, still guides, O Christ, to Thee.

O make Thy Church, dear Savior, a lamp of purest gold,
To bear before the nations Thy true light as of old.
O teach Thy wandering pilgrims by this their path to trace,
Till, clouds and darkness ended, they see Thee face to face.
WILLIAM WALSHAM HOW (1823–1897)

SAVIOR OF THE NATIONS, COME

There are periods in church history when the church forgot how to sing.

Ambrose of Milan lived in such a period, but he changed it. In the late 300s a fierce cultural struggle was taking place. Although the government of the Roman Empire was officially Christian, pagan ways were still strong. As bishop of Milan, Ambrose strengthened the church in many ways, opposing pagan ideas by standing up to emperors, and introducing many hymns for his congregation to sing.

This is one of those hymns; in it he is teaching the people the theological truth of the incarnation of the Son of God. It is interesting that an early translation of this Ambrose hymn was made by Martin Luther, another leader who strengthened the church through singing. When we consider the "Savior of the nations" who reigns eternally, we certainly have a lot to sing about.

Scriptures: John 1:1-3, 14; Philippians 2:5-11; 1 John 1:1-3
Themes: Incarnation, Trinity, Praise

Savior of the nations, come,
Virgin's Son, make here Thy home!
Marvel now, O heav'n and earth,
That the Lord chose such a birth.

Not of flesh and blood the Son,
Offspring of the Holy One;
Born of Mary ever blest
God in flesh is manifest.

Wondrous birth! Oh, wondrous Child
Of the virgin undefiled!
Though by all the world disowned,
Still to be in heav'n throned.

From the Father forth He came
And returneth to the same,

Captive leading death and hell.
High the song of triumph swell!

Thou, the Father's only Son,
Hast o'er sin the vict'ry won.
Boundless shall Thy kingdom be;
When shall we its glories see?

Praise to God the Father sing.
Praise to God the Son, our King,
Praise to God the Spirit be
Ever and eternally.

AMBROSE OF MILAN (340–397)
Translated into German by Martin Luther (1483–1546)
Translated into English by William M. Reynolds (1812–1876)

TELL ME THE STORY OF JESUS

Almost everyone loves to listen to stories. In this gospel song, Fanny Crosby, the blind hymnwriter, asks to be told the story of Jesus, and in the process of asking, she tells the story of Jesus herself.

The first verse tells of his birth with the choir of angels singing. The second verse tells of his ministry on earth, despised, afflicted, homeless, rejected, and poor, and the third verse tells of his death and resurrection, concluding with the wonderful line, "Love paid the ransom for me."

Many people today don't know that wonderful story. We often find it easier to talk about our church, but maybe people are really saying, "Tell me the story of Jesus." So let's tell them that story.

Scriptures: Acts 1:7-9; Acts 26:22-23; 1 Corinthians 15:3-4
Themes: Jesus' Ministry, Incarnation

Tell me the story of Jesus,
Write on my heart every word;
Tell me the story most precious,
Sweetest that ever was heard.
Tell how the angels in chorus
Sang as they welcomed His birth,
"Glory to God in the highest!
Peace and good tidings to earth."

Tell me the story of Jesus,
Write on my heart every word;

Tell me the story most precious,
Sweetest that ever was heard.

Fasting alone in the desert,
Tell of the days that are past,
How for our sins He was tempted,
Yet was triumphant at last.
Tell of the years of His labor,
Tell of the sorrow He bore,
He was despised and afflicted,
Homeless, rejected and poor.

Tell of the cross where they nailed Him,
Writhing in anguish and pain;
Tell of the grave where they laid Him,
Tell how He liveth again.
Love in that story so tender
Clearer than ever I see:
Lord, may I always remember
Love paid the ransom for me.

FANNY JANE CROSBY (1820–1915)

THE LIGHT OF THE WORLD IS JESUS

This gospel song is a commentary on the writings of John. The Gospel begins, as this song begins, by talking about the whole world being in darkness and Jesus coming as the Light. The chorus contains the line, "Once I was blind, but now I can see," that is almost a direct quote of the blind man who was healed by Jesus. In that story Jesus declares that he is the Light of the world. The second stanza of this gospel song comes from John 12 as well as from John's first epistle, and the last stanza is taken from the last chapters of the book of Revelation, which were also written by the apostle John.

If there were any doubt, Jesus declared boldly as he was teaching in the Temple, "I am the light of the world. If you follow me, you won't have to walk in darkness, because you will have the light that leads to life" (John 8:12).

Scriptures: John 1:5; John 8:12; John 9:5; Revelation 21:23
Themes: Light, Blindness, Salvation

The whole world was lost in the darkness of sin,
The Light of the world is Jesus;
Like sunshine at noonday His glory shone in,
The Light of the world is Jesus.

Come to the Light, 'tis shining for thee;
Sweetly the Light has dawned upon me;
Once I was blind, but now I can see;
The Light of the world is Jesus.

No darkness have we who in Jesus abide,
The Light of the world is Jesus;
We walk in the Light when we follow our Guide,
The Light of the world is Jesus.

Ye dwellers in darkness with sin blinded eyes,
The Light of the world is Jesus;
Go, wash at His bidding, and light will arise,
The Light of the world is Jesus.

No need of the sunlight in heaven we're told,
The Light of the world is Jesus.
The Lamb is the Light in the City of gold,
The Light of the world is Jesus.

PHILIP PAUL BLISS (1838–1876)

THE SANDS OF TIME ARE SINKING

There are two stories woven together in this hymn. The author of this hymn, Anne Ross Cousin, was in her home, sewing, when an idea struck her. She had just finished reading a biography of Samuel Rutherford, a seventeenth-century Scottish Covenanter. Not only had he lived a remarkable life, but he had said many remarkable and eminently quotable things. She decided to weave the sayings together and make a hymn out of them.

The other story, of course, is that of Samuel Rutherford, who was banished from the town and church he loved because he refused to conform to the established church of the time. When he got his summons to appear before Parliament and answer the charges, he was ill and dying. He responded, "I have been summoned to appear before a higher court; that first summons I must answer." He died a few days later. His last words were "Glory to my Creator and Redeemer forever! Oh, for arms to embrace Him. Oh, for a well-tuned harp! Glory! Glory dwelleth in Immanuel's land."

So Anne Cousin wove her hymn tapestry around his words, closing each stanza with the words "glory, glory dwelleth in Immanuel's land." Anne Cousin didn't know how famous her hymn would become. It was the favorite hymn of evangelist Dwight L. Moody and was also sung at the bedside of Charles Haddon Spurgeon just before he died.

Scriptures: Psalm 24:7; John 17:3-5; Hebrews 12:3
Themes: Christlikeness, Holiness, Heaven

The sands of time are sinking, the dawn of heaven breaks;
The summer morn I've sighed for—the fair, sweet morn awakes.
Dark, dark hath been the midnight, but day-spring is at hand,
And glory, glory dwelleth in Immanuel's land.

O Christ, He is the fountain, the deep sweet well of love!
The streams on earth I've tasted more deep I'll drink above:
There to an ocean fulness His mercy doth expand,
And glory, glory dwelleth in Immanuel's land.

O I am my Beloved's, and my Beloved's mine!
He brings a poor vile sinner into His "house of wine."
I stand upon His merit—I know no other stand,
Not e'en where glory dwelleth in Immanuel's land.

The Bride eyes not her garment but her dear Bridegroom's face;
I will not gaze at glory but on my King of grace,
Not at the crown He giveth but on His pierced hand:
The Lamb is all the glory of Immanuel's land.

ANNE ROSS COUSIN (1834–1906)

THE SON OF GOD GOES FORTH TO WAR

This hymn was written by an Anglican clergyman for St. Stephen's Day, when liturgical churches remember the first Christian martyr. The hymn pictures Jesus Christ leading an army and asks several times who follows in this train (or procession) of soldiers?

The first stanza says that Christ's army is made up of men and women who are not afraid to suffer pain and bear their cross—in other words, men and women like Saint Stephen. It is Stephen who is depicted in the second stanza. In Acts 7, Stephen sees Jesus standing at God's right hand

and Stephen prays for his murderers. In the third stanza, we see that the twelve apostles join the procession. They were "the chosen few on whom the Spirit came." And the fourth stanza lists people of all ages, men and women, boys and girls, in robes of white around the throne. The number of those who have given their life for Jesus Christ continues today.

In 1812, Reginald Heber, the author of this hymn, was in a comfortable parish in England. Then he responded to a call to go to India. At the age of forty-two, he died and was buried in India. He had followed in the train of Christ's procession.

Scriptures: Acts 7:57-60; Ephesians 6:10-20; 1 Timothy 6:12; Revelation 7:9-10
Themes: Martyrdom, Conflict, Courage

The Son of God goes forth to war, a kingly crown to gain:
His blood-red banner streams afar: who follows in His train?
Who best can drink His cup of woe, triumphant over pain?
Who patient bears His cross below, He follows in His train.

The martyr first, whose eagle eye could pierce beyond the grave,
Who saw His Master in the sky and called on Him to save—
Like Him, with pardon on his tongue in midst of mortal pain
He prayed for them that did the wrong: Who follows in His train?

A glorious band, the chosen few on whom the Spirit came,
Twelve valiant saints, their hope they knew, and mocked the
    cross and flame—
They met the tyrant's brandished steel, the lion's gory mane.
They bowed their necks the death to feel: Who follows in their train?

A noble army, men and boys, the matron and the maid,
Around the Savior's throne rejoice, in robes of light arrayed—
They climbed the steep ascent of heav'n thru peril, toil and pain:
O God, to us may grace be given to follow in their train!

REGINALD HEBER (1783–1826)

WHO IS THIS SO WEAK AND HELPLESS?

Christianity is a faith full of great irony. We honor our great Creator, Lord of heaven and earth, great Judge of all. But when he appears on earth, he is born among cattle, a baby in a borrowed bed. He grows up as a working man and wanders as a homeless preacher. He dies a criminal's death, abandoned by most of his closest followers. This is the God we serve.

William Walsham How's hymn brilliantly displays this irony. The first four lines of each stanza ask for the identity of this poor, mistreated person. The final four lines answer in the most glorious terms.

Some people still don't understand this irony. Even Christians get caught up in the world's idea of greatness. We often seek the glamour of a glory-filled life. But that was not our Lord's pattern, as How reminds us. Bishop How himself practiced what he preached: He was known for his ministry to the poor in some of England's worst communities and was called the "Poor Man's Bishop."

Scriptures: 1 Corinthians 1:26-30; 2 Corinthians 8:9; Philippians 2:5-11
Themes: Humility, Life of Christ, Deity of Christ

Who is this so weak and helpless,
Child of lowly Hebrew maid,
Rudely in a stable sheltered,
Coldly in a manger laid?
'Tis the Lord of all creation,
Who this wondrous path hath trod;
He is God from everlasting,
And to everlasting God.

Who is this, a Man of Sorrows,
Walking sadly life's hard way,
Homeless, weary, sighing, weeping
Over sin and Satan's sway?
'Tis our God, our glorious Savior,
Who above the starry sky
Now for us a place prepareth,
Where no tear can dim the eye.

Who is this? Behold Him shedding
Drops of blood upon the ground!
Who is this, despised, rejected,
Mocked, insulted, beaten, bound?
'Tis our God, who gifts and graces
On His Church now poureth down;
Who shall smite in holy vengeance
All His foes beneath His throne.

Who is this that hangeth dying
While the rude world scoffs and scorns,

Numbered with the malefactors,
Pierced with nails, and crowned with thorns?
'Tis the God who ever liveth
'Mid the shining ones on high,
In the glorious golden city,
Reigning everlastingly.

WILLIAM WALSHAM HOW (1823–1897)

WONDERFUL GRACE OF JESUS

In 1917, young pastor Haldor Lillenas and his wife were settling into a ministry at the Nazarene church in Auburn, Illinois. After buying a house in nearby Olivet, they had little money left to furnish it. Though they were both hymnwriters, they couldn't afford a piano. Then Lillenas found a "wheezy little organ" in a neighbor's home and paid five dollars for it. He wrote a number of songs on that instrument, including this one.

This song, with its rolling melody and climbing chorus, became very popular at evangelistic meetings. Lillenas used it in his own evangelistic crusades, and others, such as the famous song leader Charles Alexander, used it often.

The message of Scripture comes through clearly here—no matter how great a sinner you are, God's grace is greater. No matter how great your guilt, God's forgiveness is greater. Praise his name!

Scriptures: Romans 5:20-21; Ephesians 2:4-7; Titus 3:5-7; Hebrews 4:16
Themes: Grace, Salvation, Justification

Wonderful grace of Jesus,
Greater than all my sin;
How shall my tongue describe it,
Where shall its praise begin?
Taking away my burden,
Setting my spirit free,
For the wonderful grace of Jesus reaches me.

Wonderful the matchless grace of Jesus,
Deeper than the mighty rolling sea;
Higher than the mountain, sparkling like a fountain,
All sufficient grace for even me;

Broader than the scope of my transgressions,
Greater far than all my sin and shame;
O magnify the precious name of Jesus,
Praise His name!

Wonderful grace of Jesus,
Reaching to all the lost,
By it I have been pardoned,
Saved to the uttermost;
Chains have been torn asunder,
Giving me liberty,
For the wonderful grace of Jesus reaches me.

Wonderful grace of Jesus,
Reaching the most defiled,
By its transforming power
Making me God's dear child,
Purchasing peace and heaven
For all eternity—
And the wonderful grace of Jesus reaches me.

HALDOR LILLENAS (1885–1959)

WORTHY IS THE LAMB

Don Wyrtzen's father, Jack Wyrtzen, directed a New York City dance band before he was converted and started the Word of Life ministries, so Don Wyrtzen grew up with music in his bones.

This worship chorus came about because Don didn't know Spanish. He was in Mexico City assisting evangelist Luis Palau in a series of crusades but didn't understand the sermons, which were in Spanish. He said, "I spent the time during the sermons writing new songs." One day he was particularly impressed with the great truth of Revelation 5:12 and wondered how it could be best set to music for our present time. He remembered the secular song "The Impossible Dream" from the musical *The Man of La Mancha* and thought a similar style might work well with these words.

Don Wyrtzen said, "God has used this song to bless and inspire his people during these past years perhaps more than any other work I have been privileged to write."

Scriptures: Isaiah 53:7; John 1:29; Revelation 5:6-13
Themes: Worship, Power, Wisdom

Worthy is the Lamb that was slain, worthy is the Lamb that was slain,
Worthy is the Lamb that was slain, to receive: power and riches
And wisdom and strength, honor and glory and blessing!
Worthy is the Lamb, worthy is the Lamb,
Worthy is the lamb that was slain, worthy is the Lamb!

DON WYRTZEN (B. 1942)

PART XVI

LOVE OF GOD

God showed how much he loved us by sending his one and only

Son into the world so that we might have eternal life through him.

1 JOHN 4:9

GOD IS LOVE; HIS MERCY BRIGHTENS

Sir John Bowring was truly a genius. Before he was sixteen, he was proficient in German, Dutch, Spanish, Portuguese, and Italian, as well as English. As an adult, he was said to be able to speak one hundred languages and to read two hundred. Twice he was elected to Parliament, and in 1854 he was appointed governor of Hong Kong. Despite his many successes, he became one of the most unpopular governors Hong Kong ever had. He was described as being "full of conceit and without any very clear idea of political principles on a grand scale."

Bowring wrote this hymn when he was thirty years old, nearly twenty-five years before he became the hated, ruthless governor. He ended each stanza with this timeless reminder: "God is wisdom, God is love." Perhaps Bowring would have been a better governor had he reminded himself often that the truth of God's love should lead us to yet another truth: As the apostle John says, "Dear friends, since God loved us that much, we surely ought to love each other" (1 John 4:11).

Scriptures: John 15:9; 1 John 4:11, 15-16
Themes: Love, God, God's Wisdom

God is love; His mercy brightens
All the path in which we rove;
Bliss He wakes and woe He lightens:
God is wisdom, God is love.

Chance and change are busy ever;
Man decays and ages move;
But His mercy waneth never:
God is wisdom, God is love.

E'en the hour that darkest seemeth
Will His changeless goodness prove;
Through the gloom His brightness streameth:
God is wisdom, God is love.

He with earthly cares entwineth
Hope and comfort from above;
Everywhere His glory shineth:
God is wisdom, God is love.

JOHN BOWRING (1792–1872)

JESUS, THY BOUNDLESS LOVE TO ME

Paul Gerhardt had been an angry young man, a student and teacher whose plans had been put on hold by the Thirty Years' War. As a young man, he had passionately argued the finer points of Lutheran theology, but with age he mellowed. His passion turned to the overwhelming love of God. He was a wandering preacher, without a parish and without a home. At thirty-five, he became a tutor in the home of a Berlin attorney and fell in love with the attorney's daughter. At the age of forty-four he took a position as pastor of a small village church. Four years later, he married his sweetheart and began publishing his hymns, including this one.

Nearly a century later, John Wesley heard Moravians singing this song in German as he sailed with them to America. Impressed by the rich hymns of the Moravians and by their deep, personal devotion, Wesley translated many German hymns, including this one, as he traveled by horse and foot throughout the southern colonies.

Scriptures: Romans 8:35-36; 1 Corinthians 13:4-7; Philippians 3:7-8; 1 John 4:10
Themes: Love, Dedication, Commitment

Jesus, Thy boundless love to me
No thought can reach, no tongue declare;
O knit my thankful heart to Thee,
And reign without a rival there!
Thine wholly, Thine alone, I'd live,
Myself to Thee entirely give.

O Love, how cheering is thy ray!
All fear before thy presence flies;
Care, anguish, sorrow melt away,
Where'er thy healing beams arise:
O Jesus, nothing may I see,
Nothing desire, or seek, but Thee!

In suffering be Thy love my peace;
In weakness be Thy love my power;
And when the storms of life shall cease,
O Jesus, in that solemn hour,
In death as life be Thou my guide,
And save me, who for me hast died.

PAUL GERHARDT (1607–1676)
Translated by John Wesley (1703–1791)

LOVE DIVINE, ALL LOVES EXCELLING

You might wonder if Charles Wesley, as author of six thousand hymns, ever got out of his study. In fact, for most of his life he was a traveling preacher—traveling on horseback. In his pocket he carried little cards on which he scribbled hymns in shorthand as he rode. As soon as he reached an inn, he would rush in and ask for a pen and ink to write down the hymns he had composed. But even that makes it sound easier than it was.

Once, when a horse threw him, he wrote in his journal, "My companion thought I had broken my neck; but my leg only was bruised, my hand sprained, and my head stunned, which spoiled my making hymns till the next day."

Although Charles Wesley had been a classical scholar at Oxford, few of his hymns reveal allusions to the classics. However, this one follows the meter of John Dryden's "King Arthur," referring to Camelot: "Fairest Isle, all isles excelling, seats of pleasure and of love." King Arthur may have dreamed of Camelot, but as Charles Wesley rode horseback from village to village, his thoughts were on Jesus, the divine love, the joy of heaven.

Scriptures: Philippians 1:6; Philippians 3:20-21; 1 John 3:16-24

Themes: Love, Sanctification, Salvation

Love divine, all loves excelling,
Joy of heaven, to earth come down;
Fix in us Thy humble dwelling;
All Thy faithful mercies crown!
Jesus, Thou art all compassion,
Pure, unbounded love Thou art;
Visit us with Thy salvation;
Enter every trembling heart.

Breathe, O breathe Thy loving spirit
Into every troubled breast!
Let us all in Thee inherit;
Let us find that second rest.
Take away our bent to sinning;
Alpha and Omega be;
End of faith, as its beginning,
Set our hearts at liberty.

Come, Almighty to deliver,
Let us all Thy life receive;

Suddenly return and never,
Nevermore Thy temples leave.
Thee we would be always blessing,
Serve Thee as Thy hosts above,
Pray and praise Thee without ceasing,
Glory in Thy perfect love.

Finish, then, Thy new creation;
Pure and spotless let us be.
Let us see Thy great salvation
Perfectly restored in Thee:
Changed from glory into glory,
Till in heaven we take our place,
Till we cast our crowns before Thee,
Lost in wonder, love, and praise.

CHARLES WESLEY (1707–1788)

LOVING-KINDNESS

When Samuel Medley was seventeen, he joined the British Navy, where he quickly picked up profanity and had no trouble finding liquor. His quick wit made him the life of the party when his ship got into port. In a naval battle he received a severe leg wound, and the surgeon told him that to save his life the leg would have to be amputated. Samuel Medley prayed earnestly and then remembered a Bible, which he had never read before, in his trunk. He began to read it.

The next morning the surgeon reexamined him and couldn't believe the change. It was nothing short of a miracle, he said. But it wasn't until Medley returned to England and was convalescing in his grandfather's home that he began to follow Christ. When he read a verse in Isaiah, where the prophet speaks of the Messiah opening blind eyes and bringing out prisoners from their prisons, he recognized that he needed spiritual sight and release from prison.

Later in life he began writing hymns—this one is his personal testimony. In his hymns, Medley liked to repeat phrases that he thought were extremely important. So in this one, we have the refrain, "Loving-kindness, loving-kindness."

In the second stanza, notice the unusual phrase "notwithstanding." As he thought over his past life, Medley was amazed that God loved him "notwithstanding all."

Scriptures: Psalm 36:7; Isaiah 42:6-7; Isaiah 63:7; Romans 5:8
Themes: Love, Salvation, Grace

Awake, my soul, to joyful lays,
And sing thy great Redeemer's praise;
He justly claims a song for me,
His loving-kindness, oh, how free!
Loving-kindness, loving-kindness,
His loving-kindness, oh, how free!

He saw me ruined by the fall,
Yet loved me not-with-standing all;
He saved me from my lost estate,
His loving-kindness, oh, how great!
Loving-kindness, loving-kindness,
His loving-kindness, oh, how great!

Tho' num'rous hosts of mighty foes,
Tho' earth and hell my way oppose,
He safely leads my soul along,
His loving-kindness, oh, how strong!
Loving-kindness, loving-kindness,
His loving-kindness, oh, how strong!

When trouble, like a gloomy cloud,
Has gathered thick and thundered loud,
He near my soul has always stood,
His loving-kindness, oh how good!
Loving-kindness, loving-kindness,
His loving-kindness, oh, how good!

SAMUEL MEDLEY (1738–1799)

O LOVE DIVINE, THAT STOOPED TO SHARE

As professor of anatomy at Harvard Medical School, Oliver Wendell Holmes was highly regarded both as a pioneer researcher and as a teacher. One day in class, he held up a portion of a skeleton and said, "These, gentlemen, are the bones on which Providence destined man to sit and view the works of creation."

As a member of the elite Saturday Club, he met regularly with brilliant men like Emerson, Longfellow, Lowell, and Agassiz, and together they sharpened their wits. With a few words, Holmes could cut to the heart of any matter.

So this poet-scientist, this humorist-philosopher, wrote a perceptive hymn about God's great love that "stooped to share." As a scientist, he recognized the God of creation, but he also knew of a God who shares our burdens and in our pain tells us that he is near and that he loves us.

Scriptures: Psalm 139:7-12; Ephesians 2:12-13; Hebrews 2:9
Themes: Love, Comfort, Sorrow

O Love divine, that stooped to share
Our sharpest pang, our bitterest tear,
On Thee we cast each earthborn care;
We smile at pain while Thou art near.

Though long the weary way we tread,
And sorrow crown each lingering year,
No path we shun, no darkness dread,
Our hearts still whispering, "Thou art near!"

When drooping pleasure turns to grief,
And trembling faith is changed to fear,
The murmuring wind, the quivering leaf
Shall softly tell us Thou art near!

On Thee we fling our burdening woe,
O Love divine, forever dear,
Content to suffer while we know,
Living and dying, Thou art near!

OLIVER WENDELL HOLMES (1809–1894)

O LOVE THAT WILL NOT LET ME GO

There is a bit of mystery connected with this hymn. George Matheson, who wrote the hymn, went completely blind when he was eighteen years old. He remained a star student in spite of his blindness. He went on to become a great preacher in the Church of Scotland, assisted by his sister, who learned Greek and Hebrew to help with his research.

Matheson wrote this hymn when he was forty years old. He described the circumstances surrounding the writing this way: "I was at that time alone. It was the day of my sister's marriage. . . . Something happened to me, which was known only to myself, and which caused me the most severe mental suffering. The hymn was the fruit of that suffering."

The mystery is this: What suffering was he writing about? Some think he was remembering the time when his fiancée broke the engagement after learning he would soon become completely blind. But perhaps it was because his devoted sister was getting married and he would be left alone.

Regardless, Matheson had discovered a love that would not let him go. And so may we, even in the darkest times of our lives.

Scriptures: John 10:14; John 15:9; Romans 8:37-39; 1 John 3:1
Themes: Love, Comfort, Fulfillment

O Love that will not let me go,
I rest my weary soul in Thee;
I give Thee back the life I owe,
That in Thine ocean depths its flow
May richer, fuller be.

O Light that foll'west all my way,
I yield my flick'ring torch to Thee;
My heart restores its borrowed ray,
That in Thy sunshine's blaze its day
May brighter, fairer be.

O Joy that seekest me through pain,
I cannot close my heart to Thee;
I trace the rainbow through the rain,
And feel the promise is not vain
That morn shall tearless be.

O Cross that liftest up my head,
I dare not ask to fly from Thee;
I lay in dust life's glory dead,
And from the ground there blossoms red
Life that shall endless be.

GEORGE MATHESON (1842–1906)

O PERFECT LOVE

Dorothy Blomfield's sister was getting married. One evening the whole family was gathered around singing hymns. After one hymn, the sister said that she'd love to have that tune sung at her wedding if only it had appropriate words. Then she turned to Dorothy and said, "What's the use of having a sister who composes poetry if she cannot write me new words to this tune?"

Dorothy took up the challenge. Grabbing the hymnal, she went into the library to begin work. The writing "was no effort whatever," she said later, "after the initial idea had come to me of the twofold aspect of perfect union—love and life—and I have always felt that God helped me write it." Fifteen minutes after retreating to the library, Dorothy emerged with the new hymn text.

Ironically, the tune that prompted the writing of this hymn is not the music used for it today. The modern tune was composed fifteen years later, in 1898, by Joseph Barnby for the marriage ceremony of Queen Victoria's granddaughter.

Scriptures: 1 Corinthians 13:4-7; Ephesians 3:17-19; Ephesians 5:25
Themes: Love, Life, Marriage

O perfect Love, all human thought transcending,
Lowly we kneel in prayer before Thy throne,
That theirs may be the love which knows no ending,
Whom Thou forevermore dost join in one.

O perfect Life, be Thou their full assurance
Of tender charity and steadfast faith,
Of patient hope and quiet, brave endurance,
With childlike trust that fears no pain nor death.

Grant them the joy which brightens earthly sorrow;
Grant them the peace which calms all earthly strife,
And to life's day the glorious unknown morrow
That dawns upon eternal love and life.

DOROTHY FRANCES BLOMFIELD GURNEY (1858–1932)

O THE DEEP, DEEP LOVE OF JESUS

The music to which the hymn is sung is called "Ton-Y-Botel." According to one story, and it is no doubt fictional, the music was found in a bottle washed up from the ocean, hence the tune title "Ton-Y-Botel." As you sing the tune, you may be reminded of the currents of the ocean.

And there is a strong link between the ocean and the words to this hymn. The author was a London businessman who traveled across the ocean many times. Samuel Francis compares the vastness of the ocean with the vastness of God's love. It is reassuring, he says, to know that God's love is underneath us and around us and leads us onward and upward. It is also motivating as we think of others on distant shores who do not know God's love. We are called to "spread His praise from shore to shore."

Even more than loving the ocean, the author enjoyed "the deep, deep love of Jesus, / Love of every love the best."

Scriptures: Job 38:8-11; Psalm 104:25-26; Psalm 107:23-32; Isaiah 11:9; Romans 8:37-39; Ephesians 3:17-19

Themes: Love of God, Comfort

O the deep, deep love of Jesus,
Vast, unmeasured, boundless, free!
Rolling as a mighty ocean
In its fullness over me,
Underneath me, all around me,
Is the current of Thy love;
Leading onward, leading homeward
To my glorious rest above.

O the deep, deep love of Jesus,
Spread His praise from shore to shore!
How He loveth, ever loveth,
Changeth never, nevermore;
How He watches o'er His loved ones,
Died to call them all His own;
How for them He intercedeth,
Watcheth o'er them from the throne.

O the deep, deep love of Jesus,
Love of every love the best;
'Tis an ocean vast of blessing,

'Tis a haven sweet of rest,
O the deep, deep love of Jesus,
'Tis a heav'n of heav'ns to me;
And it lifts me up to glory,
For it lifts me up to Thee.

SAMUEL TREVOR FRANCIS (1834–1925)

OF THE FATHER'S LOVE BEGOTTEN

Since its inception, the church has been troubled by heresy. One of the most enduring heresies has been Arianism, which teaches that Jesus is not God by nature but was a created being.

Aurelius Prudentius, the author of this hymn, lived at a time when Arianism threatened the church. A Spaniard by birth, he became a lawyer and later a provincial governor in Spain. After his conversion he devoted himself to the service of the church and to the writing of sacred poetry. He wrote about 385 poems, most of them written for personal devotional use.

In this hymn he presents a poetic defense for an orthodox confession of Jesus' divinity and coeternal relationship with God the Father. We can be thankful for God's many faithful saints throughout history who, like Prudentius, have passed on to us the true Christian faith.

Scriptures: John 1:1-3; Philippians 2:6; Colossians 1:16-18
Themes: Trinity, Praise, Deity of Christ

Of the Father's love begotten,
Ere the worlds began to be,
He is Alpha and Omega,
He the source, the ending He;
Of the things that are, that have been,
And that future years shall see,
Evermore and evermore.

O ye heights of heaven, adore Him;
Angel hosts, His praises sing;
Powers, dominions, bow before Him,
And extol our God and King;
Let no tongue on earth be silent,
Every voice in concert ring,
Evermore and evermore.

Christ, to Thee with God the Father,
And, O Holy Ghost, to Thee,
Hymn and chant and high thanksgiving,
And unwearied praises be:
Honor, glory, and dominion,
And eternal victory,
Evermore and evermore.

AURELIUS CLEMENS PRUDENTIUS (348–CA. 413)
Translated by John Mason Neale (1818–1866) and Henry W. Baker (1821–1877)

SWEET PEACE, THE GIFT OF GOD'S LOVE

Two stories are behind this hymn. First, Peter Bilhorn was singing at a camp meeting, and a friend jokingly said that he wished Bilhorn would write a song that he could sing with his voice, which apparently wasn't very good. Bilhorn asked him for some suggestions, and the friend said, "Oh, any sweet piece." Bilhorn smiled and thought that "sweet piece" spelled p-e-a-c-e might make a good gospel song. He wrote the idea in his notebook.

The second story took place the following winter when Bilhorn was traveling west from Chicago by train toward Iowa with another member of Dwight L. Moody's evangelistic team. Near Wheaton, Illinois, the passengers felt a jolt, and the train came to a stop. Bilhorn and the other Moody associate got out to see the problem. A woman had been struck, and her mangled body lay in the ditch in a pool of blood. It was an awful sight.

The associate said to Bilhorn, "You know that is all Jesus Christ left on this earth. His body was resurrected, but his blood was left to atone for our sins."

Bilhorn responded, "Yes, and that is what gives me sweet peace; His blood atones for my sin." Back on the train, Bilhorn wrote the song "Sweet Peace, the Gift of God's Love."

Scriptures: Romans 5:1; Ephesians 2:14-15; Colossians 1:20
Themes: Peace, Love, Atonement

There comes to my heart one sweet strain,
A glad and a joyous refrain; I sing it again and again—
Sweet peace, the gift of God's love.

Peace, peace, sweet peace! Wonderful gift from above!
O wonderful, wonderful peace! Sweet peace, the gift of God's love.

Thru Christ on the cross peace was made,
My debt by His death was all paid; no other foundation is laid
For peace, the gift of God's love.

When Jesus as Lord I had crowned,
My heart with this peace did abound; in Him the rich blessing I found—
Sweet peace, the gift of God's love.

In Jesus for peace I abide,
And as I keep close to His side, there's nothing but peace doth betide
Sweet peace, the gift of God's love.

PETER PHILIP BILHORN (1865–1936)

THE LOVE OF GOD

This hymn has an amazing history. Part of it can be traced back almost a thousand years to a Jewish hymn written in Aramaic by Meir Ben Isaac Nehorai, a cantor in Worms, Germany. It was to be sung at a Jewish festival, just before the reading of the Ten Commandments. The words were later found scribbled on the wall of a patient's room in an insane asylum.

Then, in the early 1900s at a Nazarene camp meeting, Pastor Frederick Lehman heard the words quoted. He was deeply stirred by them and decided to adapt them into a hymn. He wrote later, "The profound depth of the lines moved us to preserve the words for future generations. One day . . . we picked up a scrap of paper and, seated upon an empty lemon box pushed against the wall, with a stub pencil, added the first two stanzas and the chorus of the song."

From a Jewish cantor in Germany, from a patient in an insane asylum, and from a Nazarene pastor seated on an empty lemon box comes this majestic hymn about the love of God.

Scriptures: Romans 8:38-39; Ephesians 3:16-19; 1 John 3:1
Themes: God's Love, Salvation, Grace

The love of God is greater far than tongue or pen can ever tell,
It goes beyond the highest star and reaches to the lowest hell;
The guilty pair, bowed down with care, God gave His Son to win:
His erring child He reconciled and pardoned from his sin.

O love of God, how rich and pure!
How measureless and strong!
It shall forevermore endure
The saints' and angels' song.

When years of time shall pass away and earthly thrones and kingdoms fall,
When men, who here refuse to pray, on rocks and hills and mountains call,
God's love so sure shall still endure, all measureless and strong:
Redeeming grace to Adam's race—the saints' and angels' song.

Could we with ink the ocean fill and were the skies of parchment made,
Were ev'ry stalk on earth a quill and ev'ry man a scribe by trade,
To write the love of God above would drain the ocean dry,
Nor could the scroll contain the whole tho'stretched from sky to sky.

FREDERICK M. LEHMAN (1868–1953)

THE WONDER OF IT ALL

Gospel singer George Beverly Shea wrote only one or two songs, and this was one of them. Shea was aboard the SS *United States* on his way to Scotland to join evangelist Billy Graham for meetings there. When another passenger found out who he was and where he was going, Shea was asked what went on in one of their crusade meetings. In his answer, he spelled out the typical program, then he came to the end, the response to the gospel invitation. Shea said, "I found myself at a loss for words." He tried to describe the response that followed Billy Graham's simple invitation but it seemed indescribable. Finally, Shea said, "What happens then never becomes commonplace, . . . watching people by the hundreds come forward. . . . Oh, if you could just see the wonder of it all."

"I think I should," replied Shea's fellow passenger. Then he wrote the words *The Wonder of It All* on the back of a card and handed it to Shea. Later that evening Shea looked at the card again and wrote the words for this song.

Scriptures: Psalm 8:1-4; Romans 11:33; Hebrews 2:6
Themes: Wonder, Love, Creation

There's the wonder of sunset at evening, the wonder at sunrise I see;
But the wonder of wonders that thrills my soul
Is the wonder that God loves me.

O, the wonder of it all! The wonder of it all!
Just to think that God loves me.
O, the wonder of it all! The wonder of it all!
Just to think that God loves me.

There's the wonder of springtime and harvest, the sky, the stars, the sun;
But the wonder of wonders that thrills my soul
Is a wonder that's only begun.

GEORGE BEVERLY SHEA (B. 1909)
© 1957 Word Music, LLC.
All Rights Reserved. Used by Permission.

PART XVII

MISSIONS AND EVANGELISM

[The Lord says,] "I will make you a light to the Gentiles,

and you will bring my salvation to the ends of the earth."

ISAIAH 49:6

BRINGING IN THE SHEAVES

Just before Alben Shaw died, he gave his son, Knowles, a prized violin and this advice: "Be good to your mother, and prepare to meet your God." Knowles, about twelve years old at the time, dropped out of school and worked hard and long to provide for his mother and two sisters on their small Indiana farm. For a little extra money, he played the violin at community parties and square dances.

In the middle of a big party, Knowles remembered the second half of his father's advice: Prepare to meet your God. He put away his fiddle, prayed for forgiveness, and attended the first church service he could find. Gradually, Knowles learned about the Christian life. When he was twenty-six, he began preaching, and two years later, he was known as the "singing evangelist" of Indiana.

One day after reading Psalm 126:5-6, which says, "They that sow in tears shall reap in joy. He that goeth forth and weepeth, bearing precious seed, shall doubtless come again with rejoicing, bringing his sheaves with him," (KJV) he wrote the gospel song "Bringing in the Sheaves."

Knowles died in a train accident when he was only forty-three years old, but in his short time of evangelistic ministry, he saw eleven thousand people make decisions for Christ. That is quite a harvest.

Scriptures: Psalm 125:5-6; Isaiah 35:10; John 4:35

Themes: Witnessing, Service, Joy

Sowing in the morning, sowing seeds of kindness,
Sowing in the noontide and the dewy eve;
Waiting for the harvest, and the time of reaping,
We shall come rejoicing, bringing in the sheaves.

Bringing in the sheaves, bringing in the sheaves,
We shall come rejoicing bringing in the sheaves.
(Repeat.)

Sowing in the sunshine, sowing in the shadows,
Fearing neither clouds nor winter's chilling breeze;
By and by the harvest and the labor ended,
We shall come rejoicing, bringing in the sheaves.

Going forth with weeping, sowing for the Master,
Tho' the loss sustained our spirit often grieves;

When our weeping's over, He will bid us welcome,
We shall come rejoicing, bringing in the sheaves.
KNOWLES SHAW (1834–1878)

CHRIST FOR THE WORLD WE SING

Until he was fifty-six, Samuel Wolcott had never written a hymn, but he ended up writing two hundred of them. Wolcott went as a missionary to Syria, but after two years he had to return to America. In the United States, he pastored churches in Rhode Island, Illinois, Massachusetts, and Ohio, but his heart was still in Syria.

While attending a YMCA convention in Cleveland, Wolcott was captivated by a huge banner with the words "Christ for the World and the World for Christ" outlined in green above the pulpit. As Wolcott left the meeting, the words for this hymn gradually took shape in his mind.

Wolcott had learned that the "world" for whom Christ died included not only those in distant lands like Syria, where he had tried to serve, but also the poor, those that mourn, the faint, the burdened, the sin-sick, and the sorrow-worn in such needy places as the major cities of America where he ministered.

Scriptures: Matthew 25:40; Acts 1:8; Romans 1:16-17
Themes: Evangelism, Missions

Christ for the world we sing;
The world to Christ we bring
With loving zeal—
The poor and them that mourn,
The faint and over-borne,
Sin-sick and sorrow-worn,
For Christ to heal.

Christ for the world we sing;
The world to Christ we bring
With fervent prayer—
The wayward and the lost,
By restless passions tossed,
Redeemed at countless cost
From dark despair.

Christ for the world we sing;
The world to Christ we bring
With one accord—
With us the work to share,
With us reproach to dare,
With us the cross to bear,
For Christ our Lord.

Christ for the world we sing;
The world to Christ we bring
With joyful song—
The newborn souls whose days,
Reclaimed from error's ways,
Inspired with hope and praise,
To Christ belong.

SAMUEL WOLCOTT (1813–1886)

FREELY, FREELY

Jimmy and Carol Owens form a songwriting team that became known to the Christian world during the Jesus People movement of the 1970s. One Sunday evening after a service, Jimmy and Carol were eating with Jack Hayford, pastor of the Church on the Way, just northwest of Los Angeles. Pastor Hayford suggested, "Why don't you write a musical about our church?" The suggestion was meant not to focus on their particular church but rather to focus on the principles of ministry that had made the church successful.

Jimmy and Carol Owens began to work on the project immediately. They saw it as "a gift from God to the universal church." Working with singer Pat Boone, they developed the *Come Together* musical. In 1973, they took the musical to England, where it was featured in four hundred presentations, often in large halls and cathedrals. Across the United States, young people of diverse churches were coming together in new ways that hadn't been experienced before.

At the heart of the jubilant *Come Together* were the simple words and melody of "Freely, Freely," written by Carol Owens and taken from the instructions of Jesus as he sent out his disciples: "Freely ye have received, freely give" (Matthew 10:8, KJV).

Scriptures: Matthew 10:7-8, 42; 2 Corinthians 9:7
Themes: Stewardship, Witnessing, Unity

God forgave my sin in Jesus' name,
I've been born again in Jesus' name;
And in Jesus' name I come to you to share His love
As He told me to.

He said, "Freely, freely you have received—
Freely, freely give; go in my name and, because you believe,
Others will know that I live."

All pow'r is given in Jesus' name,
In earth and heav'n in Jesus' name;
And in Jesus' name I come to you to share His pow'r
As He told me to.

CAROL OWENS (B. 1931)

FROM GREENLAND'S ICY MOUNTAINS

In 1819 a royal letter was sent to all parishes of the Church of England authorizing a collection to be taken to aid "The Society for the Propagation of the Gospel in Foreign Lands." Reginald Heber's father-in-law had asked him to preach at his Sunday evening service. After the royal letter came, the father-in-law asked if Reginald knew an appropriate hymn that could be used to promote a special missionary offering. Heber couldn't think of one, so he went into a corner of the room for twenty minutes. When he returned, he showed three stanzas to his father-in-law. His father-in-law liked them, but Heber wasn't quite satisfied. He wrote a fourth stanza to give a more triumphant ending to the hymn.

When he wrote the hymn, Heber didn't know that India did not have coral strands, nor did he realize he would soon be appointed bishop of Calcutta, India, where he served for the rest of his life. The Christian church was just waking up to the missionary challenge when Heber wrote this hymn, but because of it, Christians in succeeding generations have been powerfully reminded that the Great Commission applies to every generation.

Scriptures: Matthew 9:37-38; Matthew 28:19-20; Acts 1:8
Themes: Missions, Stewardship, Salvation

From Greenland's icy mountains,
From India's coral strand,
Where Afric's sunny fountains
Roll down their golden sand;
From many an ancient river,
From many a palmy plain,
They call us to deliver
Their land from error's chain.

What though the spicy breezes,
Blow soft o'er Ceylon's isle;
Though ev'ry prospect pleases,
And only man is vile?
In vain, with lavish kindness,
The gifts of God are strown;
The heathen, in his blindness,
Bows down to wood and stone.

Can we, whose souls are lighted
By wisdom from on high,
Can we to men benighted
The lamp of life deny?
Salvation! O salvation!
The joyful sound proclaim,
Till earth's remotest nation
Has learned Messiah's name.

Waft, waft, ye winds, His story,
And you, ye waters, roll,
Till, like a sea of glory,
It spreads from pole to pole:
Till o'er our ransomed nature
The Lamb, for sinners slain,
Redeemer, King, Creator,
In bliss returns to reign.

REGINALD HEBER (1783–1826)

GIVE ME A PASSION FOR SOULS

When Herbert Tovey attended Moody Bible Institute in Chicago in the early 1900s, students were required to witness to someone at least once a week. For some students this was difficult. It meant going out on the streets of Chicago and giving out a gospel tract or actually talking to someone about their faith. It was easier to stay in the dormitory and talk with fellow students.

Herbert Tovey may have felt that way too. At least he was aware that even when he was passing out a gospel tract or quoting a Bible verse to someone on the street, he often didn't care about that person as he should.

Herbert Tovey wrote many gospel songs after this one. "Give Me a Passion for Souls" was one of his first, but it was the heartfelt prayer of a Bible school student. Many of us have echoed the same prayer.

Scriptures: Acts 1:8; Colossians 4:6; 1 Peter 3:15-16
Themes: Conversion, Witnessing, Salvation

> Give me a passion for souls, dear Lord, a passion to save the lost;
> O that Thy love were by all adored, and welcomed at any cost.
>
> *Jesus, I long to be winning men who are lost, and constantly sinning;*
> *O may this hour be one of beginning the story of pardon to tell.*
>
> Though there are dangers untold and stern confronting me in the way,
> Willingly still would I go, nor turn, but trust Thee for grace each day.
>
> How shall this passion for souls be mine? Lord, make Thou the answer clear;
> Help me to throw out the old life-line to those who are struggling near.
> HERBERT GEORGE TOVEY (1888–1972)

JESUS SAVES

Priscilla Owens of Baltimore was a public school teacher for forty-nine years and a Sunday school teacher for fifty years. Evidently she loved to teach children.

One year the Sunday school of Baltimore's Union Square Methodist Church was asked to prepare a special missionary service. The church leaders needed a missionary song, one that children as well as adults could sing. They didn't want something somber because they wanted it to be as exciting as missionary service is.

Priscilla Owens got the job of writing the special missionary song. It may have been the only song she ever wrote, but it has now been sung around the world, and the message is just as true now as when she wrote it: "Jesus Saves! Jesus Saves!"

Scriptures: Psalm 96:2-3; Mark 16:15; Romans 1:16
Themes: Salvation, Missions, Witnessing

We have heard the joyful sound: Jesus saves! Jesus saves!
Spread the tidings all around: Jesus saves! Jesus saves!
Bear the news to ev'ry land, climb the steeps and cross the waves;
Onward! 'tis our Lord's command; Jesus saves! Jesus saves!

Waft it on the rolling tide; Jesus saves! Jesus saves!
Tell to sinners far and wide: Jesus saves! Jesus saves!
Sing, ye islands of the sea; echo back, ye ocean caves;
Earth shall keep her jubilee: Jesus saves! Jesus saves!

Sing above the battle strife, Jesus saves! Jesus saves!
By His death and endless life, Jesus saves! Jesus saves!
Sing it softly thro' the gloom, When the heart for mercy craves;
Sing in triumph o'er the tomb—Jesus saves! Jesus saves!

Give the winds a mighty voice—Jesus saves! Jesus saves!
Let the nations now rejoice—Jesus saves! Jesus saves!
Shout salvation full and free; highest hills and deepest caves;
This our song of victory—Jesus saves! Jesus saves!

PRISCILLA J. OWENS (1829–1907)

JESUS SHALL REIGN

Isaac Watts once said that his aim was to see "David converted into a Christian." He meant singing the Psalms was good, but it would be better if they were infused with the gospel. He felt some Psalms were unsuitable for Christian worship because they were written before the cross of Christ and the completion of God's redemption and revelation.

The great missionary hymn "Jesus Shall Reign" is based on Psalm 72. There was no great missionary effort when Watts wrote these words. Not until sixty years later did William Carey—the father of the modern missionary movement—set sail for India. Today, by means of radio and literature, as well as through the work of faithful missionaries, Christ's Kingdom has "spread from shore to shore," and "people and realms of ev'ry tongue / Dwell on His love with sweetest song."

Scriptures: Psalm 50:1-6; Psalm 72:8-14; Zechariah 14:9; Revelation 11:15
Themes: Missions, Praise, Victory

Jesus shall reign where'er the sun
Does his successive journeys run;
His kingdom spread from shore to shore,
Till moons shall wax and wane no more.

To Him shall endless prayer be made,
And endless praises crown His head;
His name like sweet perfume shall rise
With ev'ry morning sacrifice.

People and realms of ev'ry tongue
Dwell on His love with sweetest song,
And infant voices shall proclaim
Their early blessings on His name.

Blessings abound where'er He reigns;
The prisoner leaps to loose his chains;
The weary find eternal rest,
And all the sons of want are blest.

Let every creature rise and bring
His grateful honors to our King;
Angels descend with songs again,
And earth repeat the loud amen!

ISAAC WATTS (1674–1748)

LET THE LOWER LIGHTS BE BURNING

One of evangelist Dwight L. Moody's favorite stories concerned a ship on Lake Erie during a violent storm. The ship was trying to enter the Cleveland harbor but all the captain could see were the upper lights from the lighthouse. Lower lights were needed to guide the ship into the channel and to warn of treacherous rocks along the shore.

"Where are the lower lights?" asked the captain.

"They must have gone out," replied the pilot.

In the darkness the pilot tried to guide the ship, but he missed the channel and crashed into the rocks. Many lives were lost, and the ship was in shambles.

Moody said, "The Master will take care of the great lighthouse. Let us keep the lower lights burning."

Songwriter Philip Bliss heard that story and wrote this gospel song to encourage all of us to make sure our lights are burning, so that "some poor fainting, struggling seaman / You may rescue, you may save."

Scriptures: Matthew 5:16; Luke 12:35; Philippians 2:15
Themes: Evangelism, Witnessing, Salvation

Brightly beams our Father's mercy
From His lighthouse evermore,
But to us He gives the keeping
Of the lights along the shore.

Let the lower lights be burning!
Send a gleam across the wave!
Some poor fainting, struggling seaman
You may rescue, you may save.

Dark the night of sin has settled,
Loud the angry billows roar;
Eager eyes are watching, longing,
For the lights along the shore.

Trim your feeble lamp, my brother;
Some poor sailor tempest tossed,
Trying now to make the harbor,
In the darkness may be lost.

PHILIP PAUL BLISS (1838–1876)

LET YOUR HEART BE BROKEN

Hymnwriters are sometimes asked to write hymns for special occasions, but that isn't always easy. Bryan Leech has been involved with sacred music since his college days. He has written many hymn texts and tunes, a musical play, and a musical adaptation of Dickens's *A Christmas Carol.* And he has served as an editor of a popular hymnal.

So Leech seemed to be a logical choice to write a hymn for World Relief Sunday. But he didn't have any good ideas. He said later, the topic "seemed like a very unpromising concept for a spiritual song." Then he remembered something that Bob Pierce, the founder of World Vision, International, often said: "Let my heart be broken by the things that break the heart of God."

Even as Jesus had compassion on the crowds that thronged about him, so we, today, need to share his compassion and have our hearts broken for the needy world.

Scriptures: Matthew 9:36; James 2:15-16; 1 John 3:17
Themes: Poverty, Stewardship, World

Let your heart be broken for a world in need—
Feed the mouths that hunger, soothe the wounds that bleed,
Give the cup of water and the loaf of bread—
Be the hands of Jesus, serving in His stead.

Here on earth applying principles of love—
Visible expression God still rules above,
Living illustration of the living word
To the minds of all who've never seen and heard.

Blest to be a blessing, privileged to care,
Challenged by the need apparent everywhere,
Where mankind is wanting, fill the vacant place,
Be the means thru which the Lord reveals His grace.

Add to your believing deeds that prove it true—
Knowing Christ as savior, make Him master too:
Follow in His footsteps, go where He has trod,
In the world's great trouble risk yourself for God.

Let your heart be tender and your vision clear—
See mankind as God sees, serve Him far and near;
Let your heart be broken by your brother's pain,
Share your rich resources—give and give again.

BRYAN JEFFERY LEECH, (B. 1931)

O ZION, HASTE

One night in 1868, a worried mother sat up with one of her children who was critically ill. She prayed to the Lord to heal her child. She realized how quickly her comfortable lifestyle was jolted by the reality of something really important, such as her children. And what is really important to God is the evangelization of the world. If God raised up her child, would she be willing to see him go out as a missionary to a continent like Africa, where David Livingstone was lost in the interior? Out of her inner wrestling with such questions, thirty-four-year-old Mary Ann Thomson wrote this hymn.

The hymn blends the messianic pronouncement of Isaiah 52 with the missionary call of Romans 10. For over a hundred years, this hymn has stirred thousands to respond to God's call.

Scriptures: Isaiah 52:7-9; Matthew 28:19; Romans 10:13-15
Themes: Witnessing, Stewardship, Dedication

O Zion, haste, thy mission high fulfilling,
To tell to all the world that God is Light;
That He who made all nations is not willing
One soul should perish, lost in shades of night.

Publish glad tidings, tidings of peace;
Tidings of Jesus, redemption, and release.

Behold how many thousands still are lying,
Bound in the darksome prison-house of sin,
With none to tell them of the Savior's dying,
Or of the life He died for them to win.

Proclaim to every people, tongue and nation
That God, in whom they live and move, is love:
Tell how He stooped to save His lost creation,
And died on earth that man might live above.

Give of thy sons to bear the message glorious;
Give of thy wealth to speed them on their way;
Pour out thy soul for them in prayer victorious;
And all thy spending Jesus will repay.

MARY ANN THOMSON (1834–1923)

PASS IT ON

Kurt Kaiser, who wrote this song, came on the music scene at just the right time, in the middle of the Jesus People revival of the early 1970s. He grew up in a Plymouth Brethren home in Chicago and was recognized as a piano virtuoso from his early years. In the early 1960s, when he was still in his twenties, he wrote orchestrations for artists like Jerome Hines, Burl Ives, and Tennessee Ernie Ford. But at the end of the decade he teamed up with Ralph Carmichael to write a musical for youth. They called it *Tell It Like It Is.*

Kaiser's goal for the musical was not just to entertain but rather to reach young people for Christ. According to the guidelines the writers had established, "the idiom had to be fresh, because the words restated in current terminology an important doctrine." Carmichael and Kaiser divided up their duties. Kaiser says, "My job was to write a 'Just As I Am' for young people. The tune came the following Sunday night after church; I was sitting in my den at home and a little fire burned in the fireplace. I looked into the fire and the thought came to me. . . . 'It only takes a spark to get a fire going.' "

Perhaps Kurt Kaiser's biggest thrill came when he saw 100,000 people at the Cotton Bowl singing his song. Kaiser recalls, "They were lighting candles off one another and the whole place was singing . . . 'It only takes a spark to get a fire going' " and then Kaiser thought, *Isn't it amazing what can happen if you take your hands off the ability God has given you and watch what happens?*

Scriptures: Matthew 5:14-16; Acts 1:8; Philippians 2:15
Themes: Witness, Love, Light

It only takes a spark to get a fire going,
And soon all those around can warm up in its glowing
That's how it is with God's love, once you've experienced it:
You spread His love to everyone, you want to pass it on.

What a wondrous time is spring—when all the trees
   are budding,
The birds begin to sing, the flowers start their blooming:
That's how it is with God's love, once you've experienced it:
You want to sing, it's fresh like spring, you want to pass it on.

I wish for you, my friend, this happiness that I've found—
You can depend on Him, it matters not where you're bound:

I'll shout it from the mountain top, I want my world to know:
The Lord of love has come to me, I want to pass it on.

PEOPLE NEED THE LORD

When you think of contemporary Christian songwriters, you might think of Nashville, Tennessee, or Southern California. Chances are, you won't think of North or South Dakota. But Greg Nelson, from North Dakota, and Phill McHugh, from South Dakota, got together in Nashville, Tennessee. Together they have written hundreds of songs.

One day, after trying to come up with new song ideas with little success, they went to lunch at a nearby restaurant. The waitress was pleasant enough, but she seemed sad and lonely. They began looking around the restaurant and noticed how many others seemed to be empty, even fearful.

As they went out to their car, they said, "You know, people need the Lord." They agreed that a song had to be written around those words. That afternoon they wrote "People Need the Lord."

Scriptures: Psalm 40:17; Isaiah 61:1; Matthew 9:12; 1 John 3:17

Themes: Conversion, Salvation, Help

People need the Lord, people need the Lord;
At the end of broken dreams, He's the open door.
People need the Lord, people need the Lord;
When will we realize people need the Lord.

RESCUE THE PERISHING

Hymnwriter Fanny Crosby, though she was blind, loved to visit rescue missions in New York City. One hot summer night, she was talking to a group of men at a mission. "I made a pressing plea," she said, "that if there was a boy present who had wandered from his mother's home and teaching, he should come to me at the end of the service. A young man of eighteen came forward and said, 'Did you mean me?'"

After Fanny Crosby prayed with the teenager, he rose from his knees and said enthusiastically, "Now I am ready to meet my mother in heaven, for I have found God."

A few days before, Fanny Crosby had been given the suggestion to write a hymn on the theme "Rescue the Perishing," taken from Luke 14:23, where the master in one of Jesus' parables tells his servant to go out into the highways and byways and bring people in. That evening, Crosby could think of nothing else but the line, "Rescue the perishing, care for the dying;" after returning home from the mission, she wrote this hymn.

Scriptures: Isaiah 61:1; Luke 14:23; 2 Peter 3:9; Jude 1:22-23
Themes: Evangelism, Witnessing, Service

Rescue the perishing, care for the dying,
Snatch them in pity from sin and the grave;
Weep o'er the erring one, lift up the fallen,
Tell them of Jesus, the mighty to save.

Rescue the perishing,
Care for the dying;
Jesus is merciful,
Jesus will save.

Though they are slighting Him, still He is waiting,
Waiting the penitent child to receive;
Plead with them earnestly, plead with them gently,
He will forgive if they only believe.

Down in the human heart, crushed by the tempter,
Feelings lie buried that grace can restore;
Touched by a loving heart, wakened by kindness,
Chords that are broken will vibrate once more.

Rescue the perishing, duty demands it—
Strength for thy labor the Lord will provide;
Back to the narrow way patiently win them,
Tell the poor wand'rer a Savior has died.

FANNY JANE CROSBY (1820–1915)

SO SEND I YOU

Margaret Clarkson couldn't get a teaching job in Toronto, so she accepted a position in an isolated logging community in northern Ontario. For a young woman in her early twenties who was prone to migraines and arthritis, it was not a good location. Margaret had grown up in a loveless home, and her parents divorced as she was beginning her teen years. So it is not surprising that loneliness hit her hard in that logging community.

One night she read John 20:21: "As my Father hath sent Me, even so send I you" (KJV). She thought of missionaries who had gone to isolated places around the world. Because of her physical problems, Margaret realized she could never go to a distant land as a missionary, but, she said, "God seemed to tell me that night that this was my mission field, and this was where he had sent me." That evening, Margaret Clarkson wrote the words to "So Send I You."

Later, she realized that there is joy in obedience, and she regretted the strong, somber tone of the hymn she had written earlier. So she wrote a more optimistic version entitled, "So Send I You, By Grace Made Strong." However, the earlier version is the one that is sung in most churches today.

Scriptures: Matthew 28:18-20; John 20:21; Acts 1:8
Themes: Missions, Service, Witness

So send I you to labor unrewarded,
To serve unpaid, unloved, unsought, unknown,
To bear rebuke, to suffer scorn and scoffing
So send I you, to toil for Me alone.

So send I you to bind the bruised and broken,
O'er wand'ring souls to work, to weep, to wake,
To bear the burdens of a world aweary
So send I you, to suffer for My sake.

So send I you to loneliness and longing,
With heart ahung'ring for the loved and known,
Forsaking home and kindred, friend and dear one
So send I you, to know My love alone.

So send I you to leave your life's ambition,
To die to dear desire, self will resign,

To labor long, and love where men revile you
So send I you, to lose your life in Mine.

So send I you to hearts made hard by hatred,
To eyes made blind because they will not see,
To spend, tho' it be blood, to spend and spare not
So send I you, to taste of Calvary.

Coda: As the Father hath sent Me, so send I you.

WORK FOR THE NIGHT IS COMING

Annie Louisa Walker wrote this song when she was eighteen years old. Born in England, she moved with her family when she was very young to the backwoods of Quebec, where this poem was written. For this teenager in primitive surroundings, work abounded, yet it wasn't something she dreaded. In fact, Annie found joy in it.

When the family moved to Ontario, Annie and her sisters started a school for girls. Many girls did not have much schooling beyond the elementary years in those days, so Annie's school was much appreciated. Later she moved back to England and worked for a cousin who was a famous British novelist.

The New Living Translation puts John 9:4 this way: "We must quickly carry out the tasks assigned us by the one who sent us. The night is coming, and then no one can work." What tasks has God assigned to you?

Scriptures: Proverbs 6:6; John 9:4; Colossians 3:23
Themes: Strength, Values, Zeal

Work, for the night is coming,
Work thro' the morning hours;
Work while the dew is sparkling;
Work, 'mid springing flow'rs.
Work, when the day grows brighter,
Work in the glowing sun;
Work, for the night is coming,
When man's work is done.

Work, for the night is coming,
Work thro' the sunny noon;
Fill brightest hours with labor,
Rest comes sure and soon.
Give ev'ry flying minute
Something to keep in store;
Work, for the night is coming,
When man works no more.

Work, for the night is coming,
Under the sunset skies;
While their bright tints are glowing,
Work, for daylight flies.
Work till the last beam fadeth,
Fadeth to shine no more;
Work, while the night is dark'ning,
When man's work is o'er.

ANNIE LOUISA COGHILL (1836–1907)

PART XVIII

PATRIOTIC

I urge, then, first of all, that requests, prayers,

intercession and thanksgiving be made for everyone—

for kings and all those in authority, that we may live

peaceful and quiet lives in all godliness and holiness.

1 TIMOTHY 2:1-2, NIV

AMERICA THE BEAUTIFUL

Along with several other professors from Eastern colleges, Katherine Bates was teaching at a new summer school in Colorado Springs when the group went to climb Pike's Peak. Since this was 1893, without the roads and trails we have today, that was quite a climb.

When Bates got to the top, she recalled, she "gazed in wordless rapture over the far expanse of mountain ranges and sea-like sweep of plains." She was in awe. That evening, in Colorado Springs, she wrote this hymn.

On her way to Colorado, Bates and the others had stopped to see the Chicago World's Fair, and, she said, Chicago was "in no small degree responsible for at least the last stanza."

Later she wrote, "If only we could couple the daring of the Pilgrims with the moral teachings of Moses, we would have something in this country that no one could ever take from us."

Scriptures: 2 Chronicles 7:14; Proverbs 14:34; Isaiah 32:16-17
Themes: Patriotic, Creation, Beauty

O beautiful for spacious skies, for amber waves of grain,
For purple mountain majesties above the fruited plain!
America, America, God shed His grace on thee,
And crown thy good with brotherhood from sea to shining sea.

O beautiful for pilgrim feet, whose stern, impassioned stress
A thoroughfare for freedom beat across the wilderness!
America! America! God mend thine ev'ry flaw,
Confirm thy soul in self-control, thy liberty in law.

O beautiful for heroes proved in liberating strife,
Who more than self their country loved and mercy more than life!
America! America! May God thy gold refine,
Till all success be nobleness, and ev'ry gain divine.

O beautiful for patriot dream that sees, beyond the years,
Thine alabaster cities gleam—undimmed by human tears!
America! America! God shed His grace on thee,
And crown thy good with brotherhood from sea to shining sea.

KATHERINE LEE BATES (1859–1929)

BATTLE HYMN OF THE REPUBLIC

Julia Ward Howe wrote these lyrics during the heart of the Civil War. She sent the words to the *Atlantic Monthly* magazine and received an honorarium of five dollars. But the money wasn't her concern. Her purpose was to provide some wholesome lyrics for the tune "John Brown's Body Lies A-Moldering in the Grave." She accomplished that and more. When President Abraham Lincoln first heard the hymn, he asked to have it sung again. Soon the entire nation was singing the song.

The text is filled with biblical allusions. The expression "grapes of wrath" refers to Revelation 14:19; the sounding trumpet is probably from Revelation 8. For the Christian, the message of this song is that God's truth is eternal. Although circumstances may appear overwhelmingly difficult, God will still accomplish his purposes, and his truth will endure.

It can be dangerous to identify political causes or even national patriotism with God's truth. Nations may rise and fall, but God's truth remains forever. "His truth is marching on."

Scriptures: Psalm 20:7; 1 Corinthians 15:24-27; Revelation 8:6; Revelation 14:19
Themes: Patriotic, Judgment, Courage

Mine eyes have seen the glory of the coming of the Lord,
He is trampling out the vintage where the grapes of wrath are stored;
He hath loosed the fateful lightning of His terrible swift sword—
His truth is marching on.

Glory! glory, hallelujah!
Glory! glory, hallelujah!
Glory! glory, hallelujah!
His truth is marching on.

I have seen Him in the watch fires of a hundred circling camps,
They have builded Him an altar in the evening dews and damps;
I can read His righteous sentence by the dim and flaring lamps—
His day is marching on.

He has sounded forth the trumpet that shall never sound retreat,
He is sifting out the hearts of men before His judgment seat;
O be swift, my soul, to answer Him! be jubilant, my feet!
Our God is marching on.

In the beauty of the lilies Christ was born across the sea,
With a glory in His bosom that transfigures you and me;
As He died to make men holy, let us live to make men free,
While God is marching on.

JULIA WARD HOWE (1819–1910)

ETERNAL FATHER, STRONG TO SAVE

This is the only hymn for which William Whiting is known. The son of a London grocer, he was befriended by a local clergyman who directed a training school in Winchester. Upon his father's death, Whiting joined the staff of the training school and was given responsibility for the education and upbringing of sixteen boys.

The boys nicknamed Whiting "Hoppy" because he had a club foot. It was not a term of derision but rather of camaraderie. "Hoppy" and his sixteen boys were a close-knit group.

When one of his boys was about to sail to America, "Hoppy" Whiting and the boys prayed for him. In the middle of the nineteenth century, crossing the Atlantic was still a perilous voyage. Besides praying for him, "Hoppy" Whiting wrote a hymn for the boys to sing: "Eternal Father, strong to save, whose arm hath bound the restless wave."

Soon it became popular far beyond Winchester. It was adopted by the sailors of the British Empire and even by the French navy. And when Winston Churchill met with Franklin Roosevelt aboard a warship on the North Atlantic during World War II, this was the hymn that Churchill requested.

Scriptures: Psalm 107:23; Mark 5:39-41; Acts 27:22-26; 2 Corinthians 11:25
Themes: Strength, God the Father, Comforter

Eternal Father, strong to save, whose arm hath bound the restless wave,
Who bids the mighty ocean deep its own appointed limits keep.
O hear us when we cry to Thee for those in peril on the sea.

O Christ, the Lord of hill and plain o'er which our traffic runs amain
By mountain pass or valley low: wherever, Lord, our brethren go
Protect them by Thy guarding hand from every peril on the land.

O Spirit, whom the Father sent to spread abroad the firmament:
O Wind of Heaven by Thy might save all who dare the eagle's flight.
And keep them by Thy watchful care from every peril in the air.

O Trinity of love and power, our brethren shield in danger's hour;
From rock and tempest, fire and foe, protect them wheresoe'er they go;
Thus evermore shall rise to Thee glad praise from air, and land and sea.
WILLIAM WHITING (1825–1878)

GOD OF OUR FATHERS

Six years before his death in 1907, Daniel Roberts wrote, "I remain a country parson, known only within my own small world." This hymn was penned while he pastored a rural church in Brandon, Vermont. He wrote it in 1876 to commemorate the one-hundredth birthday of the Declaration of Independence, and it was sung for the first time at Brandon's Fourth of July celebration.

Because the people of Brandon enjoyed the hymn, Roberts submitted it to the committee planning the centennial celebration for the U.S. Constitution. The committee chose it as the official hymn for the occasion and sent it to the organist at St. Thomas Episcopal Church in New York City to compose an original tune. The new tune, with a dramatic trumpet fanfare, was introduced in 1892 in New York City at the four-hundredth anniversary of the discovery of America by Christopher Columbus.

Scriptures: Psalm 33:12; Psalm 44:1-4; Proverbs 14:34
Themes: Patriotic, Peace, Guidance

God of our fathers, whose almighty hand
Leads forth in beauty all the starry band
Of shining worlds in splendor through the skies,
Our grateful songs before Thy throne arise.

Thy love divine hath led us in the past;
In this free land by Thee our lot is cast;
Be Thou our ruler, guardian, guide, and stay,
Thy Word our law, Thy paths our chosen way.

From war's alarms, from deadly pestilence,
Be Thy strong arm our ever sure defense;
Thy true religion in our hearts increase,
Thy bounteous goodness nourish us in peace.

Refresh Thy people on their toilsome way;
Lead us from night to never-ending day;
Fill all our lives with love and grace divine,
And glory, laud, and praise be ever Thine.

DANIEL CRANE ROBERTS (1841–1907)

MY COUNTRY 'TIS OF THEE

Twenty-four-year-old Samuel Smith, who had just graduated from Harvard, had a reputation for being able to speak fifteen languages. That's why composer Lowell Mason handed him a collection of some German songs for children. Mason didn't know German, and he didn't know if any of the songs would be worth translating, but he wanted Smith to check them out for him.

Here's the way Smith tells it: "One dismal day in February 1832, about half an hour before sunset, I was turning over the leaves of one of the music books, when my eye rested on the tune which is now known as 'America.' I liked the spirited movement of it. . . . I glanced at the German words and saw that they were patriotic and instantly felt the impulse to write a patriotic hymn of my own, adapted to that tune. Picking up a scrap of waste paper which lay near me, I wrote at once, probably within half an hour, the hymn 'America.' " The following Fourth of July it was sung publicly for the first time.

What Smith didn't realize was that the British had been using the same tune for a hundred years to sing "God Save the King."

Scriptures: Psalm 33:12; 1 Timothy 2:1-3; 1 Peter 2:13
Themes: Church, Creation, Patriotic

My country, 'tis of thee, sweet land of liberty,
Of thee I sing: land where my fathers died,
Land of the pilgrim's pride,
From ev'ry mountain side let freedom ring!

My native country, thee, land of the noble, free,
Thy name I love: I love thy rocks and rills,
Thy woods and templed hills;
My heart with rapture thrills like that above.

Let music swell the breeze, and ring from all the trees
Sweet freedom's song: let mortal tongues awake;

Let all that breathe partake;
Let rocks their silence break, the sound prolong.

Our fathers' God, to Thee, Author of liberty,
To Thee we sing: long may our land be bright
With freedom's holy light;
Protect us by Thy might, great God, our King!

SAMUEL FRANCIS SMITH (1808–1895)

THE STAR-SPANGLED BANNER

Francis Scott Key was an attorney in Washington, D.C., when the War of 1812 broke out. Although he is best known for writing "The Star-Spangled Banner," he also wrote several hymns and was a leader in the organization of the American Sunday School Union.

In 1812, President James Madison asked Key to try to negotiate the release of a physician who had been taken prisoner by the British. The British admiral granted Key's request for a visit, but because an attack on Fort McHenry and Baltimore was about to be made, Key was detained aboard his truce boat.

Key paced the deck all night. As dawn brought some shafts of light, he could see "the broad stripes and bright stars" of the flag flying over the fort. That day he went back to the city and wrote the first draft of "The Star-Spangled Banner" on the back of a letter. Before the day was over, the anthem was printed and circulated all over Baltimore. The flag that was waving over Fort McHenry that night is still on display in Baltimore.

Scriptures: Psalm 33:12; Proverbs 14:34; 1 Peter 2:13-14
Themes: Patriotic, Courage, Conflict

O say, can you see, by the dawn's early light,
What so proudly we hailed at the twilight's last gleaming,
Whose broad stripes and bright stars, thru the perilous fight,
O'er the ramparts we watched, were so gallantly streaming?
And the rockets' red glare, the bombs bursting in air,
Gave proof thru the night that our flag was still there.
O say, does that star-spangled banner yet wave
O'er the land of the free and the home of the brave?

O thus be it ever, when free men shall stand
Between their loved homes and the war's desolation!

Blest with victory and peace, may the heav'n-rescued land
Praise the Pow'r that hath made and preserved us a nation!
Then conquer we must, when our cause it is just;
And this be our motto: "In God is our trust!"
And the star-spangled banner in triumph shall wave
O'er the land of the free and the home of the brave!

FRANCIS SCOTT KEY (1779–1842)

PART XIX

PRAYER AND CONSECRATION

Don't worry about anything; instead, pray about everything.

Tell God what you need, and thank him for all he has done.

PHILIPPIANS 4:6

APPROACH, MY SOUL, THE MERCY SEAT

John Newton used to say, "Keep your relationship with God honest and personal." He always remembered the days when he was a slave trader, living a life of debauchery. After his conversion, he lived in constant amazement that God could love him. The well-known hymn "Amazing Grace" is his personal testimony.

When Newton became a minister, he started writing hymns. He never considered himself a poet, but he often wrote hymns for his midweek Bible study and prayer service. This was probably one of those hymns.

Unlike many hymnwriters of his day, Newton frequently used the pronoun *I* in his hymns, reflecting his deep and personal relationship with God. He often expressed his questions and fears, as he does in this hymn. In his prayer life, Newton regularly struggled with the doubts thrown at him by Satan, but he knew that he belonged to Christ and that ultimately Christ was the Victor.

Scriptures: Nehemiah 1:4-7; Daniel 9:4-19; Hebrews 4:14-16
Themes: Prayer, Confession, Comfort

Approach, my soul, the mercy seat
Where Jesus answers prayer;
There humbly fall before His feet,
For none can perish there.

Thy promise is my only plea;
With this I venture nigh:
Thou callest burdened souls to Thee,
And such, O Lord, am I.

Bowed down beneath a load of sin,
By Satan sorely pressed,
By war without, and fears within,
I come to Thee for rest.

Be Thou my shield and hiding place
That, sheltered near Thy side,
I may my fierce accuser face
And tell him Thou hast died.

O wondrous love! to bleed and die,
To bear the cross and shame,
That guilty sinners, such as I,
Might plead Thy gracious Name!

JOHN NEWTON (1725–1807)

BE THOU MY VISION

Between A.D. 500 and 700 the Irish church was synonymous with missionary fervor. One historian commented that their missionary effort was "the one all-absorbing national thought and passion." Irish missionaries labored from Scotland to Switzerland. One of these missionaries was Columba of County Donegal. His biographer wrote, "Certain spiritual songs, which had never been heard before, he was heard to sing." He was known as one of the poets of the Irish church.

"Be Thou My Vision" is anonymous, but it comes from the seventh or eighth century, shortly after the time of Columba of Donegal. It is filled with various titles for God. The word *vision* is used to indicate not only what we focus on but also what we strive for. As we strive for a goal, we gain a long-range perspective that helps us see today's disappointments as trivial when compared to the heavenly vision.

Scriptures: Psalm 16:2-11; Philippians 3:12; Colossians 3:1; Hebrews 12:1
Themes: Jesus Christ, Vision, Presence of God

Be Thou my Vision, O Lord of my heart;
Nought be all else to me, save that Thou art—
Thou my best thought, by day or by night,
Waking or sleeping, Thy presence my light.

Be Thou my Wisdom, and Thou my true Word;
I ever with Thee and Thou with me, Lord;
Thou my great Father, and I Thy true son,
Thou in me dwelling, and I with Thee one.

Riches I heed not, nor man's empty praise,
Thou mine inheritance, now and always;
Thou and Thou only, first in my heart,
High King of heaven, my treasure Thou art.

High King of heaven, my victory won,
May I reach heaven's joys, O bright heaven's Sun!
Heart of my own heart, whatever befall,
Still be my Vision, O Ruler of all.

IRISH HYMN (8TH CENTURY)
Translated by Mary Elizabeth Byrne (1880–1931)
Versified by Eleanor Henrietta Hull (1860–1935)

WORDS USED BY PERMISSION OF THE EDITOR'S LITERARY ESTATE, AND CHATTO & WINDUS, LTD.

BEFORE THY THRONE, O GOD, WE KNEEL

William Boyd Carpenter, bishop of Ripon, England, wrote this hymn for Christians whose consciences needed tenderizing. It is much like the words in Psalm 139:23: "Search me, O God, and know my heart." There is so much packed into this hymn of confession that it is difficult to sing.

Our lives become so busy that we lose track of sins that are accepted as normal by our society. Bishop Carpenter speaks of our need to be delivered "from love of pleasure, lust of gold, from sins which make the heart grow cold." We need to take time to kneel humbly before our holy God, to search our hearts before him, and to ask him to "give us a conscience quick to feel."

Scriptures: Psalm 51:1-3; Psalm 139:23; 1 John 1:9
Themes: Confession, Forgiveness, Renewal

Before Thy throne, O God, we kneel;
Give us a conscience quick to feel,
A ready mind to understand
The meaning of Thy chastening hand;
Whate'er the pain and shame may be,
Bring us, O Father, nearer Thee.

Search out our hearts and make us true;
Wishful to give to all their due.
From love of pleasure, lust of gold,
From sins which make the heart grow cold,
Wean us and train us with Thy rod;
Teach us to know our faults, O God.

For sins of heedless word and deed,
For pride, ambitious to succeed,
For crafty trade and subtle snare
To catch the simple unaware,
For lives bereft of purpose high,
Forgive, forgive, O Lord, we cry.

Let the fierce fires which burn and try
Our inmost spirits purify:
Consume the ill; purge out the shame;
O God, be with us in the flame;
A newborn people may we rise,
More pure, more true, more nobly wise.

WILLIAM BOYD CARPENTER (1841–1918)

CHANGE MY HEART, O GOD

Some songs are written in a study, some in a home, and some on a quiet beach. But "Change My Heart, O God" was written in a car in the middle of Southern California traffic not far from Disneyland.

Eddie Espinosa was driving to work one day, and he prayed as he drove. "I wanted to get closer to God," he says, "but there were things in my life that weren't pleasing to God." Then he said aloud, "God, do something. I need you to change my heart."

"In the middle of traffic," he says, "I began singing a song that I didn't know. It was almost like I was taking dictation. It just blew me away."

He reached for a scrap of yellow paper, and when he stopped at a traffic signal, he began scribbling as quickly as possible. He tried to keep the tune in mind until he got to work. That night he taught it to a Bible study group that met in his home. A member of the group told their pastor that Eddie had written a song, and soon "Change My Heart, O God" was known nationally, then internationally.

Scriptures: Psalm 51:10; Jeremiah 24:7; Romans 7:18-25
Themes: Renewal, Adoration, Revival

Change my heart, O God, make it ever true.
Change my heart, O God, may I be like You.
You are the potter, I am the clay.
Mold me, make me; this is what I pray,
Change my heart, O God.
Writer: Eddie Espinosa

FILL MY CUP, LORD

We sometimes think that hymns are written when the author is having a mountaintop experience, enjoying personal fellowship with God, and feeling blessed by God. That wasn't the case for Richard Blanchard.

A Methodist pastor of a large Florida church that had a television ministry, Blanchard was busy all the time. Once he was asked by a young couple to officiate their wedding, and he agreed to do so if they would come in for premarital counseling. They met with him for their first session but didn't show up on time for their second meeting. Blanchard was irritated, and he told his secretary, "I'll wait for thirty minutes and then I'm leaving." They were upsetting his entire schedule for the day.

He left his office and went into a Sunday school classroom. There he sat down at a piano and started to play. Soon the Lord gave him, much to his amazement, a song: "Fill My Cup, Lord."

Blanchard said later, "When I was not in the mood to be used of God, God was in a mood to use me."

Scriptures: Isaiah 44:3; John 4:13-14; John 7:38
Themes: Seeking God, Salvation, Holy Spirit

Like the woman at the well I was seeking
For things that could not satisfy;
And then I heard my Savior speaking:
"Draw from My well that never shall run dry."

Fill my cup, Lord—I lift it up, Lord!
Come and quench this thirsting of my soul;
Bread of heaven, feed me till I want no more—
Fill my cup, fill it up and make me whole.

There are millions in this world who are craving
The pleasure earthly things afford;
But none can match the wondrous treasure
That I find in Jesus Christ, my Lord.

So, my brother, if the things this world gave you
Leave hungers that won't pass away,
My blessed Lord will come and save you,
If you kneel to Him and humbly pray.

Richard Blanchard
© 1959 Word Music, LLC

FILL THOU MY LIFE, O LORD MY GOD

A visitor walked into Horatius Bonar's church in Edinburgh, Scotland, and asked, "Is Bonar the hymnwriter still alive? I always understood he was a medieval saint." This confusion may be understandable. After all, Bonar had written hymns for more than fifty years, and some of them are reminiscent of the monastic hymns of Bernard of Cluny.

But Bonar was not a monk, shut away from the hard realities of life.

He began his ministry in the slums, writing hymns for children. He was deeply involved in a movement of evangelicals that pulled out of the national church of Scotland to form the Free Church. And through it all, he worked incessantly. One biographer wrote, "He was unbelievably immersed in work." He loved to travel; he loved his family.

Although his life was busy and filled with the cares of family and congregation, he prayed that, most of all, his life might be filled with "praise in every part."

Scriptures: Ephesians 3:19; Hebrews 13:15; 1 Peter 4:10-11
Themes: Consecration, Service, Praise

Fill Thou my life, O Lord my God,
In ev'ry part with praise,
That my whole being may proclaim
Thy being and Thy ways.

Not for the lip of praise alone,
Nor e'en the praising heart
I ask, but for a life made up
Of praise in ev'ry part;

Praise in the common things of life,
Its goings out and in,
Praise in each duty and each deed,
However small and mean.

Fill ev'ry part of me with praise;
Let all my being speak
Of Thee and of Thy love, O Lord,
Poor though I be, and weak.

So shalt Thou, Lord, from me, e'en me,
Receive the glory due,
And so shall I begin on earth
The song forever new.

So shall no part of day or night
From sacredness be free:
But all my life, in ev'ry step,
Be fellowship with Thee.

HORATIUS BONAR (1808–1889)

HIGHER GROUND

Johnson Oatman seemed to be having a midlife crisis. He felt he was locked into his father's mercantile business in Medford, New Jersey. It was a good business and he wasn't unhappy in it, but he was a bit restless. Oatman wanted to do something that could reach out and touch more people for the Lord. He became an ordained Methodist minister and preached in churches in central New Jersey, but his commitment to his father's business kept him from becoming a pastor. He was still not content with his vocation.

When he was thirty-six, Oatman apparently found his talent. He began writing gospel songs. Within a few years the world was singing his songs, including "Count Your Blessings," "No, Not One," and "Higher Ground." In camp meetings across the country "Higher Ground" became a favorite. It expresses the desire of most Christians, and it certainly expresses the desire of a restless Johnson Oatman, who was pressing on the upward way.

Scriptures: Matthew 6:33-34; Luke 9:62; Philippians 3:14
Themes: Holiness, Sanctification, Perseverance

I'm pressing on the upward way,
New heights I'm gaining ev'ry day;
Still praying as I'm onward bound,
"Lord, plant my feet on higher ground."

Lord, lift me up and let me stand,
By faith, on Heaven's tableland.
A higher plane than I have found;
Lord, plant my feet on higher ground.

My heart has no desire to stay
Where doubts arise and fears dismay;
Tho' some may dwell where these abound,
My prayer, my aim, is higher ground.

I want to live above the world,
Tho' Satan's darts at me are hurled;
For faith has caught the joyful sound,
The song of saints on higher ground.

I want to scale the utmost height,
And catch a gleam of glory bright;

But still I'll pray till Heav'n I've found,
"Lord, lead me on to higher ground."

JOHNSON OATMAN JR. (1856–1922)

HOW LONG HAS IT BEEN?

In southern gospel music circles, Mosie Lister is a legend. Perhaps the song that is most often associated with him is "How Long Has It Been?"

Born into a musical family in Georgia, Lister disappointed his parents because he seemed to be tone-deaf. But they got him to practice violin, and gradually he learned to distinguish pitches. However, he wanted to do more than distinguish pitches; he wanted to write songs.

Lister came to fame as he worked with southern gospel quartets, arranging, writing, singing, and producing. But Lister was concerned about some people who had drifted far away from the Lord. Long ago, they had told God that they loved him, but they hadn't given God much thought in recent years. He thought about writing a song asking the question: "How long since you really prayed?"

Then, he recalls, "All of a sudden I realized that this was what I needed to say. I just started writing as fast as I could." In ten minutes he had it finished. Within five years, more than a million copies of the song in sheet music had been sold.

George Beverly Shea, Billy Graham's beloved soloist, often closed his concerts by singing this song: "How Long Has It Been?"

Scriptures: Psalm 50:15; Jeremiah 33:3; Romans 10:13

Themes: Invitation, Prayer, Conversion

AUTHOR: MOSIE LISTER (B. 1921)

©1956, 1969, Mosie Lister songs. Rights administered by the Copyright Company, Nashville, TN.

I AM PRAYING FOR YOU

Twenty-three-year-old Samuel Clough of Dublin, Ireland, wrote the words to this hymn, printed them up on a leaflet, and circulated the sheets to his friends at church. Fourteen years later, Ira Sankey, who was the music director for evangelist Dwight L. Moody, happened to see the leaflet with Clough's poem. The Moody-Sankey team had just arrived in Ireland for the first time, and Ira Sankey was looking, as always, for some homegrown hymns to sing at their crusades.

When Sankey saw these words, he quickly set them to music. Soon they were being sung not only all over Ireland, Scotland, and England but also all over America.

Scriptures: Ephesians 1:16-17; Colossians 4:12; James 5:16
Themes: Prayer, Witnessing, Conversion

I have a Savior, He's pleading in glory,
A dear, loving Savior, tho' earth friends be few;
And now He is watching in tenderness o'er me,
And oh, that my Savior were your Savior, too!

For you I am praying, for you I am praying,
For you I am praying, I'm praying for you.

I have a Father; to me He has given
A hope for eternity, blessed and true;
And soon He will call me to meet Him in heaven,
But oh, that He'd let me bring you with me, too!

I have a robe; 'tis resplendent in whiteness,
Awaiting in glory my wondering view;
Oh, when I receive it all shining in brightness,
Dear friend, could I see you receiving one, too!

When He has found you, tell others the story,
That my loving Savior is your Savior, too;
Then pray that your Savior will bring them to glory,
And prayer will be answered—'twas answered for you!

SAMUEL O'MALLEY CLOUGH (1837–1910)

I MUST TELL JESUS

Some people seem to have an endless stream of heartaches and painful experiences. Elisha Hoffman knew one such person in Lebanon, Pennsylvania. One day when Pastor Hoffman visited her, he found her extremely discouraged. When he asked her what was wrong, she unburdened herself to him, and as she finished she asked, "Brother Hoffman, what shall I do? What shall I do?"

The pastor quoted some verses from Scripture and then said, "You cannot do better than to take all of your sorrows to Jesus. You must tell Jesus."

For a moment the woman said nothing. Then her face lit up, her eyes sparkled, and she responded: "Yes, I must tell Jesus, I must tell Jesus."

On his way home Hoffman couldn't forget the joy on that woman's face when she said, "I must tell Jesus." So as soon as he got home, he wrote the words of this gospel song, "I Must Tell Jesus."

Scriptures: 2 Timothy 4:17; Hebrews 10:21-22; 1 Peter 5:7
Themes: Prayer, Tribulation, Sorrow

I must tell Jesus all of my trials;
I cannot bear these burdens alone;
In my distress He kindly will help me;
He ever loves and cares for His own.

I must tell Jesus! I must tell Jesus! I cannot bear my burdens alone;
I must tell Jesus! I must tell Jesus! Jesus can help me, Jesus alone.

I must tell Jesus all of my troubles;
He is a kind, compassionate Friend;
If I but ask Him, He will deliver,
Make of my troubles quickly an end.

Tempted and tried I need a great Savior,
One who can help my burdens to bear;
I must tell Jesus, I must tell Jesus;
He all my cares and sorrows will share.

O how the world to evil allures me!
O how my heart is tempted to sin!
I must tell Jesus, and He will help me
Over the world the victory to win.

ELISHA ALBRIGHT HOFFMAN (1839–1929)

I WILL CALL UPON THE LORD

Michael O'Shields was a traveling Bible teacher in west Texas and Oklahoma. That is a lot of territory to cover, but the need to make a living and the meager offerings required him to travel a lot.

The Bible studies were conducted in homes, quite often in farmhouses. The people seemed hungry for good Bible teaching, and Michael was thrilled to be used by the Lord in this way, but he was newly married and he needed to bring home some money for groceries. He recalls one time driving two hundred miles from Oklahoma to Abilene, Texas, for a Saturday night meeting and returning with an offering of twelve dollars.

The long trips, however, gave Michael time to write some songs, which he introduced to those attending the Bible studies. "I Will Call upon the Lord" was one of those songs. Michael did plenty of calling on the Lord during those days of meager offerings, so it was certainly his heartfelt cry. But this song served another purpose. It begins with the men singing a line, and the women echoing. Some of the farmers to whom Michael introduced the song didn't have great voices, but Michael didn't care. By having the men begin the song, they were taking leadership in worship. Soon the song became a favorite.

Scriptures: Psalm 18:3-36; Psalm 55:16; Isaiah 55:6
Themes: Prayer, Praise, Worship

I will call upon the Lord who is worthy to be praised.
So shall I be saved from my enemies. I will call upon the Lord.
The Lord liveth, and blessed be the Rock,
And let the God of my salvation be exalted.
(Repeat the last 2 lines.)

MICHAEL O'SHIELDS
© 1994 by MCA Music Publishing/ Sound III, Inc.
All rights reserved by Universal Music Corporation/ASCAP
Used by permission. All rights reserved.

I WOULD BE LIKE JESUS

As the twentieth century was about to dawn, there was great interest in living a consistent Christian life in the workplace as well as in church on Sunday. The novel *In His Steps* by Charles Sheldon had just been published and people were asking the question that characters in that book were asking, "What would Jesus do?" How does a Christian apply the teachings of Christ to modern living?

This was the concern of songwriter James Rowe, who wrote this gospel song early in the twentieth century. Rowe had come to America from England in 1890 and had settled in Albany, New York. Coming to America, he had thought that he would enjoy a richer, more prosperous life. But he found it wasn't satisfying. "Earthly pleasures" may have called him, but he was no longer enthralled by them. Now his prayer was to be like Jesus.

Scriptures: Romans 8:29; Ephesians 2:10; 1 Peter 2:21
Themes: Jesus, Commitment, Christlikeness

Earthly pleasures vainly call me, I would be like Jesus;
Nothing worldly shall enthrall me, I would be like Jesus.

Be like Jesus, this my song, in the home and in the throng;
Be like Jesus all day long; I would be like Jesus.

He has broken ev'ry fetter, I would be like Jesus;
That my soul may serve Him better, I would be like Jesus.

All the way from earth to Glory, I would be like Jesus;
Telling o'er and o'er the story, I would be like Jesus.

That in Heaven He may meet me, I would be like Jesus;
That His words "Well done" may greet me, I would be like Jesus.

JAMES ROWE (1865–1933)

IN THE GARDEN

Austin Miles had a job as a pharmacist and a hobby as a photographer, but in his church he was known as the song leader and occasionally a songwriter. On his first songwriting effort, a publisher not only offered him a contract but also offered him a job as an editor.

It all went well for Miles in the music business, until one day his boss told him that he needed a special kind of song for their next hymnal. It had to be "sympathetic in tone, breathing tenderness in every line; one that would bring hope to the hopeless, rest for the weary, and downy pillows in dying beds."

It was a tall order, but Austin Miles opened his Bible to his favorite chapter, John 20, and tried to re-create the scene with his photographer's eye. He recalled it this way: "I seemed to be standing at the entrance of a garden, looking down a gently winding path, shaded by olive branches. A woman in white, with head bowed, walked slowly into the shadows. It was Mary."

Then the words came to him, and he wrote as quickly as he could the words that we now have as the song "In the Garden."

Scriptures: Matthew 28:5-9; John 15:15-16; John 20:16
Themes: Comfort, Peace, Hope

I come to the garden alone,
While the dew is still on the roses,
And the voice I hear, falling on my ear,
The Son of God discloses.

And He walks with me, and He talks with me,
And He tells me I am His own;
And the joy we share as we tarry there,
None other has ever known.

He speaks, and the sound of His voice
Is so sweet the birds hush their singing,
And the melody that He gave to me,
Within my heart is ringing.

I'd stay in the garden with Him
Tho' the night around me be falling,
But He bids me go; thro' the voice of woe
His voice to me is calling.

C. AUSTIN MILES (1868–1945)

IN THE HOUR OF TRIAL

Life had been difficult for James Montgomery. His parents died when he was twelve. He was so distressed that he couldn't do his schoolwork, so he was asked to leave school. Finally, he got a job with a newspaper. It sounded like a good opportunity, but when the editor had to flee the country to avoid prosecution, the twenty-three-year-old James became the new editor. When he commemorated the fall of the Bastille in his editorials, he was fined, imprisoned, and called "a wicked, malicious and seditious person."

James knew what trouble was like. However, years later the British government honored him for his advocacy of humanitarian causes, especially the abolition of slavery.

This hymn was written after he read the story of Peter in the Gospels: "[Jesus said,] I have pleaded in prayer for you, Simon, that your faith should not fail" (Luke 22:32).

Scriptures: Luke 22:32; John 16:33; 1 Corinthians 10:13; Hebrews 2:14-15, 18
Themes: Trials, Jesus, Care

In the hour of trial, Jesus, plead for me;
Lest by base denial, I depart from Thee.
When Thou seest me waver, with a look recall,
Nor for fear or favor suffer me to fall.

With forbidden pleasures would this vain world charm,
Or its sordid treasures spread to work me harm;
Bring to my remembrance sad Gethsemane,
Or, in darker semblance, cross-crowned Calvary.

Should Thy mercy send me sorrow, toil, and woe,
Or should pain attend me on my path below,
Grant that I may never fail Thy hand to see:
Grant that I may ever cast my care on Thee.

When my last hour cometh, fraught with strife and pain,
When my dust returneth to the dust again,
On Thy truth relying, through that mortal strife:
Jesus, take me, dying, to eternal life.

JAMES MONTGOMERY (1771–1854)
Altered by Frances A. Hutton (1811–1877)

INTO THE WOODS

For the Southern poet Sidney Lanier, life was a struggle. He fought with the Confederate Army in the Civil War, was captured, and was imprisoned under miserable conditions at Point Lookout, Maryland. When he was released at the end of the war, Lanier was seriously ill. He recovered briefly and then had a breakdown at the age of thirty. Lanier became a lecturer in English literature at Johns Hopkins University in Baltimore, but weakened by tuberculosis, he had to retreat to the mountains.

He continued to write poetry and essays, establishing himself as a major Southern writer. But he knew he was getting weaker and that his life would be short. Lanier spent more time reading about the last days of Jesus Christ and how the Lord had retreated to the Mount of Olives and to the garden of Gethsemane.

So it was in Lanier's own dark night going into the woods that he wrote these masterful words about the experience of his Savior. He died at the age of thirty-nine.

Scriptures: John 18:1, 11; John 19:2-5
Themes: Good Friday, Sorrow, Suffering of Christ

Into the woods my Master went, clean forspent, forspent;
Into the woods my Master came, forspent with love and shame.
But the olives they were not blind to Him,
The little gray leaves were kind to Him,
The thorn-tree had a mind to Him, when into the woods He came.

Out of the woods my Master went, and He was well content;
Out of the woods my Master came, content with death and shame.
When death and shame would woo Him last,
From under the trees they drew Him last,
'Twas on a tree they slew Him last, when out of the woods He came.

SIDNEY LANIER (1842–1881)

JUST A CLOSER WALK WITH THEE

"Just a Closer Walk with Thee" was probably the favorite southern gospel song of the twentieth century, yet no one knows who wrote it or when it was written. It became known nationally in the 1930s when African-American churches held huge musical conventions. In the 1940s southern gospel quartets featured it in all-night gospel-singing rallies. In the 1950s Elvis Presley set sales records with it on a 45 RPM single. In the 1960s Tennessee Ernie Ford made the charts with it. And by the time the 1970s had ended, more than a hundred artists had recorded the song.

Its history probably goes back to an unknown writer in the slave fields of the South before the Civil War. Southern black church choirs kept the hymn alive until World War II.

But while the song is indebted to the African-American experience for its soul, people of every background can identify with it because it presents the humble prayer of every Christian's heart, and humble prayer is the kind that God honors.

Scriptures: Psalm 91:1-2; Mark 1:16-18; 1 John 2:6
Themes: Comfort, Guidance, Personal Relationship

I am weak but Thou art strong;
Jesus, keep me from all wrong;
I'll be satisfied as long
As I walk, let me walk close to Thee.

Just a closer walk with Thee,
Grant it, Jesus, is my plea,

Daily, walking close to Thee,
Let it be, dear Lord, let it be.

Through this world of toil and snares,
If I falter, Lord, who cares?
Who with me my burden shares?
None but Thee, dear Lord, none but Thee.

When my feeble life is o'er,
Time for me will be no more;
Guide me gently, safely o'er
To Thy kingdom shore, to Thy shore.

AUTHOR UNKNOWN

JUST A LITTLE TALK WITH JESUS

During the Great Depression of the 1930s, Cleavant Derricks was pastor of a small African-American church in Alabama. "Rev," as everyone liked to call him, wrote songs, and while his church members loved to sing them, he didn't think they would be of any interest to anyone else.

The church needed new hymnals because the ones it had were ragged and torn, and some had disappeared, as hymnals sometimes do. So "Rev" found the name and address of the publisher in Dallas and decided to see the publisher about getting some more hymnbooks. Of course, he didn't have any money, but some of his church members encouraged him to take some of his songs with him. So he did.

The publisher wasn't excited about most of Revelation's songs, but there were two that merited a closer look. When the publisher asked him what he wanted in return for the two songs, he said he thought that fifty hymnals would be fair. So Rev went home with fifty new hymnals, and the publisher got the rights to "Just a Little Talk with Jesus." Within three years, it had become one of America's most beloved southern gospel songs.

Scriptures: Romans 12:12; 1 Thessalonians 5:17; Hebrews 4:16
Themes: Prayer, Trust, Difficulty

I once was lost in sin but Jesus took me in,
And then a little light from heaven filled my soul;
It bathed my heart in love and wrote my name above,
And just a little talk with Jesus made me whole.

Now let us have a little talk with Jesus;
Let us tell Him all about our troubles.
He will hear our anguished cry; He will answer by and by.
Now when you feel a little prayer is turning,
And you feel a little fire is burning,
You will know a little talk with Jesus makes it right.

Sometimes my path seems dreary without a ray of cheer,
And then the cloud about me hides the light of day;
The mists in me rise and hide the starry skies,
But just a little talk with Jesus clears the way.

I may have doubts and fears, my eyes be filled with tears;
But Jesus is a friend who watches day and night.
I go to Him in prayer; He knows my every care,
And just a little talk with Jesus makes it right.

CLEAVANT DERRICKS
© 1937 Bridge Building (BMI)
All rights reserved. Used by permission.

LEAVE IT THERE

African American pastor Charles Tindley knew what it was like to have problems. He was born into slavery before the Civil War, and his parents died when he was only five years old. But Charles Tindley taught himself how to read and write, traveled to Philadelphia, and enrolled in night school. He took correspondence courses from a seminary and graduated as an expert linguist in both Hebrew and Greek.

To support himself, he worked as a caretaker in a Methodist church in Philadelphia. Years later, when he was fifty-one, he returned to the church as its pastor. Under his ministry, the church membership increased to 12,500.

Once one of his members came to him for counsel. She was loaded down with troubles, and she didn't know what to do. Tindley advised her, "Put all your troubles in a sack; then take them to the Lord and leave them there."

After the woman left, Tindley went to his study and penned the words to this gospel song: "Take your burden to the Lord and leave it there."

Scriptures: Psalm 42:5; Isaiah 26:3-4; 1 Peter 5:7
Themes: Comfort, Hope, Prayer

If the world from you withhold of its silver and its gold,
And you have to get along with meager fare,
Just remember, in His Word, how He feeds the little bird;
Take your burden to the Lord and leave it there.

Leave it there, leave it there;
Take your burden to the Lord and leave it there;
If you trust and never doubt, He will surely bring you out;
Take your burden to the Lord and leave it there.

If your body suffers pain and your health you can't regain,
And your soul is almost sinking in despair,
Jesus knows the pain you feel, He can save and He can heal;
Take your burden to the Lord and leave it there.

When your enemies assail and your heart begins to fail,
Don't forget that God in heaven answers prayer;
He will make a way for you and will lead you safely thro';
Take your burden to the Lord and leave it there.

When your youthful days are gone and old age is stealing on,
And your body bends beneath the weight of care;
He will never leave you then, He'll go with you to the end;
Take your burden to the Lord and leave it there.

CHARLES A. TINDLEY (1851–1933)

LORD, I HAVE SHUT THE DOOR

William Runyan started playing the organ for his church when he was twelve years old and became a pastor and evangelist in Methodist churches in Kansas when he was twenty-one, but he didn't start writing hymns until he was forty-five.

You might think that a man raised in Methodist camp meetings might like boisterous hymns of praise, but Runyan isn't known for that. He wrote the music for hymns such as "Great Is Thy Faithfulness" and "Teach Me Thy Will, O Lord."

"Lord, I Have Shut the Door" is based on the words of Jesus in Matthew 6:6, "When you pray, go away by yourself, shut the door behind you, and pray to your Father in private." Prayer is not a time to show off to others how much religious language we know. It is a time to humble ourselves before God. Finding a place of solitude may not be easy, but in such a place, it is easier for us to hear God speak to us. We can talk to God anytime and anywhere, but some places are too noisy for us to hear God talk to us. That's why we need to "shut the door."

Scriptures: 1 Kings 19:11-12; Psalm 46:10; Matthew 6:6
Themes: Prayer, Communion, Submission

Lord, I have shut the door, speak now the word
Which in the din and throng could not be heard;
Hushed now my inner heart, whisper Thy will,
While I have come apart, while all is still.

Lord, I have shut the door, here do I bow;
Speak, for my soul attent turns to Thee now.
Rebuke Thou what is vain, counsel my soul,
Thy holy will reveal, my will control.

In this blest quietness clamoring cease;
Here in Thy presence dwells infinite peace;
Yonder, the strife and cry, yonder, the sin:
Lord, I have shut the door, Thou art within!

Lord, I have shut the door, strengthen my heart;
Yonder awaits the task—I share a part.
Only through grace bestowed may I be true;
Here, while alone with Thee, my strength renew.

WILLIAM M. RUNYAN

LORD, LISTEN TO YOUR CHILDREN PRAYING

Ken Medema is one of those amazing people who never let a handicap get them down. Though blind, he got a master's degree in music from Michigan State University and worked as a music therapist at Fort Wayne State Hospital. He has traveled the country giving concerts, and he has written several musicals in addition to his songs.

It was while he was working as a music therapist in New Jersey that he asked his youth fellowship to join with him in prayer for a young man who was hospitalized. After praying, Medema began to hum and then sing the chorus impromptu. The group then joined in softly as they continued in a mood of prayer for the young man.

Scriptures: Psalm 5:1-3; Colossians 4:2-3; James 5:13-16
Themes: Prayer, Blindness, Waiting on God

> Lord, listen to your children praying,
> Lord, send your Spirit in this place;
> Lord, listen to your children praying,
> Send us love, send us pow'r, send us grace.

Words: Ken Medema

© 1973 by Hope Publishing Co.

LORD, SPEAK TO ME

When Frances Havergal was a child, her father nicknamed her "Little Quicksilver." She had a quick and hungry mind and as a child memorized long passages of Scripture. Her mother died when Frances was only eleven, but one of the last things her mother said to her was, "Pray God to prepare you for all he is preparing for you."

Shortly before she wrote this hymn at the age of thirty-six, she wrote in a letter, "I am always getting surprised at my own stupidity. . . . If I am to write to any good, a great deal of living must go to a very little writing." About the same time, she also wrote, "I feel like a child writing. You know a child will look up at every sentence and ask, 'What shall I say next?' This is what I do. Every line and word and rhyme comes from God."

She called this hymn "A Worker's Prayer" and wrote what she had learned to be the secret of Christian service: It is not what we do in our own strength; it is how we respond to God's work within us. God speaks to us so we may speak to others; he seeks after us so we may seek after others.

Scriptures: Romans 14:17; 2 Corinthians 5:20; 2 Timothy 2:1-2, 15
Themes: Prayer, Service, Witness

> Lord, speak to me, that I may speak
> In living echoes of Thy tone;
> As Thou hast sought, so let me seek
> Thy erring children lost and lone.
>
> O teach me, Lord, that I may teach
> The precious things Thou dost impart;
> And wing my words, that they may reach
> The hidden depths of many a heart.

O fill me with Thy fullness, Lord,
Until my very heart o'erflow
In kindling thought and glowing word
Thy love to tell, Thy praise to show.

O use me, Lord, use even me,
Just as Thou wilt and when and where;
Until Thy blessed face I see,
Thy rest, Thy joy, Thy glory share.

FRANCES RIDLEY HAVERGAL (1836–1879)

MAKE ME A CAPTIVE, LORD

George Matheson is best known for the hymn "O Love that Wilt Not Let Me Go," but this hymn is equally as powerful. It is full of paradoxes: Matheson writes that the only way to be free is to be a captive of the Lord; the only way to conquer is to give up your sword; the only way to be strong is to recognize your weakness; the only way to become a ruler is to give up your crown; and the only way to stand tall is to lean on Jesus.

George Matheson's life was full of paradoxes too. By the time he was eighteen, he was almost blind, yet he had a brilliant record as a student at the University of Glasgow. He became a minister at a beautiful summer resort, which of course he could not see, but hundreds vacationed there just to hear him preach. He preached with an open Bible that he couldn't read in front of him, but he didn't need to read because he memorized all his sermons. In fact, as he preached he looked directly at his audience and many of his parishioners had no idea that he was blind.

The idea for this hymn came from Paul's epistles. While chained to his Roman guards, Paul wrote much about freedom. But he also talked about being a prisoner and a bondservant of Jesus Christ.

Scriptures: 2 Corinthians 12:10; Galatians 5:1; Ephesians 3:1
Themes: Submission, Holiness, Obedience

Make me a captive, Lord, and then I shall be free;
Force me to render up my sword, and I shall conqueror be.
I sink in life's alarms when by myself I stand;
Imprison me within Thine arms, and strong shall be my hand.

My heart is weak and poor until its master find;
It has no spring of action sure, it varies with the wind;

It cannot freely move till Thou hast wrought its chain;
Enslave it with Thy matchless love, and deathless it shall reign.

My power is faint and low till I have learned to serve;
It wants the needed fire to glow, it wants the breeze to nerve;
It cannot drive the world, until itself be driven;
Its flag can only be unfurled when Thou shalt breathe from heaven.

My will is not my own till Thou hast made it Thine;
If it would reach a monarch's throne it must its crown resign;
It only stands unbent, amid the clashing strife,
When on Thy bosom it has leant and found in Thee its life.

GEORGE MATHESON (1842–1906)

MAKE ME A SERVANT

You have probably heard the expression, "You had better watch out what you pray for; God might give it to you."

That's the way it was with Kelly Willard. Kelly had been playing piano and composing music for some of the biggest names in country music, and after her marriage to Dan Willard, she began her career as a soloist. But her rise to fame left her feeling a bit guilty. Kelly had lost something along the way, so she began praying, "Make me a servant, Lord" and wrote up her prayer as a song.

God answered her prayer. How? She became pregnant. Kelly's first response to the news of her pregnancy was, "What is this, God, your idea of a joke?" But soon she realized that God had answered her prayer through motherhood!

Scriptures: John 12:26; 1 Corinthians 9:19; Philippians 2:7
Themes: Servanthood, Submission, Prayer

The lyrics are inspired by John 13:14-16.

KELLY BAGLEY WILLARD (B. 1956)
Rights administered by the Copyright Company, Nashville, TN.

MAY THE MIND OF CHRIST, MY SAVIOR

All of us want to be more like Jesus, but where do we start? Kate Wilkinson said we should start with Paul's words to the Philippian believers: "Let this mind be in you, which was also in Christ Jesus" (Philippians 2:5, KJV). But how does the mind of Christ become part of us? This hymn directs us to Colossians 3:16 for the answer: "Let the word of Christ dwell in you richly" (NIV). The third stanza returns to Philippians for this promise: "God's peace . . . will guard your hearts and minds" (4:7).

Christian growth results from obeying God's Word.

Kate Wilkinson combined two passions in her life: She was deeply involved in a ministry to girls and the Keswick Deeper Life movement. So this hymn, which was published when Kate was sixty-six years old, combines simplicity in communicating with the girls and spiritual depth that she found in the Keswick movement.

Scriptures: Philippians 2:5; Philippians 4:7; Colossians 3:16
Themes: Word of God, Peace

May the mind of Christ, my Savior,
Live in me from day to day,
By His love and pow'r controlling
All I do and say.

May the word of God dwell richly
In my heart from hour to hour,
So that all may see I triumph
Only through His pow'r.

May the peace of God my Father
Rule my life in ev'rything,
That I may be calm to comfort
Sick and sorrowing.

May the love of Jesus fill me
As the waters fill the sea;
Him exalting, self abasing—
This is victory.

May I run the race before me,
Strong and brave to face the foe,
Looking only unto Jesus
As I onward go.

May His beauty rest upon me
As I seek the lost to win,
And may they forget the channel,
Seeing only Him.

KATE B. WILKINSON (1859–1928)

NEAR TO THE HEART OF GOD

In Chicago, Cleland McAfee had just received word that his brother and sister-in-law had lost both of their daughters to diphtheria within twenty-four hours. He was grief-stricken. He was asked to say some words at the funeral and also to sing a solo. He couldn't think of anything to say or to sing. But his mind went to verses in Psalms that brought comfort and rest to those who sought refuge in the Lord. As he meditated further, he wrote the words and music to this simple hymn, "Near to the Heart of God."

At the double funeral, outside the darkened, quarantined house of his brother, Cleland McAfee with a choking voice sang this hymn publicly for the first time. The following Sunday, his church choir sang it from their pastor's handwritten copy.

Scriptures: Psalm 34:18; Psalm 46; Psalm 94:19; Hebrews 4:16
Themes: Comfort, Rest, Peace

There is a place of quiet rest
Near to the heart of God,
A place where sin cannot molest,
Near to the heart of God.

O Jesus, blest Redeemer,
Sent from the heart of God,
Hold us who wait before Thee
Near to the heart of God.

There is a place of comfort sweet
Near to the heart of God,
A place where we our Savior meet,
Near to the heart of God.

There is a place of full release
Near to the heart of God,
A place where all is joy and peace,
Near to the heart of God.

CLELAND BOYD MCAFEE (1866–1944)

THE COMPLETE BOOK OF HYMNS

NEARER, MY GOD, TO THEE

Sarah Adams had to say farewell often, and it was always hard. Her mother had died when Sarah was only five—that was her first farewell. At thirty-two, as an actress playing Lady Macbeth in London's Richmond Theater, she said farewell to the stage. She wanted to continue, but her health was failing. The health of her sister was also poor, and Adams feared the day when she would have to bid her farewell. She began to question her faith. Why did God seem so far away?

When Adams's pastor asked her and her sister to help him prepare a hymnal, the two responded eagerly, writing thirteen texts and sixty-two new tunes. As the sisters were finishing their work, their pastor mentioned that he was planning a sermon about Jacob's dream of a ladder ascending to heaven and he needed an appropriate hymn. Adams soon completed the five stanzas of "Nearer, My God, to Thee." In her own life, she learned that each step we take—even the difficult and painful farewells—only draws us nearer to God.

Scriptures: Genesis 28:10-15; Psalm 119:148-152; James 4:8
Themes: Dedication, Service, Death

Nearer, my God, to Thee, nearer to Thee!
E'en though it be a cross that raiseth me;
Still all my song shall be, nearer, my God, to Thee,
Nearer, my God, to Thee, nearer to Thee.

Though like the wanderer, the sun gone down,
Darkness be over me, my rest a stone;
Yet in my dreams I'd be nearer, my God, to Thee,
Nearer, my God, to Thee, nearer to Thee.

There let the way appear steps unto heav'n;
All that Thou sendest me in mercy giv'n;
Angels to beckon me nearer, my God, to Thee,
Nearer, my God, to Thee, nearer to Thee.

Then, with my waking thoughts bright with Thy praise,
Out of my stony griefs, Bethel I'll raise;
So by my woes to be nearer, my God, to Thee,
Nearer, my God, to Thee, nearer to Thee.

SARAH FLOWER ADAMS (1805–1848)

580

NEARER, STILL NEARER

Lelia Naylor was only a child when she felt her need of a Savior. A sensitive child, she had felt very much alone after her father died. In her Methodist church in McConnelsville, Ohio, Lelia went forward to the altar and prayed three different times, but she didn't feel as if anything had happened. Then one time as she knelt at the altar, she recalled, "A man came and laid his hand on my head and said, 'Why, little girl, God is here and ready to forgive your sins.' " That made the difference, so she accepted God's forgiveness.

When Lelia was nineteen, she married Charles Morris, and together they established a Christian home. When she was thirty, at a summer camp meeting in Mountain Lake Park, Maryland, Lelia rededicated her life to God. "I just opened my heart," she said, "to let his Holy Spirit come in. He filled me with joy and gladness." After that, she wrote more than 1,500 hymns, including "Nearer, Still Nearer," which she wrote when she was thirty-six. But Lelia didn't take the credit. She said, "I am just a channel. I open my mind and let the story flow through. I am not the author. I am only a channel."

Scriptures: 2 Chronicles 15:2; Colossians 3:1-4; James 4:8
Themes: Holiness, Sanctification, Christlikeness

Nearer, still nearer, close to Thy heart,
Draw me, my Savior, so precious Thou art;
Fold me, O fold me close to Thy breast,
Shelter me safe in that "Haven of Rest,"
Shelter me safe in that "Haven of Rest."

Nearer, still nearer, nothing I bring,
Naught as an off'ring to Jesus my King;
Only my sinful, now contrite heart,
Grant me the cleansing Thy blood doth impart,
Grant me the cleansing Thy blood doth impart.

Nearer, still nearer, Lord, to be Thine,
Sin, with its follies, I gladly resign,
All of its pleasures, pomp and its pride,
Give me but Jesus, my Lord crucified,
Give me but Jesus, my Lord crucified.

Nearer, still nearer, while life shall last,
Till safe in glory my anchor is cast;

Thro' endless ages, ever to be,
Nearer, my Savior, still nearer to Thee,
Nearer, my Savior, still nearer to Thee.

LELIA NAYLOR MORRIS (1862–1929)

NOW THE DAY IS OVER

Sabine Baring-Gould would never have guessed that he would be best remembered for his children's hymns. After all, he wrote eighty-five books in areas as diverse as religion, travel, folklore, mythology, history, fiction, biography, sermons, and popular theology. He wrote the fifteen-volume *Lives of the Saints*. He edited a quarterly review of ecclesiastical art and literature. The British Museum displays more titles by him than by any other writer of his time. But he loved children, so we remember him for songs like "Onward Christian Soldiers" and "Now the Day is Over."

After graduating from Cambridge, Baring-Gould started a church in his tiny two-floor apartment. "Soon," he said, "the congregation filled the room and the stairs and the kitchen. . . . The singing had to bump down the stairs, fill the kitchen, and one strain of the tune after another came up irregularly through the chinks of the floor."

In the crowded and noisy church setting, the clergyman introduced this peaceful hymn based on Proverbs 3:24: "When you lie down, you will not be afraid; when you lie down, your sleep will be sweet" (NIV).

Scriptures: Psalm 4:8; Psalm 139:11-12; Proverbs 3:24
Themes: Comfort, Evening Prayer, Rest

Now the day is over,
Night is drawing nigh,
Shadows of the evening
Steal across the sky.

Jesus, give the weary
Calm and sweet repose;
With Thy tend'rest blessing
May our eyelids close.

Grant to little children
Visions bright of Thee;

Guard the sailors tossing
On the deep blue sea.

Thro' the long night-watches,
May Thine angels spread
Their white wings above me,
Watching round my bed.

When the morning wakens,
Then may I arise,
Pure and fresh and sinless
In Thy holy eyes.

SABINE BARING-GOULD (1834–1924)

O TO BE LIKE THEE!

When people were introduced to Thomas O. Chisholm, the author of this hymn and "Great Is Thy Faithfulness," he would often say, "Aw, I'm just an old shoe!"

Born in a Kentucky log cabin in 1866, Chisholm was self-educated and began teaching in a rural school when he was sixteen. At the age of twenty-seven, the Kentucky farm boy wrote this hymn, "O to Be Like Thee!" He served on the staff of the *Pentecostal Herald* in Louisville until his health broke. He was accepted as a traveling preacher in the Methodist church, but once again health problems caused him to resign. Regretfully he had to leave the ministry. Eventually he became a life insurance agent in Vineland, New Jersey.

Throughout his life he displayed many of the characteristics that he praised in Jesus in the hymns he wrote. Chisholm, who described himself as an old shoe, was perhaps more like Christ than he realized.

Scriptures: Romans 8:29; Ephesians 2:10; 1 John 3:1-2
Themes: Holiness, Discipleship, Dedication

O to be like Thee! blessed Redeemer,
This is my constant longing and prayer;
Gladly I'll forfeit all of earth's treasures,
Jesus, Thy perfect likeness to wear.

O to be like Thee! O to be like Thee,
Blessed Redeemer, pure as Thou art!

Come in Thy sweetness, come in Thy fullness—
Stamp Thine own image deep on my heart.

O to be like Thee! full of compassion,
Loving, forgiving, tender and kind;
Helping the helpless, cheering the fainting,
Seeking the wand'ring sinner to find.

O to be like Thee! while I am pleading,
Pour out Thy Spirit, fill with Thy love;
Make me a temple meet for Thy dwelling,
Fit me for life and heaven above.

THOMAS OBEDIAH CHISHOLM (1866–1960)

OPEN MY EYES, THAT I MAY SEE

God calls us to employ all our senses as we strive to seek and serve him. We must keep our entire beings—our bodies and our souls—tuned to God's every communication and prompting. In our busy lives we often miss the quiet promptings of God's Spirit. And when we do hear God speak, we often ignore the message. "I'm too busy now," we say. "I have more important things to do." This hymn calls us to watch, listen, and act on what we have seen and heard, sharing it with others.

Clara Scott, the writer of this hymn, was a music teacher who composed a great deal of instrumental and vocal music. She began teaching music when she was only eighteen at a small high school in rural northwestern Iowa, and that is where she spent most of her life. But God expanded her ministry through her instrumental and vocal compositions. She became known for her book of anthems, *The Royal Anthem Book*, which was published in 1882. Her eyes and ears were open to God's leading, and she was ready to obey. We should be ready to do the same.

Scriptures: 2 Kings 6:17; Psalm 40:8; Psalm 119:17-20; James 1:22
Themes: Prayer, Holy Spirit, Guidance

Open my eyes, that I may see
Glimpses of truth Thou hast for me;
Place in my hands the wonderful key
That shall unclasp and set me free.
Silently now I wait for Thee
Ready, my God, Thy will to see;

Open my eyes—illumine me,
Spirit divine!

Open my ears, that I may hear
Voices of truth Thou sendest clear;
And while the wave-notes fall on my ear,
Ev'rything false will disappear.
Silently now I wait for Thee,
Ready, my God, Thy will to see;
Open my ears—illumine me,
Spirit divine!

Open my mouth, and let it bear
Gladly the warm truth ev'rywhere.
Open my heart and let me prepare
Love with Thy children thus to share.
Silently now I wait for Thee,
Ready, my God, Thy will to see;
Open my heart—illumine me,
Spirit divine!

CLARA H. SCOTT (1841–1897)

OPEN OUR EYES, LORD

Every speaker has times when he feels that he is speaking to a brick wall.
Youth speakers often experience this when addressing young people.
How can God possibly speak to a group when their eyes and ears are
closed? Bob Cull felt that way when he was speaking to an audience of
young people in a Christian school in Hawaii. As long as he was entertaining them, it was okay, but when he started drawing them to Jesus
Christ, he lost them.

He felt defeated and wondered if it was hopeless. But the Lord seemed
to encourage him to write a prayer song to "reach closed-hearted people." After praying about it for half an hour, he says, "the song, like an
answer to my prayer, fell into my head." Since that time, it has been
translated and recorded in dozens of different languages.

Scriptures: Psalm 119:18; Matthew 9:27-31; Luke 24:31-32
Themes: Worship, Waiting on God, Prayer

ROBERT CULL (B. 1949)
Rights administered by the Copyright Company, Nashville, TN.

PRAYER IS THE SOUL'S SINCERE DESIRE

When the Reverend Edward Bickersteth was writing his *Treatise on Prayer,* he turned to newspaper editor James Montgomery to write a hymn about prayer that he could use in his book. Today Rev. Bickersteth's volume has been forgotten, but the newspaperman's hymn is still being sung.

This hymn is a theological definition in poetic form. What is prayer? Bickersteth may have said it more completely, but Montgomery defined it simply. (Montgomery later said he received more praise for this hymn than anything else he had written.)

Many years after he retired, Montgomery continued to conduct family prayer meetings in his home. After he closed one such meeting, he walked quietly to his room. The next day he was found unconscious on the floor and later died. As he had written in this hymn, prayer is the Christian's "watchword at the gates of death; he enters heaven with prayer."

Scriptures: Matthew 6:5-8; Luke 11:1-4; Colossians 4:2; 1 Thessalonians 5:17
Themes: Prayer, Dedication

Prayer is the soul's sincere desire,
Unuttered or expressed,
The motion of a hidden fire
That trembles in the breast.

Prayer is the burden of a sigh,
The falling of a tear,
The upward glancing of an eye,
When none but God is near.

Prayer is the simplest form of speech
That infant lips can try;
Prayer the sublimest strains that reach
The Majesty on high.

Prayer is the contrite sinner's voice,
Returning from his ways,
While angels in their songs rejoice
And cry, "Behold, he prays!"

Prayer is the Christian's vital breath,
The Christian's native air,
His watchword at the gates of death;
He enters heaven with prayer.

O Thou, by whom we come to God,
The Life, the Truth, the Way;
The path of prayer Thyself hast trod:
Lord, teach us how to pray!

JAMES MONTGOMERY (1771–1854)

PRECIOUS LORD, TAKE MY HAND

Thomas Dorsey was successful in Chicago nightclubs, but as a Christian he was urged to use his musical talent for the Lord. In 1932 he was invited to go to St. Louis and lead the music for a large revival meeting. He hesitated to agree because his wife was pregnant. He didn't want to leave her with the time for delivery so close, but he made the trip.

The second day of the revival meetings, he got a telegram. The baby had been born, but his wife had died in childbirth. He rushed back to Chicago and held the baby in his arms. Only a few hours later, his infant son died too. Both mother and baby were buried in the same casket.

Dorsey was devastated. He was trying to serve God, and this is what happened. In anger, he told the Lord, "God, you aren't worth a dime to me right now."

A few weeks later, still depressed, he sat down at the piano, and the words and music simply came to him. With tears streaming down his face, he sang, "Precious Lord, Take My Hand."

Scriptures: Psalm 27:9-11; Isaiah 41:13; John 10:3-4
Themes: Comfort, Hope, Guidance

THOMAS A. DORSEY (1899–1965)
Rights administered by Unichappell Music, Inc.

SEARCH ME, O GOD

At the age of twenty-four, evangelist J. Edwin Orr wrote this hymn following an Easter evangelistic campaign in New Zealand.

During that campaign in 1936, revival fell on the people of New Zealand. Midnight services had to be added to accommodate the crowds; many were converted, and revival fires spread across the island nation. The key to this revival was the public confession and reconciliation of believers, based on the verse in Psalm 139 that begins, "Search me, O God." As hearts were cleansed, the Holy Spirit moved in power.

As Orr was about to leave New Zealand, four Maori girls came and sang him their native song of farewell. Impressed by the tune and still stirred by the revival he had witnessed, young Orr quickly scribbled the stanzas of this hymn on the back of an envelope as he waited in the post office of Ngaruawahia, New Zealand.

Orr, a brilliant man who would go on to earn doctorates from universities in Europe, Asia, Africa, and America, studied revival movements for the next fifty years and chronicled them in numerous books.

Scriptures: Psalm 51:7; Psalm 139:1-2, 23-24; 1 John 1:9
Themes: Confession, Dedication, Surrender

Search me, O God, and know my heart today;
Try me, O Savior, know my thoughts, I pray.
See if there be some wicked way in me;
Cleanse me from every sin, and set me free.

I praise Thee, Lord, for cleansing me from sin;
Fulfill Thy Word, and make me pure within.
Fill me with fire, where once I burned with shame;
Grant my desire to magnify Thy name.

Lord, take my life, and make it wholly Thine;
Fill my poor heart with Thy great love divine.
Take all my will, my passion, self and pride;
I now surrender, Lord—in me abide.

O Holy Ghost, revival comes from Thee;
Send a revival, start the work in me.
Thy Word declares Thou wilt supply our need;
For blessings now, O Lord, I humbly plead.

JAMES EDWIN ORR (1912–1987)

SPEAK, LORD, IN THE STILLNESS

God revealed himself mightily to the prophet Elijah, sending fire to burn the sacrifice on Mount Carmel. But later, as Elijah moped on Mount Horeb, the Lord taught him an important lesson. There was a wind, an earthquake, and a fire—but the Lord was not in any of these. Then came a still, small voice. That was how God chose to speak to his prophet.

The same is true today. We long for fire from heaven to silence skeptics once and for all, but God doesn't usually work that way. Long ago he revealed himself as a helpless baby sleeping in a dirty feeding trough, and today he speaks quietly to ordinary people like you and me—if only we are still enough to listen.

Written in South Africa by a missionary from England, this hymn is not only an excellent reminder for us in church worship services but also in our times of personal devotions.

Scriptures: 1 Samuel 3:9; Job 4:16; Psalm 62:1
Themes: Prayer, Surrender, Dedication

Speak, Lord, in the stillness,
While I wait on Thee;
Hushed my heart to listen
In expectancy.

Speak, O blessed Master,
In this quiet hour,
Let me see Thy face, Lord,
Feel Thy touch of power.

For the words Thou speakest,
"They are life" indeed;
Living Bread from heaven,
Now my spirit feed!

All to Thee is yielded,
I am not my own;
Blissful, glad surrender,
I am Thine alone.

Fill me with the knowledge
Of Thy glorious will;
All Thine own good pleasure
In my life fulfill.

EMILY MAY GRIMES (1868–1927)

SWEET HOUR OF PRAYER

According to one account, the author of this hymn was a blind preacher and curio-shop owner in Coleshill, England. He carved ornaments out of ivory or wood and sold them in his small store. He also wrote poetry. One day, when a local minister stopped at the store, William Walford, the blind shop owner, mentioned that he had composed a poem in his head. He asked the minister to write it down for him. Three years later, the minister visited the United States and gave the poem to a newspaper editor.

Unfortunately, no one knows what happened to William Walford of Coleshill. Researchers have found a William Walford, a minister in Homerton, England, who wrote a book on prayer that expresses many of the same thoughts that are given in this poem. That may be the true author.

But the identity of the hymnwriter is not as important as knowing a God who hears and answers prayer. In our hymns, *prayer* is frequently rhymed with *care*. This is appropriate, for whenever we are aware of care, we should be equally aware of prayer. God cares about us, and that motivates us to pray.

Scriptures: Deuteronomy 34:1; Matthew 7:11; Matthew 21:22; Ephesians 6:18
Themes: Prayer, Comfort, Hope

Sweet hour of prayer! sweet hour of prayer!
That calls me from a world of care,
And bids me at my Father's throne
Make all my wants and wishes known;
In seasons of distress and grief,
My soul has often found relief,
And oft escaped the tempter's snare,
By thy return, sweet hour of prayer!

Sweet hour of prayer! sweet hour of prayer!
The joys I feel, the bliss I share
Of those whose anxious spirits burn
With strong desires for thy return!
With such I hasten to the place
Where God my Savior shows His face,
And gladly take my station there,
And wait for thee, sweet hour of prayer!

Sweet hour of prayer! sweet hour of prayer!
Thy wings shall my petition bear
To Him whose truth and faithfulness
Engage the waiting soul to bless;
And since He bids me seek His face,

Believe His Word and trust His grace,
I'll cast on Him my every care,
And wait for thee, sweet hour of prayer!

WILLIAM W. WALFORD (1772–1850)

TEACH ME TO PRAY, LORD

In the Gospel of Luke, one of the disciples said to Jesus, "Lord, teach us to pray" (11:1). Prayer is so simple, yet we realize there is much to learn. A new Christian prays, but soon he gets frustrated, and he doesn't know if there is something wrong with him, something wrong with prayer, or something wrong with God. Prayer is the greatest privilege in the world, yet when you call people together to pray, few Christians come.

The author of this song, Albert Reitz, was pastor of the Rosehill Baptist Church in Inglewood, California, when he wrote it. There had just been a Day of Prayer sponsored by the Evangelical Prayer Union of Los Angeles; it was a wonderful experience to meet with Christians of various denominations to pray for the city. They prayed for power, and they asked God to do great things in their growing city. The next morning, in his study, Pastor Reitz was still thinking about that united prayer meeting, and as he said, "The Lord gave the words and the music then followed."

Scriptures: Luke 11:1-4; John 15:7-8; Ephesians 1:18-19
Themes: Prayer, God's Power, Commitment

Teach me to pray, Lord, teach me to pray;
This is my heart cry day unto day;
I long to know Thy will and Thy way;
Teach me to pray, Lord, teach me to pray.

Living in Thee, Lord, and Thou in me;
Constant abiding, this is my plea;
Grant me Thy power boundless and free:
Power with men and power with Thee.

Power in prayer, Lord, power in prayer,
Here 'mid earth's sin and sorrow and care;
Men lost and dying, souls in despair—
O give me power, power in prayer.

My weakened will, Lord, Thou canst renew;
My sinful nature Thou canst subdue

Fill me just now with power anew,
Power to pray and power to do!

Teach me to pray, Lord, teach me to pray;
Thou art my Pattern day unto day;
Thou art my surety now and for aye;
Teach me to pray, Lord, teach me to pray.

ALBERT SIMPSON REITZ (1879–1966)

THE LORD'S PRAYER

Albert Hay Malotte had made a mess of his life, and now, like the Prodigal, he was returning home. Albert had been a choir boy and had studied music in Philadelphia, but he had left home and spent his money. Now he had to wire his father for money for train fare home. On the way home he thought about his father, the Prodigal Son, and the Lord's Prayer, which begins, "Our Father."

That was the beginning of the song that is now a classic. For several years he kept thinking about it. In those years, Walt Disney had hired him for the ballet *Little Red Riding Hood,* and Albert composed the scores for fifteen animated films. He had become a success. But he still had some unfinished business.

The next time he went home, he finished the song that had been on his mind for years, and he called for his parents to listen and be his first audience. When he finished singing it for them, there was silence, then sobbing. They threw their arms around him but could not speak. Their beloved prodigal had sung for them "The Lord's Prayer."

Scriptures: Matthew 6:9-13; Luke 11:1-4; Luke 18:13
Themes: Prayer, Worship, God the Father

Our Father which art in heaven, Hallowed be thy name.
Thy kingdom come, Thy will be done in earth, as it is in heaven.
Give us this day our daily bread.
And forgive us our debts, as we forgive our debtors.
And lead us not into temptation, but deliver us from evil:
    For thine is the kingdom, and the power, and the glory,
    for ever. Amen.

ALBERT HAY MALOTTE (1895–1964)

PART XX

RESURRECTION AND VICTORY

"Why are you looking among the dead for someone who is alive?

He isn't here! He is risen from the dead!"

LUKE 24:5-6

BECAUSE HE LIVES

The late 1960s were dark days for Bill and Gloria Gaither. Both of them were struggling with health problems, and Gloria was pregnant with their third child. The world around them was swirling with news of the Vietnam War, civil unrest, the drug culture, and violence in the streets. Was this any kind of world in which to raise a family?

Discouraged and disheartened, they looked for signs of hope. One day in the spring, Bill walked out of his office to inspect a newly paved parking area. Construction workers had covered it with several coats of asphalt. Bill was satisfied with the job that was done, but as he turned, he noticed a tiny blade of grass poking through the layers of rock and tar to reach into the sunlight.

In early summer the baby was born, and when Bill and Gloria brought their child home, they wrote this song of joy, remembering the blade of grass that prospered even in a hostile environment. More important, they remembered that their baby could indeed face uncertain days because Christ lives.

Scriptures: John 14:29; Ephesians 2:4-7; Philippians 3:10

Themes: Hope, Easter, Resurrection

God sent His Son, they called Him Jesus,
He came to love, heal, and forgive;
He lived and died to buy my pardon,
An empty grave is there to prove my Savior lives.

Because He lives, I can face tomorrow;
Because He lives all fear is gone;
Because I know He holds the future,
And life is worth the living just because He lives.

How sweet to hold a new-born baby,
And feel the pride, and joy he gives;
But greater still the calm assurance,
This child can face uncertain days because He lives.

And then one day, I'll cross the river,
I'll fight life's final war with pain;
And then as death gives way to victory,
I'll see the lights of glory and I'll know He lives.

WILLIAM J. (B. 1936) AND GLORIA GAITHER (B. 1942)

CHRIST AROSE

It's hard to match this hymn for sheer drama. The first stanza begins dismally, then strikes a note of hope, and then the chorus explodes with joy. The music itself comes rising up from the depths and celebrates on high.

Robert Lowry wrote both the words and music to this hymn in 1874. At the time, he was professor of literature at Bucknell University, in Pennsylvania, and pastor of a nearby church. He had written other hymn tunes and texts as he practiced his passion for poetry and song. "Sometimes the music comes and the words follow," he explained once. "I watch my moods, and when anything strikes me, whether words or music, no matter where I am, at home, on the street, I jot it down. My brain is sort of a spinning machine, for there is music running through it all the time."

In 1874, as he was having his devotions around Easter, Lowry was impressed with the simple words, "He is not here, but is risen." He moved quickly to the little pump organ in his living room, and the words and music came quickly. What a joyous hymn!

Scriptures: Luke 24:6-7; John 19:41-42; Acts 2:22-24; Romans 6:8-9
Themes: Resurrection, Easter, Victory

Low in the grave He lay,
Jesus my Savior!
Waiting the coming day,
Jesus my Lord!

Up from the grave He arose,
With a mighty triumph o'er His foes;
He arose a Victor from the dark domain,
And He lives forever with His saints to reign,
He arose! He arose!
Hallelujah! Christ arose!

Vainly they watch His bed,
Jesus my Savior!
Vainly they seal the dead,
Jesus my Lord!

Death cannot keep his prey,
Jesus my Savior!
He tore the bars away,
Jesus my Lord!

ROBERT LOWRY (1826–1899)

CHRIST JESUS LAY IN DEATH'S STRONG BANDS

In his death on the cross, Christ bound himself with the chains of sin and death. In his resurrection from the tomb, Christ broke those chains for himself and for us all. Martin Luther celebrates Christ's conquest over sin and death in this rousing Easter hymn. The reformer was deeply aware of the spiritual battle won by Christ on that first Easter. Luther was also aware of the ongoing spiritual battle every believer must face. He once felt Satan's oppressive presence so keenly that he threw an inkpot at it. An ink spot still decorates the wall of his room in Wartburg Castle!

Luther believed that singing hymns was one of our best weapons against Satan and his evil forces. He once said, "The devil, the originator of sorrowful anxieties and restless troubles, flees before the sound of music almost as much as before the Word of God." By celebrating Christ's victory through song, we can continue to wage war against sin and death and begin to experience Christ's resurrection power in our lives.

Scriptures: Acts 2:24; Ephesians 1:18-20; 1 Peter 1:3-5
Themes: Resurrection, Easter, Victory

Christ Jesus lay in death's strong bands
For our offenses given;
But now at God's right hand He stands,
And brings us life from heaven;
Wherefore let us joyful be,
And sing to God right thankfully
Loud songs of Alleluia! Alleluia!

It was a strange and dreadful strife
When life and death contended;
The victory remained with life;
The reign of death was ended;
Stripped of power, no more he reigns,
An empty form alone remains;
His sting is lost forever! Alleluia!

So let us keep the festival
Whereto the Lord invites us;
Christ is Himself the joy of all,
The Sun that warms and lights us;
By His grace He doth impart
Eternal sunshine to the heart;
The night of sin is ended! Alleluia!

Then let us feast this Easter Day
On the true bread of heaven;
The Word of grace hath purged away
The old and wicked leaven;
Christ alone our souls will feed;
He is our meat and drink indeed;
Faith lives upon no other! Alleluia!

MARTIN LUTHER (1483–1546)
Translated by Richard Massie (1800–1887)

CHRIST THE LORD IS RISEN TODAY

This hymn was sung for the first time in a deserted iron foundry in London, England. That iron foundry, which became the first Wesleyan chapel, is known as the Foundry Meeting House.

Charles Wesley, who along with his brother John launched the Methodist movement, had just been converted a year earlier and was already writing hymns. This was one of his earliest, and it was written for the first service in that old iron foundry building.

Today this Resurrection hymn is regarded as one of the greatest and most beloved of the many hymns that Charles Wesley wrote. Yet his brother John wasn't convinced this hymn deserved to be preserved for posterity. When John was seventy-seven years old, he collected what he considered his brother's best hymns into a new Methodist hymnal, but this hymn was omitted. It wasn't until fifty years later that another editor found this great hymn and included it in a new Wesleyan hymnal. We say, "Alleluia!" for that unknown Methodist editor.

Scriptures: Luke 24:5-7; 1 Corinthians 15:20; Revelation 1:17-18
Themes: Eternal Life, Easter, Hope

Christ the Lord is risen today, Alleluia!
Sons of men and angels say, Alleluia!
Raise your joys and triumphs high, Alleluia!
Sing, ye heavens, and earth reply, Alleluia!

Lives again our glorious King, Alleluia!
Where, O death, is now thy sting? Alleluia!
Once He died, our souls to save, Alleluia!
Where's thy victory, boasting grave? Alleluia!

Love's redeeming work is done, Alleluia!
Fought the fight, the battle won, Alleluia!
Death in vain forbids Him rise, Alleluia!
Christ hath opened paradise, Alleluia!

Soar we now where Christ has led, Alleluia!
Following our exalted Head, Alleluia!
Made like Him, like Him we rise, Alleluia!
Ours the cross, the grave, the skies, Alleluia!

CHARLES WESLEY (1707–1788), AND OTHERS

HAIL THE DAY THAT SEES HIM RISE

Within a year of his conversion in 1738, Charles Wesley wrote three great hymns to celebrate special days of the church: "Hark! the Herald Angels Sing" for Christmas, "Christ the Lord Is Risen Today" for Easter, and "Hail the Day That Sees Him Rise" for Ascension Day.

Charles Wesley is well-known, but Martin Madan, who had a role in Wesley's hymns, has almost been forgotten. The fearless evangelism of Charles Wesley and his brother John, the founders of the Methodist church, attracted many. Madan was one of these who was converted through the preaching of the Wesleys and later became a preacher himself. He also became interested in music, and although he left no song that we now sing, he edited many of Charles Wesley's hymns for inclusion in his hymnal. Madan liked to insert *alleluias* into hymns, and it was probably he who put them into both this hymn and "Christ the Lord Is Risen Today."

Scriptures: Luke 24:50-53; Acts 1:9-11; Ephesians 4:8
Themes: Ascension, Resurrection, Victory

Hail the day that sees Him rise, Alleluia!
To His throne above the skies; Alleluia!
Christ, the Lamb for sinners giv'n, Alleluia!
Enters now the highest heav'n. Alleluia!

There for Him high triumph waits; Alleluia!
Lift your heads, eternal gates, Alleluia!
He hath conquered death and sin, Alleluia!
Take the King of glory in! Alleluia!

See, He lifts His hands above! Alleluia!
See, He shows the prints of love! Alleluia!

Hark! His gracious lips bestow, Alleluia!
Blessings on His church below. Alleluia!

Lord, beyond our mortal sight, Alleluia!
Raise our hearts to reach Thy height, Alleluia!
There Thy face unclouded see, Alleluia!
Find our heav'n of heav'ns in Thee! Alleluia!

CHARLES WESLEY (1707–1788)

HE LIVES

By training, Alfred Ackley was a cellist who had studied at the Royal Academy of Music in London. But he was also a minister of the gospel, serving Presbyterian churches in Pennsylvania and California.

The gospel song "He Lives" was written after a question was posed to Ackley by a young Jewish student: Why should I worship a dead Jew?

Ackley answered quickly, "He lives! I tell you he is not dead, but lives here and now! Jesus Christ is more alive today than ever before. I can prove it by my own experience, as well as the testimony of countless thousands."

Ackley talked to the man further and then went home to reread the Resurrection stories of the Gospels. As he read, the words "He is risen" struck him with new meaning. Then, from the combination of the scriptural evidence, his own heart, and the experience of the innumerable cloud of witnesses, he sat down at the piano and wrote the song. He once said, "The thought of his ever-living presence brought the music promptly and easily."

Scriptures: Matthew 28:6; Philippians 3:10; Revelation 1:18
Themes: Resurrection of Christ, Hope, Joy

I serve a risen Savior, He's in the world today;
I know that He is living, whatever men may say;
I see His hand of mercy, I hear His voice of cheer,
And just the time I need Him He's always near.

He lives, He lives, Christ Jesus lives today!
He walks with me and talks with me along life's narrow way.
He lives, He lives, salvation to impart!
You ask me how I know He lives? He lives within my heart.

In all the world around me I see His loving care,
And tho' my heart grows weary I never will despair,

I know that He is leading thru all the stormy blast;
The day of His appearing will come at last.

Rejoice, rejoice O Christian, lift up your voice and sing
Eternal hallelujahs to Jesus Christ the King!
The hope of all who seek Him, the help of all who find,
None other is so loving, so good and kind.

HE'S ALIVE

Son of a seminary professor, raised in Sunday school and singing in the church choirs, Don Francisco seemed to have had a good start in life. But when he was fourteen, he started experimenting—with things such as philosophy, psychology, and drugs. Walking the streets of Los Angeles and San Francisco, he got an education in the ways of the world. He started singing in nightclubs, doing yoga, and practicing meditation. Don Francisco was looking for something, but he couldn't find it.

Eastern philosophy wasn't satisfying to him, and he didn't know where to turn. He says, "I heard the Lord speak to me in an almost audible voice saying, 'I am Jesus, and I am alive in your heart. Read my Word and do it.' "

"I am Jesus, and I am alive." These remarkable words caused a remarkable change in Don Francisco's life. He dedicated himself to the Lord and to Christian music. Within two years his first Christian album was released.

"He's Alive" is the story of the apostle Peter as he experienced that first Resurrection morning. But it is also Don Francisco's story as he heard Jesus say to him, "I am Jesus, and I am alive."

Scriptures: Mark 16:7; John 11:25-26; John 20:1-10

Themes: Resurrection of Christ, Crucifixion, Deity of Christ

He's alive! He's alive, He's alive and I'm forgiven;
Heaven's gates are open wide.
He's alive, He's alive, oh He's alive and I'm forgiven;
Heaven's gates are open wide
He's alive, He's alive, Hallelujah, He's alive.

I KNOW THAT MY REDEEMER LIVES

Every once in a while, a verse jumps out of the Old Testament and takes on a new meaning. Job lost his fortune, family, and much of his health. In a stunning display of faith, he expresses his only remaining hope: "I know that my Redeemer lives, and he will stand upon the earth at last" (Job 19:25). The words find an uncanny fulfillment in Jesus.

Jesus gave his life to redeem us, to buy us back from our slavery to sin. His death was the price for our freedom. But that's not the bottom line, thank God. As the sun rises on Easter morning, we can say with Job, "I know that my Redeemer lives." He lives! Death could not hold him. He lives, to finish salvation's work in me.

Hymnwriter Samuel Medley had been a midshipman in the British Royal Navy and was converted after reading a sermon by Isaac Watts. In his hymns Medley often repeated words and phrases. Here, what's repeated is the most important concept: "He lives. . . . He lives. . . . He lives."

Scriptures: Job 19:25-27; Acts 2:32; 1 Corinthians 15:20-22
Themes: Resurrection, Easter, Praise

I know that my Redeemer lives:
What joy the blest assurance gives!
He lives, He lives, who once was dead;
He lives, my everlasting Head!

He lives to bless me with His love;
He lives to plead for me above;
He lives my hungry soul to feed;
He lives to help in time of need.

He lives and grants me daily breath;
He lives and I shall conquer death;
He lives my mansion to prepare;
He lives to bring me safely there.

He lives, all glory to His name;
He lives, my Savior, still the same;
What joy the blest assurance gives:
I know that my Redeemer lives!

SAMUEL MEDLEY (1738–1799)

JESUS CHRIST IS RISEN TODAY

You might confuse this hymn with Charles Wesley's "Christ the Lord Is Risen Today"—the theme is the same, the structure is similar, and Wesley also had a hand in this hymn. But this hymn is based on a medieval Latin text.

Alleluia is the perfect word for Easter Sunday. It simply means "Praise the Lord." It is used throughout Scripture (especially in Psalms and Revelation) to glorify God for the mighty acts he has done. And what mightier act is there than this: the resurrection of Christ from the dead.

Interestingly, this hymn speaks more about Christ's death than his new life. Both are vital aspects of God's redeeming work. Christ endured the cross *and* rose from the dead. His death and resurrection are inseparable, and hymn singers exult in all of it. Alleluia!

Scriptures: Acts 2:32; 1 Peter 3:18; Revelation 1:17-18
Themes: Resurrection, Praise, Easter

Jesus Christ is risen today, Alleluia!
Our triumphant holy day, Alleluia!
Who did once, upon the cross, Alleluia!
Suffer to redeem our loss. Alleluia!

Hymns of praise then let us sing, Alleluia!
Unto Christ, our heavenly King, Alleluia!
Who endured the cross and grave, Alleluia!
Sinners to redeem and save. Alleluia!

Sing we to our God above, Alleluia!
Praise eternal as His love, Alleluia!
Praise Him, all ye heavenly host, Alleluia!
Father, Son, and Holy Ghost. Alleluia!

LATIN HYMN (14TH CENTURY)
Translated in Lyra Davidica, *1708*
Stanza 2 from John Arnold's Compleat Psalmodist, *1749*
Stanza 3 by Charles Wesley (1707–1788)

JESUS LIVES, AND SO SHALL I

Two of the finest minds in eighteenth-century Germany were greatly influenced by the same poetry teacher at the University of Leipzig. The young students were Johann Goethe, who became one of Germany's greatest writers, and Gotthold Lessing, who achieved fame as both a dramatist and a literary critic. The poetry teacher was Christian Gellert. Gellert had wanted to become a minister like his father, but his poor health made that impossible. Instead he became an instructor in poetry at the university, and in that position he was greatly loved by his students.

When Gellert was forty-two years old, he published this poem, which really is the Christian's hope. In the upper room, Jesus promised his disciples, "Because I live, you also will live" (John 14:19, NIV).

Without Christ, human life is merely prolonged dying. Everything decays. But Jesus gives us eternal life, and that radically changes our life on earth. Not only do we have eternity to look forward to, but we have the power to live in right relationship with God and others now in our daily lives.

Scriptures: John 14:19; Acts 2:24; 1 Corinthians 15:17-19, 51-55
Themes: Resurrection, Death

Jesus lives, and so shall I:
Death, thy sting is gone forever!
He for me hath deigned to die,
Lives the bands of death to sever.
He shall raise me from the dust:
Jesus is my hope and trust.

Jesus lives and reigns supreme:
And, His kingdom still remaining,
I shall also be with Him,
Ever living, ever reigning.
God has promised—be it must:
Jesus is my hope and trust.

Jesus lives—and by His grace,
Vict'ry o'er my passions giving,
I will change my heart and ways,
Ever to His glory living.
Me He raises from the dust:
Jesus is my hope and trust.

Jesus lives—I know full well
Naught from Him my heart can sever,
Life nor death nor pow'rs of hell,
Joy nor grief, henceforth forever.
None of all His saints is lost:
Jesus is my hope and trust.

Jesus lives—and death is now
But my entrance into glory;
Courage, then, my soul, for thou
Hast a crown of life before thee.
Thou shalt find thy hopes were just:
Jesus is my hope and trust.

CHRISTIAN FURCHTEGOTT GELLERT (1715–1769)
Translated by Philip Schaff (1819–1893)

RISE AGAIN

David Wilkerson, of *The Cross and the Switchblade* fame, had asked twenty-two-year-old Dallas Holm to be the soloist and song leader in his youth crusade ministry. Before long, they felt a praise band should be started too.

Dallas realized he had a challenge: He needed new material. He told himself, "I need to get busy and write some songs." For a while his mind was blank—he couldn't come up with anything. Then he prayed, and part of his prayer was, "Lord, if You were singing, what would You sing?"

Usually songs are written about Jesus or addressed to Jesus, but Dallas Holm, as crazy as it sounds, imagined Jesus on a street corner, playing a guitar and singing. What would he be singing about? Then the song came to Dallas. He says, "God wrote the song, and I just delivered the message."

Scriptures: Matthew 28:5-10; Mark 15:22-32; Acts 2:22-24
Themes: Resurrection of Christ, Joy, Worship

Go ahead, drive the nails in my hands;
Laugh at me where you stand:
Go ahead, and say it isn't me
The day will come when you will see!

'Cause I'll—rise again;
Ain't no pow'r on earth can tie me down;
Yes, I'll rise again.

Go ahead, and mock my name;
My love for you is still the same;
Go ahead and bury me;
But very soon I will be free!

Go ahead and say I'm dead and gone,
But you will see that you were wrong.
Go ahead, try to hide the Son,
But all will know that I'm the One!

'Cause I'll come again;
Ain't no pow'r can keep me back;
Yes, I'll come again.

Dallas Holm

THE DAY OF RESURRECTION

This no doubt is one of the oldest hymns in church hymnals. Not too much is known about exactly when in the life of John of Damascus this hymn was written. But it is said that John of Damascus started his hymnwriting with a funeral hymn for a fellow monk. The monk wasn't dead yet, but everyone, including John, thought death was near. So John prepared his song and was singing it loudly in his room, testing it out. Suddenly the monk for whom it was written burst into the room and scolded John for raising such a racket. Tradition says that John was expelled from the monastery for causing this disturbance, but the Lord told the abbot in charge that John would be doing great things with music, so the abbot welcomed John back.

And John did do great things, collecting, writing, and organizing the great hymns of the Greek-speaking church. This hymn is taken from an Easter liturgy still used in the Greek Orthodox Church.

Scriptures: Luke 24:46-49; Acts 2:24; 1 Corinthians 15:56-57
Themes: Resurrection, Joy, Victory

The day of resurrection!
Earth, tell it out abroad;
The passover of gladness,
The passover of God.
From death to life eternal,

From earth unto the sky,
Our Christ hath brought us over
With hymns of victory.

Our hearts be pure from evil,
That we may see aright
The Lord in rays eternal
Of resurrection light;
And listening to His accents,
May hear, so calm and plain,
His own "All hail!" and, hearing,
May raise the victor strain.

Now let the heavens be joyful!
Let earth her song begin!
Let the round world keep triumph,
And all that is therein!
Let all things seen and unseen
Their notes in gladness blend,
For Christ the Lord hath risen,
Our joy that hath no end.

JOHN OF DAMASCUS (8TH CENTURY)
Translated by John Mason Neale (1818–1866)

THE STRIFE IS O'ER

Note the pattern of this hymn: Each stanza makes three statements followed by *Alleluia*. The first statement shows how the forces of evil tried to conquer Christ but were beaten. The second gives us a positive expression of what has occurred. Christ wins, he rises, and he opens heaven and frees slaves. The third shows how we respond with songs and shouts of joy: Alleluia!

The richness of the text is matched by the majesty of the music, written by the sixteenth-century composer Giovanni de Palestrina. He was a devout Roman Catholic who created many wonderful sacred works still used in churches and secular settings.

The Bible describes the work of Christ in many different ways, and Christian writers through the ages have elaborated on all these ideas. God exercised his power on our behalf when he raised Christ from the dead. Death has no ultimate power over us because we are risen with Christ. Alleluia!

Scriptures: Acts 2:22-24; 1 Corinthians 15:55-57; Revelation 19:1-2
Themes: Resurrection, Victory, Easter

The strife is o'er—the battle done,
The victory of life is won;
The song of triumph has begun:
Alleluia!

The pow'rs of death have done their worst,
But Christ their legions hath dispersed;
Let shouts of holy joy outburst:
Alleluia!

The three sad days have quickly sped,
He rises glorious from the dead;
All glory to our risen Head!
Alleluia!

He closed the yawning gates of hell,
The bars from heav'n's high portals fell;
Let hymns of praise His triumphs tell:
Alleluia!

Lord, by the stripes which wounded Thee,
From death's dread sting Thy servants free,
That we may live and sing to Thee:
Alleluia!

LATIN HYMN
Symphonia Serenum Selectarum, 1695
Translated by Francis Pott (1832–1909)

VICTORY IN JESUS

Eugene M. Bartlett is a legendary name in southern gospel circles. Born in 1885, he taught in singing schools throughout the South and founded the Hartford Music Company in 1918. He brought gospel music into churches large and small.

In 1939, when he was fifty-four, Bartlett had a serious stroke. Partially paralyzed, he was virtually confined to a bedroom. No more could he travel and encourage churches in their singing. No more could he teach students, as he loved to do.

But he could still study the Bible. Writing was laborious; he struggled to put words down on paper and to put notes down on a score. But that's the way he wrote his last song, "Victory in Jesus," a song filled not only with hope and cheer, but also with solid theology gleaned from his Bible study.

Scriptures: John 15:16; Romans 5:8; 1 Corinthians 15:57; 1 John 5:4
Themes: Victory, Hope, Salvation

I heard an old, old story, how a Savior came from glory,
How He gave His life on Calvary to save a wretch like me;
I heard about His groaning, of His precious blood's atoning,
Then I repented of my sins and won the victory.

O victory in Jesus, my Savior, forever,
He sought me and bo't me with His redeeming blood,
He loved me ere I knew Him, and all my love is due Him,
He plunged me to victory beneath the cleansing flood.

I heard about His healing, of His cleansing pow'r revealing,
How He made the lame to walk again and caused the blind to see;
And then I cried, "Dear Jesus, come and heal my broken spirit,"
And somehow Jesus came and bro't to me the victory.

I heard about a mansion He has built for me in glory,
And I heard about the streets of gold beyond the crystal sea;
About the angels singing, and the old redemption story,
And some sweet day I'll sing up there the song of victory.

EUGENE M. BARTLETT (1885–1941)

PART XXI

SALVATION

God saved you by his grace when you believed.

And you can't take credit for this; it is a gift from God.

Salvation is not a reward for the good things

we have done, so none of us can boast.

EPHESIANS 2:8-9

A CHILD OF THE KING

When Harriett Buell walked home from her Methodist church in Manlius, New York, one Sunday morning, she was still thinking about her pastor's sermon. In the afternoon she wrote down all four stanzas of "A Child of the King." She wanted to share the blessing that she had received, so she sent the poem to her denominational magazine. A few months later, her poem was published, and Harriett thought that was the end of it.

But without her knowledge, a music teacher saw the poem in the magazine and wrote music for it, and soon Harriett's song was being sung all around the country.

When Harriett wrote the song, it was entitled, "The Child of a King." But more recently, in order to put more emphasis on the greatness of our King and the fact that he has many children, the title has been changed to "A Child of the King."

Scriptures: Psalm 50:10-11; Romans 8:16-17; 1 Corinthians 2:9; 1 John 3:2
Themes: Assurance, Trust, Christian Living

My Father is rich in houses and lands;
He holdeth the wealth of the world in His hands!
Of rubies and diamonds, of silver and gold,
His coffers are full—He has riches untold.

I'm a child of the King!
A child of the King!
With Jesus my Savior,
I'm a child of the King!

My Father's own Son, the Savior of men,
Once wandered o'er earth as the poorest of them:
But now He is reigning forever on high,
And will give me a home in heav'n by and by.

I once was an outcast stranger on earth,
A sinner by choice and an alien by birth;
But I've been adopted; my name's written down—
An heir to a mansion, a robe, and a crown.

A tent or a cottage, why should I care?
They're building a palace for me over there!
Who exiled from home, yet still I may sing;
All glory to God, I'm a child of the King.

HARRIETT E. BUELL (1834–1910)

AMAZING GRACE

The tombstone of John Newton, the author of this hymn, tells his story: "John Newton, clerk, once an infidel and libertine, a servant of slavers in Africa, was, by the rich mercy of our Lord and Savior Jesus Christ, preserved, restored, pardoned, and appointed to preach the faith he had so long labored to destroy." Those words were written by John Newton himself, and they are a testimony to God's transforming power.

After years as a hardened slave trader, Newton met Jesus Christ, and his life was dramatically turned around. Throughout his years of ministry, God's amazing grace remained central to his thinking. When it was suggested he retire at the age of eighty-two due to poor health and a failing memory, he responded, "My memory is nearly gone, but I remember two things: that I am a great sinner, and that Christ is a great Savior."

Scriptures: John 1:16-17; Romans 5:20-21; Ephesians 2:6-9
Themes: Grace, Salvation, Conversion

Amazing grace! how sweet the sound—
That saved a wretch like me!
I once was lost but now am found,
Was blind but now I see.

'Twas grace that taught my heart to fear,
And grace my fears relieved;
How precious did that grace appear
The hour I first believed!

The Lord has promised good to me,
His word my hope secures;
He will my shield and portion be
As long as life endures.

Through many dangers, toils and snares
I have already come;
'Tis grace hath brought me safe thus far,
And grace will lead me home.

When we've been there ten thousand years,
Bright shining as the sun,
We've no less days to sing God's praise
Than when we'd first begun.

JOHN NEWTON (1725–1807)
Stanza 5 by John P. Rees (1828–1900)

BELIEVE ON THE LORD JESUS CHRIST

Harry Clarke had overcome a lot in his life. Born in Wales, he was an orphan from his early years, and he struggled to survive as a teenager. He finally got to America, where he was converted. Salvation, he discovered, wasn't really complicated at all. It was quite simple, and he wanted to tell the world about it. So one of the first things he did after his conversion was write a simple chorus. He was not a great poet, but he could recognize a good tune and could put some words to it.

Clarke sent a music publisher a tune and a chorus for a song called "Believe on the Lord Jesus Christ." The publisher wanted more; a few stanzas to go with the chorus. Harry Clarke couldn't give them more, so the publisher sent Clarke's chorus to Avis Christiansen, a poet, to supply the verses.

Clarke's chorus gives the apostle Paul's answer on how to be saved. Avis Christiansen's verses give the question.

Scriptures: Acts 16:31; Romans 10:9-10; Ephesians 2:8-9
Themes: Conversion, Salvation, Decision

"What must I do?" the trembling jailor cried,
When dazed by fear and wonder;
"Believe on Christ!" was all that Paul replied,
"And thou shalt be saved from sin."

Believe on the Lord Jesus Christ,
Believe on the Lord Jesus Christ,
Believe on the Lord Jesus Christ,
And thou shalt be saved!

What must I do! O weary, trembling soul,
Just turn today to Jesus;
He will receive, forgive and make thee whole—
Christ alone can set thee free.

His blood is all thy plea for saving grace,
The precious fount of cleansing!
O come, accept His love, behold His face,
And be saved forevermore.

HARRY D. CLARKE (1888–1957) AND AVIS B. CHRISTIANSEN (1895–1985)

FREE FROM THE LAW

Mrs. Philip Bliss had probably given her songwriter husband the usual Christmas presents in previous years, but she had no ideas for Christmas 1871. So she asked a friend, "What shall I give my husband for a Christmas present?"

The friend made a strange suggestion—at least it may seem strange to us today. She suggested a bound volume of a British magazine called *Things New and Old*. So that's what Mrs. Bliss got for her husband that Christmas.

After he received the magazine and began reading it, Philip Bliss noticed an article that related Romans 8, which says there is no condemnation for those who are in Christ Jesus, to Hebrews 10, which says we are redeemed "once for all." That was all he needed to get started on a new gospel song

A year later, evangelist Dwight L. Moody was using the song in his first visit to Scotland. Because the hymn was so scriptural and in perfect agreement with Scottish Reformed teaching, it paved the way for Moody's evangelistic messages.

Scriptures: Romans 5:15; Romans 8:1; Hebrews 10:10
Themes: Law, Grace, Salvation

Free from the law, O happy condition,
Jesus hath bled, and there is remission;
Cursed by the law and bruised by the fall,
Grace hath redeemed us once for all.

Once for all, O sinner, receive it,
Once for all, O brother, believe it;
Cling to the Cross, the burden will fall,
Christ hath redeemed us once for all.

Now are we free—there's no condemnation,
Jesus provides a perfect salvation;
"Come unto Me," O hear His sweet call,
Come, and He saves us once for all.

"Children of God," O glorious calling,
Surely His grace will keep us from falling;
Passing from death to life at His call,
Blessed salvation once for all.

PHILIP PAUL BLISS (1838–1876)

GRACE! 'TIS A CHARMING SOUND

Grace led Philip Doddridge to take some surprising steps in his life. He was a gifted student, but he turned down a scholarship to train for the ministry in the Church of England. He chose instead to side with the Dissenters, the nonconformists who emphasized personal commitment to Christ over institutional loyalty. He went to a Dissenter college, trusting God to provide "new supplies each hour." Later he pastored a Congregational church.

He wrote about 370 hymns in his lifetime, never seeing any of them published. Friends would copy them and use them in their churches, but the hymns were not formally produced until four years after Doddridge's death.

Grace sometimes works like that too. In his goodness, God may grant us anonymity. He may delay the rewards of public acclaim until after we die. He may delay other rewards as well. This hymn conveys the author's strong awareness of heaven—the place where God's grace is most at home. On earth, grace is the faint underscoring of our lives. In heaven, it echoes through the halls!

Scriptures: Ephesians 2:8-10; Hebrews 4:16; 1 Peter 5:10
Themes: Grace, Salvation, Hope

Grace! 'tis a charming sound,
Harmonious to the ear;
Heaven with the echo shall resound,
And all the earth shall hear.

Grace first contrived the way
To save rebellious man;
And all the steps that grace display
Which drew the wondrous plan.

Grace led my roving feet
To tread the heavenly road;
And new supplies each hour I meet,
While pressing on to God.

Grace all the work shall crown,
Through everlasting days;
It lays in heaven the topmost stone,
And well deserves the praise.

PHILIP DODDRIDGE (1702–1751)

HE LIFTED ME

Charles Gabriel, the writer of this gospel song, was the most popular gospel-song composer in the Billy Sunday evangelistic era. An Iowa farm boy, he taught himself to play the family's reed organ. Soon he began composing gospel songs, but he would have been surprised how far his gospel songs would go.

On a chilly Thursday afternoon in London, the scholarly editor of the Church of England newspaper was asked to preach in a poorer section of London at the anniversary of an old church. The church had once catered to a large middle-class congregation, but now the neighborhood had changed for the worse. On a Thursday afternoon, the Anglican clergyman didn't expect too many people to be there. Instead, the church was packed with five hundred people.

The preaching service came first, then there was tea, and then there was an informal meeting with lots of singing. The highlight was the singing of "He Lifted Me." The song leader asked various groups to sing a stanza, beginning with the youth and then the women, followed by the men. The editor, who had never heard the song before, was overwhelmed. It wasn't just the boisterous volume; it was also the expressions on their faces as they sang: "And from the depths of sin and shame / Thro' grace He lifted me." Later he wrote, "I saw the glow in their faces and heard the passion of their voices, and I felt, 'Here is the true Christian apologetic.'"

Scriptures: Psalm 40:2-3; Isaiah 61:10; 2 Corinthians 5:17
Themes: Salvation, Crisis, Conversion

In loving-kindness Jesus came
My soul in mercy to reclaim,
And from the depths of sin and shame
Thro' grace He lifted me . . .

From sinking sand He lifted me,
With tender hand He lifted me,
From shades of night to plains of light,
Oh, praise His name, He lifted me!

He called me long before I heard,
Before my sinful heart was stirred,
But when I took Him at His word,
Forgiv'n He lifted me . . .

His brow was pierced with many a thorn,
His hands by cruel nails were torn,
When from my guilt and grief, forlorn,
In love He lifted me . . .

Now on a higher plane I dwell,
And with my soul I know 'tis well;
Yet how or why, I cannot tell,
He should have lifted me . . .

CHARLES HUTCHINSON GABRIEL (1856–1932)

LET THY BLOOD IN MERCY POURED

When we come to Christ, a transaction takes place, and this hymn beautifully captures that transaction. We receive Jesus, and Jesus receives us.

In a way, each time we come to worship, we review this transaction. In the worship service we hear again of the amazing sacrifice of Christ. We hear how he gave up his heavenly glory to become a man. We hear how he loved us enough to die for us. We hear of the power of his resurrection and the Spirit who now lives in us, empowering us each day. We hear of the promise of eternal life.

But we should also be renewing our vows to the Lord. We should take every opportunity—our songs, our offerings, our words to others, our attentive listening, our standing, our sitting, our kneeling, or our proceeding—to remind ourselves that we belong to the Lord and will live for him. We are not our own; we were bought with a price—the precious blood of Jesus.

Scriptures: Romans 5:6-8; 1 Corinthians 6:19-20; 1 Peter 1:18-19
Themes: Cross, Consecration, Love

Let Thy blood in mercy poured,
Let Thy gracious body broken,
Be to me, O gracious Lord,
Of boundless love the token.

Thou didst give Thyself for me,
Now I give myself to Thee.

Thou didst die that I might live;
Blessed Lord, Thou cam'st to save me;
All that love of God could give,
Jesus by His sorrows gave me.

By the thorns that crowned Thy brow,
By the spear wound and the nailing,
By the pain and death, I now
Claim, O Christ, Thy love unfailing.

Wilt Thou own the gift I bring?
All my penitence I give Thee;
Thou art my exalted King,
Of Thy matchless love forgive me.

GREEK HYMN (6TH–9TH CENTURY?)
Translated by John Brownlie (1859–1925)

MY FAITH HAS FOUND A RESTING PLACE

The pioneering radio preacher Donald Grey Barnhouse used to ask, "When you get to the pearly gates and God asks, 'What right do you have to come into my Heaven?' what will you say?" This song is an answer to that question.

Some might flash their church membership cards or dangle their perfect-attendance Sunday school pins before the Master. Some might spout the theology they have learned or present their résumés packed with good deeds. "You should let me in because I would be an asset to your community. I would sing alto in your choir, and I could help out with the youth group."

But God does not run heaven like a country club or a successful corporation. We cannot get in on our own qualifications. The door is barred to all who try to earn their entry. But it swings wide open for the simple saint who affirms in faith, "I need no other argument, / I need no other plea; It is enough that Jesus died, / And that He died for me."

Scriptures: John 6:37-39; Titus 3:4-7; 1 John 5:13
Themes: Faith, Assurance, Trust

My faith has found a resting place—
Not in device or creed:
I trust the Ever-Living One—
His wounds for me shall plead.

I need no other argument,
I need no other plea;
It is enough that Jesus died,
And that He died for me.

Enough for me that Jesus saves—
This ends my fear and doubt;
A sinful soul I come to Him—
He'll never cast me out.

My heart is leaning on the Word—
The written Word of God:
Salvation by my Savior's name—
Salvation through His blood.

My great Physician heals the sick—
The lost He came to save;
For me His precious blood He shed—
For me His life He gave.

ELIZA EDMUNDS HEWITT (1851–1920)

MY SINS ARE BLOTTED OUT, I KNOW

Merrill Dunlop, who had recently graduated from Moody Bible Institute in Chicago, was crossing the Atlantic on a liner called *The Leviathan* when the idea for this gospel song, "My Sins Are Blotted Out, I Know," came to him. He says he was reading the verse in Micah 7 that says God tramples our sins under his feet and throws them into the depths of the ocean. Then Dunlop looked around at the dimensions of the sea, and, he says, "I meditated upon it and what the Bible says about our sins—buried in those depths—removed—blotted out. Then, making it personal, I said, 'My sins are blotted out, I know.' The melody came almost simultaneously with the words." He jotted down the chorus as he walked the deck.

Dunlop went on to become a noted pianist, organist, and composer of gospel songs, but this song, perhaps his first, was his personal testimony.

Scriptures: Isaiah 44:22; Micah 7:18-19; Acts 3:19
Themes: Forgiveness, Atonement, Salvation

What a wondrous message in God's Word!
My sins are blotted out, I know!
If I trust in His redeeming blood,
My sins are blotted out, I know!

My sins are blotted out, I know!
My sins are blotted out, I know!

They are buried in the depths of the deepest sea;
My sins are blotted out, I know!

Once my heart was black but now, what joy,
My sins are blotted out, I know!
I have peace that nothing can destroy,
My sins are blotted out, I know!

I shall stand some day before my King,
My sins all blotted out, I know!
With the ransomed host I then shall sing:
"My sins are blotted out, I know!"

MERRILL DUNLOP
© 1927 New Spring (ASCAP)
All rights reserved. Used by permission.

NOR SILVER NOR GOLD

When James M. Gray wrote a song, he made sure there was good theology behind it. And for good reason—Gray was a theologian. He taught Bible at Moody Bible Institute in Chicago even before it became Moody Bible Institute. He became dean there and later the president. He was also one of the original editors of the *Scofield Reference Bible.*

This gospel song is based on 1 Peter 1:18-19, which in the King James Version says, "Ye were not redeemed with corruptible things, as silver and gold, . . . but with the precious blood of Christ." Kidnapped, but now redeemed.

Scriptures: Romans 6:23; Titus 3:5-6; 1 Peter 1:18-19
Themes: Salvation, Conversion, Death of Christ

Nor silver nor gold hath obtained my redemption,
Nor riches of earth could have saved my poor soul;
The blood of the cross is my only foundation,
The death of my Savior now maketh me whole.

I am redeemed, but not with silver; I am bought, but not with gold;
Bought with a price, the blood of Jesus, precious price of love untold.

Nor silver nor gold hath obtained my redemption,
The guilt on my conscience too heavy had grown;
The blood of the cross is my only foundation,
The death of my Savior could only atone.

Nor silver nor gold hath obtained my redemption,
The holy commandment forbade me draw near;
The blood of the cross is my only foundation,
The death of my Savior removeth my fear.

Nor silver nor gold hath obtained my redemption,
The way into heaven could not thus be bought;
The blood of the cross is my only foundation,
The death of my Savior redemption hath wrought.

JAMES MARTIN GRAY (1851–1935)

NOT WHAT THESE HANDS HAVE DONE

When Horatius Bonar was called to lead the great Chambers Memorial Church in Edinburgh, people wondered if he would change his style. But he didn't. A visitor to his church once wrote, "His voice was low, quiet, and unimpressive. Once he paused and addressed the Sunday school children who sat by themselves on one side of the pulpit. He is just like his hymns—not great, but tender, sweet, and tranquil."

This is one of those hymns. No doubt it was inspired by the words of Paul to Titus: "He saved us, not because of the righteous things we had done, but because of his mercy" (Titus 3:5). Paul wrote to the Ephesians, "Salvation is not a reward for the good things we have done, so none of us can boast" (Ephesians 2:9). A hard worker like Bonar might have been tempted to think his deeds were worth something to God, but he knew better. He knew that God wants us to come to him humbly, as little children, trusting completely in what he has accomplished through Jesus Christ.

Scriptures: Isaiah 64:6; Ephesians 2:4-7; Titus 3:5
Themes: Salvation, Grace, Peace

Not what these hands have done
Can save this guilty soul;
Not what this toiling flesh has borne
Can make my spirit whole.

Not what I feel or do
Can give me peace with God;
Not all my prayers and sighs and tears
Can bear my awful load.

Thy work alone, O Christ,
Can ease this weight of sin;
Thy blood alone, O Lamb of God,
Can give me peace within.

Thy grace alone, O God,
To me can pardon speak;
Thy power alone, O Son of God,
Can this sore bondage break.

I bless the Christ of God,
I rest on love divine,
And with unfaltering lip and heart,
I call this Savior mine.

HORATIUS BONAR (1808–1889)

NOTHING BUT THE BLOOD OF JESUS

Robert Lowry, who wrote this hymn, wore many hats. He was a professor of literature at Bucknell University for a while, and he served as pastor of churches in Pennsylvania, New Jersey, and New York. He liked to write music for gospel songs, and he worked with Fanny Crosby and others as a lyricist. Occasionally he would write both words and music as he did for the triumphant Easter hymn "Low in the Grave He Lay" and this one, "Nothing but the Blood of Jesus."

There's a simplicity about this tune. It has a five-note range, the basses have only two notes to sing, and the guitar players have just two basic chords. But Lowry might say that it is simple because salvation is simple. We try to complicate it, to add more chords and harmonies to it, but salvation is really "nothing but the blood of Jesus."

Scriptures: Matthew 26:28; Romans 5:9; Hebrews 9:22
Themes: Crucifixion, Sins, Salvation

What can wash away my sin?
Nothing but the blood of Jesus;
What can make me whole again?
Nothing but the blood of Jesus.

Oh! precious is the flow that makes me white as snow;
No other fount I know, nothing but the blood of Jesus.

For my pardon this I see—
Nothing but the blood of Jesus;
For my cleansing, this my plea—
Nothing but the blood of Jesus.

Nothing can for sin atone—
Nothing but the blood of Jesus;
Naught of good that I have done—
Nothing but the blood of Jesus.

This is all my hope and peace—
Nothing but the blood of Jesus;
This is all my righteousness—
Nothing but the blood of Jesus.

ROBERT LOWRY (1826–1899)

O HAPPY DAY

Few church songs have gone through such a variety of renditions as this one. Philip Doddridge would never have recognized the Hawkins' Youth Choir's African-American arrangement, which put the song on the charts in the late 1960s.

Doddridge went through a lot of changes himself. His mother was a Lutheran, but both his mother and his father died by the time he was thirteen. Orphaned, he went to live with a Presbyterian minister. Later he studied in an Anglican school but decided instead to become a Congregational minister.

Although he wrote many hymns, Doddridge was reluctant to have any of them published. So "O Happy Day" wasn't put into print until 1755, four years after his death. The refrain was not added until a hundred years later when an anonymous author added, "Happy day, happy day, when Jesus washed my sins away," and set it to a popular tune of the day.

We have a feeling that Doddridge wouldn't have minded, as long as the theology wasn't changed. " 'Tis done: the great transaction's done; I am my Lord's, and He is mine." That's enough to make all of us sing, "O happy day."

Scriptures: Psalm 40:16; Isaiah 61:10; Philippians 4:4
Themes: Testimony, Salvation, Joy

O happy day that fixed my choice on Thee, my Savior and my God!
Well may this glowing heart rejoice, and tell its raptures all abroad.

Happy day, happy day, when Jesus washed my sins away!
He taught me how to watch and pray and live rejoicing every day.
Happy day, happy day, when Jesus washed my sins away!

O happy bond, that seals my vows to Him who merits all my love!
Let cheerful anthems fill His house, While to that sacred shrine I move.

'Tis done: the great transaction's done; I am my Lord's, and He is mine;
He drew me and I followed on, charmed to confess the voice divine.

Now rest, my long-divided heart; fixed on this blissful center, rest;
Nor ever from my Lord depart, with Him of ev'ry good possessed.

PHILIP DODDRIDGE (1702–1751)

REDEEMED

Fanny Crosby didn't start writing hymns until she was forty, but she made up for lost time. Only a rare few have matched the number of Christian songs she's written. Blinded in infancy because of a doctor's error, Crosby demonstrates no bitterness in her songs. We find nothing but joy and longing for the Lord. "Redeemed and so happy in Jesus" is not just a line that sounds good in a hymn, it's the story of Crosby's life. Blinded to the light of this world, Fanny Crosby had a light shining in her soul.

Love is another major topic in Crosby's work. She regularly marvels at God's love: "His love is the theme of my song." Only as we come face to face with the overwhelming love of God can we begin to love others fully. As John says, "We love each other because he loved us first" (1 John 4:19). And Jesus said that the world would recognize his disciples by the love they had for one another.

Scriptures: Psalm 107:1-2; Ephesians 1:7; 1 Peter 1:18-21
Themes: Redemption, Love, Joy

Redeemed, how I love to proclaim it!
Redeemed by the blood of the Lamb;
Redeemed through His infinite mercy,
His child, and forever, I am.

Redeemed, redeemed,
Redeemed by the blood of the Lamb.
Redeemed, redeemed,
His child, and forever, I am.

Redeemed and so happy in Jesus,
No language my rapture can tell;
I know that the light of His presence
With me doth continually dwell.

I think of my blessed Redeemer,
I think of Him all the day long;
I sing, for I cannot be silent;
His love is the theme of my song.

I know I shall see in His beauty
The King in whose law I delight;
Who lovingly guardeth my footsteps,
And giveth me songs in the night.

FANNY JANE CROSBY (1820–1915)

SAVED, SAVED, SAVED

Oswald J. Smith, the author of this hymn, became one of the greatest missionary statesmen of the twentieth century. But when he was in his twenties, he seemed to be a failure at everything he touched.

He had resigned from his church in Toronto and felt his ministry was over. He had submitted some hymns to a music publisher in Chicago, but nothing seemed to be happening with them.

However, in 1919, a large evangelistic campaign came to Toronto, and Oswald Smith wanted to help out. He was out of work, so he had plenty of time on his hands. He volunteered to usher at the meetings but was turned down. He offered to do personal work with those who responded to the gospel invitation, but his offer was ignored. So he decided to sell hymnbooks in the aisles. *Maybe*, he thought, *God could use me that way.*

Then one night, when the auditorium was filled with 3,400 people, the song leader announced that they were going to sing a new hymn called "Saved." Smith couldn't believe it; he had written that song! The song leader pointed at him and said, "That young man down there wrote this hymn." As his hymn was sung, it seemed as though the voices would raise the roof. That night, God spoke to Smith again: "I knew he was not going to put me on the shelf."

Scriptures: Romans 10:13; Ephesians 2:8-9; Titus 3:5-6
Themes: Salvation, Atonement, Assurance

Saved! saved! saved! my sins are all forgiv'n;
Christ is mine! I'm on my way to heav'n;
Once a guilty sinner, lost, undone,
Now a child of God, saved thro' His Son.

Saved! I'm saved thro' Christ, my all in all;
Saved! I'm saved, whatever may befall;
He died upon the cross for me, He bore the awful penalty;
And now I'm saved eternally—I'm saved! saved! saved!

Saved! saved! saved! by grace and grace alone;
Oh, what wondrous love to me was shown,
In my stead Christ Jesus bled and died,
Bore my sins, for me was crucified.

Saved! saved! saved! oh, joy beyond compare!
Christ my life, and I His constant care;
Yielding all and trusting Him alone,
Living now each moment as His own.

OSWALD J. SMITH (1889–1986)

THY WORKS NOT MINE, O CHRIST

There is religion, and then there is faith. Religion is humanity reaching for God. Different religions in their different ways try to reach their god or gods. Rituals, lifestyles, and philosophies are all aimed at attaining the favor of deity.

Faith, by contrast, is merely taking the hand of God, who is reaching out to us. We enter into a relationship that is his doing, not ours. This is the Good News of Christianity. Some people take the elements of Christianity and try to make a religion out of them, but it is, pure and simple, a matter of faith—receiving what God has done.

That's why we need strong and simple songs like this one. Horatius Bonar, the greatest of the Scottish hymnwriters, emphasized correct doctrine in his hymns, but it was doctrine that throbbed with warmth and life. In this hymn he stresses that it was what Christ did—his works not ours, his pains not ours, his cross not ours, and his righteousness not ours—that has purchased our eternal salvation. So Bonar echoes a recurring strain in Scripture: "No righteousness avails / Save that which is of Thee."

Scriptures: 2 Corinthians 5:21; Ephesians 2:8; Titus 3:4-7
Themes: Cross, Righteousness, Atonement

Thy works, not mine, O Christ,
Speak gladness to this heart;
They tell me all is done;
They bid my fear depart.

To whom, save Thee, who canst alone
For sin atone, Lord, shall I flee?

Thy pains, not mine, O Christ,
Upon the shameful tree,
Have paid the law's full price
And purchased peace for me.

Thy cross, not mine, O Christ,
Has borne the awful load
Of sins that none in heav'n
Or earth could bear but God.

Thy righteousness, O Christ,
Alone can cover me:
No righteousness avails
Save that which is of Thee.

HORATIUS BONAR (1808–1889)

YE MUST BE BORN AGAIN

When George Stebbins heard a sermon on Christ's words to Nicodemus, "You must be born again" (John 3:7), he said that should be made into a gospel song. With just a little moving around, the words would fall into a rhythmical form, he thought. But Stebbins was a musician and not a songwriter, so he called on local pastor William Sleeper to help him. He told him his idea, and in a few days Sleeper came up with the text.

About ten years later, the superintendent of a boys' school was walking along a street in St. Joseph, Missouri. He saw a cluster of young men. At first, he was suspicious; clusters of young men often meant trouble. But as he got closer, he noticed they were singing. When he got closer yet, he understood the words: "Ye must be born again." He stopped and asked, "What does it mean to be born again?"

A young man explained and then invited him to a meeting inside a nearby building. The school superintendent says, "I accepted the invitation, and after the service, I acknowledged Christ as my Savior. Through the influence of that hymn, my soul was awakened."

Scriptures: John 3:3; 2 Corinthians 5:17; 1 Peter 1:23
Themes: Salvation, Conversion, Invitation

A ruler once came to Jesus by night,
To ask Him the way of salvation and light;
The Master made answer in words true and plain,
"Ye must be born again."

"Ye must be born again,
Ye must be born again;
I verily, verily, say unto thee,
Ye must be born again."

Ye children of men, attend to the word
So solemnly uttered by Jesus the Lord;
And let not this message to you be in vain,
"Ye must be born again."

Oh, ye who would enter that glorious rest,
And sing with the ransomed the song of the blest;
The life everlasting if ye would obtain,
"Ye must be born again."

A dear one in heaven thy heart yearns to see,
At the beautiful gate may be watching for thee;
Then list to the note of this solemn refrain,
"Ye must be born again."

WILLIAM TRUE SLEEPER (1819–1904)

PART XXII

TESTIMONY

"I know this: I was blind, and now I can see!"

JOHN 9:25

ALL MY LIFE LONG (SATISFIED)

George Beverly Shea, who has been associated with evangelist Billy Graham for many years, tells this story from when he was eight years old. As he and his father were walking in the small college town of Houghton, New York, his father pointed out a tall, elderly lady. "She writes hymns," his father said.

When the boy got home, he told his mother about meeting Clara Tear Williams and the fact that "she writes hymns." His mother smiled and went to the piano. Then she found a hymnal with one of Clara Tear Williams's hymns. It was "All My Life Long."

Shea never forgot that day. When he became a teenager and began to sing solos, this was one of the first solos he sang. He continued to sing it often through the years, because as he says, the hymn addresses a person's fundamental needs—a need for security, a need to be loved, and a need to find identity.

Scriptures: Psalm 107:9; John 6:35; John 7:37
Themes: Salvation, Holiness, Joy, Satisfaction

All my life long I had panted for a drink, from some clear spring,
That I hoped would quench the burning of the thirst I felt within.

Hallelujah! I have found Him Who my soul so long has craved!
Jesus satisfies my longings—thru His blood I now am saved!

Feeding on the husks around me, till my strength was almost gone,
Longed my soul for something better, only still to hunger on.

Well of water ever springing, bread of life so rich and free,
Untold wealth that never faileth, my Redeemer is to me.

CLARA TEAR WILLIAMS (1858–1937)

ASHAMED OF JESUS

It is hard to imagine that this hymn was written by Joseph Grigg when he was only ten years old. His parents were poor, and he grew up to be a mechanic. Later Grigg became an assistant pastor of a Presbyterian church. When he died at age forty, an elegy that called him "the friend of the poor, the charm of the social circle, and the attractive and useful preacher" was written for him.

When he was ten years old, Grigg heard a sermon on Mark 8:38, where Jesus said, "Whosoever therefore shall be ashamed of me and of my words . . . of him also shall the Son of man be ashamed" (KJV). For the ten-year-old, it was unbelievable that someone who called himself a Christian would be ashamed of Jesus, so he wrote, "Jesus, and shall it ever be a mortal man ashamed of Thee? / Ashamed of Thee, whom angels praise, whose glories shine thro' endless days."

It's almost unbelievable that a ten-year-old could write such profound lines, but it is even more unbelievable that adult Christians could be ashamed of Jesus.

Scriptures: Mark 8:38; Romans 1:16; 2 Timothy 1:7-13
Themes: Witnessing, Christian Living, Courage

Jesus, and shall it ever be a mortal man ashamed of Thee?
Ashamed of Thee, whom angels praise, whose glories
   shine thro' endless days.

Ashamed of Jesus, I never, I never will be;
For Jesus, my Savior, is not ashamed of me.

Ashamed of Jesus! Sooner far let evening blush to own a star;
He sheds the beams of light divine o'er this benighted soul of mine.

Ashamed of Jesus! That dear Friend, on whom my hopes of heav'n depend.
No! when I blush, be this my shame, that I no more revere His name.

Ashamed of Jesus! Yes, I may when I've no guilt to wash away;
No tear to wipe, no good to crave, no fears to quell, no soul to save.
JOSEPH GRIGG (1728–1768)

HE HAS MADE ME GLAD

The author of this song was no stranger to difficulty. Leona Bruce Von Brethorst was a child of Appalachia. She was one of eleven children, and she often went to school without shoes.

After high school, she moved to Detroit, Michigan, to work in a defense plant during World War II. After the war, she relocated to California, where she got married and had two children. But her husband left her before the older child was three years old.

Leona was crushed. She battled depression and took odd jobs so she and her children could have food to eat.

Her church was a stabilizing force in her life, and she was asked to be a worship leader. At first she laughed at the idea, but she agreed even though she said, "I don't know a note of music or how to play any instrument."

Depression struck Leona again when her children left home, and she was devastated by loneliness. She began to spend more time in prayer and Bible reading. One day after reading in Chronicles about the dedication of the Temple and how the glory of the Lord filled the place, and after reading Psalm 100 about entering his courts with thanksgiving in my heart, she realized that thanksgiving is the key to knowing the joy of the Lord. It was then that she wrote "He Has Made Me Glad." She sang the song the following Sunday for her Sunday school class, and people have been singing it ever since.

Scriptures: 2 Chronicles 5:11-14; Psalm 92:4; Psalm 100:4; Psalm 122:1

Themes: Joy, Praise, Thanksgiving

LEONA VON BRETHORST (B. 1923)
Rights administered by the Copyright Company, Nashville, TN.

HE KEEPS ME SINGING

Luther Bridgers, a twenty-six-year-old Methodist pastor in Kentucky with a gift of evangelism, was sometimes asked to lead revival campaigns in other churches.

That is what happened one week in 1910. While he was preaching in another Kentucky town, his wife and children were staying with her parents in Harrodsburg. In the middle of the week of revival meetings, Bridgers received word that disaster had struck. Fire had broken out in his in-laws' home, and his wife and three young sons were trapped inside. They had burned to death.

He was in shock, disbelieving what had happened, but when he returned to Harrodsburg, the four caskets were the grim reality. As he recovered from the trauma, he began examining what he still had to hold onto. His answer was, "Jesus, Jesus, Jesus." Soon the song emerged. One stanza says: "Tho' sometimes He leads thro' waters deep, / Trials fall across the way, / Though sometimes the path seems rough and steep, / See His footprints all the way."

Scriptures: Isaiah 52:9; Acts 16:25; Ephesians 5:19

Themes: Comfort, Name of Jesus, Joy

There's within my heart a melody,
Jesus whispers sweet and low,
Fear not, I am with thee, peace, be still,
In all of life's ebb and flow.

Jesus, Jesus, Jesus, sweetest name I know,
Fills my ev'ry longing, keeps me singing as I go.

All my life was wrecked by sin and strife,
Discord filled my heart with pain,
Jesus swept across the broken strings,
Stirred the slumb'ring chords again.

Feasting on the riches of His grace,
Resting 'neath His shelt'ring wing,
Always looking on His smiling face,
That is why I shout and sing.

Tho' sometimes He leads thro' waters deep,
Trials fall across the way,
Tho' sometimes the path seems rough and steep,
See His footprints all the way.

Soon He's coming back to welcome me
Far beyond the starry sky;
I shall wing my flight to worlds unknown,
I shall reign with Him on high.

LUTHER B. BRIDGERS (1884–1948)

HE TOUCHED ME

Bill Gaither was an unknown twenty-seven-year-old high school teacher in Indiana when evangelist Dale Oldham invited him to play the piano at a revival meeting fifty miles away, so he was honored.

The service was memorable. Dale's son, Doug Oldham, provided the special music. Many people responded to the invitation. After the service, Bill, Dale, and Doug talked about how they had all felt the presence of the Holy Spirit. In fact, they felt that, during the meeting, the hand of Jesus had touched them. Just before the three separated, Dale said to Bill, "You should write a song that says, 'He touched me, oh, he touched me.'"

The next morning, Bill wrote the song. Within a week Doug Oldham was singing it in concerts, and soon he made a recording of it. Others recorded it, from the Imperials quartet to Elvis Presley, who won a Grammy for his recording.

The song launched Bill Gaither's music career. Gaither felt that the song was successful simply because it expresses everyone's testimony who comes to Jesus: "I had no hope, I was done. Then the hand of Jesus touched me."

Scriptures: Matthew 14:36; Matthew 20:34; Luke 5:13
Themes: Salvation, Joy, Testimony

Shackled by a heavy burden, 'neath a load of guilt and shame;
Then the hand of Jesus touched me, and now I am no longer the same.

He touched me, O, He touched me,
And O, the joy that floods my soul;
Something happened, and now I know,
He touched me and made me whole.

Since I met this blessed Savior, since He cleansed and made me whole;
I will never cease to praise Him, I'll shout it while eternity rolls.

WILLIAM J. GAITHER (B. 1936)
© 1963 William J. Gaither, Inc. All rights controlled by Gaither Copyright Management.
Used by permission.

HEAVEN CAME DOWN

In the field of gospel music, John W. Peterson has worn many hats. He has written more than one thousand gospel songs and tunes; he has composed about thirty cantatas, which have sold nearly ten million copies; he has edited and compiled many hymnals; and he has served as president of the Singspiration music company.

In the summer of 1961, he led the singing at the Montrose Bible Conference in Montrose, Pennsylvania. When he invited people in the audience to give personal testimonies, an elderly gentleman got to his feet. Peterson recalls it like this: "As he spoke, his face glowed, especially when he rehearsed that night when he came to Jesus Christ. The way he expressed it was: 'Heaven came down and glory filled my soul.'"

Those words grabbed Peterson, so he jotted them down. What a wonderful theme for a song. Later that week, he wrote the song, both words and music.

Scriptures: Psalm 21:1; Isaiah 61:10; Acts 16:34; 1 Thessalonians 1:6
Themes: Praise, Salvation, Joy

O what a wonderful day, day I will never forget;
After I wandered in darkness away, Jesus my Savior I met.
O what a tender, compassionate Friend He met the needs of my heart;
Shadows dispelling, with joy I am telling, He made all the darkness depart!

Heaven came down and glory filled my soul,
When at the cross the Savior made me whole;
My sins were washed away and my night was turned to day
Heaven came down and glory filled my soul!

Born of the Spirit with life from above into God's family divine;
Justified fully thru Calvary's love, O what a standing is mine!
And the transaction so quickly was made when as a sinner I came,
Took of the offer of grace He did proffer He saved me
    O praise His dear name!

Now I've a hope that will surely endure after the passage of time;
I have a future in heaven for sure, there in those mansions sublime.
And it's because of that wonderful day when at the cross I believed;
Riches eternal and blessings supernal from His precious hand I received.

JOHN WILLARD PETERSON (B. 1921)
©1961, Renewed 1989 by John W. Peterson Music Company
All rights reserved. Used by permission.

HE'S EVERYTHING TO ME

If contemporary Christian music has a founder, it may be Ralph Carmichael, the author of this song. Carmichael's influence on Christian music spanned the second half of the twentieth century. He won an Emmy in 1949 and recorded a number of CDs in the 1990s.

He was music director of Billy Graham's early films, which brought him to the attention of Hollywood. He eventually wrote and arranged pop tunes for singers such as Nat King Cole, Perry Como, and Bing Crosby. He worked with the *I Love Lucy* TV show and composed for the long-running *Bonanza* series.

His folk-rock musicals in the 1960s introduced pop music styles into Christian music, and today many of his songs are included in our hymnals, including "He's Everything to Me."

In the late 1960s, Carmichael realized that "many kids were calling me old-fashioned." So he started writing tunes with a beat in order to communicate with that day's youth. The words of this song are based on the apostle Paul's personal testimony in Philippians 3:7-9: "Because of what Christ has done . . . for his sake I have discarded everything else," a testimony that will never go out of date.

Scriptures: Ephesians 3:8-12; Philippians 3:7-9; Colossians 1:16-17
Themes: Commitment, Praise, Worship

In the stars His handiwork I see, on the wind He speaks with majesty,
Tho'He ruleth over land and sea, what is that to me?
I will celebrate nativity, for it has a place in history:
Sure, He came to set His people free—what is that to me?

Till by faith I met Him face to face and I felt the wonder of His grace,
Then I knew that He was more than just a God who didn't care,
That lived away out there and now He walks beside me day by day,
Ever watching o'er me lest I stray, helping me to find that narrow way—
He's everything to me.

RALPH CARMICHAEL
© Bud John Songs, Inc.
All rights reserved. Used by permission.

I AM NOT SKILLED TO UNDERSTAND

No doubt there were many things that Dora Greenwell could not understand. She was born into a well-to-do English family, but her father died and economic problems made it necessary for the family estate to be sold. She struggled with fragile health as she lived alone in London. Why hadn't God given her an easier life? She worked with handicapped and mentally retarded children. Why did they have to suffer so?

When she was thirty-nine, Greenwell wrote her first book, *The Patience of Hope.* She was beginning to see how important patience is for dealing with life's hard questions. But she didn't want to dwell on the unanswered questions; she preferred to think about God's glorious exclamations (those passages in Scripture that begin with *how, what,* or *why* and extol the greatness of God) and his sovereign plan of salvation. So when she compiled her book *Songs of Salvation,* she included this poem: "I am not skilled to understand / What God hath willed, what God hath planned; / I only know at His right hand / Stands One who is my Savior."

Scriptures: 2 Samuel 22:3; Romans 5:8; 2 Corinthians 5:21; Hebrews 2:17-18
Themes: Trust, Confidence, Salvation

I am not skilled to understand
What God hath willed, what God hath planned;
I only know at His right hand
Stands One who is my Savior.

I take Him at His word and deed:
"Christ died to save me," this I read;
And in my heart I find a need
Of Him to be my Savior.

That He should leave His place on high
And come for sinful man to die,
You count it strange? so once did I
Before I knew my Savior.

And O that He fulfilled may see
The travail of His soul in me,
And with His work contented be,
As I with my dear Savior!

Yes, living, dying, let me bring
My strength, my solace, from this spring;
That He who lives to be my King
Once died to be my Savior!

DORA GREENWELL (1821–1882)

I STAND AMAZED IN THE PRESENCE

In the early 1900s, Charles H. Gabriel was the king of gospel music. Gabriel wrote the words and music for a number of hymns used by popular evangelists of his day such as Billy Sunday and his song leader, Homer Rodeheaver.

Gabriel's hymns reflect a change in the style of gospel music. In the 1800s, hymns were deeply theological and often meditative. But with the revivals of Moody and Sunday, Christians learned to love songs that were fun to sing, highly energetic, and easy to remember. Perhaps Gabriel's most popular hymn is "O That Will Be Glory for Me," with its rousing chorus. He also wrote "Send the Light," a stirring missionary call with a tune that drives the singer halfway across the ocean.

These songs, like "I Stand Amazed in the Presence," focus on a simple emotion and celebrate it. In this case, it is raw amazement at the magnitude of Christ's sacrifice. We love this song because we can identify with it. How can we help but "stand amazed" in his presence? How marvelous! How wonderful!

Scriptures: Matthew 26:43; Luke 22:41; Romans 5:6-8; Ephesians 3:18-19
Themes: Love of Christ, Passion, Gethsemane, Praise

I stand amazed in the presence
Of Jesus the Nazarene,
And wonder how He could love me,
A sinner, condemned, unclean.

How marvelous! how wonderful!
And my song shall ever be:
How marvelous! how wonderful
Is my Savior's love for me!

For me it was in the garden
He prayed, "Not My will, but Thine";
He had no tears for His own griefs,
But sweat drops of blood for mine.

In pity angels beheld Him,
And came from the world of light
To comfort Him in the sorrows
He bore for my soul that night.

He took my sins and my sorrows,
He made them His very own;
He bore the burden to Calv'ry,
And suffered and died alone.

When with the ransomed in glory
His face I at last shall see,
'Twill be my joy thru the ages
To sing of His love for me.

CHARLES HUTCHINSON GABRIEL (1856–1932)

I WILL SING OF MY REDEEMER

It's not easy to keep the Christian faith bottled up. Throughout history, various rulers have tried to keep Christians from preaching the gospel but with little success. Ancient Rome would not have minded if Christians had just kept to themselves, privately enjoying their faith. But Christianity doesn't work that way. As the apostles told the authorities in Jerusalem, "We cannot stop telling about everything we have seen and heard" (Acts 4:20).

Philip Paul Bliss, the author of this gospel song, was the song leader for evangelist Major Daniel W. Whittle. Whittle, who had been taken prisoner during the Civil War, was converted while imprisoned by reading the New Testament. A few years after he got out of the army, he became an evangelist, and he asked Philip Bliss to be his song leader. Three years later, however, Bliss and his wife died in a train accident. This hymn text was found in Bliss's trunk. James McGranahan, who succeeded Bliss as Whittle's song leader, wrote the music.

Scriptures: Acts 4:20; Ephesians 1:6-8; Philippians 1:7
Themes: Witness, Praise, Salvation

I will sing of my Redeemer
And His wondrous love to me;
On the cruel cross He suffered,
From the curse to set me free.

Sing, O sing of my Redeemer,
With His blood He purchased me;
On the cross He sealed my pardon,
Paid the debt and made me free.

I will tell the wondrous story,
How, my lost estate to save,
In His boundless love and mercy,
He the ransom freely gave.

I will praise my dear Redeemer,
His triumphant pow'r I'll tell,
How the victory He giveth
Over sin and death and hell.

I will sing of my Redeemer
And His heav'nly love to me;
He from death to life hath bro't me,
Son of God with Him to be.

PHILIP PAUL BLISS (1838–1876)

I WILL SING OF THE MERCIES OF THE LORD

The words of this chorus come from Psalm 89:1: "I will sing of the mercies of the LORD for ever" (KJV).

The composer of the tune and the author of the lyrics are uncertain. Fred Fillmore and James Fillmore were brothers living in the Cincinnati area. Both of them were ministers and traveling music teachers, teaching piano, organ, and singing in Ohio, Indiana, Kentucky, Tennessee, and elsewhere. Together they started a music company called the Fillmore Brothers Publishing Company, and they published a magazine that contained some of the new songs they wrote.

Since James wrote more music than Fred did, it had been assumed that this song should be credited to James, but recently someone found the melody in one of Fred's collections of gospel songs. Whoever wrote it, the song had been forgotten until it was rediscovered in the late 1950s, when youth groups, Sunday schools, and vacation Bible schools started singing it again.

Scriptures: Psalm 89:1; Lamentations 3:22; 2 Corinthians 1:3

Themes: Love, Witnessing, Praise

I will sing of the mercies of the Lord forever,
I will sing, I will sing.
I will sing of the mercies of the Lord forever,
I will sing of the mercies of the Lord.
With my mouth will I make known
Thy faithfulness, Thy faithfulness,
With my mouth will I make known
Thy faithfulness to all generations.

FRED AUGUSTUS FILLMORE (1856–1925) AND/OR JAMES HENRY FILLMORE (1849–1936)

I WILL SING THE WONDROUS STORY

The year was 1886. The place was North Adams, Massachusetts. Twenty-one-year-old Peter Bilhorn, who had just been converted the previous year, approached evangelist Francis Rowley after a church service. Young Bilhorn was eager to use his musical talents for the Lord. "Why don't you write a hymn?" he asked the evangelist. "And I will set your words to music."

Rowley didn't know if he could write a good hymn, and he didn't know if young Bilhorn could compose a good tune, but he said he would try. The following night he came back with this gospel song. It originally began, "Can't you sing the wondrous story?" For Bilhorn, who was a singer as well as a pianist and organist, it was an ideal personal testimony. Just a couple of years earlier, he had started his music career singing in Chicago taverns, so he understood the line "I was lost but Jesus found me—found the sheep that went astray." Bilhorn wrote the music, and the following year the song was published.

Bilhorn went on singing the wondrous story the rest of his life, writing two thousand songs, designing a lightweight folding organ for evangelistic use, assisting evangelists like Billy Sunday, and ministering around the world with Christian music.

Scriptures: Psalm 23:4; Luke 15:4-7; Revelation 15:3
Themes: Jesus, Saints, Evangelism

I will sing the wondrous story of the Christ who died for me—
How He left His home in glory for the cross of Calvary.

Yes, I'll sing the wondrous story
Of the Christ who died for me,
Sing it with the saints in glory,
Gathered by the crystal sea.

I was lost but Jesus found me—found the sheep that went astray,
Threw His loving arms around me, drew me back into His way.

Days of darkness still come o'er me, sorrow's paths I often tread;
But the Savior still is with me—by His hand I'm safely led.

He will keep me till the river rolls its waters at my feet;
Then He'll bear me safely over, where the loved ones I shall meet.

FRANCIS HAROLD ROWLEY (1854–1942)

I'D RATHER HAVE JESUS

When the mother of George Beverly Shea put a poem on their family piano, she had no idea what would happen. Most likely she wanted her son to read the words and make some changes in his life's direction. It looked as if he were heading for a career singing popular music on NBC. He had impressed everyone who heard him, and he admits that he was lured by the possibilities.

But then he saw the poem on the piano, and he was moved by the words. He sat down at the piano and started singing a tune that seemed to fit the words. Shea didn't know it at the time, but his mother was listening in the next room, and she asked him to sing it in church the next day. So the words by Rhea Miller and the tune by George Beverly Shea were cemented together.

Bev Shea's life direction changed because of that hymn. A few years later he became associated with evangelist Billy Graham and sang the hymn around the world.

Scriptures: Matthew 16:24-26; Philippians 1:21; Philippians 3:8
Themes: Dedication, Commitment

I'd rather have Jesus than silver or gold;
I'd rather be His than have riches untold;
I'd rather have Jesus than houses or lands,
I'd rather be led by His nail pierced hand.

Than to be the king of a vast domain
Or be held in sin's dread sway,
I'd rather have Jesus than anything
This world affords today.

I'd rather have Jesus than men's applause;
I'd rather be faithful to His dear cause;
I'd rather have Jesus than world-wide fame,
I'd rather be true to His holy name.

He's fairer than lilies of rarest bloom;
He's sweeter than honey from out the comb;
He's all that my hungering spirit needs,
I'd rather have Jesus and let Him lead.

RHEA F. MILLER (1894–1966)

IN MY HEART THERE RINGS A MELODY

This gospel song was born on a hot summer day in Texas. Elton Roth was directing the music for evangelistic services in a cotton-mill town, and one afternoon he took a walk to see the big cotton mill outside of town. It was a long walk for a hot day, so when he returned to town, he looked for some shade. Then he saw a church on the corner.

This is the way he tells it: "The door being open, I went in. There were no people in the pews, no minister in the pulpit. Everything was quiet, with a lingering sacred presence. I walked up and down the aisle and began singing, 'In my heart there rings a melody,' then hurried into the pastor's study to find some paper. I drew a staff and sketched the melody, remaining there for an hour or more to finish the song, both words and music."

That evening at an open-air meeting, he introduced it to some two hundred boys and girls. They sang it enthusiastically, and the adults joined in to sing it again. Roth was thrilled with the response to the new song. "It seemed," he says, "my whole being was transformed into song."

Scriptures: Psalm 100:2; Isaiah 51:3; Ephesians 5:19
Themes: Music, Salvation, Joy

I have a song that Jesus gave me,
It was sent from heav'n above;
There never was a sweeter melody,
'Tis a melody of love.

In my heart there rings a melody,
There rings a melody with heaven's harmony;
In my heart there rings a melody;
There rings a melody of love.

I love the Christ who died on Calv'ry,
For He washed my sins away;
He put within my heart a melody,
And I know it's there to stay.

'Twill be my endless theme in glory,
With the angels I will sing;
'Twill be a song with glorious harmony,
When the courts of heaven ring.

Words: Elton Roth

IT IS NO SECRET

Stuart Hamblen lived life in the fast lane. A cowboy singer and a Hollywood actor with his own radio show, he spent his nights drinking, gambling, and partying. Then evangelist Billy Graham came to town, and Hamblen invited him to be on his radio show. Hamblen enjoyed the time and accepted Graham's invitation to come to the crusade the next night. When the closing invitation was given at Graham's crusade, Hamblen walked forward to receive Jesus Christ.

Newspapers spread the word quickly: Hamblen had hit the sawdust trail. Then one day as he was walking on a Hollywood street, actor John Wayne stopped him and asked, "Is it true what happened to you?" Hamblen replied, "I guess it's no secret."

John Wayne laughed and said, "That sounds like a song to me."

As they parted, Hamblen told his friend, "You know, John, what God has done for me, he can do for you." That night Stuart Hamblen wrote the words to his personal testimony, "It Is No Secret."

Scriptures: Mark 5:19; Acts 1:8; Acts 26:26-29
Themes: Testimony, Witness, Invitation

The chimes of time ring out the news
Another day is through;
Someone slipped and fell,
Was that someone you?

You may have longed for added strength
Your courage to renew;
Do not be disheartened
For I bring hope to you.

It is no secret what God can do;
What He's done for others He'll do for you.
With arms wide open He'll pardon you;
It is no secret what God can do.

There is no night, for in His light
You'll never walk alone,
Always feel at home
Wherever you may roam;

There is no power can conquer you,
While God is on your side.

Just take Him at his promise
Don't run away and hide.

IT TOOK A MIRACLE

By the time John W. Peterson got to Bible school soon after World War II, he had already experienced a few miracles in his life. An air force pilot, he had regularly flown the "China Hump" and had survived the dangers of that military duty. But in this song, John Peterson is talking about a different kind of miracle.

While he was a student at Moody Bible Institute in Chicago, missionaries often came to the school and told of their experiences and how God miraculously changed lives in their ministries. To Peterson this was the greatest miracle of all—the miracle of God transforming a sinner into a new creation in Jesus Christ. One day after hearing a missionary talk about God miraculously changing lives, John Peterson couldn't get it out of his mind. Soon words of the chorus took shape in his mind, and as soon as he could, he rushed to a practice room in the music building of the school and completed the melody. Later he added the verses.

Since that time, John Peterson has written more than 1,100 songs and thirty-four cantatas that have sold more than eight million copies. All that might be called pretty miraculous, but John Peterson would still say that the greatest miracle of all is when God saves a soul.

Scriptures: 2 Corinthians 5:17; Ephesians 2:13-19; 1 Peter 2:9-10
Themes: Salvation, Conversion, Miracles of Christ

My Father is omnipotent, and that you can't deny;
A God of might and miracles—'tis written in the sky.

It took a miracle to put the stars in place,
It took a miracle to hang the world in space;
But when He saved my soul, cleansed and made me whole,
It took a miracle of love and grace.

Tho' here His glory has been shown, we still can't fully see
The wonders of His might, His throne—'twill take eternity.
The Bible tells us of His pow'r and wisdom all way thru,
And ev'ry little bird and flow'r are testimonies too.

JOHN WILLARD PETERSON (B. 1921)
© Copyright 1948, renewed 1976 by John W. Peterson Music Co.
All rights reserved. Used by permission.

JESUS IS ALL THE WORLD TO ME

Newspapers called Will Thompson the "millionaire songwriter." In his home state he was called the "Bard of Ohio." He had gone to New York and had made it big; his secular songs were selling like hotcakes.

But Will really didn't care about his secular success. He cared about Jesus Christ, so he began writing gospel songs. He realized that a major evangelist such as Dwight L. Moody would never get to smaller towns, so he loaded an upright piano onto a two-horse wagon and took the gospel into the Ohio countryside.

He was in his fifties when he wrote "Jesus Is All the World to Me," his lifetime testimony. He would rather introduce Jesus Christ to a small hamlet in Ohio than to be known as a major songwriter in New York City.

Scriptures: 1 Corinthians 2:2; Galatians 6:14; Philippians 3:8-11
Themes: Jesus Christ, Commitment, Peace

Jesus is all the world to me, my life, my joy, my all;
He is my strength from day to day, without Him I would fall.
When I am sad, to Him I go, no other one can cheer me so;
When I am sad He makes me glad, He's my Friend.

Jesus is all the world to me, my Friend in trials sore;
I go to Him for blessings, and He gives them o'er and o'er.
He sends the sunshine and the rain, He sends the harvest's golden grain;
Sunshine and rain, harvest of grain, He's my Friend.

Jesus is all the world to me, And true to Him I'll be;
Oh, how could I this Friend deny, when He's so true to me?
Following Him I know I'm right, He watches o'er me day and night;
Following Him, by day and night, He's my Friend.

Jesus is all the world to me, I want no better friend;
I trust Him now, I'll trust Him when life's fleeting days shall end.
Beautiful life with such a Friend; beautiful life that has no end;
Eternal life, eternal joy, He's my Friend.

WILL LAMARTINE THOMPSON (1847–1909)

LOVE LIFTED ME

Sometimes hymns are reborn. "Amazing Grace" is rediscovered with every generation. "O Happy Day" was given new life in the 1970s. "Love Lifted Me," written by James Rowe a century ago, was resurrected by singers such as Ray Stevens, B. J. Thomas, and Kenny Rogers, who made successful recordings of it in the 1970s.

James Rowe came to America from England in 1890 and took a job with the railroad and later, the Hudson River Humane Society. He found he had a knack for writing both serious and humorous verses for greeting cards and eventually went into business working with his artist-daughter to produce material for greeting card publishers.

While secular artists who have adapted this hymn emphasize the word *love*, James Rowe emphasized Jesus Christ. It is the love of Jesus Christ that can lift us, not the garden variety of love.

Scriptures: Psalm 18:16; Psalm 40:1-3; Ephesians 2:4-6
Themes: Love, Salvation, Conversion

I was sinking deep in sin, far from the peaceful shore,
Very deeply stained within, sinking to rise no more;
But the Master of the sea heard my despairing cry,
From the waters lifted me, now safe am I.

Love lifted me! Love lifted me!
When nothing else could help, Love lifted me.

All my heart to Him I give, ever to Him I'll cling,
In His blessed presence live, ever His praises sing;
Love so mighty and so true merits my soul's best songs;
Faithful loving service, too, to Him belongs.

Souls in danger, look above, Jesus completely saves;
He will lift you by His love out of the angry waves;
He's the Master of the sea, billows His will obey;
He your Savior wants to be, be saved today.

JAMES ROWE (1865–1933)

NOW I BELONG TO JESUS

During the Depression years, insecurity was a major problem. Finding a job and keeping it was not easy. Norman Clayton, the writer of this gospel song, worked on a dairy farm, in a New York City office, in a commercial bakery, and in his father's construction business. On the side he was a church organist, a position he took at the South Brooklyn Gospel Church when he was twelve years old.

But despite the insecurity in the world around him, Clayton knew he had security with Jesus Christ. He belonged to Jesus, and Jesus belonged to him. Clayton made it a practice to memorize Scripture and let the Scripture come out in his songs.

Scriptures: Romans 8:35; Romans 14:8; Colossians 1:27

Themes: Salvation, Assurance, Comfort

Jesus my Lord will love me forever,
From Him no power of evil can sever;
He gave His life to ransom my soul—now I belong to Him!

Now I belong to Jesus, Jesus belongs to me—
Not for the years of time alone, but for eternity.

Once I was lost in sin's degradation;
Jesus came down to bring me salvation,
Lifted me up from sorrow and shame—now I belong to Him!

Joy floods my soul, for Jesus has saved me,
Freed me from sin that long had enslaved me;
His precious blood He gave to redeem—now I belong to Him!

NORMAN J. CLAYTON

O FOR A THOUSAND TONGUES TO SING

The original title of this hymn was "For the Anniversary Day of One's Conversion"; Charles Wesley wrote it on May 21, 1749, the eleventh anniversary of his own conversion. Before they were converted, John and Charles Wesley were dubbed "methodists" because of the methods of spirituality they had introduced in their club at Oxford, the Holy Club. But later John and Charles met the German Moravians, who loved to sing, were very missions-minded, and emphasized a personal conversion experience.

One of the Moravian leaders, Peter Bohler, once said, "Oh, Brother Wesley, the Lord has done so much for my life. Had I a thousand tongues, I would praise Christ Jesus with all of them." This was the inspiration for Charles Wesley to build a hymn to celebrate the date of his conversion.

Charles had known from childhood that Jesus died on the cross to pay the penalty for sin. But on May 21, 1738, he accepted and applied it personally—"His blood availed for me."

Scriptures: Psalm 145:2-3; Psalm 150:6; Isaiah 35:4-6
Themes: Praise, Joy, Forgiveness

O for a thousand tongues to sing my great Redeemer's praise,
The glories of my God and King, the triumphs of His grace!

My gracious Master and my God, assist me to proclaim,
To spread thro' all the earth abroad the honors of Thy name.

Jesus! the name that charms our fears, that bids our sorrows cease,
'Tis music in the sinners' ears; 'tis life, and health, and peace.

He breaks the power of canceled sin, He sets the prisoner free;
His blood can make the foulest clean; His blood availed for me.

He speaks, and listening to His voice, new life the dead receive;
The mournful, broken hearts rejoice; the humble poor believe.

Hear Him, ye deaf; His praise, ye dumb, your loosened tongues employ;
Ye blind, behold your Savior come; and leap, ye lame, for joy.

CHARLES WESLEY (1707–1788)

O, HOW HE LOVES YOU AND ME

Kurt Kaiser has won all sorts of awards for his composing, conducting, and arranging, including the Lifetime Achievement Award by the American Society of Composers, Authors, and Publishers. He has written scores of tunes in virtually every kind of musical style and has written more than four hundred songs.

Where do his ideas come from? He says, "Through the years I have been in the habit of keeping my ears tuned to things that people say, a phrase that may give me an idea for a song. I'll write it down quickly . . . and file it away in a special place in my office. Occasionally I will pull these things out and look at them."

One day he came across this line, "O, how he loves you and me." He began to think about that phrase, and in fifteen minutes he had written the entire song. It's a simple song, but God has used it to touch millions of hearts.

Scriptures: John 15:12-13; Romans 5:8; 1 John 3:16
Themes: Love, Crucifixion, Worship

O, how He loves you and me. O, how He loves you and me;
He gave His life, what more could He give?
O, how He loves you; O, how He loves me;
O, how He loves you and me.

Jesus to Calv'ry did go, His love for mankind to show;
What He did there brought hope from despair:
O, how He loves you; O, how He loves me;
O, how He loves you and me.

KURT KAISER

O, HOW I LOVE JESUS

What's in a name? If that name is Jesus, a great deal is in a name. Because this chorus is so well-known, we think the theme of this song is our love for Jesus. But it isn't. We think of the last five words of the chorus—"because he first loved me"—and we think that the song is about Jesus's love for us. That's closer, but that still isn't it.

Actually, the verses of this song were written by British clergyman Frederick Whitfield around 1855, and he probably never heard the chorus. The chorus is a nineteenth-century American folk song that was sung in many camp meetings of the time.

So what's the song about? It's about Jesus' name. In verse 1, we praise the name of Jesus. In verse 2, we remember that he was named Jesus because he would save his people from their sins. In verse 3, we recall that Jesus gives us daily hope and help, and in verse 4, the name of Jesus reminds us that he bears our sorrows and our pain.

Yes, it's no wonder we love Jesus. After all, he first loved us.

Scriptures: John 14:23; Philippians 2:9-11; 1 Peter 1:8; 1 John 4:19
Themes: Love, Jesus Christ, Comfort

There is a name I love to hear,
I love to sing its worth;
It sounds like music in mine ear,
The sweetest name on earth.

O, how I love Jesus, O, how I love Jesus,
O, how I love Jesus, because He first loved me!

It tells me of a Savior's love,
Who died to set me free;
It tells me of His precious blood,
The sinner's perfect plea.

It tells me what my Father hath
In store for ev'ry day,
And tho' I tread a darksome path,
Yields sunshine all the way.

It tells of One whose loving heart
Can feel my deepest woe,
Who in each sorrow bears a part,
That none can bear below.

FREDERICK WHITFIELD (1829–1904)

SINCE JESUS CAME INTO MY HEART

It's hard to think that this joyful gospel song was written after a father had buried his youngest son. Rufus McDaniel's son Herschel was greatly loved by his parents, so when his life was taken away at an early age, it was heart-wrenching for both mother and father.

But Rufus McDaniel felt the best way to honor his son was to write a gospel song full of joy and hope. Such a song would not only lift him and his wife out of their melancholy but also be a suitable remembrance for their son Herschel.

So Rufus McDaniel, a pastor in southern Ohio, wrote this gospel song that speaks of a hope that is steadfast and sure, as well as a light in the valley of death. The joy was there for Rufus because Jesus had come into his heart.

Scriptures: Isaiah 35:10; Luke 15:6-7; Acts 16:34
Themes: Salvation, Joy, Hope

What a wonderful change in my life has been wrought
Since Jesus came into my heart!
I have light in my soul for which long I had sought,
Since Jesus came into my heart!

Since Jesus came into my heart,
Since Jesus came into my heart,
Floods of joy o'er my soul like the sea billows roll,
Since Jesus came into my heart.

I have ceased from my wand'ring and going astray,
Since Jesus came into my heart!
And my sins, which were many, are all washed away,
Since Jesus came into my heart!

I'm possessed of a hope that is steadfast and sure,
Since Jesus came into my heart!
And no dark clouds of doubt now my pathway obscure,
Since Jesus came into my heart!

I shall go there to dwell in that City, I know,
Since Jesus came into my heart!
And I'm happy, so happy, as onward I go,
Since Jesus came into my heart!

RUFUS MCDANIEL (1850–1940)

THEE WILL I LOVE, MY STRENGTH

John and Charles Wesley sailed across the Atlantic to America as ministers and missionaries of the Church of England. They were devoutly following the letter of the law in regard to Christian teaching, but the spirit was missing. They had not yet been converted.

On the boat trip to America, the Wesleys met a group of Moravian Christians who impressed them greatly. There was great joy in their faith, and they were always singing. It may have been during that Atlantic crossing that the Wesleys were introduced to this hymn by Johann Scheffler.

But it wasn't until 1738, back in England, that John Wesley himself felt the "sacred fire" within him. His faith was no longer just an agenda of spiritual activities. Now he could sing, "Thee will I love, my joy, my crown."

Scriptures: Matthew 3:11; Luke 10:25-28; John 21:15
Themes: Love, Worship, Thankfulness

Thee will I love, my strength, my tow'r,
Thee will I love, my joy, my crown,
Thee will I love with all my pow'r
In all my works and Thee alone,
Thee will I love 'til sacred fire
Fills my whole soul with pure desire.

I thank Thee uncreated Sun
That Thy bright beams on me have shined;
I thank Thee, who hast overthrown
My foes, and healed my wounded mind:
I thank Thee whose enlivening voice
Bids my freed heart in Thee rejoice.

Uphold me in the doubtful race,
Nor suffer me again to stray;
Strengthen my feet with steady pace
Still to press forward in Thy way:
That all my pow'rs, with all their might,
In Thy sole glory may unite.

Thee will I love, my joy, my crown;
Thee will I love, my Lord, my God;
Thee will I love, beneath Thy frown
Or smile, Thy sceptre or Thy rod;
What though my flesh and heart decay,
Thee shall I love in endless day.

JOHANN SCHEFFLER (1624–1677)
Translated by John Wesley (1703–1791)

YESTERDAY, TODAY, AND TOMORROW

This song, both words and music, were really written by Don Wyrtzen, the son of evangelist Jack Wyrtzen, but there is a story behind why Don's father is officially credited with writing the words. His father, Jack Wyrtzen, began the Word of Life youth outreach with conference and school facilities in Schroon Lake, New York, as well as missionary outreaches around the world.

One day, Jack's son, Don, who is well-known as a composer, saw an outline of a sermon that his father had preached. The title of the sermon was "Three Days in the Life of the Christian." Don developed the song based on that sermon and then put his father's name down as the author. But the father said that all the credit should go to his son. Jack said, "He developed the theme. I don't really know why he put my name on it. I think when we get to heaven, the Lord will give him credit for the entire hymn."

Maybe one could say that yesterday Jack preached the sermon, today his son Don wrote the hymn, and tomorrow the Lord will give Don credit for the entire hymn. But maybe not. We do know that yesterday, Christ died for us, today he lives for us, and tomorrow he is coming again for us.

Scriptures: 1 Corinthians 15:3-4; 1 Thessalonians 4:16-17; Hebrews 13:8
Themes: Crucifixion, Return of Christ, Invitation

> Yesterday He died for me, yesterday, yesterday,
> Yesterday He died for me, yesterday,
> Yesterday He died for me, died for me—this is history.
>
> Today He lives for me, today, today,
> Today He lives for me, today,
> Today He lives for me, lives for me—this is victory.
>
> Tomorrow He comes for me, He comes, He comes,
> Tomorrow He comes for me, He comes,
> Tomorrow He comes for me, comes for me—this is mystery.
>
> O friend, do you know Him? Know Him? Know Him?
> O friend, do you know Him? Know Him?
> O friend, do you know Him? Do you know Him? Do you know Him?
> Jesus Christ the Lord, Jesus Christ the Lord, Jesus Christ the Lord.

Written by: Don Wyrtzen/Jack Wyrtzen
© 1966 New Spring (ASCAP)
All rights reserved. Used by permission.

PART XXIII

THANKSGIVING

Enter his gates with thanksgiving; go into his courts with praise.

Give thanks to him and praise his name.

PSALM 100:4

COME, YE THANKFUL PEOPLE, COME

Many Christians are in the habit of giving thanks before meals. It is said that Henry Alford also gave thanks after meals, standing and offering his gratitude to God for the blessings just received. He also did this at the end of the day. Indeed, Alford was one of the "thankful people" that he writes about in this hymn.

But this song isn't just about thanksgiving for what God has done. It is also about work completed, a job well done. It is about aching muscles and full barns, sun-reddened faces and meals of plenty. It was written to be used at harvest festivals in villages throughout England. Each village observed a celebration whenever it brought in its harvest, and Alford, one of the leading churchmen in England in the nineteenth century, provided this hymn of thanks. It was originally called "After Harvest."

Scriptures: 1 Chronicles 16:8-9; Psalm 92:1; Psalm 146:7-11
Themes: Thanksgiving, Creation, Second Coming

Come, ye thankful people, come,
Raise the song of harvest home;
All is safely gathered in,
Ere the winter storms begin;
God, our Maker, doth provide
For our wants to be supplied;
Come to God's own temple, come,
Raise the song of harvest home.

All the world is God's own field,
Fruit unto His praise to yield;
Wheat and tares together sown,
Unto joy or sorrow grown;
First the blade, and then the ear,
Then the full corn shall appear;
Lord of harvest, grant that we
Wholesome grain and pure may be.

For the Lord our God shall come,
And shall take His harvest home;
From His field shall in that day
All offenses purge away,
Give His angels charge at last
In the fire the tares to cast,

But the fruitful ears to store
In His garner evermore.

Even so, Lord, quickly come,
Bring Thy final harvest home;
Gather Thou Thy people in,
Free from sorrow, free from sin,
There, forever purified,
In Thy presence to abide;
Come, with all Thine angels, come,
Raise the glorious harvest home.

HENRY ALFORD (1810–1871)

COUNT YOUR BLESSINGS

The song "Count Your Blessings" was written by Johnson Oatman Jr. His father, Johnson Oatman Sr., a prominent businessman in the small town of Lumberton, New Jersey, was the best singer in church and probably in the whole community.

Johnson Oatman Jr. worked in his father's business all his life. He also became ordained as a Methodist preacher, so he often preached in one of the small Methodist churches in the area. But he could never sing like his father could sing.

However, when he was thirty-six years old, Oatman counted his blessings and discovered another talent. He could write songs, and for the next three decades he wrote four or five new gospel songs each week. He didn't want any money for them, but his publisher insisted, so Oatman finally agreed to accept one dollar per song.

Scriptures: Psalm 28:7; Psalm 103:1-5; Ephesians 1:3
Themes: Thanksgiving, Praise, Joy

When upon life's billows you are tempest-tossed,
When you are discouraged, thinking all is lost,
Count your many blessings, name them one by one,
And it will surprise you what the Lord hath done.

Count your blessings, name them one by one;
Count your blessings, see what God hath done;
Count your blessings, name them one by one;
Count your many blessings, see what God hath done.

Are you ever burdened with a load of care?
Does the cross seem heavy you are called to bear?
Count your many blessings, ev'ry doubt will fly,
And you will be singing as the days go by.

When you look at others with their lands and gold,
Think that Christ has promised you His wealth untold;
Count your many blessings, money cannot buy
Your reward in Heaven, nor your home on high.

So, amid the conflict, whether great or small,
Do not be discouraged, God is over all;
Count your many blessings, angels will attend,
Help and comfort give you to your journey's end.

JOHNSON OATMAN JR. (1856–1922)

GIVE THANKS

Some people may say, "You wouldn't be able to give thanks to God if you had the problems I have."

Well, consider the story of Henry Smith, the man who wrote the worship song "Give Thanks." Despite a degenerative eye disease, Smith made it through college and even through seminary, but soon he was declared legally blind. Unable to get a pastorate or any long-term employment, he went back home and worked at various odd jobs to support himself.

What did the future hold for Henry Smith? He says, "I remember being extremely thankful, and I remember my pastor quoting 2 Corinthians 8:9, that Christ, though he was rich, became poor for our sakes that we might become rich in him. So Henry wrote a song about the situation: "Give Thanks."

Today Henry runs a recording studio and plays bass for his church worship team. Because of his lack of eyesight, he depends on his memory to get the right chords. Regarding his blindness, he says, "It slows me down, but it doesn't stop me." Give thanks.

Scriptures: 2 Corinthians 8:9; Ephesians 5:20-21; Philippians 2:7-8
Themes: Thankfulness, Praise, Worship

Give thanks with a grateful heart, give thanks to the Holy One;
Give thanks because He's given Jesus Christ, His Son.
And now let the weak say, "I am strong!"
Let the poor say, "I am rich because of what the Lord has done for us."
Give thanks.

HENRY SMITH JR.
© 1978 BY INTEGRITY'S HOSANNA! MUSIC / ASCAP
All rights reserved. Used by permission

NOW THANK WE ALL OUR GOD

With the exception of "A Mighty Fortress is Our God," this is the most widely sung hymn in Germany. Like many other great hymns, it was forged in the crucible of the Thirty Years' War.

Martin Rinkart was the only pastor in the walled city of Eilenberg. Many refugees fled there, hoping the walls would protect them, only to see the city overrun by Swedes, then by Austrians, and then by Swedes again. In the crowded conditions, hunger and plagues were chronic problems. In 1637 Rinkart conducted funerals for five thousand residents—including his wife. So when he prays, "Guide us when perplexed," he is not talking about minor inconveniences.

Yet thanksgiving erupts from this stately song. The tune, by Johann Cruger, was introduced with the text in 1644 while the war still raged. It has a majesty and a resolve that few other works can match. We can thank God even during the most trying times. We can know God is with us "in this world and the next."

Scriptures: Psalm 147; Isaiah 12:4-6; Romans 8:35-37
Themes: Thanksgiving, Praise, Guidance

Now thank we all our God
With heart and hands and voices,
Who wondrous things hath done,
In whom His world rejoices;
Who, from our mothers' arms,
Hath blessed us on our way
With countless gifts of love,
And still is ours today.

O may this bounteous God
Through all our life be near us,

With ever joyful hearts
And blessed peace to cheer us;
And keep us in His grace,
And guide us when perplexed,
And free us from all ills
In this world and the next.

All praise and thanks to God
The Father now be given,
The Son, and Him who reigns
With them in highest heaven,
The one eternal God,
Whom earth and heaven adore;
For thus it was, is now,
And shall be evermore. Amen.

MARTIN RINKART (1586–1649)
Translated by Catherine Winkworth (1827–1878)

SONGS OF THANKFULNESS AND PRAISE

Christopher Wordsworth took after his father, who was a scholar, and his uncle, who was the famous poet William Wordsworth. Christopher became a school headmaster, a church vicar, and eventually a bishop in the Church of England. As a Greek scholar, he wrote a commentary on the Bible. But his uncle's poetic spark was in him, too, and he wrote more than a hundred hymns for church use.

Wordsworth tried to combine teaching and poetry in his hymns. He wanted his hymns to teach about Jesus and to call those who sang them to praise him. This hymn, for instance, succinctly surveys Christ's early ministry—from birth to baptism, from temptation to first miracle. But as it teaches about the person of Christ, it also calls us to praise him.

The key word in this hymn is the word *manifest.* God made himself manifest—in other words, he revealed himself—in Jesus. For this he deserves our constant praise.

Scriptures: John 1:14; Romans 16:25-26; 1 Timothy 3:16
Themes: Thanksgiving, Praise, Life of Christ

Songs of thankfulness and praise,
Jesus, Lord, to Thee we raise,
Manifested by the star

To the sages from afar;
Branch of royal David's stem
In Thy birth at Bethlehem;
Anthems be to Thee addressed,
God in man made manifest.

Manifest at Jordan's stream,
Prophet, Priest, and King supreme;
And at Cana, wedding guest,
In Thy Godhead manifest;
Manifest in power divine,
Changing water into wine;
Anthems be to Thee addressed,
God in man made manifest.

Manifest in making whole
Palsied limbs and fainting soul;
Manifest in valiant fight,
Quelling all the devil's might;
Manifest in gracious will,
Ever bringing good from ill;
Anthems be to Thee addressed,
God in man made manifest.

CHRISTOPHER WORDSWORTH (1807–1885)

THANKS TO GOD FOR MY REDEEMER

It is easy to thank God for roses. It is much harder to thank him for the thorns. This hymn offers a mature approach to thanksgiving, showing appreciation for pain and pleasure, joy and sorrow.

August Storm wrote this hymn in 1891 while still a young man of twenty-nine. He worked for the Salvation Army in Sweden and published this hymn in the organization's periodical, *The War Cry*. The Salvation Army has always specialized in reaching out to the poor and troubled, so Storm probably saw more than his share of pain and sorrow, as well as the joy and pleasure of lives turned to Christ.

Just eight years after writing this hymn, Storm was stricken with a back problem that left him crippled for the rest of his life. He managed to continue his Salvation Army work, and he maintained a thankful spirit even during this most difficult time. If anything, his troubles gave more power and credibility to his sermons and writings.

Scriptures: Psalm 105:1-4; Ephesians 5:20; 1 Thessalonians 5:18
Themes: Thanksgiving, Trials, Hope

Thanks to God for my Redeemer,
Thanks for all Thou dost provide!
Thanks for times now but a memory,
Thanks for Jesus by my side!
Thanks for pleasant, balmy springtime,
Thanks for dark and dreary fall!
Thanks for tears by now forgotten,
Thanks for peace within my soul!

Thanks for prayers that Thou hast answered,
Thanks for what Thou dost deny!
Thanks for storms that I have weathered,
Thanks for all Thou dost supply!
Thanks for pain and thanks for pleasure,
Thanks for comfort in despair!
Thanks for grace that none can measure,
Thanks for love beyond compare!

Thanks for roses by the wayside,
Thanks for thorns their stems contain!
Thanks for home and thanks for fireside,
Thanks for hope, that sweet refrain!
Thanks for joy and thanks for sorrow,
Thanks for heav'nly peace with Thee!
Thanks for hope in the tomorrow,
Thanks through all eternity!

AUGUST LUDWIG STORM (1862–1914)
Translated by Carl E. Backstrom (1901–?)

WE GATHER TOGETHER

No one knows who the author of this hymn was, but we can trace it to
the Netherlands in the first quarter of the seventeenth century. The
Dutch were praying for freedom from Spanish oppression. One Dutch
city after another had been captured and sacked by the Spanish armies.
Many citizens had been exiled.

But a few years later, the Spanish overlords were being driven out.
Night was ending; the dawn was coming. This hymn was written to give

thanks for the victory that was almost in sight. For these Dutch believers, "the wicked oppressing" were the Spaniards, who would "now cease from distressing." There was no doubt that God should receive the glory for the victory.

Life is often like that. The victory may still be around the corner, but that should not keep us from giving thanks. For Holland, a golden age of prosperity—of world exploration, of artists like Rembrandt and scientists like Leeuwenhoek—was only a few decades away. And blessings like these are merely a foretaste of what God has for us in the future.

Scriptures: Psalm 67:1-4; John 16:33; Colossians 4:2
Themes: Thanksgiving, Praise, Guidance

We gather together to ask the Lord's blessing;
He chastens and hastens His will to make known;
The wicked oppressing now cease from distressing,
Sing praises to His name: He forgets not His own.

Beside us to guide us, our God with us joining,
Ordaining, maintaining His kingdom divine;
So from the beginning the fight we were winning:
Thou, Lord, wast at our side, all glory be Thine!

We all do extol Thee, Thou Leader triumphant,
And pray that Thou still our Defender wilt be.
Let Thy congregation escape tribulation:
Thy name be ever praised! O Lord, make us free!

NETHERLANDS FOLK HYMN
Translated by Theodore Baker (1851–1934)

WE PLOW THE FIELDS

Matthias Claudius had no intention of writing a hymn. A German journalist, he was merely writing a poem about a group of peasants gathering for a banquet. The seventeen-stanza poem, originally entitled "Paul Erdmann's Fest," depicts friends coming over to Paul Erdmann's house and enjoying themselves. It praises both Paul Erdmann for his hospitality and God as the ultimate source of the feast.

Jane Campbell, a British music teacher, made the free translation of this poem into its present English form. She contributed it to a new hymnal in 1861, along with some other translations from German. Since that time, it has become a favorite harvest hymn in many churches. The hymn gained new popularity when John Michael Tebelak and Stephen Schwartz included it in their 1960s musical *Godspell*.

In any era the sentiments are valid. God has given us all the good things we have, and he deserves our thanks.

Scriptures: Isaiah 55:10-11; Acts 14:17; James 1:17-18
Themes: Thanksgiving, Creation, Praise

We plow the fields and scatter
The good seed on the land,
But it is fed and watered
By God's almighty hand.
He sends the snow in winter,
The warmth to swell the grain,
The breezes and the sunshine,
And soft, refreshing rain.

All good gifts around us
Are sent from heaven above;
Then thank the Lord,
O thank the Lord for all His love.

He only is the Maker
Of all things near and far;
He paints the wayside flower,
He lights the evening star.
The winds and waves obey Him,
By Him the birds are fed;
Much more, to us His children,
He gives our daily bread.

We thank Thee then, O Father,
For all things bright and good:
The seedtime and the harvest,
Our life, our health, our food.
Accept the gifts we offer
For all Thy love imparts,
And, what Thou most desirest,
Our humble thankful hearts.

MATTHIAS CLAUDIUS (1740–1815)
Translated by Jane M. Campbell (1817–1878)

PART XXIV

TRIALS AND TEMPTATIONS

Dear brothers and sisters, when troubles come your way,

consider it an opportunity for great joy.

JAMES 1:2

BE YE GLAD

Michael Blanchard needed one more song for the album called *Love Lives On*, which he and his wife, Greta, were assembling. The year was 1979, and the world news was not good. The United States was absorbed with the Iranian hostage crisis. Genocide abounded in Cambodia, and boat people were going through excruciating suffering. Blanchard had all this on his mind when he was reading Psalms in the New English Bible.

As he read, a small phrase seemed to jump out at him: "Be ye glad." Blanchard says, "The song wrote itself. It came out real fast. I can't take much credit, except for being his conduit."

Blanchard had no idea that "Be Ye Glad" would become popular. He said, "A song that I think is going to be a winner lays there like an egg." But this song, which talks of our brokenness and God's great love, touched the hearts of listeners. Blanchard said, "No one is immune from brokenness, but there is a larger, forgiving love that transcends our present state. And that is what the gladness is all about."

Scriptures: Psalm 97:12; John 16:20; 1 Peter 1:3-9
Themes: Joy, Salvation, Praise

In these days of confused situations,
In these nights of a restless remorse;
When the heart and the soul of a nation
Lay wounded and cold as a corpse.
From the grave of the innocent Adam
Comes a song bringing joy to the sad;
Oh, your cry has been heard and the ransom
Has been paid up in full, be ye glad.

Oh, be ye glad, be ye glad. Ev'ry debt that you ever had
Has been paid up in full by the grace of the Lord,
Be ye glad, be ye glad, by ye glad.

Now from your dungeon a rumor is stirring,
You have heard it again and again;
Ah, but this time the cell keys they're turning
And outside there are faces of friends.
And tho' your body lay weary from wasting,
And your eyes show the sorrow they've had;

Oh, the love that your heart is now tasting
Has opened the gate, be ye glad.

MICHAEL BLANCHARD
© 1980 New Spring (ASCAP)
All rights reserved. Used by permission.

CHRISTIAN, DOST THOU SEE THEM?

John Mason Neale got in trouble with church leaders in England because he liked formal, high-church liturgy and worship, and the church leaders didn't. So although Neale was a brilliant scholar who knew twenty languages, he was assigned the job of caretaker of an almshouse for old men. Neale didn't mind because this job gave him time to translate ancient hymns into English.

This hymn is one of them, either written by or in the spirit of Saint Andrew of Crete. Each stanza depicts a different way in which the Christian can be attacked by evil. The first verse talks about visible temptation, the second about spiritual temptation—pride, jealousy, and so on—and the third about temptation that comes to us as we listen to voices in the world around us. In the fourth verse, the Lord is speaking, offering encouragement to us who struggle to pray.

Scriptures: 1 Corinthians 10:13; Ephesians 6:16; 2 Peter 2:9
Themes: Temptation, Trials, Prayer

Christian, dost thou see them on the holy ground,
How the powers of darkness compass thee around?
Christian, up and smite them, counting gain but loss,
In the strength that cometh by the holy cross.

Christian, dost thou feel them, how they work within,
Striving, tempting, luring, goading into sin?
Christian, never tremble, never be downcast;
Gird thee for the battle, watch and pray and fast.

Christian, dost thou hear them, how they speak thee fair,
"Always fast and vigil, always watch and prayer?"
Christian, answer boldly, "While I breathe I pray."
Peace shall follow battle, night shall end in day.

"Well I know thy trouble, O my servant true.
Thou art very weary; I was weary too.
But that toil shall make thee some day all mine own,
And the end of sorrow shall be near my throne."

Translated by John Mason Neale (1818–1866)

FIGHT THE GOOD FIGHT

Too many of us are spiritually flabby, often avoiding spiritual conflict instead of facing it. That was certainly not the apostle Paul's style, nor was it John Monsell's. Monsell was a gifted Irish clergyman who could hold his congregation spellbound as he spoke. He had an enthusiastic and charismatic personality and a quick wit, and he advocated "more fervent and joyous" singing in his church. He once told his congregation, "We are too distant and reserved in our praises."

This hymn was written to accompany the reading of Ephesians 4:17-32, where Paul outlines the nature of new life in Christ. But Monsell's hymn has allusions to many other passages of Scripture as well. Stanza 1 refers to 1 Timothy 6:12 and Philippians 4:1; stanza 2 to Hebrews 12:1, John 14:6, and Philippians 3:14; stanza 3 to 1 Peter 5:7; and stanza 4 to Galatians 6:9, Mark 5:36, John 6:29, and Colossians 3:11. By the time you have finished the last stanza, you have had an excellent Bible study.

Scriptures: Philippians 4:1; 1 Timothy 6:12; 1 Peter 5:7
Themes: Conflict, Courage, Trust

Fight the good fight with all thy might!
Christ is thy strength, and Christ thy right.
Lay hold on life, and it shall be
Thy joy and crown eternally.

Run the straight race through God's good grace;
Lift up thine eyes, and seek His face.
Life with its way before us lies;
Christ is the path, and Christ the prize.

Cast care aside, lean on thy Guide;
His boundless mercy will provide.
Trust, and thy trusting soul shall prove
Christ is its life, and Christ its love.

Faint not nor fear, His arms are near;
He changeth not, and thou art dear.
Only believe, and thou shalt see
That Christ is all in all to thee.

JOHN SAMUEL BEWLEY MONSELL (1811–1875)

MY SOUL, BE ON THY GUARD

The old adage "Practice what you preach" applies to songwriters, too. Unfortunately, George Heath didn't take his own advice.

Heath was a pastor in a Presbyterian church in Devonshire, England, when this hymn was written. In it he warns Christians about being too casual about their faith. Be on your guard, he urges. Watch, fight, and pray. Renew the battle every day, and ask for God's help constantly.

However, Heath, the author of this hymn, was removed as pastor of his church because he was "proven unworthy," and dismissed "for cause." We don't need to know the details, but it seems as if George Heath had become careless, the very thing he had warned against in his hymn. There is no Christian that is immune from temptation; Satan, the Bible says, is like a roaring lion, looking for victims to devour.

Scriptures: Matthew 26:41; 1 Corinthians 9:26-27; 1 Peter 5:8
Themes: Conflict, Armor, Sins

My soul, be on thy guard—ten thousand foes arise.
The hosts of sin are pressing hard to draw thee from the skies.

O watch and fight and pray; the battle ne'er give o'er,
Renew it boldly ev'ry day, and help divine implore.

Ne'er think the victory won, nor lay thine armor down;
The work of faith will not be done till thou obtain thy crown.

Fight on, my soul, till death shall bring thee to thy God;
He'll take thee, at thy parting breath, to His divine abode.

GEORGE HEATH (1750–1822)

STAND BY ME

Born in slavery before the Civil War, Charles Tindley was a remarkable man. He taught himself to read as a teenager, attended night school, and completed seminary work by correspondence. As a Methodist pastor, he built a Philadelphia church, with ten thousand active members on its membership list. A strong biblical preacher, he also reached out to the community, organized food and clothing drives, and built a soup kitchen in the church basement. He walked into bars and witnessed for Jesus Christ.

Six-feet-four-inches tall, Charles was an imposing leader, and when he spoke, people listened. He knew that most African-Americans felt trapped in hopeless situations and were regarded as second-class citizens, so many of the songs he wrote tried to encourage people in their Christian lives.

This song is one example: "When the world is tossing me like a ship upon the sea, / Thou who rulest wind and water, stand by me."

Scriptures: Matthew 28:20; John 16:33; Hebrews 13:5
Themes: Suffering, Comfort, Peace

When the storms of life are raging, stand by me,
When the storms of life are raging, stand by me;
When the world is tossing me like a ship upon the sea,
Thou who rulest wind and water, stand by me.

In the midst of tribulations, stand by me.
In the midst of tribulations, stand by me;
When the hosts of hell assail, and my strength begins to fail,
O Thou mighty God of battles, stand by me.

In the midst of faults and failures, stand by me,
In the midst of faults and failures, stand by me;
When I do the best I can, and my friends misunderstand,
Thou who knowest all about me, stand by me.

When I'm growing old and feeble, stand by me;
When I'm growing old and feeble, stand by me;
When mine eyes grow dim in death and I draw my latest breath,
O Thou God of all the ages, stand by me.

CHARLES A. TINDLEY (1851–1933)

THROUGH IT ALL

A gifted musician, Andrae Crouch has had many honors and successes in life, but he has also had his share of heartaches. In one church where he appeared, the first four rows walked out when he appeared on the platform. They hadn't known that he was African American. At another engagement the church couldn't find housing for him until one member volunteered a room next to his chicken coop.

But "Through It All" wasn't written as a result of such experiences. It came after he had purchased a ring for a young woman who often sang with his group. He recalls, "We were working three days at a church in Northern California and I had picked out that time to ask her to be my companion in life." The first night his fiancée-to-be didn't show up. She didn't come the next night either.

On the third night she came, gathered the group together, and announced that she was in love and planning to get married. Her husband-to-be would not be Andrae Crouch; she had someone else in mind. After the service, the heartbroken Crouch drove five hours back to his home. His mind went to David in the Old Testament and how David had been directed both by God's rod and God's staff. In this time of personal anguish, Crouch wrote "Through It All."

Scriptures: Psalm 23:4; John 16:33; Romans 5:1-5
Themes: Guidance, Trust, Comfort

Through it all, through it all,
I've learned to trust in Jesus, I've learned to trust in God;
Through it all, through it all,
I've learned to depend upon His Word.

ANDRAE CROUCH (B. 1942)

YIELD NOT TO TEMPTATION

The author of this song, Horatio Palmer, conducted choirs and taught music theory. As a choir director, he began the Church Choral Union, which grew to twenty thousand voices. Once Palmer directed the group in a concert at New York's Madison Square Garden, but for the occasion he had to restrict the size of his choir to four thousand voices.

He was perhaps best known for his textbooks in music theory, books that every serious student of music was required to study. In fact, it was when he was working on an exercise in music theory for one of his books that an idea for a hymn suddenly came to him. He put aside his music theory as quickly as he could and jotted down the words and music to "Yield Not to Temptation."

Many of us know how to live the Christian life in theory, but when the subtle temptation comes, we find it easier to submit to the temptation. Palmer knew what to do, not only in theory, but also in practice: "Ask the Savior to help you, / Comfort, stengthen, and keep you; / He is willing to aid you / He will carry you through."

Scriptures: Matthew 26:41; 1 Corinthians 10:13; James 1:14-16
Themes: Temptation, Sins, Strength

Yield not to temptation for yielding is sin;
Each victory will help you some other to win;
Fight manfully onward, dark passions subdue;
Look ever to Jesus—He'll carry you through.

Ask the Savior to help you,
Comfort, strengthen, and keep you;
He is willing to aid you
He will carry you through.

Shun evil companions, bad language disdain,
God's name hold in rev'rence, nor take it in vain;
Be thoughtful and earnest, kind-hearted and true;
Look ever to Jesus—He'll carry you through.

To him that o'er-cometh God giveth a crown;
Thru faith we will conquer tho'often cast down;
He who is our Savior our strength will renew;
Look ever to Jesus—He'll carry you through.

HORATIO R. PALMER (1834–1907)

BIBLIOGRAPHY

Bailey, Albert Edward. *The Gospel in Hymns.* New York: Charles Scribner's, 1950.

Barrows, Cliff, et al. *Crusader Hymns and Hymn Stories.* Minneapolis: Billy Graham Evangelistic Association, Hope Publishing, 1966, 1967.

Bence, Evelyn. *Spiritual Moments with the Great Hymns.* Grand Rapids, MI: Zondervan, 1997.

Benson, Louis F. *Studies of Familiar Hymns, Second Series.* Philadelphia: Westminster Press, 1923.

Blanchard, Kathleen. *Stories of Favorite Hymns.* Grand Rapids, MI: Zondervan, 1940.

Bonner, Clint. *A Hymn Is Born.* Nashville: Broadman Press, 1959.

Brown, Theron, and Hezekiah Butterworth. *The Story of Hymns and Tunes.* New York: American Tract Society, 1906.

Christensen, Phil, and Shari MacDonald. *Celebrate Jesus.* Grand Rapids, MI: Kregel, 2003.

———. *Our God Reigns.* Grand Rapids: Kregel, 2000.

Colquhoun, Frank. *Sing to the Lord.* London: Hodder and Stoughton, 1988.

Davis, Paul. *Inspirational Hymn and Song Stories of the Twentieth Century.* Greenville, SC: Ambassador Publications, 2001.

Draper, James. *More Than a Song.* Chicago: Moody, 1970.

Emurian, Ernest K. *Living Stories of Famous Hymns.* Boston: W. A. Wilde, 1955.

———. *Sing the Wondrous Story.* Natick, MA: W. A. Wilde, 1963.

———. *Stories of Christmas Carols.* Grand Rapids, MI: Baker, 1958, 1967.

Hart, William J. *Unfamiliar Stories of Familiar Hymns.* Boston: W. A. Wilde, 1940.

Houghton, Elsie. *Christian Hymn Writers.* Glamorgan, Wales: Evangelical Press of Wales, 1982.

Hubbard, W. L. *History of American Music.* Toledo: Irving Squire, 1908.

Hughes, Charles W. *American Hymns Old and New.* New York: Columbia University Press, 1980.

Hustad, Donald P. *Dictionary-Handbook to Hymns for the Living Church.* Carol Stream, IL: Hope Publishing, 1978.

Hywel-Davies, Jack. *Morning Has Broken.* London: Fount Paperbacks, 1991.

Asimakoupoulos, Greg, ed. *Give Thanks with a Grateful Heart.* Brentwood, TN: Integrity Publishers, 2002.

Johnson, Carl G. *Miracles and Melodies.* Grand Rapids, MI: Baker, 1970.

Konkel, Wilbur. *Living Hymn Stories.* Minneapolis: Bethany, 1971.

———. *Stories of Children's Hymns.* Minneapolis: Bethany, 1967.

Osbeck, Kenneth W. *Amazing Grace.* Grand Rapids, MI: Kregel, 1990.

———. *101 Hymn Stories.* Grand Rapids, MI: Kregel, 1982.

———. *101 More Hymn Stories.* Grand Rapids, MI: Kregel, 1985.

Paine, Silas H. *Stories of the Great Hymns of the Church.* New York: Little and Ives, 1926.

Petersen, William J., and Randy Petersen. *The One Year Book of Hymns.* Carol Stream, IL: Tyndale, 1995.

Reynolds, William. *Songs of Glory.* Grand Rapids, MI: Zondervan, 1990.

Rizk, Helen Salem. *Stories of the Christian Hymns.* Boston: Whittemore, 1964.

Routley, Erik. *Hymns and Human Life.* London: John Murray, 1952.

Rudin, Cecelia Margaret. *Stories of Hymns We Love.* Chicago: John Rudin, 1934, 1951.

Sanford, Don. *Popular Hymn Stories.* Grand Rapids, MI: Zondervan, 1957.

Sankey, Ira D. *My Life and the Story of the Gospel Hymns.* New York and London: Harper and Brothers, 1906–1907.

Shea, George Beverly. *Then Sings My Soul.* Grand Rapids, MI: Revell, 1968.

Smith, H. Augustine. *Lyric Religion: The Romance of Immortal Hymns.* New York: D. Appleton-Century Company, 1931.

Smith, Jane Stuart, and Betty Carlson. *Favorite Women Hymn Writers.* Wheaton, IL: Crossway, 1990.

Terry, Lindsay. *Stories behind 50 Southern Gospel Favorites, Vol. 1.* Grand Rapids, MI: Kregel, 2002.

———. *The Sacrifice of Praise.* Nashville: Integrity, 2002.

Wells, Amos R. *A Treasury of Hymn Stories.* Grand Rapids, MI: Baker, 1945.

INDEX OF HYMN TITLES

INDEX OF AUTHORS, TRANSLATORS, ARRANGERS, AND SOURCES

INDEX OF AUTHORS, TRANSLATORS, ARRANGERS, AND SOURCES

INDEX OF THEMES

Books in the Complete Book Popular Reference Series

The Complete Book of Bible Trivia contains more than 4,500 questions and answers about the Bible.

The Complete Book of Christian Heroes is an in-depth popular reference about people who have suffered for the cause of Christ throughout the world.

The Complete Book of When and Where focuses on more than 1,000 dates that illustrate how God has worked throughout history to do extraordinary things through ordinary people.

The Complete Book of Zingers is an alphabetized collection of one-sentence sermons.

The Complete Book of Who's Who in the Bible is your ultimate resource for learning about the people of the Bible.

The Complete Book of Bible Basics identifies and defines the names, phrases, events, stories, and terms from the Bible and church history that are familiar to most Christians.

The Complete Book of Bible Secrets and Mysteries serves up secrets and mysteries of the Bible in a fun, entertaining way.

The Complete Book of Bible Trivia: Bad Guys Edition, an extension of Stephen Lang's best-selling book *The Complete Book of Bible Trivia*, focuses on facts about the "bad guys" in the Bible.

The Complete Book of Hymns is the largest collection of behind-the-scene stories of the most popular hymns and praise songs.

The Complete Book of Wacky Wit is filled with more than 1,500 humorous sayings to live by.